Using Quattro® Pro 3

Using Quattro® Pro 3

Stephen Cobb

Osborne **McGraw-Hill**

Berkeley New York St. Louis San Francisco
Auckland Bogotá Hamburg London Madrid
Mexico City Milan Montreal New Delhi Panama City
Paris São Paulo Singapore Sydney
Tokyo Toronto

Osborne **McGraw-Hill**
2600 Tenth Street
Berkeley, California 94710
U.S.A.

Osborne **McGraw-Hill** offers software for sale. For information on translations, software, or book distributors outside of the U.S.A., please write to Osborne **McGraw-Hill** at the above address.

Using Quattro® Pro 3

234567890 DOC 9987654321

ISBN 0-07-881736-6

Contents at a Glance

Contents

Acknowledgments

Many thanks to my patient editors at Osborne, Liz Fisher and Wendy Goss, who stuck with this project across the months and across the miles to Scotland. Thanks also to Nan and Art in Scotts Valley for their valuable assistance. To Chey, Erin, Dorothy, and Briah go my thanks for the endless encouragement and unconditional good cheer.

Introduction

This book is a complete guide to Quattro Pro 3, the powerful presentation spreadsheet from Borland International. As a Quattro Pro 3 user you will enjoy numerous state-of-the-art features, such as multiple spreadsheets with dynamic linking between them and sophisticated graphing capabilities, including a complete drawing and slide show facility. There are also such helpful features as an undo key, complete mouse support, and direct access to database files from such programs as Paradox. By learning to use Quattro Pro 3, you will be mastering one of the best implementations of desktop computer power.

About This Book

If you are new to electronic spreadsheets, the best approach is to read this book chapter-by-chapter. Topics are presented in a natural order of progression, based on years of experience in conducting spreadsheet training seminars. By following the examples, learning Quattro Pro 3 is made easy. Users who are experienced with other spreadsheets can probably skim the first chapter and note the special features of Quattro Pro 3. If you just want to read about certain topics, you can turn straight to the chapters that interest you and examine the examples to see how Quattro Pro 3 is applied to typical spreadsheet tasks as well as more advanced applications like desktop presentations. The index allows you to use the book as a complete reference to Quattro Pro 3's commands and features.

Armed with this book and Quattro Pro 3 you can tackle such tasks as budget projection, financial recordkeeping, statistical analysis, and custom applications development, including slide shows and automated presentations. You will quickly learn a system of commands that is logical, accessible, and easily customized.

How This Book Is Organized

The first chapter introduces you to the basics of spreadsheets and points out important capabilities and features of Quattro Pro 3. You are also introduced to the basic concepts of the program's operation, such as entering data and using the menu system. Chapter 2 demonstrates the operation of the main spreadsheet commands, while Chapter 3 discusses database management.

In Chapter 4 you will find a detailed examination of how to use the built-in functions that give Quattro Pro 3 its tremendous mathematical capabilities. In Chapter 5 a comprehensive spreadsheet-building exercise brings together and reviews elements from earlier chapters as well as Quattro Pro 3's printing and preview features. The chapter also explores techniques for developing presentation-quality spreadsheets with visual enhancements. Chapter 6 demonstrates many of the customizable aspects of the program, such as international currency, date formatting, and color display. Chapter 7 discusses data storage in detail, proceeding from the basics of disk storage to such advanced topics as password file protection. Handling multiple windows and spreadsheet linking is discussed in depth. You will also see how Quattro Pro 3's File Manager simplifies hard disk management. The program's ability to read data from such programs as 1-2-3, Reflex, dBASE, and Paradox is also described.

Chapter 8 presents an in-depth discussion of Quattro Pro 3's extensive graphics capabilities with numerous tips for effective chart making. Chapter 9 explains how to manipulate date- and time-related information. It also describes advanced techniques for regression analysis, backward solving of equations, matrix arithmetic, frequency distribution, and what-if tables, and demonstrates the use of XY graphs. Quattro Pro 3 commands for transforming text data into paragraphs and values are illustrated with numerous examples in Chapter 10, which covers the string functions and parse feature.

For users seeking to streamline their work, Chapter 11 provides tips on the use of Quattro Pro 3 shortcuts. The simple technique of recording keystrokes in macros is described along with other methods of macro creation. Step-by-step examples lead you through each method. Chapter 12 shows you how to automate tasks with special macros. The command language of Quattro Pro 3 is discussed with examples of how it can be used to create worksheet-specific menus. You will also find tips on creating and modifying user interfaces and developing linked spreadsheet applications. In Chapter 13 you will find more examples of Quattro Pro 3's unique features, including the graph annotator, slide shows, and Paradox access, showing how these can be applied to typical office tasks.

Appendix A offers ideas for setting up Quattro Pro 3 on a hard disk system. Appendix B offers tips for networking with Quattro Pro 3. Appendix C has tips for problem solving and printer support.

The Look of Quattro Pro 3

Ever since the first version of Quattro was introduced, one of the hallmarks of the program has been its flexible interface. Whether it is simply a matter of changing the screen colors, or a complete reorganization of the menu system, the program can be customized so that commands are presented as effectively as possible for as many different types of users as possible. For example, mouse users get a mouse palette, but those without a mouse do not.

With the release of Quattro Pro 3 this flexibility has been taken a step further. The WYSIWYG display mode gives you accurate on-screen details of your work, such as typestyles, charts, and graphics. The WYSIWYG mode also gives you attractive command "buttons" with a three-dimensional sculpted look. Not every PC, however, can display this feature and Quattro Pro 3 was designed to run on a wide range of different systems to give as much computing power to as many users as possible. If you have a VGA or EGA display you will be able to use WYSIWYG, if not you can still use the Quattro Pro 3 spreadsheet in character mode and display full-screen graphs.

Since Quattro Pro 3 has many different faces, the pictures used in this book to illustrate how Quattro Pro 3 works were created on a variety of displays. In the early chapters the most basic display mode is used most of the time. This allows you to concentrate on the contents of the display rather than its appearance. However, whenever the graphics capabilities of Quattro Pro 3 are being illustrated, more complex graphics screens are used. Since full-page color graphics are not feasible in a book of this type, there will be some situations where the illustrations fail to show the program's capabilities. There may be times when the style of display used in the book differs from what you have on your monitor but the important point is that the contents will essentially be the same.

A Final Note

If you are using an earlier version of Quattro Pro, such as Quattro Pro 2, the majority of the instructions in the book will be accurate. However, it is strongly recommended that you take advantage of Borland's very reasonable upgrade plan to get Quattro Pro 3. You will find that the added features and improved performance are well worth it.

Besides being a powerful business tool, Quattro Pro 3 is a lot of fun to work with, and to write about. Here's hoping that you enjoy using Quattro Pro 3.

1 *Getting Started*

Chapter 1 tells you what Quattro Pro 3 is and how to start using it for a variety of tasks. It introduces the basic concepts of Quattro Pro 3, thereby helping you build a foundation for the many procedures you will learn in the rest of the book. By the end of this chapter you will have learned how to enter data, create formulas, and store your work. The chapter begins with a look at the main features and benefits of Quattro Pro 3.

What is Quattro Pro 3?

Quattro Pro 3 is a spreadsheet program with integrated database management and graphic presentation capabilities. *Spreadsheet, database,* and *graphics* refer to ways of organizing and analyzing information. A spreadsheet arranges information in columns and rows like a columnar pad. A database management program stores information in fields and records. A graphic presentation program presents information visually, as in pie charts, bar graphs, diagrams, and slide shows.

Quattro Pro 3 is the latest version of a program for DOS-based PCs, which has been steadily improved since it was first introduced by Borland International in 1987. The following sections review the general features of a modern electronic spreadsheet, as well as summarize the specific benefits of Quattro Pro 3.

Electronic Spreadsheet

An electronic spreadsheet program adds computer power to the simple but effective method of arranging information used by accountants for centuries: the columnar pad. Instead of writing numbers on a paper pad, you enter them on a computer screen. Instead of calculating numbers on a calculator, you tell the spreadsheet program to calculate them for you. Instead of putting the columnar pad in a filing cabinet or desk drawer, you tell the program to store your work in a file, known as a worksheet, on a computer's disk. When you want a paper report, you tell the program which columns and rows you want to send to your computer's printer.

When you load a Quattro Pro 3 worksheet on a state-of-the-art personal computer, you immediately see how the column and row arrangement is translated into a screen image. This is shown in Figure 1-1, where you can see a worksheet recording how many people taking Northern flights were in First, Business, and Coach class for each of four quarters. The capital letters across the top of the worksheet identify the columns; the numbers down the left side of the worksheet identify the rows. The collection of words and numbers you see in Figure 1-1 is referred to as a model, since it describes, or models, a particular set of circumstances, in this case, the passenger volume on certain airline routes.

Each junction of a spreadsheet column and row produces a box, or cell, into which you can enter a number or text. The column letters and row numbers are combined to give each cell a unique address. In Figure 1-1 you can see that the word Northern has been entered in column A, row 1, known as cell A1. The number 125 has been entered in cell B5.

The numbers in row 9 are the results of calculations that add up the three figures for each quarter. The numbers in column F are totals of each of the three classes of travel. Because these totals are calculations, changing the number in B5 will cause the totals to change.

In Figure 1-2 you can see that 125 has been altered to 137. You can also see that three other numbers changed: the total for Qtr1, the total for First, and the grand total in cell F9. When you calculate with a spreadsheet, you do not have to use an eraser to make changes. In fact, Quattro Pro 3 has a key that can undo any change.

As a spreadsheet program, Quattro Pro 3 offers a full range of features, including the following:

■ 256 columns and 8192 rows, that is, more than two million cells, per worksheet

■ Several worksheets loaded and displayed at the same time

■ Links between worksheets to enable you to build consolidated worksheets

■ More than 100 built-in formulas, known as functions, to simplify calculations

■ Background calculation to enable you to keep working while formulas are being calculated

■ The ability to create large spreadsheets on modest computer hardware

■ The ability to display spreadsheets on screen exactly as they will appear when printed out

■ Direct exchange of files with other spreadsheet programs, including Lotus 1-2-3 Release 2.2

Figure 1-1. *Typical Quattro Pro 3 worksheet*

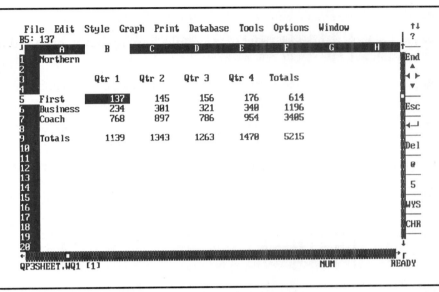

Figure 1-2.   *Worksheet in Figure 1-1 with different numbers*

Is What You See What You Get?

You probably noticed that Figure 1-2 looks quite a bit different from Figure 1-1, even though both screens show the same worksheet. In Figure 1-2 you still have the column and row arrangement, but you cannot see the grid of lines identifying the columns and rows. This is because of the fact that Quattro Pro 3 draws the spreadsheet differently on different computers.

More powerful computers, with what are known as EGA and VGA displays, have the ability to display greater detail. When you load Quattro Pro 3 on one of these computers, the program automatically takes advantage of this ability to provide extra detail. This ability is known as the WYSIWYG mode of display. WYSIWYG is an acronym for what you see is what you get; it refers to the ability to show on screen an exact image of what Quattro Pro 3 will print when the time comes to produce a report from the spreadsheet. In Figure 1-3 you can see a report printed from the worksheet in Figure 1-1. Note that the actual shape and style of the letters in the report match the screen displayed in WYSIWYG mode in Figure 1-1.

The display mode in Figure 1-2 is called character mode because the screen is composed from a fixed set of characters. Even lines drawn on the

Northern					
	Qtr 1	Qtr 2	Qtr 3	Qtr 4	Totals
First	125	145	156	176	**602**
Business	234	301	321	340	**1196**
Coach	768	897	786	954	**3405**
Totals	**1127**	**1343**	**1263**	**1470**	5203

Figure 1-3. *Printed report*

screen are made up of characters. There are 25 lines of characters in Figure 1-2, with 80 characters on each line. Even though some PCs cannot display Quattro Pro 3 in WYSIWYG mode, even the oldest PCs can display it in character mode. This allows Quattro Pro 3 to run on a wide range of equipment.

Another feature of character mode is that it is easier to reproduce when you want to print the actual screen as it appears on the monitor, rather than a report like the one in Figure 1-3. A WYSIWYG screen contains a lot of detail that is clear when displayed on a 14-inch monitor, but that becomes hard to read when shrunk to fit the printed page. Since the role of screens in this book is to make things clear, most of the illustrations use character mode screens. WYSIWYG screens are, however, used when features specific to WYSIWYG operations are being discussed.

Later in this chapter, in the section "Of Mice, Menus, and Macros," the commands for switching between display modes will be discussed. Users of some PCs will have more than two choices for display mode. Special modes that allow more columns and rows to be placed on the screen are available. Users of color monitors can change the colors used by Quattro Pro 3 to display the various parts of the screen.

When you want to print your work, Quattro Pro 3 offers a variety of typefaces or fonts, plus underlining, line drawing, and shading. It even has a command that automatically shrinks large reports so they fit on a single page. In Figure 1-4 you can see a 12-month expense projection printed on a single page. In summary, the WYSIWYG features Borland has incorporated in Quattro Pro 3 are as follows:

■ Adjustable display modes, including WYSIWYG for EGA and VGA users.

■ Wide selection of screen and print fonts automatically generated by the program using Bitstream fontware technology in addition to the fonts in your printer.

■ Choice of colors and shading for all parts of the screen, plus conditional colors such as negative values in red.

■ Options to display/hide spreadsheet gridlines, column and row headings, and zero values. In Figure 1-5 you can see Quattro Pro 3 in WYSIWYG mode with the column and row headings and gridlines turned off.

■ Print To Fit command, which scales down reports to fit on the page.

■ Ability to place live charts and graphic images in spreadsheets, as shown in Figure 1-5, as well as print combined charts and graphs.

■ Line drawing, boxes, shading, and bullet characters to dress up spreadsheet reports.

■ A screen preview mode that lets you inspect each page of a report before you send it to the printer.

Hardware Factors

Now that you have seen that Quattro Pro 3 works on a wide range of PC displays, also note that Quattro Pro 3 can be loaded on just about any hardware configuration. The term "hardware configuration" is a way of saying "collection of equipment," and Quattro Pro 3 can run on any IBM-compatible PC that has a hard disk and at least 512K of RAM. The expression "512K of RAM" refers to the size of the memory area used by a PC to hold programs and data temporarily while they are being used.

Information and the space it takes up in a computer system is measured in bytes; one byte is roughly the amount required to hold one character. One kilobyte, or K, is 1,024 bytes, so 512K means 524,288 bytes. In fact 512K is exactly one half of a megabyte, which is 1,024K. Although 512K

Quattro Vadis Travel – Total Amount: $103,407

Expenses – Monthly Growth Factor of: 1.015

	JAN	FEB	MAR	APR	MAY	JUN	JUL	AUG	SEP	OCT	NOV	DEC	YEAR
POLK ST.													
Lease	350	355	361	366	371	377	383	388	394	400	406	412	4,564
Phones	230	233	237	241	244	248	251	255	259	263	267	271	2,999
Telex	110	112	113	115	117	119	120	122	124	126	128	130	1,435
Electric	120	122	124	125	127	129	131	133	135	137	139	141	1,565
Res. Rent	500	507	515	523	531	539	547	555	563	572	580	589	6,521
VAN NESS													
Lease	500	507	515	523	531	539	547	555	563	572	580	589	6,521
Phones	250	254	258	261	265	269	273	277	282	286	290	294	3,260
Telex	150	152	155	157	159	162	164	166	169	172	174	177	1,956
Electric	225	228	232	235	239	242	246	250	253	257	261	265	2,934
Res. Rent	835	848	860	873	886	900	913	927	941	955	969	984	10,889
UNION SQ.													
Lease	1,200	1,218	1,236	1,255	1,274	1,293	1,312	1,332	1,352	1,372	1,393	1,414	15,649
Phones	300	304	309	314	318	323	328	333	338	343	348	353	3,912
Telex	250	254	258	261	265	269	273	277	282	286	290	294	3,260
Electric	205	208	211	214	218	221	224	228	231	234	238	241	2,673
Res. Rent	890	903	917	931	945	959	973	988	1,003	1,018	1,033	1,048	11,607
EMBARCADERO													
Lease	900	913	927	941	955	970	984	999	1,014	1,029	1,044	1,060	11,737
Phones	275	279	283	288	292	296	301	305	310	314	319	324	3,586
Telex (AUG)	0	0	0	0	0	0	0	150	132	155	157	169	773
Electric	0	0	0	0	0	0	0	0	0	0	0	0	0
Res. Rent	580	589	598	606	616	625	634	644	653	663	673	683	7,564
TOTALS	7,870	7,988	8,108	8,229	8,353	8,478	8,605	8,884	9,018	9,153	9,290	9,430	103,407

Figure 1-4. *Results of the Print To Fit feature*

might sound like a lot, all of the files required to run a powerful program like Quattro Pro 3 actually take up several megabytes of space on disk. You can tell this from the fact that Quattro Pro 3 is supplied on several floppy disks, each of which can store at least 360K worth of information.

You might wonder how Quattro Pro 3 is able to operate in a relatively small amount of RAM when it consists of several megabytes of program files. The answer is that it uses a clever piece of software technology developed by Borland and christened VROOM, which stands for Virtual Runtime Object Oriented Memory Manager. In simple terms this mouthful of technospeak means that only those parts of Quattro Pro 3 needed for the task at hand are loaded into memory. Although Quattro Pro 3 can perform many different tasks, it only works on one or two at a time. Since the program code for only those one or two tasks is loaded into memory, that leaves room for spreadsheets. Moreover, whereas many programs are divided into several parts, called overlays, the code that makes up Quattro Pro 3 consists of hundreds of small program modules. The VROOM

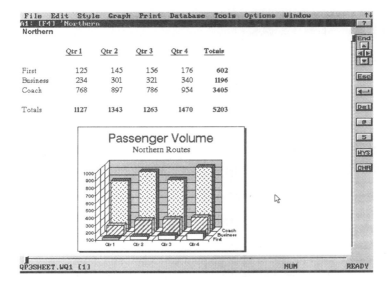

Figure 1-5.   *Customized Quattro Pro 3 display*

technology swiftly shuffles these in and out of memory as needed so the impression you get is that the entire program is on hand as soon as you issue a command.

Memory Matters

When you are working with Quattro Pro 3, your computer's RAM contains one other thing besides your spreadsheet and the Quattro Pro 3 program modules: the disk operating system, or DOS. This is the piece of software that controls basic computer operations such as arranging files on disk. In fact, it is only after you have loaded DOS that a program like Quattro Pro 3 can communicate with your hardware. When you tell your computer to load Quattro Pro 3, it is actually DOS that carries out this command. When you tell Quattro Pro 3 to store a worksheet in a disk file, it is DOS that handles the nuts and bolts of the operation. Quattro Pro 3 and other programs, such as WordPerfect and Paradox, that work through the operating system to apply your hardware to practical tasks are referred to as applications.

Quattro Pro 3 works with all versions of PC-DOS and MS-DOS numbered 2.0 or higher and any other compatible operating system, such as DR-DOS. Quattro Pro 3 does not require you to use any software besides DOS. Some applications, such as Microsoft Excel, do require you to use additional software; that is, to load DOS, then to load what is called an operating environment, which provides the font, mouse, and printer control the application requires. For example, Excel requires the Windows operating environment. This imposes an additional burden on your hardware, requiring more RAM. Quattro Pro 3 provides its own font, mouse, and printer support; at the same time, however, it can be operated within the Windows environment if you desire.

Having said that Quattro Pro 3 works with 512K of RAM, it must be said that 640K is preferable, and you will get even better performance if you have expanded memory. This is extra memory beyond 640K that meets the requirements of the Expanded Memory Specification, or EMS. If you plan to make extensive use of the WYSIWYG mode, several megabytes of expanded memory will substantially improve performance, plus let you create much larger spreadsheets than are possible with only 640K. Quattro Pro 3 can use up to 8 megabytes of EMS memory. For more about EMS see Appendix A.

There is an important distinction to be made between disk storage and random access memory, or RAM. The RAM in your computer is the area that holds program files while you use them plus the data on which the program is working, such as the worksheet file you saw in Figure 1-1. The information in RAM constantly changes while you use your computer and is wiped out when you turn off the computer.

The disks you use, either the removable floppy disks or the fixed disks, known as hard disks, within the computer, store information permanently. This means that when you turn off the computer the information in disk files stays there ready for the next time you need it. That is, unless there is a physical problem with the disk, the files should remain as you left them until the next time you need them. Quattro Pro 3 requires that you have five megabytes of free disk space on your hard disk before it can be installed.

When information is being stored on a disk it is said to be written into a file. When it is retrieved, it is read from the disk. The process of reading and writing is known as disk access and is one of the few aspects of computing that requires moving parts. This means that accessing information on disk is much slower than working with it in RAM. It also means that hard disks, which spin very fast, access data quicker than floppy disks. The other advantage of hard disks is that they store much more information than floppy disks and can accommodate the files required by a program like Quattro Pro 3.

The most important nonmoving part of your computer is the central processing unit, or CPU, the single chip that is at the heart of the PC's electronics. There are basically four levels of CPU, known by code numbers, each one more powerful that its predecessor. Quattro Pro 3 works well with all four of them:

8088	Found in the first IBM PC and the PC XT
80286	Introduced in the IBM AT
80386	Introduced in the Compaq 386
80486	Found in newer systems

To summarize the hardware requirements of Quattro Pro 3, they are a PC with

■ At least 512K RAM

■ DOS 2.0 or later

■ Five megabytes of available hard disk space

In Table 1-1 you can see the features available in Quattro Pro 3 according to the display system on your PC. As far as printing goes, Quattro Pro 3 supports a wide range of dot-matrix, laser, postscript, and letter-quality printers. For graphics, it supports a range of popular plotters. Bitstream fonts are supported on laser, ink jet, and dot-matrix printers; nine fonts are included with the program.

Adapter	Monitor	Features
VGA Plus	High resolution color	WYSIWYG Character modes 132 column mode Adjustable colors Graph View/Annotate
Plain VGA	High resolution color	WYSIWYG Character modes Adjustable colors Graph View/Annotate
Plain VGA	Black/white/gray	WYSIWYG Character modes Adjustable gray scale Graph View/Annotate
EGA	Medium resolution color	WYSIWYG Character modes Adjustable colors Graph View/Annotate
EGA	Black and white	WYSIWYG Character modes Black/white palette
CGA	Color	Character mode Adjustable colors Graph View/Annotate
Hercules mono	Monochrome	Character mode Adjustable attributes Graph View/Annotate
IBM PC mono	Monochrome	Character mode Adjustable attributes

Table 1-1. *Features According to Display System*

Beyond the Spreadsheet

Although the ability to enter, calculate, and print out figures quickly is the main appeal of an electronic spreadsheet and the principal reason this type of software enjoyed a rapid rise in popularity during the 1980's, modern spreadsheets go much further than that. As do competing products such as Lotus 1-2-3 and Microsoft Excel, Quattro Pro 3 offers database management and graphics.

Database Management   A database is a collection of information organized in a meaningful way. Anything from a telephone directory to a filing cabinet of medical records can be considered a database. Database management is the electronic storage and organization of such information. A database involves grouping pieces of information as records and organizing them into fields. For example, in Figure 1-2 the figures for the three classes of passenger could be sorted alphabetically by name or numerically by the largest total as shown in Figure 1-6.

Another aspect of database management is the ability to locate specific information. For example, in Figure 1-7 you can see a list of employees. Using the database commands in Quattro Pro 3, you can find all employees earning above a certain amount. You can even copy their names to a separate part of the worksheet, then sort them. The database features of Quattro Pro 3 are summarized as follows:

■ Sorting on up to 256 keys

■ Querying on simple and complex criteria, with record extraction from separate worksheets and even foreign files, including dBASE and Paradox databases

■ Direct reading and writing of foreign database files, including Reflex, Paradox, and dBASE

■ Direct links with Paradox, including hot-key switching into Quattro Pro 3 from Paradox and use of Paradox SQL Link

Graphs   The value of pictures in conveying information has been appreciated for thousands of years, and computers make it easy to create graphs and charts that greatly speed up our assimilation of facts and figures, as well as help us understand their implications. In Quattro Pro 3

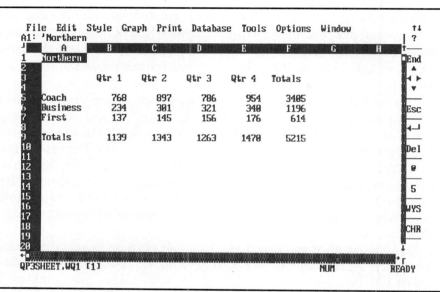

Figure 1-6. *Sorted worksheet*

File Edit Style Graph Print Database Tools Options Window
D1: (C0) [W12] @SUM(D5..D20)

	A	B	C	D	E	F
1	Employee		Total Salary:	$404,773		
2	Database		Total Sales:	4,141,248		
3						
4	I.D. #	Last Name	First Name	Salary	Sales	Date of Hire
5	10701	Rue	Mick	$24,234.00	301,793	02/22/85
6	10702	Wading	Les	$27,357.00	331,968	06/17/85
7	10703	Figone	Fred	$22,238.00	241,263	07/29/85
8	10704	Jones	Karen	$18,141.00	321,607	08/07/85
9	10705	Forte	Steve	$33,282.00	200,935	06/25/85
10	10706	Baxter	Andrew A.	$26,469.00	210,937	05/02/86
11	10707	Torres	Lisa	$23,453.00	251,404	03/12/90
12	10708	Abenojar	Bill	$29,036.00	221,265	11/27/85
13	10710	Chang	Charly	$24,489.00	330,152	12/28/89
14	10711	Ruess	Berni	$23,337.00	181,115	07/15/85
15	10712	Willock	Sam	$23,175.00	201,980	12/09/85
16	10713	McKenna	Sharon	$22,350.00	301,053	03/02/87
17	10714	Muller	Mario	$33,366.00	300,506	10/28/85
18	10715	Kobuchi	Joseph	$19,436.00	310,702	05/26/86
19	10716	Matsumoto	Owen	$30,863.00	201,704	04/02/87
20	10717	Romfo	Erin	$24,347.00	231,942	04/04/87

EMPLOYEE.WQ1 [1]   NUM   READY

Figure 1-7. *Employee database*

there are simple commands that draw a graph from numbers and words you entered into your spreadsheet. Whenever the numbers in the spreadsheet change, the graph is updated. Graphs can be pasted into the spreadsheet, as was shown in Figure 1-5, or viewed full screen, as shown in Figure 1-8.

The limitations of black-and-white on paper do not do justice to the vibrant colors seen on a good computer monitor, but you can see that the use of an image is effective in conveying information, in this case the trend in passenger volume figures shown in earlier examples. The type of graph in Figure 1-8, a three-dimensional ribbon chart, is one of more than a dozen chart styles Quattro Pro 3 offers. Unlike some programs, Quattro Pro 3 does not require you to load additional software to get this graph-making capability. Designing and printing graphs are managed entirely within the Quattro Pro 3 program.

Sometimes, what you need to make a point is a text chart consisting of a bulleted list of points, as shown in Figure 1-9. A bulleted list can also be created in Quattro Pro 3, even though the list does not use numbers. The purpose of Quattro Pro 3 is to allow you to present information effectively, regardless of the type of information with which you work. Moreover,

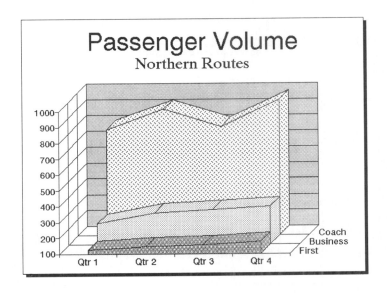

Figure 1-8.   *Full-screen graph*

Take Over Air Lines

Your airline for the roaring 90s

❏ *Aggressive*
    ☑   Acquired Sky High Shuttle, May 1989
    ☑   Reduced costs by 50% in 12 months
❏ *Efficient*
    ☑   Best "on-time" record in 89 and 90
    ☑   Lowest lost luggage claims
❏ *Committed to Profits*

Figure 1-9. *Text chart printed from Quattro Pro 3*

Quattro Pro 3 images can be saved in special files ready to be processed by slide bureaus.

Sometimes you want your presentations to have character and style; that is, you want them to use more than just words. For this reason, Quattro Pro 3 provides the Graph Annotator, a complete drawing package with which you can embellish charts or draw freehand illustrations. A variety of predrawn artwork, known as clip art, is included with Quattro Pro 3, ready to be pasted into your own designs. You can see the Graph Annotator at work in Figure 1-10.

These days computers are not only used to create paper illustrations and 35 mm slides, they are used to make presentations on a large screen or overhead display system. With Quattro Pro 3 you can put together a series of graphs that are then displayed one after another at your command or by simple user input. A variety of visual effects can be used to fade from one slide to another, and sound effects can be added to create a full presentation environment. The graphic features in Quattro Pro 3 can be summarized as follows:

■ Wide range of chart types, including three-dimensional charts

■ Fast Graph command to draw graphs from spreadsheet data automatically

■ The Graph Annotator to embellish graphs with freehand drawings and clip art

■ Comprehensive slide show facility complete with graph buttons, a variety of fade in/fade out styles, and digitized sound effects; you can see a slide show in progress in Figure 1-11.

Of Mice, Menus, and Macros

Now that we have discussed what Quattro Pro 3 is and some of the things it can do, it is time to look at how you relate to the program, that is, how

Figure 1-10.   *Chart being enhanced in Graph Annotator*

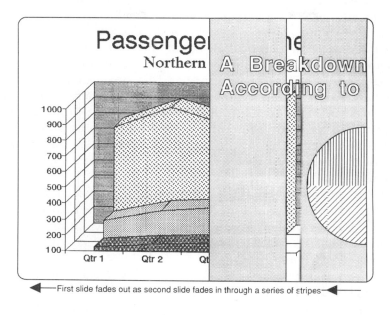

First slide fades out as second slide fades in through a series of stripes

Figure 1-11. *Sliding from one graph to the next*

you tell Quattro Pro 3 what you want it to do. The way you issue instructions to a program is known as the program interface. In this, as in so many other areas, Quattro Pro 3 is extremely flexible.

You have already seen that Quattro Pro 3 provides different screen modes to match the abilities of different equipment. The program also offers different interfaces for different users. For example, if you have an EGA or VGA system and know how to load Quattro Pro 3 on your computer, you can try the following experiment, which switches Quattro Pro 3 between WYSIWYG and character modes. If you do not yet know how to load Quattro Pro 3, see the instructions given later in this chapter. If you do not have an EGA or VGA system, you can follow the text and illustrations. Note that even if you think you will always use WYSIWYG mode, it is helpful to know how to access character mode since this mode is less work for the computer and therefore Quattro Pro 3 will run faster in it.

Across the top of the Quattro Pro 3 screen is a list of items: File, Edit, Style, and so on. This top line of the screen is known as the menu bar and provides a simple but effective way of issuing commands to Quattro Pro 3. To use the menu, press the F3 key or the slash key (/), which is usually below the question mark. Either F3 or / activates the menu bar. When you press F3 or /, the first item on the bar, File, becomes highlighted. You can move this highlighting by pressing the RIGHT ARROW key on your keyboard. To select an item, highlight it, then press ENTER. To cancel a selection, press the ESCAPE key. You can also select an item by pressing the F3 or / key, then typing the first letter of the menu item, for example, **O** for Options. Try this now; you will see the Options menu appear, as shown in Figure 1-12.

There are many items on the Options menu. To select one, you can type its first letter or you can move the highlighting to the item and press ENTER. Select Display Mode; you will see the menu shown in Figure 1-13 (unless your system can only use one mode). This is referred to as the Options Display Mode menu.

Now, if you are currently using WYSIWYG mode, select 80 × 25. If you are currently in character mode, choose WYSIWYG. When you make a choice from the Options Display Mode menu, the screen will be redrawn and the Options menu will reappear. You put the Options menu away by pressing ESCAPE or typing **Q** for Quit.

You can see that Quattro Pro 3 offers you several ways of interacting with the program. You have two keys you can press to activate the menu, F3 or /. You have two ways of selecting menu items, highlight and enter or type letter. You have two ways of leaving a menu, ESCAPE or Quit.

If you have a mouse installed on your computer, Quattro Pro 3 offers even more ways of issuing commands. On the right-hand side of the screen in Figure 1-13 you can see a series of boxes. These constitute what is called the mouse palette, and Quattro Pro 3 has full support for mouse users. In computer terms a mouse is an input device, a means of providing the computer with information by pointing at objects on the screen. Typically, you roll the mouse around the desktop to cause a pointer to move around the screen. When the pointer on the screen is pointing at an object you want to select, you press a button on the mouse and the object is selected.

To use the mouse palette to switch between character and WYSIWYG modes, you simply click on the button labeled WYS for WYSIWYG and click on the one that says CHR for character mode. You can also use the

Figure 1-12. *Options menu*

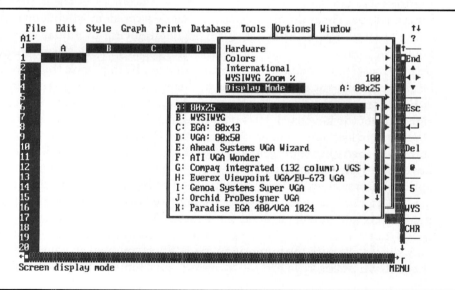

Figure 1-13. *Options Display Mode menu*

mouse to pick the desired option from the menu system. You select an item from the menu bar by pointing to it and clicking the mouse button. You can click anywhere outside a menu to put it away.

At appropriate points throughout the book you will find tips on using a mouse with Quattro Pro 3. Later in the book you will read how to modify the mouse palette to include your favorite commands. You will also learn how to use the Edit Menus command to customize the Quattro Pro 3 program menus. Beyond this, you will learn how to write and record macros that automate common tasks and organize them into your own set of menus. Now, however, it is time to take a look at the main keystrokes that operate Quattro Pro 3 and to begin working with the program.

Main Keys

All of Quattro Pro 3's features can be controlled from the keyboard. There are several different PC keyboard layouts in use today. As you can see in Figure 1-14, the basic differences are in the placement of the cursor and function keys. These differences should not be a problem when learning or using Quattro Pro 3. Although it might be annoying to adjust from one keyboard to another, you should realize that the keys work the same, even if their locations are different. For this reason, in this book the keys will be referred to by the names that are on them, rather than by their location.

For example, the key marked ESC or ESCAPE may be on the left or the right side of the keyboard. However, pressing ESCAPE does the same thing whether the location is left or right. Quattro Pro 3 uses the ESCAPE key the same way many other programs do, to let you change your mind. After you have selected an option from a menu, pressing ESCAPE lets you deselect the option. Keys used extensively by Quattro Pro 3 are shown in Table 1-2.

Quattro Pro 3 uses the cursor-movement keys extensively for highlighting options and moving around the screen. These are the arrow keys: UP, DOWN, LEFT, and RIGHT. These keys may be found in a separate group or may share keys with the numeric keypad. When you turn on your computer the arrow/number keys are set to arrows, just like the alphabet keys are

Figure 1-14.   *Alternative keyboard layouts*

set to lowercase. Use the SHIFT key to produce numbers instead of arrows, or lock in numbers by tapping the NUM LOCK key. This process is the same as using either SHIFT for the capital letters *A* through *Z* or locking in capital letters with the CAPS LOCK key. Full use of the cursor-movement keys is discussed when you begin working the first example in this chapter.

Quattro Pro 3 makes effective use of the function keys, labeled F1, F2, and so on. These keys are either down the left side or across the top of the keyboard, depending on the layout. The function keys as used in Quattro Pro 3 are listed in Table 1-3, and they will be explained as they are used in the examples.

Key	Purpose
ENTER	Enter data into worksheets; select highlighted menu items; confirm block coordinates and other settings
ESCAPE	Cancel changes on the edit line; exit a menu; return you to READY mode; unlock block coordinates
BACKSPACE	Remove characters to the left on the edit line; unlock block coordinates; return beginning coordinate to current cell
DELETE	Delete cell contents; remove current character from edit line
INS	Control OVERSTRIKE mode when editing
SHIFT	Used to get the upper half of any key, including capitals *A* through *Z*, symbols such as $, and numbers on the numeric keypad
CAPS LOCK	Type *A* through *Z* as capital letters without shifting; does not affect any other keys
NUM LOCK	Lock numeric pad into numbers; lock out cursor movement with those keys
SCROLL LOCK	Switch between Move and Size when adjusting windows
CTRL	Used with certain keys to execute commands, such as CTRL-BREAK, which stops macro execution, CTRL-D, which prepares cell for data entry, and CTRL-ENTER, which assigns shortcuts
PRINT SCREEN	Print current screen; this key will not print graphs
@	Precedes built-in formulas, the @functions
/	In READY mode activates the menu; in formulas used for division
\	Used as cell fill command to repeat characters; also used in naming instant macros
+	Both plus keys are used to begin formulas and perform addition. The plus key on the numeric keypad expands menus
*	Used for multiplication sign
—	Used for subtraction; the minus key on the numeric keypad contracts menus

Table 1-2. *Keys Frequently Used in Quattro Pro 3*

Key	Regular	ALT	SHIFT
F1	Help	Previous Help	
F2	Edit	Macro Menu	Debug
F3	Menu/Choice	Function List	Macro Commands
F4	Absolute		
F5	Goto	Undo	Pick Window
F6	Pane	Zoom	Next Window
F7	Query	All Select	Select
F8	Table		Move (in File Manager)
F9	Calc		Copy (in File Manager)
F10	Graph		Paste (in File Manager)

Note also ALT-N, which selects window *N*.

Table 1-3.   *Function Keys*

Starting Quattro Pro 3

A great deal of effort went into making Quattro Pro 3 an easy program to start on almost any computer. There are two steps: installing the program (something you only need to do once) and issuing the command that begins the program (something you do at the start of every Quattro Pro 3 session). Most hard disk drive systems have a hard disk drive that is called C and a floppy disk drive that is called A. To install Quattro Pro 3 you place disk 1 of the program disk into drive A and *log on* to that drive. This means that you make drive A the *active drive,* which is done by typing A : and pressing ENTER at the DOS prompt. The DOS prompt will probably look like C> or C:\> and then change to A> or A:\> when you execute this command.

With drive A active, type **INSTALL** and press ENTER to initiate the installation process. When the program files are copied onto the hard disk you will need to answer some questions about your system. Having answered these, Quattro Pro 3 will be installed and ready to use. To load

Quattro Pro 3 from the DOS prompt, type **Q** and press ENTER when you are in the QPRO directory. You will either see a screen like the one shown in Figure 1-15 or, if your computer is using the WYSIWYG mode, a screen like the one in Figure 1-16. The screen in Figure 1-16 has been annotated to show the terms used by Quattro Pro 3 for the main part of the working area. You are now ready to start working with the program. Next time you use your system, type **CD\QPRO** followed by **Q** to run the program, where QPRO is the name of the directory in which Quattro Pro 3 has been installed. If Quattro Pro 3 is installed in a different directory, apply the correct name instead of QPRO.

Startup Problems

If you do not know what the DOS prompt is or how to get to it, or if you have difficulty following the installation process described here, or if you do not get a screen similar to the ones shown in Figure 1-15 or 1-16, you should consult Appendix A. If you want to customize such things as the way Quattro Pro 3 handles your screen or the menu structure, consult

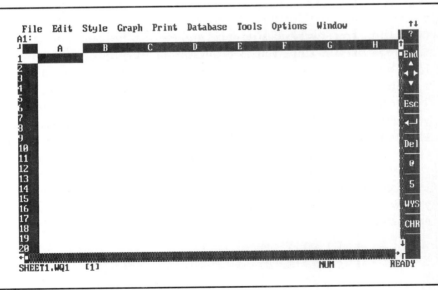

Figure 1-15. *Opening screen: character mode*

Chapter 6, "Working with Defaults." If you have a black-and-white monitor, you should start the INSTALL program using a special command or "switch" that makes the screens easier to read. You should enter INSTALL /B instead of just INSTALL.

Starting and Leaving Quattro Pro 3

As you have seen, you can start Quattro Pro 3 by typing **Q** at the DOS prompt. This is the basic method of starting the program on a hard disk. The command can be incorporated into a hard disk menu system, or

Figure 1-16. *Opening screen: WYSIWYG mode*

Quattro Pro 3 can be started automatically, as soon as your system is turned on or reset. The procedures for setting up these methods are explained in Appendix A. You can instruct Quattro Pro 3 to load a worksheet as soon as the program loads. Commands for doing so are explained in Chapter 6.

When you type **Q** and press ENTER the program loads into memory. This takes a matter of seconds, depending on the type of hardware you are using. You are then presented with the opening screen (shown in Figures 1-15 and 1-16). Leaving the program can be done in several ways and is discussed in the section "Saving and Ending" later in this chapter. Normally, you will want to store the work you have done in a file on disk. However, if you do not need to store any of your work, you can simply turn off the computer or restart it. If you want to go directly back to the DOS prompt, you can type **/** followed by **F** for File and then **x** for Exit. If you have done any work that has not been saved on disk, you will be prompted to confirm the Exit command.

Spreadsheet Concepts

This section introduces the basic concepts of spreadsheets and prepares you for the next chapter. Some brief examples demonstrate how to enter and calculate numbers with Quattro Pro 3 and familiarize you with the special keys and the menu system.

The Worksheet Area

When you first load Quattro Pro 3 you have an empty electronic work space called a *worksheet* in which to place numbers, words, and instructions (formulas and calculations). As you can see in Figures 1-15 and 1-16, there is a line of letters near the top of the screen and a list of numbers down the side. The letters represent a series of columns and the numbers a series of rows. The intersection of each column and row forms a rectangle, a box into which you put information. These boxes are called *cells*. One of them is highlighted when you start the program. This highlighted cell is called A1 because it is in column A on row 1. Every cell has a name based on its location, or *coordinates,* just like a map. You move from cell to cell to lay out information. When you first start Quattro Pro 3 you are in cell A1. If you were to enter information at this point, it would be placed in cell A1. The cell you are in is called the *current cell.*

The highlighting that marks the cell you are in is called the *cell selector.* It can be moved with the cursor keys or the arrow keys. When you move the cell selector, the horizontal and vertical borders indicate which column and row you are in, using reverse highlighting. Your exact location is recorded at the top left of the screen. A guide to your relative location within the worksheet is provided by the vertical and horizontal scroll bars on the right and bottom of the worksheet.

Worksheet Size

The worksheet is very large; the columns continue off the side of the screen through column Z. Farther columns are numbered AA through AZ, then BA through BZ, and so on. After repeating the alphabet nine and a half times, you get to the last column, IV, a total of 256 columns. The rows go beyond 20 down to 8192. Multiplying the columns and rows together gives you a total of over two million cells. Obviously your monitor can show you only a small portion of this huge work area at a time. Since the monitor can only show you about one ten thousandth of the total area of the worksheet, the screen acts like a cockpit window, showing you different parts of the worksheet as you move the cell selector around.

Quattro Pro 3 provides important information around the edge of the screen. When you are using Quattro Pro 3, the horizontal and vertical borders, the top menu bar and command line, and the bottom status area work like a dashboard or control panel. They display important information and messages. The status of the CAPS LOCK, NUM LOCK, and SCROLL LOCK keys is shown at the bottom of the screen. The *mode indicator* shows you a variety of messages about the current task. At the top of the screen the *cell identifier* shows the contents of the current cell, its display format, and its width setting.

Movement Keys

To explore the work area, press the RIGHT ARROW key once. You will see the highlighting move to the next cell to the right, B1. You are now in cell B1. Press the DOWN ARROW key once and you will be in cell B2. Notice that in the top-left corner your current location is being monitored. This is very helpful, since eyeballing your location is notably prone to error, particularly after several hours at the screen.

Your keyboard has the ability to repeat keystrokes and will do so if you lean on, rather than just tap, a key. Throughout the rest of this book you should take the term *press* to mean lightly tap rather than push and hold down. To see the keyboard repeat feature in action, press the DOWN ARROW key and hold it for two seconds. You will see the cell indicator move quickly down the screen and the numbers at the left will scroll by rapidly. You can see that you are dragging the screen with you to view a different area of the spreadsheet. Now try pressing the HOME key. It takes you back to A1.

The UP, DOWN, LEFT, and RIGHT ARROW keys move you one cell in each of their respective directions. Used with the CTRL key, the RIGHT and LEFT ARROW keys move a screen at a time across the worksheet. You hold down the CTRL key, then press the arrow key. A similar effect can be achieved with the TAB and SHIFT TAB keys, respectively. The PAGE UP and PAGE DOWN keys move you a screen at a time up and down the worksheet. The HOME key always places you in A1 (unless you are using locked titles, described in the next chapter). The END key followed by the UP, DOWN, LEFT, or RIGHT ARROW key takes you to the last cell in that direction. The last cell means the last occupied cell in a row or column and the first occupied cell if the next cell is empty. Do not use the END key like the CTRL key; you press END and then the arrow key.

The INSERT and DELETE keys are often grouped with the cursor keys. Pressing DELETE removes the contents of the current cell. Pressing INSERT changes the way that the EDIT mode works and allows you to add text to the middle of a value or label without typing over other characters.

Types of Information

Quattro Pro 3 categorizes all information into one of two types of data: values or labels. To oversimplify, values are numbers and calculations, and labels are words or text. Quattro Pro 3 treats the two categories of data differently. By looking at the first character of each new entry into the worksheet, Quattro Pro 3 determines the appropriate category for that data—value or label.

Values

To see how to enter information into Quattro Pro 3 and how the program recognizes values, try the following exercise. With the cell selector in cell A1, type **789** from the row of numbers at the top of the keyboard. Do *not* press ENTER or any other key; just observe what has happened. Notice that the number 789 has not yet been placed into the worksheet. Instead, it is on the top command line, which is now acting as the edit or input line. The cursor is flashing after the number 9. At this point you can either continue to type or use the BACKSPACE key to erase what you have typed. Also notice that a change has taken place in the bottom status area. The mode indicator now says VALUE. This tells you that Quattro Pro 3 is reading what you have typed as a value. If you pressed the ENTER key prematurely or otherwise caused the number to leave the top line of the screen, just type **789** again and observe what happens before you press ENTER.

Mode Indicator

You can now place the number 789 into the worksheet. To do so, press the ENTER key and observe that the number disappears from the edit line and is placed into the worksheet in the cell you are highlighting, as shown in Figure 1-17. The cell identifier in the top status area now lists the contents of the cell. While the cell identifier might seem like a duplication of effort, you will see in a moment that what Quattro Pro 3 shows you in the cell identifier is sometimes different from what it displays in the worksheet. The cell identifier shows the exact content of the cell as Quattro Pro 3 reads it.

When you have pressed ENTER you will also see that the mode indicator returns to READY. Notice that the numbers you have entered are placed on the right-hand side of the cell. Quattro Pro 3 normally aligns numbers

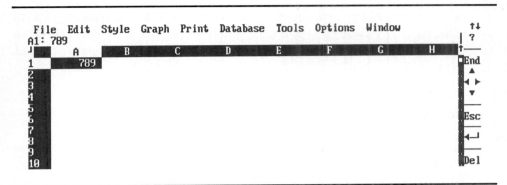

Figure 1-17.   *The first value entered in A1*

evenly with the right of the column. This is referred to as *flush-right alignment.*

Locking Capitals

Now that you are back in the READY mode, you can move to another cell. Press the RIGHT ARROW key once and you will be in cell B1. Here you will enter a label. Before you type, take a look at your keyboard and locate the CAPS LOCK key. This key allows you to type in capital letters without using the SHIFT key. Many people find it convenient to type labels all in capitals. Press the CAPS LOCK key once and notice the bottom status area reflects this change with the message CAPS. When you are locked into capitals, the letters *A* through *Z* are automatically typed as capitals. However, you must still use the SHIFT key to access symbols and commands that are on the upper half of the keys.

Labels

In a moment you are going to type the word *BASE* because you will use Quattro Pro 3 to figure out the full price of a car from, among other things, the base price. When you type the letter **B**, notice that the mode indicator says LABEL. Also notice that the word is being typed on the edit line so you can change it with the BACKSPACE key if you make an error. Type **BASE**, press ENTER, and observe the cell identifier at the top of the screen. In front of the word you typed is an apostrophe ('). The apostrophe was automatically placed there by Quattro Pro 3 as a reminder that this is a label. Although you are not likely to confuse this particular label with a number, later you will encounter instructions that look like labels but are in fact values.

The apostrophe not only tells you that this is a label but also signifies that this is a left-aligned label. Labels can either be left-aligned, right-aligned, or centered in the column. Right-aligned labels are preceded by a quotation mark ("). Centered labels begin with a caret (^), which is the shifted 6 on the keyboard. Rather than make you type one of the three label align characters (', ", or ^) before every label, Quattro Pro 3 will assume one of them. This is the *default label alignment* and, as you can see, it is left-aligned. Later you can change the default or change the alignment of a block of labels. To enter a label aligned differently from the default, just type the desired alignment before the text of the label. If you want the label to begin with one of the alignment characters, use two of them. Thus, entering **"Right On"** will actually produce a right-aligned label that reads "Right On".

Entering with Arrows and the Mouse

You will now enter another label directly below BASE. This will be the word PREP, for dealer preparation costs, but you will use a slightly different method to enter it into the cell. First press DOWN ARROW to move to cell B2, and then type **PREP**. It will appear on the edit line like the numbers **789** and **BASE** did before. Now press the DOWN ARROW key again. Doing so enters the label and moves you down to the next row. This can be a very useful feature if you want to enter a series of labels or numbers. The direction keys will enter what you are typing and move you in a particular direction with one keystroke. For this reason it is important not to press the cursor keys when you are entering information into an empty cell. Practice this method of entering by typing **TAX** and then pressing the DOWN ARROW key, followed by **TOTAL** and the DOWN ARROW key. The results will look like Figure 1-18.

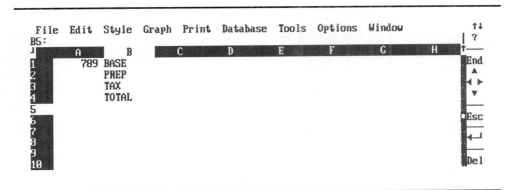

Figure 1-18.   *Entered data*

If you are using a mouse with Quattro Pro 3, you will see what you type on the Edit line preceded by [Enter] [Esc]. Click on [Enter] to confirm your entry. Click on [Esc] to cancel what you have typed. Alternatively, you can click on the Enter arrow or one of the cursor arrows in the mouse palette to make an entry or click on the Esc button in the palette to cancel an entry.

Editing Cells

Changing worksheet entries and correcting mistakes is one of the most important procedures you will need to know. In this example, 789 is a ridiculously low price for a car, so you need to change it. Press HOME; you will be highlighting cell A1 and the number 789. To change a cell entry completely, just type a new entry. Type **8000** and press ENTER. Do *not* put commas in the thousands when entering numbers in Quattro Pro 3; they will be put in later. The new number completely replaces the old one.

What if you want to modify the contents of the cell, rather than completely replace them? For example, you might want to change 8000 to 8095 to reflect a price increase. When you do not need to completely change a cell, you can change part of it using the Edit key, F2. In this case, you press F2 while your cell selector is in A1. When you do so, the contents of the cell are returned to the edit line as shown in Figure 1-19. Press BACKSPACE to back over the last two zeroes, and type **95**. Now press ENTER to see the

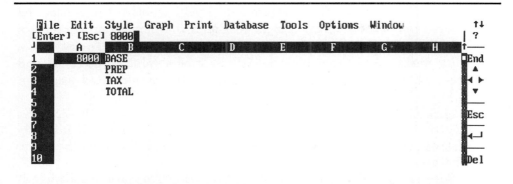

Figure 1-19. *Editing a cell*

modified contents returned to the cell. Note that if you using a mouse with Quattro Pro 3 you will see [Enter] [Esc] on the edit line when you are editing. You can click on [Enter] to confirm the contents as they exist on the edit line, or you can click on [Esc] to cancel the editing and restore the cell contents as they were before you began editing.

Suppose you now want to add a figure for dealer preparation costs to the worksheet. First press DOWN ARROW once. You will be in cell A2. Type the number **567**, and enter it into the cell by pressing the DOWN ARROW key. You are now in cell A3 and ready to do some math with Quattro Pro 3.

Instructions and Formulas

In cell A3 you want a figure for the tax that must be paid on the base price of the car. Assume that the tax rate is 10% or 0.1. The figure you want in cell A3 is 8095×0.1. You want Quattro Pro 3 to calculate this for you, so you are going to type an instruction into cell A3 that will tell the program to multiply the number in cell A1 by 0.1 and place the answer in cell A3. Note that you are not going to tell the program simply to multiply the number 8095 by 0.1. Quattro Pro 3 can do that, but that is not the true power of a spreadsheet. What you want to do is establish a relationship between the cells so that, even if the number in A1 changes, the relationship will remain and A3 will continue to give you 0.1 times the content of

A1. The instruction will be entered as **.1*A1** . Quattro Pro 3 uses the asterisk for a multiplication sign. Although the instruction contains a letter as well as numbers, the program considers the decimal point to be a *value indicator* and so reads what follows it as a value. Type **.1*A1** and press ENTER. You will immediately see the tax figure calculated, as shown in Figure 1-20.

Look at the cell identifier in the second line of the screen. Notice that Quattro Pro 3 is not concerned about the actual number in cell A3. It simply records the relationship between the two cells. This will remain the same, whatever number is in cell A1.

Suppose that the base price goes up. Press HOME to move to 8095 in cell A1. Change it by typing **8900**, the new price, and pressing ENTER. Instantly, Quattro Pro 3 updates cell A3. If you move the cell selector down to cell A3 and look at the cell identifier, you will see that the cell contents have not changed. They are still the same formula you entered before.

Now you want to calculate a total price for the car including the base price, preparation costs, and tax. You will need to add several cells together. To do this, first place the cell selector in the cell that is to contain the answer—in this case, cell A4. Now you will type an instruction that tells Quattro Pro 3 that this cell will contain the sum of cells A1, A2, and A3. You might think that you could type **A1+A2+A3**, and this is almost correct. However, instructions involving only cell references need special treatment because Quattro Pro 3 will read the letter *A* as a label. To get around this and to make sure that Quattro Pro 3 knows that what you are typing is a value, type a plus sign first and then the cell reference. Make

Figure 1-20.   *Calculation entered*

sure the cell selector is in A4, and then type the formula **+A1+A2+A3** and press ENTER.

The Function Instruction

If you decided to take out a loan to finance the full price of this car, you might want to calculate how big a monthly payment you would have to make. A loan payment calculation involves three pieces of information. Labels for these three items will be typed into column D, starting in D1. Move the cell selector to D1. Then, using the DOWN ARROW key to enter them, type the three labels **PRINCIPAL, INTEREST,** and **TERM.** Also type one more label, **PAYMENT,** and then move back up to cell E1 where you will enter the principal amount. Your screen should look like Figure 1-21. The amount you want to finance is the total price from cell A4. Instead of typing the number again, simply type **+A4** and press ENTER. This establishes a relationship between these two cells so that whatever is in cell A4 is also in cell E1.

Now move the cell selector to E2. Here you want to enter the rate of interest you will pay. This needs to be expressed as a rate per period of the loan. Suppose you are going to make monthly payments. You need to enter the amount of interest you will pay in one month. If the bank is charging 12% per annum (A.P.R.), the rate is 0.01, or 1%, per month. Type **.01** in cell E2 and press DOWN ARROW to go to cell E3. In this cell type the term, the number of months for the loan, say **36**, and press DOWN ARROW.

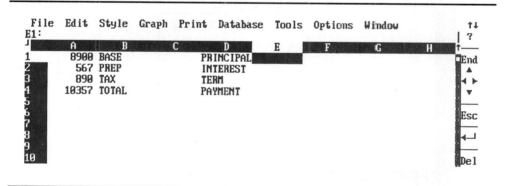

Figure 1-21. *More labels entered*

A formula for the payment will be entered in cell E4. You do not need to know the actual formula. Quattro Pro 3 knows exactly how to calculate a loan payment if it is given the principal, interest, and term because it has a special built-in function. In fact there are dozens of built-in functions covering most common calculations. Press the Function Choices key, ALT-F3, and you will see a list of these pop up over the worksheet, as in Figure 1-22. Press PAGE DOWN and you will see more of these formulas. Press PAGE DOWN until you see the function you need, @PMT. Highlight the @PMT function and press ENTER. The function will be typed on the edit line for you and the menu of choices will disappear. Notice that the name of the function is preceded by the @ sign (shifted number 2 on the keyboard). This is a special code that helps Quattro Pro 3 distinguish functions from other entries. This gives rise to the term *@functions* for the built-in formulas that use this code.

The @PMT function needs to know the amounts for principal, interest, and term of the loan. This information is presented to the function within parentheses so the next character that you type needs to be the open parenthesis, (. Now type **E1,E2,E3)** and press ENTER. These three entries are called *arguments*—cell numbers in this case. Most functions require some sort of argument to operate.

Figure 1-22. *Functions list*

You do not have to use the Function Choices key to create this formula. You can press ESCAPE to remove the Choices menu and return to the READY mode. With the cell selector in E4, you could simply type the entire formula **@PMT(E1,E2,E3)** and press ENTER to place it into the cell. Either method is acceptable and produces the monthly payment, as shown in Figure 1-23.

To give you an idea of how flexible a spreadsheet can be, you can now try some changes to the assumptions that produce the answer in E4. For example, if you were considering a more expensive model you could type the new price in A1 and immediately see the new payment in E4. To make payments less expensive each month, type in a longer term, such as 48 months, into E3.

Using the Menu System

The manipulation of facts and figures in cells is only part of the power of Quattro Pro 3. A whole range of commands arranged in a series of menus and submenus can be accessed through the menu bar at the top of the screen by pressing the MENU key, which is the forward slash key. Type **/**,

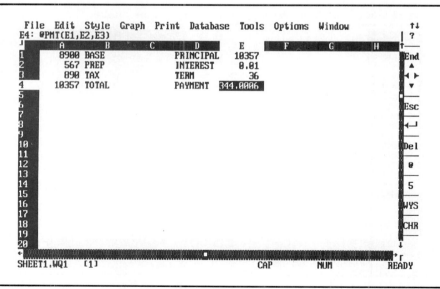

Figure 1-23.   *The monthly payment*

and you will see that the menu bar is activated, with the first option, File, highlighted. You can use the RIGHT ARROW key to highlight Edit, and continue across the bar to highlight each of the items in turn. Notice that the word MENU appears in the mode indicator at the lower right of the screen. An explanation of what each of the items does is given on the bottom row of the screen.

Now type **F** or DOWN ARROW and the first menu, File, will be pulled down, as shown in Figure 1-24. The items you see listed in the box are the categories of file operation that Quattro Pro 3 offers. The words across the bottom of the screen tell you what the option on the menu does. For example, in Figure 1-24 the item "New" is highlighted. You can see that this opens a new spreadsheet window. You can pull down each of the menus in turn by pressing the RIGHT ARROW key with the File menu visible. If you keep pressing RIGHT ARROW or LEFT ARROW you will return to the File menu.

You can select any item on a menu by typing the highlighted letter, which is usually the first letter. Alternatively, you can first press DOWN ARROW to put the menu bar on the desired option and then press ENTER. Try moving the highlight to the word Utilities and you will see the message "Access DOS, the file manager, for settings for compressing files." Notice

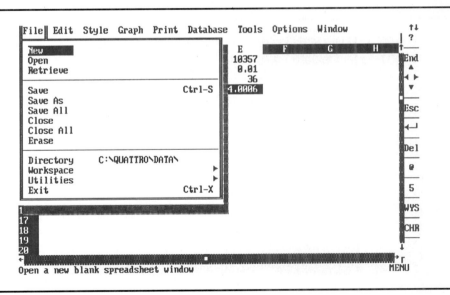

Figure 1-24.   *The File menu*

that this menu item has a small triangle next to it. This means that a submenu will appear when this item is selected. Select the Utilities option and you will see DOS Shell, File Manager, and SQZ! Press CTRL-BREAK to go back one step in the menu system. You leave the menu completely by pressing ESCAPE until you are back in the READY mode.

Saving and Ending

Having completed this series of calculations, you may decide to take a break. You need to think about where the information you have created is located. So far, all of the work you have been doing is in the computer's memory. The only problem with this is that the memory is only as good as the power to your computer. If you accidentally pull the plug or suffer an electrical failure, the memory's contents are lost. You must transfer the data to permanent storage on disk. This has to be done on a regular basis and should always be done before you leave your PC unattended.

Type / to bring up the menu and then type **F** for File. Now type **S** for Save and you will see a prompt like the one in Figure 1-25. You can type

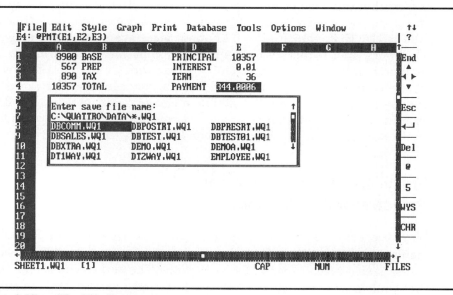

Figure 1-25.   *The File Save prompt*

in a name for the file into which you want Quattro Pro 3 to store this worksheet. The name can be any eight letters or numbers, like QLOAN101, but no spaces are allowed within the name (QLOAN_MY is acceptable). Although you can use some punctuation in file names, not all punctuation characters are valid in file names. For this reason, it is best to avoid punctuation when naming files. For complete details on file naming, see Chapter 7. When you have typed the name, press ENTER.

Note that the first time you save a spreadsheet the program will suggest storing it on the same drive and directory you started the program from, typically C:\QPRO or C:\QUATTRO. You may want to avoid storing data files among program files. To change this before saving the file, select Directory from the File menu and type the name of a data file directory for a hard drive system. Then press ENTER. From now on until you restart the program, Quattro Pro 3 will save spreadsheets to this directory rather than to the directory occupied by the program files.

To make this change permanent, you can type / and select Options, Start-up, and then Directory. Enter the desired drive and directory and press ENTER, and then press ESCAPE to return to the Options menu. Now select Update, which will place your choice in a small file on the disk. Quattro Pro 3 refers to this configuration file every time you load the program.

Now that you have saved your work, you can either turn off your system or return to DOS by typing / to activate the menu and selecting File followed by Exit. Quattro Pro 3 knows if you have not saved changes to your work and, if this is the case, will prompt you to confirm the Exit command. If you do not want to stop working with Quattro Pro 3 but want to begin a fresh file after saving the last one, you can clear the worksheet area by typing /, selecting File, and then Erase. Again, Quattro Pro 3 will prompt for confirmation if you have not saved changes to the worksheet on the screen. For more information on file saving, see Chapter 7.

Entry, Movement, and Menu Selection with a Mouse

With the excellent mouse interface built into Quattro Pro 3 and the increasing popularity of these devices you may well want to try using a mouse to select cells, commands, and actions. The first step is to make sure that your mouse and mouse driver are installed correctly. If the mouse is installed, then Quattro Pro 3 will place a *mouse pointer* on the screen for you. This is a small rectangle if you are displaying Quattro Pro 3 in character mode, or a small arrow if you are using graphics mode. If you are having trouble seeing the mouse pointer, just move the mouse and you should see the pointer move on the screen. If a mouse pointer fails to appear, check the installation instructions that came with the mouse and the mouse notes in Appendix A of this book.

In Figure 1-25 you can see the mouse palette on the right of the screen. This is the way it appears in character mode. Clicking on Esc is the same as pressing ESCAPE, and clicking on the crooked arrow is the same as pressing ENTER. Mouse actions consist of pointing, clicking, and dragging. *Pointing* means placing the mouse pointer over a specific object on the screen. *Clicking* means pressing and then quickly releasing the mouse button when you are pointing to an object. Quattro Pro 3 uses just one mouse button; if your mouse has more than one button, use the button on the left. *Dragging* means pointing to an object and then holding down the mouse button while moving the mouse. For example, you can point to cell B2 and then drag the mouse pointer to cell D10 to highlight cells B2 through D10. When you release the mouse button the cells remain selected.

The mouse can be very powerful when using Quattro Pro 3. For example, to delete the contents of a cell you can click on the cell, and then click on Del in the mouse palette to pick Delete. To erase a group of cells you can drag the highlight across the cells in question and then click on Del. You can use the mouse to pick menu items by clicking on the item you want. Any command that requires a group of cells to be selected will accept cells highlighted by dragging with the mouse. To dismiss a pull-down menu you do not have to press ESCAPE—you can just click anywhere on the worksheet.

Quattro Pro 3 allows you to preselect cells for some commands such as formatting. Thus you can highlight a block of cells using the mouse, and then use the Style Numeric Format command to assign a format to all of the cells. The selected cells are automatically assumed to be the ones to which you want to apply the command.

Parts of Quattro Pro 3 consist of lists, which you can navigate with the mouse. You can see a list *scroll bar* on the right of the file list in Figure 1-25. The worksheet scroll bars and the rest of the mouse palette are described in detail in Appendix A. In general this book assumes that mouse users are among the more adventurous and will probably discover for themselves what the mouse can do. In order to avoid the book getting too long and unwieldy there are not separate mouse instructions for every activity. However, when the mouse has a particularly useful or important role to play, then appropriate references are made and the palette is displayed.

Spreadsheet Practice

To practice data entry, you can type in the values and labels shown in Figure 1-26. This particular model is a record of passenger volume figures for Take Over Airlines, Inc., over a four-year period. Four main destinations are served by Take Over Airlines (TOA) and the volume figures are listed by destination.

In a new worksheet, move down to A4 where you will enter the title Cities. Type **Cities:** and press RIGHT ARROW to enter this label and prepare to type the first year of the model in cell B4. Later in this book you will learn several different ways of handling dates and calendar information in Quattro Pro 3, including sophisticated date arithmetic. In this situation you can simply type **1989** and press RIGHT ARROW to enter it and move to C4 for the next year.

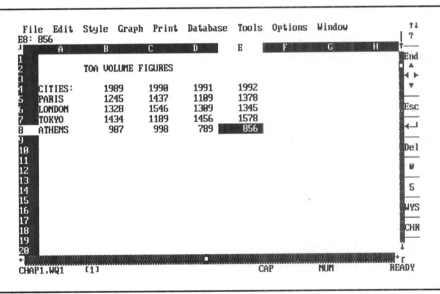

Figure 1-26.   *The TOA volume figures*

However, instead of typing 1990, this time you will create the year by adding one to the previous year. This is the formula 1+B4, which does not need an additional plus sign in front of it because 1 is a value indicator. Type **1+B4** and press RIGHT ARROW. Now type **1+C4** and again press RIGHT ARROW. Then type **1+D4**, and this time press ENTER. You can return to B4, update that cell to 1990, and see the other years change automatically. In the next chapter you will see that there are shortcuts to entering a series of similar formulas such as the ones used here for the years.

Now go to cell A4 and enter the city names. The DOWN ARROW key will work well for this. Follow the city names with the numbers shown in Figure 1-26. These numbers will be used in several later examples. When you are done entering all of the cities and their data, save this information in a file named CHAP1.WQ1. You will then be able to recall the file for use in Chapter 2.

2 *Spreadsheet Commands*

Chapter 1 introduced the Quattro Pro 3 spreadsheet and told you how it can be used. In the example at the end of that chapter you saw how the Quattro Pro 3 screen acts like a pilot's control panel, providing you with valuable information and status reports as you navigate around the huge worksheet. You also experimented with the basics of entering data and saved your work to a disk file for later retrieval. In this chapter you will find spreadsheet commands explored in depth with practical examples.

Starting a Spreadsheet Session

When you load Quattro Pro 3 you are presented with a worksheet *window,* called window [1]. This window contains an empty worksheet that is a grid of more than two million cells. You can enter new information into this blank worksheet, or if you have already stored a spreadsheet, you can retrieve it from disk. The empty worksheet that is presented when you first load Quattro Pro 3 is called SHEET 1. Its file name is SHEET1.WQ1. The worksheet name appears in the status line at the bottom-left corner of the screen, as you can see in Figure 2-1. This is the default name—the name that Quattro Pro 3 will use unless you issue instructions to the contrary.

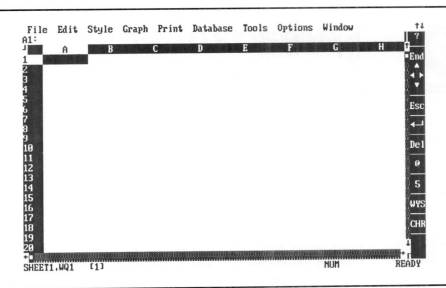

Figure 2-1.   *The opening screen*

Multiple Windows

An important distinction to bear in mind when using Quattro Pro 3 is between worksheets and worksheet windows. In Figure 2-2 you can see four different worksheets: SHEET1.WQ1, REVENUE.WQ1, EX-PENSE.WQ1, and PROFIT.WQ1. Each worksheet is in a separate worksheet window: SHEET1.WQ1 is in window [1], REVENUE.WQ1 is in window [2], EXPENSE.WQ1 is in window [3], and PROFIT.WQ1 is in window [4]. However, it is important to distinguish between the window and the worksheet that occupies it. For example, PROFIT.WQ1 could just as easily appear in window [2], with REVENUE.WQ1 in window [4]. The number of the window in which a particular worksheet appears is determined by the order in which the worksheets were created or read from disk.

This distinction becomes clearer as you consider a typical work session with Quattro Pro 3, which begins by opening window [1] and filling it with a fresh SHEET1. At any time during your work on SHEET1, you can use the File New command to open up a second worksheet window containing a second empty worksheet. This second worksheet is initially called

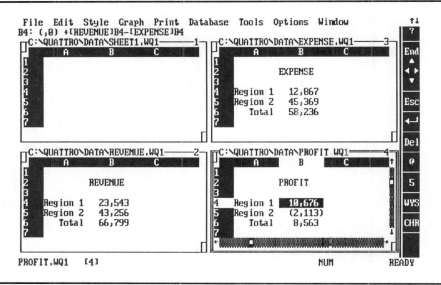

Figure 2-2.   *Several worksheets*

SHEET2.WQ1, and it appears without your having to close the first. The second worksheet is as large as the first, and it is positioned on the top of the first, obscuring it like a document placed on top of another in a pile, as shown in Figure 2-3. Note the number 2 in square brackets on the status line, which is telling you that this is the second worksheet window that you have open.

When you have several worksheet windows open, you can display them all on the screen at once by using the Window Tile command. The effect was shown in Figure 2-2 and can also be seen in Figure 2-4, where two windows are open. This arrangement is referred to as *tiling*. An alternative method of showing that more than one window is open is to use *stacking*. You can see the effect of the Window Stack command in Figure 2-5.

Only one worksheet window at a time can be the *current window*, which is the one you are actively using. This window contains the worksheet or document that will be affected by the commands you issue, and its name appears on the lower left of the screen. The current worksheet window is also marked by double lines around it, instead of single, so you can see that QSOUTH.WQ1 is the active document and window [1] the active window in Figures 2-4 and 2-5.

Figure 2-3. *Second worksheet on top of first*

Figure 2-4. *Two windows tiled*

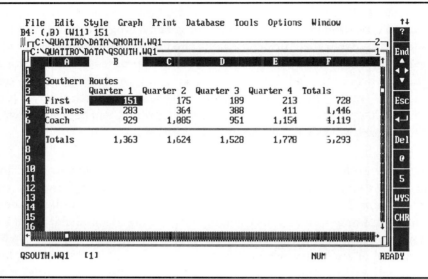

Figure 2-5.   *Two windows stacked*

Bringing Back Stored Files

When you use the File New command to create a fresh worksheet, you open
a new document, and the contents of those documents that are already
open are not affected. If you want to work on a spreadsheet that you have
already stored on disk you have two commands to choose from: File Open
and File Retrieve.

Opening Files   The File Open command opens up a new worksheet
window and reads a file from disk into it. Because this command does not
affect any of the other windows or their contents it is a safe way to read
existing files from disk. However, there are disadvantages to reckless use
of File Open. If you open too many new windows without closing ones you
are not using, you will burden your computer unnecessarily. Not only will
you notice that your system response time slows down, but opening more
windows than you really need makes it difficult to keep track of your work.

Retrieving Files   When you use the File Retrieve command to read a
worksheet file from disk, you bring it into the current worksheet window,

replacing all two million cells of the worksheet that is already occupying the current window. This means you erase anything that was entered into the current worksheet prior to issuing the File Retrieve command. For this reason, you should be sure to save any work in progress before performing the retrieval operation. When working on one spreadsheet you may decide that you would like to see a different spreadsheet. Fortunately, Quattro Pro 3 is keeping track of your work and will prompt you before overwriting the current worksheet, as shown in Figure 2-6.

The Transcript Feature   In addition to prompting before overwriting or erasing data, Quattro Pro 3 has a "disaster recovery" facility called *Transcript*. This feature keeps track of your keystrokes—both data entries and commands—and stores them in a special log file on disk. If you suffer a power loss or if you accidentally delete some data, as in the case of a hasty retrieval of another worksheet, you can recall the lost data by replaying your actions from the Transcript log. Refer to Chapter 7 for details on using Transcript.

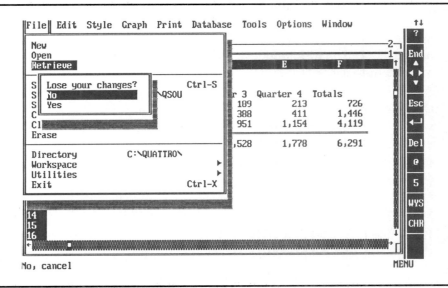

Figure 2-6.   *Lose changes prompt*

Using the File List

Suppose that you have started Quattro Pro 3 and decide to retrieve a
worksheet stored on disk. You do this by typing / to activate the menu and
pressing ENTER to select File. When you select Retrieve from the File menu,
a list of previously saved worksheet files appears, as shown in Figure 2-7.
This is an alphabetical list that grows as you add more files. The maximum
number of files you can see is 12. Any more files must be scrolled into view
with the cursor-movement keys or mouse manipulation of the scroll bar on
the right of the box.

You pick one of these files by using the cursor-movement keys to
highlight the name and then pressing ENTER. Alternatively, you can type
the file name and press ENTER.

A copy of the file is read from the disk into the computer's memory. In
Figure 2-8 you can see the retrieved TOA worksheet from Chapter 1. Notice
that the cell selector is on the same cell on which you left it when the file
was stored to disk. This feature allows you to return to the point where
you left off. If you leave the cell selector on the fringe of your worksheet
and then retrieve the file some time later, you may be confused about the

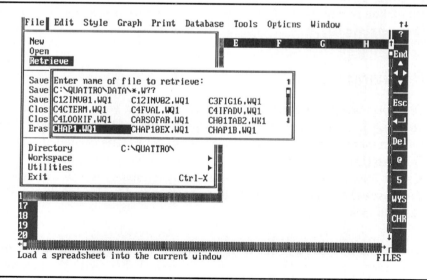

Figure 2-7.   *File Retrieve command*

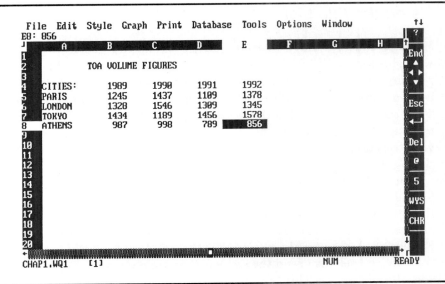

Figure 2-8. *Retrieved worksheet*

location of the cell selector. For this reason, some people prefer to press HOME before saving their work so that the worksheet looks familiar when they retrieve it.

Resaving Files

Once you begin to make changes to a worksheet, you should save the file on a regular basis. You do this because the copy of the worksheet that you have in memory disappears if the power to your PC is turned off. Although Quattro Pro 3 can recover your work using its Transcript feature, it is still a good idea to save your files regularly, perhaps every 15 minutes. This decreases the amount of rebuilding that Transcript has to do should you suffer a loss of power.

Automatic File Save When you save a worksheet you must decide whether to overwrite the old version of the worksheet with the new version or to put the new version in a new file and give it a different name. To save a worksheet over the top of the original version you type / and then select File and Save (/FS). Quattro Pro 3 uses the file name that appears in the lower left of the screen, which is the default file name.

Prompted File Save As   To save the current worksheet to a new file name, you use File Save As (/FA). A prompt will appear asking you for the file name to use. The existing, or default, name from the lower left of the screen is displayed, as shown in Figure 2-9. At this point you can accept the name by pressing ENTER or by clicking the mouse button.

   Accepting the default name might seem like the same action as using the File Save command. However, with both File Save and File Save As, Quattro Pro 3 will check to see whether a file of the same name exists on disk. If it does, then you will be prompted as shown in Figure 2-10. Your choices are Cancel, Replace, and Backup. Generally you will want to replace the older version until the worksheet design is complete. Then you may want to save different sets of numbers in different files, in which case you pick Cancel and repeat the File Save As command, entering a new name instead of the default name.

   To change the default file name in the save file prompt you can just type the name you want. This will automatically replace what is already there.

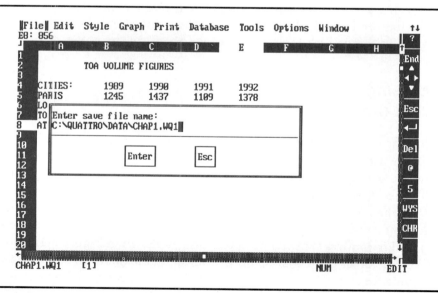

Figure 2-9.   *File Save As command*

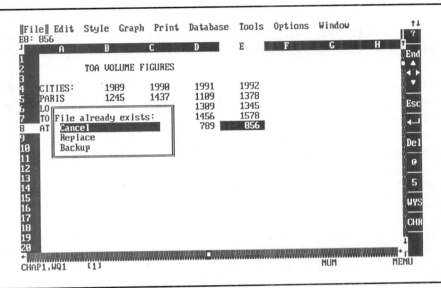

Figure 2-10. *"File already exists" prompt*

Alternatively, you can edit the default file name by pressing the Edit key (F2), followed by other editing keys to change the name. The keys that you can use are listed in Table 2-1. When the name is typed correctly you can press ENTER or click the mouse button to confirm the name.

Erasing Worksheets
And Closing Windows

When you have saved a spreadsheet and want to build a new one, you can either use the File Erase command to clear the entire worksheet window, or you can open a fresh worksheet window with the File New command. To clear the worksheet window, type / and select File followed by Erase. If there has been no change to the worksheet since you saved it, you will get a clean work area immediately. If there are unsaved changes, you are asked to confirm that you want to erase, as shown in Figure 2-11. Quattro Pro 3 asks for confirmation of several commands like this one that could have a drastic effect. In this case the File Erase command erases all two

Key	Action
LEFT ARROW	Moves cursor 1 character left
RIGHT ARROW	Moves cursor 1 character right
HOME	Moves cursor to first character
END	Moves cursor to the right of last character
TAB	Moves cursor 5 characters to the right
CTRL-RIGHT ARROW	Moves cursor 5 characters to the right
SHIFT-TAB	Moves cursor 5 characters to the left
CTRL-LEFT ARROW	Moves cursor 5 characters to the left
DELETE	Deletes character at cursor
INSERT	Toggles between INSERT and OVERSTRIKE modes
BACKSPACE	Deletes character to left of cursor
ESCAPE	Cancels editing
ENTER	Enters contents of edited cell
DOWN ARROW	Enters contents of edited cell
UP ARROW	Enters contents of edited cell
PAGE DOWN	Enters contents of edited cell
PAGE UP	Enters contents of edited cell

Note: If you add a math sign to the end of a formula in EDIT mode, you can use the cursor-movement keys or mouse for the pointing method of formula writing. You can do this after typing a math sign in the middle of a formula if you press F2 before pointing.

Table 2-1.   *Role of Keys in EDIT Mode*

million cells from memory. Note that the File Erase command does not affect files that are stored on disk. To delete files from disk you use the File Utilities command described in Chapter 7.

When you use File Erase to clear a worksheet window, you do not close the window. The window remains open and the file name in the lower-left corner of the screen remains as it was before the File Erase command was issued. The command to close a window is File Close. This reduces the number of open windows by closing the current window. For example, in Figure 2-2 the File Close command would close PROFIT.WQ1, leaving three windows open. When you give the File Close command and you have unsaved changes in the worksheet currently occupying the window, Quattro Pro 3 will ask you for confirmation before carrying out the command.

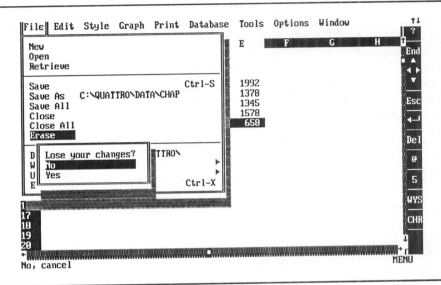

Figure 2-11.   *File Erase prompt*

Getting Down to Work

Now that you know how Quattro Pro 3 handles opening and closing your work area, the next few sections discuss the ways in which the program handles worksheet defaults and data entry.

Worksheet Defaults

In a program as flexible as Quattro Pro 3, you can change many aspects of the way the program works. For example, the columns can be from 1 to 254 characters wide. However, the program gives a new worksheet some basic settings known as the *defaults*. A default is what the program does, or assumes, unless you tell it differently. For example, you have seen that the name of the worksheet in the current worksheet window is referred to as the default file name.

In a new worksheet the default columns are wide enough to accommodate nine characters; labels are aligned on the left; and the format for showing numbers is the *General format*. The General format shows numbers with no commas in the thousands and no decimal places (unless they are entered or calculated by a formula). A calculation resulting in many decimal places is shown in the General format with as many decimal places as will fit in the cell. (Changing the worksheet to other formats is described in detail later in this chapter in the section entitled "Format Commands.")

When you start working on a spreadsheet, you can change the default settings for that worksheet; for example, you can make all columns ten characters wide. (The commands for controlling columns are discussed later in this chapter.) You can also change the defaults permanently so that you always have columns that are ten characters wide. You can change other default settings of the program such as colors and displayed items. (Chapter 6 explains how to make these changes.)

Data Entry

As discussed in Chapter 1, there are two types of data in a spreadsheet: values and labels. There are also two methods of entering data into the spreadsheet, whether you are entering values or labels. You can either type your entry and press ENTER, which puts the data into the cell and leaves that cell highlighted; or you can type your entry and press a cursor-movement key, which enters the data and moves you in the direction of the key you pressed. In both cases, you put the cell selector on the cell where you want to enter the data before you begin typing. The labels and numbers in Figure 2-12 were entered by pointing to the first row of the column, typing the first entry, pressing DOWN ARROW, typing the next entry, pressing DOWN ARROW, and so on.

Canceling an Entry

At times you will need to change or cancel an entry as you type it. One common situation in which this occurs is when you start typing a piece of new data and realize that your cell selector is pointing to the wrong cell, possibly one that already has data in it. Data that you type first appears on the input line near the top of the screen. Pressing ENTER or an arrow key or clicking on Enter at this point will place the data from the input line into the wrong cell. If there is already data in the cell, the new data will replace the old, and you will have to re-enter the old data. If the cell is

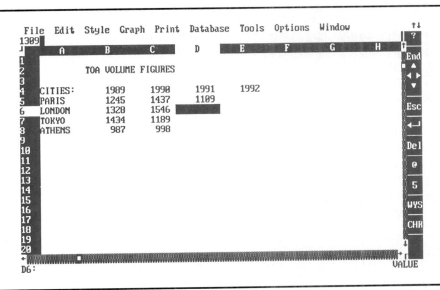

Figure 2-12. *Entering data*

empty but is the wrong cell for the new data, you will have to remove the incorrect entry. Fortunately, Quattro Pro 3 lets you change your mind before you enter what is on the input line. If you press ESCAPE or click on Escape, whatever you have typed is removed from the input line, and you are back in the READY mode. Then you can move the cell selector to the correct location.

If you start typing a new piece of data in the right place but make an error or a spelling mistake, use the BACKSPACE key to back the cursor over the data on the input line until you have erased the error, and then resume typing. Remember, you should *not* press the LEFT ARROW key to go back and correct mistakes while typing a new entry. Doing so will enter the data into the cell.

Cell Editing

After you have entered data, the data appears on the input line whenever the cell is selected. You can change the contents of a cell in several ways. Which method you use will depend upon the type of change you need to make. The following paragraphs explain the different ways of editing, using the data in Figure 2-12 as an example.

Re-Entry When you re-enter data into a cell, the contents of the cell are changed. The simplest method of re-entry is to type the new data over the old, completely replacing it. For example, if you place the cell selector on the word *LONDON*, type **ROME**, and press ENTER, the entire word *LONDON* will disappear, not just the first four letters.

The Edit Key If you want to change the label *LONDON* to *LONDON-HEATHROW*, you can avoid retyping the entire entry by using the Edit key (F2). When you place the cell selector on a cell and press F2, the contents of the cell are returned to the input line and the mode indicator displays EDIT. The status line at the bottom of the screen changes to show you what cell you are editing and what was in the cell before it was entered. With the cell contents back on the input line you can now add to the cell contents and place the revised entry back in the worksheet by pressing ENTER. (Mouse users can assign the Edit key to one of the three user-defined mouse buttons on the mouse palette, as described in Chapter 6.)

When you are in EDIT mode several keys perform differently. Pressing HOME moves the cursor to the left side of the entry. Pressing END places the cursor back on the right side. You can also move around the contents of the cell with the LEFT and RIGHT ARROW keys. Thus, if you mistakenly entered **LUNDON - EATHROW**, you could press F2 to edit the cell, press the LEFT ARROW key until your cursor is under the erroneous *U*, and then press the DELETE key to remove it, as in the following:

LUNDON - EATHROW to LNDON - EATHROW

You could then type **O** to insert it into the text to the left of the cursor.

LONDON - EATHROW

You would then move to the right with the RIGHT ARROW key to put the cursor under the *E*. There you would type **H** to complete the editing. You can press ENTER regardless of where your cursor is within the data, and the revised information will be placed back into the cell from the input line.

While you are editing a cell in EDIT mode, you are also in INSERT mode, where what you type is inserted into the text instead of replacing what was there before. However, you can get into OVERSTRIKE mode by pressing the INSERT key. When you press INSERT during editing, the message OVR appears in the status area at the bottom of the screen. Quattro Pro 3 automatically reverts to INSERT mode when you leave EDIT mode. Table 2-1 lists the keys you can use in EDIT mode.

Cell Delete   There will be times when you will want to erase the entire contents of a cell. The correct way to clear out a cell is with the Cell Delete key, or DELETE. Simply put the cell selector in the cell you want to erase and press DELETE or click on Del in the mouse palette. If you want to erase a whole group of cells, you can use the Extend key (SHIFT-F7) and select the cells before pressing DELETE, as explained in the section "Block Editing Commands" later in this chapter.

You may already know another method of erasing a cell that is used in other spreadsheet programs that do not have a Cell Delete key. You place the cell selector on the cell you want to delete and press the SPACEBAR and ENTER. With this method it appears that the cell has been emptied. But the cell identifier displays an apostrophe, which begins a label. You have replaced what was in the cell with a blank label. This method of cell deleting is a bad habit to get into, since the cell is not really emptied. It can also affect some calculations that include those cells. Blank cells are hard to find since there is nothing to see in them unless you first place the cell selector on one and observe the cell identifier. Consequently this method of blanking cells should be avoided.

Edit/Calc   When you enter a formula into a cell, what you see on the worksheet is the value that results from that formula. However, Quattro Pro 3 records the formula and displays it in the cell identifier when you highlight the cell that contains the formula. The formula remains dynamic; that is, the value it displays will change when cells or functions referenced in the formula change. At times you will want to "freeze" the results of a formula and convert the formula to the value it created. One way to do this is to edit the cell. When you press F2 to edit a cell that contains a formula, the formula is placed on the input line. You press the Calc key (F9) to convert the formula to its result. You then press ENTER to place the value in the worksheet and replace the formula.

For example, suppose you are assembling passenger volume figures for TOA, and you are missing the number of passengers for Paris in the first year of the table. If you are in a hurry, you might decide to estimate the

Paris number in Figure 2-12 by multiplying the numbers for London by a fraction. In cell B5 you enter **0.89∗B6**. However, if you leave cell B5 dependent on B6, someone might see that it is a formula and not a real number. You simply highlight B5, press F9, and then press ENTER to replace the formula with the actual number it created. In Chapter 3 you will read how to convert whole blocks of formula cells into their values by using the Edit Values command.

Automatic Editing

If you enter data that Quattro Pro 3 cannot read, pressing ENTER to place the data in a cell will result in a beep and possibly a message box on the screen. For example, Quattro Pro 3 does not accept numbers that contain commas. In Figure 2-13 you can see the effect of entering **1,000**. The "Invalid character" message appears and the mode indicator has changed to ERROR. You can press ENTER or ESCAPE to remove the message. Quattro Pro 3 will automatically place you in EDIT mode. It will also point out your error by placing the cursor at the first mistake it reads in what you have tried to enter. In this case, the program will place the cursor under the superfluous comma so that you can press DELETE to remove it. The corrected data can then be placed into the cell with ENTER. If you press ESCAPE three times at a data-entry error message, you will completely cancel the erroneous entry.

Quattro Pro 3 not only tries to show you where the error lies, but gives you different error messages depending upon the type of error. For example, if you were trying to calculate a loan payment (as was shown in Chapter 1) but you misspelled the @PMT function as **@PAYMENT**, you would get the "Unknown @-function" message. Many errors in data entry give rise to the "Invalid cell or block address" message, which indicates that the program is attempting to read what you have typed as a formula. This error arises when you want to enter an address, such as **123 Main St.**, a problem dealt with later in this chapter.

Format Commands

The difference between the numbers you see in the left and right halves of Figure 2-14 is a result of a change in the Numeric Format. This feature

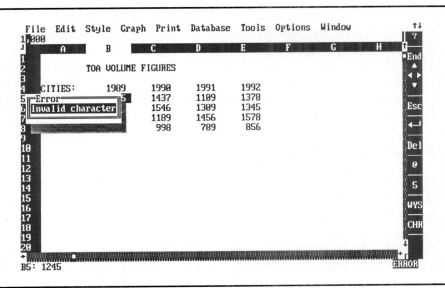

Figure 2-13.   *"Invalid character" error*

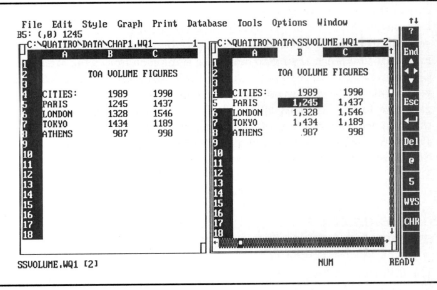

Figure 2-14.   *Two formats*

determines how your numbers look. You will recall that Quattro Pro 3 does not permit commas in numbers when you enter them. Commas, leading dollars signs, parentheses for negative numbers, and the number of decimal places are all functions of the Numeric Format.

Numeric Formats

The appearance of numbers in the worksheet is controlled by the program through the Numeric Format. In fact, the ability to change the way a number is displayed is a very powerful aspect of Quattro Pro 3, saving you a lot of typing and retyping. Quattro Pro 3 initially uses the General format for numbers. This format shows decimal places only when you enter them or when you enter formulas that result in values with decimal places. The program calculates as many as 15 decimal places. When a formula creates a number with decimal places, the decimals are displayed until the complete number is shown or until the cell is filled, whichever comes first. For example, given the following cells, the General format will show cell D4 as **2.5**, cell D5 as **3.333333**, and cell D6 as **0.333333**.

B4:	5	C4: 2	D4: +B4/C4	=	2.5
B5:	10	C5: 3	D5: +B5/C5	=	3.333333
B6:	1	C6: 3	D6: +B6/C6	=	0.333333

Because this format results in the decimal place appearing at a different position in the column, you may want to use a different format for values such as dollars and cents.

Default Format

The Numeric Format used by Quattro Pro 3 can be changed for a part of the worksheet or for all of it. If all or most of the numbers in a worksheet are dollars, you might want to choose the Currency format as your default format. To change the overall, or *global*, format, type /, select Options, Formats, and then Numeric Format. The menu you see in Figure 2-15 shows all of the Numeric format choices. They are listed with examples in Table 2-2.

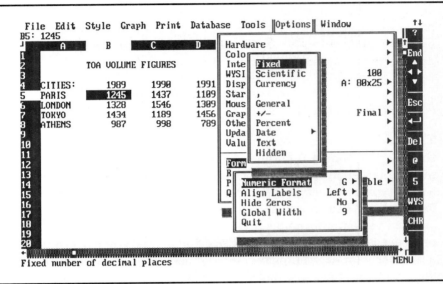

Figure 2-15.   *Numeric Format choices*

Format Name	Description of Format
Fixed	No commas in 1000s, negatives in parentheses, user-defined decimal places: 2000.99 (2000.99)
Scientific	Exponential notation, negatives in parentheses, user-defined decimal places: 2.00E+03 (2.00E+03)
Currency	User-defined currency prefix, commas in 1,000s, negatives in parentheses, user-defined decimal places: 2,000.99 ($2,000.99)
, (Financial)	Commas in 1,000s, negatives in parentheses, user-defined decimal places: 2,000.99 (2,000.99)
General	Varies decimal places; uses exponential notation for large numbers; negatives preceded by minus sign (−)
+/−	Represents positive numbers as plus signs (+), negatives as minus signs (−) for simple bar charts
Percent	Divides contents by 100; uses % sign as suffix
Date	Various options, described in Chapter 9, including formats for time values
Text (Formulas)	Displays formulas in cells rather than their values

Table 2-2.   *Format Choices*

Some of the formats require that you indicate how many decimal places should be used. If you select such a format, a prompt automatically appears, as shown in Figure 2-16. As you can see, the options are from 0 to 15. Formats such as Fixed and Currency suggest two decimal places, but you can type your choice over this before pressing ENTER or clicking the Enter button to confirm the format selection.

Style and Numeric Format

Changing the default or options format affects the appearance of all values in the worksheet, except for those cells formatted with the Style Numeric Format command. In Figure 2-17 you can see the effect of changing the global format to Currency with 0 decimal places. Notice that the years, which are actually just numbers, are also changed to currency. Quattro Pro 3 needs to be told that there is a block of cells that must be formatted differently. Cells formatted separately from the default format are not affected by changes to the default format.

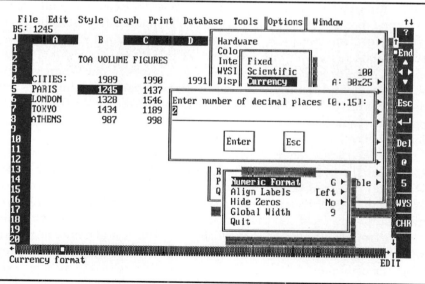

Figure 2-16. *Decimal place prompt*

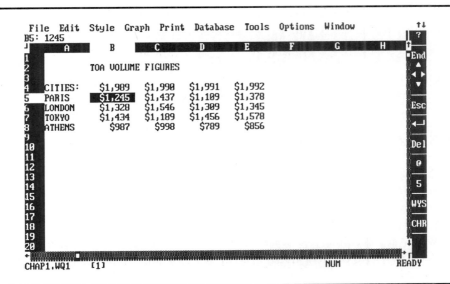

Figure 2-17.   *Global format change*

Formatting individual cells or groups of cells is the task of the Style commands, one of which is Numeric Format. This command allows you to specify a special format for one or more cells that is different from the whole worksheet. You normally begin a Style command by placing the cell selector on the cell you want to change or in the top-left corner of the group of cells if there is more than one cell to be worked on. When you type /, select Style, and then pick Numeric Format, you have the same format options as on the Default menu. There is one other item on this menu—the option to reset the format. You use this option when you want a manually formatted cell to revert to the default format.

The Fixed and General formats work well for entering years because they omit the commas. When you choose the Fixed format you must tell Quattro Pro 3 that there are to be no (0) decimal places for these years. When you press ENTER to confirm the format, you will have to perform one more step: You must tell the program to which cells this format applies.

Quattro Pro 3 assumes that when you enter the format command you want to format at least the cell where the cell selector is located when you start the command. In this case, this would be referred to as block B4..B4, meaning all the cells from B4 to B4. To extend this range you use the cursor keys, pointing out the cells to be included. If you press END and then RIGHT ARROW, you can extend the highlight to the last active cell on the right, in this case E4. This is a very handy use of the END-arrow key combination. The highlighting extends over the cells and the block is now B4..E4. When you have told Quattro Pro 3 the block to which the format applies, you press ENTER and, as you can see from Figure 2-18, all the cells within the block are changed. You can also type the coordinates of the cells you want to affect, rather than pointing them out. Notice that the input line tells you that cell B4 has a Fixed format with 0 decimal places assigned to it (F0). The full list of format identifiers is provided in Table 2-3.

When you have formatted cells with the Style command, they will retain their format even if the Options Format is changed. To remove a format applied with the Style command, use the Reset option on the Style Numeric Format menu.

Format Considerations

When a format change establishes the number of decimal places that can be displayed, Quattro Pro 3 rounds the number for display purposes only.

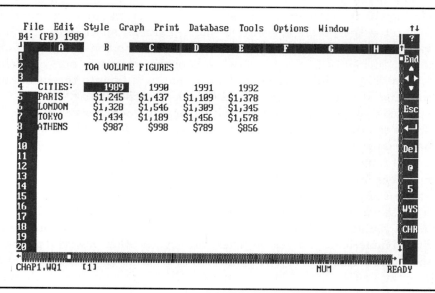

Figure 2-18. *Years formatted*

Code	Format
F0-F15	Fixed (0-15 decimal places)
S0-S15	Scientific (0-15 decimal places)
C0-C15	Currency (0-15 decimal places)
,0-,15	Comma/Financial (0-15 decimal places)
G	General (variable decimal places)
+	+/− (the bar graph format)
P1-P15	Percentage (0-15 decimal places)
D1-D5	Date formats
T	Text
D6-D9	Time formats
H	Hidden

Table 2-3. *Format Identifiers*

However, it remembers the number to 15 decimal places, even if the format says 0 decimal places are to be displayed. In Chapter 4 you will find a discussion of the @ROUND function, which causes the program to round numbers permanently.

The default width of Quattro Pro 3 columns is nine characters. To distinguish the numbers in adjacent cells and prevent them from appearing to run together, there is always a single character space to the right of a value entry. This means that a 9-character column can accept only eight digits. In Figure 2-19 you see what happens when you apply a default format that produces numbers longer than will fit into the 9-character columns. If you turn **1989** into **$1989.00**, the cell shows ********* to let you know you need to widen the column or change the format. Figure 2-20 shows the result of widening the columns. With wider columns the numbers reappear. (Widening columns is discussed later in this chapter.)

Use numeric formats to avoid worrying about the appearance of your numbers. In this way you can concentrate on building your spreadsheets and writing formulas. By setting the correct default format, you will not need to waste time changing the appearance of separate blocks of cells. When you do need to distinguish a group of cells from the whole, use the Style Numeric Format option. There are several other powerful options on the Style menu. The Style Alignment command is discussed later in this chapter, and the Style Line Drawing and Shading commands are discussed in Chapter 5.

Figure 2-19. *Asterisk effect*

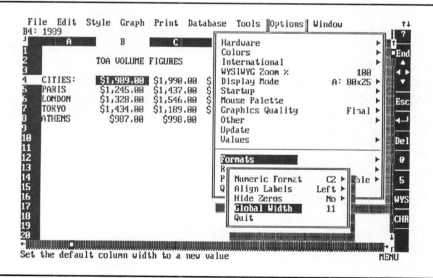

Figure 2-20. *The effect of widening columns*

Values

You have already seen that Quattro Pro 3 distinguishes between values and labels by the first character of a new cell entry. Anything that begins with one of the following characters is treated as a value:

0 through 9 . + - (@ # $

These items are called *value indicators*. If you do not begin an entry with one of these characters, the program will treat the entry as a label. Occasionally, you will need to enter data that looks like a number but is not. (Overcoming this problem is discussed in the "Wrong Numbers" section in a moment.)

Cell References

Whenever you enter instructions or formulas involving both numbers and cells, such as **1.1∗A1**, the number can be typed first. This lets Quattro Pro 3 know that what follows is a value. When formulas consist of cell references only, such as **A3+A4**, you obviously cannot do this; you must add a value indicator at the beginning of the entry. In the last chapter you saw that this can be a plus sign, as in **+A3+A4**. The plus sign does not alter the value of the cell reference it precedes. You can also use a parenthesis to begin a value entry, as in **(A3+A4)**. Parentheses are excellent value indicators when you need to control the order of calculation, as in **(A2+A3)∗(B2+B3)**. However, for every opening parenthesis there *must* be a closing parenthesis. You may find it easier to use the single + for simple formulas. The + on the numeric keypad can be typed without using the SHIFT key.

Big Numbers

You will occasionally need to enter a large number into a Quattro Pro 3 worksheet. Given the General display format and the default column width of nine characters (eight digits), entering the number **123456789** results in **1.2E+08** being displayed in the worksheet. The cell identifier lets you know that the number 123456789 is still stored. What you are seeing is the scientific notation (1.2×10 to the power of 8). Widening the column to ten characters will restore the number to its normal appearance. If you work with numbers in the millions and billions, you can set Exponential as the default format and see all of your numbers in the 1.0E+01 style. The Fixed, Currency, and Commas formats all show asterisks instead of converting a number too big for a cell into an exponential notation.

Wrong Numbers

Sometimes you need to work with numbers that are not values. For example, if you type a list of phone numbers into a spreadsheet and you type **555-1212** and press ENTER, you will get **-657** in the cell. This occurs because Quattro Pro 3 reads the *5* as meaning a value is coming and performs math on the entry, reading it as *555 minus 1212*. To overcome this problem you must precede a wrong number with one of the label indicators described in the "Labels" section of this chapter. For example, the apostrophe is used to indicate a label aligned on the left of the cell. Thus **'555-1212** will enter the phone number as a left-justified label. To enter several numeric labels, you can use the Database Data Entry Labels command, described in Chapter 3.

Another common example of a wrong number is a street address, for example, *123 Main Street*. In this case, if you type **123 Main Street** without a label indicator in front of it, Quattro Pro 3 will give you the error message "Invalid cell or block address" because it expects either a cell coordinate or a value since you began with the value 1. When you press ENTER, the program will cause a beep and will automatically switch you to EDIT mode so that you can correct the error. This often occurs when you type a formula or a number incorrectly; for example, if you omit a closing parenthesis or type a comma in a number.

When you are placed in EDIT mode, Quattro Pro 3 places the cursor where it thinks the problem lies, which is usually the first character that caused the confusion. Thus, typing **1:00 A.M.** will cause Quattro Pro 3 to put the cursor under the colon. In this case you can simply press HOME to place the cursor at the head of the entry to type the required label indicator. Remember that in EDIT mode you use ENTER to put the data into the cell. If you want to retype the entire entry, press ESCAPE to leave EDIT mode and return to READY mode.

Number Series

Quattro Pro 3 provides several methods for entering a series of numbers—for example, 101, 102, 103, and so on. Such series are often needed to number consecutive columns and rows, as in the numbering of inventory items and their locations shown here:

You can fill a group of cells with consecutive numbers automatically. You choose the starting number, the interval between numbers, and the ending number; for example, starting at 101, incrementing by 1, and ending at 105, as in the inventory item numbering. The command that performs this special form of value entry is called Edit Fill. This command is discussed in detail in Chapter 3.

Another method of numbering consecutively is achieved with formulas. Consider the row of years required in the table of volume numbers seen earlier in Figure 2-12. They appear as

1989 1990 1991 1992

These numbers can be created with a simple formula. If **1989** is in cell B4, then C4 can be **1+B4**. Cell D4 can be **1+C4** and cell E4 can be **1+D4**. You see

1989 1990 1991 1992

but the cells contain

1989 1+B4 1+C4 1+D4

When the years are entered this way, you need only type a new year over **1989** and all the other years will adjust accordingly. For example, changing B4 to **1991** would produce the following:

1991 1992 1993 1994

In the section of this chapter entitled "Edit Copy" you will learn how to copy formulas such as the ones used here to quickly create a series of related values.

Formulas

Much of the power of a spreadsheet lies in its formulas. When you are simply adding cells together or calculating internal rate of return on an investment, the ability to establish a relationship between cells gives you tremendous number-crunching ability. Quattro Pro 3's built-in formulas, such as the one used to calculate a loan payment in Chapter 1, are discussed in depth in Chapter 4. There you will learn how formulas are put together and entered in the spreadsheet.

Entering Formulas

So far you have seen formulas created by looking at the worksheet and deciding which cells are involved. For example, you know that the total of the three items shown here is going to be +A1+A2+A3:

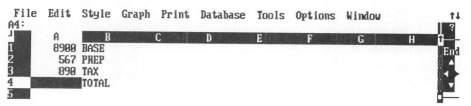

You might want to use this example to try the pointing method of entering formulas. This method begins with the plus sign or a value, if there is one in the formula. In VALUE mode, you use the arrow keys to highlight the first number you want in the formula. The program types the cell address for you.

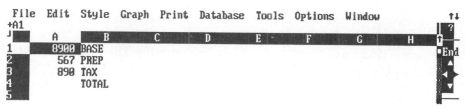

Now type the next math sign, another plus, and the cell selector moves back down to the cell in which you are building the formula. The basic procedure is math sign, point, math sign, point.

You can now point to the next cell that needs to go into the formula. It, too, is added on the edit line at the top of the screen as you build the formula.

Type another math sign, **+** in this case, and the process is repeated for the third cell. The formula reads **+A1+A2+A3**. You now press ENTER to place it in the cell. This method is very useful when you have lots of cells scattered throughout the spreadsheet and you cannot remember the cell location of a particular number.

The pointing method can be used effectively with formulas that involve functions, as in the case of the loan payment shown following, where the procedure is partially complete. The user placed the cell selector in E4, typed **@PMT(**, pressed the UP ARROW key to highlight E1, and then pressed a comma and moved the cell selector up to E2.

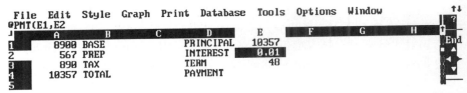

A second comma was pressed while E2 was highlighted, and the pointer moved to the third cell needed by the formula, E3. At E3 the closing parenthesis was typed to complete the formula. The ENTER key was then pressed to place the finished formula into the cell.

Mouse Formulas

You can use the mouse very effectively when building formulas. The basic procedure is to select the cell in which you want to create the formula, and then type a math character and click on the cell you want to place into the formula. You can then type the next math character, click another cell, and so on. You can click the Enter button to place the completed formula into the cell. When you need a formula to refer to a block of cells, you click on the top-left corner of the block and then drag the highlighting across to the lower-right corner.

Formula Errors

If you make what Quattro Pro 3 considers to be an error when creating a formula, using either the typing or the pointing method, pressing ENTER to place the formula in a cell will result in a beep and an error message. Sometimes these can be quite specific, such as "Missing right paren" when you fail to close a pair of parentheses. Press ENTER at the message and the program will place you in EDIT mode and point out your error by placing the cursor at the first mistake it reads in what you have tried to enter. For example, entering **@PMT(E1,E2,E3,)** will cause the program to place the edit cursor under the superfluous third comma so that you can press DELETE to remove it. You can then re-enter the corrected formula.

Functions and Blocking

There is an alternative method of adding the three items in cells A1 through A3 one at a time, as with the formula +A1+A2+A3. The alternative is to consider these cells as part of a group, or *block*, and then apply a function that adds them to the block's contents. The function that does this is @SUM. Like the @PMT function, the @SUM function consists of the @ sign followed by the function name, SUM, followed by the parentheses containing the cells to which the function is applied. In this case, the block is made up of cells A1 through A3 inclusive. The completed formula is thus **@SUM(A1..A3)**. If you were to type this formula into a cell and press ENTER, you would see that Quattro Pro 3 records this as **@SUM(A1.A3)**, but adds an extra period to make it easier to see. You never need to type the second period.

Instead of typing the formula you can use the pointing method. You place the cell selector in the cell that is to contain the formula and type **@SUM** and a left parenthesis, (. Then you point to the first cell in the block of cells to be summed, in this case, A1. While you are pointing to this first cell you type a period (.) to anchor this cell as the beginning of the block. The appearance of the double dots signifies that the cell reference is anchored, as shown in the following illustration.

Next you use the arrow keys to expand the highlighting to the other cells that are to be included in the block. This is sometimes referred to as *painting* the block. If you anchor the beginning of the block in the wrong cell, press ESCAPE to unlock that cell and move to another. When you have highlighted all the cells to be summed, type the closing parenthesis. The completed formula is placed in the original cell when you press ENTER. The completed formula in this case is @SUM(A1..A3), meaning the sum of all values in cells A1 through A3 inclusive.

The blocking method of formula writing works well for large areas of cells that need to be included in a formula like @SUM. Using a previous example, the total TOA volume figures can be summed by this blocking method, as shown in Figure 2-21.

There are some rules for blocking cells. The most important rule is that *the block must be rectangular.* The cell in which you anchor the beginning point of the block is usually the top cell in a column of cells or the left cell in a row. If the block includes cells from more than one column or row, you can begin the painting process in the top-left corner of the block, although any corner will do. The "Block Editing Commands" section of this chapter explains blocks in greater detail. That section also describes how to assign names to blocks of cells to make writing formulas even easier.

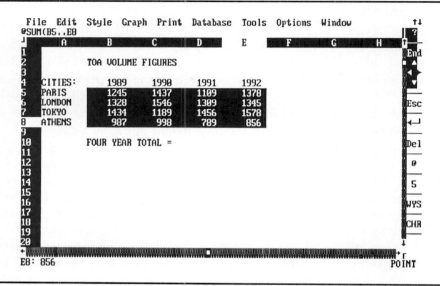

Figure 2-21.　*Blocking method*

Labels

Although spreadsheets are thought of as number-crunching tools, the role played by labels is very important. Labels tell you and anyone else using the worksheets what the numbers mean. You should never fall into the trap of entering numbers and formulas without first placing appropriate labels to indicate what the numbers represent. Quattro Pro 3 creates a label whenever a new cell entry begins with one of the following *label indicators:*

A through Z ' " ^ { [! / < > : ; ! ~ ? }] _) = & %

In addition to these characters, a space at the beginning of an entry also tells the program that you are typing a label. There is a special label character, the vertical bar, which can be used for printing instructions, as described in Chapter 5.

Aligning Labels

You have seen that by default Quattro Pro 3 aligns labels on the left and puts an apostrophe in front of the text to remind you that this is a label. You can center a label in the column by starting the label with the caret sign (^), the symbol on the 6 key. You place a label flush right by preceding it with the double quotation mark ("). You can see left-, center-, and right-justified versions of the TOA city names in Figure 2-22.

The label-alignment characters can be inserted in several ways. You can make all labels right, left, or centered by default. Type / to activate the menu and pick Options, followed by Formats and Align Labels. Select the alignment you prefer. Once selected, this format remains in effect for the current session of Quattro Pro 3. You can also make this the permanent default by selecting the Update command from the Options menu.

To vary individual labels from the default label alignment setting, type the desired prefix preceding the text of the label. For example, if your default is left alignment, you can create a centered label as an exception by preceding it with the ^. To right-justify an individual label, type the double quote before the label text.

To vary a group of cells from the default alignment you use the Style Alignment command. This command also allows you to change the alignment of numbers, which can be positioned on the left or in the center of a column, as well as on the right where they normally appear. To change the alignment of a group of cells, type / to activate the menu and pick Style. Now select Alignment and you will see the four choices: General, Left, Right, and Center. When you pick any of these you will be prompted to

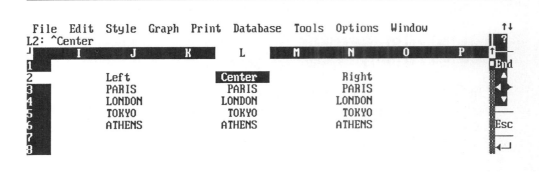

Figure 2-22.   *Alignment examples*

specify the block of cells you want to affect. After selecting the cells, press ENTER to confirm the change.

You can use General alignment to reinstate the usual alignment of labels on the left and numbers on the right. The Left, Center, and Right alignments apply to all values and numbers in the cells you select.

Long Labels

Quattro Pro 3 labels can contain as many as 254 characters. You seldom need them this long, but you need to know how the program acts upon labels wider than one column. In Chapter 10 you will see wide labels wrapped into a rectangular area on the spreadsheet to let you compose text for letters, memos, and notations on spreadsheet models. For now, consider the title typed in cell B2 of Figure 2-23. When a label like this is entered, Quattro Pro 3 gives no indication that it will exceed the 9-character width of the cell. However, when you press ENTER to put this label into the cell, you see that it does exceed the cell width. The label is still legible and will print when you print this worksheet. From the cell identifier you can see that all of the title is considered as the contents of cell B2.

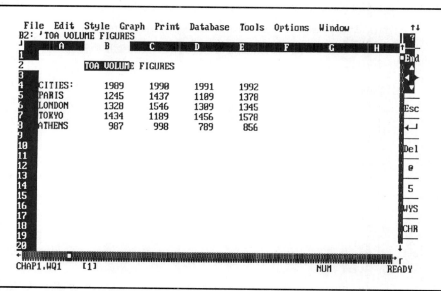

Figure 2-23. *Long label*

Long labels simply borrow space from adjacent cells to display their contents. Placing the cell selector in C2 and referring to the cell identifier at the top of the screen will show you that there is nothing in this cell. Cell C2 is empty. The contents of cell B2 simply flow over into that display area.

Unfortunately, this presents a problem when you want to enter a long label to the left of an occupied cell, as would be the case if you changed the label **CITIES:** to **DESTINATION**. Figure 2-24 shows the effect of entering **DESTINATION** in cell A4. The cell to the right of A4 is occupied and Quattro Pro 3 cannot display the full label. However, the missing letters are not lost, as you can see from the status line.

The solution to this problem is either to abbreviate the label, for example, change it back to **CITIES:**, or to make the column wider. Normally, you will choose to widen the column using the column commands. There may be times when you will choose to shorten the label, particularly if you are trying to keep the worksheet small or if you want the entries in a column to be more consistent in width.

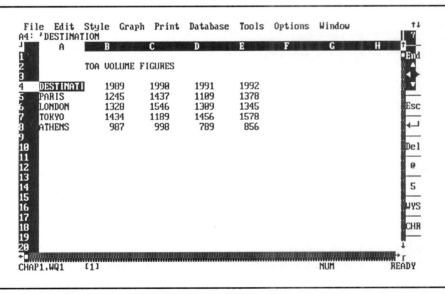

Figure 2-24.   *Label overflow*

Lines and Repeating Labels

If you want to create the impression of a line across a spreadsheet as a visual divider, you can enter a line or lines into a separate row. Figure 2-25 shows equal signs used for a dividing line. To create a dividing line, you fill a cell with a single character or a sequence of characters. Instead of typing enough characters to fill the column, you use the backslash, which is the Cell Fill command. The \ is followed by the characters you want to repeat. Thus, **\=** produces

=========

* produces

****

and **\+=** produces

+=+=+=+=+=

This technique is a lot quicker than manually entering a series of symbols. The Cell Fill command has an added advantage: when columns are altered in width, the command keeps the correct number of characters in the cell.

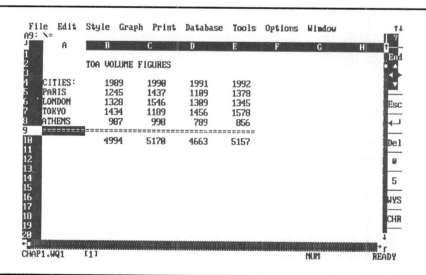

Figure 2-25.   *The equal sign line*

An alternative method of adding lines and dressing up your spreadsheet is provided by the Style commands described in Chapter 5. You can use Line Drawing to add lines, Shading to shade areas of the worksheet, and a Font that underlines cell entries.

Dates and Times

One category of information that deserves special attention is date and time calculations. Quattro Pro 3 is very adept at handling dates and times and performing mathematics upon them. If you look at a date—for example, April 1, 1992—you can see that it is part text and part number. For a computer program to handle a date as something that has value, the date must be converted to a number. However, for easy reading, a date has to be displayed as text.

If you were to type April 1, 1992 and press ENTER, you would have created a label, since the letter A is a label indicator. However, if you press CTRL-D before typing the date and then type the date in any of the following formats, Quattro Pro 3 will convert the date to a number, but display it as a date:

	Date	Format
1.	01-Apr-92	DD-MMM-YY
2.	01-Apr	DD-MMM
3.	Apr-92	MMM-YY
4.	04/01/92	MM/DD/YY
5.	04/01	MM/DD

If you type the date using format 2 or 5, Quattro Pro 3 assumes the current year. Format 3 assumes the first day of the month. A date entered in one of these styles preceded by CTRL-D will be recorded as a serial number, thus allowing you to perform date arithmetic with it. Quattro Pro 3 does this by calculating the number of days between the date and the end of the last century. Using the first day of the century as day 1, any two dates can be compared and the difference calculated.

You can see the power of this function if you use Quattro Pro 3 to answer the simple question: How many days have you been alive? In a new worksheet you can answer this question by following these steps:

1. In A1 press CTRL-D and then type your birth date in the form day, month, and year, using the appropriate one- or two-digit representation of dd/mm/yy, as in 12/25/52.

2. Press DOWN ARROW to enter the date and move down to the next cell.

3. In A2 press CTRL-D and then type today's date in the same format. Press DOWN ARROW to enter the date and move down to the next cell.

4. In A3 type **+A1-A2** and press ENTER. This is the number of days from your birth date to today.

If you look at the cell identifier while the cell selector is in cell A2, you will see a number. That number is the number of days from the turn of the century to the date in A2. In the next chapter you will see that many applications of Quattro Pro 3's database capabilities utilize date arithmetic. For a complete discussion of dates in Quattro Pro 3, refer to Chapter 9.

Working with Columns

There are several useful commands that you can apply to the columns from which the worksheet is built. You can add new columns, delete columns, and hide columns. You can also change the width of columns in several ways. You can issue a command that automatically adjusts column widths based on the data that you have entered in the columns.

Current Column Width

A little earlier in the chapter we tried to enter the label **DESTINATION** in cell A4, but found that the entire label could not fit because the cell to the right of A4 was occupied. The best solution to a problem like this is to widen the column. Type **DESTINATION** in cell A4 to try this. The column your cell selector is occupying is the current column. To widen the current column, type **/** to activate the menu and then select Style followed by Column Width. You are prompted for a width setting and reminded that the column can be from 1 to 254 characters wide. The current width is also shown, and you can see arrows in either side of the column letter, reminding you which column is being adjusted.

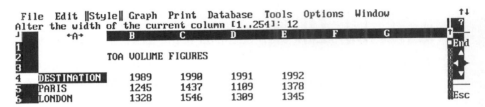

Initially, the default width of 9 is shown when you first enter this menu. You can either type the number of characters for the width, or press the RIGHT or LEFT ARROW key to widen or narrow the column on the screen. The width number changes as you do this. The arrow method lets you visually adjust the width until it is suitable. When the column is an appropriate width, in this case 12, press ENTER to confirm it and to return to READY mode. For the word *DESTINATION*, a column width setting of 12 is sufficient.

The column width changes for the full length of the column. You cannot mix cells of varying widths within a column. When you have manually set the width of the current column, Quattro Pro 3 shows you a width reminder in the cell identifier of any cell in the column. In this case the notation is [W12]. This is helpful if you change numerous columns in a worksheet.

Block Widths

In Figure 2-26 the format of the volume figures for the TOA example has been changed, and the columns look cramped. In a case like this you do not need to set the width of each column. You can change the width of several columns at once by using the Block Widths option on the Column menu. Picking this option gives you several options that affect a group of columns. You can pick Set Width, Reset Width, or Auto Width. If you select Set Width, the program prompts you for the location of the columns to be altered. You indicate a block of columns in the same way that you mark blocks for other purposes: by extending the range with the cursor keys or

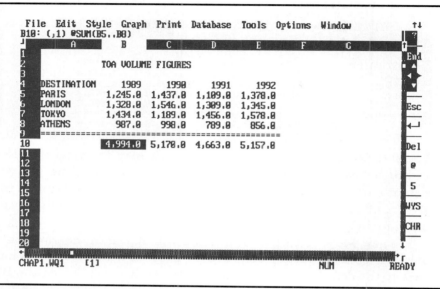

Figure 2-26.   Cramped columns

the mouse. For example, here you can see that the RIGHT ARROW was used
to increase the block:

```
File   Edit ‖Style‖ Graph  Print  Database  Tools  Options  Window        ↑↓
Enter block of columns: B10..E10                                          ?
         A        B        C        D      E        F      G         ↑
1                                                                        End
2             TOA VOLUME FIGURES                                          ◄
3                                                                         ►
4   DESTINATION    1989     1990     1991     1992
5   PARIS       1,245.0  1,437.0  1,109.0  1,378.0
6   LONDON      1,328.0  1,546.0  1,309.0  1,345.0                       Esc
7   TOKYO       1,434.0  1,189.0  1,456.0  1,578.0
8   ATHENS        987.0    998.0    789.0    856.0                        ↵
9   ==========================================================
10             4,994.0  5,170.0  4,663.0  5,157.0                       Del
```

When the block is selected you press ENTER or click the Enter button, and
the prompt changes to ask for a width. You can type the desired width
setting as you do when using the regular Column Width command explained earlier.

```
  File  Edit ‖Style‖ Graph  Print  Database  Tools  Options  Window        ↑↓
Alter the width of columns [1..254]: 12                                      ?
 J        A          ←B→        ←C→        ←D→        ←E→        F           End
1
2                 TOA VOLUME FIGURES                                          ▲
3                                                                            ◄ ►
4 DESTINATION      1989        1990       1991       1992                     ▼
5 PARIS          1,245.0     1,437.0    1,109.0    1,378.0                   Esc
6 LONDON         1,328.0     1,546.0    1,309.0    1,345.0
7 TOKYO          1,434.0     1,189.0    1,456.0    1,578.0                    ↵
8 ATHENS           987.0       998.0      789.0      856.0
9 ====================================================================       Del
10                4,994.0     5,170.0    4,663.0    5,157.0
```

You can also use the LEFT and RIGHT ARROW keys to adjust the column width. Notice the arrows in the column heading reminding you which columns are being adjusted. When you press ENTER to confirm the width setting, all columns within the block (except any whose width has been set individually) will change to the new width.

The new width setting of the columns will appear in the input line, as in [W12] for 12 characters wide. If you want to change a group of columns back to the default column width you use the Reset option on the Block Width menu. This allows you to select a number of columns at once that need their individual width settings released.

Automatic Column Widths

Quattro Pro 3 allows you to set up columns that adjust their width automatically to compensate for changes in the data entered. For example, a column of city names may look like it only needs 12 characters, but along comes Blue Ridge Summit and you need to change the width to at least 16. By using the Auto Width option on the Block Width menu you can alter the width of a column or group of columns to accommodate the widest entry plus a specific number of characters, from 0 to 40. Thus you can enter the number 2 to automatically expand or contract each column in the block so that each is two characters wider than the largest entry.

Global Width

You can assign specific widths to individual columns, either one at a time or in groups, but you may want to change all of the column widths at once. To make a global change to the column widths you type / and select Options, Format, and then Global Width. Select the new width either by typing the desired number of characters or by pressing the LEFT or RIGHT ARROW key. Press ENTER or click the Enter button to confirm the setting.

A default column width change does not change those columns that have been set individually. For example, if column A was set to 12 it would remain at 12 when you changed the global width, whatever global width you chose. This is a very useful feature since it preserves the effort you have made setting certain columns correctly. However, there may be times when you want a column to revert to the global setting. To do this, place the cell selector in the column you want to reset. Type / to activate the menu, select Style and Reset Width. The column will now take its width measurement from the default setting. Use the Reset Width command on the Block Width menu to cause a group of columns to revert to the default width.

Hiding and Exposing Columns

You can tell Quattro Pro 3 to hide a column from display for purposes of improved appearance or confidentiality. The formulas in the worksheet operate as usual when a column is hidden. The full use of this feature is covered in Chapter 5.

Inserting and Deleting Columns

At times you will have entered data only to find you need an extra column. A new column is easy to create. Just pick Insert from the Edit menu and you will be asked if you want to insert Rows or Columns. Pick Columns and you will be asked to indicate the number of columns you want inserted. Columns are added to the left of the current column. Press ENTER to insert one column. Press the RIGHT ARROW key once for each additional column you want to add, and then press ENTER. The new columns are added down all 8192 rows of the worksheet, so you should consider if there is any unseen data that will be affected at the time of the insert. You can press END, DOWN ARROW and END, UP ARROW while inserting a column in order to view lower and upper areas of the worksheet before you press ENTER to confirm the insertion.

Deleting columns works in the same way; you pick Delete from the Edit menu, and then Columns. Highlight the columns you want to delete. Deleting removes all the data in those columns so it should be used with care. Check areas above and below the current screen for valuable data that might be deleted with the column. Note that the integrity of formulas in the worksheet is preserved whenever you insert columns or rows.

Working with Rows

You can use the Insert and Delete commands to manipulate spreadsheet rows. There will be times when you have entered data only to find you need an extra row. Just select Insert from the Edit menu, and then pick Rows. You will be asked to indicate the number of rows you want inserted. New rows are added above the current row. Press ENTER to insert one row. Press the DOWN ARROW key once for each additional row you want to add, and then press ENTER. New rows are added across all 256 columns of the worksheet, so you must consider if there is any unseen data that will be affected at the time of the insert. You can press CRTL-LEFT ARROW and CRTL-RIGHT ARROW while inserting a row in order to view other areas of the worksheet before you press ENTER to confirm the insertion.

The Delete command works the same way; you pick Delete from the Edit menu, followed by Rows. You then highlight the rows you want to remove. The Delete Rows command removes all the data in those rows across all 256 columns so it should be used with care. Check the areas to the left and right of the current screen for valuable data that might be deleted with the rows.

Block Editing Commands

You have seen that the Insert and Delete commands on the Edit menu work with rows and columns. There are other Edit commands, such as Copy and Move, that are applied to a group of cells known as a block. These are among the most powerful and useful commands in the program, so it is important to be sure what constitutes a block. A block of cells is anchored in one cell and extended beyond that in any direction while maintaining a rectangular grouping to the cells. You can refer to a block of cells by any two diagonal coordinates. The diagram in Figure 2-27 shows what is and is not a block.

Edit Copy

One of the most useful abilities of a computer is its capacity for copying information. This capability is used in Quattro Pro 3 to produce unlimited copies of standard worksheets, such as weekly expense report models, that have to be used again and again. The Edit Copy command as it applies to a block of cells is particularly useful when creating any model where the same labels, numbers, or formulas are used more than once.

Simple Copy   Consider the formulas mentioned earlier for producing a series of years by adding 1 to the previous year, starting with **1989** in B4:

	B	C	D	E
Row 4	1989	1+B4	1+C4	1+D4

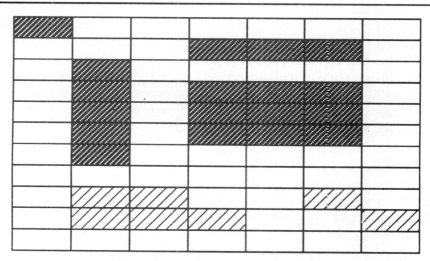

Heavily hatched cells constitute valid ranges
Lightly hatched cells are not considered ranges

Figure 2-27.   *Blocks acceptable to Quattro Pro 3*

When you create a formula like this in cell C4, which says **1+B4**, you are in effect telling Quattro Pro 3 to add 1 to the cell on the left. The formulas **1+C4** and **1+D4** actually mean the same thing. You can copy the formula from C4 to D4 and E4. To do this, place the cell selector in the cell to be copied and pick Copy from the Edit menu. You will be prompted for the "Source block of cells," meaning "which group of cells do you want to copy?" Quattro Pro 3 assumes you want to include the current cell and shows **C4..C4**. You can then do one of the following:

■ Accept this cell reference by pressing ENTER.

■ Reject it with BACKSPACE or ESCAPE.

■ Use the cursor keys or mouse to highlight additional cells to be copied.

■ Type the coordinates of the cell(s) you want to copy.

To copy C4, you can just press ENTER to accept that cell as the block to be copied. When you do this a new prompt appears: "Destination for cells." This prompt asks for the cells you are going to copy into, in this case **C4..E4**. You can indicate this by typing **C4.E4**. Alternatively you can type a period to anchor the beginning point of the block at C4 and then press RIGHT ARROW to include the other cells through to E4. (You could use **D4.E4** as the destination, but it does not matter if you copy the formula over the cell it is in. This is quicker when you are using the pointing method.) Having indicated the destination cells, press ENTER. Quattro Pro 3 will copy the formula as instructed and convert each new formula relative to its location. This ability to address cells in a relative manner makes this kind of copying very useful. In Chapter 5 you will read about the difference between a relative cell address and an absolute one.

Large Copies   The Edit Copy command works for much larger groups of cells and for labels as well as values. In Figure 2-28 the example TOA figures are highlighted for copying. The cell selector was placed on A4 before the Edit Copy command was issued. The highlighting was then extended, or painted to E8. (The END-RIGHT ARROW and END-DOWN ARROW key combinations work well to paint a solid block of cells like this.) The arrangement of labels and years in A4 through E8 will be duplicated by the Edit Copy command in order to prepare for a revenue calculation for the same cities and years. Figure 2-29 shows the destination being pointed

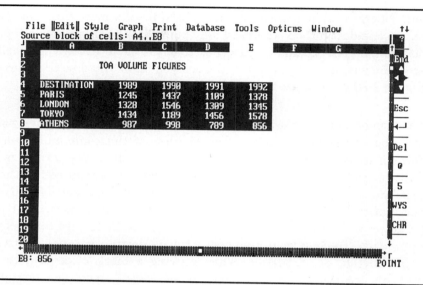

Figure 2-28. *Copying a block*

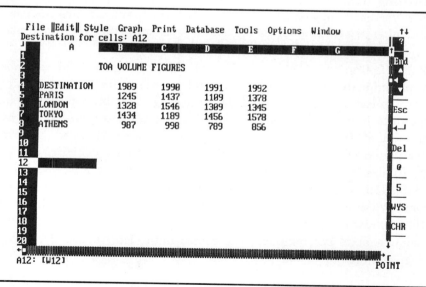

Figure 2-29. *Destination indicated*

out. When the Edit Copy command is used to copy more than one source cell to one destination, you need only point out the upper-left cell of the destination. The command assumes that you have enough free cells to accommodate a block the size of the one you highlighted as the source. In Figure 2-30 you can see the results of the Edit Copy command.

The Copy Keys   You will use the Edit Copy command extensively when building spreadsheet models. The rhythm of the command keys will become second nature. To copy one cell to many cells, the pattern is Edit Copy (to pick the command), ENTER (to accept the current cell as the one to be copied), point (move the cell selector to select the upper-left cell of the destination block), anchor (type a period to lock in this coordinate), point (to select the rest of the destination block), and ENTER (to complete the command). To copy from many cells to one destination, use Edit Copy, point, ENTER, point, ENTER. When copying a block of several cells to multiple locations, use Edit Copy, point, ENTER, point, anchor, point, ENTER. To save you the trouble of selecting the Copy command from the Edit menu, Quattro Pro 3's shortcut feature has Edit Copy assigned to a single key combination, CTRL-C. You can therefore use CTRL-C as a quick way to commence the Copy command.

Always remember that the Edit Copy command does not check for existing data in the destination cells. You can actually lose data by inadvertently copying over it. Use caution the first few times you use Copy and always save the worksheet before performing large copy operations.

Formula Copies   Cells B13 through E16 of Figure 2-30 can now be replaced with calculations that determine revenue for TOA by multiplying the figures in the upper half by an average amount for each ticket. A formula is written in B13, multiplying the volume figure in B5 by the amount of 500; the formula is 500*B5. The results of this and the formulas for London (450*B6), Tokyo (700*B7), and Athens (550*B8) are shown in Figure 2-31. To copy this block to the other columns, you highlight **B13..B16** as the source of the copy and highlight **B13..E13** as the destination. When a column block is copied over several columns, you point out the top row of the new locations. Quattro Pro 3 assumes you have space below that to accommodate the copied data. The results are shown in Figure 2-32.

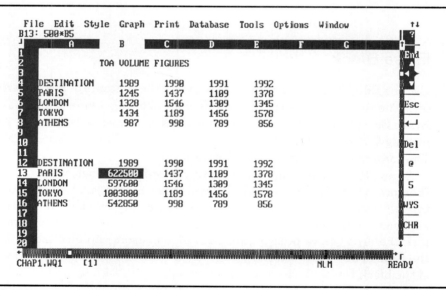

Figure 2-30.   *Completed copy*

```
 File  Edit  Style  Graph  Print  Database  Tools  Options  Window      ↑↓
 B13: 500*B5                                                              ?
  ┘        A        B        C        D        E        F        G       ↑
  1                                                                      End
  2            TOA VOLUME FIGURES                                         ◀
  3                                                                       ▶
  4     DESTINATION    1989     1990     1991     1992                    ▼
  5     PARIS          1245     1437     1109     1378
  6     LONDON         1328     1546     1309     1345
  7     TOKYO          1434     1189     1456     1578                   Esc
  8     ATHENS          987      998      789      856                   ◀┘
  9
 10                                                                      Del
 11
 12     DESTINATION    1989     1990     1991     1992                    @
 13     PARIS         622500    1437     1109     1378
 14     LONDON        597600    1546     1309     1345                    5
 15     TOKYO        1003800    1189     1456     1578
 16     ATHENS        542050     998      789      856                   WYS
 17
 18                                                                      CHR
 19
 20                                                                       ↓
  ←                                                                      ┐r
 CHAP1.WQ1    [1]                                      NLM          READY
```

Figure 2-31.   *New formulas in B13..B16*

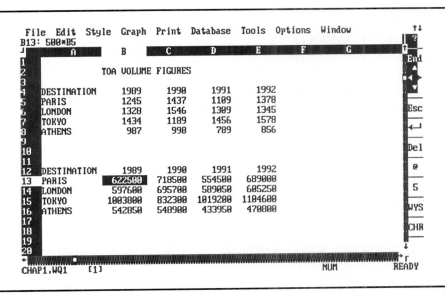

Figure 2-32. *The formulas copied*

Erase Block

Use the Edit Erase Block command to delete the contents of more than one cell. The DELETE key is the best method for deleting single cells, but Edit Erase Block works effectively on large areas that need to be cleared. After picking the command, highlight the block to be modified and press ENTER. The contents of all selected cells are erased.

As an alternative to using the menu you can simply select the cells and then press DELETE. To select the cells with the mouse you just click on the top-left corner of the block and drag across to highlight them. With the keyboard, you press the Extend key (SHIFT-F7) and use the cursor keys to pick the area before pressing DELETE. Mouse users can also make use of the Extend key when selecting large areas. Click on the top-left corner cell of the block you want to select, and then press SHIFT-F7. Quattro Pro 3 will extend the block to the next cell you click on. Although the program has an Undo key (ALT-F5), you should use the combination of cell selection and the DELETE key with care.

Search and Replace

Quattro Pro 3 offers a very useful Edit command called Search & Replace. Normally associated with word processing programs, the term *search and replace* refers to a program's ability to search for every instance of one thing and replace it with another. For example, if you had used *NEW YORK* many times throughout a worksheet and were then told it should be *NEWARK*, you might think you had to move to each cell that says *NEW YORK* and type **NEWARK** over it. Instead, you can highlight the area of the worksheet containing the words you want to change and have Quattro Pro 3 search and replace within that block to make the changes for you.

In the example shown in Figure 2-33 you can see an earnings report for commodity brokers. You want to increase the salary of all brokers making a Base of 25.00 to 28.00. From the Search & Replace menu you first choose Block to highlight the area of the spreadsheet to be searched. Include all cells that you need to change. In this case the block will be C4.C20. This is recorded in the menu, as shown in Figure 2-34. Then pick Search String to enter the characters you want Quattro Pro 3 to search for. These can be

```
 File  Edit  Style  Graph  Print  Database  Tools  Options  Window       ↑↓
A1: [W17] 'Broker listing                                                 ?
┘           A              B          C          D          E        F
1    Broker listing                                                      ●End
2
3           Last Name      First Name    Base      Sales
4    Rue               Mick           24.00    300.00                   Esc
5    Wading            Les            27.00    330.00
6    Figone            Fred           22.00    240.00
7    Jones             Karen          25.00    320.30
8    Forte             Steve          33.00    200.00                   ↵
9    Baxter            Andrew A.      26.00    210.00
10   Torres            Lisa           25.00    250.00                   Del
11   Abendjar          Bill           29.00    220.00
12   Herzberg          Brian          27.00    310.00                   @
13   Chang             Charly         25.00    330.00
14   Ruess             Berni          23.00    100.00                   5
15   Willock           Sam            25.00    200.00
16   McKenna           Sharon         22.00    300.00                   WYS
17   Muller            Mario          33.00    300.00
18   Kobuchi           Joseph         25.00    310.00                   CHR
19   Matsumoto         Owen           30.00    200.00
20   Romfo             Erin           24.00    230.00
S&R01.WQ1   [1]                                            NUM     READY
```

Figure 2-33.   *The Search & Replace example*

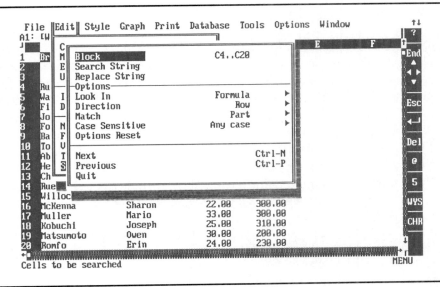

Figure 2-34.   *The recorded block*

letters, numbers, math signs within formulas, or any character or string of characters you have entered into the cells. In this case, 25 will work fine, since the rest of the number will remain the same. Pick Replace String to enter the characters to replace the ones you are searching for, in this case, 28. If you do not wish to replace the searched for item but rather delete it, leave this section blank. Such an operation would be appropriate if you wanted to change *LONDON HEATHROW* to just *LONDON*, searching for *HEATHROW* and replacing with nothing. The Search & Replace options allow you to fine tune the operation. They are listed in Table 2-4.

To proceed with the search and replace operation, choose Next and Quattro Pro 3 will highlight the first cell it finds that contains the characters you are searching for. You then must make a choice, as shown in Figure 2-35. You pick Yes to replace this instance of 25.00. Choosing No leaves this case as it is, for example, if there is an exception to the pay upgrade. Selecting All tells Quattro Pro 3 to proceed with an automatic search and replace from this point on. Do not pick All unless you are certain about what will happen. If you are not careful about limiting the block to be searched, you could change instances of the search characters you did not anticipate.

The Edit option is a very handy one, allowing you to interrupt the search and replace to edit a particular cell that has been found, for example, if you wanted to use 29 for one of the entries. The Quit option tells Quattro Pro 3 to stop the process before all instances have been changed. If you choose this option, the last cell found becomes the current cell. After the last instance of the search characters has been reached and your decision

Type Option	Action
Look In:	
Formula	Looks for search string within formulas, cell references, block names, and so on. A search for 2 finds 2*2, B2, B52s, and so on, but does not find 6*7.
Value	Values the formula in each cell and looks for the search string in the result. Converts formula to value if result contains search string. Thus a search for 2 with 5 as a replace string will find 6*7 and convert it to 45.
Condition	Allows you to set a condition in the search string, such as +B2>12, where B2 is the first cell in the search block. The search finds all cells with a value greater than 12.
Direction:	
Row	Searches the block from the current cell proceeding row by row.
Column	Searches the block from the current cell proceeding column by column.
Match:	
Part	Searches for partial cell entries, so that a search string of **mar** would find **martian** and **market**.
Whole	Requires that the match be the entire cell contents, except for the label indicator, so that a search string of **mar** would not locate a cell containing **mars**.
Case Sensitive:	
Any-case	Does not require a match in cases, so that a search string of **erin** would find **Erin** and **ERIN**.
Exact-case	Requires that the match be exact as far as case is concerned. A search string of ERIN would not find **Erin**.

Note: A search initiated with Next moves forward through the block from the current cell, whereas a search initiated with Previous moves backward. Both choices search the entire block.

Table 2-4. *Search & Replace Options*

File ‖Edit‖ Style Graph Print Database Tools Options Window

	A	B	C	D	E	F
1	Broker listing					
2						
3	Last Name	First Name	Base	Sales		
4	Rue	Mick	24.00	300.00		
5	Wading	Les	27.00	330.00		
6	Figone	Fred	22.00	240.00		
7	Jones	Karen	25.00	320.00		
8	Forte	Steve				
9	Baxter	Andrew A.				
10	Torres	Lisa				
11	Abenojar	Bill				
12	Herzberg	Brian				
13	Chang	Charly				
14	Ruess	Berni				
15	Willock	Sam				
16	McKenna	Sharon	22.00	300.00		
17	Muller	Mario	33.00	300.00		
18	Kobuchi	Joseph	25.00	310.00		
19	Matsumoto	Owen	30.00	200.00		
20	Ronfo	Erin	24.00	230.00		

Replace this string:
Yes
No
All
Edit
Quit

C7: (,2) 25   MENU

Figure 2-35. *Search choices*

has been entered, Quattro Pro 3 returns to the READY mode. The next time you use the Search & Replace command for this worksheet in this session, it will remember the settings that you entered. In fact, the Search & Replace command will remember the settings even if you move to a different worksheet window, allowing you to repeat the same operation on similar spreadsheets, one after another. If you need to change the settings you can simply pick the Options Reset command.

Edit Move

You will occasionally need to move a group of cells from one location to another. If you need a few extra columns or rows in a spreadsheet, you can sometimes use the Edit Insert command to accomplish the changes you want. At other times you will be able to use the Edit Delete command to remove extra space, but these commands do not work well in crowded spreadsheets, and at times you will need to move a group of cells. The Edit

Move command requires that you highlight the cells to be moved and then indicate their destination. Note that any cell entries within the area they are being moved to will be overwritten by the moved cells.

The Edit Move command preserves the integrity of the formulas within the block. Relative cell references are preserved correctly. Thus, the following line of cells moved from row 4 to row 6 would be adjusted as shown:

	B	C	D	E
Row 4	1989	1+B4	1+C4	1+D4
Row 6	1989	1+B6	1+C6	1+D6

There are some situations in which Edit Move does affect the way your formulas work. These are explained in Chapter 5. As a safety precaution, save your worksheet before a large block move so that you can retrieve the unchanged version if the effects of the move are not what you had anticipated. Large block moves will take several moments for the computer to complete. The mode indicator will flash WAIT until the operation is over.

Edit Names

If there is a block of cells that you work with frequently, you can save time by attaching a name to the block. For example, the figures for TOA passenger volume over the 4-year period may need to be totaled, and that total may then need to be used in several ways. By calling the cells in the block B4..E8 by the name TVF (for TOA Volume Figures), you can enter the formula **@SUM(TVF)** to get an immediate total for all the numbers in those cells. Likewise, you can use **@AVG(TVF)** to get the average volume. You can see these formulas at work in Figure 2-36. One of the great advantages to using these names is that you are less prone to error when writing formulas. It is easier to type **TVF** than **B4.E8**. If you typed **B5.E8** by mistake, Quattro Pro 3 would not know you missed a line of numbers. But if you typed **TVD** by mistake, the program would beep and tell you that the name had not been found.

To name a block of cells, place the cell selector on the top-left cell of the group to be named, activate the main menu, select Edit, and then select Names. Select Create to assign a new name. Type the name at the prompt,

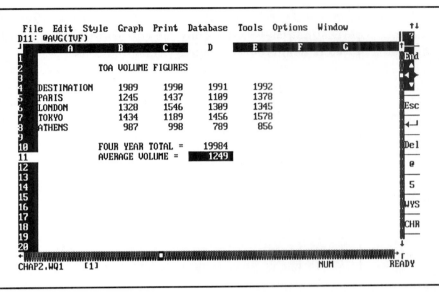

Figure 2-36. *The block name in use*

as shown in Figure 2-37, and press ENTER. You will then be able to highlight the block of cells to be included, just as you do with other Edit commands. Press ENTER to complete the operation.

Once you have created a name, you can refer to it in formulas. Press the F3 key to show a list of Block Names, as shown in Figure 2-38. In this example you can see that several other names besides TVF have been created. You can copy a name from the list into a formula by highlighting the name and pressing ENTER. You can move to a named block by the Goto key (F5) and typing or inserting the name of the block and then pressing ENTER.

The next time you use the Edit Name Create command you will see the names that have been created listed alphabetically. Use the Delete command to delete redundant block names; that is, to remove the names from the cells. You do not actually delete the named cells. The Labels command allows you to assign names from labels in the spreadsheet, a technique described in Chapter 11. The Reset command deletes all block names at once. (Quattro Pro 3 requires that you confirm this action with a Yes / No response in order to avoid accidental loss of names settings.) The Make

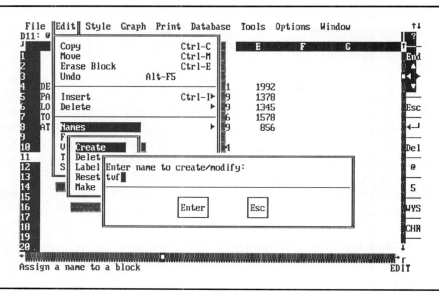

Figure 2-37. *The Edit Names Create command*

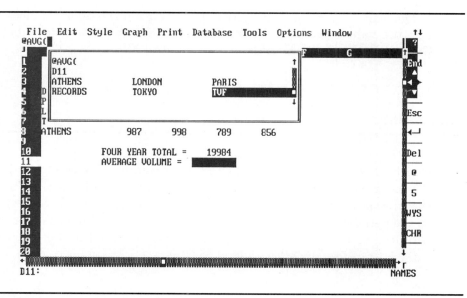

Figure 2-38. *Selecting a named block*

Table command will print a list of the block names together with their cell coordinates in an area of the spreadsheet you designate. This task is best done in an area set aside for worksheet housekeeping, as described in Chapter 11.

As you might imagine, the names you use for blocks must follow certain rules. They can contain as many as 15 characters. You can use the letters *A* through *Z* and numbers 0 through 9 as well as punctuation characters. The names should bear some meaningful relationship to the contents of the cells, but at the same time they should not be too long. This would negate some of the convenience of using them. Block names should not be the same as any valid cell reference. For example, do not use R88 for the Rome 1988 figures because there is a cell called R88 on row 88 in column R. Using R_88 or 88R would be better. You can use any number of block names and the blocks can overlap. For example, you could separately name each city's four years or each year's five cities.

Other Edit Commands

The Edit Fill command is a way of producing a column or row of sequential numbers. You can use it to number lists, create a range of values, and so on.

The Edit Values command turns all formulas in the cells you block out into the values produced by the formulas. Edit Values is described in Chapter 3, along with Edit Transpose and Edit Fill.

Calculating

Quattro Pro 3 is designed to update the answers to all formulas quickly. Whenever you enter new information, the program checks to see whether the new data affects any other cells. Cells containing formulas that depend on the new data are automatically updated. There may be times when you will need to alter the way information is calculated, either for the whole worksheet or for only a few cells.

Replacing a Formula with Its Result

At times you may find it necessary to replace the formula in a cell with the number that is the answer to that formula. This could be necessary when you have used the @RAND function, one of the built-in functions that produces random numbers. Many of the examples in this book were created with @RAND to produce values for hypothetical spreadsheets. After the @RAND function has produced a number, you may want to replace the formula with the value it created. To do this to one cell, highlight that cell, press the Edit key (F2) and then press the Calc key (F9). This will replace the formula in a single cell with a value.

Recalculation

Quattro Pro 3 normally calculates the result of a formula when the formula is entered. The program does this *in the background,* meaning that the calculation proceeds while you are working on the worksheet. The default mode of calculation is Background, which can be changed. Occasionally, you may want the program to make you wait until recalculation is finished before allowing you to continue using the worksheet. When you change an entry in a cell used by a formula, the result is automatically recalculated. You can select Recalculation from the Options menu to change the Mode setting from Background to Automatic. However, you will find that as your worksheet begins to increase in size a noticeable amount of time will pass before the recalculations are completed under Automatic mode.

You can turn off the Background recalculation feature in Quattro Pro 3 and avoid the delays involved in Automatic mode. If you pick Manual from the Mode choices offered by the Options Recalculation command you can stop Quattro Pro 3 from doing any calculation until you have finished a series of entries. If you change to Manual mode and make a change to the worksheet you will see the message CALC on the status line. This reminds you that the worksheet is not up to date. You can then press the Calc key (F9) to recalculate formulas all at once. Alternatively, you can return to either Background or Automatic recalculation, which causes Quattro Pro 3 to update the worksheet as soon as you select another cell or make another entry.

Manual recalculation tells Quattro Pro 3 to recalculate formulas only in the following situations:

- When the formulas are entered or edited

- When you press the Calc key (F9)

- When you turn Automatic or Background recalculation back on

Manual recalculation is sometimes useful when you are entering a lot of data and do not want to see the results until all the data is entered. If enough calculated cells are affected, the data entry will be faster with recalculation set to Manual, so that recalculation occurs only after all the data is entered. However, the Background mode of calculation will generally allow you to keep entering data and get up-to-date results in your spreadsheet, without noticeable performance lags or the risks involved in assuming an uncalculated worksheet to be correct.

Protecting Your Work

After you have expended a lot of time and effort getting information into your worksheet, it is a good idea to take steps to protect it. If you work in an office with several people, possibly sharing a computer with them, someone may retrieve a spreadsheet you have been working on and unwittingly damage it by entering new data over complex formulas. As a precaution against this, you can *protect* all or part of a worksheet to prevent new data from being entered.

Global Protection

To protect the entire worksheet you select Protection from the Option menu, followed by Enable. This is effective immediately and you will see the letters **PR** in the cell status area for each cell to remind you that the cell is protected. While you can still move around the spreadsheet, if you try to change the contents of a protected cell, Quattro Pro 3 responds with a beep and the error message "Protected cell or block." You will need to press ENTER or ESCAPE to remove the message. You will not be allowed to enter data into any cell unless it has been specifically unprotected, as described in a moment. If you save the worksheet with protection enabled, anyone who retrieves it will be prevented from changing any data until protection is turned off through the same menu.

Partial Protection

As you develop spreadsheet models that perform useful functions in your business, you may want to have some data entry work done by people who are inexperienced with Quattro Pro 3. Suppose you are maintaining inventory records. You want the inventory clerk to update the inventory levels for a hundred items. The clerk is not an experienced Quattro Pro 3 user and you are worried that numbers will be entered over labels and so on. In this case, you can apply protection to the entire worksheet and then remove protection from the column where the numbers will be entered.

You can protect the entire worksheet with the Options Protection command, and then unprotect certain cells. You use the Style Protection command to do this. When you pick Protection from the Style menu you are asked whether you want to Protect or Unprotect. Choose Unprotect and you are prompted for a group of cells to change. When you select the cells and press ENTER to confirm the command those cells will be marked U in the cell status area. You are free to change these cells. If you later decide that you want to protect these unprotected cells you use the Style Protection Protect option.

Note that Quattro Pro 3 allows you to assign different colors to protected and unprotected cells. This is one of the many customizable features of the program that are discussed in Chapter 6. You will find more information on protection in Chapter 5. The development of unprotected input blocks using selective protection is also covered in Chapter 3.

Printing

The basic procedure for printing from the Quattro Pro 3 spreadsheet is to point out the block of cells to be printed and tell the program to print them.

To do this you use the Block command from the Print menu, followed by the Spreadsheet Print command. However, the variable factors such as the size of the paper in the printer and the size of the block of cells to be printed will often need to be adjusted to produce the desired results. This process is described in detail in Chapter 5.

3 *Database Commands*

A database is a collection of information arranged in a meaningful way. Whether the information is laid out in a table of columns and rows or consists of a collection of separate forms, almost anything from a phone book to medical records to an inventory list can be considered a database.

Quattro Pro 3 as a Database

Programs designed to handle large amounts of information are called *database-management software*. In this chapter you will read about the database-management capabilities of Quattro Pro 3: how they enable you to enter, store, and then manipulate collections of data. Quattro Pro 3 has two database functions: sorting and selecting data. These two functions are referred to as a *database sort* and a *database query*. The sort capability lets you reorder your data according to your specifications. The ability to query a collection of data means that you can ask the program to locate selected data. For example, the program can search the inventory database in Figure 3-1 for all inventory items that have the number 2 in the Bin# column. The query function also lets you extract information such as a list of all inventory items priced less than $1000. Many different software packages offer some level of database management. These programs can be divided into two groups: relational and simple.

```
 File  Edit  Style  Graph  Print  Database  Tools  Options  Window          ↑↓
A5: [W8] 110001                                                              ?
 J      A    B          C                  E        F       G
1                                                                          End
2             TOA - Repair Shop Inventory Listing                          ▲
3                                                                         ◄┤ ├►
4      Item#  Bin#      Description         Price  Purchased InStock        ▼
5      110001    9 Cone Machelle, Left    1,675.70  08/10/91     34
6      110002    5 Cone Machelle, Right   1,675.70  07/14/91     23       Esc
7      110003    1 Forward Bulkhead Unit    428.06  07/28/91      2
8      110004    2 Cone Machelle, Upper   1,675.70  09/00/91      5        ◄┘
9      110005    2 Cone Machelle, Lower   1,675.70  08/24/91      9
10     110006    2 Machelle, Retaining Flange 71.23 08/29/91      5        Del
11     110007    5 Cover Clamp               7.19   07/28/91     24
12     110008    3 Wheel Brackets, Front  1,122.36  09/03/91     21        @
13     110009    3 Wheel Brackets, Rear   1,225.84  08/29/91      7
14     110010   10 Wheel Brackets, Clip      57.36  08/01/91      4        5
15     110011   11 Wheel Brackets, Wing Right 1,096.09 07/19/91  16
16     110012    8 Wheel Brackets, Valve Stem   4.38 09/02/91     8        WYS
17     110013    6 Wheel Brackets, Wing Left 1,223.20 08/21/91    4
18     110014   12 Wheel Brackets, Valve Rod  165.70 08/15/91    27        CHR
19     110015    4 Wheel Brackets, Seal       29.59  09/17/91     34
20     110016    7 Wheel Rim Seals             4.38  09/07/91     32
                                                                       ┌
INVENT1.WQ1  [1]                                        NUM           READY
```

Figure 3-1.   *Inventory database*

Relational Databases

A *relational database* is one that can relate the data in several different files based on common elements. These programs can handle large amounts of data. Many of these programs also have a command language that can be used to compose complex sets of instructions in order to present users with complete menu-driven applications. Such programs are referred to as *programmable relational databases*. Examples of these kinds of databases are Ashton-Tate's dBASE series and Paradox from Borland International.

Quattro Pro 3 is not a relational database. However, it can keep a sizable amount of related information in one worksheet: more than 8000 records with as many as 256 fields, each one of which can be over 250 characters in length. Because Quattro Pro 3 is memory-based, it quickly performs database operations like sort and find. Its database commands follow the same pattern as the spreadsheet commands, so you can perform database-management tasks without learning a new program. You have all the power of Quattro Pro 3's built-in functions and graphics on hand to help analyze your data. Furthermore, Quattro Pro 3 can read data from dBASE, Paradox, and other relational databases and export files to them as well. The adaptable user interface and macro command language of Quattro Pro 3 also make customized menu-driven applications a powerful possibility.

Simple Databases

The personal-computer equivalent of card files, simple databases are designed to make creating, sorting, and searching records as easy as possible. Simple databases, however, usually lack the graphics and math capabilities found in Quattro Pro 3. For this reason, if you are learning Quattro Pro 3 for spreadsheet work anyway, you will also want to use it for simple database applications. In this way, you can easily add database-management capabilities to your repertoire of computer skills without learning another program, as well as keep all of your data in the same format.

The Quattro Pro 3 Database

Quattro Pro 3's fast and flexible spreadsheet makes it an excellent place to put together lists of information. There are just a few rules to follow in order for your lists to work with the program's database commands. These rules concern the fields and records by which the database is organized.

Fields

All information in a database is categorized by fields. Fields are the categories into which each set of facts, called a record, is broken down. In Quattro Pro 3, each field is a separate column, and each field has a name, which is placed at the top of the column. A Quattro Pro 3 database is composed of a series of consecutive columns. Each column typically contains consistent types of data; for example, each column should contain either all values, all labels, or all dates. Each column should have a unique title.

First	Last	City	State
Fred	Jones	Bend	OR
Bill	Jones	Butte	MT
Frank	James	Hill	SD
Tim	White	Dallas	TX

Acceptable fields and records

First	Last	City	State
Fred	Jones	Bend	OR
Frank	James	Hill	SD
Tim	White	Dallas	TX

Blank row causes problems

First	Last	City	State
======	======	======	======
Bill	Jones	Butte	MT
Frank	James	Hill	SD
Tim	White	Dallas	TX

Row of labels causes problems

Name	Name	City	State
Fred	Jones	Bend	OR
Bill	Jones	Butte	MT
Frank	James	Hill	SD
Tim	White	Dallas	TX

Invalid duplicate field names

Figure 3-2. *Acceptable and unacceptable fields, rows, and columns*

Records

Each set of facts about one item in a database is a record. Records correspond to each line on a list or to each card in a card file. In a Quattro Pro 3 database, each complete set of facts occupies one row. The rows of records are placed one after another with no empty rows between them. There should not be a blank row above the first record. Figure 3-2 shows a model of an acceptable record layout.

Limits

Since a Quattro Pro 3 database consists of a block of consecutive rows and named columns, some limits apply to the database dimensions. The maximum number of fields is 256, the total number of columns. The maximum number of records is the total number of rows minus one row for the field names: 8191. The maximum field size is 253 characters, which is also the maximum column width minus 1 for the label identifier. As you might imagine, you will probably run out of memory before you get to the limits of Quattro Pro 3's database capacity. For more on memory size and usage, see Chapter 7.

Database Creation

The Quattro Pro 3 database is not a special area of the program. As far as Quattro Pro 3 is concerned, any data entered into a worksheet and falling within the definition of consecutive rows and named columns is a database. You may already have created a database while working on a spreadsheet.

Spreadsheets as Databases

Consider the TOA volume figures used as an example in Chapters 1 and 2. The numbers for each city occupy one row; thus, each row is a record. The columns containing the years plus the city names are the fields. This data can be rearranged with the Database Sort command, so that the cities are in alphabetical order, as shown in Figure 3-3.

Types of Data

Your entries in a database may be labels or values. The labels can be left-, right-, or center-aligned because their alignment will not affect the operation of the database commands. In the examples in Figures 3-3 and 3-4, the city names are labels. The values can be numbers, or they can be formulas and dates. However, the numbers in columns C through E of Figure 3-4 are formulas for projected revenue, each year being the previous year incremented by a growth formula. In Figure 3-5, the formulas are shown in Text format. You can see in the upper half of the figure that each row is based on a different growth factor. Cells containing formulas can be sorted based on the results of the formulas. In Figures 3-4 and 3-5 the cities are sorted in descending order according to revenue in the final year of the projection.

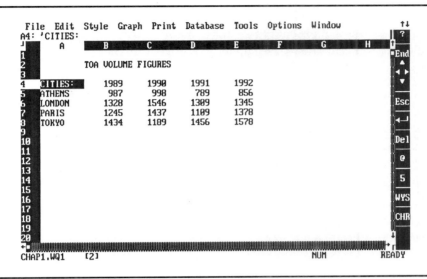

File Edit Style Graph Print Database Tools Options Window
A4: 'CITIES:

A	B	C	D	E	F	G	H
		TOA VOLUME FIGURES					
CITIES:	1989	1990	1991	1992			
ATHENS	987	998	789	856			
LONDON	1328	1546	1309	1345			
PARIS	1245	1437	1109	1378			
TOKYO	1434	1109	1456	1578			

CHAP1.WQ1   [2]   NUM   READY

Figure 3-3.   *Cities in alphabetical order*

File Edit Style Graph Print Database Tools Options Window
C5: (,0) [W12] 1.15*B5

A	B	C	D	E	F	G
		TOA VOLUME FIGURES				
DESTINATION	1989	1990	1991	1992		
PARIS	1,245	1,432	1,647	1,893		
LONDON	1,328	1,461	1,607	1,760		
TOKYO	1,434	1,534	1,634	1,734		
ATHENS	987	1,036	1,088	1,143		
	TOA VOLUME FIGURES GROWING		115.00%			
DESTINATION	1989	1990	1991	1992		
TOKYO	1,434	1,649	1,896	2,181		
LONDON	1,328	1,527	1,756	2,020		
PARIS	1,245	1,432	1,647	1,893		
ATHENS	987	1,135	1,305	1,501		

CHAP3FOR.WQ1 [2]   NUM   READY

Figure 3-4.   *Projected volume*

Figure 3-5. *Formulas exposed*

If the formulas you use refer only to other cells on the same row within the Sort Block, then sorting cells containing formulas does not pose a problem. However, if you have formulas in a database that refer to cells outside the database, such as a cell containing the rate of growth, you must make those cell references *absolute*. This means that if cell E12 contains the rate of growth by which the volume figures are incremented from year to year, the formula in C15 must be +B15*$E$12, as shown in Figure 3-5. Placing the dollar sign in front of the column and row references prevents the coordinate from changing depending upon its position. Thus, you can safely sort the block of cells A15 through E18 while retaining the rate of growth shown in cell E12. (Absolute referencing of cells is described in detail in Chapter 5.)

Quattro Pro 3's numeric dates, described in detail in Chapter 9, are particularly important in databases since many collections of information include dates. In many cases, records will need to be sorted or selected according to dates. Consider the inventory listing for the TOA repair shop shown earlier in Figure 3-1. The date that items entered the inventory is

```
   File  Edit  Style  Graph  Print  Database  Tools  Options  Window        ↑↓
A5: [W8] 110002                                                              ?
     A        B              C              E        F         G           End
1                                                                          ▲
2              TOA -  Repair Shop Inventory Listing                      ◄ ►
3                                                                          ▼
4    Item#  Bin#      Description        Price  Purchased InStock
5    110002    5 Cone Nachelle, Right    1,675.70  07/14/91    23
6    110011   11 Wheel Brackets, Wing Right 1,096.09 07/19/91  16         Esc
7    110007    5 Cover Clamp                7.19  07/28/91    24
8    110003    1 Forward Bulkhead Unit    428.06  07/28/91     2          ↵
9    110010   10 Wheel Brackets, Clip      57.36  08/01/91     4
10   110001    9 Cone Nachelle, Left     1,675.70  08/10/91    34          Del
11   110014   12 Wheel Brackets, Valve Rod 165.70  08/15/91    27
12   110013    6 Wheel Brackets, Wing Left 1,223.20 08/21/91   4           @
13   110005    2 Cone Nachelle, Lower    1,675.70  08/24/91     9
14   110006    2 Nachelle, Retaining Flange 71.23  08/29/91     5           5
15   110009    3 Wheel Brackets, Rear    1,225.84  08/29/91     7
16   110012    8 Wheel Brackets, Valve Stem  4.38  09/02/91     8          WYS
17   110008    3 Wheel Brackets, Front   1,122.36  09/03/91    21
18   110016    7 Wheel Rim Seals            4.38  09/07/91    32          CHR
19   110004    2 Cone Nachelle, Upper    1,675.70  09/08/91     5
20   110015    4 Wheel Brackets, Seal      29.59  09/17/91    34
INVENT1.WQ1  [1]                                         NUM        READY
```

Figure 3-6.   *Inventory sorted by date*

an important part of material and asset management. The same information is sorted by date in Figure 3-6 to show the oldest items on hand.

Problem Data

Many databases contain non-numeric numbers, that is, numbers that are
entered as labels. A typical example is ZIP codes in addresses. If you enter
01234 as a number, it will appear as **1234** in the cell because a leading 0
in a number does not register. You get around this problem and the ones
created by 9-digit ZIP codes, telephone numbers, and part numbers that
contain letters as well as digits by entering these figures as numbers
preceded by label prefixes. If you do not do so, the ZIP code **94109-4109**
entered as a number would result in **9000** because Quattro Pro 3 will read
the dash as a minus sign. Note that when you enter telephone numbers
with area codes, beginning the entry with a square bracket will make it a

label, as in **[800] 555-1212**. Quattro Pro 3 can still sort and search for numbers even if they are entered as labels.

The distinction between values and labels gives rise to another data entry problem, one that is immediately apparent when you try to enter a typical street address, such as 10 Downing Street. Quattro Pro 3 takes its cue from the first character of the entry, in this case the number 1. This is a value and it leads Quattro Pro 3 to assume that what follows is also a value, an assumption that proves erroneous when you type the rest of the address and attempt to enter it. You will get the rather ironic error message "Invalid cell or block address." As with numbers such as ZIP codes, the answer is to place a label prefix at the beginning of any alphanumeric entry that is not a formula.

Remembering to type a label prefix in front of a non-numeric number gets very tedious and can give rise to data entry errors. To overcome this problem, Quattro Pro 3 allows you to designate certain cells in a spreadsheet as Labels Only. To do this you use the Data Entry option on the Database menu. When cells are designated Labels Only, anything you enter into them will be automatically preceded by a label prefix. The Data-Entry option also allows you to restrict entries to Dates Only, a means of avoiding errors in date fields. (Restricting data types is discussed in detail toward the end of this chapter, under the heading "Data Entry Techniques.")

Transpose

You may find that you often need to reorganize information in a spreadsheet so that you can work with it as a database. For example, you might want the TOA volume figures listed with the years as rows and the cities as columns. This can be done with the Edit Transpose command.

After selecting Transpose from the Edit menu, you highlight the cells involved and press ENTER. You can see the result of transposing in Figure 3-7. (Note that the city names were center-aligned in row 10.) The Edit Transpose command is particularly useful when importing data from other programs. It is not effective if your data contains formulas, since the cell references are thrown off by the rearrangement. However, if you convert the formulas to their corresponding values before transposing, the values are not affected by the move. You can use the Edit Values command to highlight a block of cells and convert them from formulas to values.

```
 File  Edit  Style  Graph  Print  Database  Tools  Options  Window        ↑↓
A10: 'CITIES:                                                              ?
⌐      A        B        C        D        E        F        G        H    ┐
1                                                                         End
2              TOA VOLUME FIGURES                                          ▲
3                                                                         ◄ ►
4  CITIES:     1989     1990     1991     1992                             ▼
5  PARIS       1245     1437     1109     1378
6  LONDON      1328     1546     1309     1345                            Esc
7  TOKYO       1434     1189     1456     1578
8  ATHENS       987      998      789      856                            ◄┘
9
10 CITIES:  PARIS    LONDON   TOKYO    ATHENS                             Del
11    1989     1245     1328     1434      987                             @
12    1990     1437     1546     1189      998
13    1991     1109     1309     1456      789                             5
14    1992     1378     1345     1578      856
15                                                                        WYS
16
17                                                                        CHR
18
19
20
+                                                                        →
CHAP1.WQ1    [2]                                          NUM        READY
```

Figure 3-7.   *Transposed block*

Column Widths

Since the requirements of a database allow only one row for each record, fields containing lengthy information may require extensive widening of the column. Notice that the Description field in Figure 3-6 had to be made significantly wider than the others. In order to compensate for widening, you can narrow the columns containing short data, such as the Bin# field in Figure 3-6. Keep in mind that you do not have to make each column wide enough to show all the data that it contains in order for Quattro Pro 3 to store long entries. However, if you want all of the data to print, you will need to expand columns prior to printing.

One solution to this dilemma is to use the Auto Width command. This command allows you to set the width of a group of columns all at once, making each column wide enough to display its longest entry, plus a fixed number of blank spaces. A typical use of this command would be after entering data into the database, but prior to printing out reports. Rather than checking each column to make sure it is wide enough, simply select a cell in the leftmost column of the database. Then type / to activate the menu and select Style, followed by Block Widths. You can now pick Auto Width and Quattro Pro 3 will prompt you to enter the extra space between columns, which is measured in characters. In most cases 2 characters is sufficient. When you type 2 and press ENTER you are prompted for the block of columns that you want to adjust. Highlight the columns with the cursor keys or the mouse and press ENTER to confirm. You will immediately see that all of the columns within the block have their column widths set automatically. You need only indicate one row within each column, but the columns must be in a contiguous block. To auto-adjust nonadjacent columns you need to issue the command for each column in turn.

Note that the Style Hide Column command, described in Chapter 5, will let you temporarily remove selected columns from view if necessary. Notice in Figure 3-6 that column D is missing. This is because column D contains original cost information and is currently hidden.

Sort

Sorting is the process of rearranging rows of information according to alphabetical or numerical order. Typically, sorting is used for placing the records in a database into a new order, as diagrammed in Figure 3-8. For example, the airline flights listed in this figure can be sorted numerically according to flight number as shown on the left, or alphabetically according to the city of their destination as shown on the right. However, you do not need field names to sort spreadsheet information with Quattro Pro 3. For example, you could sort the list of things to do shown in Figure 3-9 according to the priority numbers, without bothering to provide any field names.

Providing Sort Information

To change the order of records in a worksheet, Quattro Pro 3 needs to know two things:

Take Over Airline Flights

Flt#	City	Departs
101	RIO	10:00
102	MADRID	08:15
103	PARIS	07:30
104	TOKYO	09:45
105	VIENNA	12:15
106	LONDON	11:20
107	ROME	08:45

SORT

Flt#	City	Departs
106	LONDON	11:20
102	MADRID	08:15
103	PARIS	07:30
101	RIO	10:00
107	ROME	08:45
104	TOKYO	09:45
105	VIENNA	12:15

From Flight # Order Sorted to Alphabetical Order by City

Figure 3-8. *Diagram of Sort*

Where the data is located	The Sort Block of cells contains the records but not the field names.
How you want the data sorted	The columns that are the keys on which to sort. You can use up to five keys.

You define the Sort Block and the sort keys by using Database menu items. Quattro Pro 3 will then remember them and allow you to resort the database after editing the records.

The Data Menu

To perform a sort you activate the menu bar, then select Database as shown in Figure 3-9. When you pick Sort from the Database menu, you are prompted in logical order for the information that Quattro Pro 3 needs to perform a sort—Block, 1st Key, 2nd Key, and so on—as shown in Figure 3-10. When you have provided this information, you select Go to activate the sort. In Figure 3-10 you can see the result of sorting the block B4..C10

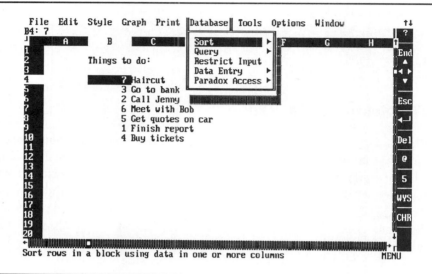

Figure 3-9.   *The Database menu*

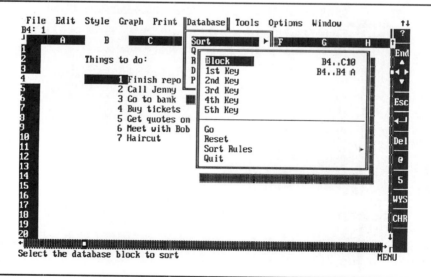

Figure 3-10.   *The Sort menu*

using B4 as the key with ascending (A) as the order. You can use Reset to move from sorting one area of a worksheet to another. Selecting Quit returns you to READY mode. This is often a quicker way to move than pressing ESCAPE several times.

The Sample Database

Figure 3-11 shows a database that will be used to demonstrate the database features of Quattro Pro 3. This figure is the TOA On-Call Roster, a list of staff members who are on standby to work. Their names and ranks, together with relevant data such as where they are based and how many days notice they must have before working, are recorded. To practice the database commands, enter this database into a blank Quattro Pro 3 worksheet. Enter the names as labels and the numbers as values. Enter dates in *MM/DD/YY* format after first pressing CTRL-D to set the date format. Although this is only a small collection of data, it is a typical

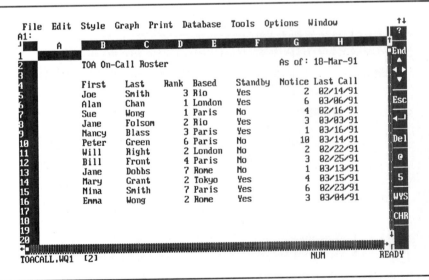

Figure 3-11. *A sample database*

Quattro Pro 3 database in form and application and will be an effective model for learning the database commands.

The Sort Block

The first item of information that Quattro Pro 3 needs in order to sort a database is the block of data to be sorted; that is, all of the fields of all of the records. This block consists of the entire database *except* for the field names. In Figure 3-11, the block of data is cells B5 through H16; all of the employee names, their locations, and so on. When you select Block from the Sort menu, you are prompted to point out the cell block containing the records. The easiest way to point out this block is to place the cell selector in the top-left corner of the block (the first record of the first field) before entering the menu system. The initial coordinate is always the cell occupied by the cell selector prior to entering the menu system. This coordinate is not locked at this point. If you are not in B5, the first field of the first record, this is the time to move there. To anchor the block, type a period. Quattro Pro 3 responds by showing you the locked cell coordinates, in this case, B5..B5.

The END Key

To complete the highlighting of the Sort Block, use the END key. Press END once and the word END appears in the lower right of the screen. Now press RIGHT ARROW. You will see the highlighting move to the last column on the right. The END message will disappear. Next press END again and then DOWN ARROW. Now the highlighting runs through to the last row, completely highlighting, or painting out, the data (cells B5..H16 in this case). Press ENTER to confirm this block, and you will be returned to the Sort menu for the next step. The END key is particularly useful in this instance because it automatically encompasses the entire block of data.

You should avoid defining the data to be sorted as just one or two fields. In other words, do not think "I am going to sort last names," but rather think of the entire database as one entity and decide, "I am going to sort the database according to last names." By defining the Sort Block, you have told Quattro Pro 3 where the data to be sorted is located. You then need to tell Quattro Pro 3 how you want the sort to be ordered.

The Sort Keys

To tell Quattro Pro 3 in what order to put the records, you select *keys*, which are devices for pointing out which column is the key to the sort. For example, to sort the TOA staff alphabetically by last name, you would select the Last Name column as the first key. If you wanted a complete sort by name so that the several Smiths were sorted by first name, you would select a second key, the First Name column. When two or more items have identical entries in the field chosen for the first key, the second key acts as a tie-breaker.

To select keys, simply pick the appropriate number from the Sort menu. As you can see, five keys can be used. This number is sufficient to sort a customer account database by first name, last name, middle initial, ZIP code, and date of last purchase. When you type **1** for the first key, you will be prompted for the column to be used, as shown here:

The cell location is not anchored; it is the initial cell your selector occupies prior to entering the menu system. Place the cell selector on the first record in the desired column; in this case it is cell C5, the first item in the Last field. There is no need to anchor the cell with a period. When you press ENTER to confirm the location, you are prompted for either Descending or Ascending order. Descending is, of course, from highest to lowest (3,2,1 or C,B,A); ascending is from lowest to highest (1,2,3 or A,B,C). Thus, to sort from A to Z you select Ascending. Remember that Quattro Pro 3 is thinking numerically, that is, A=1 and Z=26. After picking Descending or Ascending, you are returned to the Sort menu. However, the data has not yet changed. You must select Go to initiate the sort. When you do so, Quattro Pro 3 reorders the database and returns you to the Sort menu. You can see the results of an Ascending sort based on C5 in Figure 3-12.

```
   File  Edit  Style  Graph  Print  Database  Tools  Options  Window      ↑↓
 B4: 'First                                                                ?
 ┘     A        B      C    D     E        F      G       H        T
 1
 2             TOA On-Call Roster                    As of: 18-Mar-91     End
 3                                                                         ▲
 4             First   Last   Rank  Based    Standby  Notice Last Call    ◄ ►
 5             Nancy   Blass    3 Paris     Yes       1  03/16/91          ▼
 6             Alan    Chan     1 London    Yes       6  03/06/91
 7             Jane    Dobbs    7 Rome      No        1  03/13/91         Esc
 8             Jane    Folsom   2 Rio       Yes       3  03/03/91
 9             Bill    Front    4 Paris     No        3  02/25/91         ←┘
 10            Mary    Grant    2 Tokyo     Yes       4  03/15/91
 11            Peter   Green    6 Paris     No       10  03/14/91         Del
 12            Will    Right    2 London    No        2  02/22/91
 13            Nina    Smith    7 Paris     Yes       6  02/23/91          @
 14            Joe     Smith    3 Rio       Yes       2  02/14/91
 15            Sue     Wong     1 Paris     No        4  02/16/91          5
 16            Emma    Wong     2 Rome      Yes       3  03/04/91
 17                                                                       WYS
 18                                                                       CHR
 19
 20
 ←                                                                        ↓
 TOACALL.WQ1  [2]                                  NUM           READY
```

Figure 3-12. *Sorted list*

Successive Sorts

If you are performing a series of sorts—for example, as you edit names and you want to check that the alphabetical order is correct—you do not need to redefine the Sort Block or the sort keys already set. Quattro Pro 3 remembers the locations of these items. For example, if you decide to add a second key column to the sort, such as the First Name column in the TOA staff database, you do not need to redefine the Sort Block. The block is retained in memory. If you pick Block and find the correct block of cells is already defined, simply press ENTER to reconfirm it. Do not press ESCAPE, since this will unlock the block coordinates.

The ability to resort a block of cells without having to redefine the sort parameters is convenient but it can pose a problem when you want to sort several different blocks of cells within the same worksheet. For example, suppose you have sorted cells B2 through E30, based on columns B and C. The 1st Key is cell B3 and the 2nd Key is cell C3. Now you want to sort another set of data, in cells H30 through M50, keyed on cell J30. There can be only one Sort Block defined at once in a Quattro Pro 3 worksheet, so you have to redefine the Sort Block setting from B2..E30 to H30..M50. You also need to redefine the 1st Key from B3 to J30. What is not so obvious is that you should not simply redefine these settings, but you should use the Reset option on the Sort menu before entering the new settings.

The reason for using Reset when changing Sort Blocks is that there is no other way to clear a sort-key setting. In the example just given, you were going from a sort where two keys were used, B3 and C3, to a sort where only one is required, 30. The Reset command is the only way to clear C3 from the second key setting, and this is something you may overlook if you do not need a second key in this particular sorting operation. If you do not do something about the second key you will get the error message "Key column outside of Sort Block." At this point you will have two choices: to define a second key that is appropriate to the new Sort Block, or to use the Reset option on the Sort menu. The Reset option affects all five keys *and* the Sort Block, so using Reset at this stage means that you lose all of your settings. For this reason you should use Reset whenever you decide to sort a separate area of a worksheet. A more radical approach to this problem is to use the multiple-worksheet capability of Quattro Pro 3. If you have two databases to sort in one worksheet you can always copy one of them to another worksheet and avoid having to reset sort settings.

Note that when you add data to the bottom of a database Quattro Pro 3 does not automatically include the added data in the Sort Block or place the data in the correct alphabetical order. For example, suppose you are adding new staff names to the bottom of the list in Figure 3-12. After adding the new names, you need to redefine the Sort Block and issue a command to sort the new records into the database.

Sort Block Expansion

Quattro Pro 3 will not automatically extend the Sort Block to cover new additions to a database *unless* you insert a row before the end of the database. Rows inserted into the worksheet within any named or recorded block of cells become part of that block. The coordinates of the block expand to accommodate the new cells. Inserted rows are added to the Sort Block if you use Edit Insert Rows with your cell selector on any row in the database except the first one. Thus, if you want to add new employees in their correct alphabetical locations within the list, you can normally do so with Edit Insert Rows. In Figure 3-13 you can see a new employee being added to the list.

```
 File  Edit  Style  Graph  Print  Database  Tools  Options  Window      ↑↓
Marvin                                                                    ?
┌───────────────────────────────────────────────────────────────────┐
│     A       B       C     D      E       F       G      H           │↑
│1                                                                    │ End
│2         TOA On-Call Roster               As of: 18-Mar-91          │ ▲
│3                                                                    │ ◄ ▼
│4         First   Last    Rank  Based   Standby  Notice Last Call    │
│5         Nancy   Blass    3 Paris    Yes        1 03/16/91           │
│6         Alan    Chan     1 London   Yes        6 03/06/91           │Esc
│7         Jane    Dobbs    7 Rome     No         1 03/13/91           │
│8         Jane    Folsom   2 Rio      Yes        3 03/03/91           │ ◄┘
│9         Bill    Front    4 Paris    No         3 02/25/91           │
│10        Mary    Grant    2 Tokyo    Yes        4 03/15/91           │Del
│11        Peter   Green    6 Paris    No        10 03/14/91           │
│12        Hank                                                        │ 0
│13        Will    Right    2 London   No         2 02/22/91           │
│14        Nina    Smith    7 Paris    Yes        6 02/23/91           │ 5
│15        Joe     Smith    3 Rio      Yes        2 02/14/91           │
│16        Sue     Wong     1 Paris    No         4 02/16/91           │WYS
│17        Emma    Wong     2 Rome     Yes        3 03/04/91           │
│18                                                                   │CHR
│19                                                                   │
│20                                                                   │ ↓
└───────────────────────────────────────────────────────────────────┘
  C12: [W8]                                                           LABEL
```

Figure 3-13. *Adding a new employee*

Rules of Order

You may wonder how Quattro Pro 3 decides exactly in what order to place the rows when the Database Sort Go command is issued. The program looks at the column that is designated as the 1st Key, sorts it, and the rest of the cells are moved according to their entries in the key column. Typically, a column will consist of all labels or all values, in which case the order is fairly easy to predict. If you have picked Ascending, then numbers go from lowest to highest and words go from those beginning with A to those beginning with Z. Dates go from the oldest to the most recent. However, there are some subtleties to alphabetical order, and some rules that Quattro Pro 3 uses to determine sort order when a key column contains a mixture of values and labels. The default sort order used by Quattro Pro 3 is an ascending sort in the order listed in Table 3-1.

There are a couple of situations to watch for where the order may not be what you expect. Accidental spaces at the beginning of a label will cause that label to be placed at the top of a list. You can change the rules slightly using the Sort Rules option on the Database Sort menu. There are two areas that you can affect, as shown in Figure 3-14. The Numbers before Labels option is either Yes or No, with No being the default. When changed to Yes, the effect is to change the order of items in Table 3-1 to 6,1,2,3,4,5.

The Label Order option can either be set to Dictionary, which is the default setting, or to ASCII. The Dictionary setting means that Quattro Pro 3 sorts labels alphabetically, with those that begin with special characters coming after those that begin with ordinary letters. In ascending order the Dictionary sort will place words with uppercase letters before identical words with lowercase letters, as in FRED, FREd, FRed, Fred, fred.

The ASCII order uses the ASCII code of the first character of the label as the basis of the sort. *ASCII* stands for American Standard Code for Information Interchange, a system of codes in which each printer or screen character has a numeric value, from 1 to 250. (You can use the @CODE function described in Chapter 9 to explore ASCII codes.) The effect of

1. Blank cells	These appear at the top of the list, even before cells that contain only blank spaces.
2. Labels beginning with spaces	These are arranged according to the number of spaces preceding the first character, with more spaces preceding fewer; then alphabetically from A to Z, according to characters after an equal number of spaces.
3. Labels beginning with numbers	These come before labels that begin with words and are arranged numerically.
4. Regular labels	These are arranged according to the alphabet, from A to Z, according to the rules in number 5.
5. Labels beginning with special characters	Such characters as @ and $ come after Z. When two labels begin with the same special character they are arranged according to the second character, so that $NEW comes before $OLD. There is a consistent order among special characters that goes, from lowest to highest: ! " # $ % & ( ) * + - . / : ; < = > ? @ [\ ] ^ ' {	} ~.
6. Numbers, from lowest to highest	This applies to the value of the number, not its formatted appearance. Thus 10 and 1.00E+01 are equal, as are 0.1 and 10.00%.

Table 3-1.   *Ascending Sort Order*

Figure 3-14. *The Sort Rules*

selecting ASCII order for sorting a list based on a column of labels is likely to be surprising if you are not familiar with ASCII. For example, all labels beginning with capital letters will come before those beginning with lowercase letters, and some special characters will also come before lowercase letters. In ascending sorts, labels beginning with numbers will precede any labels beginning with letters.

You can also alter the sort order by using a Sort Table. The use of a Sort Table allows you to determine the priority given to foreign characters. To use a Sort Table, select Options from the main menu and then choose International. This feature is described in Chapter 6.

Applying the Sort

Having seen Quattro Pro 3's ability to sort information, you are ready to consider some applications of this feature. Placing data in order can be especially useful when you are attempting to analyze or report it.

Analytical Sorting

Suppose you have a list of sales statistics for a company's sales force. Instead of having them arranged alphabetically, you may want to sort these numbers according to the Total column to see which people are turning in the best overall performance. To see who is selling more of a particular product you could sort by the product column. Later in this chapter you will learn how to find specific records within a database using the Data Query command, but it is important to bear in mind that simply sorting data makes it easy to find your way around it and to draw conclusions from it.

Prereport Sorting

In addition to analyzing a database, sorting is useful when you are creating reports from a database. A budget report will look better if the offices are placed in some order rather than arranged haphazardly. If you were a manager using the database of TOA on-call personnel, you might need to produce lists of TOA staff who are available to work at any given time. Placing the list in alphabetical order makes it easier to read as well as more professional looking.

A related use of the Sort command is to tidy up data entry errors. For example, it is quite possible to enter the same record into a database several times. Duplicate records can be found by sorting the database and then browsing through it.

Nondatabase Sorting

A further application of the Sort command was mentioned earlier: sorting lists that are not databases. This means that you can use the Sort command when building or organizing a spreadsheet project that is not intended to be a database. For example, suppose you are creating a budget and are entering figures for a number of expense categories, as shown in Figure 3-15. You might decide that they will look better in numerical order, from largest to smallest, so you use the Sort command to arrange them that way. The quick way to do this is as follows:

1. Select the cells: Using SHIFT-F7 and the cursor keys or the mouse, highlight from cell A4 down through B14. This will probably leave the cell selector in B14, which is fine.

2. Issue the Database Sort Block command: This will pick up A4..B14 as the Sort Block.

3. Pick 1st Key and press ENTER: This will select B14 as the 1st Key, which is what you want. Press ENTER.

4. Now pick Go. This will produce a descending list, as shown in Figure 3-16. Note that you do not have to type **D** since this is the default sort order.

In this example there are two shortcuts: preselecting the Sort Block, and using a cell other than the first cell in the column as the sort key. You can also see that you do not need field names for a sort to work. If you now decide that an alphabetical list might be better, you can change the 1st Key to any cell from A4 through A14 and pick A as the sort order.

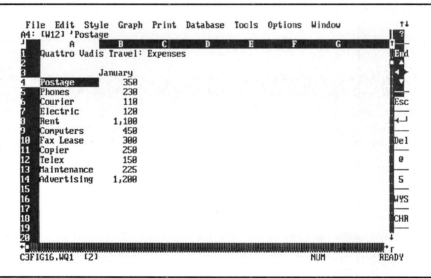

Figure 3-15.   *Expenses before sorting*

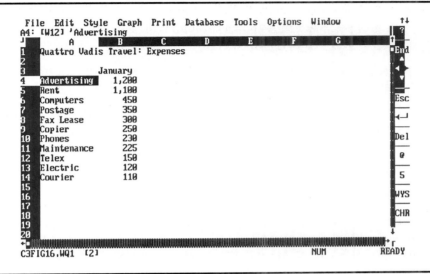

Figure 3-16. *Expenses after sorting*

Sort Saving

When the sort operation is performed, a large amount of information is moved. Unless you are very sure of the effects of the sort, you should always save a worksheet before sorting. Another safeguard is to make sure that the Undo feature is enabled. (Select Options, Other, Undo, and Enable.) This will allow you to reverse the effect of a sort just by pressing the Undo key (ALT-F5).

Sort Precautions

As mentioned earlier, do *not* think of sorting one column in a database, because information will become detached from its records and cannot be put back together. To guard against unwanted changes to data, always save the file before a sort. That way, if the sort produces an effect you do not want, you can retrieve the presort file. You might also want to check the Sort Block setting on the Sort menu before issuing the Go command.

If you cannot see the Sort Block coordinates on your menu, press the Expand key (+) on the numeric pad. This will give you a wide version of the menu, showing the settings.

Reordering with Edit Fill

Although records in a database may not be in numeric or alphabetic order, the order in which they are entered may be significant. If this is the case, you can insert a column to the left of the database and fill it with a series of numbers that correspond to each of the records. You can do this easily with the Edit Fill command. For example, you could add a Record# column to the database shown in Figure 3-11.

You can type a field name such as Record# on the same row as the other database field names. Then you can place the cell selector below the field name on the same row as the first piece of data in the database. When you select Edit Fill, you will be asked to define a block of cells to fill. Anchor this block in the current cell by typing a period and extend the highlighting down the worksheet. You must highlight down to and including the row of the last record. To do this quickly, press RIGHT ARROW, then END and DOWN ARROW, and then LEFT ARROW. This action takes the highlighting into the first column currently occupied by data, down to the last row of data, and then back into the original column you want to fill, as shown in Figure 3-17. Using the END key on completed columns and rows is a quick way of getting around.

When you press ENTER to confirm the fill block, Quattro Pro 3 prompts you for a start number. You can use the suggested default of 0 or any other number, such as 1001. Then press ENTER and you will be prompted for the increment. You will usually select 1, although you can use decimals or units larger than 1. After entering the increment, you must specify the ending number. Simply type a number that is larger than the largest number you want in the block you are filling, and Quattro Pro 3 will stop at the end of the block. Alternatively, if you know the ending number you need, you can type that number. (The default ending number of 8191 comes from numbering all the rows from 0 to 8191.) You can see the completed Edit Fill in Figure 3-18.

If you include this column of numbers in the Sort Block, you can always resort the database on this column, which will restore the original order of records. Note that Edit Fill can also produce a horizontal series of numbers if you define a row as the fill block. You can even fill a rectangle with a series of values if you pick a rectangular fill block.

Figure 3-17. *Defining the block to be filled*

Figure 3-18. *Completed Edit Fill*

Database Printing

As introduced in Chapter 2, printing information from Quattro Pro 3 involves defining the block of cells to be printed. To print a database, you simply need to define the database as the block of cells to be printed. Quattro Pro 3 arranges the data on pages according to the quantity of information and the size of the page. To print the data in sorted order, be sure to use the Sort Go command before you issue the Print Spreadsheet command.

Quattro Pro 3's print commands are covered in detail in Chapter 5. Several commands are pertinent to printing databases. Using field names as a heading that will appear across the top of each page is very useful when the list runs onto several pages. Multiple-page listings will also benefit from headers that number the pages.

Once you have defined a print block, Quattro Pro 3 continues to print from those same cells without your having to redefine them. Thus you can sort, print, and then resort and print without having to redefine the print block.

You may want to add a separator line printed at the top of your database below the field names, like this:

First Last Rank Based Standby Notice Last Call

You can use the Line Drawing option on the Style menu to create a line like this, placing the line on the bottom of the field name cells. This avoids having to add an extra line to the database, which could get sorted into the rest of the data.

Making Inquiries

Quattro Pro 3 can not only sort a collection of data in a worksheet, but, with the Database Query feature, it can also locate specific records or groups of records. Having located records, you can browse through and edit them. You can even copy matching records to a separate list. (The Database Query feature is not the same as the Edit Search & Replace feature described in the last chapter.)

Lines of Questioning

As an example of the Database Query feature, imagine you are the personnel manager at TOA. You need to find employees at a specific location and then you want to know which employees are available. You can phrase this need as a question or query. A typical query would be "Find employees based in Rome who are available." Using the TOA on-call database for this management function, you can address this query to the program. The conditions you place on requests to find specific data in Quattro Pro 3 are called *criteria*. In this example, the criteria can be expressed as "Find all employees whose records have Rome in the Based column and Yes in the Standby column." When given this command in the appropriate manner, Quattro Pro 3 will respond either by highlighting records that match the criteria, or by placing a list of matching records in a separate area of the worksheet.

In order to find data that matches certain conditions or criteria, Quattro Pro 3 needs to know two things:

Where the data is located	The Query Block contains the entire database including the field names
Which data to find	The Criteria Table is used to specify the criteria of your search, that is, what data to match

After you have given Quattro Pro 3 these two pieces of information, the program locates matching records by highlighting them. If you provide a third piece of information, called an *Output Block,* Quattro Pro 3 extracts a list of items and places the list in that area of the worksheet.

Where Data Is Located

To undertake any query operation, you first need to tell Quattro Pro 3 about the Query Block, that is, which block of cells contains the data you want to search. If you have just sorted the database, you might think that you have already answered the question "Where is the data?" After all, the Sort menu asked you to define a block of data. However, while the procedure used in a query is similar to that used in a sort, there is a difference: The Query Block includes the field names; the Sort Block does not.

To define the Query Block, select Database from the menu bar and then Query and you will see the menu shown in Figure 3-19. When you select Block, Quattro Pro 3 prompts you to point out the cells containing the database records. This is the entire database, including the field names. When you first pick Block, the prompt for the cells containing the database records is not anchored, and you should move the cell selector to the top-left corner of the database if it is not already there. Anchor the cell by typing a period. Just as in sorting operations, you can use the END key very effectively to highlight the Query Block. Press END and then RIGHT ARROW. Press END again and then DOWN ARROW. This will highlight the entire database. Press ENTER to confirm this block. Now you are ready to tell Quattro Pro 3 what records you want to find.

Note that you do not have to include the entire database in the block to be searched. You can leave off some records from the bottom of the block. However, you must include field names for the columns you are searching.

Figure 3-19. *The Query menu*

Which Data to Find

To tell Quattro Pro 3 which data you are looking for you establish a *Criteria Table*. In its simplest form a Criteria Table consists of a field name above a piece of data. For example, suppose you want to find all personnel in the sample database who are based in London. The Criteria Table would be as follows:

Based   (this is the field name)
London   (this is the data to match)

You enter this information into cells of your worksheet. You then tell the program the location of that criteria and ask it to locate the records. Quattro Pro 3 does this by trying to match what you have specified in the criteria to each row of the appropriate column in the Query Block. In this example, the program looks in the field or column that is called or headed by the word *Based*. The program checks for the text *London*. When a match for such text is found, the entire record that contains the matching text is highlighted.

The data that you ask Quattro Pro 3 to match can consist of formulas as well as simple text or value entries. You can also use multiple criteria, checking up to 256 fields at once.

Creating a Criteria Table

A typical Criteria Table is shown in Figure 3-20. As you can see, it consists of two field names, with values from those fields entered beneath them. This particular table is being set up to locate anyone based in Rome who is on standby. This means that Quattro Pro 3 will look in two fields, Based and Standby. The program will look for *Rome* in the first field and *Yes* in the second. Only when it encounters a record that meets both of these criteria will it accept the record as a match.

To build a Criteria Table, you type the field names of the columns in which you want to match data, followed by the data you want to match, in a separate area of the worksheet. The actual positioning of the Criteria Table on the spreadsheet is not critical to performance of the Locate operation, but the Criteria Table should be set apart from the database in

Figure 3-20. *Setting the Criteria Block*

an unused portion of the worksheet. However, there are some practical factors regarding location that you should consider. Do not place the Criteria Table directly to the right or left of the database if you expect to be deleting records or rows from the database with the Edit Delete Row command. Do not remove the Criteria Table too far from the database as you will be needlessly consuming memory.

You define the Criteria Table to Quattro Pro 3 by selecting Criteria Table from the Query menu. You highlight the appropriate block of cells and press ENTER, as shown in Figure 3-20. Be careful not to include any blank lines in the Criteria Table, since this will cause Quattro Pro 3 to find everything in the database. If the entries beneath the field names in a Criteria Table are all on the same line, as they are in Figure 3-20, then the relationship between them is AND. This means that a record must meet both criteria to be included in the Locate operation. If the entries are on separate lines, the relationship is OR, and the program locates records that match any one of the criteria. For example, the following arrangement selects everyone who is based in Rome, plus everyone who is on standby:

Based	Standby
Rome	
	Yes

Locating Data

When you have defined the Query Block and the Criteria Table, you are returned to the Query menu. To find the records meeting your criteria, select the Locate command. Locate causes Quattro Pro 3 to highlight the first item meeting your criteria. As you can see from Figure 3-21, this highlighting bar runs the full length of the record. You can then move to the next record that meets the criteria by pressing the DOWN ARROW key. When you get to the last matching record and try to go further, Quattro Pro 3 will beep. You can move back up through the records with the UP ARROW key and continue to browse through the matching items by using the UP and DOWN ARROW keys. The END key takes you to the last record, while HOME takes you to the first. If there are no records meeting your

Figure 3-21. *Results of Locate*

criteria, Quattro Pro 3 will beep in response to the Locate command and return to the Query menu. This is an opportunity to check that you have specified the criteria correctly.

Notice that the cursor flashes within the Locate highlight bar and that you can move it across the bar with the RIGHT and LEFT ARROW keys. The cursor moves from column center to column center. To completely change any cell on the Locate bar, place your cursor in the appropriate column, type the new entry, and press ENTER. Alternatively, you can press F2 and edit the cell contents, returning them to the cell with the ENTER key.

After you have used Locate, you return to the other areas of Quattro Pro 3 by pressing ESCAPE. If you entered from the Query menu, ESCAPE takes you back to the Query menu, where you can make changes. If you entered the query by pressing F7—described in a moment—ESCAPE takes you directly to READY mode. One handy key that takes you from any mode or menu back to READY mode, regardless of how you got there, is CTRL-BREAK.

The Locate feature is very useful for quick searches when you do not want to print out a separate list, for example, to perform a quick check of a specific item in stock or an employee record. If you want to copy the records that have been located to another part of the worksheet, or to another worksheet, then you need the Extract command, which is described later in this chapter.

Advanced Criteria

So far you have seen that a Criteria Table offers a simple but effective way of indicating the parameters of your search for data. You can take the Criteria Table even further by using formulas and block names to create detailed search specifications.

Assigning Names

You may have noticed an option on the Database Query menu called Assign Names. This allows you to give block names to each cell in the second row of your database, using the field names in the first row. Why would you want to do this? You have already seen that you can query your database without carrying out this operation. The value of the Assign Names command appears when you start to develop more sophisticated search criteria. So far, you have seen how to search for something that is an exact match, telling Quattro Pro 3 to match *Rome* and *Yes*. When you come to search for a range of values, such as *Rank greater than 5*, then block names come in very handy.

The Assign Names command is very easy to use. After you have defined the Query Block, just select Assign Names. You will not see anything happen. However, if you quit from the Query menu and use the Edit Names Create command you will see a list of the block names you have just created. If you press the Expand key (+) you will see the cell coordinates listed next to the names, as shown in Figure 3-22. You can then use these names in search formulas. Note that block names are stored in capital letters. In fact, Quattro Pro 3 is not at all case-sensitive when it comes to the Query command. A query based on *YES* also finds *yes* and *Yes*. When you put together Criteria Tables and formulated criteria it will not matter if you refer to field names in upper- or lowercase.

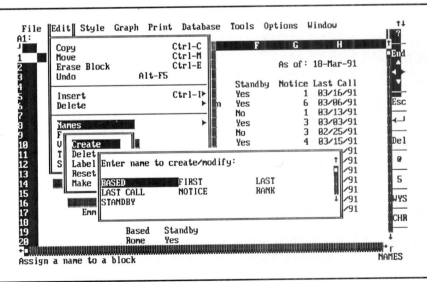

Figure 3-22. *Names Create list after Assign Names*

Formulated Criteria

You can enter numbers and labels into a Criteria Table and you can also use formulas. These formulas use *logical operators*. They also use the block name associated with each column by the Assign Names command. Thus, you could enter **+RANK>5** in the Rank column of a Criteria Table to find all persons with a rank greater than 5.

Each Criteria Table formula includes three elements: Field, Comparison Operator, and Value. These tell Quattro Pro 3 which field contains the value you are attempting to match, whether you want to match an exact value or a range of values, and the value itself. For example, suppose you need to find all staff with a Rank above 5. This can be expressed as +Rank>5. Note that the plus sign is used here because this is a formula. Rank is the field name, > is the comparison operator (meaning greater than), and 5 is the value. The comparison operators you can use are as follows:

>	Greater than (+Rank>5 means 6,7,8, and so on)
<	Less than (+Rank<5 means 4,3,2, and so on)
>=	Greater than or equal to (+Rank>=5 means 5,6, and so on)
<=	Less than or equal to (+Rank<=5 means 5,4,3, and so on)
<>	Not equal to (+Rank<>5 means anything other than 5)
=	Equal to (+Rank=5 means only 5)

Note that you generally will not use an expression like +Rank=5 unless it is part of a larger formula, since there is no need to use a formula if the criterion is a single case. Simply use 5 as the criterion.

Since Quattro Pro 3 lists all named blocks for you, you can create formulas using block names with the List key (F3). For example, to create the formula +RANK>5 you first type + and press F3. Select RANK from the list by highlighting it and pressing ENTER. Now you can type **>5** and press ENTER to complete the formula. This avoids typing errors such as incorrect spelling of block names.

Complex Formulated Criteria

To place additional qualifications on the criteria you use for querying items, you can add logical operators, which set up more categories to match. The logical operators shown here set up two or three criteria for the personnel list:

AND   as in Based="Rome"#AND#Rank>5

OR   as in Based="Rome"#OR#"Paris"

NOT   as in Based="Rome"#AND#Rank>5#NOT#First="Joe"

The logical operator must be placed in the formula within # signs as shown in the examples. You create multiple conditions with logical operators to make your search more specific. For example, if you wanted to locate all staff based in Paris with a rank greater than 5, you would type **+BASED="paris"#AND#RANK>5** as shown here:

Notice that the field name in the Criteria Table is Based but the Based field is not the only one referred to in the formula. In fact, you can use any field name from your database when you are using formula criteria that reference named cells in the database. For example, in the next illustration you can see a formula referencing Rank and Notice that has been entered under the field name Last.

Criteria Techniques

A quick way to create and use a Criteria Table is to copy the entire set of field names to a new location and then define those names and the row

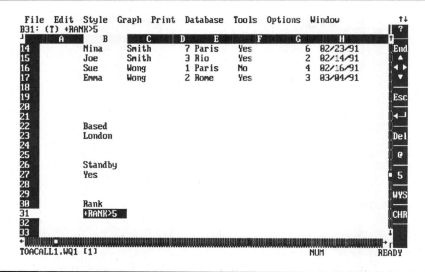

Figure 3-23. *Three separate Criteria Tables*

beneath them as the Criteria Table. Enter the data you want to match under the appropriate field name prior to a search and then delete it when the search is completed. You do not have to have an entry in every column of the Criteria Table for it to work.

You can also set up more than one set of cells to be used as criteria in a worksheet. Although only one block at a time can be specified as the Criteria Table, you can quickly switch settings by using block names. For example, in Figure 3-23 you can see three different sets of criteria located in blocks B22..B23, B26..B27, and B30..B31. These blocks have been called CRIT1, CRIT2, and CRIT3 respectively. Suppose you have just performed a Locate operation with B22..B23, otherwise known as CRIT1, as the Criteria Table and now you want to use CRIT2. You simply type / to activate the menu, select Database, Query, and then Criteria Table. When prompted for the Criteria Table coordinates you press F3 for a list of block names. Highlight CRIT2, as shown in Figure 3-24, and press ENTER to confirm. You can now select Locate to perform the search on CRIT2. Note that when you use a named block for your Criteria Table, the name of the block (rather than the coordinates) appears in the menu settings, as shown in Figure 3-25.

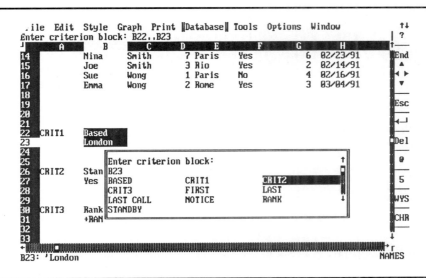

Figure 3-24.   *Selecting named Criteria Block*

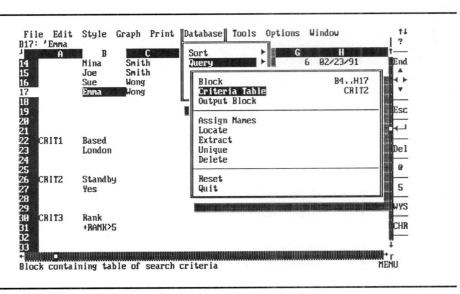

Figure 3-25.   *Named Criteria Table setting*

Matching Text

If what you are looking to match in a criterion is a piece of text—that is, something that has been entered as a label—and you want to incorporate it in a formula, you must place it in double quotes. For example, "paris" will find *PARIS, Paris,* and *paris.* When you use the comparison operators with labels, Quattro Pro 3 interprets > as meaning higher in the alphabet. This means that you can use these operators with non-numeric fields like ZIP codes to specify codes equal to or greater than, say, 94100, which would be written as +ZIP>"94100".

To add scope to your searches for a text match, you can use *wildcards.* These are the question mark (?), the asterisk (*), and the tilde (~). The question mark stands for any character in that position in a string, as in *V?LE,* which would find *VALE, VOLE, VILE,* and so on. The asterisk means anything from this character to the end of the label, as in *VERN*,* which would find anything beginning with *VERN,* like *VERNAL, VER-NON,* and so on. Tilde means "not," as in *~Paris,* which would find anything but *Paris.*

Repeating a Query

The F7 key will repeat the last query you performed. Suppose you have to look up different employee records on a regular basis, and you have a Criteria Table with Last and First as headings. You would type the name of the employee you were looking for under the Last Name and First Name headings in the Criteria Table and select Locate. The next time you needed to look up an employee's record, you would type the name of the employee in the Criteria Table and press F7. The same Criteria Table and Query Locate are used, but with the new entry in the Criteria Table. In this way you can find a succession of employees from a long list with relative ease.

After performing a Query Locate, you will get the same results again when you press F7 if you are working in the same spreadsheet during the same session. If you last performed a Query Extract, which will be discussed next, then Extract is performed the next time you press F7.

Query Extract

So far you have seen that Quattro Pro 3 is adept at locating records in a database. At some point you will probably want a list of items matching your criteria. You do this once you have established the database and the criteria. You can then place the list anywhere in the worksheet.

Providing the Data

You create a list of data selected from a Quattro Pro 3 database by using the Extract command, which copies data meeting your criteria into a separate area of the spreadsheet. The Extract command needs the following four pieces of information.

Where the data is located	The Query Block
What to extract	The Criteria Table
Where to output	The cells in which to place the extracted data
What data to output	The field names of the desired columns

If you have already used the Locate feature, you will have used the first two items. The last two involve moving to an empty part of the worksheet and typing in the names of the fields you want reported.

The Output Block

Once you have decided which pieces of information you want and where to have Quattro Pro 3 output the matching records you can extract the information. For example, in Figure 3-26 you can see the results of the Extract function, using the fields Last and Last Call. This figure shows the names of the staff that meet the criteria plus the date they were last called.

There is no limit to the number of fields you can include in the Output Block, and you do not need to include fields that were part of the criteria. Of course, as you can see from Figure 3-27, you can include all fields in the output if you want to.

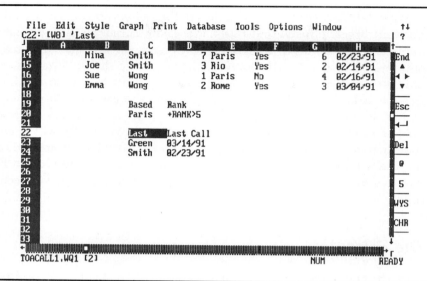

Figure 3-26. *Extract results*

File Edit Style Graph Print Database Tools Options Window

B22: 'First

	A	B	C	D	E	F	G	H	
14		Nina	Smith		7 Paris	Yes		6 02/23/91	End
15		Joe	Smith		3 Rio	Yes		2 02/14/91	▲
16		Sue	Wong		1 Paris	No		4 02/16/91	◄ ►
17		Emma	Wong		2 Rome	Yes		3 03/04/91	▼
18									
19			Based	Rank					Esc
20			Paris	+RANK>5					
21									◄┘
22		First	Last	Rank	Based	Standby	Notice Last Call		
23		Peter	Green	6 Paris	No	10 03/14/91			Del
24		Nina	Smith	7 Paris	Yes	6 02/23/91			@
25									
26									5
27									
28									
29									WYS
30									
31									CHR
32									
33									

TOACALL1.WQ1 [2]   NUM   READY

Figure 3-27. *Extracting full record*

When you have entered the names of the fields you want reported, you must next record the Output Block. Place your cursor on the leftmost field name and select Output from the Query menu. Anchor the cell you are in and press END and RIGHT ARROW to include all of the field names. Press ENTER to confirm the output block. You may want to extend the Output Block of cells. If you do not extend it beyond the row of field names, you will be telling Quattro Pro 3 that it can use any number of rows below the field names for the output. If you press PAGE DOWN once, you will be saying that there are 20 lines available, and Quattro Pro 3 will highlight this area. As your worksheets get crowded, it is a good idea to limit the Output Block like this so that the program is prevented from outputting over occupied cells.

The Extract

With the Output Block defined, select Extract to tell Quattro Pro 3 to place the items identified by your criteria into the output cells. Quattro Pro 3 uses the last criteria you defined; either the Formula Criteria or the Criteria Table from which to select the items. When you have performed the extract, the data can be printed, copied, or further manipulated. As with the Locate command, you can repeat the last query with F7. Thus, you can change the name of the city you are looking for, for example, and press F7 to get a new list.

Note that when Quattro Pro 3 extracts numbers from the database to an output range, they are only numbers. Formulas in the database are converted to their numeric value upon extraction.

Unique Records

When creating large databases it is not unusual for duplicate records to occur, particularly if more than one person is using the database. However, any sort of the database should reveal duplicates, which can then be deleted as required. When you extract records from a database and two identical records match the criteria, you will get both records in the output list.

There may be situations in which you want to extract only the unique values in one or more fields. For example, suppose you have a database of wines classified according to Country, Region, and Year. You want a list of all regions of France represented in the database. You can use a criteria of Country=France and an output field with the heading Region. When you issue the Extract command, however, the resulting list will contain one region name entry for every record that has France in the Country field, meaning there will be many duplicates in the list. In a situation like this, when what you want is each unique region name listed only once, use the Unique option on the Database Query menu. The Unique option lists any item that will be identical to another item in the output block once. In other words, the Unique option lists unique values, whereas the Extract option lists all values.

Sorting Extracted Data

Extracted data is a series of consecutive columns and rows; in fact, by extracting data you have created a new database. This database can now be sorted. If you were asked to provide a list of all the staff, you would want the list alphabetized or put in some other order. You can do this by defining the Sort Block as the output data minus the field names. Remember that Quattro Pro 3 remembers the last Sort Block and keys you used, so it is wise to select the Reset command from the Sort menu before performing a sort on a new block.

Deleting Records

When you are cleaning up or maintaining a database, you may need to get rid of records. One way of doing this is to find the record and then delete it with the Edit Delete Row command. However, this has the possibly negative side effect of removing any data that is on the same row as the deleted record, all the way across the worksheet. Quattro Pro 3 has an automated alternative, called Query Delete, that does not interfere with cells outside the database.

The Query Delete command has the effect of an Edit Erase operation on cells containing records to be deleted, followed by an Edit Move to close up blank cells in the database. At the same time it adjusts the Database Query Block setting to make sure it is correct.

To use this command you set the criteria for the records you want deleted and then select Delete instead of Locate or Extract. You will be prompted to confirm this action since the program removes cells from the worksheet.

Query Delete can be dangerous; be careful that your criteria are correct before using this command and perform a File Save beforehand. You can always perform a Query Locate before a Query Delete, just to make sure that your criteria are working as intended. Another safeguard is to make sure that the Undo feature is enabled (by selecting Options, Other, Undo, and Enable). This will allow you to reverse the effect of Query Delete just by pressing the Undo key (ALT-F5).

Databases and Multiple Worksheets

You can see that managing a database requires several elements in addition to the data itself. Querying the database requires a Criteria Table. An Output Block is required for an Extract to be performed. One way to manage these elements is to divide them between worksheets. For example, you can keep the database in one worksheet and the Criteria Table and Output Block in a separate worksheet. You can see this arrangement in Figure 3-28 where two worksheets, DATABASE and REPORT, are tiled side by side. The REPORT worksheet is where the user is specifying the criteria and extracting the data.

With the REPORT worksheet active you set the Query Block by defining the cells occupied by data in the DATABASE worksheet. When you get the prompt "Enter database block," use SHIFT-F6, the Next Window key, to make DATABASE the active worksheet; then highlight the database cells. When you confirm this, the setting in the Query menu will look something like: [DATABASE]B4..H17. Keeping the REPORT worksheet active, you proceed to define the Criteria Table and Output Block using cells in the REPORT worksheet. You can see that this has been done in Figure 3-29.

To extract data from the DATABASE worksheet into REPORT you make REPORT the active worksheet and then issue the Extract command. Records from DATABASE that meet the criteria in REPORT will be copied into REPORT. You can also use the Locate command from REPORT. In this case, Quattro Pro 3 takes you to the DATABASE worksheet and shows you the selected records there. When you leave FIND mode you are returned to the REPORT worksheet.

An extension of the multiple-worksheet approach would be to have several different worksheets for reporting on the same database. This

Figure 3-28. *Extracting from a separate file*

Figure 3-29. *Settings for extracting from a separate file*

would allow you to switch criteria simply by making a different worksheet window active before executing the query.

Working with Foreign Databases

While many users find that a Quattro Pro 3 worksheet is the ideal place to keep track of their data, no one expects all of the world's databases to be available in Quattro Pro 3 format. Because there is so much useful data stored in databases created by other programs, Borland gave Quattro Pro 3 the ability to read files created by popular database programs. This means that you can use the Data Query command to inspect data in a database file created by another program such as dBASE or Paradox. You can establish criteria in your worksheet that refer to fields in the foreign file. Using the Extract command you can read a selection of data from the foreign file into a Quattro Pro 3 worksheet.

You can also use Quattro Pro 3 to update a foreign database. For example, suppose that your company uses Paradox to maintain a central database of expenses, and that you keep track of your expenses in a Quattro Pro 3 worksheet. You can store your expense records in a file that can be saved as a Paradox database. You can read about querying of foreign databases in Chapter 13, which covers the importing and exporting of Paradox data.

Data Entry Techniques

Spreadsheets used as databases take far more keystrokes than regular spreadsheets, where the bulk of the entries are created by formulas that are copied. In addition, databases often need extensive editing to be kept current. If you are maintaining a sizable database, you may wish to employ a typist to edit or input the data. There are some steps you can take to make the work easier for someone unfamiliar with Quattro Pro 3.

Input Form

If you are having someone who is not well versed in spreadsheets perform data-entry for you, you can make an input form to assist them. The first step is to protect the entire spreadsheet. To do this you issue the Options Protection command and select Enable. This prevents any data from being altered. Then you can use the Style Protection command to Unprotect those cells where the data will be entered or edited. When you are ready to have someone work on the database you can issue the Restrict Input command from the Database menu. You highlight a block of the worksheet that includes the unprotected cells. When you press ENTER this area becomes the *Input Block*. User access is now limited to any unprotected cells in the Input Block. The diagram in Figure 3-30 shows how the Input Block and unprotected cells work together to create a *mask* over the worksheet.

The effect of the Restrict Input command is considerable. The message INPUT appears in the mode indicator. The cursor keys will not take you outside of the defined Input Block of cells and will only move to those cells within the Input Block that are unprotected. You can type data and press

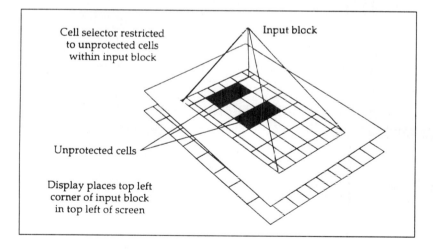

Figure 3-30. *Diagram of input range*

ENTER, or edit data with F2 and re-enter it. The program menu is not available, so typing / begins a new label instead of activating the menu.

To break out of the INPUT mode you press ESCAPE or ENTER while the INPUT message is displayed. This means that it is very easy to override the Restrict Input command. In fact, the command is most effective when used in macros that further control the user's access to commands, as described in Chapter 12.

Data Control

Earlier in this chapter, mention was made of the need to type a label prefix when entering non-numeric numbers such as ZIP codes. Another chore for data-entry workers is making sure that dates are entered as dates. To overcome this problem, Quattro Pro 3 allows you to designate certain cells in a spreadsheet as Labels Only. To do this you use the Data Entry option on the Database menu. When you select the Labels Only command, you highlight an area—usually a field or column—to be affected by the command. From then on, anything entered into those cells will be automatically preceded by a label prefix. You will see the word *Label* in front of the cell address on the input or status line, as shown in Figure 3-31, to remind you that the cell has a forced data type.

The default label prefix, usually the apostrophe for left-alignment, is now added to what you type into a label cell. If the cells you selected with

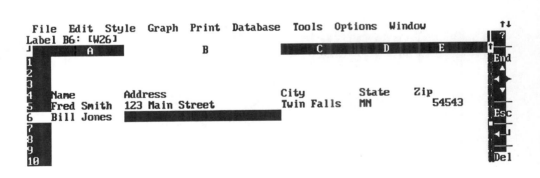

Figure 3-31. *Forced data type: Label*

the Labels Only command already contain numbers or formulas entered as values, then these retain their status. However, if you edit and then re-enter one of these cells it will be converted to a label.

The Database Data Entry command also allows you to restrict entries to Dates Only, a means of avoiding errors in date fields. You will see the word *Date* in front of the cell address in the input and status lines to remind you that what you enter must be a date. Cells selected by the Dates Only command will accept dates typed in any of the standard date formats, which are described in detail in Chapter 9.

4 Formulas and Functions in Depth

In previous chapters you have seen that Quattro Pro 3 understands several formulas of varying complexity, from a simple formula that adds cells to a complex one that calculates a loan payment. In this chapter you will see the ways in which formulas can be applied to typical spreadsheet operations and the many built-in formulas, or functions, that Quattro Pro 3 provides to enhance your formulas.

Formulas Are Instructions

While the word *formula* may remind many people of algebra and science classes, in the context of Quattro Pro 3 the term simply means an *instruction* written in a form that the program can understand. As you have seen, the way you give Quattro Pro 3 instructions can be as straightforward as "add cell A1 and cell A2." In fact, even complex instructions follow a consistent arrangement, or *syntax*. As you learn to manipulate formulas, you will want to use the program's built-in functions for more complex calculations. Quattro Pro 3 offers nearly a hundred functions. Most of these functions follow the same format as the functions in 1-2-3, although Quattro Pro 3 provides some functions that are not available in 1-2-3 Release 2, or even in Release 3.

Formula Formats

Simple Quattro Pro 3 formulas combine values—like numbers or cells containing numbers—with operators, such as the division sign or the plus sign. The formula in cell H7 of Figure 4-1 can be diagrammed like this:

H7 = H5	*	H6
Value	Operator	Value

If cells H5 and H6 were named as blocks, the formula could be diagrammed like this:

H7 = Width	*	Length
Value	Operator	Value

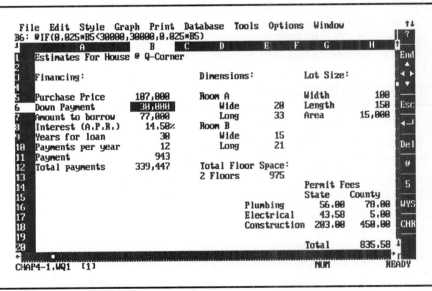

Figure 4-1.   *Example of formulas*

Quattro Pro 3 formulas are algebraic in format. Thus, within a formula you can use other formulas separated, or *delimited*, by pairs of parentheses, as in the following:

E13 = ((E6*E7)+(E9*E10))*2

This formula in E13 means "multiply E6 by E7, add that to the product of E9 multiplied by E10, and then double the answer." The formula could calculate the total floor area of a two-story house with two rooms on each floor whose width and length were in cells E6 through E10.

When you ask Quattro Pro 3 to make decisions about the data to be calculated, several elements are required, as in this formula:

B6 = @IF(0.25*B5<30000,30000,0.25*B5)

This formula tells Quattro Pro 3 that the down payment in B6 should be 25% of the purchase price in B5, unless the product of those two values comes to less than 30,000, in which case B6 should be 30,000. This formula is used in Figure 4-1 to calculate the down payment. The buyer must pay at least 25% of the purchase price and no less than $30,000.

An expense report that breaks down expenses for each week by type might contain the formula

G13=@IF(@SUM(WEEK)=@SUM(TYPE),@SUM(TYPE),@ERR)

This formula says that G13 will have one of two possible answers, depending on a decision made by the @IF function. If the sum of the block of cells called WEEK is equal to the sum of the block of cells called TYPE, the program should insert that sum; otherwise, it should give an error message (@ERR). By the end of this chapter you will be able to read such formulas and compose them with Quattro Pro 3's formula syntax and functions.

Notice that none of the previous formulas have spaces entered in them. No spaces is a general rule in all Quattro Pro 3 formulas. Also note that the program capitalizes cell references, block names, and function names. It does not matter if you enter these as upper- or lowercase letters; Quattro Pro 3 will store and display them in uppercase.

Acceptable Values

The values in a Quattro Pro 3 formula can be cells containing values, as in +H5*H6. They can be a block of cells containing values, either stated as coordinates as in +G16..G18+H16..H18, or described by block names, as in STATE+COUNTY. They can also be functions like @PMT, which was used in Chapter 1 to calculate a car loan payment. The same function is used in Figure 4-1 to calculate a mortgage payment in cell B11. Note the use of a separate cell for number of payments per year. You can calculate the total payments to be made on a 30-year loan if you multiply the number of payments by the calculated payment amount, using the formula +B9*B10*B11. The many Quattro Pro 3 @functions that can be used in formulas are described later in this chapter.

Values in Quattro Pro 3 formulas can also be constants. A *constant* is a number, date, or piece of text that you enter directly, such as the 1 in 1+B3. Constants are used in formulas for projections; for example, a formula to figure projected sales might be Sales*1.1. A constant is also used in calculations like finding the circumference of a circle (2*@PI*Radius).

Operators and Priorities

There are many different operators that you can use in Quattro Pro 3 formulas. First, there are the standard arithmetic operators: add (+), subtract (–), multiply (*), and divide (/). Another operator, the exponent (^), produces powers of a number. In Chapter 3 you saw how you can set search conditions using logical operators, such as the greater-than sign in Rank > 5. All of the operators recognized by Quattro Pro 3 are listed in Table 4-1, where the order of operations in a formula is also shown. If all the operators are the same, as in 2*3*4 (=24), the calculation is performed from left to right. You can affect the order of calculation by using parentheses, as in these two calculations:

2*3+4=10
2*(4+3)=14

When you nest calculations within several parentheses, the inner-most calculations are performed first. Earlier you saw the formula

((E6*E7)+(E9*E10))*2. This arrangement of parentheses means that the E6*E7 and E9*E10 calculations will occur first, then the two products will be added together, and finally that sum will be multiplied by the 2 that stands outside the parentheses. Actually, the two inner sets of parentheses are not necessary because, as is shown in Table 4-1, * will occur before +.

Using Formulas

Much of a spreadsheet's power clearly lies in formulas. Whether you are simply adding two cells together or calculating the sum of the year's depreciation of an asset, the ability to establish a relationship between cells gives you tremendous number-crunching ability.

Operator	Used for	Priority
&	Placing text in string formulas	1
#AND#	Logical AND formulas	1
#OR#	Logical OR formulas	1
#NOT#	Logical NOT formulas	2
=	Equal in conditional statements	3
<>	Not equal in conditional statements	3
<=	Less than or equal to	3
>=	Greater than or equal to	3
-	Subtraction	4
+	Addition	4
*	Multiplication	5
/	Division	5
-	Negation (preceding a formula)	6
+	Positive (preceding a formula)	6
^	Exponentiation (to the power of)	7

Table 4-1. *Operators and Order of Precedence, 7 Being Highest*

Methods for Creating And Entering Formulas

You can create formulas in several ways. First, there is the literal method: you look at the worksheet and decide which cells are involved; then you type their addresses into the formula. For example, you can see that the total of the state permit fees in Figure 4-1 is going to be +G16+G17+G18. You can type this formula directly and Quattro Pro 3 will accept it, unless you type an invalid coordinate. The formula will be correct if the cells you have described are the correct cells for the formula.

For the more cautious spreadsheet user and the less adept typist, there is the pointing method of entering formulas. This method begins with the + sign or other value indicator, which places Quattro Pro 3 in VALUE mode. You then use the arrow keys to highlight the first cell you want in the formula. You have seen that, when you do this, Quattro Pro 3 types the cell address for you. You can then type the next math sign or value indicator, and the cell selector will move back down to the cell in which you are building the formula. The basic sequence is math sign, point, math sign, point. You can point to each cell that needs to go into the formula, and it is added on the edit line at the top of the screen as you build the formula. Place the completed formula into the original cell with the ENTER key. This method is very useful when you have lots of cells scattered throughout the spreadsheet and cannot remember the location of a particular number.

You can use the pointing method effectively with formulas that involve functions, as in the case of the loan payment. Separate each argument of the @PMT function by a comma. After you initiate the formula by entering **@PMT(** move the cell selector to the cell containing the first argument. Then enter a comma to add that location to the formula and return the cell selector to the cell in which the formula is originating. When you then point out the cell for the second argument and type another comma, that location is pulled into the formula, and the cell selector is returned to the original cell. Lastly, point out the third and final argument, and with the cell selector on the third cell, type the closing parenthesis, which completes the formula. The cell selector is now back at the original cell. You can incorporate additional values into the formula by pressing the desired math sign (as in * to multiply this payment by a cell or number). Otherwise, press the ENTER key to place the completed formula in the cell.

Formulas and Blocks

Some formulas and functions use blocks of cells. You can enter blocks by typing the diagonal coordinates of the block directly as you create the formula. Alternatively, you can use the pointing method to block out the cells to be included, anchoring the upper-left corner by typing a period and then using the DOWN and/or RIGHT ARROW as necessary to complete the highlighting of the block.

Results of Entering a Formula

After you have entered a formula, the cell displays the *result* of the formula, not the formula itself. However, the cell identifier still displays the formula, not the value, whenever you highlight a cell that contains a formula. You may not want the value generated by the formula to be *dynamic* and therefore change when the worksheet is recalculated. To *fix* a value, you can convert the formula to the value it produces. This can be done in two ways. Press F2 while highlighting the cell containing the formula, and the formula is placed on the edit line at the top of the screen. Then press the Calc key (F9), and the formula is turned into its result. You can then place this result into the cell with the ENTER key. Alternatively, you can use the Edit Values command, described in Chapter 2, to convert a block of cells from formulas to values.

Named Blocks

Naming blocks with the Edit Name command is very useful when you are developing formulas, because you can use block names instead of cell coordinates. Even attaching a name to a single cell is productive. It is often easier to type LENGTH * WIDTH than H5*H6, particularly if you are composing the formula in Q33. You do not need to check where these elements are and do not need to take the time to point them out. Furthermore, if you type H555*H6 by mistake, Quattro Pro 3 will not tell you that this is an error. But if you try to enter an invalid block name, the program will beep and place you in EDIT mode so that you can correct the mistake. Many people find that block names are easier to use than cell coordinates for groups of cells. Consider the columns of permit fees in Figure 4-2. It is

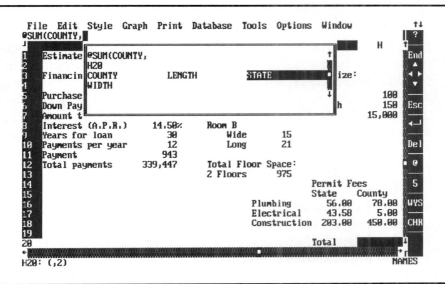

Figure 4-2. *Block choices*

much easier to type @SUM(STATE) than @SUM(G16..G18). The benefits of block names rapidly increase as you create more formulas. Thus, the formula @SUM(STATE,COUNTY) is much easier to type than typing the formula @SUM(G16..G18,H16..H18), particularly because you can press the Choices key (F3) to pop up a list of block names from which to choose.

Formulas and Mice

Instead of pointing and highlighting with the arrow keys, you can use the mouse to indicate cell addresses when building formulas. You can type a math sign and then click on a single cell to pull it into a formula, or you can click and drag to define a group of cells. If you use the F3 key to list block names, you can expand the list by clicking anywhere on the top row of the box. The expanded list shows the actual coordinates of the blocks:

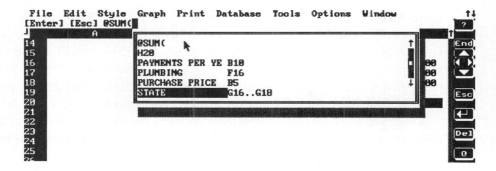

Click on the up and down arrows to page sections of the list into view. You can click on any name in the list to paste it into the formula you are building on the edit line.

If you use the ALT-F3 key combination to list functions, as described later in this chapter, you can use the mouse pointer to scroll the list of functions. You can click on any function in the list to paste it into the formula you are creating on the edit line. You can simulate ALT-F3 by clicking on the @ sign in the mouse palette.

Editing Formulas

If there is a mistake in a formula that you are creating, such as a misspelled block or function name or an invalid cell reference or unrecognized symbol, Quattro Pro 3 will not accept the formula when you press ENTER. Instead, it will beep and display a message. When you press ENTER or ESCAPE to acknowledge the message, the program changes to EDIT mode and attempts to position the edit cursor near the error you have made. Formulas are always edited on the input line and are placed there either by Quattro Pro 3 when it rejects a formula, or by you when you need to change a previously entered formula. To initiate editing a formula, you highlight the cell and press F2 to enter EDIT mode. The formula will be displayed on the edit line.

Common Formula Errors

If you spell a formula correctly but used improper elements within it, Quattro Pro 3 displays an error message. The exact message will depend upon the error. For example, entering @SUM(B2..TC12) earns the response "Invalid Character" since there cannot be a cell TC12. When you see a message of this type, check the formula to find the error. The program attempts to put the cursor near the error, so look there first. You may have neglected to close a pair of parentheses or quotations, or omitted the @ sign before a function name. A list of error messages is provided in Table 4-2.

A common mistake is to enter spaces between the elements of a formula. Although the documentation occasionally appears to show spaces, they are

Message	Problem/Solution
Formula too long	You exceeded the limit of 254 characters in a formula; break formula into several subformulas
Incomplete formula	You left something out; check for operators not followed by arguments
Invalid argument type	You have tried to use an argument that does not fit the @function you are using; check the syntax of the argument
Invalid cell or block address	You entered something that is being read as a nonexistent cell reference or block name; check that you have typed formula correctly and defined all block names used in the formula
Invalid character	You used a character that does not fit the syntax; check for trailing commas, other punctuation that is out of place
Missing arguments	You forgot to supply an argument where one is expected; check your entry
Missing operator	You forgot to separate values or functions with an operator; check your entry
Missing right parenthesis	You opened one more set of parentheses than you closed; check for missing right parenthesis or extra left parenthesis
Syntax error	You have made an error that does not fall into the other categories; check spelling of your entry and syntax requirements of the functions you are using
Too many arguments	You have supplied more arguments than the function can accept; check syntax and punctuation of what you entered
Unknown @function	You used a function name that is not recognized; check spelling and try using Choice list

Table 4-2.   *Common Entry Error Messages*

generally not allowed in formulas. Unlike 1-2-3, Quattro Pro 3 does sometimes allow spaces in formulas, although you do not need to type any. To be on the safe side, however, you would do best to avoid spaces completely.

Named blocks must be spelled correctly. You can press the Choices key (F3) to select from a list of block names when writing formulas. As you can see from the box in the upper-right corner of Figure 4-2, the list makes block names very easy to use. The main advantage of using the F3 key for placing block names in formulas is to avoid typographical errors.

You may succeed in entering a formula only to see the message CIRC appear among the status indicators. This message tells you there is a circular reference in your formula, meaning that the formula refers to itself. You cannot ask Quattro Pro 3 to multiply the current cell by 1.1 and to put the answer in the current cell. This kind of problem, which usually becomes apparent as soon as you see what you have attempted to do, is solved by retyping the formula. If you see the CIRC message and cannot determine which cell is producing it, then you can use the Options Recalculation command to find out. The menu that the Options Recalculation command gives you shows the location of the circular reference. You can then pick Quit to leave the menu and edit the cell in question.

A somewhat similar problem is to refer to a block in your formula that is as yet unnamed. When this happens, you must stop typing the formula to name the block. This is especially annoying when the formula is complex and lengthy. You can avoid the problem by defining a named block as soon as you create it and by using the Choices key (F3) to select block names.

One trick to save the typing you have already done on a rejected formula is to press HOME when Quattro Pro 3 places you in EDIT mode and then type an apostrophe. This will allow you to enter the formula as a label and then review it. When you edit the formula and are ready to re-enter it as a value, press HOME and then DELETE to remove the apostrophe before pressing ENTER.

Functions Are Built-in Formulas

Quattro Pro 3 provides you with the basic building blocks of complex formulas in the form of functions. These built-in formulas are specially coded commands that facilitate typical calculations. Using functions, you do not have to enter lengthy instructions.

Function Arguments

Some functions simply generate values by themselves. For example, @PI gives the value of pi. The date function @NOW tells you what your PC thinks the current date and time is. However, most functions require additional information, called arguments. For example, the principal, interest, and term required by the @PMT function are said to be the arguments of @PMT. Some functions require just one argument, like @SUM, which only needs to know what block of cells you want to sum. Others, such as @PMT, require several arguments.

The arguments required by functions can be broken down into three types: *numeric,* such as cells containing numbers, as in @PMT(E1,E2,E3); *block,* such as a block of cells being summed with @SUM(B1..B3), or a named block, such as @SUM(TOTAL SALES); and *string,* a label or piece of text entered into a cell, entered into a function in quotes, or produced by another function.

Some functions can accept more than one argument, in which case the arguments are separated by commas, as in @SUM(B1..B3,C1..C3,E1..E3). This function totals the first three rows of columns B, C, and E. Numeric functions can reference a mixture of cell coordinates and block names, as in @PMT(E1, INTEREST, TERM). Functions are often combined with operators and values in formulas, just like any other formula element.

Function Syntax

There are about a hundred functions and several ways of classifying them. In addition to the distinction between numeric and string functions, which closely follows that between values and labels, functions can be grouped by the type of work they apply to: financial, date, logical, and so on. However, all Quattro Pro 3 functions are always entered in the same basic format, using a standard arrangement of parts, or *syntax:*

■ Functions begin with the leading @ sign.

■ Next is the name of the function, typed in upper- or lowercase or a combination and spelled accurately.

■ The arguments, when required, follow the function name enclosed in parentheses.

■ With more than one argument, you must separate the arguments by commas; the arguments must be in proper order.

■ There should be no spaces between the @ and the function name. (There may be spaces between the components, the left parenthesis, the arguments, and the commas, but they are not required.)

A function combined with any arguments is a *function statement*. If you try to enter a function statement that contains an error—for example, an incorrectly spelled function name—Quattro Pro 3 will beep and place the entry on the edit line. It will attempt to place the edit line cursor in the area of the mistake. This can be very helpful if you have omitted a comma between arguments or left a pair of parentheses unclosed. See Table 4-2 for a list of error messages.

The Functions Key

One way to prevent errors like misspelled function names is to use the Functions key (ALT-F3). Pressing ALT-F3 when you are in either VALUE mode or EDIT mode pops up a list of the functions, as shown in Figure 4-3. You can then browse through this list with the arrow keys, moving a page at a time with PGUP or PGDN. When you see the function that you need, highlight it and press ENTER to place it onto the edit line. This avoids mistyping the name. Mouse users can use the scroll bar on the right side of the list to view the functions.

You can also look up a function by spelling part of the name. When the function list appears, press the Edit key (F2), and you will see the message "Search for: *" appear in the status line at the bottom of the screen. Just start typing what you can remember of the name and the list box will move to the closest match. For example, if you type **P**, then you will be taken to the first function beginning with *P*, which is PAYMT. Type **M** and you will get to PMT. To back up a step press BACKSPACE and you will move back to PAYMT. Press ENTER to confirm your selection.

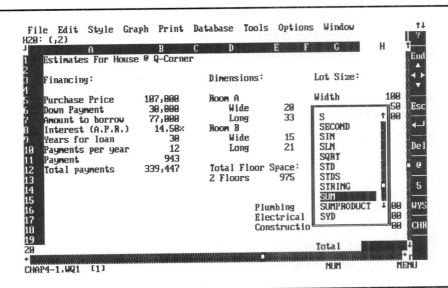

Figure 4-3.   *The function choices*

Mastering Functions

It would be hard to memorize Quattro Pro 3's more than 90 functions. By using a few simple techniques, however, you can make full use of them.

First, you should *always assume there is an appropriate function*. Chances are that the calculation you want to perform is one that many other spreadsheet users need to perform, so it is probably provided by Quattro Pro 3. Sometimes you may need to combine several functions in one formula to do the job. Occasionally, you will need to use an intermediate cell to produce part of the answer before completing the calculation in another cell. Remember that columns can be hidden from the display and printed reports so that extra columns for calculations need not affect the way the worksheet looks.

It is a good idea to use the Functions key (ALT-F3) to look up and enter functions. The Functions key not only prevents typos but also reminds you of the wide range of functions that can be used. You may realize that there is a quicker way to solve your formula. When you are constructing formulas containing block names, use the Choices list (F3) to make sure you use correctly defined block names.

You will also want to save particularly useful function statements. When you come up with a good formula that you are likely to use often, you might consider saving the worksheet under a different name to keep a copy of the formula for reference. Chapter 7 discusses how to save portions of a spreadsheet to separate files and how to combine several files into one. This technique allows you to build a library of useful functions. You can also print useful formulas by highlighting the appropriate cell and pressing the PRTSC key. This will print the information from the whole screen, including the cell identifier.

If you follow these guidelines and are prepared to spend some time experimenting with and reading about functions, you will find that they offer tremendous power. A complete examination of each function is beyond the scope of this book. With three pages per function, this chapter alone would grow to 300 pages. What you will find in the rest of this chapter is a series of discussions on different sets of functions grouped according to their practical roles. Examples are given in most cases together with references to other parts of the book where the functions are used.

Aggregate Functions

Aggregate functions perform some of the most commonly used calculations in spreadsheet work. In addition to @SUM, which was used in Chapter 2, this group includes functions that aggregate a block of cells, count the contents and average the block, find the largest and smallest numbers in the block, and determine degree of variance. These functions also work with several different blocks at once or with numerous individual cells.

Sum

The @SUM function is one of the most frequently used functions. In Figure 4-4, @SUM is used to add the values in a block of cells—the earnings of a group of commodity brokers. You can use @SUM to total columns, rows, and blocks including columns and rows. All that @SUM needs to know is the coordinates of the block to be summed. Its syntax is

@SUM(*Block*)

The block does not need to have values in every cell; the empty cells will be ignored. The @SUM function works well with block names. For example, @SUM(TOTAL) will give the total of values in the block of cells named TOTAL. In Figure 4-5 you can see an expense report where this feature is used to arrive at the total expenses for one week. The block named TOTAL is cells B5 through F15. You can sum several different blocks at once if you separate them by a comma, as in @SUM(TA,TD), which would sum two blocks, one named TA, the other TD.

There are several advantages to using @SUM to add up cells, rather than a "cell+cell+cell" formula. Rows or columns entered within a summed block are automatically included in the block. For example, consider these two approaches to adding up values.

B2:	100		B2:	100
B3:	200	or	B3:	200
B4:	300		B4:	300
B5:	===============		B5:	==========
B6:	@SUM(B2..B4)		B6:	+B2+B3+B4

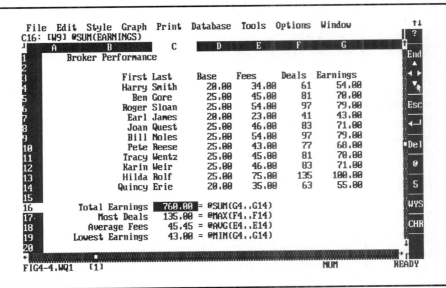

Figure 4-4. @SUM function

```
 File  Edit  Style  Graph  Print  Database  Tools  Options  Window        ↑↓
D19: @SUM(TOTAL)                                                            ?
        A        B        C        D        E        F        G
1                                                                         End
2              Monday   Tuesday  Wednesday Thursday Friday   Totals        ▲
3                                                                        ◄ ►
4     Meals                                                                 ▼
5        B'fast   3.45     0.00     3.89     4.76     5.98    18.08
6        Lunch    5.00     8.95     6.74     5.78    18.96    45.43      Esc
7        Dinner   0.00    23.87     5.89    13.45     0.00    43.21
8     Travel                                                                ←┘
9        Air      0.00   143.89     0.00     0.00   148.00   291.89
10       Mileage  0.00     0.00     0.00     0.00     3.50     3.50      Del
11       Parking  0.00     0.00    12.00    12.00    12.00    36.00
12       Taxi     0.00     0.00     0.00     0.00     0.00     0.00      @
13    Miscellaneous
14       Supplies 34.00    0.00     6.00     0.00     3.00    43.00       5
15       Other    0.00     0.00     0.00    23.87     0.00    23.87
16    ============================================================       WYS
17              50.45   176.71    34.52    59.86   191.44   512.98
18                                                                        CHR
19                      Total =    512.98
20
FIG4-6.WQ1   [2]                                         NUM       READY
```

Figure 4-5. *The sum in the expense report*

In the example on the left it will not matter if you need to insert an extra
row into the spreadsheet to include another value in the calculation. For
example, if you place the cell selector on row 4 and issue the Edit Insert
Row command to include one more row, cells B4, B5, and B6 become cells
B5, B6, and B7. The formula that was in B6 but is now in B7 becomes
@SUM(B2..B5). If you enter a new value in B4 it will be included in the
@SUM calculation.

The same is not true if you have used the cell+cell method of adding.
Here you can see the results for both of the examples above, after a row
and a new value of 250 was inserted at B4:

B2:	100		B2:	100
B3:	200		B3:	200
B4:	250	or	B4:	250
B5:	300		B5:	300
B6:	===============		B6:	=========
B7:	@SUM(B2..B5)		B7:	+B2+B3+B5

Inserting new rows within the summed range increases the range to include the new cells. Individually referenced cells are not automatically added to + formulas.

The integrity of the @SUM formula is preserved if you insert a row at B2 because the whole set of numbers is moved down. However, because Quattro Pro 3 inserts new rows above the current cell, the new B2 would not be included in the @SUM formula. If you were to enter a value into B2 at that point it would not be included in the sum. If you insert a row into the original example at B5, then the accuracy of the formula is preserved, but again, the new cell is not included. As a rule, then, you add a cell to a summed column if you insert the row while selecting the second cell of the block, or the last cell, or any cell in between.

Since it is quite natural to add numbers to the bottom of a list, you might want to include the row below the last number when you create an @SUM formula. For instance, you could include cell B6 in the @SUM argument in the last example. Then you could place the cell selector on row 6 below the last number, insert a new row, and have that row be included in the summed block. When Quattro Pro 3 finished calculating, the labels in the block would have a value of 0, and thus would not affect the answer.

Sum Product

A function that is new with Quattro Pro 3 is @SUMPRODUCT. This function is used to sum up the results of multiplication between blocks of cells. For example, here you have two sets of numbers in two columns and you want to know what you get if the pairs of numbers that are on the same row are multiplied together, and the results added up:

When you multiply 10 by 30 you get 300. When you multiply 20 by 40 you get 800. Add together 300 and 800 and you get 1100, which is the answer returned by @SUMPRODUCT. For its arguments the @SUMPRODUCT function requires two blocks of equal size, separated by a comma. This

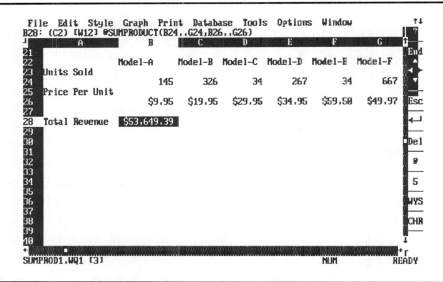

Figure 4-6. *@SUMPRODUCT function*

function does not work if any of the cells in the blocks are empty. As you can see from Figure 4-6, the blocks can be either columns or rows, as long as their dimensions are equal.

Count

The @COUNT function counts the number of items or nonempty cells in a block of cells. This function is useful for such projects as inventory tracking, since @COUNT can tell you how many entries there are in a column, and thus how many inventory items there are in a list. You simply need to tell the function the location of the cells to be counted. The syntax is

@COUNT(*Block*)

Note that Quattro Pro 3 includes labels when calculating @COUNT. Thus the count for a summed range that includes a line of labels might be greater than you expect. For example, the following arrangement results in an answer of 6 when summed, an answer of 4 when counted.

B1:	2		B1:	2
B2:	2		B2:	2
B3:	2		B3:	2
B4:	============		B4:	===========
B5:	@SUM(B1..B4)		B5:	@COUNT(B1..B4)

Only if cell B4 was empty would the count be 3.

Average

@AVG is used to give the average of values in a block of cells. You can see the usefulness of this function in Figure 4-4, where it was used to calculate the average of fees earned by brokers. The function is simply

@AVG(*Block*)

Like @SUM, the @AVG function works well with columns, rows, and larger blocks, particularly if you use a block name. However, label cells are used in calculating the average. Essentially, the @AVG function combines @SUM with @COUNT; you could say that @AVG=@SUM /@COUNT. Since @COUNT gives a value of 1 to a label, the arrangement seen here would produce 6 when summed, but 1.5 when averaged.

B1:	2		B1:	2
B2:	2		B2:	2
B3:	2		B3:	2
B4:	======		B4:	======
B5:	@SUM(B1..B4)		B5:	@AVG(B1..B4)

Only if cell B4 were empty would the average of the values, 2, be correctly determined by @AVG.

Maximum

Shown earlier in Figure 4-4, this function will find the largest value in a specified block:

@MAX(*Block*)

Like the @SUM function, @MAX works well with block names. In Figure 4-4, for example, the block name DEALS was used for the cells in column F. The @MAX function is useful when evaluating projections, since it can tell you the largest number that results from a change in assumptions.

You can also use @MAX with single cells if you separate them with commas. Thus @MAX(B5,G3,K7) will tell you the largest amount in those three cells. This is handy when you want to perform a tax-form calculation and need to enter the larger of the numbers on two rows. You can also use @MAX to compare a cell to a number. Thus @MAX(G5,10) will return the value in G5 if it is greater than 10; otherwise, you will get the value 10. This is also useful for tax calculations, when a subtraction results in a negative number but you must enter 0 instead of the negative number. The formula @MAX(G5,0) will return either the value in G5 or 0, whichever is greater. If G5 is negative the result is 0.

Minimum

Corollary to the @MAX function, the @MIN function returns the smallest value in a block of cells:

@MIN(*Block*)

This function can be used to identify low levels in projections and inventory lists. You can also use @MIN and @MAX to determine the highest and lowest balances for a customer's credit or checking account.

Standard Deviation

This function returns the standard deviation for a given block of cells that represent a population of data:

@STD(*Block*)

The standard deviation of a set of values is a measure of how much variation there is from the average of the values. The standard deviation is the square root of the variance. If you want to compute sample standard deviation, use the @STDS function, but be aware that this function is unique to Quattro Pro 3 and is not compatible with earlier programs.

Variance

The @VAR function returns a measure of variance for a block of cells, that is, the amount of variation between individual values and the mean of the population.

@VAR(*Block*)

The result of this function is the square of the standard deviation of the same set of values. To calculate variance for a sample rather than a population, use @VARS, but bear in mind that this function is unique to Quattro Pro 3 and is not compatible with earlier programs.

Arithmetic Functions

These functions affect the way numbers are calculated. They are often used when the outcome of a formula needs to be modified; for example, the outcome should be rounded, or a negative number should be turned into a positive number.

Absolute

To arrive at the absolute value of a number, you use the @ABS function. The syntax is

@ABS(*Value*)

For example, the formula @ABS(B5) returns the absolute value of the contents of B5. The absolute value of a number is its positive equivalent, so if B5 is −1.5, @ABS(B5) equals 1.5.

Integer

At times you need to drop the decimal places from a number, rather than round them up or down. This can be done with the @INT function. Its syntax is

@INT(*Value*)

Thus, the formula @INT(B5) returns 2, when cell B5 contains 2.75. The value is stripped of digits following the decimal place, rather than rounded up to 3.

Modulus

You use the @MOD function when you need the number that is left after two other numbers are divided. This returns the remainder of X divided by Y, as in

@MOD(X,Y)

Thus, the formula @MOD(B5,5) returns 1 when B5 contains the value 36. This function is very useful when you need to figure shipping factors. You could use, for example,

@MOD(*Cases In Order,Cases Per Truck*)

to determine how many cases will be left after a large order has been put on the trucks. Note that using zero as the value for Y is not valid since you cannot divide by zero. Doing so will produce an ERR message in the formula cell.

Random

When you need a random number in a cell you can use @RAND. This function takes no argument:

@RAND

@RAND produces a uniformly distributed random number greater than or equal to 0 and less than 1. You normally want to combine it with a formula to produce a random number within a certain range. You do this by putting the high end and the low end of the range, separated by a minus sign, in a pair of parentheses and then multiplying that by the @RAND function added to the low-end number. Thus, a random number from 3 to 12 would be produced by

(12-3)*@RAND+3

If you need to get a whole number from the @RAND function, you will need to use @INT or @ROUND.

Although random numbers might not seem to be very useful in a program that is designed to help you organize and accurately analyze information, they can be useful when you want to fill cells with numbers to test a spreadsheet design. Several of the models in this book were created from random numbers.

The @RAND function returns a new random number every time the worksheet recalculates. This can cause problems if you are trying to use the function to create values used elsewhere in the worksheet. Data generated by @RAND can be fixed by using the Edit Values command to change the formula to a value. This allows you to hide the fact that the numbers you have created with @RAND are just random numbers.

Round

For some records, you may need to have the numbers displayed and printed to be rounded. Quattro Pro 3 retains up to 15 decimal places in calculations that result in fractions. When you use a display format that sets the number of decimal places to less than 1, these fractions are not displayed but are still active. This produces a visual problem when numbers containing fractions are summed but formatted for a small fixed number of decimal places. As the fractions accumulate, the total appears incorrect. Thus, if the numbers here in column B were the result of calculations, and they were shown in Fixed format with 0 decimal places in column C, the total would look wrong:

B		C	
B1	3.33	C1	3
B2	3.33	C2	3
B3	3.33	C3	3
Total	10	Total	10

To solve this problem, the numbers being totaled need to be rounded with @ROUND. The format of the function is as follows:

@ROUND(*X,Y*)

The function rounds off the value of X using Y as the number of digits to round to. The value of Y should be between –15 and +15 and should be an integer (whole number). Quattro Pro 3 will round X to an integer. The effect on the preceding example is shown here:

B1 @ROUND(3.33,0)	=	3
B2 @ROUND(3.33,0)	=	3
B3 @ROUND(3.33,0)	=	3
Total		9

You can combine @ROUND with @RAND to produce a whole number within a specified range, as in the following formula:

@ROUND(((48-18)*@RAND+18),0)

This produces a number from 18 to 48 with no decimal places.

Exponent

The @EXP function returns the value of *e* (a constant, approximately 2.7182818) raised to the power of X, as in

@EXP(*X*)

where X is a numeric value less than or equal to 709. Thus, if X is 2, then *e* will be squared. This function is the inverse of a natural logarithm, @LN. If the value of X is greater than 709.85, then the @EXP function returns ERR.

Square Root

You can find the square root of a number or formula in Quattro Pro 3 with the @SQRT function. This function uses the syntax

@SQRT(*Value*)

For example, @SQRT(B5) returns the square root of the value in B5. Square roots of negative numbers produce the response ERR. Use the negation operator or the @ABS function to make the value a positive number.

One typical application of @SQRT is in the calculation of the hypotenuse, or slope, of a triangle. For example:

@SQRT(*Base*Base+Height*Height*)

Log and Log Base

The @LN(*X*) and @LOG(*X*) functions return the log base *e* of *X* and the log base 10 of *X*, respectively. Thus, @LN(100) equals 4.60517 and @LOG(100) equals 2. If the value of *X* is less than or equal to 0, these functions return the ERR message in the cell in which they were applied.

Database Functions

When you want to find the total of a column, you normally use the aggregate function @SUM. Likewise, to calculate the average of a column of numbers, you use the @AVG function. If you want to sum selected records, however, such as the fees for all brokers in the south, you would turn to the database functions shown in Figure 4-7. In the lower half of the figure you can see the seven database functions typed out in formulas. To the right are the answers that those formulas produce. In the upper half of the screen are some of the records referred to in the formulas as well as a small Criteria Table. The database functions use several of the concepts discussed in Chapter 3 such as Query Block and Criteria.

The basic operation of a database function is to tell Quattro Pro 3 which block of cells is involved, which column of the block you want the function applied to, and which records to include based on the Criteria Table. For example, in Figure 4-7 @DAVG averages only the records for column 4 (Earnings) specified by the Criteria Table, in this case where Region = South. All database functions have the same syntax. In the case of @DAVG it is

@DAVG(*Block,Column,Criteria*)

Block is the cell block containing the database, the rectangular group of consecutive rows and named columns that constitute a database, including the field names at the top. *Column* is the number of the column containing the field you want to average, with the first column as 0, the second as 1, and so on. *Criteria* is a cell block containing search criteria.

The @DAVG function averages selected field entries in a database. It includes only those entries in the column number specified whose records meet the chosen criteria. Criteria refers to the coordinates of a block containing a Criteria Table that specifies search information, as in I8..I9. This is the Criteria Table for all the formulas in the lower half of Figure 4-7, which analyze the earnings for all brokers in the South region. (Criteria Tables were described in detail in Chapter 3.) The field specified in the criteria and the field being averaged need not be the same; you can average earnings for all brokers in the South Region, or average fees for all brokers earning over 45. The field averaged is that contained within the column you specify with the column number. You can specify all or part of a database as the block, but field names must be included for each field you include in the block. All of the other database functions use the same three arguments: *Block, Column,* and *Criteria*.

Maximum Value

The @DMAX function finds the maximum value of selected field entries in a database. It includes only those entries in the specified column whose records meet the criteria in the Criteria Table. Its syntax is

@DMAX(*Block,Column,Criteria*)

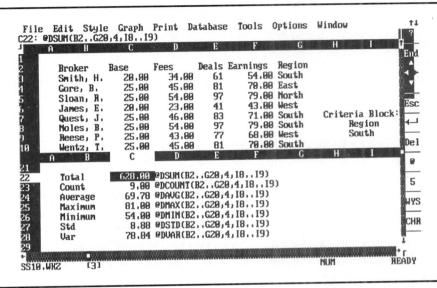

File Edit Style Graph Print Database Tools Options Window

C22: @DSUM(B2..G20,4,I8..I9)

	Broker	Base	Fees	Deals	Earnings	Region		
	Smith, H.	20.00	34.00	61	54.00	South		
	Gore, B.	25.00	45.00	81	70.00	East		
	Sloan, R.	25.00	54.00	97	79.00	North		
	James, E.	20.00	23.00	41	43.00	West		
	Quest, J.	25.00	46.00	83	71.00	South	Criteria Block:	
	Noles, B.	25.00	54.00	97	79.00	South	Region	
	Reese, P.	25.00	43.00	77	68.00	West	South	
	Wentz, T.	25.00	45.00	81	70.00	South		

	Total	620.00	@DSUM(B2..G20,4,I8..I9)
	Count	9.00	@DCOUNT(B2..G20,4,I8..I9)
	Average	69.78	@DAVG(B2..G20,4,I8..I9)
	Maximum	81.00	@DMAX(B2..G20,4,I8..I9)
	Minimum	54.00	@DMIN(B2..G20,4,I8..I9)
	Std	8.88	@DSTD(B2..G20,4,I8..I9)
	Var	78.84	@DVAR(B2..G20,4,I8..I9)

SS18.WK2   [3]   NUM   READY

Figure 4-7. *Database formula example*

@DMAX is a very useful function when you are analyzing a large group of numbers, such as the broker earnings reports for each of four regions. Instead of sorting through the records and manually choosing which ones to compare to find the largest earnings number for brokers in one region, the @DMAX function does that for you. You might also find @DMAX useful for determining the largest figure in the earnings column for all brokers who had earnings greater than a certain level. This would give you some basis with which to compare the higher-earning brokers.

Minimum Value

@DMIN finds the minimum value of selected field entries in a database. It includes only those entries in the specified column whose records meet the criteria in a Criteria Table. Its syntax is

@DMIN(*Block,Column,Criteria*)

You can use this function for such applications as inventory tracking. If one column in your inventory database is called Quantity On Hand and another is called Required Delivery Time, you can have @DMIN show the smallest current quantity on hand for all inventory items that need less than ten days' delivery time. By watching this number as inventory is added or deleted from the database, you will know when ordering is required.

Standard Deviation Measure

The @DSTD function finds the standard deviation value of selected field entries in a database. It includes only those entries in the specified column whose records meet the criteria in a Criteria Table. Its syntax is

@DSTD(*Block,Column,Criteria*)

If you want to compute sample standard deviation, use the @DSTDS function, but be aware that this function is unique to Quattro Pro 3 and is not compatible with earlier programs.

Sum Value

The @DSUM function totals selected field entries in a database. It includes only those entries in the specified column whose records meet the criteria in the Criteria Table. Its syntax is

@DSUM(*Block,Column,Criteria*)

This function will quickly return you such useful answers as the total earnings paid to brokers in one region.

Variance Measure

The @DVAR function calculates variance for selected field entries in a database. It includes only those entries in the column specified whose records meet the criteria in the Criteria Table. Its syntax is

@DVAR(*Block,Column,Criteria*)

To calculate variance for a sample rather than a population, use @DVARS, but bear in mind that this function is unique to Quattro Pro 3 and is not compatible with earlier programs.

Financial Functions

The functions provided for financial calculations in Quattro Pro 3 are extensive. You can calculate annuities, mortgage payments, present values, and numerous other figures that would otherwise require a lengthy formula to be composed. There are some basic terms and conditions common to all Quattro Pro 3 financial functions. Table 4-3 lists the arguments that Quattro Pro 3 financial functions require and the abbreviations used for them. These abbreviations are used in the following descriptions.

Argument	Definition
Rate	Interest rate, per period as defined in Nper, should be greater than –1
Nper	Number of periods—for example, 12 months or 1 year; an integer greater than 0
Pv	Present value; an amount valued today
Pmt	A payment; a negative cash flow amount
Fv	Future value; an amount to be accumulated
Type	Either 0 or 1. Type indicates the difference between ordinary annuity (0) and annuity due (1). Argument of 0 means payments made are at the end of each period; 1 means they are made at the beginning. The default assumption is that type = 0

Table 4-3. *Financial Function Arguments*

Old Style Functions	New Style Functions
@CTERM(*Rate,Fv,Pv*)	@NPER(*Rate*,0,-*Pv,Fv*,0)
@FV(*Pmt,Rate,Nper*)	@FVAL(*Rate,Nper,-Pmt*,0,0)
@PMT(*Pv,Rate,Nper*)	@PAYMT(*Rate,Nper,-Pv*,0,0)
@PV(*Pv,Rate,Nper*)	@PVAL(*Rate,Nper,-Pmt*,0,0)
@RATE(*Fv,Pv,Nper*)	@IRATE(*Nper*,0,-*Pv,Fv*,0)
@TERM(*Pv,Rate,Fv*)	@NPER(*Rate,-Pmt*,0,*Fv*,0)

*Note that negative arguments indicate cash flows assumed to be negative.

Table 4-4.   *Older Functions and New Alternatives**

Quattro Pro 3 stipulates that when interest rates are required in financial function arguments, they must be stated as a percentage per period. For example, when figuring monthly loan payments with the @PMT or @PAYMT functions, the interest argument must be stated as percentage per month.

A connoisseur of spreadsheet programs might describe the financial functions in Quattro Pro 3 as a subtle blend of the best from 1-2-3 and Excel. While retaining "backward" compatibility with 1-2-3 Release 2 and Quattro 1.0 and Quattro Pro 2, Quattro Pro 3 allows more sophisticated financial calculations, using optional arguments for the timing of payments. In Table 4-4 you can see the older functions and the improved alternatives. Unless you are creating worksheets that need to be compatible with older programs you will probably want to employ the new Quattro Pro 3 functions.

Payment Functions

There are several financial functions that relate to loan payments. They are @PMT, @PAYMT, @IPAYMT, and @PPAYMT. They will be considered as a group since they serve as a good example of the power and flexibility provided by Quattro Pro 3's financial functions. For example, the @PAYMT function can be used to perform several different calculations, depending upon the number of arguments provided.

@PMT   As you saw in Chapter 1, the @PMT function calculates the amount required to pay back a loan in equal payments based on a given principal or amount borrowed, a rate of interest, and a loan term. The format of the function is

@PMT(*Pv,Rate,Nper*)

Present value (*Pv*) is the principal, the amount being borrowed. *Rate* is the interest being charged, and number of payments (*Nper*) is the life of the loan. The values for *Pv, Rate,* and *Nper* can be numeric constants, numeric fields, or formulas that result in a number. Note that *Rate* must be greater than −1 and *Nper* cannot be zero.

Figure 4-8 shows a loan calculation worksheet, which demonstrates the argument requirements of the @PMT function. Since the rate is requested in percentage per period but is normally quoted as an annual percentage rate, the loan payment formula divides the contents of cell M4 by 12. Likewise, the term of the loan (*Nper*) is stated in years in M3 for convenience and then multiplied by the payments per year (12) in the formula.

```
 File  Edit  Style  Graph  Print  Database  Tools  Options  Window            ↑↓
M5: (,2) @ROUND(@PMT(M2,M4/12,M3*12),2)                                          ?
J      I        J          K            L          M                          End
1
2              Principal                      15,000.00
3              Term, in years                      5.00
4              Interest rate (%A.P.R)             8.00%
5              Monthly payment                   309.92
6              Total of payments              18,595.20                       Esc
7              Total interest paid             3,595.20
8                                                                              ↵
9
10     PMT    Paid in    Paid in      Cumulative  Remaining                    Del
11·    #      Interest   Prinicipal   Interest    Balance
12                                                                             @
13     1   +M2*$M$4/12  +$M$5-J13   +J13        +M2-K13
14     2   +M13*$M$4/12 +$M$5-J14   +L13+J14    +M13-K14                       5
15     3   +M14*$M$4/12 +$M$5-J15   +L14+J15    +M14-K15
16     4   +M15*$M$4/12 +$M$5-J16   +L15+J16    +M15-K16                       WYS
17     5       104.07      205.85     535.23     13,985.63
18     6       102.56      207.36     637.79     13,778.27                     CHR
19     7       101.04      208.88     738.83     13,569.39
20     8        99.51      210.41     838.34     13,358.98                     ↓
←                                                                            ↵
CHAP4PMT.WQ1 [3]                                                 NUM        READY
```

Figure 4-8.   *Loan calculation worksheet*

This value could be adjusted for quarterly (4), semiannual (2), or annual (1) payments.

@PAYMT   A more sophisticated function for calculating loan payments and other values is @PAYMT. In its simplest form, the @PAYMT function works like @PMT to return the size of payment required to amortize a loan across a given number of periods, assuming equal payments at a constant rate of interest. However, the first difference between the two functions is apparent in the order and number of arguments they use. The format of the @PAYMT function is

@PAYMT(*Rate,Nper,Pv,Fv,Type*)

The function's purpose can be defined as determination of the fully amortized mortgage payment for borrowing present value amount at rate percent of interest per period over a specified number of periods.

You can use a numeric constant, a numeric field, or a formula that results in a number for the principal (*Pv*), *Rate*, and term (*Nper*) arguments. Note that the interest rate must be greater than −1 and that the term cannot equal 0. The last two arguments, future value (*Fv*) and *Type*, are optional and are discussed in a moment. Figure 4-9 shows an example of the @PAYMT function being used to calculate the payment required to repay $26,000 over 36 months when borrowed at 12.00% A.P.R. Here is where you can see the second major difference between the @PMT and @PAYMT; the latter produces a negative value. The reason for this is the financial assumption that a payment is a negative item from a cash flow point of view.

In the example in Figure 4-9 column B is used to identify the figures in column C. Note that the interest rate is stated as 12% in cell C11, meaning 12.00% per year. It is then divided by 12 when used as the *rate* argument in the @PAYMT function statement in cell C14. This is to comply with the Quattro Pro 3 requirement that *rate* be stated as interest per period. You could use an expanded model like the one in Figure 4-10 to make this calculation even more explicit.

Future Value and @PAYMT   The optional future value argument in an @PAYMT function statement is used when you apply the @PAYMT function to the task of calculating the size of payments you need to make each month to accumulate a specific sum of money in the future. For example,

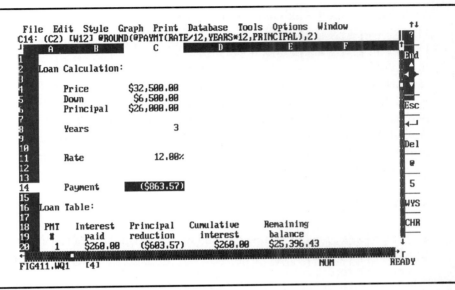

Figure 4-9.   *@PAYMT for loan calculation*

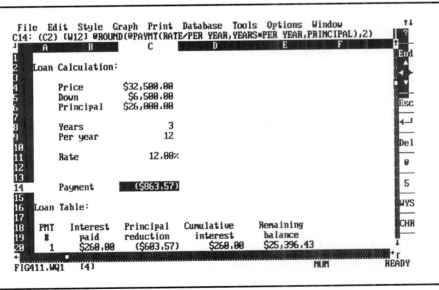

Figure 4-10.   *Expanded loan model*

suppose you want to accumulate $26,000 to purchase a new car. You are going to put away an amount of money every month for two years. That money will earn 8.00% interest. How large does the monthly payment have to be? You can see the answer calculated in Figure 4-11.

In this example, the argument cells in column C have been named according to the labels in column B, using the Edit Names Create Labels command (described in Chapter 11). Note that when you use the future value argument you cannot just omit the present value argument. A zero is commonly used as a place-holder for the present value argument, as in

@PAYMT(*Rate*/12,*Nper*,0,*Fv*,*Type*)

You might also note in Figure 4-11 the calculation of principal paid into the account and the amount of interest earned. These calculations are not automatically carried out by Quattro Pro 3 but provide a useful perspective on the @PAYMT function. Economists might note that a $26,000 car loan at 12.00% for two years costs approximately $1224 per month while a two-year savings plan at 8.00% to obtain the same amount costs $996. However, the borrower gets the use of the car for two years and possibly a

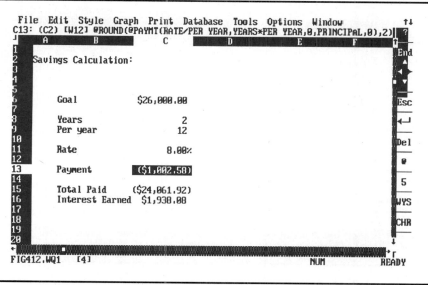

Figure 4-11. *Savings plan with type argument of 0*

tax deduction as well, while the saver gets a tax bill and will probably need more than $26,000 to buy the same car at the end of the plan.

The Type Argument   In Figure 4-11 you can see the other optional argument for the @PAYMT function: *Type*. Quattro Pro 3 can calculate interest based on two types of repayment arrangements. The program assumes, as do many consumer loans, that the payment is due at the end of the loan period. In other words, the first payment is due one month from when you receive the principal of the loan, and at the end of each one-month period after that. This assumption is type 0. If you omit a *type* argument, Quattro Pro 3 will assume type 0. The alternative type, based on having the payment due at the beginning of each loan period, is type 1. You can force this assumption by including 1 as the *type* argument, as shown in the revised loan payment plan in Figure 4-12. You can see that the amount of each payment is less under a type 1 loan. Of course, the practical effect of going to a type 1 loan is to reduce the term of the loan by one period and pay the first payment from the proceeds of the loan, a practice once followed by some banks.

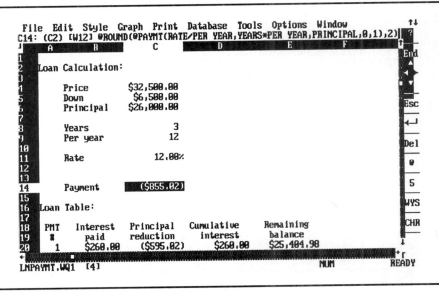

Figure 4-12.   *Loan plan with type argument of 1*

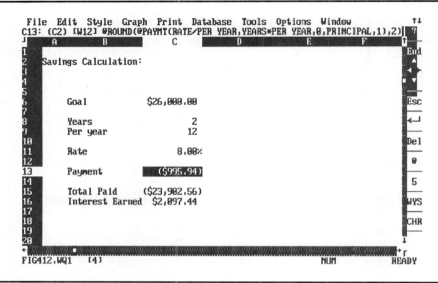

Figure 4-13. *Savings plan with type argument of 1*

In Figure 4-13 you can see the effect of going to type 1 on a future value savings plan calculation. Here the effect is positive since it assumes that you begin the savings plan by making the first deposit. In Figure 4-11 the assumption was that the payment on the plan was at the end of the period, thus requiring larger payments to achieve the same goal. You can see that the *type* argument is likely to be 0 for such calculations as loans, but 1 for such items as annuities and savings plans.

Loan Tables You may want to see a table of payments for a mortage loan, showing the split between interest and principal and the amount of principal left unpaid. A table of payments can be laid out below the mortgage calculations, as shown in Figure 4-14. Notice the formula for the payment in E7. The term of the loan is stated in years in cell E5 and then multiplied by 12 to produce monthly payments in E7. Also note that the @ROUND function is used to round the payment to the nearest cent (two decimal places). This is necessary when you are performing real-world loan calculations rather than just estimates.

```
 File  Edit  Style  Graph  Print  Database  Tools  Options  Window        ↑↓
E7: (,2) [W12] @ROUND(@PMT(E4,E6/12,E5*12),2)                               ?
⌐    A        B         C          D          E          F              ◄ End
1                                                                          ▲
2            Mortgage Table                                                ◄ ►
3                                                                          ▼
4            Principal                           80,000.00
5            Term, in years                             25
6            Interest rate (%A.P.R)                  11.50%                 Esc
7            Monthly payment                       813.18
8            Total of payments                  243,954.00                ◄┘
9            Total interest paid                163,954.00
10                                                                         Del
11  PMT  Paid in     Paid in    Cumulative  Remaining
12   #   Interest    Prinicipal Interest    Balance                        @
13   1     766.67      46.51       766.67   79,953.49
14   2     766.67      46.51     1,533.33   79,906.97                      5
15   3     766.67      46.51     2,300.00   79,860.46
⌐    A        B         C          D          E          F              WYS
310  298    766.67      46.51   228,466.67   66,139.03
311  299    766.67      46.51   229,233.33   66,092.51                    CHR
312  300    766.67      46.51   230,000.00   66,046.00
313
CHAP417.WQ1  [4]                                         NUM       READY
```

Figure 4-14.   *Mortgage table*

The loan payment table consists of five columns, starting with the payment number, which runs from 1 to 300. The Window Options Locked Titles command has been used to show the bottom of the table as well as the top. (This command is described in the next chapter.) Column B calculates the amount of each payment that is interest, while column C shows the amount paid to reduce the principal. In column C a running total of interest is maintained while the declining principal is tracked in column E. You can see the formulas that make up this table in Figure 4-15. Notice the use of the @IF function in columns B, C, and D. (The @IF function is discussed in detail later in the chapter.) The @MAX function is used in column E to produce a zero value when the loan is completely amortized.

The total figures in E8 and E9 show the total interest and principal payments respectively. You might notice that the total principal reduction is actually $5.17 more than the amount of the loan. This is a result of the need to accept payments in dollars and whole cents. As any banker knows, there are several ways of dealing with this kind of minor imbalance in a loan amortization. (You might want to experiment with these using Quattro Pro 3; for example, the actual payment required to retire the sample loan in exactly 300 payments is 1560.905236.)

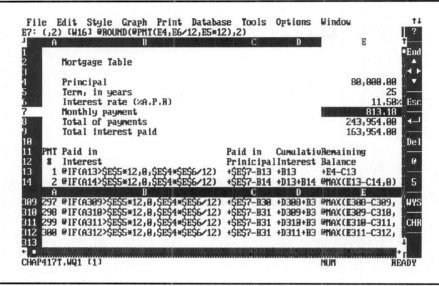

Figure 4-15. *Mortgage table formulas*

Finally, it should be noted that the method of calculating the remaining balance on the loan shown in Figure 4-14 is simple interest, the method commonly used by banks for mortgages and personal loans. Some lending institutions use the rule of 78 to determine the amount left unpaid. This method uses a system like sum-of-the-years, shown later in the discussion of the @SYD function, to determine interest.

@IPAYMT and @PPAYMT There may be times when you want to figure out how much of a loan payment is going toward interest and how much toward principal. Quattro Pro 3 has functions for both of these calculations. The interest portion of a payment is calculated with @IPAYMT while the principal portion is calculated with @PPAYMT. Of course, if you already know the size of the payment you can easily calculate these amounts from a loan table, or you can take the result of @IPAYMT away from the amount of the payment to get the result of @PPAYMT. However, both @IPAYMT and @PPAYMT can be used without first figuring the payment amount. They return the portion of the total payment for a specific payment, for example, for the thirtieth payment of thirty-six. The form of both functions is the same:

@IPAYMT(*Rate,Period,Nper,Pv,Fv,Type*)

and

@PPAYMT(*Rate,Period,Nper,Pv,Fv,Type*)

where *Rate* is the interest rate, *Period* is the period of the loan you are calculating interest for, *Nper* is the total number of periods in the loan, and *Pv* is the principal of the loan. Quattro Pro 3 will assume the *Fv* argument to be zero if not supplied, and that *Type* is zero unless otherwise specified. The *Fv* argument is used when calculating an accumulated future amount.

To apply the @IPAYMT argument to the loan in Figure 4-15 and get the interest portion of the 297th payment you would use the formula:

@IPAYMT(E6/12,297,E5*12,E4)

The result would be −45.9621, which is a few cents different from the result in the loan table, due to the rounding of the payment in the table. Despite this minor discrepancy, the @PPAYMT and @IPAYMT functions are handy for a number of lending related calculations.

@NPER   A great function for window shoppers is the @NPER function, which calculates the number of payments required to pay off a loan at a given payment amount. Suppose you want to buy a $10,000 car and can afford $200.00 per month. If the going rate of interest on car loans is 13% you would use the formula

@NPER(0.13/12,-200,10000)

to calculate that just over 72 payments are required to pay off the loan. Note that the payment argument is entered as a negative value since it is a negative cash flow item. The @NPER function uses the form

@NPER(*Rate,Payment,Pv,Fv,Type*)

and returns ERR if the *Payment* amount is not enough to amortize the loan. (As you might expect, the *Payment* amount must at least equal the interest rate per period times the principal.) The *Type* argument is used to indicate whether the payments are being made at the beginning or end of the period. The default, assumed if you omit the final argument, is 0, meaning at the end of the period.

The optional *Fv* argument is used when you want to calculate the payments required to create a future sum of money. For example, to calculate how many payments of $200 per month are required to reach a lump sum of 50,000 when you are earning 10% interest per year and have $2000 already invested, you would use the following:

@NPER(0.1/12,-200,-2000,50000,0)

The answer is roughly 132 payments. Note that this changes to 131 if you change the final argument from 0 to 1 to indicate that the payments are made at the beginning of the period. Also note that the current balance is a negative amount, as are the payments.

@TERM   An alternative function to use if you have a target figure or goal in mind for your investments is @TERM. Like @NPER, this function calculates how long it will take a series of equal, evenly spaced investments to accumulate to a target amount based on a steady rate of interest. The syntax of the @TERM function is

@TERM(*Payment,Rate,Fv*)

This function does not offer a present value or type argument and is provided in Quattro Pro 3 essentially for backward compatibility.

@CTERM   The @CTERM function calculates the number of periods it takes for a single investment to grow to some future amount. The @CTERM function has the following format:

@CTERM(*Rate,Fv,Pv*)

Rate is a numeric value representing the fixed interest rate per compounding period. The *Fv* argument is a numeric value representing the future

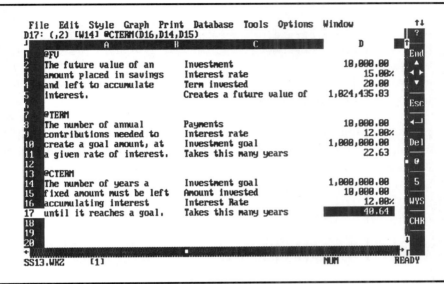

Figure 4-16.   *The @CTERM function*

value that an investment will reach at some point. The *Pv* argument is a numeric value representing the present value of the investment.

In Figure 4-16 you can see that the goal of reaching $1 million from an initial investment of $10,000 earning 12% per year will take 41 years to achieve.

Investment Functions

Quattro Pro 3 offers several financial functions that assist in the task of evaluating investments. These are @PV, @PVAL, @NPV, @FV, @FVAL, @RATE, @IRATE, and @IRR, and they are discussed in the following sections.

The Importance of Present Value   When you are evaluating a potential investment it helps to know the present value of the investment. Suppose you have been offered an investment opportunity that promises to pay you $1050 after one year if you invest $1000 now. You know that simply putting the $1000 in a good savings account will turn that $1000 into $1060, so the

investment does not seem worthwhile. To put it another way, the investment promises a 5% yield whereas you can get 6% elsewhere. Another way
of comparing the promised yield of an investment with your estimate of
realistic alternative yields is to *discount* the payment from the investment.
If the discounted value is greater than the amount you are considering
investing, then the investment is a good one. Another term for the discounted value is *present value*.

Consider the present or discounted value of a venture offering a 12-
month return of $1050 on an initial investment of $1000. You would take
the $1050 and divide it by the number of payments plus the rate of return
on the alternative investment, in this case 6%. The formula is thus
1050/(1+.06) and the answer, the present value of $1050 received a year
from now discounted at a rate of 6%, is $991. Since the present value of
the promised return is less than the price of the investment, $1000, the
investment is not a good one. To use Quattro Pro 3 for this kind of analysis,
you use the @PV and @PVAL functions, which can handle investments
promising more than one annual payback amount.

@PVAL   @PVAL returns the present value of an investment based on
periodic and constant payments and a constant interest rate. The function
has the following format:

@PVAL(*Rate,Nper,Pmt,Fv,Type*)

Payments (*Pmt*), interest *Rate*, and term (*Nper*) can be numeric constants,
numeric fields, or formulas that result in a number. Interest must be
greater than or equal to −1. The future value (*Fv*) and *Type* arguments are
optional.

An example of a @PVAL calculation is shown in Figure 4-17. The
promised return on an investment of $150,000 is five annual payments of
$25,000. Entering the payments, the discount rate, and the term into the
@PVAL function in B6 you get the result $158,821.18, the most you should
consider investing to get the promised return. Note that Quattro Pro 3
treats payments as negative values. The entry of -B4 in the @PVAL
statement causes the function to return a positive value for the present
value rather than a negative value.

Since the present value of the promised return is shown to be greater
than the proposed investment amount, you might want to approve the

Figure 4-17.   *The @PVAL function*

investment. However, while the @PVAL function allows you to take the time value of money into account when comparing investment opportunities, you must still bear in mind less readily quantifiable factors such as risk. Typically the discount rate represents a zero risk alternative such as CDs or Treasury notes.

Suppose that an investment of $100,000 was going to pay a lump sum of S150,000 at the end of the five years, rather than installments of $30,000. This can be calculated using the optional future value argument of the @PVAL function, as in

@PVAL(0.12,5,0,-150000)

The result is $85,114.03, considerably less than the amount of the proposed investment, indicating that the investment is not a good one. This makes sense since you are deprived of the use of the money until the end of the investment period. You would have to get over $190,000 at the end of five years for the use of your $100,000 to exceed the return from the 12% discount rate. Note that the 0 in the @PVAL statement represents the missing present value argument.

While the future value option makes the @PVAL function more versatile, most @PVAL calculations do not use the other optional argument, *type*. Quattro Pro 3 assumes that the payments from the investment will be made at the end of the periods, not at the beginning. To change the assumption to the beginning, include the argument 1 for type, as in

@PVAL(0.12,5,-30000,0,1)

The result of this formula is $121,120.48, indicating that the investment is more attractive if the return is paid at the beginning of the periods.

@PV   Another way to calculate the present value of a simple annuity—that is, a regular series of equal payments—is to use the @PV function, which takes the form

@PV(*Payment,Rate,Nper*)

The arguments can be numeric constants, numeric cells, or a formula that results in a number. Interest must be greater than –1.

An example of this calculation is shown in Figure 4-18. The promised return is five annual payments of $30,000, or $150,000. Entering the payments, the discount rate, and the term into the @PV function gives you the result of $108,143.29, the most you should consider investing to get the promised return. The @PV function allows you to take the time value of money into account when comparing investment opportunities. However, the @PV function is mainly included for backward compatibility with programs like 1-2-3.

Net Present Value   A function closely related to @PVAL is @NPV, which calculates the *net present value* of returns on an investment, based on a discount rate. The net present value of an investment should be greater than zero, otherwise it offers no better return than investing at the

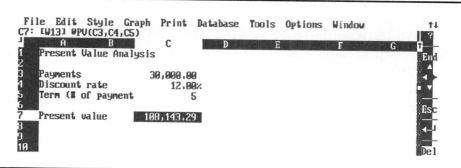

Figure 4-18.   *Present value*

discount rate. Whereas @PVAL assumes equal amounts of cash flow from the investment or a single lump sum, the @NPV function handles unequal amounts returned from the investment, using the format

@NPV(*Rate,Block,Type*)

where *Rate* is the discount rate of interest and *Block* is cells containing the cash outlay and flows from the investment. Typically, the first value in the block is the amount invested, and further amounts are returns on the investment. The stream of cash is assumed to be constant, that is, at regular intervals, but the amounts can vary. For example, suppose you are promised three annual payments of $30,000, $40,000, and $50,000, in return for your investment of $100,000. The net present value of this proposition is calculated with the formula

@NPV(0.12,B1..B4)

The first argument is the discount rate of 12%. The second argument is the block of cells containing the values 100,000, 30,000, 40,000, and 50,000. The result is less than zero (–5,122.78 in fact), which suggests that this is not a good investment.

Suppose you are still interested in the investment and counter with a demand for returns of $35,000, $45,000, and $50,000. When you enter these in cells B2..B4, the result is positive (2422.09), suggesting that the investment is now much more profitable. In Figure 4-19 you can see a worksheet used to evaluate a further proposal that offers payments over a period of four years in return for an initial investment of $110,000. Note that you can state the @NPV value arguments as a range, rather than as separate cells.

With all financial functions, including @NPV, you need to pay attention to Quattro Pro 3's assumptions about timing. In 1-2-3 Release 2.0, the @NPV function has no type argument to alter the timing assumption. Quattro Pro 3 allows you to specify a type argument, which can be either 0 or 1, depending on whether the cash flows are at the beginning or end of the period. If you do not specify a type argument, Quattro Pro 3 assumes payment at the end of the period in @NPV calculations. This means that the model shown in Figure 4-19 actually represents putting out $110,000 one year from the beginning of the project and receiving the first payment

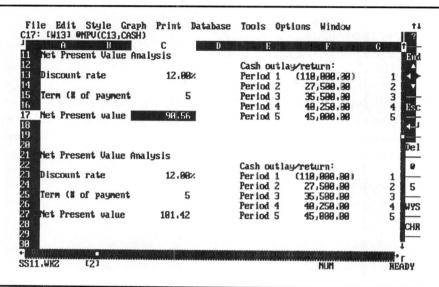

Figure 4-19. *@NPV calculations*

of $27,500 at the end of the second year. It is more likely that you will want to base calculations upon paying out the funds for the investment at the beginning of the first period and receiving the first payment in return at the beginning of the second period. To accommodate this assumption you can either specify a type argument of 1 or take the initial investment out of the @NPV argument and place it at the end of the formula, as in Figure 4-19 where the range of returns is F24..F27. The initial outlay is placed in cell F23 and subtracted from the result of the @NPV function. The result shows that the investment is slightly better under the new assumptions.

@IRATE   Suppose you are considering two investments. One offers to pay you four annual payments of $1000 in return for your investment of $3000. The other offers 48 monthly payments of $80 for the same $3000. You might want to calculate a rate of return for both of these investments in order to see which is the better deal. The rate at which your $1000 is expected to grow is the compound growth rate, calculated by the @IRATE function, using this format:

@IRATE(*Nper,Pmt,Pv,Fv,Type*)

The last two arguments are optional. In the case of the first investment the formula would be

@IRATE(4,1000,-3000)

The result is an annual rate of return percentage, since the Nper argument is entered as years. In this case the result is .125898325, or 12.59% when expressed with just two decimal places. The rate of return of the second investment is expressed as

@IRATE(48,80,-3000)

The result is .010562829, or 1.06%, which is a monthly rate of interest since the Nper argument is expressed in months. To calculate an annual rate of return for the second investment you would use

@IRATE(48,80,-3000)*12

The result is 12.68%, which is marginally better than the first investment despite the fact that it pays less cash (48*$80=$3840 as opposed to $4000).

The @IRATE function arrives at its answer by performing a net present value calculation. Quattro Pro 3 guesses at the rate of return on the investment and figures the net present value of the investment at the guess rate. If the resulting net present value is greater than zero, the program guesses a higher rate and recomputes the net present value. If the guess rate results in a net present value lower than zero, a lower rate is used. In fact, the rate of return on an investment is the percentage that most closely results in a net present value of zero. Quattro Pro 3 repeats, or iterates, the calculation until it arrives at the correct rate or has completed 20 iterations. If it does the 20 iterations without getting the right rate you will get an error message.

@RATE   An alternative to the @IRATE function is the @RATE function, which takes the following form:

@RATE(*Fv,Pv,Nper*)

The @RATE function returns the rate of interest required to grow a present value sum into a specified target value over a stated term. This function is mainly provided for backward compatibility with earlier programs.

Internal Rate of Return   When you want to compare the payback you will receive from different investments, you can use the @IRR function to calculate the internal rate of return. This function uses the format

@IRR(*Guess,Block*)

where *Guess* is your estimate of what the answer will be and *Block* is a reference to a range of cells containing amounts of cash flow. Typically, the first number in the range will be a negative one, indicating the initial payment or investment. The @IRR function assumes that the payments occur at the end of the period. This function works much like the @IRATE function except that, like the @NPV function, it can handle a range of unequal cash flows.

Generally, an investment is attractive if it shows an internal rate of return greater than the rate you can obtain elsewhere, the rate known as comparison or hurdle rate. The @IRR function can be seen at work in Figure 4-20, where three different investments are compared. The third one offers the best return as it results in the highest @IRR. Notice that the formula in I12 does not include a guess argument. This is because the guess argument is optional and only required if Quattro Pro 3 has difficulty reaching an @IRR result. If you enter an @IRR formula and get an error in return, try altering or adding the guess argument, using a percentage close to what you would estimate the return to be.

@FVAL   To see what a series of payments will be worth over time, given that they earn interest, you use the @FVAL function. This is shown in Figure 4-21, where the @FVAL function returns the future value of the annual retirement fund contribution of $10,000, which earns 15% per year. The @FVAL function has the following format:

@FVAL(*Rate,Nper,Payment,Pv,Type*)

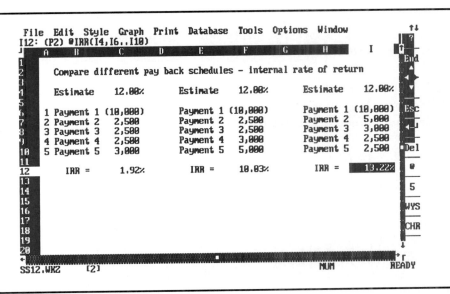

Figure 4-20.   *@IRR calculations*

Rate is a numeric value greater than 0, representing periodic interest rate. *Nper* is a numeric value, representing the number of periods of the investment. *Payment* is a numeric value, representing the amount of equal payments to be made. The @FVAL function calculates the future value of an investment where the payment is invested for a number of periods at the specified rate of interest per period. You can use @FVAL to see the effects of regular savings plans and evaluate such investments against

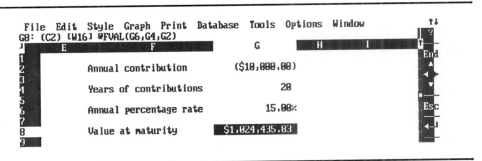

Figure 4-21.   *The @FVAL function*

alternative uses of funds. You can use the *Pv* argument to indicate an existing value in the program and the *Type* argument to indicate whether the payment is made at the beginning or end of the period. For example, you might want to put $1,000 into a savings account at the beginning of each of seven years, and you would like to know what the account would be worth at the end of the seven years. The account earns 8.5% per year, so the formula would be

@FVAL(.085,7,-1000,0,1)

which returns the answer of $9,830.64. If the account already had $2,500 in it when the plan began, the formula would be

@FVAL(.085,7,-1000,-2500,1)

which returns the answer of $14,255.99. If you decided to make the payments at the end of each period the formula would be

@FVAL(.085,7,-1000,-2500,0)

which yields $13,485.85.

@FV Another function for calculating future value is @FV. This function is shown in Figure 4-22, where it returns the future value of an annual retirement fund investment of $2,500, earning 12.5% per year over a 10-year term. The @FV function has the following format:

@FV(*Payment,Rate,Nper*)

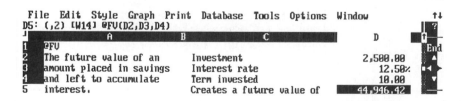

Figure 4-22. *The @FV function*

Payment is a numeric value representing the amount of equal payments to be made. *Rate* is a numeric value greater than 0 representing periodic interest rate. *Nper* is a numeric value representing the number of periods of the investment. While you can use @FV to see the effects of regular savings plans and evaluate such investments against alternative uses of funds, it is mainly provided in Quattro Pro 3 for backward compatibility. The assumption in @FV is that the payments are made at the beginning of the period.

Depreciation Functions

Quattro Pro 3 offers three different methods for calculating depreciation, all of which are shown in Figure 4-23. These methods are used because most goods lose value over time, and most state and federal tax laws allow businesses to deduct some of this lost revenue from taxable income.

Straight-Line Depreciation   The straight-line method results in an equal amount of depreciation per period:

@SLN(*Cost,Salvage,Life*)

This is the simplest form of depreciation.

File Edit Style Graph Print Database Tools Options Window						↑↓
C6: (,2) [W12] @SLN(C1,C2,C3)						?
A	B	C	D	E	F	
1 Value to depreciate		11,785.00				End
2 Salvage value		1,340.00				▲
3 Estimated life		5.00				◄ ►
4						▼
5 Period		@SLN	@DDB	@SYD		
6 1 Year		2,089.00	4,714.00	3,401.67		Esc
7 2 Year		2,089.00	2,828.40	2,785.33		
8 3 Year		2,089.00	1,697.04	2,089.00		◄┘
9 4 Year		2,089.00	1,018.22	1,392.67		
10 5 Year		2,089.00	187.34	696.33		Del

Figure 4-23.   *Depreciation*

Sum-of-Years Depreciation The @SYD function uses a method called the Sum-of-Years-Digits to vary the rate at which depreciation is taken. This function requires knowing the year for each calculation, and takes the form:

@SYD(*Cost,Salvage,Life,Period*)

An interesting application of the @SYD function is in the computation of a loan payout based on the "rule of 78," which results in a larger payoff for loans than the simple interest calculation shown earlier in Figure 4-15. The rule of 78 payout table is shown in Figure 4-24.

Double-Declining-Balance Depreciation The @DDB function calculates depreciation based on the double-declining method, using the following elements:

@DDB(*Cost,Salvage,Life,Period*)

```
 File  Edit  Style  Graph  Print  Database  Tools  Options  Window        ↑↓
B13: (,2) @IF(A13>E$3,0,@ROUND(@SYD($E$7,0,$E$3,A13),2))                    ?
        A        B          C           D           E        F      G
 1
 2               Principal                       25,000.00                 End
 3               Term, in months                    48.00                   ▲
 4               Interest rate (%A.P.R)              8.80%                   ◄ ►
 5               Monthly payment                   619.75                   ▪ ▼
 6               Total of payments              29,748.00                  Esc
 7               Total interest paid             4,748.00
 8                                                                          ◄┘
 9               Payout based on rule of 78
10      PMT      Interest   Principal   Cumulative  Remaining              Del
11       #       paid       reduction   interest    balance
12                                                                          @
13       1         193.80     425.95       193.80   24,574.05
14       2         189.76     429.99       383.56   24,144.06               5
15       3         185.72     434.03       569.28   23,710.03
16       4         181.68     438.07       750.96   23,271.96              WYS
17       5         177.65     442.10       928.61   22,829.86
18       6         173.61     446.14     1,102.22   22,383.72              CHR
19       7         169.57     450.18     1,271.79   21,933.54
20       8         165.53     454.22     1,437.32   21,479.32               ↓
←     ■                                                                    →┌
CHAP4PMT.WQ1 [2]                                          NUM           READY
```

Figure 4-24. *Loan payout based on rule of 78*

As in all of the depreciation functions, *Cost* is a numeric value representing the amount paid for an asset. *Salvage* is a numeric value representing the worth of an asset at the end of its useful life. *Life* is a numeric value representing the expected useful life of an asset. *Period* is a numeric value representing the time period for which you want to determine the depreciation expense. The @DDB function determines accelerated depreciation values for an asset, given the initial cost, life expectancy, end value, and depreciation period.

Accelerated Cost Recovery Most tax calculations no longer use the three methods of depreciation just described, but rather a method known as the Accelerated Cost Recovery System (ACRS). The rate of depreciation allowed by ACRS varies each year of the asset's life and depends on when the asset was placed in service. There is no ACRS function in Quattro Pro 3, but you can use the @INDEX function to create IRS tables of depreciation rates, based on the month placed in service and the year of the asset's life. @INDEX is a logical function, described in the next section.

Logical Functions

Quattro Pro 3 provides a variety of functions that can be very useful in situations where logical arguments need to be entered into fields.

@IF

The @IF function instructs Quattro Pro 3 to choose between two actions based on a condition being either true or false. Suppose that you are budgeting quarterly revenue and expenditures for a computer store, using a spreadsheet like that shown in Figure 4-25. You have gotten good results from spending 5% of all sales revenue on advertising. Thus, advertising is normally Sales*0.05. However, you know that money spent on advertising beyond a certain dollar amount is not effective (say, $110,000, expressed as 110.00 in the model).

What you want to do is to budget your advertising expenditures with a ceiling of 110. You can do this by adding the @IF function to the advertising

File   Edit Style Graph Print Database Tools Options Window   ↑↓
B17: (,2) @IF(0.05*B10<110,0.05*B10,110)   ?

	A	B	C	D	E	F	
1							End
2		Quarter 1	Quarter 2	Quarter 3	Quarter 4		▲
3							◄
4	SALES (000s)						▼
5							
6	PC Systems	1,205.00	1,325.50	1,458.05	1,603.86		Esc
7	Monitors	210.00	231.00	254.10	279.51		
8	Printers	532.00	585.20	643.72	708.09		◄┘
9							
10	TOTAL	1,947.00	2,141.70	2,355.87	2,591.46		▭Del
11							
12							@
13	EXPENSES (000s)						
14							5
15	Salaries	194.70	214.17	235.59	259.15		
16	Bonuses	48.68	53.54	58.90	64.79		WYS
17	Advertising	97.35	107.09	110.00	110.00		
18	Other	58.41	64.25	70.68	77.74		CHR
19							↓
20	TOTAL	399.14	439.05	475.16	511.68		

C4IFADV.WQ1 [2]   NUM   READY

Figure 4-25.   *Store budget*

expense formula to tell Quattro Pro 3 that if Sales*0.05 is less than 110, Advertising=Sales*0.05; otherwise, Advertising=110. In the spreadsheet this is written as

@IF(0.05*B10<110,0.05*B10,110)

The format of the @IF function is as follows:

@IF(*Condition,True,False*)

This syntax means that if the condition is true, then the response is that stated in the *True* argument. Otherwise, the result is that stated in the *False* argument. True and false results can be constants, value or label cells, or other formulas, and can be any type of data.

The @IF function is extremely versatile because it allows the spreadsheet to become intelligent, that is, to do one of two things based on a condition that you establish. This can be used in numerous situations in a typical worksheet. For example, you can use @IF to test the integrity of a

```
   File  Edit  Style  Graph  Print  Database  Tools  Options  Window      ↑↓
G17: (,2) @IF(@SUM(TD)=@SUM(TA),@SUM(TD),@ERR)                            ?
        A        B        C        D        E        F        G        End
1
2                Monday   Tuesday  Wednesday Thursday Friday   Totals      ▲
3
4  Meals                                                                   ▼
5     B'fast       3.45     0.00     3.89     4.76     5.98    18.08    Esc
6      Lunch       5.00     8.95     6.74     5.78    18.96    45.43
7     Dinner       0.00    23.87     5.89    13.45     0.00    43.21
8  Travel
9       Air        0.00   143.89     0.00     0.00   148.00   291.89    Del
10  Mileage        0.00     0.00     0.00     0.00     3.50     3.50
11  Parking        0.00     0.00    12.00    12.00    12.00    36.00    @
12     Taxi        0.00     0.00     0.00     0.00     0.00     0.00
13 Miscellaneous
14  Supplies      34.00     0.00     6.00     0.00     3.00    43.00    5
15     Other       0.00     0.00     0.00    23.87     0.00    23.87
16 ========================================================================WYS
17              50.45   176.71    34.52    59.86   191.44   512.98
18                                                                       CHR
19                      Total =   512.98
20
SS09.WK2    [2]                                           NUM         READY
```

Figure 4-26. *The expense report*

spreadsheet, as in the expense report worksheet shown in Figure 4-26. Anyone who has filled out expense reports knows that the sum of the rows should equal the sum of the columns. When you lay out this kind of report in Quattro Pro 3, the calculation is done for you. However, you should never assume that just because the work is done electronically it is always done correctly. The @IF formula in cell G17 says that if the sum of the columns (TD) equals the sum of the rows (TA), the cell should contain the sum of the columns; otherwise, it should contain an error message (produced by the @ERR function) to show that a mistake has been made. When a mistake has been detected, the ERR message appears as a label in cell G17.

Suppose Quattro Pro 3 detects an error. You review the spreadsheet. Close examination reveals that someone typed a number over a formula in column G. This caused the sum of the columns to be incorrect. When the erroneous value is replaced by the correct formula, the ERR message will disappear and the expense report will be correct.

When you want to apply several conditions to a calculation, you can *nest* @IF statements. For example, in a large report you may want to allow a small margin of error in the figures. In the case of Figure 4-26 this would not exactly be appropriate, but you could amend the statement in G17 to read as follows:

@IF(@SUM(TD)>@SUM(TA)*1.01,@ERR,
@IF(@SUM(TA)>@SUM(TD)*1.01,@ERR,
@SUM(TD,TA)/2))

This tells Quattro Pro 3 that if the total down exceeds 101% of the total across, there is an error. Likewise, if the total across exceeds 101% of the total down, there is an error. Otherwise, the answer should be the average of the total down and the total across. If the figures are entirely accurate, the answer will be accurate. Otherwise, the answer will be within 1% of the correct total.

Another example of nesting @IF statements is shown in the formula used in Figure 4-27 to calculate commissions based on a percentage (4% to 6%) of sales. The statement in D5 reads

@IF(C5<40000,0.04*C5,@IF(C5<50000,0.05*C5,C5*0.06))

This formula says that if the sales in C5 are less than $40,000, the commission will be 4% (0.04) of sales; otherwise, if sales are greater than

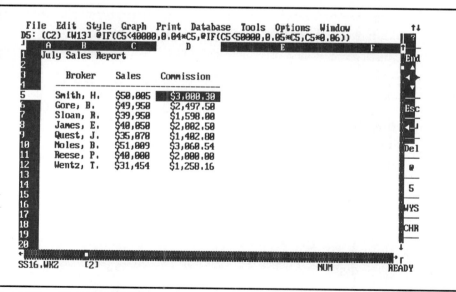

Figure 4-27.   *Nested @IF statement*

or equal to $40,000 but less than $50,000, the commission will be 5%. If sales are greater than or equal to $50,000, the commission will be 6%. The nesting of @IF statements takes a little planning, but if you write out the statement first, you can usually frame the actual formula to fit most conditional situations. The @IF function can return labels as well as values. For example, in the broker transaction record shown in Figure 4-28, the word *Yes* in cell K9 is the result of an @IF formula. The record needs to show if special handling is required. This is based on the amount of the transaction, shown in H11. The formula in K9 states @IF(H11>20000,"Yes","No"). Thus the word *Yes* is returned in this case because the amount in H11 is greater than 20,000.

The name of the broker could also be entered with an @IF formula that looks for the broker number entered in H6 and responds with one of three names, like this:

@IF(H6=3,"Sloan, R.",@IF(H6=2,"Doe, J.",
@IF(H6=1,"James, E.",@ERR)))

This formula will result in the ERR message if the broker number is not 1, 2, or 3.

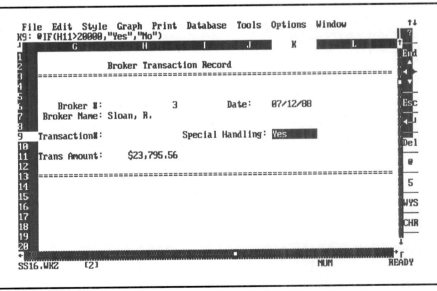

Figure 4-28.   *Label Yes*

Lookup Tables

When you want to make a formula dependent on a range of conditions, you have an alternative to nesting @IF functions. You can have Quattro Pro 3 refer to a table of conditions, called a *lookup table*. This is a vertical or horizontal list of numbers or labels that you can use to look up related numbers or labels. Figure 4-29 shows a commission table that offers a simple way to determine the rate based on a broader range of sales levels. The vertical list of sales levels in column E and related commission rates in column F show the rate applicable to any given level of sales. Any sales amount below \$35,000 earns a commission of 3.50%. Sales from \$35,000 to \$35,999 earn 3.75%, and so on. The bottom of the table shows that sales of \$50,000 and up earn 8.00%. This table of numbers, consisting of cells E3 through F19, have been named TABLE with the Block Advanced Create command. In cell D3 the formula reads

@VLOOKUP(C3,\$TABLE,1)*C3

This means that the vertical lookup function is invoked to look up the value of cell C3 in the block of cells named TABLE in column 1. The value that

Figure 4-29. *Lookup table*

is found in the table, in this case the commission rate of 8%, is then multiplied by cell C3 to calculate the commission amount.

The syntax of the vertical lookup function is thus

@VLOOKUP(*Index,Table,Column*)

The *Index* is the cell containing the value you are looking up in the table. The *Table* should be consecutive columns of values. The *Column* is the column in the table that the formula should look to for its result. The column numbering is 0 for the first column, 1 for the next column to the right, and so on. In the example, the contents of C3 and column 0 of the lookup table must be values. The column 0 values must be a consecutive range. However, the contents of column 1 and any additional columns in the table can be labels.

The lookup table can be laid out horizontally, as shown in Figure 4-30. The formula in H5 uses the @HLOOKUP function. This example supposes that each broker has a number and writes that number on sales transaction slips. A clerk then records the slips in the format shown in Figure 4-30. As the clerk enters the broker number, Quattro Pro 3 looks up that number in the horizontal table of names. (Parts of the table are shown on screen in Figure 4-30 for the purposes of illustration.) The first row of a horizontal table is row 0; successive rows are numbered 1, 2, 3, and so on. The syntax of the @HLOOKUP function is

@HLOOKUP(*Index,Table,Row Number*)

Row 0 must be a series of values or an alphabetical list of labels. Successive rows can be values or labels. Row 1, which the formula references in this case, is a set of labels.

Note that you do not have to use a block name for the lookup table reference in the formula. None was used in Figure 4-30. However, a block name makes it easier to refer to the cells of the table than typing I13..P14, particularly if you want to copy the formula containing the reference to the table and thus need to make the cell references absolute, as in $I$13..$P$14. A reference to a block name can be made absolute simply by preceding it with a dollar sign, as in $TABLE.

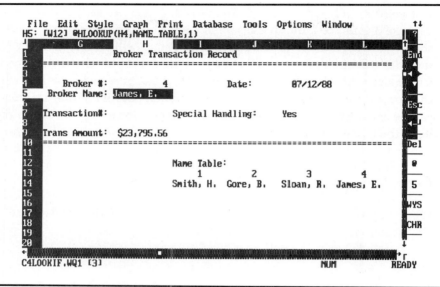

Figure 4-30. *Horizontal lookup table*

Choose

A function directly comparable to a lookup table is @CHOOSE, which selects its responses based on a number. For example, if there were just a few brokers, you could use the @CHOOSE function in place of @HLOOKUP in cell H5 of Figure 4-30. If there were just four brokers, the formula in H5 could read

@CHOOSE(H4,"Smith, H.","Gore, B.","Sloan, R.","James, E.")

The number entered in cell H4 would thus determine the name placed into H5. The syntax of the @CHOOSE function is

@CHOOSE(*X, Case0, Case1,...,Casen*)

If *X* equals 1, *Case0* is used. If *X* equals 2, *Case1* is used, and so on. The value of *X* must be a number between 1 and the total number of results in the argument. Values of *X* outside that range will cause an error. If *X* includes a decimal, Quattro Pro 3 rounds off the value. The *X* value can be a numeric constant, a cell, or a formula, as in the previous example, where this function is a compact way of handling small lists of results. The results can be constants or formulas of any data type. However, all results must have the same data type.

Error

When you want a cell to reflect an error you can use the @ERR function. This function takes no arguments; it is simply entered as

@ERR

@ERR returns the value ERR in the current cell and, in most cases, also creates the ERR message in any other cells that reference the cell in which you created the ERR condition. The exceptions to this are @COUNT, @ISERR, @ISNA, @ISNUMBER, @ISSTRING, @CELL, and @CELL-POINTER formulas. These formulas do not result in ERR if they reference a cell that contains ERR. The ERR value resulting from this function is the same as the ERR value produced by Quattro Pro 3 when it encounters an error.

@NA

The @NA function works the same as @ERR except that it returns the value NA, which distinguishes it from the ERR message that Quattro Pro 3 uses when a formula is typed incorrectly.

Index

The @INDEX function is a hybrid of the vertical and horizontal lookup tables. For this function you state the column number and row number for a value set in a table of values. The function has the syntax

@INDEX(*Range,Column,Row*)

There are a number of interesting applications for this function, including the accelerated depreciation schedule shown in Figure 4-31. This is a table of the allowed rates of depreciation for real property placed in service before March 15, 1984. The months are numbered across the top and the years of asset life are listed down the side. By answering the questions in rows 2 through 5 in column E, you provide the index data needed for the formula used in J5: @INDEX(A9..M17,E4,E5). The number 7 in E4 is the column coordinate; the number 4 in E5 is the row coordinate. The cell at which they intersect, H13, contains the value 9% returned by the @INDEX formula. Note that the number of the indexed block corresponds to the numbers you assign to the header column and row, not the 0, 1, 2, 3 numbering used in the @VLOOKUP function.

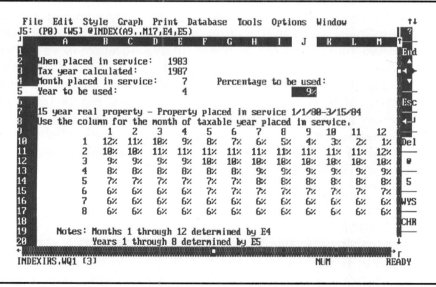

Figure 4-31. *ACRS with @INDEX*

True and False

If you want to give a value to a conditional statement, you can use the @TRUE and @FALSE functions to provide a 1 and a 0, respectively. These functions require no arguments and are discussed in depth in Chapter 13.

The @IS Functions

You will notice a series of functions in the Functions list (SHIFT-F3) beginning with @IS. They are @ISERR, @ISNA, @ISNUMBER, and @ISSTRING. Used in a variety of situations, these functions relate to errors and nonvalues for numbers and dates. They are described in detail in Chapter 13.

String Functions

A particularly powerful group of Quattro Pro 3 functions are those that help you manipulate strings. This is not an electronic version of marionetes, but rather a sophisticated way of handling sequences of characters or text. To Quattro Pro 3, a *string* is a sequence of characters with no numerical value. This can be words, like *Quattro Pro 3*, or a group of characters, like *'123*, since they are preceded by a label prefix. The words *John* and *Doe* entered into separate cells can be pulled together, or *concatenated*, by string formulas. As you can see in Figure 4-32, you can use string functions to create text from spreadsheet entries. The string functions can convert numbers to strings and vice versa. Because string functions relate directly to the way in which Quattro Pro 3 handles text, they are included in Chapter 10, "Managing Text."

Special Functions

The complex set of functions referred to as miscellaneous or special functions are used in advanced worksheets and are explained in Chapter

```
     File  Edit  Style  Graph  Print  Database  Tools  Options  Window        ↑↓
B11: [W11] +B3& "&A3& works in the   "&C3& office."                           ?
 J        A         B          C        D        E        F         G        ↑
1   Last Name First Name Location Salary    Sales     Years OJ Birthday        End
2   ======================================================================    ▲
3   Doe        John      Boston      22      240        4     09-Feb-40        ◀
4   Ferrari    Wanda     New York    23      180        7     01-Dec-56        ▼
5   Overndout  Roger     Seattle     19      310        9     07-May-39
6   Pitts      Cheri     San Diego   27      330        3     15-Mar-42        Esc
7   Paluka     Joseph    San Fran    26      210        5     09-Jun-50        ◀┘
8   Farmer     Fanny     Chicago     30      200       10     29-Jan-32
9   Graph      Otto      San Diego   32      170       11     01-Sep-31
10                                                                            Del
11  John Doe works in the   Boston office.
12  Wanda Ferrari works in the  New York office.                              @
13  Roger Overndout works in the  Seattle office.
14  Cheri Pitts works in the  San Diego office.                              5
15  Joseph Paluka works in the  San Fran office.
16  Fanny Farmer works in the  Chicago office.                              WYS
17  Otto Graph works in the  San Diego office.
18                                                                          CHR
19
20
                                                                            ↓
SS17.WK2       [3]                                       NUM              READY
```

Figure 4-32.   *String example*

13, where they are shown applied to practical situations. These functions are @@, @CELL, @CELLINDEX, @CELLPOINTER, @COLS, @ROWS, @CURVALUE, @FILEXISTS, @MEMAVAIL, @MEMSAVAIL, @NUM-TOHEX, and @HEXTONUM.

Trigonometric Functions

If you work with geometry and trigonometry, Quattro Pro 3 offers many useful functions. While these are mainly used in engineering and scientific applications, they can be very handy in many situations.

Pi

The @PI function provides the value of pi to 11 decimal places. For calculations that require the value of pi, you can type **@PI**. The @PI function takes no argument; it simply returns the value 3.14159265359. The formula to calculate the circumference of a circle is thus 2@PI*Radius. The area of a circle can be calculated by combining @PI and the exponent function, @PI*(Radius^2), which calculates pi times the square of the radius.

Degrees and Radians

Another application of @PI is to convert radians to degrees. In Quattro Pro 3 as well as 1-2-3, the trigonometric functions like @SIN and @COS produce answers in radians. You can use pi to express angles measured in radians as degrees, and to convert degrees to radians, using the following formulas:

$$1 \text{ Radian} = \frac{360°}{pi \times 2} \quad \text{or } 180/pi$$

$$1 \text{ Degree} = \frac{pi \times 2 \times radian}{360} \quad \text{or } pi/180$$

For trigonometric functions in 1-2-3, you must use 180/@PI and @PI/180 to make the necessary conversions from radians to degrees and vice versa. However, Quattro Pro 3 has two functions called @DEGREES and @RADIANS that simplify this conversion.

@DEGREES   Used to convert radians to degrees, the @DEGREES function is an alternative to using *180/@PI when you need to calculate an angle measurement. The syntax is @DEGREES(X), where X is a measurement in radians. You can see an example of this in Case 3 of Figure 4-33, where an angle is calculated by the @ASIN function from the measurements of two sides of a right-angled triangle.

@RADIANS   Used to convert degrees to radians, this function is an alternative to multiplying by @PI/180. The syntax is @RADIANS(X), where X is a measurement in degrees. You can see an example of this in Case 1 of Figure 4-33, where the @TAN function is being used to calculate the length of one side of a triangle.

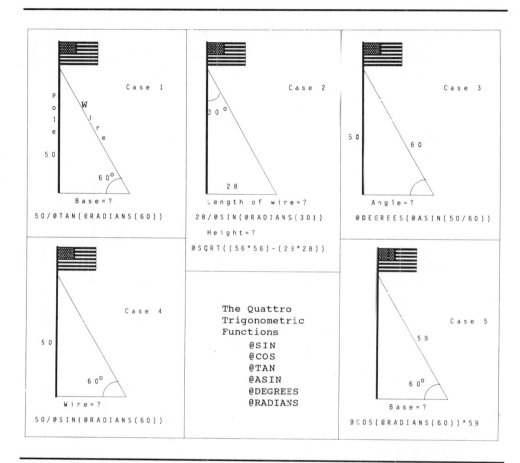

Figure 4-33. *Flagpole example*

Sine, Cosine, and Tangent

These three functions—expressed as @SIN(X), @COS(X), and @TAN(X) —
return the trigonometric sine, cosine, and tangent of X, an angle measured
in radians. You can convert an angle measured in degrees to one expressed
in radians by using the @RADIANS function. Thus, @SIN(@RADIANS(60))
returns the sine of a 60-degree angle. A result in radians can be con-

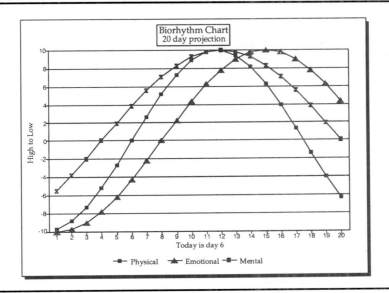

Figure 4-34.   *Sine curves on biorhythm chart*

```
 File  Edit  Style  Graph  Print  Database  Tools  Options  Window      ↑↓
D6: [W11] 10*@SIN(C6*@PI/11.5)                                            ?
       A            B       C         D           E          F          ↑
  1  Subject's birthday 12/04/80                                        End
  2  Today's date      11/19/91        BIORHYTHM CHARTING                ▲
  3  Days projected       20                                           ◄─ ─►
  4                                                                      ▼
  5              Today >  Tday-Bday  Physical   Emotional   Mental
  6         1  11/14/91    3,997     (9.79)     (10.00)     (5.56)      Esc
  7         2  11/15/91    3,998     (8.88)      (9.75)     (3.83)      ◄┘
  8         3  11/16/91    3,999     (7.31)      (9.01)     (1.95)
  9         4  11/17/91    4,000     (5.20)      (7.82)      0.00       Del
 10         5  11/18/91    4,001     (2.70)      (6.23)      1.95
 11         6  11/19/91    4,002     (0.00)      (4.34)      3.83        @
 12         7  11/20/91    4,003      2.70       (2.23)      5.56
 13         8  11/21/91    4,004      5.20       (0.00)      7.07
 14         9  11/22/91    4,005      7.31        2.23       8.31        5
 15        10  11/23/91    4,006      8.88        4.34       9.24
 16        11  11/24/91    4,007      9.79        6.23       9.81       WYS
 17        12  11/25/91    4,008      9.98        7.82      10.00
 18        13  11/26/91    4,009      9.42        9.01       9.81       CHR
 19        14  11/27/91    4,010      8.17        9.75       9.24
 20        15  11/28/91    4,011      6.31       10.00       8.31        ↓
BIOSOFT.WQ1  [3]                                          NUM         READY
```

Figure 4-35.   *The biorhythm worksheet*

verted to degrees with the @DEGREES function, so that the formula @DEGREES(@ACOS(a/b)) returns the angle between a and b expressed in degrees. These functions are shown in the problems in Figure 4-33.

Inverse

The inverse trigonometric functions— expressed as @ASIN(X), @ACOS(X), @ATAN(X) —save you from having to create them from the @COS, @SIN, and @TAN functions. They return an angle measured in radians, given its sine, cosine, or tangent. The @ATAN2(X,Y) function calculates a 4-quadrant arctangent from the X and Y coordinates of a point.

Trigonometric Applications

Of course, there are a wide variety of ways in which the trigonometric functions can be used. You can use them to generate curves that show one set of values plotted against another. An example of this is a biorhythm chart, which is used to plot levels of physical, emotional, and mental energy on a time scale. The @SIN function is used to generate the curve shown in Figure 4-34, a simple biorhythm chart. The worksheet from which this was calculated is shown in Figure 4-35. The current date and the subject's birthdate are recorded and then extrapolated for the three different cycles: 22 days for the physical level, 28 for the emotional level, and 32 for the mental level.

Solving Formulas

There are often situations in which you know the solution to a formula and want your spreadsheet to find the factors that should be input to reach that solution. For example, you might know the terms at which you can borrow money and the amount you can afford to repay each month. In other words, you know the answer and two of the three arguments for the @PMT formula. What you want to know is how much you can afford to borrow, the principal argument. Quattro Pro 3 can tell you this using a command called Solve For. Located on the Tools menu, Solve For is described in Chapter 9, along with the What-If command that creates a table of possible results based on one or two variable inputs.

5 Building, Viewing, And Printing

In previous chapters you saw several methods of entering information into Quattro Pro 3. You have seen how formulas are created and copied to produce extensive spreadsheets from a few simple entries. You have also seen how data is organized in the worksheet so that the worksheet can be treated like a database. This chapter reviews the process of building a spreadsheet model and explains the commands for viewing information on the screen and for printing it on paper.

Building a Typical Worksheet

This chapter provides step-by-step instructions for creating a sample worksheet. You can use the techniques presented here to build a typical spreadsheet model. You will see how to organize and print the worksheet as well as how to dress it up with Style commands. You can perform these steps yourself as a practical exercise, or you can use them as a reference when building your own models.

Suggestions made here offer approaches you can take when using Quattro Pro 3's features. These are methods that have been effective, but they are not rules. As you become more experienced with Quattro Pro 3, you may develop other techniques that are more suited to the particular demands of your work.

227

Basic Design

The first sample worksheet presented in this chapter is a 12-month expense projection for a group of travel agencies. Part of the expense projection is shown in Figure 5-1. Five expense items are calculated for each of several agencies:

Lease	The rent of the office space
Phones	The cost of telephone service
Telex	The cost of Telex services
Electric	The monthly utility bill
Res. Rent	The monthly charge for renting airline reservations terminals

The January figures are multiplied by a growth factor to produce the February figures. In each successive month the expenses increase by the

```
 File   Edit   Style   Graph   Print   Database   Tools   Options   Window          ↑↓
B4: (,0) 350                                                                         | ?
     A           B       C       D       E       F       G                          ⊤──
1                                                                                   ▐End
2             JAN     FEB     MAR     APR     MAY     JUN                            ▐  ▲
3   POLK ST.                                                                            ◄ ►
4       Lease    350     354     357     361     364     368                            ▼
5       Phones   230     232     235     237     239     242                         ──
6       Telex    110     111     112     113     114     116                         Esc
7       Electric 120     121     122     124     125     126                         ──
8       Res. Rent 500    505     510     515     520     526                         ←┘
9   VAN NESS                                                                         ──
10      Lease    500     505     510     515     520     526                         Del
11      Phones   250     253     255     258     260     263                         ──
12      Telex    150     152     153     155     156     158                          @
13      Electric 225     227     230     232     234     236                         ──
14      Res. Rent 835    843     852     860     869     878                          5
15  UNION SQ.                                                                        ──
16      Lease  1,200   1,212   1,224   1,236   1,249   1,261                         WYS
17      Phones   300     303     306     309     312     315                         ──
18      Telex    250     253     255     258     260     263                         CHR
19      Electric 205     207     209     211     213     215                         ──
20      Res. Rent 890    899     908     917     926     935                          ↓
SHEET1.WQ1   [1]                                             NUM          READY
```

Figure 5-1. *The basic model*

same factor. The growth factor ensures that the company running the agencies budgets sufficient funds to cover rising expenses.

Building Principles

In general, the best approach to building spreadsheets is to enter data in the following order:

■ *Labels* You use labels to identify the contents and arrangement of the model. Do not worry about the exact titles for columns and rows, since you can change them later. Also, do not worry about the width of columns, since these too can be adjusted after most of the model has been built.

■ *Numbers* Numbers make up the basic data in a worksheet. As you enter the numbers you will get a general idea of the dimensions of the model.

■ *Formulas* Enter the first few formulas and make sure they work before copying them. Do not worry about the format of the results.

■ *Formats* When you know what kind of numbers you are using, make any necessary format changes. Use the Options Formats Numeric Format command for the most common format and Style Numeric Format for exceptions. Add any special alignment to labels with the Style Alignment command.

■ *Widths* Adjust column widths as needed. Use a global setting (Options, Formats, Global Width) for the most common width and adjust other columns individually (Style, Column Width).

You will proceed more quickly working in this order than if you spend a lot of time adjusting formats and column widths before most of the data is entered. You will probably need to readjust some widths and formats after the model is completed. Whether you build the model column by column or row by row depends upon the kind of data with which you are working.

Although this is the general order of building spreadsheets, there are a few exceptions to keep in mind. If you know you will need to copy a label and that the label will eventually have an alignment different from the default, you should align the label before copying. The same is true of cells that contain values with special formats. Set Style Numeric Format before copying, since the Edit Copy command copies a cell's format as well as its contents. The sample model will be built column by column; the column of labels will be followed by the starting values and then the first column of formulas. The first formula column will then be copied to the rest of the columns. This approach follows the natural progression of the data and will require the least number of keystrokes.

Entering and Reusing Labels

Whenever possible you should use the Edit Copy command to reuse labels that you have already entered into the worksheet. Doing so saves time and also avoids inconsistent spellings and typos. Make sure you check your data before copying it. If the labels are specially aligned, apply the alignment command before copying to reduce the need for later adjustments.

For example, to copy the labels for the sample worksheet, follow these steps:

1. Use the DOWN ARROW key to move the cell selector to cell A3. Then type the following labels in column A. The label in capital letters is the name of the office, which is followed by five categories of expenses incurred by that office. Enter all six lines as left-aligned labels:

   POLK ST.
   Lease
   Phones
   Telex
   Electric
   Res. Rent

2. To offset the expense categories from the office names, right-align the expenses. With your cell selector in A4, select Style Alignment and choose Right Align.

3. When prompted for the block to be modified, you can use the END and arrow keys shortcut: Press END and then press DOWN ARROW. This will highlight all of the labels in one step.

4. Press ENTER to confirm A4..A8 as the block to be right-aligned.

5. From the menu pick Style and then Column Width; type **12** and press ENTER to widen the column to 12 characters and better separate the labels. The results will appear as shown in Figure 5-1.

Note that the Style Alignment command deletes the current label prefix and replaces it with the one you specify: left ('), right ("), or center (^).

Straight Block Copy

After aligning the labels through row 8 of column A, you need to enter the name of the second office, **VAN NESS**. With this done, you can reuse the expense category labels from cells A4 through A8.

1. Move the cell selector up to A4 and select Edit Copy. Quattro Pro 3 assumes that the Source Block begins at A4, where your cell selector was located when you issued the command. This coordinate is already anchored as the beginning point of the Source Block, as indicated by the double dots in A4..A8.

2. Highlight the other expense labels with the DOWN ARROW key. If you want to use END and DOWN ARROW, be sure to press UP ARROW once to exclude cell A9.

3. Press ENTER to confirm A4..A8 as the Source Block.

4. To indicate the correct destination for this block, press DOWN ARROW to move the cell selector to A10.

5. Press ENTER to confirm the destination. The labels, complete with right-alignment indicators, will be copied into position for the second office. Your cell selector will be left in A4. Use END and then DOWN ARROW to move to the last cell of the model.

Reverse Copy

Now type the name of the third office, **UNION SQ.**, at A15 and press DOWN
ARROW to enter it into the cell and move to A16. To copy the expense labels
from the second office to the third, you can use a technique known as *reverse
copy*. As a spreadsheet grows, you might find it inconvenient that the Copy
command leaves the cell selector in the top-left cell of the block you copied
from. This can be particularly cumbersome when copying across several
screens of the worksheet. Reverse copy solves this problem, because it
invokes the Copy command from the block's destination, in this case, A16.

1. Select Edit Copy. Initially the suggested Source Block, which will be
   locked in at A16, is represented by A16..A16. Press ESCAPE to unlock
   this block. The display at the top of the screen changes to A16 only.

2. Move the cell selector up to the expense label in A10 and type a period
   to anchor this as the beginning point of the Source Block.

3. Highlight the other expense labels through A14 with DOWN ARROW and
   press ENTER.

4. Because you started the copy from A16, Quattro Pro 3 assumes that
   this is where you want the block of labels copied to.

There is no need to lock the destination point; simply press ENTER to
confirm it. Column A will appear as it does in Figure 5-1.

Entering the Months

Since this worksheet is a 1-year projection divided into months, you need
to enter the names of the months across the worksheet. While these
headings do not have to be entered at this point, they do make the model
easier to develop. Place the cell selector on row 2 and, starting in column
B, type **JAN** and then press RIGHT ARROW. Then type **FEB** and press RIGHT
ARROW. Type **MAR** and so on through to **DEC**. After **DEC**, move to cell N2
and enter **YEAR** for the year-end totals that will eventually be created.
When entering a series of labels like this, you can appreciate the usefulness
of the arrow method for entering data. In Chapter 13 you will read how to
enter the same month headings with Quattro Pro 3's date arithmetic

feature. Having entered these headings, use the Style Alignment command to center the labels in B2 through N2.

Beginning Values

All projections must have a starting point. In the case of a budget such as the one you are building here, the January figures are based on the actual figures for the last month of the previous year. This data is entered in column B, as shown in Figure 5-2. Again, you can make use of the arrow method as you enter the list of numbers.

Total Calculation

After you enter the figures for the first three offices, the worksheet should look like the one shown in Figure 5-2. You now need to add a fourth office, **EMBARCADERO**, as shown in Figure 5-3. Enter the office name and then copy down the expense categories and enter the starting figures. Note that the Embarcadero office has no figure for electricity, since this is included

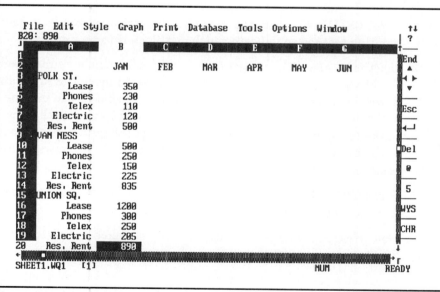

Figure 5-2.   *The January numbers*

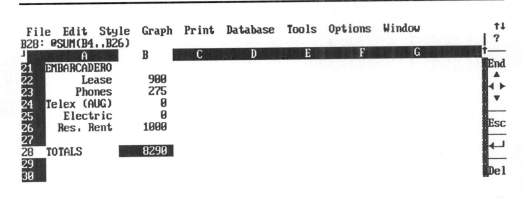

Figure 5-3.   *The EMBARCADERO numbers and January total*

in the rent. Also note that the Telex system will not be installed until August, so the label in cell A24 is edited to read Telex (AUG).

At the bottom of column B you can see a formula that sums the January expenses for all four offices. Enter the label **TOTALS** in A28, and move to B28 to create the formula, which will use the @SUM function.

1. Type **@SUM(** to begin the formula. You are now ready to use the pointing method to indicate which cell block is to be summed.

2. Use the UP ARROW key to get to B4, and anchor the beginning point of the block by typing a period. You now need to move the highlighting down the column. There is a quick way to do this. If you use the END and DOWN ARROW keys, your highlighting will go only to the next gap in the rows, in this case, cell B8. This is not the quickest way to move to the bottom of a column that is not made up of solid rows of data. A better method is to move your cell selector to a solid column of data.

3. Press LEFT ARROW, and your cell selector will be in a column (column A) that contains consecutive rows of data.

4. Now press END and DOWN ARROW. Doing so takes you directly to row 26. Do not press ENTER yet.

5. In essence you have hitched a ride on a block of occupied cells that is continuous in your desired direction. You now need to press RIGHT

ARROW to move back into the original column. The highlighting will appear in B4..B26.

6. Complete the formula with the closing parenthesis and then press ENTER. The ride-hitching method is very useful as you are building a model, since often you need to move the cell selector to the end of the model in a row or column that is not yet completely filled. However, you must always remember to come back to the original column or row before completing the maneuver.

7. With the cell selector still in B28, select Edit Copy and press ENTER. Then press RIGHT ARROW and ENTER to complete copying the formula to C28, ready to sum the February figures in column C.

Copying Formulas

The figures that occupy column C are actually formulas that multiply the expenses in column B by a factor that increases them. These formulas are repeated across the model so that a steady month-to-month increase in expenses is built into the budget. Although in practice lease payments rarely increase on a gradual monthly basis, the overall effect will be to allocate sufficient funding for probable long-term lease cost increases.

The formula in C4 is 1.01 times the value in the cell one column to the left, or 1.01*B4. You need to enter this formula in C4 now, leaving your cell selector in C4, since the formula will be copied down the column, making each cell in column C 1.01 times the value in the cell to the left. To perform the copy, follow these steps:

1. Select Edit Copy. The Source Block will be C4..C4, which Quattro Pro 3 is already suggesting. Press ENTER to confirm this.

2. The quickest way to point out the destination for the copy is to press a period while the cell selector is still in C4. This anchors the beginning point of the block in C4, and you can use the DOWN ARROW key to highlight down to C26. This is shown in Figure 5-4.

3. Press ENTER to confirm C4..C26 as the destination cells. This will complete the copy process. Including the source cell C4 in the destination causes that cell to be copied over itself, but this causes no problems.

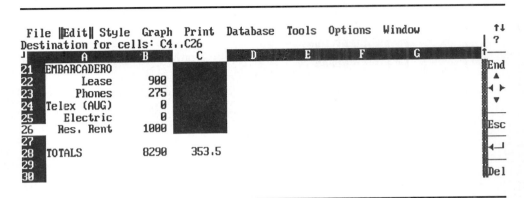

Figure 5-4.   *Destination highlighting*

Note that each cell in column C from rows 4 to 26 is 1.01 times the value of the corresponding cell in column B. One small problem is that the rows without expenses in column B are also multiplied in column C. You can easily remove these rows by erasing the contents of cells C9, C15, and C21. Simply highlight each one in turn and press the DELETE key to remove its contents. Do that now.

Copying Columns

Since you have already copied the @SUM formula from the bottom of column B to the bottom of column C (from B28 to C28), you can copy the whole of column C, from rows 4 through 28, to columns D through M to complete the projection for 12 months. The following steps will perform the copy for the column.

1. With your cell selector in C4, select Edit Copy. The Source Block needs to be expanded downward. Press PAGE DOWN and you will move the highlighting to C24. Press the DOWN ARROW key a few more times to include C28. Press ENTER to confirm C4..C28 as the Source Block.

2. Move the cell selector to D4 and anchor it with a period. Press UP ARROW twice, and you will be able to hitch a ride to the end of the model using the line of months in row 2.

3. Press END and then RIGHT ARROW. The highlighting will move to column N, which is labeled YEAR. Then press LEFT ARROW once and DOWN ARROW twice so that the highlighted Destination Block is row 4 of all of the month columns, D4..M4.

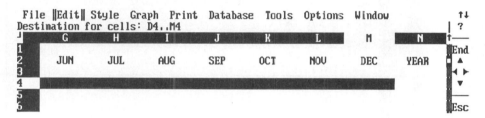

4. Quattro Pro 3 will assume that row 4 and the area below it, down as far as row 28, are available for copying into. If you want to be sure, move the highlighting down to line 28 to correspond with the Source Block and to view the full range of destination cells. However, this is not essential since you are working on a new worksheet and therefore know that nothing has already been entered. Press ENTER to confirm the destination of the copy.

The impressive results of this copy are shown in Figure 5-5. You have seen the speed with which Quattro Pro 3 reproduces a set of formulas. Since much of the work you do with numbers requires repetition of the same calculations, you will probably use the Copy command a great deal in your own spreadsheets.

Saving Your Work

At this point you can issue the File Save As command to give the worksheet a name and store the work you have done so far. When you issue the File

Figure 5-5.   *The completed copy*

Save As command for a worksheet that has not yet been saved, you are provided with a list of files in the current directory, as shown in Figure 5-6. Enter an appropriate name, such as QVBUDG01, simply by typing at the prompt. There is no need to type the extension as WQ1 is automatically added at the end of the file name. Press ENTER to confirm the name, and your work so far will be stored in a file called QVBUDG01.WQ1. You can see this name on the left of the status line at the bottom of the screen. As you continue to build the worksheet and improve it, you can quickly save further changes to the same file with the File Save command.

Display Format

After a large copy operation, you will probably want to fine-tune some of the results. As you can see in the example, the appearance of many of the numbers leaves something to be desired. This is because they are displayed in the General format, which shows as many decimal places as it takes to complete the calculation or fill the cell. When the growth factor produces

```
‖File‖ Edit  Style  Graph  Print  Database  Tools  Options  Window              ↑↓
C4: 1.01*B4                                                                       ?
 ⌐        A          B         C         D         E         F         G
 1                                                                             ┃End
 2                  JAN       FEB       MAR       APR       MAY       JUN       ┃ ▲
 3        POLK ST.                                                             ┃◄ ►
 4          Lease    350      353.5  357.035  360.6054  364.2114  367.8535     ┃ ▼
 5          Phones   230      232.3  234.623  236.9692  239.3389  241.7323
 6                                                              664  115.6111  Esc
 7        ┌─ Enter save file name: ──────────────────────┐     725  126.1212
 8        │ C:\QUATTRO\DATA\*.WQ1                       □ │     302  525.505   ◄┘
 9      VA│ ADDLIST.WQ1    ADM1324.WQ1    ADMIN.WQ1      │
10        │ ARMF5MAC.WQ1   ARROWS.WQ1     ARWMAC11.WQ1   │     302  525.505   Del
11        │ ASCIIMAP.WQ1   ATOAYEAR.WQ1   BASICOPI.WQ1  ↓│     151  262.7525
12        │ BIOSOFT.WQ1    C11DEBUG.WQ1   C12INV01.WQ1   │     906  157.6515    @
13        └──────────────────────────────────────────────┘     359  236.4773
14        Res. Rent   835    843.35  851.7835  860.3013  868.9043  877.5934    5
15        UNION SQ.
16          Lease    1200     1212   1224.12  1236.361  1248.725  1261.212    WYS
17          Phones    300      303    306.03  309.0903  312.1812  315.303
18          Telex     250     252.5   255.025  257.5753  260.151  262.7525    CHR
19          Electric  205    207.05  209.1205  211.2117  213.3238  215.4571
20        Res. Rent   890     898.9   907.889  916.9679  926.1376  935.3989    ↓
 ←░░░░░░░░░░■░░░░░░░░░░░░░░░░░░░░░░░░░░░░░░░░░░░░░░░░░░░░░░░░░░░░░░░░░░░░░░░►  ↑r
 SHEET1.WQ1    [1]                                              NUM          FILES
```

Figure 5-6.   *Saving the file*

lengthy fractions, the cell fills with many decimal figures. To correct this and format the numbers consistently, you can use the Style Numeric Format command, and select the Comma format for the value cells of the model. This format places a comma in the thousands and lets you limit the number of decimal places displayed, in this case to zero places.

1. Place your cell selector in B4, the top left of the range of cells that need to be reformatted. Select Style Numeric Format. You will see the menu shown in Figure 5-7.

2. Pick the Comma format by typing a comma (,).

3. This format assumes that you want two decimal places, but you can easily change that to zero by typing **0** and pressing ENTER.

4. You will then be prompted for the block of cells to be formatted. Press PAGE DOWN and then DOWN ARROW several times to include the last line of the model. Press END and then RIGHT ARROW to include a range of cells that extends all the way to the last column of the model. Press ENTER to confirm this block.

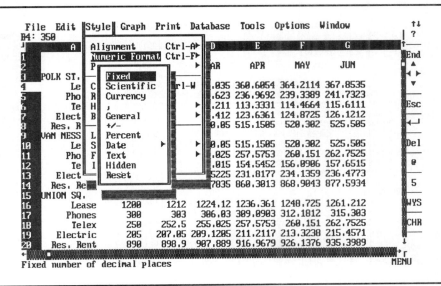

Figure 5-7. *Setting a format*

The results are very tidy and can be seen back in Figure 5-1. Notice that the decimal places are rounded by the Display format, rather than truncated. If you later change the format to display several decimal places, Quattro Pro 3 will reveal the decimal digits that the zero decimal format removed from view. Now try placing your cell selector in one of the cells that has a lot of decimal places, such as E4. You will see from the cell identifier in the bottom status area that the real content of the cell is the formula 1.01*D4, together with the format notation (,0) for Comma format, zero decimal places. A cell will still produce decimal places, however, if you change the format to display them.

Summing the Rows

Now you are ready to perform the last calculation needed to complete the model in column N, which will hold the totals for each expense category over the 12-month period. These totals will be a series of @SUM formulas, the first of which you enter in N4.

1. In cell N4 type **@SUM(**. Press END and LEFT ARROW, and then END and LEFT ARROW again to move to the extreme left of the model. Now press RIGHT ARROW once so that you are in cell B4. Type a period to anchor the beginning point of the block in this cell.

2. Press END and then RIGHT ARROW to include all the cells in the range B4..M4. Type the closing parenthesis to complete the formula and press ENTER to place the formula in N4.

3. To sum all the rows in the model, select Edit Copy with the cell selector still in N4. Press ENTER to accept N4..N4 as the Source Block.

4. Type a period to anchor N4 as the start of the Destination Block and press PAGE DOWN. Press the DOWN ARROW key several more times to include the last row of the model, 28, the one that sums all the columns. Press ENTER to confirm the copy.

5. The formula in cell N28 is actually the grand total of all the expenses, since it sums the row of column totals. You will find several cells in column N containing zeros, because the formula copied into them is inappropriate. Simply delete these with the DELETE key.

You may have noticed that the Comma format has not yet been applied to the figures in column N. You will probably want to do so to make them consistent with the rest of the model. With your cell selector on N4, select Style Numeric Format and select comma (,). Type **0** to indicate the number of decimal places. Use PAGE DOWN and DOWN ARROW to extend the highlighting through N28 before pressing ENTER to complete the operation.

Using and Viewing the Model

Having built the model, you are almost ready to use it. However, before going any further you should make sure that the latest changes are stored. Assuming that you have used the File Save As command to give the worksheet an appropriate file name, issue the File Save command to update the file. If you have not yet used the File Save As command see the earlier section, "Saving Your Work."

From a practical point of view the model has several uses. The basic use is to determine the total expenses for the year based on the assumed beginning values and growth factor. Any change to the values in column B will alter the entire model. As soon as the new amount is entered, the change affects the totals across the model and the grand total in N28.

The following sections explore commands that are useful in navigating the completed spreadsheet and viewing it. How much of the spreadsheet can be seen at any one time with depend on the display mode you are using, so the different display modes are described as an aid to working with the model.

Advanced Maneuvers

Quattro Pro 3 has a number of commands that enable you to move around the spreadsheet and change its appearance. When the spreadsheet begins to grow and becomes complex, you will want to exercise greater control over its appearance and also use some shortcuts to maneuver about in it.

END **Keys**   You have already seen that the END keys can be a great help during copy operations. Now that the model is built, END and RIGHT ARROW move you to the right side of the model. Be sure to have your cell selector on a completed row of data before using this combination. Asking Quattro Pro 3 to go to the end of the right side of a blank line means you end up in column IV. Simply press HOME, or END and LEFT ARROW to return to the worksheet area.

Goto   You may have noticed that the arrow keys are not always the most efficient way to move to a specific location, particularly if that location is some distance from your current position. For this reason, you will often want to use the Goto key (F5). When you press F5, you are prompted for the location you want the cell selector moved to. Quattro Pro 3 will show the destination cell as a default in the top left of the screen. Simply type in the coordinates of your destination and press ENTER. The cell selector will be placed in the new cell. Unless the destination cell is very close to A1, this move may disorient you at first; for example, when you are using Goto to move to the bottom-right corner of the model. If you use Goto to get to N28, Quattro Pro 3 shows just one cell, N28, on the screen. To get around this and to avoid having to remember cell coordinates, you can use block names.

Block Names   Obviously, remembering cell coordinates in large models becomes increasingly difficult. Here, Edit Names can be a great help. You can attach a name to a single cell or group of cells just for the purpose of moving it around. After you have attached a name to the group of cells with Edit Names Create, you can type the block name at the Goto prompt. Or, you can use the F3 key to list the block names, highlight the destination, and press ENTER to insert it on the Goto prompt line.

If the block name refers to a group of cells, your cell selector will be placed in the cell that is at the top-left corner of the block. That cell will be placed in the top left of your screen. For example, one way of quickly moving to a view of the lower-right section of the example spreadsheet would be to name cells K20..N28 as the block TOTAL. You could then press F5 and type **TOTAL** as the address you want to go to. Press ENTER, and you would be placed in the position shown in Figure 5-8, where cell K20 is in the top-left corner of the screen.

You will also find this technique useful if you are constantly working between the home position at A1 and another location. You can label the second location HOME and move there by pressing F5, typing **HOME**, and pressing ENTER. Alternatively, the F3 key can be used with the F5 key to

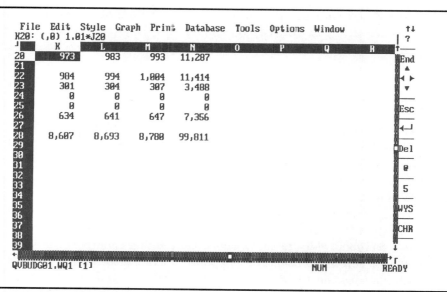

Figure 5-8.   *Results of Goto*

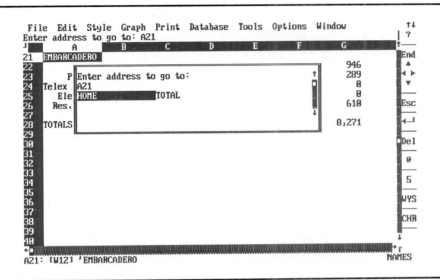

Figure 5-9. *Using F3 with F5*

display block names as shown in Figure 5-9. Note that the list of cell names is alphabetical. For this reason, cells that are frequently referenced should be labeled with names that will appear at the top of the alphabetized list.

Windows Within a Worksheet

In the course of using the model, you will encounter several situations that call for further Quattro Pro 3 commands. For example, you have already found that you cannot see the YEAR total column when you are viewing the JAN column. Quattro Pro 3 provides a simple method for letting you see two parts of the same spreadsheet at the same time. You split the screen either horizontally or vertically into two parts, called windows.

Quattro Pro 3 uses the term *window* for two different features. *Worksheet window* refers to the space within which each spreadsheet is displayed when more than one is open. You can also have a *split window* within a worksheet window. In each split window you can view a different part of the worksheet. As you move the cell selector in one window you can scroll the view in the other, or you can remove the synchronization from the windows to view each window independently.

To try using windows with the example, first position the cell selector in column E and select Window, followed by Options. The first five options are Horizontal, Vertical, Sync, Unsync, and Clear. The Horizontal and Vertical options refer to the direction of window splitting. You can see the Window menu in Figure 5-10. The Sync and Unsync options allow you to switch between the default mode of synchronized split windows and the alternative, unsynchronized mode. The split occurs at the current position of the cell selector, which is why you moved to column E before issuing the command. The Clear option closes the second window. Select Vertical, and the screen will appear divided, as shown in Figure 5-11. You can move between split windows by pressing the Windows key (F6). Press it several times, and you will see that it toggles between windows.

Initially, the split windows are synchronized. With a vertical split this means that pressing UP or DOWN ARROW will scroll the worksheet on both sides of the split. You can see that the row numbers in the dividing line match those in the left border. With a horizontal window, this means that RIGHT or LEFT ARROW will move the worksheet on the top and bottom halves

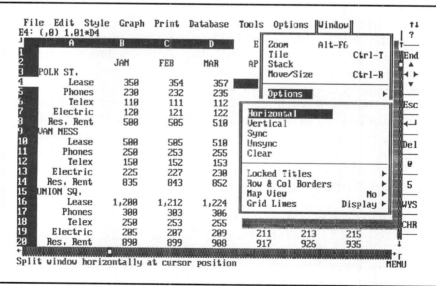

Figure 5-10. *Windows Options menu*

```
        File  Edit  Style  Graph  Print  Database  Tools  Options  Window      ↑↓
        D4: (,0) 1.01*C4                                                        | ?
        J        A       B       C        D         E       F       G       ↑─────
        1                                                      1             ■End
        2                JAN     FEB      MAR       2  APR     MAY     JUN    □  ▲
        3    POLK ST.                               3                          ◄ ►
        4        Lease   350     354      357       4  361     364     368       ▼
        5        Phones  230     232      235       5  237     239     242
        6        Telex   110     111      112       6  113     114     116    Esc
        7        Electric 120    121      122       7  124     125     126
        8        Res. Rent 500   505      510       8  515     520     526    ◄┘
        9    VAN NESS                               9
        10       Lease   500     505      510      10  515     520     526    Del
        11       Phones  250     253      255      11  258     260     263
        12       Telex   150     152      153      12  155     156     158    @
        13       Electric 225    227      230      13  232     234     236
        14       Res. Rent 835   843      852      14  860     869     878    5
        15   UNION SQ.                             15
        16       Lease  1,200   1,212   1,224      16 1,236   1,249   1,261   WYS
        17       Phones  300     303      306      17  309     312     315
        18       Telex   250     253      255      18  258     260     263    CHR
        19       Electric 205    207      209      19  211     213     215
        20       Res. Rent 890   899      908      20  917     926     935    ↓
        QUBUDG01.WQ1 [1]                                         NUM         READY
```

Figure 5-11.   *A vertical split*

of the screen, and the column letters in the dividing line will match those in the top border. Figure 5-12 shows the effect of unsynchronizing the windows. To unsynchronize windows, select Window Options Unsync. Place the cell selector on the right of the screen and move down to the bottom line of the budget. The budget is unmoved on the other side. You can see that the row numbers in the dividing line no longer match those in the left border. To clear windows, select Window Option Clear.

Note that when you are using a horizontal window column, width changes in one window will not immediately affect the other window. However, when you clear the horizontal window, changes in column width will take effect throughout the worksheet.

Titles

You can see from Figure 5-12 that when you are using windows the column headings disappear if the right side of the worksheet is moved down. In fact, you may have found this to be a problem when working without

```
 File  Edit  Style  Graph  Print  Database  Tools  Options  Window        ↑↓
B8: (,0) 500                                                             | ?
⌐    A        B      C      D    12      L       M       N      ⌐End
1                                  12     166     167    1,902    End
2             JAN    FEB    MAR    13     249     251    2,854    ▲
3   POLK ST.                       14     922     932   10,590    ◄ ►
4        Lease   350    354    357  15                            ▼
5        Phones  230    232    235  16   1,326   1,339  15,219
6        Telex   110    111    112  17    331     335   3,805    Esc
7        Electric 120   121    122  18    276     279   3,171
8        Res, Rent 500  505    510  19    226     229   2,600    ↵
9   VAN NESS                        20    983     993  11,287
10       Lease   500    505    510  21                            Del
11       Phones  250    253    255  22    994    1,004  11,414
12       Telex   150    152    153  23    304     307   3,408    @
13       Electric 225   227    230  24      0       0       0
14       Res, Rent 835  843    852  25      0       0       0     5
15  UNION SQ.                       26    641     647   7,356
16       Lease  1,200  1,212  1,224 27                            WYS
17       Phones  300    303    306  28   8,693   8,780  99,811
18       Telex   250    253    255  29                            CHR
19       Electric 205   207    209  30
20       Res, Rent 890  899    908  31                            ↓
←                                                               ► r
QUBUDG01.WQ1 [1]                                         NUM    READY
```

Figure 5-12. *Unsynchronized windows*

windows, as in Figures 5-8 and 5-9. As you move to the lower areas of the worksheet and the month labels disappear, it becomes difficult to know which months you are viewing. Knowing where you are is particularly important when you have to update cells in the middle of a large spreadsheet.

The solution is to *freeze* certain rows and columns so that titles do not disappear. To freeze titles, place the cell selector in the top left of the area you want to move, as diagrammed in Figure 5-13. When you use the Window Options Locked Titles command, you can choose Horizontal, which freezes the area above the cell selector; Vertical, which freezes the area to the left of the cell selector; or Both, which locks areas above and to the left of the cell selector.

In the sample spreadsheet, place the cell selector in B3 and select Window Options Locked Titles. You want to pick Both, so that both the months and the expense categories stay on the screen while you scan the model. When you pick your Titles choice, you are returned to the spreadsheet. Now press TAB and PAGE DOWN. Notice that the column and row headings remain on the screen. The effect of moving the cell selector after

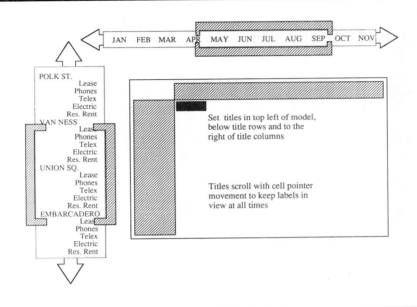

Figure 5-13. *Diagram of titles*

fixing titles is shown in Figure 5-14, where cell I24 is being updated to reflect the anticipated August installation of Telex in the EMBAR-CADERO office. You can see how much easier this is with titles visible

		APR	MAY	JUN	JUL	AUG	SEP	
2								▲
21	EMBARCADERO							◀ ▶
22	Lease	927	937	946	955	965	975	▼
23	Phones	283	286	289	292	295	298	
24	Telex (AUG)	0	0	0	0	150	152	Esc
25	Electric	0	0	0	0	0	0	
26	Res. Rent	598	604	610	616	622	628	↵
27								
28	TOTALS	8,108	8,190	8,271	8,354	8,588	8,674	Del

Figure 5-14. *Effect of fixing titles*

than without them. After making the change to this cell, press HOME and you will see that this is now B3, the cell in which you performed the title lock.

You may wonder how you can change headings if you are locked out of those cells. You can do this with the Goto key (F5). Press F5 and type the address of the title cell you want to edit, then press ENTER. The cell is placed on the edit line for you to change. Press F2 to edit the cell, and then press ENTER to place the cell contents back in the cell. To put the updated title back into place, press PAGE DOWN, TAB, and then HOME.

Locking titles works well when a model has been built and only the data is being updated. However, you may need to unlock the titles when making major changes to the spreadsheet. To clear the titles, select Window Options Locked Titles Clear.

Hiding Columns

At times the data you see on the screen is not the data you need. You may even rearrange titles and windows and the spreadsheet will still not be to your liking. In such cases, you might want to try hiding certain columns with the Style Hide Column command. Quattro Pro 3 lets you place selected columns in the background and closes up the ones in the foreground. This is diagrammed in Figure 5-15. Thus, you can pick and choose which columns to view. The Style Hide Column command is also useful when you are dealing with confidential data or arranging a worksheet prior to printing. The hidden data is not lost, and hidden formulas continue to be active.

To hide the first six months of the sample model, place the cell selector on any row in column B and select Style Hide Column. Your choices are Hide or Expose. Choose Hide and then anchor the beginning column by typing a period; press RIGHT ARROW to move the highlighting through to column G. When you press ENTER, the columns disappear from view and cannot be accessed. To return the columns to view, simply select Style Hide Column Expose. Asterisks next to the column letters indicate the columns that are currently hidden.

To return columns to the display, simply highlight them and press ENTER. If you press ESCAPE and do not select any columns, the marked columns remain hidden. The column width and format remain unaffected by the hide-and-expose process. When you carry out any command using the POINT mode to indicate cell references, Quattro Pro 3 temporarily

Normal
View of
Columns

Columns
C and E
Hidden

Spreadsheet
View of
Columns

Figure 5-15.   *The Style Hide Column command*

reveals hidden columns, marked by asterisks, so that they can be considered in the command. For example, if you use the Edit Move or Edit Copy command or formulas built with the point method, the columns will be temporarily revealed so you can correctly complete the operation.

Adding Rows

Occasionally you will need to add more rows to your model. In the sample model you need room for a title across the top. You do so by inserting several rows at the top of the spreadsheet. This will not affect any of the calculations in the model. With the cell selector in row 1, select Edit Insert Row to insert just one row. You would normally press ENTER, but to add four rows you press the DOWN ARROW key three times. When you press ENTER you will insert a total of four rows.

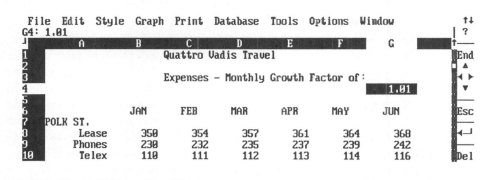

Figure 5-16. *Titles for the worksheet*

Adding Titles

There is no Quattro Pro 3 command for centering a title over a model. You have to center titles yourself. To begin, try typing the name of the travel company, **Quattro Vadis Travel**, in cell C1. This can be moved later. Below this, in cell C3, type **Expenses - Monthly Growth Factor of:** and press ENTER. In cell G4 the actual figure for the growth factor, 1.01, has been entered as a number, as shown in Figure 5-16.

Further Views

These include the use of windows and locking titles. A further technique is available to users of some graphics display adapters such as the Video-7 VRAM VGA card. This is one of a number of high resolution display adapters that Quattro Pro 3 works with on more than the usual number of spreadsheet columns on screen. Typically your screen can display 80 characters on a line. This is referred to as 80 column mode (the columns refer to characters on the screen, not actual worksheet columns). With high resolution adapters it is possible for Quattro Pro 3 to display 132 characters or screen columns. This enables a full year's worth of numbers to be viewed at once, including titles and totals.

To enable 132 column display on your system requires the right combination of program settings and hardware. Make sure all of your work is saved before attempting to use this feature for the first time. Select Options from the main menu, then choose Display Mode. If the display adapter in your system supports graphics, you should see a list of options beginning with A:80x25. Below this there may be other modes listed according to the name of the specific display adapter. Select the adapter that most closely matches your system. If the adapter supports 132 column mode it will be listed among the options when you select the adapter. Some adapters support several variations of 132 column mode.

In Figure 5-17 you can see the travel office budget displayed in 132x28 mode. It may take several tries to hit upon a mode that works with your hardware. If the screen becomes unreadable after selecting a display mode press ENTER to re-select the Display Mode option, then enter A or B to return to either normal text or normal graphics mode. When you have found a setting that works on your system you can use the Options Update command to record the change for the next session. For more on using the Options menu, refer to the next chapter.

As you can see from Figure 5-17, it takes 14 worksheet columns, A through N, to display a whole year plus titles and totals. Even in 132x28 mode the actual worksheet area on display is not large enough to show 14 columns at the default width of 9 characters wide. Consequently, the view in Figure 5-17 was created by altering widths from the default setting, as follows:

Column	Width
B through G	8
H	10
I through M	8
N	11
A	13

You may need to make other changes to your worksheet files in order to make the most of 132 column mode. You will find that multiple windows can be more effectively utilized with more of each window displayed. In 132x28 mode you can actually tile 27 separate windows, but each window is really too small for practical use. However, six or seven windows can be tiled and still reveal useful sections of worksheet in each one.

File Edit Style Graph Print Database Tools Options Window
A1: [W13]

	A	B	C	D	E	F	G	H	I	J	K	L	M	N
1					Quattro Vadis Travel – Total Amount: $100,576									
4				Expenses – Monthly Growth Factor of:			1.01							
6		JAN	FEB	MAR	APR	MAY	JUN	JUL	AUG	SEP	OCT	NOV	DEC	YEAR
7	POLK ST.													
8	Lease	350	354	357	361	364	368	372	375	379	383	387	390	4,439
9	Phones	230	232	235	237	239	242	244	247	249	252	254	257	2,917
10	Telex	110	111	112	113	114	116	117	118	119	120	122	123	1,395
11	Electric	120	121	122	124	125	126	127	129	130	131	133	134	1,522
12	Res.Rent	500	505	510	515	520	526	531	536	541	547	552	558	6,341
13	VAN NESS													
14	Lease	500	505	510	515	520	526	531	536	541	547	552	558	6,341
15	Phones	250	253	255	258	260	263	265	260	271	273	276	279	3,171
16	Telex	150	152	153	155	156	158	159	161	162	164	166	167	1,902
17	Electric	225	227	230	232	234	236	239	241	244	246	249	251	2,854
18	Res.Rent	835	843	852	860	869	878	886	895	904	913	922	932	10,590
19	UNION SQ.													
20	Lease	1,200	1,212	1,224	1,236	1,249	1,261	1,274	1,287	1,299	1,312	1,326	1,339	15,219
21	Phones	300	303	306	309	312	315	318	322	325	328	331	335	3,805
22	Telex	250	253	255	258	260	263	265	268	271	273	276	279	3,171
23	Electric	205	207	209	211	213	215	218	220	222	224	226	229	2,600

BIGPIC.WQ1   NIIM   READY

↑ →
?
End
▲
◄ ►
▼
Esc
↵
Del
@
5
6
7

You may have noticed that the menu items in Figure 5-17 do not stretch all the way across the menu bar. This means that most menu activity will normally be concentrated on the left side of the screen. However, it is possible to use this menu area should you wish to employ 132 column mode all of the time and need to add menu items with the Edit Menus feature, described in Chapter 12. While not available on all systems, the 132 column mode in Quattro Pro 3 is a useful feature for those looking to expand the horizons of their workspace and get a better view of the big picture. Bear in mind that 132 column mode is a character mode, not a graphics mode, and does not use the WYSIWYG feature.

The WYSIWYG feature can be used to view a larger area of worksheet without resorting to 132 column display. When you are in WYSIWYG mode, you can use the WYSIWYG Zoom% command on the Options menu to select a percentage less than 100 in order to shrink the display. For example, in Figure 5-18 you can see the sample worksheet displayed at 75%. Alternatively, you can assign a smaller font to the worksheet, as described later in this chapter, which will reveal more of the worksheet in WYSIWYG mode. For example, in Figure 5-19, you can see the worksheet, at 100% zoom, in a 10 point font.

Updating the Model

Having built the model and explored several ways of making it easier to view, you may want to update it to reflect a revised estimate of how much costs will rise. Recall that all of the expenses in columns C through M are based on a factor of 1.01. This was done by copying the formula 1.01*B4 from C4 to all the other cells. To change the growth basis of the spreadsheet to 1.005, you could write a new formula. The new starting location is C8, and you could enter 1.005*B8 in C8 and then copy it to all the other cells. That would involve several steps, however, and you would have to repeat all those steps every time you wanted to see the effect of a different factor. As you will see, this is not necessary with Quattro Pro 3.

Problems with Relatives

Since the growth rate is stated in G4, you might be tempted to write a new formula (+G4*B8) in C8 and copy it to all the other cells. That way you

Figure 5-18. *WYSIWYG zoom set at 75%*

Figure 5-19. *Worksheet in 10 point font*

could simply change the factor in G4 and it would be reflected throughout the budget. This approach can run into problems, however. Remember that entering a formula like 1.01*B8 in C8 means that B8, the cell to the left of C8, is multiplied by 1.01. When you copy this formula to D8, D8 becomes 1.01*C8, 1.01 times the cell to the left of D8. The formula +G4*B8 means the cell that is up four rows and over four, times the cell to the left. If you copy this formula from C8 to D8, you get +H4*C8, the cell that is up four rows and over four times the cell to the left. Since H4 is empty, the answer is 0. The same would apply to all other cells in the row if you copied the formula across the row, as you can see here in Figure 5-20. If you copy a formula and the answer is an unexpected zero, move the cell selector to the first offending cell and check the contents in the cell identifier. In the case of D8 in Figure 5-20, it is **+H4*C8** as predicted.

Absolute Solutions

The solution to the relative problem is to make any references to fixed cells absolute. Thus, you can say that C8 is absolutely G4 times B8. You indicate this in the formula by placing a dollar sign in front of the coordinates. Thus, $G$4*B8 can be copied anywhere, and the result will always be G4 times the cell to the left, since the formula was created to the right of B8.

There are two ways to make a cell reference absolute: You can type the dollar signs yourself, or—with the cursor next to the cell reference on the edit line—press the Absolute, or Abs key (F4). Quattro Pro 3 will add dollar signs for you. In fact, if you keep pressing F4, the program will show you the four possible cell references:

$G$4	Absolutely column G row 4
$G4	Absolutely column G, but any row
G$4	Any column, but absolutely row 4
G4	Completely relative

In the case of the sample model, type the formula **$G$4*B8** into C8. Then copy the formula across the columns to M8, taking care not to copy over the very last cell on row 8, since that holds the @SUM formula. Then copy

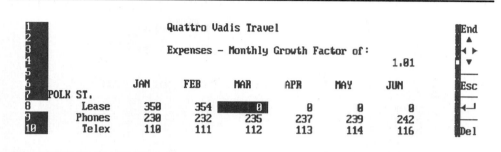

Figure 5-20. *Formula copied across a row*

C8..M8 down to C9..M30. (You will create several extra rows of zeros that you can remove with Edit Erase.) You will find that the formula works correctly now, and you can update the rate in G4, perhaps to 1.015, and see all of the affected cells change.

You can use the Abs key (F4) in either the pointing method of building formulas or while editing a formula. The absolute reference is necessary whenever you are writing formulas that are going to be copied but need to be referred to as a specific cell or block of cells in their new locations. A typical example of this is a rate, growth factor, or other spreadsheet assumption referenced to a cell outside the model.

Referencing the Total

Perhaps you would like the title of the model to reflect the total expenses for the year. This is easily done by adding a formula to cell G2. Simply type **+N32** and enter it into G2. This will pull the grand total from N32 into G2, as shown in Figure 5-21. You can edit the label in D1 to match the illustration. To produce the dollar sign on the figure in G2, you would format that cell in Currency format with zero decimal places using the Style Numeric Format command.

Having improved and expanded the model, you are almost ready to print it. However, before going any further you should make sure that the latest changes are stored. Assuming that you have used the File Save As command to give the worksheet an appropriate filename, you can issue the

```
1 ▓               Quattro Vadis Travel - Total Amount:            □End
2 ▓                                                  $103,407      ▲
3 ▓               Expenses - Monthly Growth Factor of:         ◄ ▶
4 ▓                                                     1.015      ▼
5 ▓
6 ▓               JAN      FEB      MAR      APR      MAY      JUN   Esc
7 ▓POLK ST.
8 ▓     Lease    350      355      361      366      371      377   ↵
9 ▓     Phones   230      233      237      241      244      248
10 ▓     Telex   110      112      113      115      117      119  ▌Del
```

Figure 5-21. *Grand total in title*

File Save command to update the file. However, at this point you might want to keep the earlier version, in which case you can use File Save As and give the improved worksheet a new name such as QVBUDG02.WQ1. If you have not yet used the File Save As command to store the worksheet you have been building, see the earlier section, "Saving Your Work."

Printing

Now that you have explored various methods for viewing and updating the spreadsheet, it is time to look at how you produce a printed copy. Quattro Pro 3 can produce anything from a simple, one-page printout to a carefully formatted multipage report with headers, footers, and other enhancements. You begin all printing, simple or complex, by selecting the Print menu from the main menu, as shown in Figure 5-22.

Basic Block Printing

While there are numerous options available for print operations in Quattro Pro 3, you can get results with just two commands, Block and Spreadsheet Print. Block is used to tell Quattro Pro 3 which cells are to be printed. As you might expect, Block on the Print menu works like any other Quattro Pro 3 Block command. You specify the desired coordinates, either by typing

Figure 5-22. *The Print menu*

them or by pointing out the cells. Use Spreadsheet Print to initiate printing once you have specified a block. Do not pick Spreadsheet Print unless you have followed the golden rule of PC printing: plug in, turn on, load up. Printing without a properly connected printer will produce an error in Quattro Pro 3.

Print Block

You can define a Print Block from any point in the spreadsheet. To see the basics of printing, try printing part of the sample worksheet. For example, suppose you want to print the first six months of the projection. The basic operation is as follows:

1. Select Print and then Block. The initial coordinate is not locked, so you can move it freely to identify the top-left corner of the range of cells to be printed.

2. Press HOME, and unless your titles are frozen, you will be moved to cell A1, which is an appropriate point at which to begin printing this spreadsheet. If your titles are frozen, use the arrow keys to move to cell A1.

3. Anchor the block coordinates at A1 by typing a period, and then press TAB to move over to column G. Now press PAGE DOWN and move down to include all the cells through G32. Press ENTER to confirm this block.

4. Check that the Destination setting on the Print menu is Printer. If necessary, change the setting to Printer. Check that the Copies setting is 1. Also check that you printer is on and loaded with paper.

5. Select Adjust Printer, and then pick Align to make sure that Quattro Pro 3 knows that your paper is positioned correctly in the printer.

```
                 Quattro Vadis Travel - Total Amount:
                                                $103,407
                 Expenses - Monthly Growth Factor of:
                                                   1.015

              JAN     FEB     MAR     APR     MAY     JUN
    POLK ST.
       Lease    350     355     361     366     371     377
      Phones    230     233     237     241     244     248
       Telex    110     112     113     115     117     119
     Electric   120     122     124     125     127     129
    Res. Rent   500     507     515     523     531     539
    VAN NESS
       Lease    500     507     515     523     531     539
      Phones    250     254     258     261     265     269
       Telex    150     152     155     157     159     162
     Electric   225     228     232     235     239     242
    Res. Rent   835     848     860     873     886     900
    UNION SQ.
       Lease  1,200   1,218   1,236   1,255   1,274   1,293
      Phones    300     304     309     314     318     323
       Telex    250     254     258     261     265     269
     Electric   205     208     211     214     218     221
    Res. Rent   890     903     917     931     945     959
    EMBARCADERO
       Lease    900     913     927     941     955     970
      Phones    275     279     283     288     292     296
    Telex (AUG)   0       0       0       0       0       0
     Electric     0       0       0       0       0       0
    Res. Rent   580     589     598     606     616     625

    TOTALS    7,870   7,988   8,108   8,229   8,353   8,478
```

Figure 5-23.   *The first report*

6. Quattro Pro 3 returns you to the Print menu, from which you can now select Spreadsheet Print.

The mode indicator will flash the word WAIT for a moment and the completed print job will emerge from the printer, looking like the printout shown in Figure 5-23.

Print Settings

When you use the basic Block and Print method, your printed output is based on the size of the Print Block you define and the current menu settings. These settings include the size of the paper and the margins that define the printing area. In other words, they are the parameters by which Quattro Pro 3 relates to a piece of paper. The defaults for these settings are shown in Figure 5-24. You can change margins and page length to accommodate different sizes of paper and type styles. You can also change the unit of measurement from lines and characters to inches or centimeters.

If you define the entire sample spreadsheet as the Print Block, from A1..N32, Quattro Pro 3's defaults produce the results shown in Figure 5-25. Note that the information flows over two pages and the second page lacks headings to explain the data. The solutions to these problems are numerous. You can increase the size of the paper, reduce the size of the type, repeat some information on successive pages, and add headers and footers. Indeed, Quattro Pro 3 has a wide range of print settings, which together give you complete control of your output.

Setting Headings

You can add missing column and row headings in a printout in much the same way as you can with the Locked Titles command when viewing a spreadsheet. You use the Print Headings command to identify columns and rows containing headings as print borders that are then repeated on each page. You must then redefine the Print Block to exclude areas included in the borders. For the sample spreadsheet, cells B1..N6 are

Figure 5-24.   *Page layout*

defined as the Top Heading in preparation for printing the entire spread-sheet. This area will repeat if any part of the printout does not fit on a single page. The Left Heading is defined as A7..A32. This heading will repeat if the printout has to divide the data. The Print Block can then be redefined as B7..N32. The results of printing with headings are shown in Figure 5-26. At this point, the results are fine except that they take up three pages. To remedy this requires further adjustments on the Layout menu, shown in Figure 5-27. Note that the Reset option on the Layout menu is used to clear your Headings.

```
                    Quattro Vadis Travel - Total Amount:
                                                $103,407
                    Expenses - Monthly Growth Factor of:
                                                  1.015

                 JAN     FEB     MAR     APR     MAY     JUN
    POLK ST.
         Lease    350     355     361     366     371     377
        Phones    230     233     237     241     244     248
         Telex    110     112     113     115     117     119
       Ele...
    Res.
    VAN NE
       P
                 JUL     AUG     SEP     OCT     NOV     DEC     YEAR

       Ele      383     388     394     400     406     412    4,564
    Res.        251     255     259     263     267     271    2,999
    UNION       120     122     124     126     128     130    1,435
                131     133     135     137     139     141    1,565
       P        547     555     563     572     580     589    6,521

       Ele      547     555     563     572     580     589    6,521
    Res.        273     277     282     286     290     294    3,260
    EMBARC      164     166     169     172     174     177    1,956
                246     250     253     257     261     265    2,934
       P        913     927     941     955     969     984   10,889
    Telex
       Ele    1,312   1,332   1,352   1,372   1,393   1,414   15,649
    Res.        328     333     338     343     348     353    3,912
                273     277     282     286     290     294    3,260
    TOTALS      224     228     231     234     238     241    2,673
                973     988   1,003   1,018   1,033   1,048   11,607

                984     999   1,014   1,029   1,044   1,060   11,737
                301     305     310     314     319     324    3,586
                  0     150     152     155     157     159      773
                  0       0       0       0       0       0        0
                634     644     653     663     673     683    7,564

              8,605   8,884   9,018   9,153   9,290   9,430  103,407
```

Figure 5-25.   *Complete spreadsheet printed on two pages*

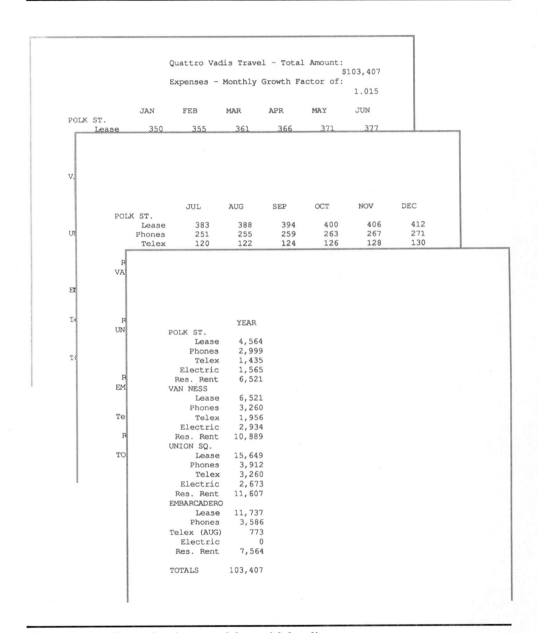

Figure 5-26. *Print of entire spreadsheet with headings*

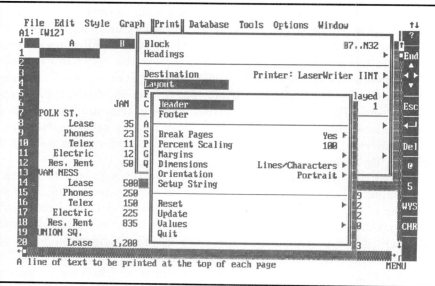

Figure 5-27. *Layout menu*

Changing Margins

Margins are a critical factor when you are adjusting print settings. For example, if you use wider paper, you must use the Print Layout Margins command to increase the right margin. There are five settings on the Layout Margins menu: Page Length, Left, Top, Right, and Bottom. The Page Length, Top, and Bottom settings deal with the length of the paper on which you are printing and the space you leave at the top and bottom of each page. The Left and Right settings determine where on the left side of the page the printing starts and how far it extends to the right (the Right setting is measured from the left edge of the page, not the Left setting).

The default unit of measure for left and right margins is characters; the default unit for Top, Bottom, and Page Length is lines. The lines/characters method of measurement, illustrated in Figure 5-24, was developed when most printers used a fixed number of characters and lines per inch, typically 10 characters per inch (10 pitch) and 6 lines per inch. Nowadays, many printers can create characters in a wide variety of sizes, usually measured in points, which gives them greater flexibility and accuracy. For this reason, Quattro Pro 3 allows you to change the unit of measurement with the Layout Dimensions command seen in the menu in Figure 5-27. The Dimensions choices are Lines/Characters, Inches, and Centimeters. Choose the dimensions best suited to your printer and to the type of reports you create. You can use the Layout Update command to make your Dimensions choice, along with the other Layout settings, permanent. Alternatively, you can choose the appropriate Dimension setting on a file-by-file basis.

If you are working with a standard 10-pitch typeface then the 15-inch-wide paper used in many wide-carriage printers calls for a right margin of 140. A sheet of 8 1/2-by-14-inch legal paper turned on its side so the width is 14 inches can use a 132- character right margin. If you reduce printer pitch you must increase margins. The condensed pitch of 17 characters per inch used on many dot matrix and laser printers allows a right margin of 140 on 8 1/2-inch-wide paper and 250 on 15-inch-wide paper. You must set the margin yourself when you change paper size or print pitch.

Altering Page Size

Most popular printers print at six lines per inch. This makes an 11-inch page 66 lines long. Quattro Pro 3 leaves a top and bottom margin of two rows plus three rows reserved for headers and footers, described in a moment. If you are working with paper that is longer or shorter than 11 inches, you must tell Quattro Pro 3 the length. If you are using Line/Characters, then an 8 1/2-by-11-inch piece of paper printed on its side is 53 lines long. You can actually tell Quattro Pro 3 you have a 33-line sheet of paper and it will treat a regular sheet of paper as though it were two sheets. This can be useful if you print a model that is less than 18 rows long.

Printer Setups

Many printers can be told to change their print style, print pitch, and other aspects by codes transmitted as part of the print data sent from the program. Quattro Pro 3 can accommodate these codes as printer setup strings, which are sent ahead of the data to set the printer. For example, most IBM and EPSON dot matrix printers respond to the characters \015 as meaning condensed print. You enter a code with the Layout Setup String command. However, in many cases it is best to choose typestyles and other print features with the Style command and allow Quattro Pro 3 to send the correct codes automatically, as described in the section on "Dressing Up Worksheets."

Writing Headers and Footers

In addition to setting parts of the spreadsheet as border headings, you can have other information repeat from page to page in a multipage Quattro Pro 3 printout by using the header and footer commands. These commands provide areas into which you type the text to be printed, along with formatting instructions that tell the program how to align the text. You can use special codes in headers and footers to print such information as the correct page number. The # sign enters the page number in a header or footer. The @ sign causes the current date, according to your PC's clock, to be printed. The straight line symbol | is used like a tab stop to position header and footer text across the line. Typing the header text with no | symbol causes Quattro Pro 3 to left-align everything. Preceding text with one | results in centering. Using two | | right-aligns the subsequent text. For example, you can use |Page# to center the text "Page" and have Quattro Pro 3 insert the correct number. You could use the following as a header:

Quattro Vadis | Report @| | Page#

to produce this result:

Quattro Vadis   Report 30-Nov-91   Page1

To remove a header or footer, simply select the Header or Footer option, then press ESCAPE followed by ENTER.

Making Page Breaks

Quattro Pro 3 automatically inserts page breaks according to the page length setting. These settings are referred to as *soft page breaks,* since they change position according to the size of the Print Block. However, you can specify *hard page breaks* to force breaks at chosen points in the printout. Hard page breaks are indicated by the | character and two colons inserted into the spreadsheet on a blank row. These characters are stored as part of the spreadsheet and are not removed until you delete them individually.

To create hard page breaks, either type them in or select Insert Break from the Style menu. When you use the Insert Break command, Quattro Pro 3 automatically inserts a blank nonprinting row that contains the page break command. If you are creating a page break manually, then create a blank row first, because any other data on a page-break row will not be printed. You should not insert page breaks in top heading cells.

Resetting Options
And Storing Defaults

When you save a spreadsheet, the print settings in effect at the time you perform the save are stored together with the worksheet data. If you need to change the print settings completely, perhaps to print out a different section of the same worksheet, you can use Reset to clear the Print Block, the borders, the margin settings, and so on.

If you will be using the same settings on a regular basis, you can incorporate them into the system defaults by selecting Update from the Layout menu. (Defaults are described in the next chapter.)

Adjusting the Printer

You may want to advance the paper in the printer by line or by page. You use the Adjust Printer menu to move the paper forward a line at a time (Skip Line). You use the Align Paper option to let Quattro Pro 3 know that the current position of the paper in the printer is correct; that is, the print head is at the top of the form. The Align command also performs the very important task of setting the page number back to 1. For example, if you print a two-page report then go to print another section on the spreadsheet, the next page will be number 3 unless you use the Align command before printing. You can use the Form Feed command to eject the current sheet of paper. This is particularly useful if you find that the last page of the printout is not automatically ejected. Note that if you want several copies of a report, you can use the Copies option to specify the number you need printed.

Unformatted Printing

Quattro Pro 3 recognizes hard page breaks and inserts others as needed, making room for headers and footers. If you need a continuous stream of print, for example, to print mailing labels, then use the Print Page Layout command and set Break Pages to No. Quattro Pro 3 will still respond to hard page breaks you have placed in the worksheet but will not print headers and footers or insert soft page breaks.

Cell Listings

What you want to print from Quattro Pro 3 is not always a neatly arranged set of numbers, but may sometimes be a quick snapshot of what is on the screen. Perhaps you also wish to include a complex formula in the cell identifier to show someone how an aspect of a model works. You can do this with the PRTSC key. Combined with SHIFT on some keyboards, the PRTSC key sends a literal picture of the cell and row numbers on the screen to your printer. This does not work when you are using graphics display mode, which requires a special screen capture program such as InSet.

If you want a list of what is in every cell in a worksheet, including the cell format and width if they differ from the global setting, select the Cell-formula option from the Print Format menu. The resulting printout will include the cells that are in the Print Block down the side of the page. This is useful for reference or for communicating with other users. An example is shown in Figure 5-28, where the cell contents are printed as they appear in the cell identifier when it is highlighted. Another user could re-create a spreadsheet design from a listing such as this.

Print Destinations

The Destination option on the Print menu determines where Quattro Pro 3 sends what you print. The default destination is Printer for Draft Mode Printing. This is the destination that you would normally use for quick spreadsheet output. You cannot use this option if you want to include graphs in your worksheet or graphic print features such as fonts and line drawing. Also, Quattro Pro 3 can perform a print to disk, represented by the File option. This operation exports data to other programs such as word processors, and is discussed in Chapter 10. The Graphics Printer option is

```
C1: 'Quattro Vadis Travel - Total Amount:
G2: (C0) +N32
C3: 'Expenses - Monthly Growth Factor of:
G4: 1.015
B6: ^JAN
C6: ^FEB
D6: ^MAR
E6: ^APR
F6: ^MAY
G6: ^JUN
A7: [W12] 'POLK ST.
A8: [W12] "Lease
B8: (,0) 350
C8: (,0) +$G$4*B8
D8: (,0) +$G$4*C8
E8: (,0) +$G$4*D8
F8: (,0) +$G$4*E8
G8: (,0) +$G$4*F8
```

Figure 5-28. *Listing cells for print block A1..G8*

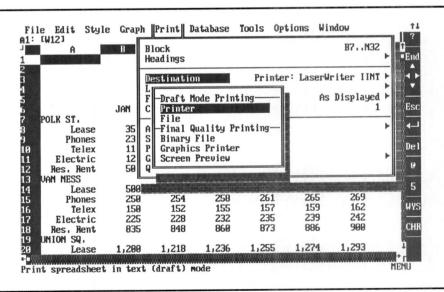

Figure 5-29. *Printer and Destination in Print menu*

used when you want to use the Style options such as fonts and line drawing in your reports. The final option is Screen Preview, which allows you to see what printed output will look like without having to put it on paper. This option is discussed later in this chapter. As you can see from Figure 5-29, Quattro Pro 3 shows you the name of the printer as well as the Destination choice in the Print menu. To change the printer model, you use the Options Hardware menu, described in the next chapter. Note that if you are using a PostScript printer the program will default to Graphics Printer.

Dressing Up Worksheets

Up to this point the appearance of the model has depended mainly on the location of the columns and rows, the alignment of the labels, and the formatting of the numbers. There are several other ways of affecting the appearance of your spreadsheets, both on the screen and on paper. Using the Style commands you can add lines and shading to your spreadsheets. You can also employ a variety of fonts to add visual appeal to your work.

Working in Graphics Mode

You can use the Line Drawing and Shading Style commands regardless of whether you have a graphics display. However, you may find it easier to work with these commands if you use WYSIWYG display mode. To do this you will need a system that supports very high-resolution graphics, such as an EGA or VGA display. The display that you will get when you choose WYSIWYG Mode will look something like Figure 5-30.

Line Drawing

Quattro Pro 3's line drawing commands work by placing lines in locations that you specify, relative to cells that you select. The lines can be single, double, or thick. They can be placed all around a cell or block of cells, or just on the top or bottom. Lines can be drawn between columns or rows, or an entire grid can be drawn. For an example of line drawing you can use

File   Edit   Style   Graph   Print   Database   Tools   Options   Window

A1: [W12]

	A	B	C	D	E	F	G	H	I	J
1			Quattro Vadis Travel - Total Amount:							
2							$103,407			
3			Expenses - Monthly Growth Factor of:							
4							1.015			
5										
6		JAN	FEB	MAR	APR	MAY	JUN	JUL	AUG	SEP
7	POLK ST.									
8	Lease	350	355	361	366	371	377	383	388	394
9	Phones	230	233	237	241	244	248	251	255	259
10	Telex	110	112	113	115	117	119	120	122	124
11	Electric	120	122	124	125	127	129	131	133	135
12	Res. Rent	500	507	515	523	531	539	547	555	563
13	VAN NESS									
14	Lease	500	507	515	523	531	539	547	555	563
15	Phones	250	254	258	261	265	269	273	277	282
16	Telex	150	152	155	157	159	162	164	166	169
17	Electric	225	228	232	235	239	242	246	250	253
18	Res. Rent	835	848	860	873	886	900	913	927	941
19	UNION SQ.									
20	Lease	1,200	1,218	1,236	1,255	1,274	1,293	1,312	1,332	1,352
21	Phones	300	304	309	314	318	323	328	333	338
22	Telex	250	254	258	261	265	269	273	277	282
23	Electric	205	208	211	214	218	221	224	228	231
	Res. Rent	890	903	917	931	945	959	973	988	1,003

QUBUDG02.WQ1 [1]   NUM   READY

Figure 5-30.   *The example in WYSIWYG mode*

the budget worksheet that has been the main subject of this chapter, and which appears in Figure 5-30. The first lines will be drawn to set apart the month headings.

The Style commands are a typical situation where the preselection feature in Quattro Pro 3 can be put to good use. You want to add a line or lines to cells A6 through N6. Keyboard users can select cell A6, press SHIFT-F7, and then press END and then the RIGHT ARROW key to select all the way through N6. Mouse users can click on A6 and then drag the highlighting through N6. Once you have selected this block of cells you can use the Style command and pick Line Drawing. The command you issue now will apply to the cells that you have preselected. You do not have to use preselection with the Style commands. If you do not, you will be prompted for the block of cells after you have issued the command, but preselection allows you to identify the cells you want to affect before having to think about the commands that you will use.

Figure 5-31.   *Line drawn below months in WYSIWYG mode*

When you pick Line Drawing you will see the Placement options listed. This menu allows you to specify where the lines will be placed in relation to the cells you have selected. You can browse through the options on this list with the UP and DOWN ARROW keys, noting the explanations that appear in the status line as you do this. The results of picking any one of these choices will appear on the screen right away, and you can make several choices from this menu before you pick Quit. For example, select Bottom and you will see a selection of line types: None, Single, Double, and Thick. Select Single for now and you will see the line drawn underneath the months, as shown in Figure 5-31. Note that the Placement menu reappears. (If you had not preselected the block to be affected you would be prompted to do so before the Placement menu returned.)

Also note that the line is difficult to see because it coincides with the spreadsheet grid lines. To solve this problem, you can use the Window Options menu to turn off the grid lines. Select Grid Lines, then Hide and

Figure 5-32. *Grid lines hidden*

the display will be changed. You can see this in Figure 5-32, where further lines have been added.

Suppose that you would like to place a line above the month labels as well. From the Placement menu select Top. Now select Single again. You will keep coming back to the Placement menu until you select Quit. Try selecting Bottom and then Double. This will put a double line below the months.

Removing Lines

If you decide that these lines are not what you want, you can pick All from the Placement menu and then pick None from the line type choices. This is the way that you erase lines: Select the cells with lines attached to them and then use All followed by None. You can also selectively remove certain lines. For example, in Figure 5-31 you could pick Bottom and then None to remove the line at the bottom of the cells.

More Line Styles

Suppose that you decide the top and bottom lines look good for the months. You pick Quit from the Placement menu to leave the Line Drawing command. Now you want to put lines between the offices. After selecting cells A13 through N13, you can put in a line that separates the two offices by using Style, Line Drawing, Top, Single, then Quit. If you repeat this command for rows 19 and 25 you will get the results shown in Figure 5-32.

Note that if you are using the character mode of display, you will see that the addition of lines also adds space to the model. These unnumbered rows that are added do not affect any formulas or block commands. You cannot select lines themselves, only the cells to which they are attached. When you use the mouse or the SHIFT-F7 key to select cells, the cell selector increases in size when it encounters a cell with a line attached so that the line is included. When you copy or move cells that have lines attached, the lines travel with the cells. In some situations it makes sense to add lines to cells early in the creation of a model, as with other Style commands, thus avoiding repetition of the Line Drawing command.

Shading

A further style improvement is to add some shading to the bottom of the model, just above the totals. Shading is inserted into cells, in this case cells A31 through N31. Select this block and then use Style, Shading, Grey. The command will insert the grey characters into the cells and quit back to the READY mode. The results are shown in Figure 5-33, which also shows the use of a different font. The font commands are described in the next section.

The Shading command does not overwrite values and labels in a cell. You can therefore select a large area and have all nonempty cells shaded at once. The Black option on the shading menu creates a much darker shading. Between the Grey and Black options you have useful tools for adding visual appeal to your documents.

You can attach lines to blocks as well as shade them. You can also put lines all the way around a large section of the worksheet. For example, you could select the entire model and then use the Outside command from the Line Drawing Placement menu to draw a line all the way around the outside of the model. If you want to create a gridwork of lines within an area of the spreadsheet you select the block and then use the Inside option from the Placement menu. This draws lines around all of the cells.

Quattro Vadis Travel - Total Amount:

$103,407

Expenses - Monthly Growth Factor of:

1.015

	JAN	FEB	MAR	APR	MAY	JUN
POLK ST.						
Lease	350	355	361	366	371	377
Phones	230	233	237	241	244	248
Telex	110	112	113	115	117	119
Electric	120	122	124	125	127	129
Res. Rent	500	507	515	523	531	539
VAN NESS						
Lease	500	507	515	523	531	539
Phones	250	254	258	261	265	269
Telex	150	152	155	157	159	162
Electric	225	228	232	235	239	242
Res. Rent	835	848	860	873	886	900
UNION SQ.						
Lease	1,200	1,218	1,236	1,255	1,274	1,293
Phones	300	304	309	314	318	323
Telex	250	254	258	261	265	269
Electric	205	208	211	214	218	221
Res. Rent	890	903	917	931	945	959
EMBARCADERO						
Lease	900	913	927	941	955	970
Phones	275	279	283	288	292	296
Telex (AUG)	0	0	0	0	0	0
Electric	0	0	0	0	0	0
Res. Rent	580	589	598	606	616	625
TOTALS	7,870	7,988	8,108	8,229	8,353	8,478

Figure 5-33.   *Shading above totals*

If you are using an HP LaserJet you can adjust the level of gray used by the Shading command. Deep in the Options menu, under Hardware Printers Fonts you will see a command called LaserJet Fonts. This is used to tell Quattro Pro 3 which LaserJet fonts you have installed in your printer. The menu has an option called Shading Level that allows you to select one of eight levels of shading, from a few percent to 100%, which is black.

Working with Fonts

Included with Quattro Pro 3 is a variety of different fonts that you can use to display and print your worksheet. Up to eight different fonts can be mixed together in one worksheet. Fonts are printed when the Print Destination is set to Graphics Printer. Fonts are visible in WYSIWYG mode and in Screen Preview.

Higher Destinations

Earlier you saw that Quattro Pro 3 offers several different destinations for your print activity. When you select Destination from the print menu you see five options split into two sections, Draft Mode Printing and Final Quality Printing, as seen earlier in Figure 5-29. The first and default option, Printer, gives you traditional spreadsheet output, plain-vanilla character text that is good for drafts of documents. The standard text characters of your printer are used. Draft Mode Printing is the quickest way to print, but it ignores the presentation- or graphics-quality printing features possessed by many of today's printers. The Graphics Printer option is used for final quality printing when you are concerned about the appearance of your reports.

Do not be confused by the term *Graphics Printer*. Selecting this option from the Destination choices does not mean that you have a graph or chart in your worksheet. When you choose Graphics Printer as the destination for your spreadsheet printing, Quattro Pro 3 applies graphics features to the output. On some printers, such as dot matrix models, this can cause printing to take quite a while. However, the results will be well worth it in terms of quality appearance.

About Fonts

What exactly are the graphics features supported by Graphics Printer? They include line drawing and shading, which have been discussed already, and also fonts. A *font* is a style of writing a set of characters. Figure 5-34 shows words printed in a number of different fonts. Most of the print examples shown so far in this chapter have used the Courier font. This is the default font of the LaserJet printer. The Printer option on the Destination menu uses whatever font is your printer's default; that is, it does not send any font information to the printer. The printer is just told what characters to print and where to place them. The exact shape of the characters is left up to the printer.

Courier is a general-purpose font that is *monospaced*, meaning that each character occupies the same width on a line. Unlike *proportional* text, such as the text you are reading now, monospaced text gives as much space to the word *fill* as it does to the word *wine*. Using proportional fonts tends to give documents a more finished and professional appearance. Some fonts have names that are proprietary because they were designed by a particular person or company. Among the better known proportional fonts are Helvetica (sometimes called Swiss) and Times (sometimes referred to as Dutch or Roman). Fonts often come in different sizes, measured in *points*. A 10-point font is about the same as elite on a typewriter. Fonts can also come in different styles: bold, italic, and underlined. In Figure 5-33 you can see the default Quattro Pro 3 font: Bitstream Swiss 12 point.

```
Courier 12 point (about 10 pitch)
```
Times or Dutch in 10 point

Times or Dutch in 12 point

Times or Dutch in 14 point italic

Helvetica or Swiss in 10 point

Helvetica or Swiss in 12 point

Helvetica or Swiss in 14 point

Helvetica or Swiss in 18 point bold

Figure 5-34.   *Sample fonts*

Font Choices

Quattro Pro 3 supports a wide range of fonts in different sizes and styles that you can use to print out your spreadsheet. You access these fonts through the Style menu. When you select Font from the Style menu you see a list of eight fonts, as shown in Figure 5-35. This is the default set of fonts provided by Quattro Pro 3.0. But if you select Edit Fonts you can change each of the fonts to your choice. For example, suppose that you want to change Font 2. You select Edit Fonts and pick Font 2, as shown in Figure 5-36, where the submenu of variables is displayed. These include Typeface, Point Size, Style, and Color. If you select Typeface, you will get a list of possibilities like the one in Figure 5-37, which is for a PostScript printer.

The choices on the Typeface list fall into several groups. There are Hershey fonts—such as Roman, Script, and Sans Serif—that are fairly simple in appearance and do not occupy much space in memory. There are also Bitstream fonts, such as Dutch and Swiss, that take up quite a bit of space but look very professional. Quattro Pro 3 allows most printers to print both of these types of fonts. There may also be fonts available for specific printers, such as the PostScript fonts shown in Figure 5-37. Many

Figure 5-35.   *Font selection menu*

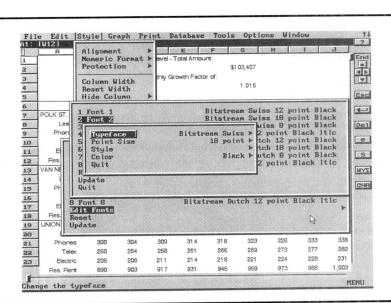

Figure 5-36. *Editing Font 2*

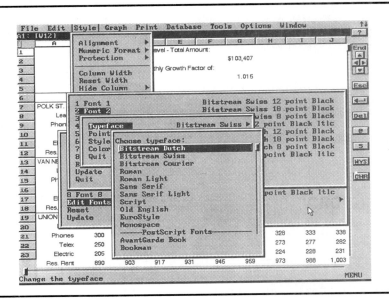

Figure 5-37. *Typeface selection*

printers like the LaserJet support print cartridges that store fonts, and Quattro Pro 3 knows about these. For more information on font selection for your printer see the "About Your Hardware" section in the next chapter.

Setting a Font

Suppose that you select Bitstream Swiss from the menu in Figure 5-37 and then select Point Size. Your choices are from 8 to 72. You pick 14 and are returned to the Font 2 menu. You decide to make this font bold, so you select Style from the list that includes Bold, Italic, and Underlined. Selecting Bold turns on this feature.

You can also turn on Italic to produce bold italic. When you have selected the style combination you want, you pick Quit. You can then select a color if you like, but remember that black and white printers cannot print color. You can now select Quit to move back in the menu tree and you will see that your choices are reflected on the Font menu under Font 2. If you create a mixture of fonts that you want to save, use the Update command on the Font menu. If you ever need to return the font selection to the default fonts, you can choose Reset from the Font menu.

You are now ready to assign a font to a section of your spreadsheet. When you select Style Font and then a number, such as 2, you are prompted for a block. When you have selected the block to be affected by the new font, press ENTER. You will see a notation of [F2] in the cell description of the affected cells. This stands for Font 2. This cell will be printed in Font 2 whenever you select Spreadsheet Print with Graphics Printer as the Destination choice. Font 2 will appear with whatever font you have selected for the second font on the font list. If you want to return a cell's font setting to Font 1, you simply select Style, Font 1, and then highlight the cell. Note that all cells of every Quattro Pro 3 worksheet are Font 1 by default. For this reason you will not see [F1] in any cells.

If you are using the WYSIWYG mode for your Quattro Pro 3 display you will see the font changes on screen while you are working on your spreadsheet. However, your ability to quickly move around the worksheet deteriorates. Quattro Pro 3 can be switched to character mode in order to keep performance levels acceptable. This means that you can have a spreadsheet that prints impressively and also calculates quickly.

To print the results of font changes in your spreadsheet you select Print, Destination, and Graphics Printer; then select Spreadsheet Print. You can see a sample of the very impressive results in Figure 5-38, which uses a different font for the spreadsheet titles. Do not use Graph Print from the

	JAN	FEB	MAR	APR	MAY	JUN
Quattro Vadis Travel - Total Amount:					$103,407	
Expenses - Monthly Growth Factor of:					1.015	
POLK ST.						
Lease	350	355	361	366	371	377
Phones	230	233	237	241	244	248
Telex	110	112	113	115	117	119
Electric	120	122	124	125	127	129
Res. Rent	500	507	515	523	531	539
VAN NESS						
Lease	500	507	515	523	531	539

Figure 5-38.   *Sample output from Graphics Printer*

Print menu because Quattro Pro 3 will try to print a graph you have defined for the spreadsheet.

Remember that you can still get a quick printout from your worksheet by selecting plain Printer from the Print Destination menu. Also remember to save your worksheet after making font changes; otherwise, they may be lost. The selections you make for Fonts 1 through 8 are specific to the worksheet in which you make them. This means that if you want to use Bitstream Swiss 14 point Bold as Font 2 in another worksheet you will have to repeat the selection process. An alternative is to establish a blank worksheet as a style sheet and use it as the starting point for a new spreadsheet whenever you want to use a particular selection of fonts.

Font Sizing

Some fonts, such as, Bitstream Dutch 10-point, are considerably smaller in height than the normal text output of most printers, which is 10 pitch (10 characters to the inch), not 10 points. You will find that you can get more lines to the inch with a 10-point font. Quattro Pro 3 will automatically adjust the printed row height for you. In some cases you will get more characters to the inch with 10-point text, but sometimes you will require wider column settings to accommodate a proportionally spaced font like Dutch 10-point.

The need for wider columns when using fonts in Quattro Pro 3 arises from the way in which the program determines width spacing when printing in graphics mode. There is no such measurement as "one character wide" when using a proportional font since all characters have their own width. Therefore, Quattro Pro 3 uses an average measurement for the font and allows for that width times the character setting of the column to determine the printed column width. Occasionally, this will not be enough. For example, the 12-character-wide column A of the sample model will probably need to be increased to accommodate the word *EMBARCADERO* which takes up a lot of space. You will need to check your column widths after setting fonts, by a test print, by using the screen preview feature described later in this chapter, or by a simple inspection if you are using WYSIWYG mode.

Font Building

To print and display an attractive font, your computer requires a lot of information. To store every point size and style for every font would require many megabytes of disk space. For this reason Quattro Pro 3 provides some fonts in a special format that stores the essence of a font in a condensed format.

When you ask Quattro Pro 3 to use a particular size and style of the font, the program extracts the font from the condensed file in a process known as *font building*. When you install Quattro Pro 3 you can select groups of fonts or you can decline font installation and perform font building only on demand. This latter approach saves a lot of disk space. When you use a particular font and font size that has not yet been built, Quattro Pro 3 will build it, resulting in a slight delay and a message box that says "Building font." Thereafter, you have access to that font and font size without the program having to repeat the building operation. However, each font is built for a particular printer, and changing printers may require Quattro Pro 3 to repeat some font building, which is done automatically.

Fonts are built on several occasions: when you select Spreadsheet Print or Graph Print, and when you view a print job with either View from the Graph menu or Screen Preview (described in a moment). An exception to this font-building process is the set of Hershey fonts. These are always available without building, and they work the same on all graphics printers. The Hershey fonts are Roman, Roman Light, Sans Serif, Sans Serif Light, Script, Old English, EuroStyle, and Monospace. Hershey fonts require very little memory, but Bitstream fonts are quite large.

Fonts and Memory

You may find that you get a memory full message when you attempt an action that requires Quattro Pro 3 to build a font. If this happens you may want to reduce the number of fonts that you are using, reduce the size of your worksheet, or otherwise conserve on memory. While a variety of fonts allows very professional-looking printouts, the cost in memory is high. Only by beefing up your system's memory can you make full use of fonts. One way to mix fonts within tight memory constraints is to use the Hershey fonts just described. These use far less memory but provide acceptable appearance for many types of printout.

Another course of action can assist you in getting good printouts without giving up fonts. Select the Graphics Quality option on the Options menu. This allows you to control the building of fonts for screen display and printing. The choices are Draft and Final. When you choose Draft, Quattro Pro 3 will only use Bitstream fonts that have already been created. A Hershey font will be substituted if the requested Bitstream font is not available. When you select Final, Bitstream fonts will be used whenever requested. New font sizes will be created whenever required. Quattro Pro 3 will switch to Draft mode if it tries to build a font and finds there is not enough memory.

Screen Previews

If you are not using WYSIWYG mode, then introducing graphic elements such as lines and fonts into your worksheets makes it difficult to tell exactly what the printed results will look like. For example, when you use a larger font for part of the spreadsheet, you need to know what effect this will have on text spacing. Quattro Pro 3 provides a screen preview feature that lets you examine very closely what your text will look like when printed. You can see fonts, lines, headers, and footers. Page breaks are revealed as well as headings. You can zoom the view to a high level of detail. You can check that your column settings are wide enough for the fonts you have chosen. The Screen Preview feature is useful even if you are operating in WYSIWYG mode since it shows how the pages will be laid out, something that WYSIWYG alone cannot do.

Using Screen Preview

When you want to see what your spreadsheet will look like when printed with the Graphics Printer option, select Destination from the Print menu and select Screen Preview. Now choose Spreadsheet Print and you will see a preview screen like the one shown in Figure 5-39. This is a representation of an 8 1/2-×-11 piece of paper with the information to be printed displayed to scale. If the text that the program is trying to show is quite small it will be "greeked," or made into symbolic characters.

A special menu across the top of the preview screen provides options to assist you in viewing your work. You can select items from the menu by their first letter, or type / and choose them by pointing and pressing ENTER. When you activate the menu with / you get explanations of the items as you highlight them.

In addition to Help and Quit, which returns you to the regular worksheet, there is a Color option to show the colors that will be printed if you have a color printer. The Previous and Next options show additional pages. By picking Ruler you can add a 1-inch grid to the display. This helps you judge the placement of text on the page.

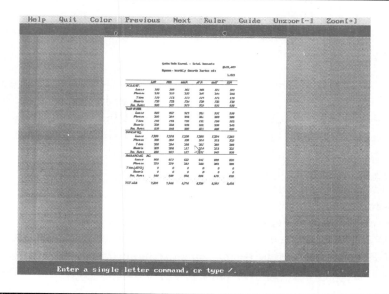

Figure 5-39.   *Preview screen*

Figure 5-40.   *Zoomed preview screen*

The Preview Zoom

To zoom you use either the plus (+) or the minus (–) key to enlarge or reduce the display. You can see the first level of zoom in Figure 5-40. Note that when you are in ZOOM mode you have a small picture of the page on the right of the screen. On this page is a box that shows you which section of the total page you are viewing. This is the guide. You can use the arrow keys to move the guide box around on the page and then press ENTER to redraw the screen with the new area enlarged. If you find the guide box obscuring your view you can select Guide from the menu to turn it off. Select Guide again and you will turn it back on.

When you have examined the preview you can pick Quit to get back to the Print menu. Select Destination and change it to Graphics Printer when you are ready to print out a final quality version of your worksheet. Select Spreadsheet Print from the Print menu to send the report to the printer.

The Finishing Touches

Whereas the Screen Preview feature allows you to see exactly what your printouts will look like before they are committed to paper, the WYSIWYG display mode allows you to see the effect of Style commands as soon as you issue them. Even these features, however, do not solve all of the problems associated with printing reports exactly as you want them. For example, the report you saw in Figure 5-26 shows one common problem: The results spread unevenly across a number of pages. The report would look much better if the results could be evenly spaced on just two pages.

Now that you have read about the various factors that control printing with Quattro Pro 3, it is time to consider how those features can work together to give you better results. Bear in mind that with the Screen Preview feature you can try any combination of print parameters without having to waste time and paper testing the results at the printer.

Shrink to Fit

The one print feature in Quattro Pro 3 that has not yet been mentioned may be just what you need to get the results you want: Print to Fit. This command automatically scales the printout so it fits on one page based on your current margin settings. In Figure 5-41 you can see the results of printing the sample worksheet after selecting Print to Fit. In fact, the Print to Fit command sends the worksheet to the printer, bypassing the Spreadsheet Print command. Print to Fit automatically selects Graphics Printer as the Destination but can be used in either WYSIWYG or character mode.

The results you get with Print to Fit will depend upon the size of the Print Block and the resolution of your printer. Quattro Pro 3 shrinks the characters down to the smallest size that will still be legible on the printer you are using. If the area of spreadsheet to be printed still will not fit on a single page, two pages are used.

The character size limit varies according to printer. Even though the characters in Figure 5-41 are very small, they are still legible. This is because they were produced by a laser printer operating at 300 dots per inch resolution. If the same block were printed with Print to Fit on a dot matrix printer operating at 180 dots per inch, the characters might not be readable. In that case Quattro Pro 3 would use two pages. Despite this

Quattro Vadis Travel - Total Amount:					$103,407								
Expenses - Monthly Growth Factor of:					1.015								
	JAN	FEB	MAR	APR	MAY	JUN	JUL	AUG	SEP	OCT	NOV	DEC	YEAR
POLK ST.													
Lease	350	355	361	366	371	377	383	388	394	400	406	412	4,564
Phones	230	233	237	241	244	248	251	255	259	263	267	271	2,999
Telex	110	112	113	115	117	119	120	122	124	126	128	130	1,435
Electric	120	122	124	125	127	129	131	133	135	137	139	141	1,565
Res. Rent	500	507	515	523	531	539	547	555	563	572	580	589	6,521
VAN NESS													
Lease	500	507	515	523	531	539	547	555	563	572	580	589	6,521
Phones	250	254	258	261	265	269	273	277	282	286	290	294	3,260
Telex	·50	152	155	157	159	162	164	166	169	172	174	177	1,956
Electric	225	228	232	235	239	242	246	250	253	257	261	265	2,934
Res. Rent	835	848	860	873	886	900	913	927	941	955	969	984	10,889
UNION SQ.													
Lease	1,200	1,218	1,236	1,255	1,274	1,293	1,312	1,332	1,352	1,372	1,393	1,414	15,649
Phones	300	304	309	314	318	323	328	333	338	343	348	353	3,912
Telex	250	254	258	261	265	269	273	277	282	286	290	294	3,260
Electric	205	208	211	214	218	221	224	228	231	234	238	241	2,673
Res. Rent	890	903	917	931	945	959	973	988	1,003	1,018	1,033	1,048	11,607
EMBARCADERO													
Lease	900	913	927	941	955	970	984	999	1,014	1,029	1,044	1,060	11,737
Phones	275	279	283	288	292	296	301	305	310	314	319	324	3,586
Telex (AUG)	0	0	0	0	0	0	0	150	152	155	157	159	773
Electric	0	0	0	0	0	0	0	0	0	0	0	0	0
Res. Rent	580	589	598	606	616	625	634	644	653	663	673	683	7,564
TOTALS	7,870	7,988	8,108	8,229	8,353	8,478	8,605	8,884	9,018	9,153	9,290	9,430	103,407

Figure 5-41. *Print to Fit*

limitation, the Print to Fit feature is a lifesaver when you are in a hurry to get a report printed and do not want to mess about adjusting all of the other parameters. Even if you have chosen a variety of fonts for the worksheet, Print to Fit scales them down to the level required to fit the results on a single page.

Whereas Print to Fit gives Quattro Pro 3 control of the shrinking process, the Percent Scaling option on the Layout menu allows you to shrink or enlarge the print block by a specified percentage. The default setting for Percent Scaling is 100%. You can enter a percentage from 1 to 1000 percent. Percentages less than 100 shrink a report to fit a smaller number of pages; percentages more than 100 expand a report to fill the printed page. Quattro Pro 3 only uses the Percent Scaling setting when you print with Spreadsheet Print. The Print to Fit command overrides the Percent Scaling setting.

Bear in mind that when Quattro Pro 3 shrinks or enlarges the print block it does not adjust the margins. This means that if you set a one-inch left margin, the report will be printed with a one-inch margin, even if you used 50% scaling. Quattro Pro 3 scales headers and footers to match the print block size. The Percent Scaling setting is saved with the worksheet file.

A Question of Widths

If the Print to Fit and Percent Scaling features do not solve your reporting problems, the next area to look at is widths. When a printout is too wide to fit on a convenient number of pages, one of the simplest techniques is to reduce the column width settings.

You have already seen that column width settings may need to be increased when you apply a font to a cell. For example, although EMBAR-CADERO may fit in 12 character in one font, it may overflow the cell in a different font. You will also find that some fonts result in numbers getting too large for the current cell width, requiring that the cell be widened to get rid of the asterisks Quattro Pro 3 uses to warn you a value cell is too narrow.

Whereas some columns may need widening, others need to be trimmed. For example, the sample model uses nine-character-wide columns for all of the monthly figures. These columns could be reduced by one or two characters. In many cases you may find that such an adjustment is enough to fit the model to the page.

You may wonder how Quattro Pro 3 handles the width or heights of rows. Normally, the height of each row is set automatically by Quattro Pro 3 according to the point size of the largest font used in that row. For example, if the labels in column A of the sample worksheet were formatted with a 14-point font and the numbers in model remained at 12 points, the row height would be determined by column A. The largest font in the row can be referred to as the key font. The height of the row is set to the point size of the key font plus some extra space for readability, determined by the particular font.

Selecting a smaller point size for the key font will result in a reduction of the length of the printout. You can manually adjust the height of a row or rows by using the Height option on the Style Block Size menu. After you tell Quattro Pro 3 the rows you want to affect, the Set Row Height command allows you to enter a size in points or to use the UP and DOWN ARROW keys to adjust the height gradually. If you set a height that is too small for the fonts on that row, the text may be cut off in the printout. To return the row height to the automatically determined setting, use the Reset Row Height option. Setting a small row height is useful when you have assigned shading to a row and want that row to be narrower than the others.

Another width-setting technique you might want to consider is to remove decimal place settings from figures. If you are displaying numbers with two decimal places, decide if these are really necessary. Reducing the decimal places allows you to reduce the column width even more (bear in mind the problem of rounded numbers versus formatted numbers, described in Chapter 4, if you decide to reduce decimal place settings).

If the report is still too wide, you might want to check the margin settings. Sometimes the left margin can be reduced and the right margin increased by just enough to fit the report onto the requisite number of pages. Also remember that if you switch to wider paper, you must change the margin settings yourself; Quattro Pro 3 cannot detect the paper change.

A Question of Orientation

One final printing option is the Orientation of the output. The choices are Portrait, Landscape, and Banner. The report printed in Figure 5-26 is an example of Portrait mode, which is the default orientation. Landscape orientation involves rotating the printout 90 degrees so it is at right angles to the print head or paper path in your printer. This is handy for printing worksheets like the example in this chapter where the number of results are wider than they are long. Indeed, a quick fix for printing the sample

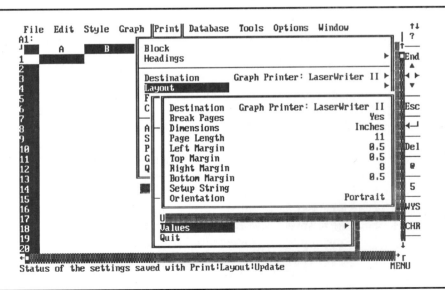

Figure 5-42.   *Layout Values display*

worksheet would be to set the orientation to landscape, then use Print to Fit.

The Banner setting allows you to print in landscape mode on continuous feed paper, such as you use in a dot matrix printer. No page breaks are placed in the report, so it flows along the entire length of the paper. This option does not work with laser or daisy wheel printers. Note that the Orientation setting for each worksheet is saved with the worksheet file. However, you can store one of the three orientations as part of the printing defaults. If you want to check the current print defaults, you can use the Values command on the Layout menu. As you can see in Figure 5-42, this presents a review of layout values stored in the default file. Press any key to clear this display. For more on default values, see the next chapter, which shows you how to adjust Quattro Pro 3's defaults to your liking.

6 *Working with Defaults*

This chapter shows you how to customize many aspects of Quattro Pro 3. In Chapter 1 you learned that the program automatically detects several aspects of your computer system and provides default settings for many commands. Quattro Pro 3's installation procedure gives you an opportunity to select some hardware defaults such as the make and model of the printer. Using the Options menu after installation, you can change the ways the program runs on your system. You can also adjust default settings of individual worksheets to fit your needs and preferences. In fact, the extent to which the details of Quattro Pro 3 can be tailored is quite exceptional. You can create customized menus and even add macros to menus. Some of these advanced features are covered in Chapter 12. However, you can begin with a number of simple changes that can make your work more efficient and more effective.

The Menu of Options

The changes to Quattro Pro 3 discussed in this chapter are made from the Options menu shown in Figure 6-1. You can see that this menu is made up of two parts. The first section consists of nine commands that deal with such basics as coloring the screen and the display mode used. The Update command stores the current settings from the first nine commands into a

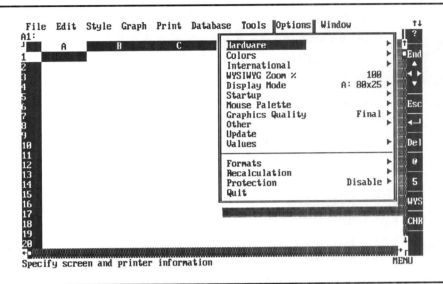

Figure 6-1.   *Options menu*

special file so that they can be used in the next session. The Values command displays a list of current default values. The second section covers three areas of default settings that apply to the current worksheet, as opposed to the program operation as a whole.

About Defaults

A computer program's defaults are what the program does unless you tell it to do something differently. Most programs have defaults of one kind or another because the program has to make some basic assumptions about how you will be using it. For example, most word processing programs arrange text between margins and tabs, and so they begin with default margin and tab settings. In the same way, Quattro Pro 3 has default column and format settings that determine how wide the columns will be and how numbers will be displayed. The starting defaults—the ones that the program uses when you first install it on your computer—are listed in Table 6-1.

Worksheet Settings

Column Width	9 characters
Format	General
Label Alignment	Left
Hide Zeroes	No
Recalculation	Background
Currency	$ prefix
Protection	Off
Font	Font 1

Program Settings

Wide Menus	Yes
Shortcuts Active	Yes
Mouse Palette	Displayed (if mouse installed)
Display Mode	Character 80 × 25 unless WYSIWYG is available
Undo	Disabled
Transcript Recording	Active
Failure Protection	100 keystrokes between saves
Expanded Memory	Spreadsheet Data
Clock	None

Table 6-1.   *Starting Defaults*

Worksheet Defaults

As you can see from Table 6-1, the defaults for Quattro Pro 3 can be divided into two categories: program and worksheet. The program defaults affect all program activity. If you use the Update command, then the changes carry over to the next session when you reload Quattro Pro 3.

The worksheet defaults are set for a specific worksheet. They do not affect new worksheets created in the same session, or in any following sessions. Thus you can display a spreadsheet called SALES.WQ1, change the default label alignment to Right, and all new labels that you enter will be automatically right-aligned. However, the next worksheet you open with File Open or create with File New will revert to left-alignment of labels. This allows you maximum control over the formatting of your worksheets without unpredictable results. Altering worksheet defaults with Quattro Pro 3 will not change formats that you have already established for specific cells.

Configuration File

The program defaults for Quattro Pro 3 are stored in the configuration file called RSC.RF. When you start the program, it reads the default settings from this file. You can update the configuration file to reflect your preferences. Suppose that you want on-screen display of the current date and time while you are working with Quattro Pro 3. You activate the menu and select Options followed by Other and then Clock. Your choices are Standard, International, or None. You pick Standard. Quattro Pro 3 returns to the READY mode, and the date and time are displayed on the status line. They remain there throughout your Quattro Pro 3 session. However, when you exit from Quattro Pro 3 and reload the program, they will not be displayed, *unless* you use the Options Update command.

To make your default selections permanent, you select the Update option from the Options menu. Selecting Update writes the current settings into the configuration file, so Quattro Pro 3 can reload them the next time you start the program. The work that you do may fall into two or more different categories so you may want to have several different sets of default choices. If you want to preserve a set of default choices, you can copy the RSC.RF file to another file, such as MY-RSC.RF, before you select Update. When the RSC.RF file is updated, the MY-RSC.RF copy will not be overwritten. This allows you to keep two different sets of defaults. You can keep many different sets of defaults in separate files and select the one you want for a particular session just prior to loading Quattro Pro 3. This process is described in Appendix A.

Format Options

The first default options discussed here are those that determine how your data appears on the worksheet. Careful manipulation of the format defaults can save a lot of time when you are applying formats to individual cells. The Formats menu contains the following options: Numeric Format, Align Labels, Hide Zeros, Global Width.

Numeric Format

The Numeric Format option allows you to determine the default format for the display of values. These choices are listed with examples in Table 6-2. Many of the formats allow you to specify the number of decimal places (from 1 to 15). While the Numeric Format option can be very convenient, saving you the trouble of formatting blocks of cells separately, you should exercise some care. For example, if you select a format with zero decimal places, and then you have to work with percentages, you might find it confusing to enter a percentage only to see Quattro Pro 3 respond by displaying 0. A percentage will appear as 0 until the cell it occupies has a format of at least one decimal place. As a rule you will not want to use a default format that has no decimal places.

Align Labels

You have seen that you can align labels and values to the left, right, or center of columns by using the Style Alignment command. The alignment of labels is determined by the leading character: ' for left, " for right, or ^ for center. To avoid starting every label with one of these signs, Quattro Pro 3 lets you select one of them as the default. Normally, this is left-aligned, but you can change it to right or center.

Making a change to Align Labels under the Options menu can save time if you think you will be using the Style Alignment command to realign most of your labels after they are entered. However, changing the default alignment does not affect labels that are already entered. Typically, you will use the Options Formats Align Labels command before you build your worksheet. If your worksheet is already built you can use the Style Alignment command to change the alignment of a whole group of labels at once. Alignment set with Style Alignment is not affected by the Options Formats Align Labels command.

Note that if you are working with long labels, these are generally easier to use if they are left-aligned. Also, the alignment of values cannot be altered with the Options Formats Align Labels command. Values in your worksheet are usually right-aligned by default, but you can use Style

Format Name	Description of Format
Fixed	No commas in 1,000s, negatives in parentheses, user-defined decimal places: 2000.99 (2000.99)
Scientific	Exponential notation, negatives in parentheses, user-defined decimal places: 2.00E + 03 (2.00E + 03)
Currency	Commas placed in 1,000s, negatives in parentheses, user-defined decimal places, user-defined currency symbol; default is $: $2,000.99
,(Financial)	Commas placed in 1,000s, negatives in parentheses, user-defined decimal places: 2,000.99
General	Varies decimal places; uses exponential notation for large numbers
+/–	Represents positive numbers as plus signs (+), negatives as minus signs (–) for simple bar charts
Percent	Divides contents by 100; uses % sign as suffix
Date	Various options, described in Chapter 9, including formats for time values
Text (Show Formulas)	Displays formulas in cells rather than their values
Hidden	Hides cell contents from view; shows contents only on the descriptor line

Table 6-2. *Format Choices*

Alignment to center- or left-align them on a cell-by-cell or block basis. String functions that create labels from values create left-aligned labels by default. You can individually center or right-align them with the Style Alignment command.

Hide Zeroes

You may have noticed that a formula resulting in zero is displayed as 0 in the worksheet. Some worksheets have a lot of zeroes in them to show that no values have yet been entered in those cells. When you are preparing a worksheet containing many zero entries, you may want to hide or suppress them. To do this, issue Options Formats Hide Zeros command and select Yes.

Bear in mind that Quattro Pro 3 will hide only true zeroes, not numbers like 0.01 that a display format of one decimal place has rounded to 0. It also does not erase the contents of cells containing zero that are hidden. The zeroes return when you change the Hide Zeroes option to No. Since many of the cells producing zeroes may actually be formulas that need to become active if certain other cells receive values, be careful not to accidentally overwrite these apparently empty cells. To prevent accidental overwriting of cells, you can use the protection commands described later in this chapter.

Global Column Width

You have already seen that the column width can be changed for a single column with the Style Column Width command, or for all columns in a block with the Block Widths command. To change the global width of the columns in the current and successive worksheets, use Options Formats Global Width.

Recalculation Options

One of the great features of a spreadsheet is that you can enter numbers and formulas and immediately see the effect of changes. This feature is known as *automatic recalculation*, the constant rechecking of all cells affected by each new entry into the worksheet. However, such a powerful feature has its drawbacks: As your worksheet grows, the time taken for each new item to be checked against the other cells increases. This recalculation time can take so long that it slows down the entry of new data. To avoid this problem Quattro Pro 3 has an added feature called *background recalculation*. This allows you to carry on working while the program is recalculating in the background. You have three options for the mode of recalculation in Quattro Pro 3: Automatic, Manual, and Background. You are presented with these options when you select Mode from the Options Recalculation menu, as shown in Figure 6-2.

Since background recalculation does your math automatically while you work on other things, you may wonder what is the point of the other two

Figure 6-2. *The Recalculation options*

choices. You use the Manual option when you do not want new worksheet entries or changes to old ones to affect other cells. This is valuable when you have a lot of data to enter into a large worksheet that is beginning to slow down Quattro Pro 3's normally fast response time. Time is saved because in manual mode, the program does not check whether a newly entered formula affects other results on the worksheet.

Although manual mode means that your spreadsheet is not always up-to-date, Quattro Pro 3 has safeguards to prevent errors. Even when you are in manual mode, however, the program will calculate a formula as it is entered. It will also recalculate formulas that are edited or copied to other cells. Although Quattro Pro 3 will not update other cells when in manual mode, it does know when you make changes to the worksheet. It reminds you that you have made changes that may affect the contents of other cells by displaying the CALC message in the status area. Whenever it is convenient, for example, after entering a new set of data, you can press the Calc key (F9), and Quattro Pro 3 will perform a complete recalculation of the worksheet. The CALC message is removed to let you know all changes have been accounted for. If you use manual mode you should make sure that before you print, save, or make decisions based on the worksheet figures, you press the Calc key (F9). Otherwise, you may be working with inaccurate data.

The automatic mode of recalculation is primarily used as an alternative to background, the difference being that automatic mode will not let you proceed with further data entry until recalculation is complete. This can be annoying when your spreadsheet begins to grow and yet you do not want to switch to manual mode.

Order of Recalculation

The way in which Quattro Pro 3 calculates your spreadsheet is based on the natural mathematical relationship between cells in formulas. This is referred to as *natural recalculation*. The least dependent cells are calculated first, on through to the most dependent. Earlier spreadsheet programs could only calculate row by row down the spreadsheet or column by column across. These methods were called row-wise and column-wise respectively, but they were not always that wise. For example, row-wise calculations can produce errors if row 5 is based on the outcome of a calculation in row 10. Users of these programs usually worked around this problem and produced spreadsheet models that worked correctly if they were calculated in the correct order, either by column or by row. As you can see when you select Order from the Recalculation menu, Quattro Pro 3 allows you to emulate these earlier programs and so can accommodate spreadsheets designed to use these methods of calculation. Unless you know a specific reason why the worksheets you are working on will not be accurate unless calculated in a specific order, you will not need this option. Most Quattro Pro 3 users can enjoy the benefits of natural recalculation.

Iteration

Many of the problems of row-wise and column-wise calculations can be solved by repeating the calculation process a number of times to take care of such dependencies. The repetition of calculation is called *iteration*. You can use the Iteration option to repeat the recalculation process as many as 255 times each time you press F9. If you have selected row-wise or column-wise as the method of calculation, you should set iteration to at least 2 to avoid errors. If you are constructing complex financial formulas containing circular cell references that require a specific number of iterations to produce a correct answer, you can enter this number on the Iteration menu.

If you are using natural recalculation, Quattro Pro 3 refers to the iteration number only if you have circular references in the worksheet. The last item on the Recalculation menu is Circular Cell. This will show you the location of a circular cell reference in the worksheet if you have the CIRC message in the bottom status area of your screen. The CIRC message means you have entered a formula into a cell that uses the result of the cell to solve the formula. For example, @SUM(A1..A5) entered into any cell from A1 through A5 would create a circular reference. Sometimes it is difficult to see what is causing a CIRC message from just viewing the spreadsheet. Use Options Recalculation to see which cell contains the circular reference.

Note that the calculation preferences you select are specific to the worksheet, and the setting is stored with the worksheet. This helps to prevent errors and inconvenience. Whenever you retrieve that large spreadsheet in which you set recalculation to Manual, the mode is already set. But when you switch to a small worksheet where you have set recalculation to Background or Automatic, the correct mode is still in operation.

Protection

To preserve the hours of work that go into making a good worksheet and to allow less proficient users to enter data into a spreadsheet without undue risk of damaging its underlying formulas, Quattro Pro 3 provides several methods of cell and worksheet protection. You saw earlier that the Style menu has a protection option that allows you to specify the protected status of specific cells and groups of cells.

When you select Protection from the Options menu you have two choices: Enable and Disable. Selecting Enable is like placing a sheet of glass over the current worksheet. You will be able to see the data but you will not be able to change it. New data cannot be placed into the worksheet, and none of the cells can be edited. Selecting Disable turns off this protection. Saving a file with protection enabled means that anyone who retrieves the worksheet will have to turn off the protection before changing the data.

If you want to allow limited changes to cells on the worksheet, for example, for data entry work, you can turn on protection with Enable and then unprotect specific cells with the Style Protection Unprotect command. In this mode you can move around in the spreadsheet but only change those cells formatted with the Style Protection Unprotect command. These cells will appear highlighted, or in a different color, making it easy for data entry personnel to locate them. You can adjust the shading of unprotected cells with the Options Colors command described later in this chapter.

Going International

Having looked at the defaults that can be established for a particular worksheet, it is time to examine those aspects of Quattro Pro 3 that can be altered for an entire session or permanently. This section begins with the International options.

Quattro Pro 3 is used in many different countries that use various notations for numbers and dates. When you select International from the Options menu, as shown in Figure 6-3, you can see that there are several areas of the program that can be changed to accommodate the needs of users in other countries. In fact, you may want to use some of the options even if you are working in the United States. For example, when you are using Quattro Pro 3 for calculations in currencies other than U.S. dollars, you may want to change the way the Currency format displays your values. The values shown in Figure 6-3 are default settings for U.S. users.

Currency

You have seen that when you first install and use Quattro Pro 3 and select the Currency format, the program displays numbers in the form of U.S. currency. The dollar sign precedes the number, as in $50. When you select Currency from the International menu, you type the character you want for the monetary symbol. You can change the symbol for currency from the dollar sign to any other character. For example, you could change it to F for French francs or £ for British pounds, as shown in Figure 6-4.

To change the symbol for the currency, simply type the character you want in the dialog box that appears, and press ENTER. You will then be asked if this is to be a prefix preceding the value or a suffix following the value. When you select one of these two options, you are returned to the International menu.

Figure 6-3.   *International options*

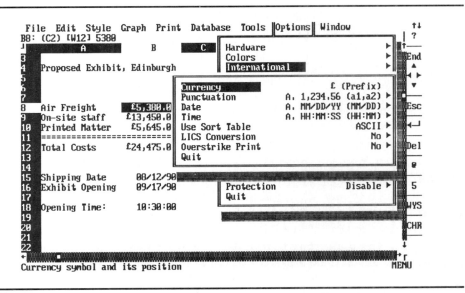

Figure 6-4.   *Using a different currency*

If the foreign character you want to use is not on your keyboard—such as the pound sign (£), which is not on American keyboards—you can choose the appropriate ASCII character from those shown in Figure 6-5. When prompted for the currency symbol, hold down the ALT key and type the number corresponding to the character you want from the numeric keypad (not the numbers across the top of the keyboard). Note that £ is 156, and 157 is the symbol used for Yen.

Punctuation

If you are preparing a French spreadsheet, you may want to make changes to the numbers in addition to changing the currency symbol. The French and other Europeans use different notations for thousands and decimals. Selecting the Punctuation option from the International menu reveals an extensive list of options, as shown in Figure 6-6. You can see that option A is the default whereas option B, which uses dots for thousands and commas for decimals, was used in the underlying worksheet.

The second column of the list of punctuation options refers to the character that is used when separating arguments in functions. Instead of

Figure 6-5. *An ASCII table*

Figure 6-6.   *Punctuation options*

commas between arguments, you can use periods, as in option F. Thus you would type **@PMT(PRINCIPAL.INTEREST.TERM)** instead of typing **@PMT(PRINCIPAL,INTEREST,TERM)**. You can also use semicolons, as in options C,D,G, and H.

Date

The way that dates are written varies greatly throughout the world. You can change the way Quattro Pro 3 displays dates in your worksheet. When you use the Style Numeric Format menu and select Date to assign a date format to a cell or group of cells, you have the following date style options:

1. DD-MMM-YY

2. DD-MMM

3. MMM-YY

4. Long International (day, month, and year)

5. Short International (day and month, or month and year)

The actual format used by items 4 and 5 will depend on the selection you make from the International menu. Normally, the Date option in the International menu is set to MM/DD/YY, which is how dates formatted with style number 4 appear. However, if you change the International Date setting to one of the other three possibilities, all dates in the current worksheet formatted with the D4 format will change to reflect the new format. These are the International date options:

1. MM/DD/YY (MM/DD)

2. DD/MM/YY (DD/MM)

3. DD.MM.YY (DD.MM)

4. YY-MM-DD (MM-DD)

You can see that each one has a long and short version. Dates formatted with the Short International format from the Style Numeric Format menu (D5) will appear in the short format shown in parentheses.

Remember that the format you select from the International Date menu is the one used by the on-screen calendar and clock display when you select International from the Clock option on the Options Other menu. This format is also used by the CTRL-D date entry command. For more discussion of dates, see Chapter 9.

Time

Just like dates, the way that times are written also varies considerably from country to country. When you are working with time values in a worksheet and want to format a value as a time, you select Time from the Style Numeric Format Date menu. These are the options:

1. HH:MM:SS (D6)

2. HH:MM (D7)

3. Long International (24-hour clock—hours, minutes, and seconds) (D8)

4. Short International (24-hour clock—hours and minutes) (D9)

These options, when applied to cells, are shown in the status line as D6 through D9. The choice you make in the Time option of the International defaults is reflected in the D8 and D9 time formats used in the worksheet, as well as in the on-screen calendar and clock display. Thus, the format you get when selecting items 3 and 4 will depend on the choice you make with the Options International Time command. Selecting Time from the International menu reveals the options shown in Figure 6-7. All of the international options for time use 24-hour notation, and each has both a long (D8) and a short (D9) form.

Other International Options

As businesses become increasingly cosmopolitan in their outlook and operations, it is necessary for software to accommodate the needs of a wider range of users. Quattro Pro 3 incorporates several enhancements in this area. These include Use Sort Table, LICS Conversion, and Overstrike Print on the Options International menu. Together with other features of

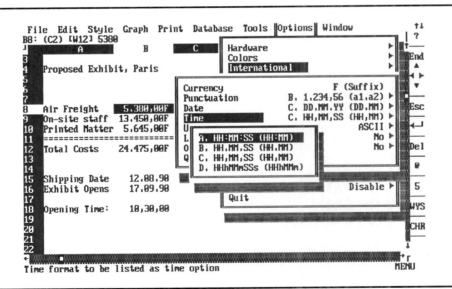

Figure 6-7.   *Time format options*

Quattro Pro 3 they should make it easier for overseas users to work with the program and for anyone to create more authentic and accurate foreign language documents.

Sort Tables

Quattro Pro 3 allows you to alter the treatment of foreign characters during Database Sort operations. The Use Sort Table command provides four options, which represent four different files with the extension SOR. These are files in which sorting order tables are stored. Select the one which is most appropriate to your needs:

ASCII.SOR   In an ascending sort this places uppercase letters before lowercase. This is because the capitals have lower ASCII values than lowercase letters. For the same reason, accented letters, which have high ASCII values, appear after z.

INTL.SOR   Short for "international," this table places uppercase and lowercase and accented letters into a continuous sequence just like that used in a dictionary: a,A,b,B,c,C and so on. A letter u with an umlaut appears with the u's as opposed to after the z's. This is the table most people will use unless they need ASCII sorting or wish to segregate certain foreign characters.

NORDAN.SOR   This is just like the international sort except that special characters used in Norway and Denmark, such as æ and ø, follow the regular alphabet.

SWEDFIN.SOR   Again, this is like the international sort except that special characters used in Sweden and Finland, such as å, follow the regular alphabet.

The SOR files used by Quattro Pro 3 are the same as those employed by Paradox and other Borland products. If you have any other SOR files in the Quattro Pro 3 program directory, then they will be included in the list displayed by the Use Sort Table command. Bear in mind that the Sort Rules command on the Database Sort menu also affects the sort order. You should coordinate the two settings. If you set Use Sort Table to ASCII you should use the ASCII setting for Label Order under Sort Rules in the

Database Sort menu. If you set Use Sort Table to anything other than ASCII, you should use the Dictionary setting for Label Order under Sort Rules in the Database Sort menu.

International Characters

There are several enhancements involving the printing of foreign characters, which are necessary for accuracy and authenticity in foreign documents.

Overstrike Print   Some printers, such as the Epson FX-80 and Diablo 630, can print accented characters *if* they are allowed to back up a space and overstrike the letter with the accent symbol. If you set Overstrike Print to Yes, this facility on your printer will be enabled. Other printers, such as the HP LaserJet, print accented letters as distinct characters and do not need this option turned on.

International Character Set   When installing Quattro Pro 3 you have the option of using an international character set as opposed to the normal U.S. character set. If you select the international set, the Bitstream fonts generated by Quattro Pro 3 will include 42 additional foreign characters. This option increases the time required to create each font and uses up more disk space. However, the international option gives you the ability to print characters that may be important if you need to prepare documents in foreign languages. The additional characters are shown in the Quattro Pro 3 manual. To switch between international and U.S. character sets you need to do the following:

1. Delete all existing font files. These files have the extension FON and are stored in the \FONTS subdirectory below the Quattro Pro 3 program directory. Enter the following command at the DOS prompt in the \FONTS directory:

   DEL *.FON

2. To change from U.S. to international rename all files with the SFO extension in the Quattro Pro 3 program directory to SFR, using the command:

   REN *.SFO *.SFR

3. To change from international to U.S. rename all SFR files in the Quattro Pro 3 program directory to SFO, using the command:

REN *.SFR *.SFO

Using LICS

The need to provide spreadsheet users with a means of representing foreign characters led Lotus to come up with a variation on standard ASCII. Known as the Lotus International Character Set, it can present a problem when reading WK1 spreadsheets into Quattro Pro 3. If you set LICS Conversion to Yes, then Quattro Pro 3 will read LICS characters into the equivalent ASCII characters when retrieving a WK1 file. Quattro Pro 3 will then convert the character back to LICS characters when saving the file in the WK1 format.

Startup Options

The Options Startup menu shown in Figure 6-8 covers several areas of Quattro Pro 3's operation that are effective when the program is first loaded. You can also use this menu to change some aspects of the way in which the menu system works.

Directory Options

In Chapter 1 you saw that the first time you use the File Save command, Quattro Pro 3 assumes you want to store your worksheet in the same area as the program files. You can use the File Directory command to change this choice for the current session. To use a new default area for storage at all times, you use the Directory option on the Startup menu. When you pick this option you get a dialog box like the one shown in Figure 6-9. The directory you set in this dialog box is the area in which you want the program to store your worksheets. It can be the name of any drive that you have available on your system, such as A:, B:, C:, D:, E:, and so on. You can

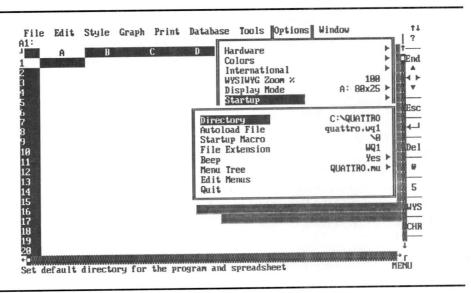

Figure 6-8. *The Startup menu*

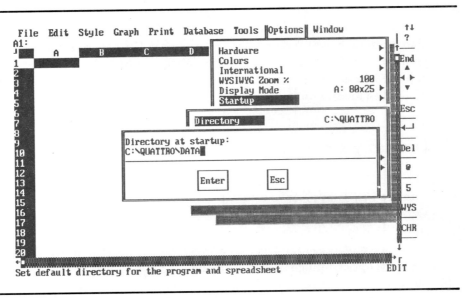

Figure 6-9. *Changing default directory*

follow the drive name with the name of the subdirectory that has been set up on that drive, such as \DATA or \QUATTRO\DATA.

If you want to use a directory that has not yet been created, use the File Utilities DOS Shell command to leave Quattro Pro 3 temporarily. This command returns you to the disk operating system, which you can use to create a directory. You can also create directories with Quattro Pro 3's File Manager, which you access from the File Utilities menu. Operating system commands are discussed in Chapter 7.

Automatic File Loading

You may find that your work with Quattro Pro 3 involves extensive use of one particular worksheet. For example, if you are almost exclusively pricing contracts, you may start with the same pricing spreadsheet every time you work with the program. To simplify your work, you can have Quattro Pro 3 retrieve a file automatically whenever the program is loaded. When you pick Autoload File from the Startup menu, you are asked to enter the name of the worksheet you want loaded whenever the program is started.

For example, if the file is a pricing spreadsheet called PRICING.WQ1, you simply type this name and press ENTER. You will immediately see the file listed on the menu. However, you must use the Update command on the Options menu to record this change and to make the autoload feature effective the next time the program is loaded. After you pick Update and reload Quattro Pro 3, the PRICING.WQ1 file will be retrieved. You can then enter the necessary data and save the new file under a different name, leaving the standard pricing worksheet unchanged on disk.

The autoload feature is always active. Whenever you load Quattro Pro 3 it looks for the file name that is recorded in the Startup menu. As you can see from Figure 6-8, the default name is QUATTRO.WQ1. If Quattro Pro 3 finds that file in the default directory when the program is loading, it retrieves the file. You can use the autoload feature either by changing the file name as just discussed, or you can save the file you want to autoload as QUATTRO.WQ1. This file can contain not only commonly used data, but it can also be a file of instructions. You could even produce a setup file for a novice Quattro Pro 3 user. You can also place macros, stored keystrokes, commands, and even custom menus in the autoload file to further assist the spreadsheet user. (If you also use 1-2-3, you can make the file called AUTO123.WK1 the autoload file name in order to use existing spreadsheets designed around this feature.)

Automatic Macro

You can designate a specific set of stored keystrokes (a macro) to be played back as soon as Quattro Pro 3 loads any spreadsheet containing the macro named in this section of the Startup menu. This autoload macro is initially called \0 (backslash zero). You can change the name to any valid macro name. (See Chapter 11 for more details on naming macros.) To supply a macro name, pick Startup Macro from the Startup menu. You can then type the name of the macro and press ENTER. Remember that to record this change to the automatic macro, you must use Update.

Each worksheet can have a macro with the designated autoload name. If you create an autorun macro in the autoload worksheet, you can have Quattro Pro 3 carry out a whole series of commands every time the program starts. This process enables you to provide automated applications for other users and is described in Chapter 12.

File Extensions

The file name used by Quattro Pro 3 when it stores your worksheets on disk consists of two parts. The first part of the name can be as many as eight characters long. The second part, separated from the first part by a period, can be three letters long and is called the *extension*. Initially, the program assigns the extension WQ1 to your worksheets. However, if you are sharing worksheets with a 1-2-3 user, you will want to save files with the WK1 extension so that 1-2-3 can read the files. You can make WK1 the default extension by selecting Extension from the Startup menu, typing **WK1**, and pressing ENTER. Note that you can always see both WQ1 and WK1 files on the file lists used by the File Open and Retrieve commands since Quattro Pro 3 looks for *.W??, which means any file name with *W* as the first letter of the extension and any other characters as the second and third. This wildcard pattern also lists files from earlier versions of Quattro, which have the extension WKQ.

To Beep or Not to Beep

If you press HOME and then press UP ARROW, **Quattro Pro 3** will beep to let you know that the key you pressed was not appropriate, because you cannot go up from the home position. The beep is designed to be helpful, and many users appreciate knowing they have pressed the wrong key when entering data and formulas. However, if you find this beep annoying, or if those around you object to it, you can turn it off by selecting Beep from the Startup menu. A small No/Yes box pops up.

You choose Yes to turn on the beep and No to turn it off. Turning off the beep can be helpful as a temporary measure when you are working on an airplane or in other close quarters where the noise of the beep would be distracting to others. If you want to keep the beep turned off in future work sessions, remember to use the Update option from the Startup menu to record your preference.

Menu Trees

As mentioned in Chapter 1, Quattro Pro 3 allows you to customize your menus. The feature of the program that does this is called the Edit Menu. A set of menus is called a *menu tree* and is stored in a file with the extension MU. You can create your own personalized menu tree and store it in an MU file. For example, if Debbie redefined her menu system, she could call it DEBBIE.MU. The Quattro Pro 3 program comes with three menu trees: QUATTRO.MU, the one that the program uses to begin with and which is pictured in most of the illustrations in this book; Q1.MU, which mimics the menus of the first version of Quattro; and 123.MU, which is designed for those who are familiar with 1-2-3 and want to operate Quattro Pro 3 with similar groupings of menu choices. You can see from the Startup menu that the current selection is QUATTRO.MU.

To activate a user menu tree other than the default QUATTRO.MU, you select Menu Tree from the Startup menu. You are presented with the following 1-2-3 menu tree, the original Quattro menu tree, and the standard Quattro Pro 3 menu tree. To change to the 1-2-3 menu tree, highlight the filename123.MU and press ENTER. You will be returned to the READY mode and the 1-2-3 menu will be in effect, as shown in Figure 6-10. To

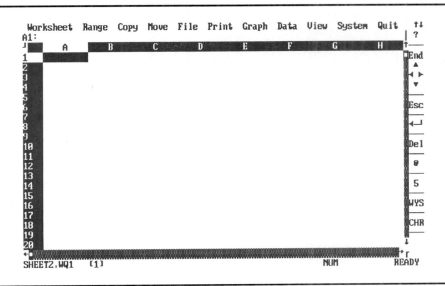

Figure 6-10.   *The 1-2-3 menu tree*

return to the Quattro Pro 3 menu, you pick Worksheet, Global, Default, Files, and Menu Tree, as shown in Figure 6-11. Then you can select the QUATTRO file from the list. You are returned immediately to the normal arrangement of menus. A change to the menu tree will remain in place after the current session only if you select Update to write the change to the RSC.RF file. To do this from the 1-2-3 menu system you select Worksheet, Global, Default, and Update. Note that the 1-2-3 menu tree shows Quattro-only commands with a small square next to them. All other menu items match those available in 1-2-3.

Edit Menus

Not only does Quattro Pro 3 allow you to choose from a range of alternative menu trees, but with the Edit Menu feature you can create your own. To alter your systems menus, select the Edit Menus command on the Options Startup menu. Suppose that you want to be able to select the Spreadsheet Print command from the File menu rather than from the Print menu. Using procedures that are described later in Chapter 12, you can use the

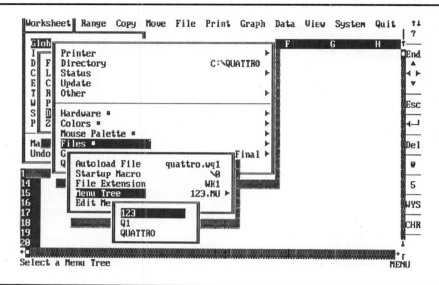

Figure 6-11.   *Using the 1-2-3 menus*

Edit Menu to redefine the File menu and change Spreadsheet Print on the Print menu to Print on the File menu.

About Your Hardware

The Hardware option on the Options menu is where you tell Quattro Pro 3 about your screen and printer. You can also use this menu to check the status of various aspects of your system, as you can see from Figure 6-12.

Screen Questions

When you installed Quattro Pro 3 on your PC you may have noticed that you did not have to specify what kind of display you were using. Quattro Pro 3 automatically detects the kind of display you have. In fact, if you are running Quattro Pro 3 on a system that has a color display and you need

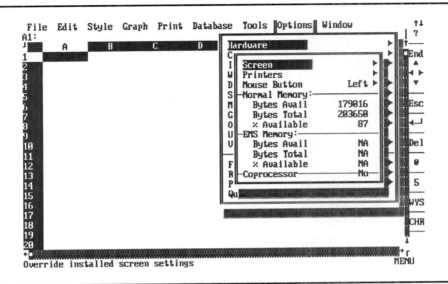

Figure 6-12. *The Hardware menu*

to move to a computer that has a monochrome display, you do not need to make any changes to the program disks.

When you pick Screen from the Hardware menu, you are presented with the menu shown in Figure 6-13. The menu has four commands besides Quit. The only time you will need to select the Screen option from the Hardware menu is if you are using a display system that Quattro Pro 3 does not know about or if you want to override the autodetect feature. If you want to change the color or shading of your display, you use the Colors command from the Options menu, rather than the Hardware command. If you want to change from character display to graphics display you use the Display Mode command described later in this chapter in the section of the same name.

Screen Type

The first Screen setting is Screen Type, and this is normally Autodetect. If your PC is displaying spreadsheets clearly, you do not need to change

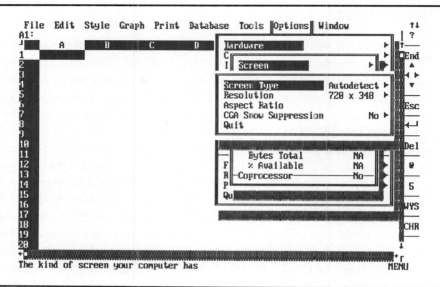

Figure 6-13. *Screen options*

the screen type. If you want to force Quattro Pro 3 to consider your display system to be a particular type, you can change to one of the listed alternatives.

Resolution

Graphic display systems create images from a collection of dots. The number of dots on a screen is referred to as the display's *resolution*. The resolution determines the sharpness of the displayed image. Resolution is measured by the number of dots across the screen and the number of lines of dots going down it, as in 640 × 200. Since some displays can operate at different resolutions, Quattro Pro 3 provides the Resolution option, which lets you choose between them. Note that you cannot change the screen resolution while in WYSIWYG mode. You must be in character mode to change resolution. The display modes are discussed in a moment.

Aspect Ratio

The ratio of the width of your monitor to its height is called the *aspect ratio*. This ratio affects the monitor's ability to show circles as truly round. Although Quattro Pro 3 can detect the display method used by your screen, it has no way of knowing the physical dimensions of the display. Dimensions vary from model to model. In fact, many models actually allow you to change the height of the screen display area, so different users of the same model can have different screen dimensions. For Quattro Pro 3 to display circles, such as those used in pie graphs, as circles and not as ellipses, you need to tell Quattro Pro 3 the aspect ratio of your screen. In some ways this is merely a cosmetic concern, since Quattro Pro 3 will print round pie graphs regardless of this setting. However, if you are using a screen capture system to make Quattro Pro 3 graphs part of a presentation, then entering the ratio can be important. When you are setting Aspect Ratio, you use the UP and DOWN ARROW keys to adjust the test circle, then press ENTER to accept the new ratios. Press ESCAPE to abort the process.

Suppressing Snow

If you are using a CGA display system, that is, one based on the old IBM Color Graphics Adaptor, you may find that certain actions in Quattro Pro 3 produce a fuzzy effect on the screen. This is referred to as "snow" and can usually be eliminated by setting CGA Snow Suppression to Yes.

About Printers

At the Hardware menu you can select Printers to let Quattro Pro 3 know about the equipment you will be using for hard copy. As you can see from Figure 6-14, you can define two printers and select one of them as the default.

When you pick 1st Printer you see the menu shown in Figure 6-15. This lists the current settings, including Make and Model. If you selected a printer during installation, it will be listed here. If you did not select a printer during installation, you can do so now by selecting the first menu item, Type of printer. If you want to define a second printer, use the 2nd Printer option on the Printers menu and select Type of printer.

Figure 6-14. *Printer options*

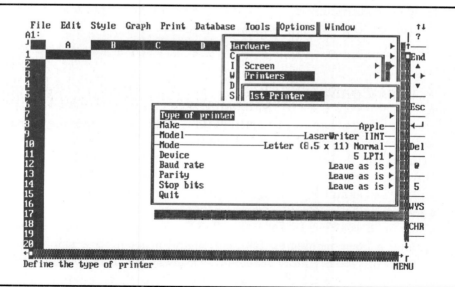

Figure 6-15. *Selecting printer type*

When you select Type of printer, you will see a list of brand names, such as Apple, EPSON, and HP. After picking the correct brand name for the printer you want to use, pick the exact model name. In some cases, such as the HP LaserJet II, you will also need to pick the print resolution that you want to use. When you have selected the type of printer, you are returned to the menu shown in Figure 6-15.

The options on this menu allow you to modify Quattro Pro 3 so that it can work with a wide range of printing devices. When you select Device you have 10 options, which represent a variety of ports on your computer. Most printers are parallel printers on port number 1, which is the first item on the list. If you are printing over a network, you may need to select LPT1 instead of Parallel-1. The EPT option sends printed output to an IBM laser printer. The PRN option sends printed output to an ASCII print file. If you pick a serial option you must select various parameters to match your printer input requirements.

Baud, Stop Bits, and Parity   If you have a serial printer, you may need to match it to Quattro Pro 3 by using settings such as Baud rate, Stop bits, and Parity. Consult your printer manual for the correct baud rate, stop bits, and parity setting. You may need to use the DOS command MODE to prepare your serial printer for use with Quattro Pro 3; this will be described in your printer manual. The Leave as is setting tells Quattro Pro 3 to use the current DOS Mode settings.

Printer Control

Having selected the correct settings on the 1st Printer menu, you return to the main Options Hardware Printers menu. Here you can choose 2nd Printer and define a completely different printer model. The Options Hardware Printer menu is also where you decide which of the two printers will be the Default Printer. Quattro Pro 3 lets you redefine printers during a session, but it needs to know which printer is the one to use. The printers are defined as either 1st Printer or 2nd Printer. For example, suppose you defined a laser printer as 1st Printer and a dot matrix printer as 2nd Printer, and you normally print on the laser. You would set Default Printer to 1st Printer. If you had to print invoices with carbon copies using the dot matrix, you would use Options Hardware Printers and select Default Printer. You would then select 2nd Printer. The 2nd Printer would remain the current printer until the end of the current session. Bear in mind that if you issue the Options Update command while Default Printer is defined as 2nd Printer, then 2nd Printer will be the default in the next session as well.

When Quattro Pro 3 is printing it needs to know how certain aspects of print operations will be controlled. These options relate to plotter operation, fonts, line feeds, and sheet feeding.

Plotter Speed   This setting allows you to slow down the speed at which the plotter pen moves if you are using a plotter. This can be helpful when you are plotting onto some materials that are apt to smudge when written on at high speed. The default setting of 0 is the fastest plotter speed. Using a higher number will slow the plotter down.

Fonts   As you saw in Chapter 5, Quattro Pro 3 provides extensive support for fonts, allowing you to print and display text in a variety of typefaces, sizes, and styles. You can print out a mixture of fonts in a worksheet report when you use Spreadsheet Print after setting the print destination to Graphics Printer. You can see a worksheet report formatted with fonts if you set the print destination to Screen Preview. You can view fonts in a graph if you use the Graph View command (F10). Graphs always print with their assigned fonts. You assign fonts to graphs with the Graph Text command, described in Chapter 8. Fonts for worksheets are assigned under the Style Font menu, discussed in Chapter 5.

Your font-printing capability depends to a certain extent on your printer. If you have installed a printer that uses font cartridges, such as the HP LaserJet, then Quattro Pro 3 allows you use the Fonts option to specify which cartridges are installed. For example, the HP LaserJet II has a left and right cartridge. When you select the Left Cartridge you get a list of possible cartridges from which to select, a list that will be familiar to users of the LaserJet. You can use the cursor movement keys to scroll down the list. To tell Quattro Pro 3 about your printer, simply highlight the name/letter of the cartridge that you have in the left cartridge slot of your printer and press ENTER. Quattro Pro 3 returns you to the Printers menu. You can repeat the process for the right cartridge if you have a set of fonts installed there. The same menu is also used to set the level of gray used when your LaserJet printer prints the Style Shading format.

The other option on the Fonts menu is Autoscale Fonts. This controls Quattro Pro 3's automatic font scaling option for graphs. The default setting is Yes, which means Quattro Pro 3 adjusts font point size to fit the dimensions of a graph. If you set this option to No, Quattro Pro 3 prints graph fonts in exact point size regardless of graph dimensions.

Auto LF Most printers today do not have an automatic line feed. Instead, the software tells the printer to advance the paper after each line of text. However, if you have a printer that adds a line feed after a line of text, you may find your output is unintentionally double spaced. If this is the case, change the Auto LF setting to Yes to solve this problem.

Single Sheet You activate this option by picking Yes from the Yes/No choice box. Picking Yes will cause Quattro Pro 3 to pause and then prompt you to insert paper in a single-sheet printer. Note that this is only required for manual feed printers; do not select Yes for this option if you are using an HP LaserJet or some other printer that continually feeds sheets from a paper tray.

Other Hardware

At the Hardware menu you can see three items with a line through them that cannot be selected. These items are simply status reports. Several Quattro Pro 3 menus use this display style to show that the items are not active choices.

Normal Memory The random-access memory, or *RAM*, in your computer is the area in which most of your work with Quattro Pro 3 takes place. The size of this area is measured in bytes, and the normal memory indicator on the status line tells you how much RAM is still available. When you turn on your PC, the RAM area is empty, but shortly after the system starts up, the core of the disk operating system (DOS) is loaded into RAM. The amount of memory DOS takes depends on the version of DOS you are using. Version 3.3 uses about 60,000 bytes or 60K (there are 1024 bytes in 1 kilobyte or 1K). When you load Quattro Pro 3 it takes up space in RAM. As you enter data into a worksheet, the amount of available RAM decreases. For example, the sample worksheet shown in Chapter 5 occupies 3K of RAM. You can monitor your use of RAM by periodically using the Options Hardware command or the @MEMAVAIL function described in Chapter 13.

Expanded Memory   A lot of computers have 640K of RAM because that is the most that can be recognized by versions of DOS up to version 3.3. However, numerous hardware and software manufacturers have designed ways of adding memory that can be recognized by programs. This is called *expanded memory,* or EMS. If you have such memory installed, Quattro Pro 3 will recognize it and report its status on the EMS section. If you have expanded memory in your PC but it is not shown on this menu, check that you have installed the drivers that came with the board. You can use the @MEMEMSAVAIL function to report available memory in a worksheet, as described in Chapter 13. For more on the types of memory and how to utilize memory effectively with Quattro Pro 3, see Appendix A.

Coprocessor   There is one computer chip inside your PC that does most of the processing of data. This chip is called the *CPU,* or *central processing unit.* Typically these units are called 8088, 80286, or 80386. However, many PCs have room for additional chips that can share the processing load. These are called *coprocessors,* and Quattro Pro 3 will detect and use one if it is installed. The most common type of coprocessor helps the CPU take care of mathematical calculations. Called numeric or math coprocessors, these units are typically named 8087, 80287, or 80387. You can see from the Hardware menu whether Quattro Pro 3 has found a coprocessor in your system. If you have a coprocessor physically installed in your system but it is not listed on the Hardware menu, recheck the installation instructions for the chip.

Display Mode

On today's PCs there are two basic technologies for displaying information on the screen: character mode and graphics mode. In character mode the display is made up of 2000 characters arranged in 25 lines of 80 characters each. This is the default mode used by Quattro Pro 3 and the one seen in most of the screens in this book. The alternative is a graphics mode known in Quattro Pro 3 as WYSIWYG, where the screen is composed of a series of dots that draw shapes, including numbers, text, and circles. The WYSIWYG mode offers advantages when it comes to drawing pictures such as charts. The disadvantage is that WYSIWYG mode requires a lot of memory and responds more slowly than character mode.

Quattro Pro 3 has the unique ability to switch between different modes of display as described in Chapter 1. This means that typical spreadsheet operations such as data entry and calculation can take place in the faster environment of character mode. However, when you want to design a high-quality report or a graph, you can switch to WYSIWYG mode. The mode that Quattro Pro 3 uses when you load the program is determined by the Options Display Mode setting. The first option on the Display Mode menu is 80x25, which is also known as character mode. The second option is WYSIWYG mode. If you use the Options Update command, then the current Display Mode selection becomes the default setting. However, the bottom two mouse buttons, WYS and CHR, allow you to switch display modes without using the Options menu or altering the default setting.

In addition to the 80x25 character mode, some EGA and VGA systems support more characters and lines, such as 80x43. If your screen is one of these, you can choose a higher density character display mode. However, such modes are not WYSIWYG and will not show font changes and grid lines.

Changing Attributes and Colors

Through the Options Colors command Quattro Pro 3 provides tremendous flexibility in the way the various elements of the program are displayed on your monitor. As you can see from Figure 6-16, a system of menus allows you to choose how each part of the screen is displayed. If your screen can display colors, Quattro Pro 3 lets you customize the colors used by the different parts of the spreadsheet. For example, you can have a brown background with the cell selector in blue with white letters, or a white background with blue letters. The number of possible combinations are far too numerous to describe. If you have a monochrome display, you can control the video attributes of the screen, choosing between Normal, Bold, Inverse, Underlined, and Empty attributes. In Figure 6-17, the first choice on the Colors menu, Menu, has been selected to show you the range of possibilities for monochrome users.

At first the ability to change shades and colors may seem somewhat frivolous. However, such changes can improve efficiency. For example,

Figure 6-16. *Setting colors*

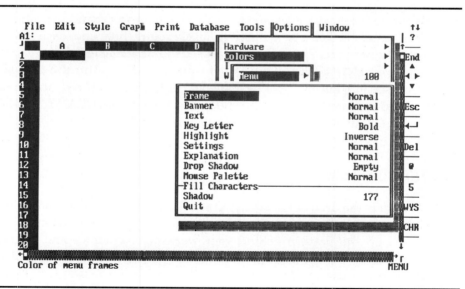

Figure 6-17. *The Menu settings*

special shading can be assigned to negative numbers, thus making them easier to locate. Labels can be displayed differently than values and make the spreadsheet easier to read. You can even tell Quattro Pro 3 to highlight values outside of specified ranges, thus alerting users to incorrect answers.

If you have a color display system or one that emulates a color system and a black-and-white or LCD screen, changing the shading can be very useful. For example, if you are using a laptop computer with an LCD screen, you will probably find the standard Quattro Pro 3 colors hard to read when they are interpreted by your system. Changing them can enhance their legibility. Even if you have a full-size color display and see Quattro Pro 3 in vibrant colors, you may not like the the default program colors.

Changing Colors

When you pick Colors from the Options menu the first item is Menu. When you choose this option you can see how Quattro Pro 3 breaks down the parts of the menu and—if you have a color monitor—the current color settings. These are shown in Figure 6-18. Suppose you want to alter the color of the menu frame. You select Frame and immediately a small paint box of colors appears with the current setting marked by a rotating cursor. By using the cursor-movement keys you can move around the paint box. Each band of color is a different background hue and each dot is a foreground shade. When you have placed the cursor on the choice you want you press ENTER. The choice is immediately reflected in the text of the menu setting, but may not be displayed until you use the Quit command to leave the menu system. Quit takes you back to the READY mode. You can adjust all of the areas listed in Table 6-3.

Fill Characters

Desktop is the area of the screen that is behind your worksheets. The Fill Characters used in Menu and Desktop refer to the way Quattro Pro 3 makes up the pattern behind your worksheet windows and menus in character mode. The pattern is simply a repetition of the shading character. You can use the ASCII chart in Figure 6-5 to choose an alternative character, and enter the number under Fill Characters.

Menu
    Frame
    Banner
    Text
    Key Letter
    Highlight
    Settings
    Explanation
    Drop Shadow
    Mouse Palette
    Fill Characters—Shadow

Desktop
    Status
    Highlight-Status
    Errors
    Background
    Fill Characters—Desktop

Spreadsheet
    Frame
    Banner
    Cells
    Borders
    Titles
    Highlight
    Graph Frames
    Input Line
    Unprotected
    Labels
    Shading
    Drawn Lines
    WYSIWYG Colors

Spreadsheet WYSIWYG
    Background
    Cursor
    Grid Lines
    Unprotected
    Drawn Lines
    Shaded Cells
    Locked Titles Text
    Titles Background
    Row and Column Labels
        Highlight
        Shadow
        Face
        Text

Conditional
    On/Off
    ERR
    Smallest Normal Value
    Greatest Normal Value
    Below Normal Color
    Normal Cell Color
    Above Normal Color

Help
    Frame
    Banner
    Text
    Keywords
    Highlight

File Manager
    Frame
    Banner
    Text
    Active cursor
    Inactive cursor
    Marked
    Cut
    Copy

Table 6-3.   *Color Settings*

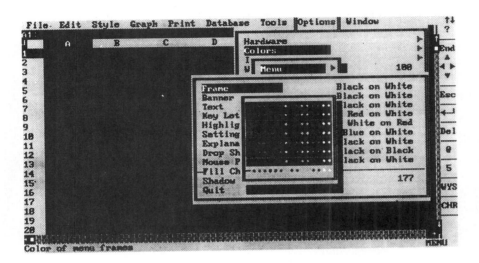

Figure 6-18. *Menu Frame colors*

Spreadsheet

The parts of the spreadsheet that you can color are listed in Table 6-3. Two areas that deserve special attention are Unprotected and Labels. The Unprotected option lets you choose a special color or shading scheme for cells that are specifically protected or unprotected. This coloring helps you distinguish these cells more clearly. Note that Quattro Pro 3's initial color and shading settings already distinguish these cells. You may also find it helpful and attractive to see cells that contain labels displayed with a different color or attribute. The Labels option allows you to do this. You can make column and row headings form a contrasting frame around the calculation areas.

Another interesting option on the Options Colors Spreadsheet menu is WYSIWYG Colors. This option, new in Quattro Pro 3, allows you to fine tune the appearance of your screen in WYSIWYG mode. The possibilities here are extensive, with all areas of the screen adjustable, as listed in Table

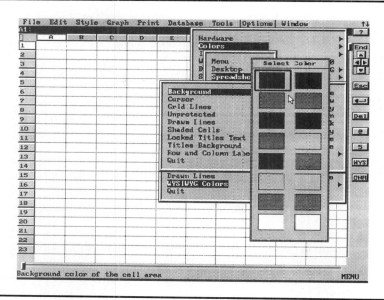

Figure 6-19. *WYSIWYG colors*

6-3. You can see the areas listed in Figure 6-19, where the user is selecting from the color palette that appears when using Options Colors in WYSIWYG mode.

Conditional

Possibly the most exciting of Quattro Pro 3's colorization options is Conditional. When you select this item from the Color menu, you see the menu shown in Figure 6-20. (Note that the settings on this menu are for a monochrome system and have been changed from the defaults for purposes of illustration.) The Conditional menu allows you to change the color or attributes of cells based on the value of their contents. Thus, negative numbers could be shown in bold, ERR cells in an eye-catching inverse, and so on. You can even set value parameters so that Quattro Pro 3 will highlight excessively high or low numbers.

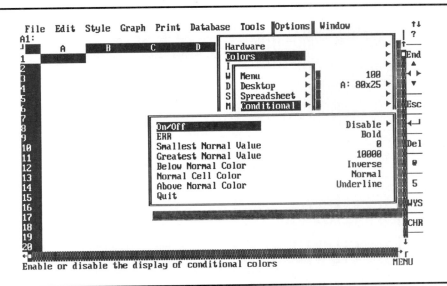

Figure 6-20. *Conditional settings*

On/Off Since the use of different colors or shadings for cells based on the value of their contents can be disconcerting to those not used to this feature, it can be turned off. When you select On/Off from the Conditional menu, you can select either Enable or Disable to activate or deactivate the conditional coloring of cells.

ERR You can bring errors to people's attention more dramatically by setting a special coloring for any cell that has the contents ERR. When the error is resolved and the ERR content is changed to a correct result, the cell color will return to normal.

Value Colors If you select Smallest Normal Value or Greatest Normal Value from the Conditional menu, you can set value limits beyond which Quattro Pro 3 alters the color of cells selected with the Normal Cell Color and Above Normal Color options. This feature is particularly helpful for data-entry personnel because it can visually alert them to data-entry mistakes that result in numbers that are outside of expected ranges.

Since a set of conditional parameters can be disabled with the On/Off option, you can easily activate it temporarily to help inexperienced users. For example, highlighting of error cells and abnormally low or high entries can be turned on to help data- entry personnel, possibly by using a macro, as will be described in Chapter 11. The conditional coloring can be turned off for more experienced users. Remember that conditional color settings, like all the other customized color settings, are not permanently stored until you use the Update option on the Default menu to write the current settings to the configuration file.

Help

You can customize the appearance of the help screens with the Help option on the Colors menu. This option divides the help screen into five areas. The Frame is the edge of the help screen; Banner is the heading for the screen; and Text is the actual wording of the help information. The Keywords are words that are used to select further help screens, and the Highlight is the shading you move around the help screen to pick keywords.

Color Palettes

The Palettes option on the Colors menu lets you select the standard color settings. This option is useful when you want to restore the original settings. When you select Palettes from the Colors menu, the choices are Color, Monochrome, Black & White, Gray Scale, and Quit. You could use this menu, for example, to temporarily switch between a customized set of colors that were stored in your RSC.RF file and the standard palette.

The Mouse Palette

If you are using a mouse you may want to alter the selections available to you in the mouse palette at the right of the screen. There are a total of seven buttons to which you can assign keystrokes. Note that these are the target areas of the palette on the right, not the actual buttons you press on your mouse.

The first four buttons are already assigned as Escape, Enter, Delete, and @, which activates the list of @ functions. You can attach whatever you want to button 5, whereas 6 and 7 are used for switching between WYSIWYG and character display modes. You can alter all of the buttons, but this is not recommended unless you are sure you know what you are doing. As you can see from Figure 6-21, the definition box for each mouse button consists of two fields: Text and Macro. The Text is a selection of three letters, such as *Esc,* or three ASCII characters that represent ENTER. You can see from Figure 6-21 that the 5th Button is marked by a **5**. The Macro field is where you tell Quattro Pro 3 what keys you want the button to type. You enter a macro code for the keystrokes, such as {ESC} for Escape, ~ for ENTER, or {BEEP} to cause a beep when you pick the inactive button 5. See Chapter 11 for more on macro codes.

As an example of expanding the mouse palette, suppose that you want clicking button 5 to be the same as pressing the HOME key. You select 5th Button and then Text. You type **Top**, or **Hom**, or any other three characters to represent *Home*. Then you press ENTER and select Macro, type

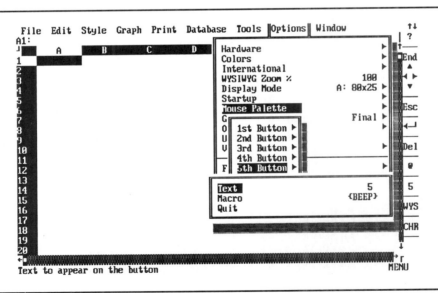

Figure 6-21. *Mouse palette settings*

{HOME}, and press ENTER. When you quit back to the READY mode you can then use button 5 to take you to the top of your worksheet.

Graphics Quality Control

The Options Graphics Quality command allows you to control when Quattro Pro 3 creates or renders Bitstream high quality fonts. Select the default setting of Final and Quattro Pro 3 will always use the Bitstream fonts you request for screen display and printing. Select Draft and Quattro Pro 3 will only use the Bitstream fonts you request if they have already been rendered. Otherwise, Quattro Pro 3 uses Hershey fonts to simulate the approximate appearance of the Bitstream fonts.

Other Options

There are several useful options grouped under the heading "Other." This is where you enable the Undo command that reverses many of the commands and actions that you perform with Quattro Pro 3. When Undo is Enabled the Undo key, ALT-F5, can undo the actions listed in Table 6-4.

The Macro command allows you to adjust screen updating during macros for faster execution. The choices are Both, Panel, Window, and None. The Both option gives the fastest macro operation, but it can make macros hard to follow when you are debugging them. The None option is the slowest. The Expanded Memory command determines what information can be placed in extra memory if you have such memory installed. See Appendix A for more on the types of memory and what you can store there.

The Clock command allows you to turn on and off the display of the date and time in the lower left corner of the screen. You can either display the date and time in Standard format or in International format, which will be the format currently in effect from the International Date and Time options. The Paradox command allows you to fine tune the use of Paradox data files over a network. You can tell Quattro Pro 3 where to look for data and for the PARADOX.NET file. For more on network operations, see Appendix B. For more on working with Paradox, see Chapter 13.

The following items can be reversed with Undo:

■ Making a new spreadsheet entry

■ Changing a spreadsheet entry

■ Deleting a spreadsheet entry

■ Deleting a named graph

■ Deleting a block name

■ Retrieving a file

■ Erasing a spreadsheet

■ Using Undo

The following cannot be reversed by Undo:

■ Command settings

■ Style and format settings

■ File Manager operations

Note that Undo always reverses the last undoable action. If you retrieve a file (undoable) then use the Style command to format cells (not undoable) then press Undo, the File Retrieve will be reversed, not the Style commands. Just press Undo again to reverse Undo.

Table 6-4. *Actions That Can and Cannot Be Reversed with Undo*

File Edit Style Graph Print Database Tools ‖Options‖ Window

Macro Recording	Logical
Default Printer	1st Printer
Startup Directory	C:\QUATTRO
Autoload File	quattro.wq1
Startup Macro	\0
File Extension	WQ1
Graphics Quality	Final
Undo	Enable
SQZ! Remove Blanks	No
Screen Type	Autodetect Driver
Clock	None
Sort Numbers Before Labels	No
Label Order	ASCII
Paradox Access Load File	ANSWER.DB
Paradox Access Autoload	Yes
International Currency	$ (Prefix)

Status of many of the settings saved with Options‖Update   MENU

Figure 6-22. *Options Value menu*

Conclusions

The Quattro Pro 3 Options menu is a powerful tool for extensive personalizing of the program. You can save a lot of time by making your preferred choices permanent program choices with the Update option. When you want a summary of the default settings, use the Options Values command. This produces the display shown in Figure 6-22. You will note two items that are not covered in the Options menu: Macro Recording and SQZ! Remove Blanks. The Macro Recording setting is determined by the Tools Macro menu, and the SQZ! settings are controlled by the File Utilities SQZ! menu.

7 *Handling Files*

In this chapter you will learn how to work with multiple windows and linked files and how to bring data into a Quattro Pro 3 spreadsheet from other programs such as dBASE and 1-2-3. Doing so enables you to share and exchange data with other users. To simplify file-management tasks Quattro Pro 3 provides a feature called the File Manager. Using the File Manager you can manipulate files and organize your hard disk without leaving Quattro Pro 3. The chapter begins with a review of the basic procedures for saving and retrieving worksheets.

The Filing Process

The File menu shown in Figure 7-1 is one of the most important menus in Quattro Pro 3. You use this menu to store and retrieve your worksheet files. You have seen that the data you enter into a worksheet window is not immediately stored in a worksheet file on disk. Instead, it is temporarily retained in the computer's memory. The memory area, the random access memory (RAM), is like an electronic desktop. Because it is electronic, the work that you do there, such as entering and calculating, is performed very quickly. By retaining most of your worksheet in memory while you manipulate it, Quattro Pro 3 can provide fast responses and rapid calculations. However, even an electronic desktop has its disad-

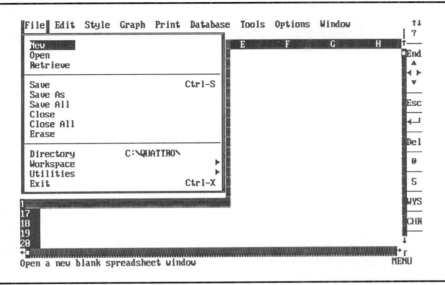

Figure 7-1. *The File menu*

vantages. The problem with RAM is that everything you have entered into it is erased when the power to your PC is turned off or interrupted. Although Quattro Pro 3 records all of your keystrokes as you work, just in case you need to recover from a disaster like a power loss, it is important to use the File menu on a regular basis to transfer a copy of the worksheet from memory to disk.

Operating System Basics

For those who do not completely understand how a computer manipulates disk storage and memory operations, this section describes what happens when you turn on your PC. The first thing a computer does when you flip on the switch is to look to the disk drives to find information stored on disks. Disks are made of the same material as cassette tapes and video cassettes. On a disk, this magnetic storage medium is laid out flat and divided into a series of concentric circles. Information is both read from and written to a disk by a moving head. This head is essentially the same as a head in a cassette tape player.

The first piece of information that the computer looks for is the operating system. On an IBM PC or PC-compatible, the operating system is called the *disk operating system,* or DOS. This system can be either PC-DOS (distributed by IBM) or MS-DOS, which is the version licensed by Microsoft to many other computer manufacturers. When the computer finds DOS, it reads the essential parts from the disk and loads them into memory. While the disk and disk drive use a combination of electronic and mechanical components, the computer's memory is purely electronic. It is a place where information can be changed much faster than on a disk. Quattro Pro 3 takes good advantage of this speed: as much of the program is loaded into memory as will fit. The amount of program in memory is adjusted to make room for data as your worksheets expand and you open more worksheet windows. This is done automatically by Quattro Pro 3—you do not have to worry about it.

The role of DOS is twofold. First, it is a flow manager, managing the flow of information in and out of the computer. When you type the letter *q,* DOS makes sure that a *q* appears on the screen and that the character is stored and printed as a *q.* When you give a command to print out data, Quattro Pro 3 passes that request on to DOS for execution. The second role for DOS is as a file manager. The information your computer uses is stored in either program files or data files. The arrangement of these files on the disk is managed by DOS. Thus, DOS actually executes your request to Quattro Pro 3 to store data on disk.

Once the computer has loaded DOS, it can start handling your information. Two important pieces of information that are usually supplied to the disk operating system at this point are the date and the time. You can type these manually or they may be read from a clock within the computer. Quattro Pro 3 uses the date and time for the optional on-screen clock display. DOS stores a record of when a file is written to the disk and displays this date and time when files are listed. This information can help you manage files.

Loading Programs

After the date and time have been entered into memory, the computer wants to know what programs you wish to execute. The way it asks you this is to display the *system prompt.* The prompt can consist of several pieces of information. The first is usually the name of the drive that the computer is using (normally C for a hard drive). The second is the *cursor*. The cursor points out where you are and where the next character you type will appear.

To start running a program, you normally type the name of the program at the system prompt and press ENTER to send the request to the disk operating system. DOS will then look on the disk for the program and begin to load it into memory. In the case of Quattro Pro 3, this means you type **Q** and press ENTER. You do not have to worry about upper- or lowercase letters when sending information to DOS, which does not distinguish between the two. When you ask Quattro Pro 3 to store information on disk and Quattro Pro 3 passes this request on to DOS, you can type the name of the file in either upper- or lowercase. However, DOS will store the name in all capital letters.

Data Entry

When you have loaded Quattro Pro 3 you are ready to enter worksheet data. When you first type labels, values, and formulas, the data is held in RAM. The program does not store the worksheet on disk as you build it. Later, you must issue a command to tell Quattro Pro 3 to store the worksheet. However, the program has a special file that contains a log of your keystrokes, and this information is recorded on disk as you type. If you suddenly lose power and RAM is erased, Quattro Pro 3 can recover your work from the keystroke log. Of course, you should save your worksheet file in the normal manner, rather than relying on rebuilding the file from the keystroke log.

Naming Files

Every file in the same directory of a disk must have a unique name. This name is composed of three parts: a file name, a period, and an optional extension. The file name consists of one to eight letters or numbers without spaces. You can use some punctuation marks in a file name, but it is usually easier to use numbers and letters rather than to try to remember which punctuation marks are acceptable. Valid punctuation characters in a file name are

( ) ! @ # $ % & - _ ' { } ~ ' ^

If you use invalid characters, DOS responds with "Invalid File Name" and so does Quattro Pro 3.

One piece of punctuation has a special role in file names: the period. It connects the file name with its extension. The extension is usually three characters long and follows the same rules as those for file names. When they are used, extensions are often chosen to distinguish between types of files. For example, Quattro Pro 3 worksheets have the extension WQ1. Earlier versions of Quattro used the extension WKQ. 1-2-3 files use WKS or WK1, depending on the version of the program (version 1 uses WKS; version 2 uses WK1). Quattro Pro 3 normally assigns an extension to the file name you create depending upon what kind of data you are saving in the file. Table 7-1 lists several Quattro Pro 3 files, showing their extensions and their use. If you want Quattro Pro 3 to save to a format that can be read by another program—for example, 1-2-3—simply enter the file name and the appropriate extension. For example, Quattro Pro 3 would save BUDGET.WK1 as a 1-2-3 file. If you want Quattro Pro 3 to use a particular extension all the time, you can enter that extension as part of the program defaults using the Options Startup File Extension command described in the previous chapter.

Copying Files

At the DOS prompt you can copy files from one disk to another, from one subdirectory of a disk to another, and from one file name to another. If you want to copy a group of files, you use special characters called wildcards to denote more than one file, as in

COPY *.WQ1 A:

This command tells the system to copy all Quattro Pro 3 spreadsheet files in the current directory of the current disk to the disk in drive A. The command

COPY SALES.W?? A:

tells the system to copy all of the worksheet files related to the SALES database (including WKS, WK1, WKQ, as well as WQ1 files) to drive A. The asterisk is used to represent a number of characters, whereas the

Name	Extension	Date	Time	Comment (added to the DOS listing)
.	<DIR>	5-26-90	7:30p	The current directory
..	<DIR>	5-26-90	7:30p	The parent directory
Q	EXE 85162	1-27-91	3:00a	A program file
QUATTRO	HLP 437784	1-27-91	3:00a	The Quattro Pro 3 help file
RSC	RF 3751	12-02-91	9:48a	The standard default file
QUATTRO	MU 253514	12-02-91	9:48a	The standard Quattro Pro 3 menus
123	MU 231848	12-01-91	2:13p	A set of 1-2-3 style menus
123	RF 3751	1-27-91	3:00a	A default file for 1-2-3 mode
Q123	BAT 19	1-27-91	3:00a	A batch file to convert to 1-2-3 mode
SWEDFIN	SOR 1637	1-27-91	3:00a	A sort file
QUATTRO	LOG 1060	12-02-91	9:48a	The Transcript log file
SALESTAT	WQ1 4013	11-20-91	10:19p	A Quattro Pro 3 worksheet file
SALESTAT	WK1 4004	11-20-91	10:30p	A 1-2-3 worksheet file
SALESTAT	WKQ 4028	11-20-91	10:30p	A Quattro 1.0 worksheet file
REPORT1	PRN 688	11-23-91	11:50a	A print file
DRUMS	SND 37920	1-27-91	3:00a	A sound file
YEN	CGM 1272	10-02-90	1:00a	A CGM art file
AIRPLANE	CLP 442	10-05-90	2:00a	A clip art file
SALES	<DIR>	5-26-90	7:44p	A sub-directory
DATA	<DIR>	5-26-90	7:44p	Another sub-directory

Table 7-1.   *A Partial Listing of Files Used by Quattro Pro 3 as They Appear in a DOS Directory Listing with Added Comments*

question mark is used to represent a single character. Thus, SALES?A.* includes SALES1A.WQ1 and SALES2A.WK1 but not SALES3.WQ1.

As shown in Table 7-1, the size of files is measured in *bytes*. This is a relative measure of electronic space. One byte is the amount of space it takes to store one character, number, space, or piece of punctuation. However, you cannot directly relate the size of a data file to the number of characters you type into it. For example, files may contain information about how the data is arranged. Quattro Pro 3 stores a typical worksheet of 1800 active cells containing over 30,000 characters in 80,000 bytes of disk space. If you use the SQZ! option described later, you can store the same worksheet in 24,000 bytes.

Since one byte is a minute unit of measurement, you will often see bytes measured in units of *kilobytes*, abbreviated as *K*. Each kilobyte is 1024 bytes. Do not worry about the extra 24; just use 1000 when converting from bytes to kilobytes. Thus, a worksheet that contains 82,944 bytes can be described as 83K in size. When files get really big they occupy megabytes. One *megabyte*, or *MB*, is 1000K, or a million bytes. The capacity of your disks is usually measured in kilobytes and megabytes. The standard 5 1/4-inch floppy disk stores 360K. The high-density 5 1/4-inch disks used in the IBM PC AT can store 1.2 megabytes. The hard-jacketed 3 1/2-inch disks used in many laptop PCs can store 720K, or 1.4 megabytes, depending on how they are formatted. Most hard disks hold at least 10 megabytes and can be several hundred megabytes in capacity.

Disks and Directories

Just as Quattro Pro 3 comes to you on disks, data created with the help of programs is also stored on disks. Information is stored on disks in files. As you work with your computer you quickly create many files. To keep these files manageable, there is a practical limit to how many files you should store on a disk. (An actual limit of 512 files per directory exists in some versions of DOS.) Large-capacity disks, particularly hard disks, are often divided into small, manageable parts called *subdirectories*. This division is much like that used in the telephone directory of a large company. The directory may list departments in its main section but not every single person in the company; each department might have its own subdirectory listing each staff member. Subdirectories are an important part of organizing your Quattro Pro 3 work on your hard disk.

Figure 7-2. *Hard drive directory system*

Handling Hard Disks

A hard disk directory system for a computer running Quattro Pro 3 and WordPerfect might look like the one shown in Figure 7-2. For your computer to find either a program file or a data file, you must specify a path for it to follow. For example, the path to the file EDITOR.DOC is \WP\LETTERS\. The path to the purchase-order entry worksheet in the SALES subdirectory of the QUATTRO directory is \QUATTRO\SALES\. You can have more than one file with the same name on the same hard disk if you keep them in separate directories. It is generally safer, however, to give each file a unique name. To identify files on a hard disk accurately, include the path to the file as part of the file name. Thus, the full name of the EDITOR.DOC file is

C:\WP\LETTERS\EDITOR.DOC

When using a hard disk you cannot, of course, be in two places at once. Normally, you begin working with a hard disk in the *root directory*. You are said to be in the root directory of a drive when you are at the uppermost level, which is signified by A:\, B:\, C:\, and so on. The directory you are in at any particular time is called the *current* or *default directory,* which simply means the one you are using. To experiment with this, you can enter the following commands from the DOS prompt. Try these commands from the DOS prompt, either before or after using Quattro Pro 3. (You can temporarily exit Quattro Pro 3 to use DOS commands by using the File Utilities DOS Shell command described later in this chapter.)

Determining the Root   You can ensure that you are in the root directory by typing **CD ** and pressing ENTER. This command tells DOS to change to the root directory. You can quickly tell which directory is the current directory by typing **CD** without the backslash at the C> prompt. DOS responds by telling you the name of the current directory.

A Better Prompt   In order to navigate a hard disk with one or more subdirectories, it is useful to change the uninformative C> prompt, which just tells you that you are using drive C, to the C:\> prompt, which tells you that you are using drive C and are in the root, or main, directory. This more informative prompt will always tell you what subdirectory you are in. For example, if you moved into a subdirectory of the root directory called DOS, the prompt would read C:\DOS>. (If your hard disk is not drive C but drive D or E or any other valid letter, just substitute that letter for C in the instructions that follow.)

To change the prompt to a more informative version, type **PROMPT P** at the C> prompt. When you press ENTER you will see the drive letter and the path ($P) to whatever subdirectory you are in, and the greater-than sign (represented by $G). Once you enter the PROMPT command, the new prompt remains in effect until you turn off or reset your computer. To get around having to re-enter the command each time you turn on your computer, you might want to add the PROMPT command to your AUTOEXEC.BAT file, as described in Appendix A, "Advanced Setups."

Working with Directories   To see the path prompt in action and to explore the directory commands, change your location to a subdirectory such as the one for Quattro Pro 3. Type **CD \QUATTRO** and press ENTER. You will see your prompt change. To change your current location back to the root directory, type **CD ** and press ENTER. To make a subdirectory directly below the root directory, type **MD \TEMP** and press ENTER. To make a subdirectory of the TEMP directory, type **MD \TEMP\MINE** and press ENTER. If you wanted to copy all the files from a disk in drive A into this new directory, you could move into the subdirectory by typing **CD \TEMP\MINE** and pressing ENTER, followed by **COPY A:*.*.** Or you could type **COPY A:*.* C:\TEMP\MINE** from the root directory.

To remove a subdirectory you must first remove all data and program files from it. If you are in a subdirectory and use the command DEL *.*, you will only delete files in that subdirectory, not across the whole disk. You can delete files from a subdirectory from anywhere. For example, if you were in the root directory, you could type **DEL \TEMP\MINE\ *.WQ1** to delete all files with the WQ1 extension in the MINE subdirectory of the TEMP subdirectory. To remove an empty subdirectory you would remove the lowest levels first. For example, type **RD \TEMP\MINE** and press ENTER, and then type **RD \TEMP** and press ENTER.

Help with DOS

Since DOS commands are not the easiest to learn and apply accurately, you may sometimes make mistakes. One of the worst is to delete the wrong file. Fortunately there is a cure. If you realize you have erased a file that you wanted to keep, do not continue to move or store additional files. Reach for a program called The Norton Utilities or another called Mace Utilities. These programs will, among other things, enable you to restore the file in most cases.

If you find the DOS directory commands difficult to use, you can use the File Manager that is a part of Quattro Pro 3. This feature, described later in this chapter, allows you to display a directory of your hard disk and copy files using a simple menu of commands.

Saving Worksheets

Having seen how your PC handles different storage areas and stores data, you can experiment with Quattro Pro 3's file-related commands. The most important of these are the ones used to save worksheets.

File Save Options

When you want to save a worksheet you can either use the File Save command or the File Save As command. The File Save command saves the current worksheet using the current name displayed in the lower-left status area of the current worksheet window. The File Save command does not give you a chance to alter the name of the file, but you are asked whether you want to overwrite the existing file with the current version. If you select Replace, the File Save command writes the current worksheet to disk. If you want to save a worksheet, plus you want the opportunity to alter the current name, then you should use the File Save As command. For Quattro Pro 3 to carry out the File Save As command and safely store a copy of your worksheet file on disk, it needs two pieces of information: where to store the data and what file name to use.

Where to Store Data

Quattro Pro 3 needs to know in which directory of which drive you want the worksheet stored. In Chapter 1 you saw that Quattro Pro 3 initially assumes that you want to save the data to the drive and directory from which you started the program. You can change this temporarily by using the File Directory command.

Suppose you have Quattro Pro 3 installed on drive C in a directory called QUATTRO. The full name of this storage area, its path, is C:\QUATTRO. However, you would like Quattro Pro 3 to store a series of worksheets on drive A. You select the Directory command from the File menu and are prompted with "Enter name of directory:" as shown in Figure 7-3. The currently selected directory is shown, in this case, C:\QUATTRO. The cursor is flashing under the first letter of this path name. Simply type the path name of the new storage area, in this case A:, and it will replace the current one. If you wanted to specify a particular directory you have created on A, you would add a backslash (\) and the name of the directory, as in **A:\WORK**. When you have typed the new directory, press ENTER. From now until you end the current session with Quattro Pro 3 (or until you use the File Directory command again to select a different area) Quattro Pro 3 will store files to and retrieve files from the new directory.

To make a more permanent change to the data directory setting, use the Options Startup Directory command (described in Chapter 6) and specify the directory you want Quattro Pro 3 to use. You must then use the Options

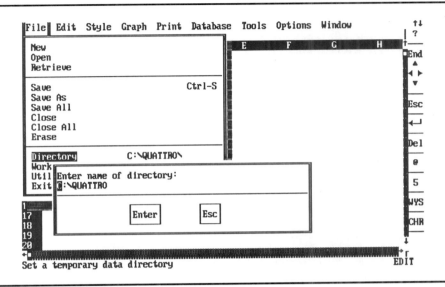

Figure 7-3. *Setting a temporary directory*

Update command to add this preference to the program's configuration file, which is read each time you load Quattro Pro 3. To store just one file to an area other than the default directory, use the File Save As command and edit the path and file name to include the desired path.

What File Name to Use

When you are ready to save a worksheet that you have built from scratch, you select File Save As. Quattro Pro 3 responds by prompting you to "Enter save file name:" as shown in Figure 7-4. This name will be from one to eight letters or numbers, following the rules described in the previous section, "Naming Files." The extension that Quattro Pro 3 places on the file name will normally be WQ1. You can use a different extension to indicate that Quattro Pro 3 should store the file in a format that can be read by a different program. This is described later in the section entitled "Special Files."

The "Enter save file name:" prompt is always followed by the current file path together with one of two additions. If the worksheet you are about to save was originally retrieved from a file on disk, you are prompted with

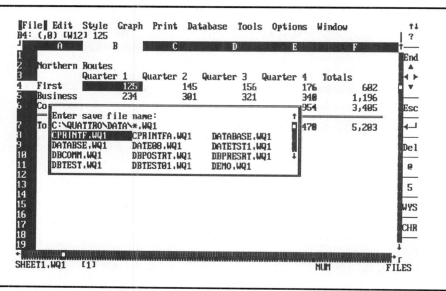

Figure 7-4. *File name list*

the name of that file, as shown in Figure 7-5. If you retrieve the file QNORTH01.WQ1 from the DATA subdirectory of the QUATTRO directory on drive C and update the figures, you will be prompted with the name

C:\QUATTRO\DATA\QNORTH01.WQ1

when you go to save the file. If you press ESCAPE at this point the suggested name will disappear and will be replaced with a generic file prompt: *.W??. This is accompanied by a list of files in the current directory.

If the worksheet you are saving has never been saved before, the "Enter save file name:" message is immediately followed by the generic name prompt, which uses a DOS wildcard as in C:\QUATTRO\DATA*.WQ1. This means any file name in C:\QUATTRO\DATA with an extension of WQ1. You also see a list of files already saved in the current directory shown in a box, as seen in Figure 7-4.

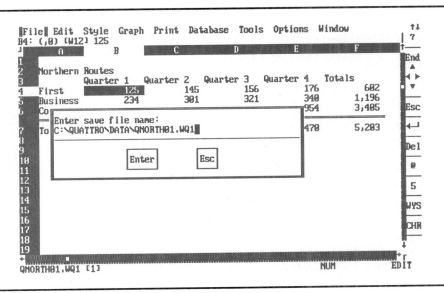

Figure 7-5. *Saving a named file*

File List

The list of file names Quattro Pro 3 shows you when saving a file allows you to see the names already in use. You can pick an existing file from this list and save the current worksheet into it, but bear in mind that doing so will replace the contents of that disk file with the worksheet you are about to store. To pick a name from the list, press RIGHT ARROW and DOWN ARROW to highlight the name. If there are more than 12 files on the list, the list scrolls as you continue to press either RIGHT or DOWN ARROW.

To search for a specific file you can press the Edit key (F2). This will return a prompt on the status line at the bottom of the screen, asking what you are searching for. This search mechanism works the same way as the name search in the function list. Just type the first character of the name you are seeking. You will either be taken to the first file in the list that begins with that character or Quattro Pro 3 will beep to let you know that there are no names that begin with the character you typed. To continue the search type the second character of the name you are looking for, and so on, until it is located. Press ENTER to use the file name you have highlighted. There are several other keys that you can use to manipulate this list, as shown in Table 7-2.

Key	Action
DOWN ARROW	Down one file
TAB	Down one file
RIGHT ARROW	Down one file
UP ARROW	Up one file
SHIFT-TAB	Up one file
LEFT ARROW	Up one file
PAGE DOWN	Down one screen
PAGE UP	Up one screen
HOME	Top of the list
END	Bottom of the list

Table 7-2. *Keys Used in File List*

If you are not sure about the name of the file you are looking for, you might find it helpful to see the date and time it was last saved to disk. This data is available by pressing the Expand key (+), using the plus on the numeric keypad. An example of the resulting display is shown in Figure 7-6. Notice that this display also includes the size of the worksheet, which is useful information when you are attempting to recall which file contains what data.

Saving Previously Named Files

If the worksheet you are saving has previously been saved and you want to resave it under the original name, use the File Save command. Alternatively, you can use the File Save As command and press ENTER when the file name prompt appears. However, if you want to save the file under a different name, you must use the File Save As command. This gives you the existing file name, which you can then edit. This is very useful when you are creating different versions of the same basic worksheet.

For example, suppose you have stored the sales figures for the first quarter of 1990 in a worksheet called 90SALE01.WQ1. You want to create a worksheet for the second quarter sales figures. You retrieve the file 90SALE01.WQ1, make the changes, and then issue the File Save As command. You want to store the new file as 90SALE02.WQ1, but you do

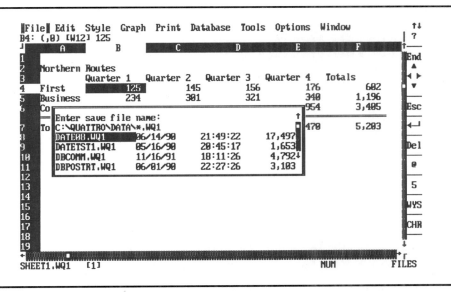

Figure 7-6. *Expanded file name list*

not want to have to retype the entire name to change the name from 90SALE01.WQ1 to 90SALE02.WQ1. Instead, you press the Edit key (F2). This allows you to use the edit keys to change the name, just as you edit entries in the worksheet. In this example, you can press SHIFT-TAB to move the cursor left five spaces, under the 1. Then press INSERT to go into OVERSTRIKE mode. This means that when you type **2** it will replace the 1, and you can press ENTER to confirm the new name.

If you use File Save As with a previously saved file and want to see the names already in use, just press ESCAPE at the default name prompt. You will get the generic file name prompt and the file list. This list includes any subdirectories of the current directory. You will find these subdirectories listed at the bottom of the file list. By highlighting a subdirectory name and pressing ENTER you can view a list of existing files in that subdirectory. If you want to save the file to a directory other than the current one, you can press ESCAPE and type the complete path name of the directory and the file name, as in

C:\QUATTRO\SALES\BUDGET.WQ1

To see what files are already in a directory other than the current one, you can press ESCAPE to clear the "Enter save file name" prompt. Then type the path name of the storage area you are interested in *together with* the generic file specification *.WQ1, and press ENTER. Quattro Pro 3 will respond with a list of files in that directory. If you do not use a file specification the program will save your file in the wrong area.

Save Confirmation

When you have the right path and file name entered for the worksheet you are about to save, press ENTER to confirm the name. If you are using either the File Save command or the File Save As command the program will not immediately save the file but will check to see if a file of the same name already exists in the current storage area. If such a file exists, Quattro Pro 3 responds with a three-line menu box offering the choices Cancel, Replace, and Backup, as shown in Figure 7-7.

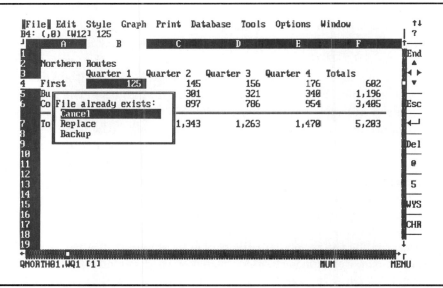

Figure 7-7. *Cancel, Replace, or Backup option*

Cancel   The Cancel option is your chance to change your mind about the save operation. Selecting Cancel will prevent the existing file from being overwritten and return you to the READY mode.

Replace   Selecting the Replace option confirms that you want to overwrite the old file. You normally use this option when you are updating a file or when you are saving successive unfinished versions of a model you are building.

Backup   The Backup option will preserve the existing file by changing the extension to BAQ and will then save the new file with the name you requested.

Saving Your Workspace

When you are working with more than one worksheet at once, as described in the next section, you may arrange multiple windows in a particular way and want to store this arrangement. Quattro Pro 3 provides the File Workspace command to store an arrangement of windows. When you issue the File Workspace command, you are asked if you want to save or restore the workspace, as shown in Figure 7-8. When you select Save you are prompted for a file name. A list of existing workspace files is displayed. The extension WSP is used for workspace files, as in RESTART.WSP. Note that the File Workspace command does not save the contents of the worksheets that are displayed in the windows; rather, it saves the size, shape, and placement of the windows, and the names of the files that are displayed in them. The workspace file is thus a collection of settings and is distinct from a regular worksheet. To save all of the open worksheets, you use the File Save ALL command. This performs a File Save for each window in turn, starting with the current window. The ususal Cancel/Replace/Backup option is given if a file has already been saved.

You can use the File Workspace Restore option when you want to recreate a particular arrangement of windows and worksheets, for example, when you start work the next day. When you select Restore you are prompted for the workspace file name, as shown in Figure 7-9. Type the name of the workspace or select from the list provided. Quattro Pro 3 will then load the files and arrange the windows as they were when the

Figure 7-8. *Workspace menu*

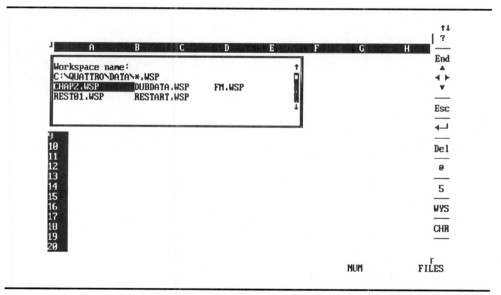

Figure 7-9. *File Workspace Restore command*

workspace was saved. Note that if any of the files included in the workspace are dependent upon linked files, you will get the Link options menu asking if you want to load supporting files. See the later section "Linking Worksheet Files" for more on responding to this menu.

The File Workspace command is very useful when you are working with multiple windows and is discussed again in the section "Multiple Worksheet Windows" later in this chapter.

Opening and Retrieving Files

When you want to bring back into memory a copy of a worksheet that you have stored on disk you can use either the Retrieve or the Open command from the File menu. Both commands assume that you want to retrieve a worksheet from the current drive and directory.

File Listing

When you select either File Retrieve or File Open, Quattro Pro 3 helps you to identify the file you want by displaying an alphabetical list of files, showing up to 12 files at once, as seen in Figure 7-10. You can use the movement keys described earlier in Table 7-2 to move down this list and highlight the file you want. If the number of worksheet files in the current storage area is greater than 12, scroll down the list. To see the date and time the files were saved as well as their size, view the expanded version of the menu, which you obtain by pressing the Expand key (+), using the plus on the numeric keypad. When you have highlighted the file you want to retrieve, press ENTER and Quattro Pro 3 will read that file into memory.

If you want to retrieve a file from a storage area other than the current one, you have several options. If you want to view files in a directory that is "higher" in the directory structure than the current directory, press BACKSPACE. This would change a prompt of C:\QPRO\DATA*.W?? to C:\QPRO*.W?? and show files in the QPRO directory which is above the QPRO\DATA directory. Alternatively, when you select File Retrieve or File Open and are prompted for a file name, you can press ESCAPE and then edit the path of the area from which you want to retrieve the file. You press ENTER to see a list of the files in that area. For example, suppose you want

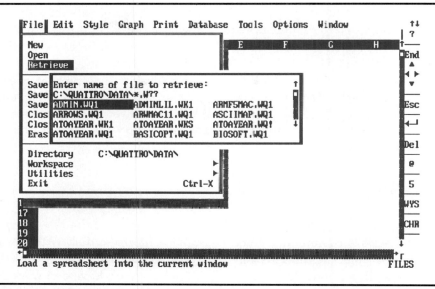

Figure 7-10.   *File Retrieve prompt*

to see all of the worksheets in the SALES subdirectory of the QUATTRO directory but the DATA subdirectory is current. The initial prompt is

C:\QUATTRO\DATA*.W??

When you press ESCAPE this changes to

C:\QUATTRO\DATA\

You can then press BACKSPACE five times so that you remove the DATA subdirectory. Now you can type in the new directory, as in

C:\QUATTRO\SALES\

and press ENTER to see all of the worksheets in this directory. Quattro Pro 3 will automatically add the *.W?? specification for you. Notice the backslash at the end of the edited prompt. If you do not include this, Quattro Pro 3 will assume that you are looking for the file SALES.WQ1 in the QUATTRO directory. When you are at a file name prompt and want to change it completely you can press CTRL-BACKSPACE. This removes the text of the prompt and allows you to type something completely different. Also note that Quattro Pro 3 lists subdirectories of the current directory at the end of the file list. This allows you to highlight a subdirectory in the file list and press ENTER to display files in that subdirectory.

If you want Quattro Pro 3 to retrieve a foreign file (one that does not have the WQ1 extension) you can type a specific extension in the edited file name prompt, such as DBF for dBASE files. If you know the exact path and file name of the worksheet you want to recover, you can type that information and press ENTER.

File Retrieve

There is an important difference between the effects of the File Open and File Retrieve commands. When you read a file from disk with the File Retrieve command the data from the file is placed in the current worksheet window. If you have just started Quattro Pro 3 you have one worksheet window open, window [1], named with the default name of SHEET.WQ1. Using File Retrieve places the data from the specified file on disk into that window. If you already have data in the current window and use the File Retrieve command, Quattro Pro 3 assumes that you want to replace the current contents of the window with the data you are going to read from disk. The data read from the file will replace all that was there before it, from cell A1 through cell IV8192.

There is the potential to lose some of your work when issuing the File Retrieve command. To prevent accidental loss of data Quattro Pro 3 checks to make sure that your work in the current window is saved. If some of your work is not saved, the program will ask whether you want to lose your changes. You will have to reply Yes or No before the File Retrieve command erases the current window contents and reads a data file from the disk. If you pick Yes, Quattro Pro 3 proceeds with the File Retrieve command, presenting a list of files from which to choose. If you pick No you are returned to the File menu where you can issue one of the Save commands to store the current worksheet before reissuing the Retrieve command.

File Open

When you issue the File Open command and select a file name Quattro Pro 3 performs two operations, the first of which is to create a new

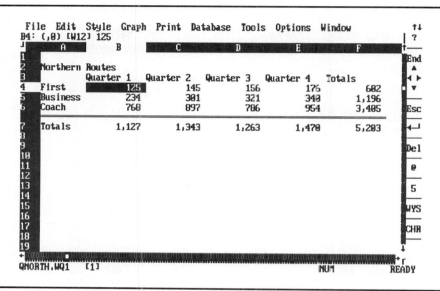

Figure 7-11. *First worksheet opened*

worksheet window. The second operation is to read the requested file into the new window. For example, in Figure 7-11 the current worksheet is QNORTH.WQ1, which is a list of passenger volumes on northern routes. This worksheet is displayed in window [1]. The user wants to work on a second set of figures for southern routes, stored in a file called QSOUTH.WQ1. The File Open command is issued and the QSOUTH.WQ1 file is specified. The immediate result is shown in Figure 7-12. The newly opened file is displayed in window [2], completely obscuring window [1]. At this point you do not know whether window [1] is still open. You can use the Next Window key (SHIFT-F6) and see whether this takes you to the other window. However, if you issue the Window Stack command you can see from the file names displayed in the window frame that two windows are opened, as shown in Figure 7-13. If you issue the File Open command again, a third window will be opened containing the worksheet you have requested. The more worksheets you work with at once, the more important the Window commands become.

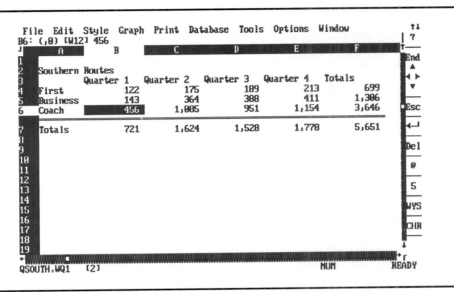

Figure 7-12.   *Second worksheet opened*

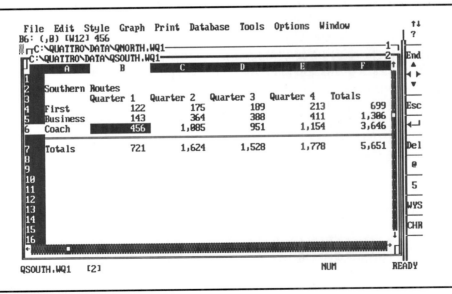

Figure 7-13.   *Stacked worksheets*

Multiple Worksheet Windows

When you have several worksheet windows open at once you will want to arrange them so that you can work effectively. For example, in Figure 7-13 two windows are open and they are stacked. You can also tile, resize, and move windows. In this section the commands for organizing multiple windows are discussed. The first commands examined are those that allow you to create multiple windows.

Opening Windows

You have seen that when you issue the File Open command Quattro Pro 3 creates a new window in which to display the requested file. You may want to create a new window without actually opening a file. For example, if you were working on the north and south worksheets shown in Figure 7-13 you might want to create a third worksheet to consolidate the two sets of numbers. To do this you would use the File New command. The result of issuing this command is shown in Figure 7-14. At first the new worksheet obscures the existing windows. The new worksheet window is numbered; in this case it is window [3]. The default file name of SHEET2.WQ1 has been assigned to the new worksheet as it was the second fresh worksheet of the current session.

If you issue the Window Stack command the new window is placed above the existing windows, as shown in Figure 7-15. Notice that the Window menu is displayed in Figure 7-15 although this menu actually disappears as soon as you issue the Stack command. Also note that when you are working in WYSIWYG mode, the Stack command does not work. To display multiple windows in WYSIWYG mode, you use the Window Tile command. This is because the WYSIWYG mode typically shows more columns and rows than character mode and therefore makes stacking redundant. If you stack windows in character mode and then switch to WYSIWYG mode, each worksheet is simply placed one on top of the other.

Closing Windows

If you keep using the File Open and File New commands, you will eventually hit Quattro Pro 3's limit of 32 windows, although you may well run

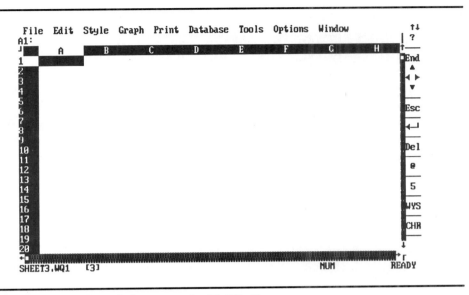

Figure 7-14.   *Fresh worksheet created with File New*

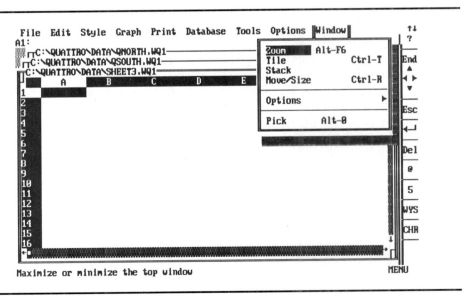

Figure 7-15.   *Window menu and stacked worksheets*

out of memory in your system before reaching that limit. Issuing the Save or Save As command does not alter this situation. This is because the Save commands store the contents of windows onto disk—they do not close the windows themselves. To close a window you need to use the File Close command or the File Close ALL command. When you request a File Close, Quattro Pro 3 checks for unsaved changes in the worksheet, and removes the window from display if none are encountered. If unsaved changes are encountered you are prompted to save them first. The File Close ALL command does this to each window in turn.

Mouse users have a quick way to close a window: click on the square on the top-left corner of the active window border. This will close the window immediately, unless there are unsaved changes to be dealt with, in which case the normal Cancel/Replace/Backup prompt appears.

When you close all windows you are left with an abbreviated Quattro Pro 3 menu that shows just one item: File. When you select File and there are no worksheets open you have five choices, as shown in Figure 7-16 and described here:

New	To open a new worksheet window
Open	To read a file from disk into a new worksheet window
Workspace	To restore a stored workspace
Utilities	To use the File Manager (from which you can open files) or the DOS Shell
Exit	To quit Quattro Pro 3

The first time that you see this reduced menu you may wonder what has happened, but as soon as you open a worksheet window the full menu will be restored.

Arranging Windows

When you have several windows open at once you have a lot of options when it comes to arranging them on the screen. When a window is first opened it occupies the whole screen. If you are in character mode, you can use the Stack command from the Window menu, shown in Figure 7-15, to tell Quattro Pro 3 to arrange all open windows one on top of another with the name of each worksheet displayed. The current window is displayed

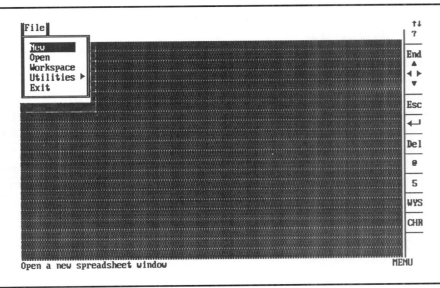

Figure 7-16.   *No worksheets open*

above the rest. Windows are numbered consecutively based on the order in which they are opened. An alternative to stacking windows is to tile them by issuing the Window Tile command. This tells Quattro Pro 3 to arrange all of the open windows on the screen at once, automatically adjusting their size to fit the available space. In Figure 7-17 the windows that were stacked in Figure 7-15 have been tiled.

You can move from window to window with the Next Window key (SHIFT-F6). To move to a window based on the number of the window, use ALT plus the window number. Thus you can move to window [3] by pressing ALT-3. The current window has a double border line around it. As you move from one window to another the cell selector jumps to a particular cell of the worksheet you are moving to. This is the cell that was active when last you left that window. You can zoom to full screen size any window that has been reduced in size. Move to that window and press the Zoom key (ALT-F6). To reduce the window to its previous state, press Zoom again.

The allocation of available display space is determined by the number of windows to be tiled. Several arrangements are shown in the diagram in Figure 7-18. Note that the order of windows after the Tile command is

Figure 7-17. *Tiled worksheets*

Figure 7-18. *Diagram of tile arrangements*

issued depends upon which window is current at the time the command is issued. The current window is placed in the top left corner of the screen.

Mouse users can move between windows by clicking the mouse on any part of the window they want to move to. To zoom a window with the mouse, just click on the pair of arrows in the top right of the screen. These will zoom the current window, or unzoom it if it is already zoomed.

When you are working with a large number of windows you can use the Window Pick command to select a specific window from a list of open windows. Figure 7-19 shows a list of windows displayed by the Window Pick command. You can highlight the one to which you want to move and press ENTER. You can also use the Pick key (ALT-0) instead of the Window Pick command to bring up this list. SHIFT-F5 will also display a pick list of windows.

Sizing Windows

For some work with multiple windows you may want an arrangement other than the tiled or stacked look. You may want to overlap certain parts of windows and obscure others. For mouse users this is very easy. To alter

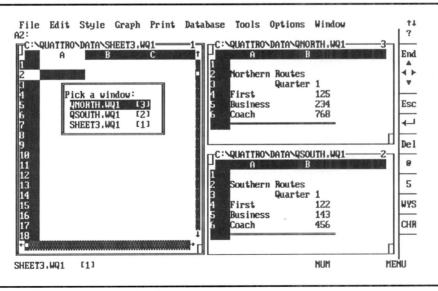

Figure 7-19.   *The window pick list (SHIFT-F5)*

the size of a window using a mouse simply place the mouse pointer on the move/size box in the lower right of the window, and then press the mouse button and drag. The window frame will change shape as you drag the mouse. When you are satisfied with the shape, release the mouse button. To move a window with the mouse, place the mouse pointer on the title of the window and then press the mouse button. The MOVE message will appear in the window and you can drag it to a new location. Release the mouse button when you reach the new location.

To move or size windows from the keyboard you use the Window Move/Size command. For example, suppose that you want to arrange the windows shown in Figure 7-19 so that they are viewed as wide horizontal strips, as shown in Figure 7-20. The first step is to make window [1] the active window. Then select Window Move/Size. A box called MOVE appears on the screen to let you know that you are in MOVE mode, as shown in Figure 7-21. Use the arrow keys to move the box within the Quattro Pro 3 Desktop. Press ENTER when the new location is reached. To change the size and shape of the window, press SCROLL LOCK after you have selected Move/Size and the MOVE box will change to SIZE, as shown in Figure 7-22. You can switch back and forth between MOVE and SIZE by using the SCROLL LOCK key.

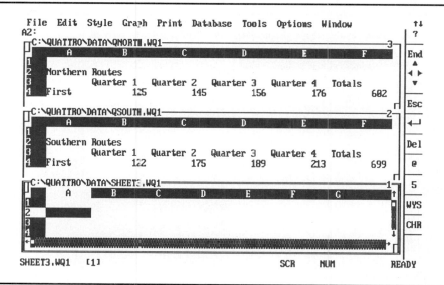

Figure 7-20. *Three worksheets arranged.*

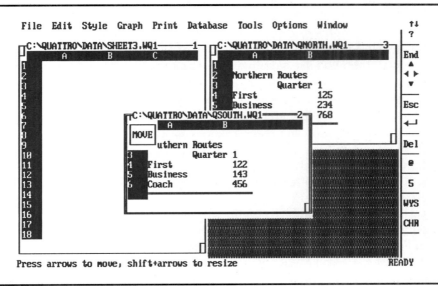

Figure 7-21.   *Window Move command*

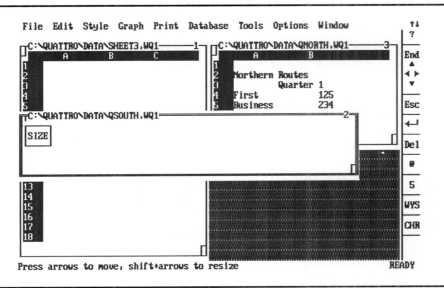

Figure 7-22.   *Window Size command*

Using Workspaces

When you have gone to a lot of trouble to set up the right arrangement of windows for your work you may well want to preserve the arrangement. As discussed earlier in this chapter, Quattro Pro 3 has a special type of file, called a workspace file, that will store information about a window arrangement, including the position of the windows and the names of the files that occupy them. To store the current arrangement of windows you issue the File Workspace command and pick the Save option. Enter an eight character file name and Quattro Pro 3 will save it with the WSP extension. These files do not save the data in worksheet files, but only the arrangement of files. Use File Save ALL to save all open files. When you issue the Files Workspace Restore command all of the windows and the files that were occupying them will be opened.

Odd Shapes and Sizes

You cannot do much work with multiple windows without realizing that Quattro Pro 3 stores the size and shape of a worksheet, as well as the data it contains, when you perform a File Save or File Save As. Just as the location of the cell selector is the same when a stored worksheet is opened as when it was last saved, so it is with the worksheet's desktop location and size. Sometimes this can be disconcerting. For example, if you have tiled a number of windows and then saved the worksheets in them, each one will be stored rather small. When you open one of these files in a later session you may not recognize it at first. There is an easy way to fix this: press ALT-F6 to zoom the window to full size. In fact, you might want to make a practice of zooming windows to full size before saving them.

Linking Worksheet Files

Beyond the advantages of just viewing several worksheets at once, Quattro Pro 3 provides the ability to link those worksheets, making data in one dependent upon data from another. This ability opens up a new realm of spreadsheet design possibilities. In some cases you will want to use this feature to split large and cumbersome worksheets into more manageable, interrelated units. Since you can copy or move data from one worksheet window to another it is easy to disassemble a large worksheet into more manageable parts. Knowing that Quattro Pro 3 supports linked formulas between files allows you to approach new projects in a different way, following more closely the traditional accounting model of consolidated sheets and supporting sheets.

You can link Quattro Pro 3 worksheets to files produced by other programs such as 1-2-3. You can pull data from several files into one graph. As mentioned in Chapter 3, when working with databases you can use multiple spreadsheets to establish multiple criteria and output ranges.

Creating a Linked File Model

Earlier in this chapter you saw two worksheets containing passenger volume figures for an airline. The figures are divided into northern and southern routes because the airline has two centers of operation, one in the north and one in the south. Suppose that you want to consolidate the figures from these two worksheets, called QNORTH.WQ1 and QSOUTH.WQ1, respectively. You could copy figures from both worksheets into a new one, perhaps called QTOTALS.WQ1. You would then have three worksheets. However, if there were changes to the figures you would have to alter two worksheets. For example, if the northern office corrected the First Class number for the fourth quarter you would need to alter the regional and the total worksheets. A better approach is to link the two regional worksheets to the totals worksheet.

To do this you first need to create the totals worksheet. This is easy to do as you can copy labels and formatting from one of the existing worksheets. To begin you open the two regional worksheets, and then use the File New command. The new window is where you will build the total worksheet. Use the Window Tile command to show all three windows at once and the effect will look like Figure 7-17. In the newly opened window you issue the Edit Copy command. When you are prompted for the Source Block of cells, press SHIFT-F6 to move to one of the regional worksheets in either window [2] or window [3]. Note that the Source Block prompt changes to the coordinates of the cell that was active the last time you used this worksheet. Also note that the full file name of the worksheet in the current window is shown in the Source Block prompt. Now you can enlarge the Source Block to cover the cells that you want to copy, in this case all of

the occupied cells of the model, A2..F7, as shown in Figure 7-23. Press
ENTER to confirm the Edit Copy command and the cells are copied from one
window into the window that was current when you issued the command.
You can see the results in Figure 7-24, where the new worksheet is being
edited to become the totals worksheet. Note that the column widths
settings are not copied from one worksheet to another, but the line drawing
style is.

Once you have changed the label in cell A2 and adjusted the column
widths to 12 with the Style Block Widths command, you are ready to
establish the links between this worksheet and the other two. The links
you create are actually formulas, so that, for example, cell B4 in the totals
worksheet is equal to cell B4 of the southern worksheet plus cell B4 of the
northern worksheet. The completed formula looks like this:

+[QSOUTH]B4+[QNORTH]B4

You can build the formula quite easily using the pointing method. With
the cell selector in B4 of the totals worksheet, type + and then press the
Next Window key. This will take you to the next window where you can

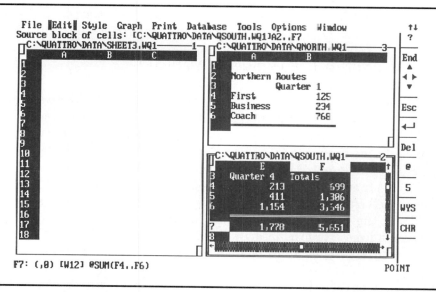

Figure 7-23.   *Copying between windows*

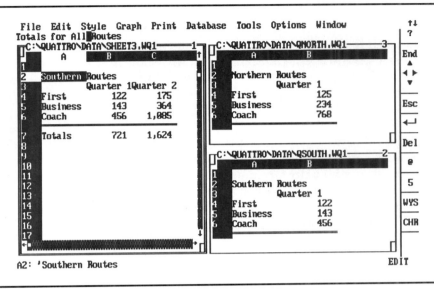

Figure 7-24. *Creating the totals worksheet*

point to cell B4 and type another **+**. You will be returned to the totals
worksheet where the formula so far on the input line will read

+[C:\QUATTRO\DATA\QSOUTH.WQ1]B4+

This looks a little intimidating because Quattro Pro 3 gives the full
worksheet name and path of the cells you are working with. These will be
abbreviated when the formula is completed. Now press Windows twice to
move to the third window where you again point to B4. Press ENTER to
complete the formula, which is shown in place in Figure 7-25.

Like other Quattro Pro 3 formulas, this one can be copied. You want
every cell from B4 through E6 to reflect the addition of the corresponding
cells in the other two worksheets. To achieve this you simply copy the
formula from B4 of the totals worksheet to the block B4..E6. The results
are shown in Figure 7-26, where the totals worksheet has been zoomed to
full screen size. Note that there was no need to adjust the formulas in
column F or those in row 7 because they are @SUM formulas based on the
columns and rows of the model.

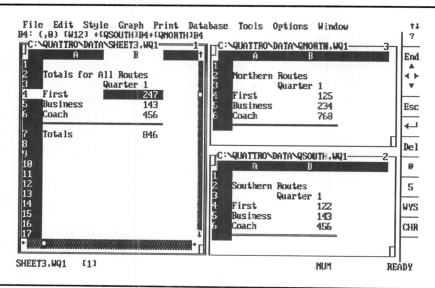

Figure 7-25. *Completed link formula*

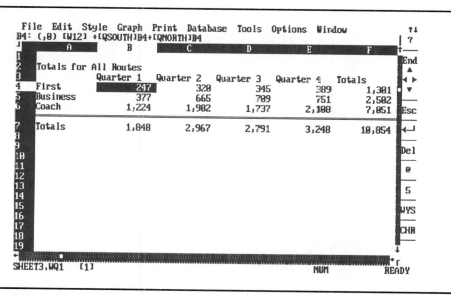

Figure 7-26. *Totals worksheet zoomed*

Working with Linked Files

Obviously, the preceding is a fairly simple example of what can be done with linked worksheets, but the principles are the same even with much larger models. Formulas that refer to cells outside of the current worksheet are called *dependent formulas*. Values that are supplied to another worksheet are called *supporting values*. Worksheets that depend upon other worksheets for values, like the one just created in this model, are called *dependent* worksheets. A worksheet that supplies values to a dependent worksheet is called a *supporting worksheet*.

When you establish a link with a supporting Quattro Pro 3 worksheet that is stored in the same directory as the dependent worksheet, then the formula you need to use is the name of the supporting worksheet enclosed in square brackets, as in [BUDGET], rather than the full path, as in [C:\NEWYORK\BUDGET.WQ1]. You can also establish links to foreign files, such as 1-2-3 worksheets. However, if the file you are linking to is not a Quattro Pro 3 file with the default extension of WQ1, then your link reference will need to include the extension. For example, suppose that you want to create a link with cell B4 in a 1-2-3 file called WEST.WK1. Entering [WEST]B4 will not work since Quattro Pro 3 will be looking for a file called WEST.WQ1. If you do enter an invalid reference in a link formula Quattro Pro 3 returns the error value NA in the cell. However, this is difficult to do because when you attempt to link to a file that Quattro Pro 3 cannot find you will be presented with an error message and a file name box, as shown in Figure 7-27. This gives you an opportunity to look up the correct file. The problem may be that the file is not in the current directory, or that the file does not have the default extension as in this case. If you press ESCAPE at the prompt in Figure 7-27 you are shown a file list that you can browse until you find the correct name. Select the correct name to complete the link.

Saving and Loading
Linked Files

When you have established a linked formula you should close the dependent file (the one containing the link formula) before closing the supporting worksheets. This is because Quattro Pro 3 links are active only when the supporting files are open. If you close the dependent worksheet before the supporting worksheets, the link formula cells will return the error value

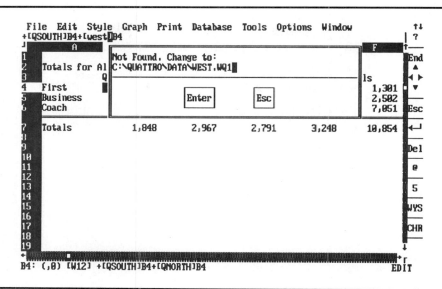

Figure 7-27. *Correcting the link file name*

NA. This NA will change to a proper value if you then open the supporting worksheets. Note that the normal procedure for saving worksheets, as opposed to closing them, is least dependent to most dependent.

When you open linked worksheets you might want to open the least dependent first, and the most dependent last. This is because when you open a dependent worksheet, Quattro Pro 3 checks to see if the supporting worksheets are open. If they are not open, the dependent worksheet cannot function correctly. However, Quattro Pro 3 knows this and will prompt you to open the supporting files, as shown in Figure 7-28.

The first option, Load Supporting, will open all worksheets referred to in formulas in the worksheet that is currently being loaded. This is a great time saver as it circumvents the need to open supporting files first. You can simply have Quattro Pro 3 do the loading for you.

The second option, Update Refs, is used to update references to unopened supporting documents. When you issue the Update Refs command, Quattro Pro 3 reads the values referred to in any link formulas in the current worksheet. The supporting worksheets do not need to be open for this command to work. This means that you can work on a dependent worksheet without opening the supporting worksheets.

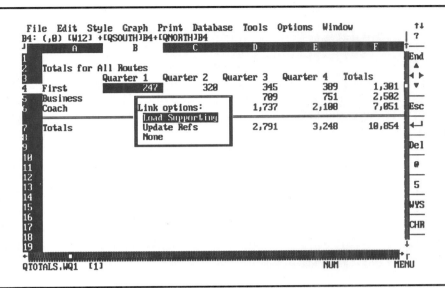

Figure 7-28. *Link options menu*

The None option tells Quattro Pro 3 to ignore the link formulas in the worksheet you are opening. This causes all formulas dependent upon links to return NA. The links can be reinstated later by using the Tools Update Links command.

Refreshing Links

After you open a dependent worksheet and decide not to open the supporting sheets—using the Update Refs command instead to read the supporting values from files on disk—you normally do not need to issue this command again. However, there is the possibility that the supporting files will be altered. For example, a colleague might give you an updated copy of a worksheet that is used to support the dependent worksheet you have loaded. If you are using Quattro Pro 3 on a network, another user might update a supporting file. If the supporting worksheet on disk is altered—perhaps by copying—Quattro Pro 3 will not necessarily know this immediately. To be sure that you are using the most recent figures in the dependent worksheet, you can use the Tools Update Links command shown in Figure 7-29 to refresh data links.

The Open command is the same as the Load-supporting option when you are retrieving a dependent worksheet. The Refresh command allows you to read linked values from a supporting worksheet, by selecting the worksheet from a list. When the list of supporting files is displayed you can select one name by highlighting it and pressing ENTER. To select more than one name from the list, highlight each name in turn and press the Extend key (SHIFT-F7). This places a checkmark by the name. You can then select other names. When all the files that you want to refresh from are checked, press ENTER. (Mouse users can simply click each file name to select it and then click the Enter button in the mouse palette.)

The Change option on the Update Links menu allows you to substitute a new supporting file for an existing one, by automatically performing a global search and replace to change the old name to a new one that you supply. The Delete option allows you to remove supporting links.

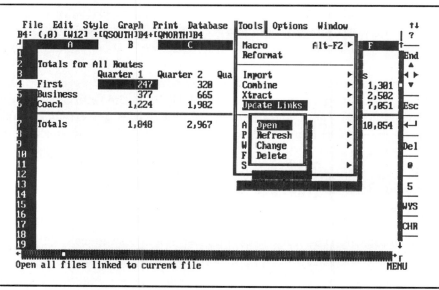

Figure 7-29. *Tools Update Links Command*

Out-of-Space Problems

When you are building a large worksheet, it is surprising how fast it can grow in size. The Edit Copy command in particular quickly generates a lot of data. This can result in space problems, both on disk and in memory.

Disk Space

When you attempt to save a file that is too large to fit in the remaining free space on your disk, Quattro Pro 3 displays a "disk full" error message. You can respond to this in several ways.

Save to a Floppy Disk   If you have been saving to a floppy disk and the current disk cannot accommodate the worksheet you are trying to save, you can retry the save after inserting a disk with more free space on it. You can use the DOS Shell command on the File Utilities menu to temporarily exit to DOS and format a fresh floppy disk if you need one. The DOS Shell command, which is described in more detail later in this chapter, does not affect your unsaved work. If you have been saving to a hard disk that has now filled up, you might consider saving to a floppy disk as a temporary measure. Remember that some floppy disks can now store over a megabyte of information.

Clean Up Your Hard Disk   If you are trying to save to a hard disk that has run out of space, you can either use DOS via the DOS Shell command or the File Manager to erase unwanted files from your hard disk. This will make more room available and help to accommodate the worksheet you are trying to save.

Convert Values   The amount of space required by formulas in a worksheet is greater than that taken up by values. If you convert numbers that are generated by formulas into their values, using the Edit Values command, then the worksheet can be stored in less space.

SQZ! the Worksheet   If saving a worksheet in the regular WQ1 format results in a "disk full" message, you might want to try the SQZ! option, described later in this chapter. You do this by using the file extension WQ! instead of WQ1. This causes Quattro Pro 3 to compress the worksheet, sometimes by as much as 75%, and thus store it in a smaller file.

Divide the Worksheet   When you attempt to save a worksheet and get a "disk full" message you may want to consider splitting the worksheet into separate, smaller worksheets. To do this you can open a new window and use the Edit Move command to move data from the current worksheet to the new one.

Memory Space

Quattro Pro 3 displays the message "memory full" when you attempt to retrieve a file that is too large to fit in currently available memory. You get a similar message when you expand the current worksheet beyond the limits of available memory. If you want to check on the amount of memory you have available, use the Options Hardware command and read the current memory status from the Hardware menu. If you have a worksheet loaded when you read the Hardware menu, you can see how much room there is for expansion. If you have a blank worksheet, you can tell how large a file you can retrieve. Quattro Pro 3 needs enough free memory to read in the file from disk and to manipulate the data within the worksheet. Thus, if you had 82,944 bytes available, you would be unwise to try and retrieve anything larger than 80,000 bytes.

When you use a command that results in the "memory full" message you should save parts of the worksheet to separate files using the Tools Xtract command. This will allow you to store the data safely so that you can redesign the worksheet, perhaps free more memory, or add more memory to the system. You can free memory by saving the current worksheet, exiting Quattro Pro 3, and removing any memory-resident programs you might have loaded.

If it was an Edit Copy command that caused the "memory full" message, you will probably find that only part of the block was copied. However, the data you had before the copy operation should still be intact. Likewise, if you tried to retrieve a file that was too large, only part of the file will be in your worksheet, but the entire file will still be safely stored on disk.

Password Protection

To prevent unauthorized access to a worksheet stored on disk, you can assign a password to the worksheet while you are saving it. Select File Save As and then type in the file name followed by a space and the letter P. When you press ENTER Quattro Pro 3 prompts you for a password. Actually, this can be several words, numbers, and spaces up to a total length of 15 characters. Pick a password that you can remember. Neither Borland nor anyone else can retrieve the data if you forget the word. No one can see the letters of the password as you type, because Quattro Pro 3 displays only a blank rectangle for each letter as shown here:

```
Enter password: ■■■■■■■■
```

When you have typed the password, press ENTER. You are then asked to verify the word by typing it again. The theory is that if you can type the word twice, you know what it is and did not make a mistake the first time you entered it. After typing the word a second time, press ENTER. The file-saving process continues as usual.

When you attempt to retrieve or open the password-protected file, you are prompted for the password. This time you need only type the password once and then press ENTER to access the file. If you type an incorrect password, Quattro Pro 3 beeps and gives you the message "Invalid password." When you save a file with password protection Quattro Pro 3 *encrypts* the file; that is, it scrambles the data to make it unintelligible, even to a sophisticated, well-trained programmer. Do not expect to be able to get the data back if you forget the password. Trying to get around the password by using the partial file retrieval command, Tools Combine, does not work either. You should leave a copy of the password in a secure place such as a locked desk drawer or in another password-protected Quattro Pro 3 file.

When you want to remove password protection from a file, you first open the file, and then use the File Save As command. Quattro Pro 3 will remind you that the file is password protected, as shown here:

```
Enter save file name:
C:\QUATTRO\DATA\AB1.WQ1 [Password protected]█

            ┌───────┐        ┌─────┐
            │ Enter │        │ Esc │
            └───────┘        └─────┘
```

You can press BACKSPACE to remove the protection message. Press ENTER to complete the file save and the file is no longer protected. Unless you remove the password protection with File Save As, the file will continue to be password protected.

If you are using Quattro Pro 3 to read 1-2-3 files, as described later in this chapter, and those files are protected by 1-2-3 password protection, Quattro Pro 3 will be able to decode the files, provided you supply the correct password. If you are sharing Quattro Pro 3 data with a 1-2-3 user, however, be sure to save your Quattro Pro 3 file as a WK1 file rather than a WQ1 file. 1-2-3 cannot read DES-encrypted files.

Using passwords can be a nuisance, so you should decide if the need for security is real. If it is, then you will want to make sure you use proper passwords. A password is of little use if it is a useless password such as *password, pass, your first name, the filename,* and so on. Believe it or not, you can buy lists of common passwords and the serious data thief is likely to guess most words that do not have the following features:

■ at least eight characters

■ a mixture of text and numbers

■ some odd characters, like @, spaces, and commas

■ a mixture of uppercase and lowercase

■ a lack of logic

While some applications are not sensitive to upper- and lowercase distinctions, Quattro Pro 3 is, which is an important point to remember when recording your passwords. The password *Fred's File* will not be accepted if it is supplied as *FRED'S FILE*, and even *Fred's file* will be rejected. To use the last feature—a lack of logical connection between the content of the file and the password protecting it—you need to be imaginative. For example, a banker might use the names of birds to protect a series of salary recommendation files. Combined with the other features, something like this would be difficult to guess:

Robin@5769

Since such a name would also be difficult to remember you must also make proper provision for recording and securing passwords. A sheet of paper locked in a drawer is usually a good technique. You can use a spreadsheet or word processor to list files and their passwords. The more paranoid might want to code the passwords on the printed listing.

Data Loss and Recovery

The best approach to prevent data loss is the same one you can use for steady monetary accumulation: save on a regular basis. This means saving every 15 minutes. You should also save your files before you do any of the following:

■ perform a file retrieve

■ exit Quattro

■ leave your PC unattended

■ move or copy a large block

■ sort data or perform an extract or block fill operation

■ combine files

However, even if you try to live by these rules, there is always a possibility that something will go wrong. Quattro Pro 3 has a built-in method of helping out.

Using Transcript

If you have lost data, you can rely on the Quattro Pro 3 *keystroke log*. This is a transcript of your recent activity that is created by a built-in feature of Quattro Pro 3 called Transcript, which automatically keeps track of your keystrokes on disk. The keystrokes are saved to a special log file with the name QUATTRO.LOG. If your machine malfunctions or you accidentally delete data, you can recall this data by replaying your actions from the Transcript log. Several thousand actions can be recorded in one log before Quattro Pro 3 copies the log to a backup file called QUATTRO.BAK and continues with a new QUATTRO.LOG. This means that between the files QUATTRO.BAK and QUATTRO.LOG you can keep an extensive record of what has been done during your Quattro Pro 3 sessions.

To gain access to the Transcript log file and review or restore keystrokes from it, use the Tools Macro command and select Transcript to display the Macros menu shown in Figure 7-30.

When you select Transcript you will see a log of data like that shown on the left in Figure 7-31. You can browse through this list with the highlight bar, which you move by means of the UP and DOWN ARROW keys. Use the PAGE UP and PAGE DOWN keys to move through this list. The line on the left side of the log groups commands that occurred since the current session started.

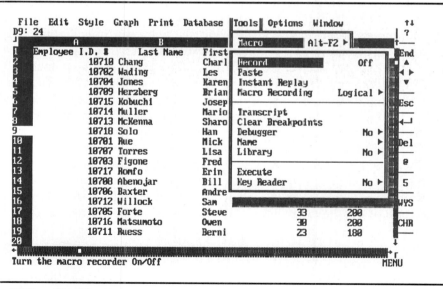

Figure 7-30.   *The Macro menu*

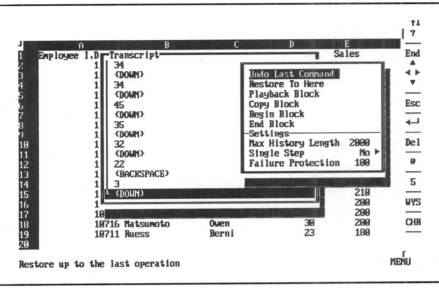

Figure 7-31.   *Transcript menu*

To use the recorded keystrokes, type / and you will see the Transcript menu shown in Figure 7-31. You use this menu to mark blocks or sections of commands for playback. Alternatively, you can have Transcript play back the commands up to the point marked by the highlight bar.

Suppose you start working with Quattro Pro 3 and have loaded Transcript. The first piece of work you do is retrieve a budget file. You are busy updating the budget numbers when there is a power outage. You have lost the changes to the budget file; however, the original file is still on the disk. When power returns you simply reload Quattro Pro 3 and run Transcript. The log file will then come up and the commands from it may be replayed. These will include the retrieval of the budget file and the changes you made. If you have lost data because of an inadvertent command, such as Edit Copy, you can run the log up to, but not including, that command. Of course, if you have enabled Undo, as described in the next section, then you can reverse the consequences of many typical spreadsheet actions. However, Transcript allows you to undo a whole series of actions, which Undo cannot.

Note the Settings part of the Transcript menu. The Max History Length determines how many lines of recorded actions will be held in the log file before it is backed up and a new one created. The Single Step option allows you to play back your Transcript commands one at a time. The Failure Protection feature determines how many keystrokes Quattro Pro 3 should wait before recording them to disk. The smaller you set this number the more complete your recovery from disaster will be. However, lower numbers also mean more frequent disk writing. For more on Transcript commands, see Chapter 12.

Activating Undo

Sometimes you can overcome errors and accidents without resorting to Transcript. If you activate Quattro Pro 3's Undo feature you can press ALT-F5 after a command to reverse its effects. This is very handy after a mistaken Edit Erase Block, or a disastrous Data Sort. To activate Undo, you use the Options Other command and select Undo. Select Enable and be sure to use the Options Update command to record this change if you want it to be in effect in the next session. You may notice a slight slowing of Quattro Pro 3's reaction time when Undo is in effect. This is due to the extra work that the program is doing to keep track of your actions, but it is a small price to pay for the ability to reverse critical actions. Table 7-3 lists actions that cannot be reversed with Undo.

Special Files

Quattro Pro 3 can read and write not only its own worksheets but also data files created by several other popular programs. If you have 1-2-3 or Symphony files on your directory, they will automatically be listed by Quattro Pro 3 because the *.W?? pattern includes WRK and WK1 files. You do not have to do anything special to retrieve one of these files. Highlight the name, press ENTER, and the file is read into Quattro Pro 3. When you go to save the file, Quattro Pro 3 will assume that you want to store it in the original format, using the same extension. For example, if you open SALES.WK1 and then use the File Save As command, the suggested name will be the same, SALES.WK1, and the file will be stored as a 1-2-3

Commands that make settings such as Sort Block (but Sort Go and Data Query Extract can be undone)

Print commands that send a document to the printer (use CTRL-BREAK to stop printing)

File menu commands

Copy, move, and delete operations in the File Manager

Format commands from the Style or Options menu

Note: To undo some commands you need to return to READY mode from the menu first. Repeat the Undo key to reverse an Undo operation.

Table 7-3.   *Actions That Cannot Be Undone*

worksheet. However, when you use the File Save As command you can alter the file name to WQ1 to match the 1-2-3 format you require.

  You can read other types of files with the File Retrieve or File Open command if you enter the full file name or alter the *.W?? prompt to *.* to list them. Files that can be read in this manner are listed in Table 7-4.

Ext.	Type of File
WKQ	Worksheets from Quattro 1.0
WKZ	Worksheet from Quattro 1.0 compressed with SQZ!
WK1	1-2-3 Release 2 worksheet
WK!	1-2-3 Release 2 worksheet compressed with SQZ!
WKS	1-2-3 Release 1 worksheet
WRK	Symphony worksheet
RXD	Reflex database
DB	Paradox database
DBF	dBASE II or III database, dBASE IV database without memo fields
SLK	Symbolic Link worksheet (Multiplan or Excel)
DIF	Data Interchange Format

Table 7-4.   *Files That Can Be Retrieved by Quattro Pro 3*

Writing to Foreign Files

You can save data into some foreign file formats simply by changing the file extension. For example, to save a file in the SYLK format that can be read by Excel, you use the File Save As command to change the worksheet extension to SLK and proceed with the save. If you want to save data from a Quattro Pro 3 worksheet to a database format such as dBASE or Paradox, you need to consider the location of the data that you are going to save. You can only save fields and records to a database format. For this reason you will probably want to use the Tools Xtract command to perform the save and specify only those cells that contain records and field names.

The Tools Xtract command allows you to save just part of a worksheet, rather than the whole thing. For example, in Figure 7-32 the cells to be exported to dBASE are A3 through E18. When you use the Tools Xtract command you must specify whether you want to save values or formulas and values. When you are storing to other worksheet formats you can save formulas, but when you are saving to a database format you will want to save values. In the figure, the Tools Xtract command was issued and the file name was entered with the DBF extension. The block of cells to be

Figure 7-32. *File Xtract to dBASE format*

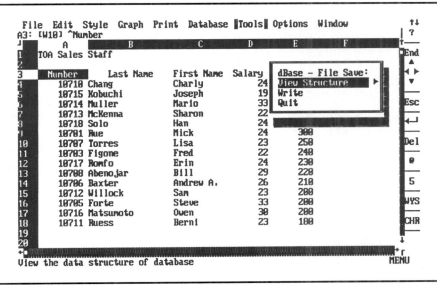

Figure 7-33.   *dBASE File Save menu*

saved was then pointed out. When you have pressed ENTER to confirm the selection of cells, Quattro Pro 3 knows you are exporting data to dBASE because of the DBF extension, and you get the opportunity to check the structure that Quattro Pro 3 has assigned to your data. You can see this from the specific format review menu displayed in Figure 7-33.

The first option on this menu, View Structure, shows the Field-name, Type, Width, and Decimals settings, as seen in Figure 7-34. Note that the field names have been altered to match the limits of field naming in dBASE. Every name has been capitalized and underlines are used in place of spaces. If a Quattro Pro 3 field name contains a punctuation character not acceptable to dBASE, the letter *A* is used instead. All unacceptable field names are thus replaced with the letters of the alphabet.

To alter settings for a particular field, you highlight the field and press ENTER. For example, you might want to change the Number field to a text field. A small menu appears from which you can select Name to change the name of the exported field, or Type to alter the type of the field. When you select Name you are prompted to edit the current name and enter the results. The Type option lists four possibilities for field types in dBASE: Text, Numeric, Logical, and Date as shown in Figure 7-35. Note that the

Figure 7-34.   *View Structure menu*

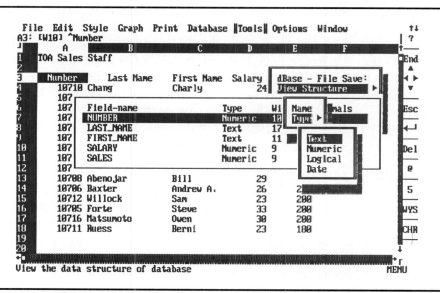

Figure 7-35.   *Changing the field type*

fifth type of data in dBASE, the Memo field, is not supported either when writing or reading from the DBF format. If you pick Numeric you are prompted for a decimal place setting. When the structure is acceptable, press ESCAPE to return to the dBASE File Save menu, shown in Figure 7-33, and select Write. This creates the dBASE file on disk.

When you are performing extracts to another database format, such as Paradox or Reflex, a menu tailored to the structural requirements of that database is presented.

Autoload Files

You may find that your work with Quattro Pro 3 involves heavy use of one particular worksheet. You can have Quattro Pro 3 retrieve a file automatically whenever the program is loaded by means of the Options Startup command (described in the previous chapter). Autoload File is the second item on the Startup menu. When you select it, Quattro Pro 3 asks you to enter the name of the worksheet that you want to have loaded whenever you start the program. When you enter the name of the file, you will immediately see the file listed on the menu. However, you *must* use the Update option from the Options menu to record this change and have the autoload feature effective the next time the program is loaded.

The autoload feature is always active. Whenever you load Quattro Pro 3, it looks for the file name recorded from the Startup menu. As you can see from Figure 7-36, the default name is QUATTRO.WQ1. If Quattro Pro 3 finds that file in the default directory when the program is loading, it retrieves the file. You can use the autoload feature either by changing the file name in the Startup menu, or you can save the file you want to autoload as QUATTRO.WQ1. Note that if you change the Autoload File setting you should use the Options Update command before ending the sessions.

Extracting from Foreign Files

You can also read selected data from foreign database files by using the Database Query command. You will recall that the Database Query command requires three pieces of information: the Query Block, the Criteria Table, and the Output Block. The Query Block is the database, the collection of information you want to query. The Criteria Table is the set of conditions that determine which records are read from the database

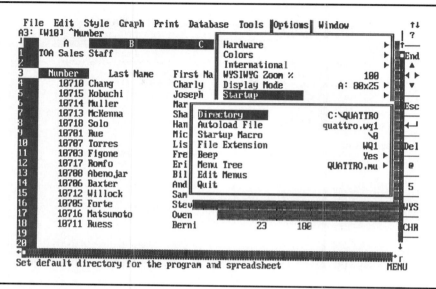

Figure 7-36. *Autoload File on the Startup menu*

by Quattro Pro 3. The Output Block is an area of a worksheet into which the selected records from the database are written.

In Figure 7-37 you can see a worksheet set up to extract records from a dBASE file. The dBASE file is called QSALES1.DBF and is stored in the current data directory. The Criteria Table in B22..B23 tells Quattro Pro 3 to look in the SALARY field of the QSALES1.DBF file for all salaries greater than 30000. Records with salaries greater than 30000 will be read into the Quattro Pro 3 worksheet below the field names in row 26. Note that the field names used in the Criteria Table and Output Block must match those in the DBF file.

When you want to extract records from a file other than the current worksheet, you refer to the file by name in the Query Block setting. In this case the setting will be [QSALES1.DBF]A1..A2. The file name requires the full path if it is in a directory other than the current data directory. The cell reference of A1..A2 is used with any foreign format file to tell

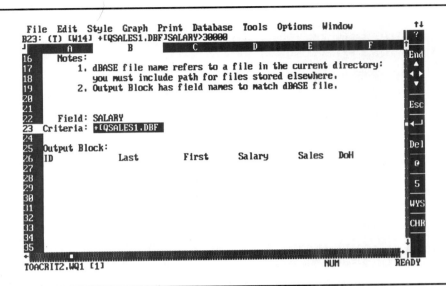

Figure 7-37. *Data Query from a dBASE file*

Quattro Pro 3 to begin at the top of that file when searching for records. The complete Database Query settings for this operation are:

Query Block:	[QSALES1.DBF]A1..A2
Criteria Table:	B22..B23
Output Block:	A26..F26

You can see the results of the Extract in Figure 7-38. Note that the link you have created here between Quattro Pro 3 and the DBF file is not dynamic and the extracted records will not be updated automatically if the DBF file is altered.

The File Manager

Quattro Pro 3's File Manager works as a shell between you and DOS to give you easy access to your files. You can use it to work with Quattro Pro 3 spreadsheet files or any other files located on either your hard disk or

```
   File  Edit  Style  Graph  Print  Database  Tools  Options  Window            ↑↓
   B22: [W13] '[UQTRANO1.DBF]SALARY
   ↓        A           B            C            D            E        F        ↑
   16    Notes:
   17          1. dBase file name refers to a file in the current directory:
   18             include path for files stored elsewhere.
   19          2. Output Block has field names to match dBase file.
   20
   21
   22    Field:  [UQTRANO1.DBF]SALARY
   23 Criteria:  +SALARY>2500                                                    ▪
   24
   25 Output Block:
   26 ID          Last_Name    First_Name    Salary      Sales   Hire Date
   27     10701 Rue          Mick          24234.00   301793.00
   28     10702 Wading       Les           27357.00   331960.00
   29     10703 Figone       Fred          22238.00   241263.00
   30     10704 Jones        Karen         18141.00   321607.00
   31     10705 Forte        Steve         33282.00   200935.00
   32     10706 Baxter       Andrew A.     26469.00   210937.00
   33     10707 Torres       Lisa          23453.00   251404.00
   34     10708 Abenojar     Bill          29036.00   221265.00
   35     10710 Chang        Charly        24489.00   330152.00           ↓
   ←       ▪                                                              →  r
   TOACRIT2.WQ1 [1]                                            NUM        READY
```

Figure 7-38.   *Completed query*

floppies. With the File Manager, you can display a list of files in any directory or disk drive and open a file by choosing its name. You can use wildcards to filter the file list, for example, *.WQ1 to display only Quattro Pro 3 spreadsheet files. You can turn this around to apply a negative filter, creating a list that shows all files except those specified in the filter. Thus, the filter [*.WQ1] shows all files except Quattro Pro 3 spreadsheet files.

File Manager also lets you sort file lists by name, extension, size, original order, or timestamp. You can display a directory tree that reveals the structure of all directories on your disk. You can move in and out of directories in the tree and use the GoTo key (F5) to search through the tree for a specific file. You can move or copy a file from one directory to another, rename files, and delete them from disk.

The File Manager Window

Quattro Pro 3's File Manager works within a File Manager window. This is like a worksheet window except that it displays only file names and subdirectories. To open a File Manager window, choose File Manager from the File Utilities menu. Quattro Pro 3 displays a window, as shown in Figure 7-39. Note that the choices in the menu bar change slightly when a File Manager window is active. The choices are now File, Edit, Sort, Tree, Print, Options, and Window (as opposed to File, Edit, Style, Graph, Print, Database, Tools, Options, and Window).

If you have not used the File Manager during the current session, the window displays information about files in the current directory. Otherwise, the directory displayed in the File Manager window is the one that was there the last time you used File Manager in the current session. Similarly, the screen position of this window is taken from the last open File Manager window.

The File Manager window shown in Figure 7-39 is actually divided into two sections. These are called *panes*. The top pane, called the *control pane*, displays prompts that allow you to make changes in four areas: drive, directory, filter, and file name. In Figure 7-39 the settings are

Drive:	C
Directory:	\QUATTRO\DATA\
Filter:	*.*
File Name:	_

You move between these items with the UP and DOWN ARROW keys. The cursor will mark which one is active. You can change the active item by pressing ESCAPE to erase the entire entry, or by pressing BACKSPACE to erase one character at a time. You can then type the new setting and press ENTER to confirm it. When you press ENTER, Quattro Pro 3 immediately reads in a new list based on your changes. When you are entering new subdirectories, be sure to precede the subdirectory in the path name with a backslash (\). For example, to view the files in D:\ SALES\REPORTS you would change Drive to D and then change Directory to \SALES\REPORTS. There is no need to enter the final backslash as Quattro Pro 3 will do that for you, changing \SALES\REPORTS to \SALES\ REPORTS\.

Underneath the control pane is the *file list pane*. This is the list of files and subdirectories in the specified directory. You can browse this list with the UP and DOWN ARROW keys as well as PAGE UP and PAGE DOWN. You can also change the directory being displayed in the File Manager window by selecting another directory from within the file list pane. If you want to see

```
 File  Edit  Sort  Tree  Print  Options  Window                    ↑↓
                                                                    ?
┌C:\QUATTRO\DATA\══════════════2─┐  ▓  D  ▓  E  ▓  F  ▓  ───
│      Drive: C                  ↑                         End
│  Directory: \QUATTRO\DATA\      ▓                         ▲
│     Filter: *.W??                   ame  Salary  Sales  ◄ ►
│  File Name: █                              24     330    ▼
│                                            19     310   ───
│  ..                                        33     300    Esc
│  123BEEP   WQ1    1,658 07/14/91           22     300   ───
│  12GROWON  WQ1    9,350 02/17/91           24     300    ←┘
│  12MJCST   WQ1    4,027 05/19/91           24     300   ───
│  1DENCRP2  WQ1   19,264 04/02/91           23     250    Del
│  1DENCRYP  WQ1   30,500 02/14/91           22     240   ───
│  1GUESS    WQ1    4,314 01/15/90           24     230     @
│  1HOUSE    WQ1    1,731 03/17/91           29     220   ───
│  1PASS     WQ1    1,474 01/15/90      A.   26     210     5
│  1PW-MJC   WQ1    2,976 04/30/91           23     200   ───
│  1STABLAN  WQ1   18,445 04/30/91           33     200    WYS
│  1STABLES  WQ1   15,178 04/24/91           30     200   ───
│  1STBYCAT  WQ1    4,090 04/25/91           23     180    CHR
│  1SYMPH    WQ1   12,715 01/28/90  ↓                     ───
│  <more>                         └
└
 C:          [2]                                 NUM      READY
```

Figure 7-39.   *File Manager window*

one of the subdirectories included on the list, just highlight it and press
ENTER. You will find subdirectories listed below file names in the file list.
If you want to see the parent directory of the current subdirectory, select
the double dots (..), which are shorthand for the parent directory.

A third pane, called the *tree pane*, is created when you use the Tree Open
command. Figure 7-40 shows a File Manager window with a tree displayed
by the Tree Open command. The tree pane now gives a visual representation of part of the directory system on the currently specified drive
(C). The section of the directory tree shown includes the current directory
and subdirectory.

Before you can work in a particular pane of the File Manager window
you must activate that pane. To activate a different pane, press the Pane
key (F6) or the TAB key. As you can see from Figure 7-39, the File Manager
window takes up half the screen when it is first displayed. You can expand
the File Manager window to fill the screen by pressing the Zoom key
(ALT-F6) or choosing the Zoom command from the Window menu. In Figure
7-41 you can see the effect of Zoom on the window in Figure 7-40. Repeat
the zoom command to unzoom the window. File Manager windows are
numbered in the same sequence as worksheet windows. You can have two

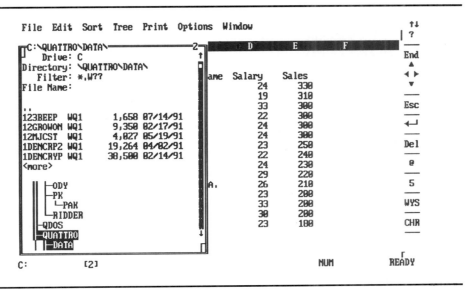

Figure 7-40.   *File Manager tree*

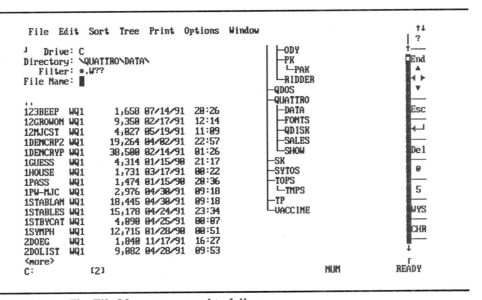

Figure 7-41.   *The File Manager zoomed to full screen*

or more File Manager windows open at the same time. Opening a second File Manager window is simply a matter of repeating the File Utilities File Manager command. The second File Manager window takes up the other half of the screen but any more File Manager windows you open will cover up the existing ones. To move between File Manager windows, use the Next Window key (SHIFT-F6). Alternatively, you can move from window to window with the ALT-*number* technique, for example, use ALT-5 to move to window [5]. You can use the Move/Size command from the Window menu to alter the size or position of File Manager windows.

To close the active File Manager window, use the File Close command. If you want to return to the worksheet you were using but do not want to close the File Manager window, press the Next Window key (SHIFT-F6). Quattro Pro 3 temporarily removes the directories from display. You can return to the File Manager window at any time with the Next Window key. Special key combinations make it easy to move around in a File Manager window or switch from one window to another. A complete list of the special File Manager keys is provided in Table 7-5.

The File Manager Menus

When you are in a File Manager window, you have access to a set of menus by typing / or pressing F3. Quattro Pro 3 activates a variation of the main menu as shown in Figure 7-39. This menu contains a subset of the usual menu commands with some new ones added.

With the File command you can create a new window or close the active one; print the file list or directory tree; update the directory display; create a directory; save a particular configuration of open windows; and temporarily exit to DOS.

The Edit command lets you copy, move, rename, duplicate, or erase files from the displayed directory. The Sort command lets you reorder the list of files by name, extension, timestamp, size, or DOS order. With the Tree command you can display the directory tree in a pane below or to the right of the file list, as well as resize the tree pane and close the tree pane.

The Print command displays a menu for printing selected files. This menu works much the same as the standard Print menu. The Options command lets you switch the file list display between names only and names and file status. You can also specify which directory is displayed initially in a File Manager window and reset many system options such as text printer and screen colors. Finally, the Window command allows you to adjust the size and position of the windows, expand the current window, or move to a different window.

Working with the Control Pane

Suppose that you want to view all 1-2-3 worksheet files in the LOTUS directory of drive E. First, make sure that the control pane of the File Manager window is active. This means that the cursor will be flashing in

General Windowing Keys

SHIFT-F5	Pick Window; accesses other windows.
ALT-0	Pick Window; accesses other windows.
F6 or TAB	Pane; activates the next File Manager window pane in the following order: control pane, file list pane, directory tree pane.
SHIFT-F6	Next Window; activates the next open File Manager window.
ALT-F6	Zoom Window; zooms an open window to full screen and back again. If the window is already expanded, this key shrinks it again, as with Window Zoom.
ALT-n	Jumps to window number n. The window number appears on the top edge of each frame.

Keys for the Control Pane

F2	Rename; prompts for a new file name, and renames the current file list selection to the file name you specify (same as Edit Rename).
F5	GoTo; finds the file name (or combination of wildcard characters) typed at the file name prompt.
ESCAPE	Clears the entry at the prompt. When you move the highlight bar away from the prompt and make no new entry, restores the original entry.
DELETE	Deletes the character under the cursor.
ENTER	Moves the cursor to the blank file name prompt or, if the cursor is at the file name prompt, opens the file or subdirectory highlighted on the file list.
HOME	Moves the cursor to the beginning of the prompt entry.

Table 7-5. *File Manager Keys*

Keys for the File List Pane

F2	Rename; renames the current (highlighted) file (same as Edit Rename).
SHIFT-F7	Select; selects the current (highlighted) file in the list so you can open, move, copy, or delete it. If the file is already selected, this key deselects it.
ALT-F7	All Select; selects all files on the list for moving, copying, or deleting. If some files on the list are already selected, deselects those files.
SHIFT-F8	Move; moves the selected files into the paste buffer, removing them from the list.
ALT-F8	Delete; erases the selected files or the highlighted file from the disk.
F9	Calc; reads the disk and refreshes the file list pane (same as File Read Dir).
SHIFT-F9	Copy; copies the selected files into the paste buffer for copying to another directory or disk, keeping them on the list.
SHIFT-F10	Paste; inserts the files in the paste buffer at the cursor position in the current directory's file list.
ESCAPE	Escape; returns all selected files to normal. Activates the control pane and moves the cursor to the file name prompt.
ENTER	Opens selected files or the file at the cursor. If the highlight bar is on the .., opens the parent directory. If the highlight bar is on a subdirectory, moves to the subdirectory.
HOME	Moves the highlight bar to the .. parent directory item.
END	Moves the highlight bar to the end of the file list.
PAGE UP	Moves the file list display up one screen.
PAGE DOWN	Moves the file list display down one screen.

In the Tree Panel

ESCAPE	Returns all selected files to normal; then activates the control pane and moves the cursor to the file name prompt.
DELETE	Deletes all selected files or the highlighted file in the file list.
F9	Calc; rereads the current disk/directory.

Table 7-5. *File Manager Keys* (continued)

one of the top four fields (press F6 or TAB to change active windows). In the drive field type **E** and press ENTER. In the directory field type **\LOTUS**. Now move to the filter prompt. The filter lets you restrict the files shown in the file list pane. This setting accepts DOS wildcards: * to take the place of any number of characters, and ? to take the place of one character. The default filter setting, *.*, displays all file names with any extension. To narrow down the files listed, you change the filter to exclude files you do not want to see. In this example, you can enter *.**WK?** to list all files with *WK* as the first two letters of their extension. This includes *WKS* and *WK1*. To be more specific, for example, to find all files beginning with *SALES*, you would enter **SALES*.***. You can also specify a negative filter to display all files except those that meet the filter specifications. To indicate a negative filter you enclose the wildcard specification in square brackets. For example, to display a list of all files except those beginning with *SALES*, enter the following specification:

[SALES*.*]

You can also combine filter specifications to create one filter. Just separate the specifications with commas. For example,

.WK?,[SALES.*]

displays all 1-2-3 spreadsheet files except for those beginning with *SALES*. The filter limits the files displayed in the File Manager window, but you can always type in the name of any file at the file name prompt to see whether it is in the current directory, regardless of whether it is shown in the list. The directory filter remains in effect until you change it, even if you change directories. To erase the current filter and return to the default of *.*, highlight the filter prompt and press ESCAPE and then ENTER.

Selecting Files

When you open the File Manager window the file name prompt is blank. At the same time, the control pane is active and the file name prompt is highlighted. You can use this prompt to open a worksheet file or look for a specific file on your disk. To open a worksheet file you type the name at the file name prompt and press ENTER. If Quattro Pro 3 finds the file, the File Manager window disappears and the worksheet is displayed. Note that if Quattro Pro 3 does not find the file you have named in the current directory, it creates a new spreadsheet with that name and displays it. For this reason you may want to locate the file in the file list, as described in a moment, rather than risk a mismatched file name entry.

If you do not know where on a disk a particular file is located you can type in the file name at the file name prompt and press the GoTo key (F5). Quattro Pro 3 searches through every directory on the disk until it finds a file with that name. It then changes the file list to show the directory containing the file you specified, with the file name highlighted and marked by a check. If there are other files with the same name, press F5 again to move to the next. If you do not know the exact name of the file, you can use wildcards to search for near matches. For example, to find a worksheet file with a name that begins with *FRED* you can start typing **FRED*.WQ1** in the file name field. As you type, Quattro Pro 3 begins looking for the file, highlighting the first file beginning with *F*, then the first one beginning with *FR*, and so on. When you have finished typing you can highlight the next matching file name by pressing F5. When the file you want is highlighted, press ENTER to open it. Table 7-5 provides a list of the special keys you can use in the control pane and their functions.

The File List Pane

The file list pane catalogs all files and subdirectories that pass through the given filter in the specified drive and directory. File names are listed first, followed by subdirectory names, in alphabetical order. The first column shows file names, the second shows file name extensions, and the third shows file size measured in bytes. The last two columns show the date and time the file was last altered. If there are more files in the directory than will fit in the pane, Quattro Pro 3 displays "<more>"at the bottom of the screen. You can press PAGE DOWN to display the next page of names or END to move to the end of the list.

Moving to the end of the list is useful since there you can find a directory status that shows the number of files in the current directory and the number of files displayed in the file list, which may be less if you have used a filter. This status line also shows how many bytes of the disk have been used together with the total number of bytes available on the disk. If you do not need datestamp and file size information you can use the Options

File List Wide View command to allow room for more file names in the list, as shown in Figure 7-42. Table 7-5 lists the special keys you can use in the file list pane.

Sorting File Lists

By default, Quattro Pro 3 lists all files and subdirectories in the file list in alphabetical order. This is the Sort Name option. To change the order of the file list you choose Sort from the File Manager menu and then select the sort order you want from the list. When you choose Name or DOS Order, Quattro Pro 3 also sorts subdirectories listed in the tree pane. You can sort by Timestamp which lists file names and subdirectories chronologically according to their timestamp, which shows when the file was last modified. The oldest file is listed first. This command sorts by time, even when the Options File List command is set to Wide View. The Extension option sorts the file list alphabetically, first by extension, then by file name. The Size option sorts file names and subdirectories by size (in bytes). The smallest file appears first in the list. This command sorts

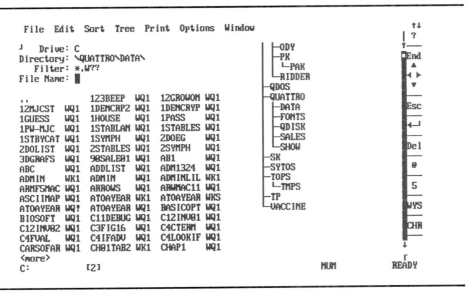

Figure 7-42. *Wide view of files*

by size, even when you have suppressed size display from the file list (with Options File List Wide View). The DOS Order option sorts file names in the same order that the DOS command DIR would list them (usually in the order of original creation).

Navigating with the File List

The Options Startup Directory setting determines which directory is displayed when you first open a File Manager window. To change the directory displayed at startup you choose Options Startup Directory, and then select either Previous (the default) to display the last directory you looked at in your last Quattro Pro 3 session, or Current to show the directory you were in when you loaded Quattro Pro 3.

If the file you want is not in the directory shown in the file list, you can access different directories by choosing subdirectories. These are normally found at the bottom of the alphabetical file list and distinguished by a backslash after the directory name. You can also move up in the directory system by using the item denoted by two dots (..), which is the parent directory of the current directory. To display files in one of the subdirectories listed in the file pane, just move the highlight bar to the directory's name and press ENTER. The directory prompt changes to show the subdirectory name, and the file pane changes to list files in that subdirectory. To move out of the current directory and into its parent directory press HOME to highlight the double dots denoting the parent directory at the top of the file list pane, and then press ENTER. Quattro Pro 3 takes you back one level in the directory and displays file names and subdirectories in the parent directory. Table 7-5 lists the keystrokes you can use in the control pane of a File Manager window.

The Directory Tree

By choosing subdirectories or the parent directory (..) item in the file list you can get to any file stored on your disk. But if you expect to traverse many directories, or if you are not sure what files are in your directories, you may want to use the directory tree, which Quattro Pro 3 can display in a third directory pane. The directory tree lists all directories and subdirectories on your disk in alphabetical order. You can move the cursor around the tree to display different directory contents in the file list pane.

When you want to use a directory tree, choose Tree from the File Manager window.

To display the directory tree just choose the Tree Open command. Quattro Pro 3 opens a tree pane below or to the right of the file pane in the File Manager window. The root directory is at the top on the far left. Subdirectories branch to the right and down. Quattro Pro 3 highlights the current directory on the tree. If there are more directories on your disk than will fit in the tree pane you can use the direction keys to scroll the list. When you use the cursor keys to move the highlight bar, Quattro Pro 3 displays files in a different directory. As you move the bar the directory prompt changes to show the name of the highlighted directory, and the file list changes to display the files in that directory.

Sizing the Tree

The first time you display a directory tree, Quattro Pro 3 divides the available File Manager window space equally between the file pane and the tree pane. You may want to give more or less space to the tree pane. To change the size of the tree pane, select Tree Resize from the File Manager menu. Quattro Pro 3 prompts you for a percentage. In future sessions, when you display the tree pane, it will be the size you last specified. Table 7-5 lists some keystrokes that let you select, delete, open, and refresh the display of file and directory information in the directory tree pane. If most of your work is in one directory, you can give more space to the file list by closing the directory tree pane. To do this use Tree Close. Quattro Pro 3 removes the directory tree and expands the file list pane to fill its space.

Printing File Information

The File Manager menu bar contains a print option. You can use this specialized Print menu to print parts of the File Manager window. The Print Block command gives you three options instead of a cell block prompt. The default option is Files, which prints a list of all files in the file list pane, even those you have to scroll to display. To print the directory tree, choose Tree. To print the file list followed by the directory tree, choose Both. You can send the output to a printer or to a file.

Managing and Loading Files

With the File Manager, you can move, copy, rename, or delete files on your disk without accessing DOS. You perform these actions from the File Manager Edit menu.

Selecting and Pasting Files

The first option on the File Manager Edit menu, shown in Figure 7-43, is Select File. This marks the highlighted file on the file list so that it stays highlighted even when you move the highlight bar away. You can use this command when you want to select a group of file names. The All Select option highlights all files on the file list, or if some files are already selected, it deselects all files.

The Copy option stores a copy of the selected files in the paste buffer. You can then paste the copy into any other directory. The Move option moves the selected files into the paste buffer and from there you can paste

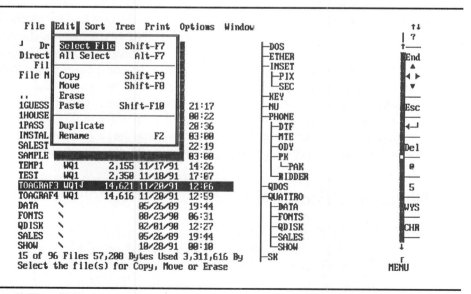

Figure 7-43.   *Edit menu*

them into another directory. The Erase option deletes the selected files from the disk. The Paste option inserts the files in the paste buffer in whatever directory you select.

The Duplicate option performs double duty, copying and renaming a file, and then storing the copy in the same or a different directory. The Rename option allows you to change the name of a file. Table 7-5 lists the special keys used in the file list pane for moving around, as well as for renaming, moving, copying, opening, and deleting files.

The first step to moving, copying, or deleting files is to select the files you want to work on. You do this with the Select and All Select keys (SHIFT-F7 and ALT-F7) or the Edit Select File and Edit All Select commands. You then use the Edit command you want, for example, Copy. Then use the file list or the directory tree to select the destination of the files you are copying. Use the Edit Paste command to place the files in this directory.

Opening Files

You can use the File Manager to open a spreadsheet file and display it in a new spreadsheet window. Just select the file name on the file list and press ENTER. Quattro Pro 3 removes the File Manager window from view and displays the spreadsheet, overlaying any existing spreadsheet windows. To open a file using a mouse, move the pointer to the file name and click the button to highlight the name; then click again to open the file.

To open several spreadsheet files at once, use the Edit Select command or SHIFT-F7 key to select each file on the file list, and then press ENTER. Quattro Pro 3 opens a new spreadsheet window for each and loads the file. Remember that you can also open a file from within the File Manager window by entering a name at the control pane's file name prompt and pressing ENTER. The name you enter does not have to be one of those displayed in the list, but it does have to be in the displayed directory.

Managing Directories

The File menu that you access from within a File Manager window contains a New command that opens a new worksheet window, and a Close command that closes the current window. The Read Dir command reads and redisplays the files on the current directory. The Make Dir command creates a new directory or subdirectory with the name and location you supply at the prompt. As in a worksheet window, the Workspace command lets you save the current setup of windows in a file or retrieve a saved workspace setup. The Utilities command allows you to open another File Manager window or access DOS without leaving Quattro Pro 3, as with the DOS Shell command on the regular File Utilities menu. The Exit command puts away Quattro Pro 3 and returns you to DOS.

The File Read command rereads the files on the specified directory and updates the file list accordingly. A typical use for this command would be when you have inserted a new disk in a floppy drive. The Calc key (F9) performs the same function as File Read, by "recalculating" the directory display.

File Manager Options

Selecting Options from the File Manager menu displays an adjusted Options menu. This menu, shown in Figure 7-44, lists some of the same system options available within a worksheet window and two options that

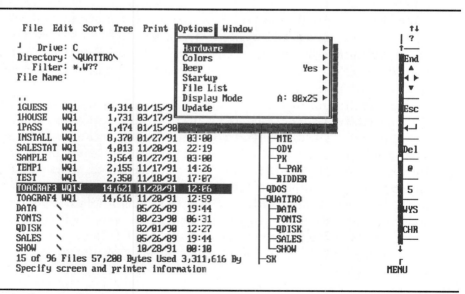

Figure 7-44. *File Manager Options*

deal directly with File Manager windows. The Hardware, Colors, Beep, Display Mode, and Update choices are the same as when you are in a worksheet window. The Start-up option contains the Menu Tree and Edit Menus commands plus a special command called Directory. This allows you to choose between a File Manager display of the directory you were in when you last used Quattro Pro 3, and the directory from which you just loaded Quattro Pro 3. The File List option displays just the file names in the file list—in several columns, or in a single column that includes size, date, and time information for each file.

Using SQZ!

A very useful file management feature that is built into Quattro Pro 3 is the ability to compress files when storing them on disk. This conserves valuable disk space. To use this feature you simply employ the file name extension WQ!. When storing files with the WQ! extension, Quattro Pro 3 uses a piece of software called SQZ! to pack the data tightly. When you retrieve a file with the WQ! extension the SQZ! program, which is contained within the main Quattro Pro 3 program, automatically unpacks the data. You can still use password protection with SQZ! files. With Quattro Pro 3 you can read compressed 1-2-3 Release 2 worksheet files that have the extension WK!, as well as compressed files from earlier versions of Quattro that have the extension WKZ.

The File Utilities SQZ! menu shown in Figure 7-45 allows you to adjust the way SQZ! operates. The Remove Blanks option allows you to increase the effectiveness of SQZ!. The Yes choice implements the added space saving of Removing Blanks. The default choice of No leaves blank cells in the compressed file. The Storage of Values option has three choices: Exact, Approximate, Remove. The Exact option retains all formulas and values in the compressed file. Leave this default setting in place if you plan to share the file with other programs. The Approximate choice retains formula results to 7 digits instead of the usual 15. The Remove option takes result values out of the worksheet and calculates results when the file is retrieved again.

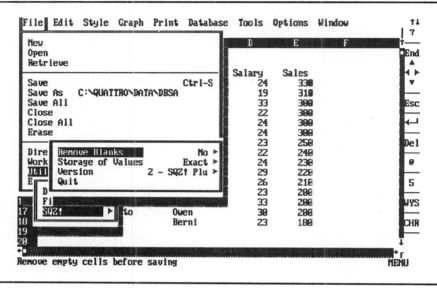

Figure 7-45. *The File Utilities SQZ! menu*

The Version option on the SQZ! menu lets you use either SQZ! or SQZ! Plus. The default is the more efficient SQZ! Plus, but if you have to pass on a file to a user who only has SQZ!, you can switch to this version. The most efficient settings for space saving are as follows:

Remove Blanks:	Yes
Storage of Values:	Remove
Version:	SQZ! Plus

To make saving in SQZ! format automatic, use Options Startup File Extension to make WQ! the default extension.

8 *Graphing*

Quattro Pro 3 offers exceptional graphics features. You can design a graph that is automatically updated when you change the numbers in the underlying spreadsheet. You can quickly create graphs with just a few keystrokes by using the Fast Graph option. You can place graphs within spreadsheets and create charts using data from multiple worksheets. But that is only the beginning. Quattro Pro 3 also offers a wide range of graphing options to produce well-designed, professional-quality graphs. In this chapter you will learn how to generate graphs from your data and apply the graphing options to improve and enhance those graphs.

Since Quattro Pro 3 provides so many options for customizing your graphs, illustrating every possible combination is beyond the scope of this book. The main options will be described, however, with suggestions for their application to your specific graphing needs.

Fast Graphs

Quattro Pro 3 can automatically generate graphs from spreadsheet numbers. This provides a quick way to make a graph; you can enter with one command the main settings from which you can develop a variety of customized graphs.

Using the Fast Graph Feature

Consider the spreadsheet in Figure 8-1. This is a record of year-to-date sales by the three agents at the Van Ness office of Quattro Vadis Travel. To make a graph of this data will take only one command. However, before issuing the command, place the cell selector in the top-left corner of the set of data to be graphed. In the case of Figure 8-1, this is D3. With D3 selected you can simply press CTRL-G, the default Shortcut for the Fast Graph feature. Alternatively, you can select Graph from the main menu and then select Fast Graph. You can see the Graph menu in Figure 8-2.

When you issue the Fast Graph command, either as a Shortcut or as a menu command, you are prompted for a Fast Graph block. This is a block of cells that includes the numbers to be graphed. Do not include totals for rows or columns of numbers being graphed—the graph commands compute totals automatically. In the case of the spreadsheet in Figure 8-1, the correct cells to include in the Fast Graph block are D3..G7. When you press ENTER to confirm this block, you are immediately presented with a graph. This can be a little alarming at first, since Quattro Pro 3 replaces the worksheet screen with a full screen display of the graph.

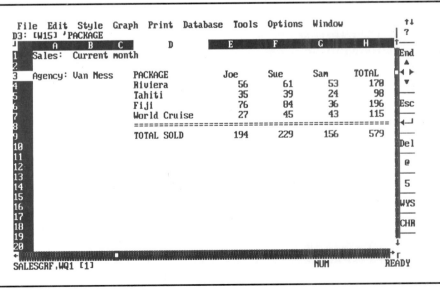

Figure 8-1. *Spreadsheet data to be graphed*

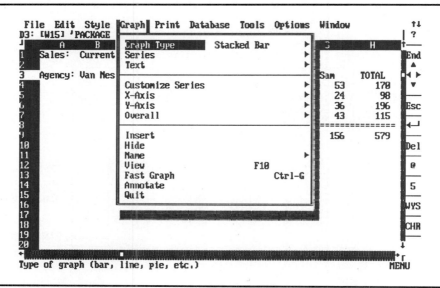

Figure 8-2. *The Graph menu*

In Figure 8-3 you can see the graph drawn by Fast Graph from the highlighted spreadsheet cells in Figure 8-1. This type of chart is called stacked-bar and it is the default graph type in Quattro Pro 3. The graph in Figure 8-3 has been annotated so that you can see the terms used by Quattro Pro 3 for the component parts of a graph. Note that the program automatically figures out how large to make the y-axis, the scale going up the left side of the graph.

The total number of products in each of the four categories of product are graphed as bars. The portion of the total sold by each agent is indicated by the three different shadings. If you have a color monitor you will see the agents differentiated by color as well. The legend box outside the main body of the graph explains which bar represents each agent. In Figure 8-3 and other figures in this chapter, the shading of the legend may not exactly match that of the main graph. This is due to the process used to reproduce the graph screen for purposes of illustration; the legend will be accurate in graphs printed and displayed by Quattro Pro 3.

To return to the spreadsheet you can press ESCAPE or the SPACEBAR. In fact, most keys will take you from the graph view back to the worksheet, but typing / while viewing a graph takes you to the *graph annotation screen.*

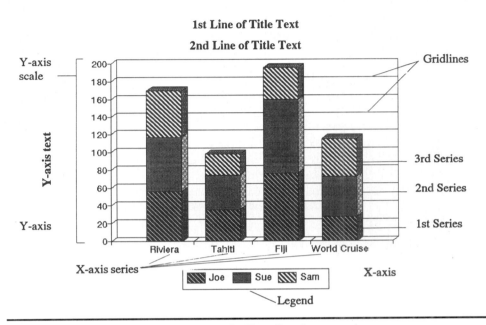

Figure 8-3. *Stacked bar graph drawn by Fast Graph*

To leave the graph annotation screen, which will be described in detail later, you type / again and then **Q** for Quit. You will be back at the graph view. You can use CTRL-BREAK to go from the annotation screen to the regular graph view, and once again to go from the regular graph view to READY mode.

Working with a Graph

As you review this first graph, note that in graph terminology the numbers for each agent constitute a series. These are measured on the y-axis, which is sometimes called the *value axis*. Each category of product is listed across the x-axis, which is sometimes called the *category axis*. Each value in the cells E4..G7 is represented by a different bar segment, which is referred to as a *data point*. The box that explains the shading is called a *legend*. Quattro Pro 3 allows you to remove the legend if it is not required (for example, when only one series of data is defined). In fact, there are many changes and embellishments you can make to this basic graph and they will be dealt with in the course of this chapter. Bear in mind, however, that making this first graph took just one command, and the results are very respectable. Furthermore, the graph you have made is dynamically linked to the data in the spreadsheet. For example, suppose that Sam actually sold 63 trips to Fiji rather than 36. You exit the graph view and change cell G6 from 36 to 63. To immediately see the difference in the graph you do not even need the menu; just press the Graph key (F10). This displays the current graph, which is the graph that the current settings generate. (Later you will see how Quattro Pro 3 stores a variety of graphs in one spreadsheet, but there is only one current graph.)

The graph of the corrected figures is shown in Figure 8-4. Notice how the y-axis has been altered to account for the increase in the size of the largest bar being graphed. If you have a printer that is capable of printing graphs you can easily print this graph. In READY mode, select Print from the main menu and then pick Graph Print. Select Destination and choose Graph Printer. Then select Go. Quattro Pro 3 should print out the graph, using the default values for size and layout. Graph printing can take

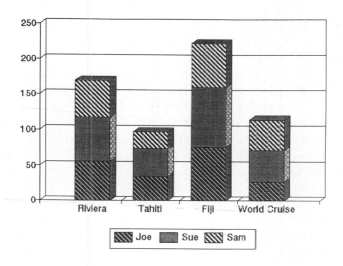

Figure 8-4.   *Corrected stacked bar graph*

several minutes, so do not be alarmed if your printer does not react for a little while.

Inserting a Graph

With Quattro Pro 3 you can insert the graph you have made into the spreadsheet that generated it. If you have either an EGA or a VGA display system, you can actually view the graph and worksheet together. On other display systems, you can insert graphs into worksheets in order to print them together on the same page, but you cannot view them together on the screen.

To insert a graph, select Insert from the Graph menu. You will be asked to specify a graph to be placed into the spreadsheet. Unless you have already defined other graphs, there will be only one graph in the list, the one that is current and appears when you press F10. This is listed as <Current Graph>. Highlight this and press ENTER. You will then be prompted for the location at which the graph is to be inserted. You might want to place the cell selector in a cell below the numbers that generate the graph. In fact, you can insert the graph over the numbers (or anywhere in the worksheet) without affecting them; in this case, cell B11 will work nicely. Anchor the block coordinates by typing a period, and then press the RIGHT and DOWN ARROW keys to move the highlighting to paint out an area of suitable size for the graph, in this case through to cell H23. This is the area that the graph will occupy. Press ENTER to complete the Graph Insert command.

Unless you have an EGA or a VGA display system and are using the WYSIWYG mode, you will not see much of a result from this command. A section of the worksheet will simply be blocked out to show the area occupied by the graph. If you have an EGA/VGA system and you want to see the graph displayed in the spreadsheet, use the Options Display mode command to select WYSIWYG or click the WYS button. The graph will be draw as the screen is rewritten. You can see the results in Figure 8-5. Notice the increased number of rows visible in WYSIWYG mode, and the improved appearance of the mouse palette and pointer. Also notice the second line of the screen, where cell B11 is especially marked as containing the current graph. In fact, this notation appears in all the cells of the block that you highlighted for the Graph Insert command. Data in any of these cells is not damaged, but it is obscured by the graph.

When you insert a graph into a spreadsheet it is dynamically linked to the data in the spreadsheet. Any changes you make to the spreadsheet

Figure 8-5. *Graph displayed in spreadsheet (WYSIWYG mode)*

entries that generated the graph are reflected in the graph. For example, suppose that the name of the World Cruise is changed to Mega-Cruise and that Joe realizes his Tahiti figure should be 53. Making these changes in the worksheet updates the graph, as you can see in Figure 8-6.

Working with Inserted Graphs

Displaying a graph in WYSIWYG mode can be quite a test of your computer's processing ability. Quattro Pro 3's response time slows down considerably when you are working in WYSIWYG mode on a spreadsheet that contains an inserted graph. Movement of the cell selector and cell editing will be slower because of the constant need to redraw the graph. You will probably want to insert graphs toward the end of the design

Figure 8-6. *Updated graph in spreadsheet (WYSIWYG mode)*

process and switch to character mode when you need to make a lot of changes to a worksheet that contains inserted graphs. To switch to character mode, click the CHR button or use the Options Display Mode command to select a character mode, such as 80x25.

Note that you can insert more than one graph in the same worksheet. Later in this chapter the procedure for naming graphs will be reviewed. When you have named a graph you can insert the named graph as well as the current graph, and the graphs will all be updated to reflect changes in the worksheet.

To remove a graph that you have inserted in your worksheet you use the Graph Hide command. This shows a list of all the graphs from which you select the one you want to remove. Highlight the graph name and press ENTER, and the graph will be removed. The graph will still be available for display.

To print a worksheet together with a graph you use the Spreadsheet Print command from the Print menu, but with the Print Destination set

Sales: Current month

Agency: Van Ness	PACKAGE	Joe	Sue	Sam	TOTAL
	Riviera	56	61	53	170
	Tahiti	53	39	24	116
	Fiji	76	84	63	223
	Mega-Cruise	27	45	43	115
	=============	======	======	======	=======
	TOTAL SOLD	212	229	183	624

Figure 8-7. *Combined spreadsheet and graph output*

to Graph Printer. You must include the graph cells (B11..H23) in the Print Block. An example of the combined output is shown in Figure 8-7. Obviously, the results of the combined print operation will depend on your printer and its capabilities; indeed, the graph-making side of spreadsheet work depends heavily on your choice of equipment. The next section reviews some of the hardware considerations in making graphs.

Graphics Equipment

Displaying and printing graphs imposes more demands on your hardware than printing spreadsheet text. As was discussed in Chapter 6, there are two different ways of displaying and printing information: character mode and graphics mode. The type of display adapter and printer that you have will affect your ability to produce graphs with Quattro Pro 3.

Graphics Display

In the character mode of display, each screen you view is made up of many separate characters typically arranged in 25 lines of 80 characters each. This is the mode shown in most of the screens in this book. The alternative is a graphics mode referred to in Quattro Pro 3 as WYSIWYG mode, where the screen is composed of a series of dots that draw shapes, including numbers, text, circles, and so on. Quattro Pro 3 can switch between different modes of display. This means that typical spreadsheet operations such as data entry and calculation can take place in the faster environment of character mode. However, when you want to design a high-quality report or a graph, Quattro Pro 3 can switch to graphics or WYSIWYG mode, shown in Figure 8-6.

If you have an IBM Color Graphics Adapter, a Hercules graphics card, an IBM Enhanced Graphics Adapter, or a VGA system, you will be able to display Quattro Pro 3 graphs on your screen when you press the F10 key and use the Annotate feature to embellish graphs. If your system does not support graphics displays, you can still create a Quattro Pro 3 graph; however, you will not be able to see the results until they are printed.

In addition, if you have an EGA or a VGA display you can also activate the WYSIWYG to display additional columns and rows in the workspace, as well as graphs that have been inserted within worksheets using the Graph Insert command. The WYSIWYG mode allows you to increase or decrease the number of spreadsheet columns and rows so that you can zoom in for greater detail or zoom out to see the bigger picture. The command for this is Options WYSIWYG Zoom%. Note that users of monochrome, Hercules, and CGA systems cannot view inserted graphs or use WYSIWYG mode.

Graphics Printing

To print a Quattro Pro 3 graph, you need a graphics *output device*; that is, a printer or plotter capable of reproducing graphics images. Most dot-matrix, laser, ink-jet, and thermal printers can produce graphs; however, daisy-wheel printers cannot produce Quattro Pro 3 graphs. Quattro Pro 3 graphs can be reproduced in color with a color printer or plotter. You initially tell Quattro Pro 3 about your graphics output device through the installation program. If you did not specify a printer then or you need to change printers, use the Hardware command on the Options menu, as discussed in Chapter 6. When you select Printers from the Hardware menu you will see that Quattro Pro 3 allows you to define two printers, 1st Printer and 2nd Printer. You define one of these two printers as the default; this is the one that is used when you issue a print command from the Print menu.

There are two ways of printing graphs with Quattro Pro 3. You can send just the graph to the printer or you can insert the graph in a spreadsheet print block and print the graph as part of the spreadsheet. As you saw from the Graph menu in Figure 8-2 there is no Print option. In Quattro Pro 3 you print graphs from the Print menu shown in Figure 8-8. As you can see, the Print menu has a Destination option. However, this affects only the direction of spreadsheet output sent to the printer with the Spreadsheet Print command, not the printing of graphs. The Graph Print command has its own Destination option, as shown in Figure 8-8.

The three options on the Graph Print Destination menu are File, Graph Printer, and Screen Preview. Graph Printer is the default selection; this is the option to use when you are sending a graph to the printer on its own, as opposed to being part of a combined spreadsheet/graph print job.

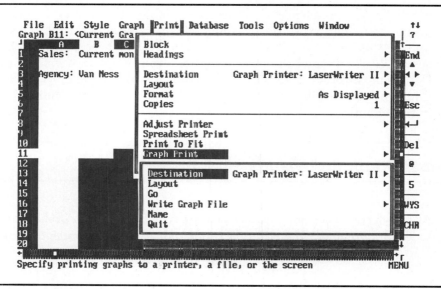

Figure 8-8.   *The Destination option*

To clarify the printing procedure, consider the following example. Suppose that your printer is an HP LaserJet. This printer is capable of printing text and graphics. Using the Options Hardware menu, you have chosen the correct model of LaserJet as 1st Printer and made sure that 1st Printer is the Default Printer. You have used Fast Graph to create a graph. You have made sure that the numbers are correct. You pressed F9 in READY mode to make sure that the spreadsheet is calculated up to date. You have pressed F10 to view the graph. The graph looks good and you want to print it. Back in READY mode you select Print from the main menu, and then Graph Print. You make sure that Graph Printer is chosen as the Destination. You check that the Layout settings are correct. You then pick Go. Quattro Pro 3 sends the graph to the Default Printer—your 1st Printer, which Quattro Pro 3 knows is a LaserJet.

Now suppose that the graph came out nicely and you want to print a quick draft of the spreadsheet that generated the graph. You pick Print from the main menu and define the Block. You check that the Destination setting on the Print menu is Printer. You check the Layout settings and then pick Spreadsheet Print. You decide you would like a presentation-quality print of the same area of the spreadsheet. You select Destination from the Print menu, change it to Graph Printer, and then select Spreadsheet Print.

Suppose that you decide to insert the graph in the spreadsheet as described earlier. You complete the Graph Insert command, define an area of cells in the spreadsheet that includes numbers, labels, and the inserted graph. You select Print from the main menu, make sure that the Destination setting is Graph Printer, and select Spreadsheet Print. Both the spreadsheet cells and the inserted graph are printed on the same page. Details of the other graph printing commands, Layout and Write Graph File, are described in the section on "Finer Points of Graph Printing" later in this chapter.

Manual Graph Commands

Although the Fast Graph feature is a powerful one, you will probably want to learn more about the different commands that you can use to create a graph. This will enable you to use the commands to create graphs from scratch and also to customize graphs that you have started with the Fast Graph feature.

To see how you use Quattro Pro 3 to build a graph from scratch, a typical scenario will be presented here. As the manager of Take Over Airlines you are called upon by the owner to review the year's performance. Immediately, you turn to the worksheet in which you have been accumulating the passenger volume figures in each of these three classes: First, Business, and Coach. This worksheet is shown in Figure 8-9. The number of passengers in each class in each of the four quarters can be easily transformed into a graph.

An example of what the numbers might look like as a graph is shown in Figure 8-10. In the following sections you will find the basic elements of building graphs described in the order in which they arise in the building process. As you have already seen in the section on Fast Graph, Quattro Pro 3 requires very little information to build a very presentable graph. However, since most elements of a graph can be customized to enhance the graph's appearance and accommodate unusual types of data, many of the menus you will use contain several options. Not all of these options will be examined as the graph is built, but they will be presented later.

Figure 8-9.   *Passenger volume by class as spreadsheet*

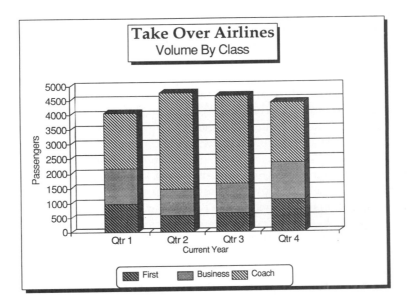

Figure 8-10. *Passenger volume by class as graph*

Preparing to Graph

The basic procedure for creating a graph with Quattro Pro 3 is to indicate the spreadsheet coordinates of the data to be graphed. Usually this data is readily available in your spreadsheet, as in the case of the sales statistics shown earlier in Figure 8-1, or the passenger statistics shown in Figure 8-9. In both cases, the numbers are in consecutive columns that form a block. In fact, Quattro Pro 3 requires that each set of values for your graph be in consecutive cells in the worksheet. Occasionally, prior to building a graph, you will need to rearrange data to comply with this requirement. You can use either the Edit Copy or Edit Move command to accomplish this, or you can develop a new spreadsheet that references the cells from the main model in a compact block suitable for graphing. In most cases, however, you will probably be graphing data that is already arranged in suitable blocks of cells.

Although the position of your cell selector prior to entering the Graph menu is not critical, you should place it near the data that is to be graphed, in this case, in cell B3 or B4. To build a graph from the spreadsheet in Figure 8-9, you first select Graph from the main menu. The Graph menu, shown earlier in Figure 8-2, shows you the main options involved in graphing. The first option, Graph Type, refers to the kind of graph that you want Quattro Pro 3 to produce. The default type is the stacked bar shown in all of the graphs so far in this chapter. When you select Graph Type, you will see a list of the available types. If you are using the graphics display mode the list of types will appear as a diagram illustrating the different possibilities with the current selection shown highlighted. In Figure 8-11 you can see the Graph Type diagram with stacked bar selected. Whichever type of list you are using, use the arrow keys to move the highlighting to the graph type you want and press ENTER to select it.

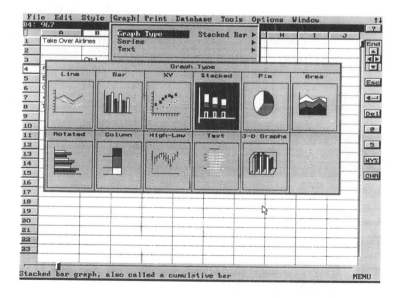

Figure 8-11.   *The Graph Type option in WYSIWYG mode*

You do not have to make your final selection of graph type before creating the graph, as the type can be changed later. Unless you have a specific type of graph in mind, leave the setting at the default stacked bar. Next, you need to tell Quattro Pro 3 the various pieces of information it needs to build the graph. Refer to Figure 8-3 for some of the basic terminology used.

Series Values

The numbers you are charting in the graph are called the *series values*. The series values must be values; they *cannot* be labels. You can graph as many as six sets of values at once. In this example, the three series values to be graphed are the volume figures for First, Business, and Coach class. When you select Series from the Graph menu, the Series menu lists 1st Series, 2nd Series, and so on. There is also a command on this menu to specify the x-axis cells; that is, the numbers or labels displayed along the x-axis to identify the different series. The Group option is used to specify more than one set of values at a time, as described in the next section.

When you select 1st Series, you are prompted to enter the cell coordinates of the first set of values. You can highlight, or paint, the cells as you do with other blocks of cells in Quattro Pro 3. First move the cell selector to make sure it is on the first value in the series; in the example in Figure 8-9 this is cell B4. Then enter a period to anchor the beginning coordinate. The screen will respond with B4..B4. Now you can select 2nd Series and use the cursor-movement keys to move to the second coordinate and highlight the column or row of values. Since values for a series must all be in consecutive cells, the END key may work well to highlight the cells you want. However, you do not need to include the total for the column or row that is being specified as a series, since Quattro Pro 3 will calculate the total of the values in the block for you. Thus, the example uses B4..E4 as the 1st Series.

If you want to change the coordinates as you are highlighting them, the ESCAPE key will unlock the coordinates so that you can begin again from the first coordinate. The BACKSPACE key unlocks the coordinates and returns the cell selector to the cell it occupied when you entered the menu system. Of course, if you know the cell coordinates, you can just type them, instead of pointing to the cells. When you press ENTER to confirm the coordinates, you are returned to the Series menu where you can indicate the next series. After you have entered all three of the series values, press ESCAPE to return to the Graph menu.

Note that the menu shows the settings for the series as you establish them, as shown in Figure 8-12. If you need to change the spreadsheet coordinates of the series values, you select Series and pick the number of the series you want to check. You will see the currently recorded block of cells highlighted. Press ENTER to confirm this block, or press ESCAPE or BACKSPACE to unlock the coordinates and redefine them. If you want to remove a series, you must use the Reset option, which is described later in this chapter.

Reading and Grouping Series Values

You may wonder why it is necessary to use the Series command when the Fast Graph command reads all of the series for you, including the x-axis. Unfortunately, the Fast Graph command does not know that it should avoid empty cells in a block. For example, Fast Graph applied to the worksheet in Figure 8-13 would produce the graph shown in Figure 8-14. You can see that there are gaps between the data points in each series, leading to greater separation between the bars. Other odd effects will occur if there are labels filling some of the empty cells, such as a line of equal signs (in row 12 in the figure).

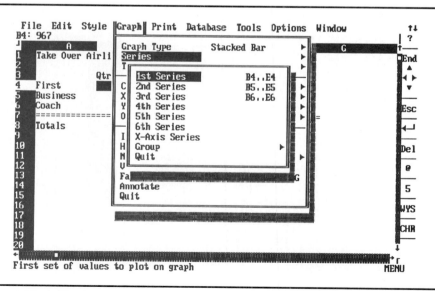

Figure 8-12. *The Series option*

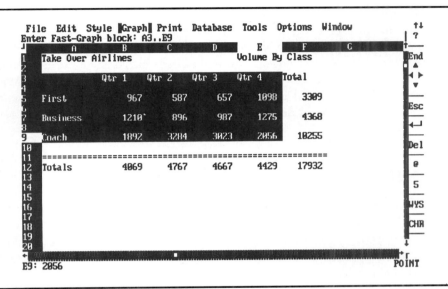

Figure 8-13.   *Spreadsheet with gaps*

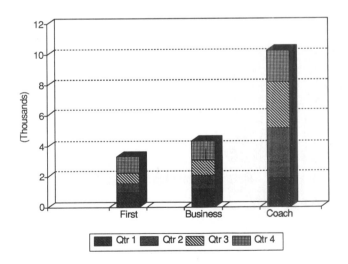

Figure 8-14.   *Fast Graph applied to the worksheet in Figure 8-13*

Another aspect of the Fast Graph command that is not immediately apparent is the way it interprets the block of data to be graphed. The series values in a block can either be read column-wise or row-wise. In the first example in this chapter the three agents, Joe, Sam, and Sue, were read as the series, and the four different packages they sold were read as the x-axis. That is, the data was interpreted column-wise because the series was read from the columns. However, you might have wanted the agents to be the x-axis and the packages the series. You can see a manually constructed graph of the same data in Figure 8-15, where Quattro Pro 3 has taken the series from the rows rather than the columns.

The individual selection of series is also a necessity when you are graphing data from multiple worksheets. For example, suppose that the data for the graph was not combined into one worksheet, but spread across several. You might have three separate worksheets, each one storing figures for a single class, as shown in Figure 8-16. In a fourth worksheet you could graph the total figures from the other three, without having to copy the data into the fourth worksheet.

To create a graph that refers to data in other worksheets, you simply use the Graph Series command and for each series move to the appropriate

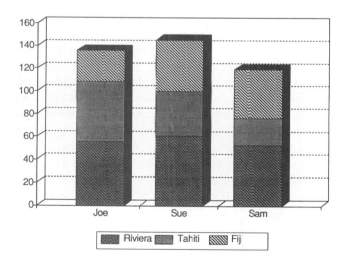

Figure 8-15.   *A row-wise reading of data*

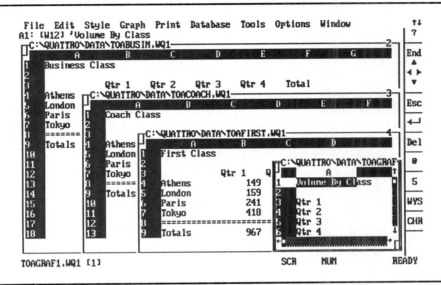

Figure 8-16.   *Three spreadsheets compiled by class*

worksheet to make the cell selection for the series values. Clearly, you need to specify each series separately for which you cannot use the Fast Graph command. Note that the current graph is the one that is displayed when F10 is pressed. In Figure 8-16 the TOAGRAF1.WQ1 worksheet is current. Also note that you can have the x-axis read from a column of values even though the series values are in rows.

There are times when you have your data series arranged conveniently but separate from the x-axis. In such cases, you can speed up series entry by choosing the Series Group option. When you choose this option you have a choice between Columns and Rows, as shown in Figure 8-17. This worksheet contains quarterly passenger numbers for Business Class travelers according to the destination city. You can assign each column of values in the block to a series, or each row. In this case, to create a quarterly graph you would use the Rows option. When you select either Columns or Rows you are prompted for a block of data (as with the Fast Graph option). However, you do not include the x-axis or labels in this block—just series values. When you have selected the block you press ENTER. No graph is automatically drawn for you, but you have accomplished in one command the equivalent of setting four series, one for each city. All you need do now to get a basic graph is to set the x-axis.

Figure 8-17. *The Group option*

X-Axis

As soon as you have provided at least one series of values, you can actually view the graph. In this case, Quattro Pro 3 will show three bars, because there are three parallel observations made about each series of data. However, until you specify the x-axis values to be displayed along the bottom of the graph, Quattro Pro 3 cannot tell you what these bars represent. The x-axis values can be numeric values or labels and should be entered before viewing the graph. This enables Quattro Pro 3 to identify the observation points along the x-axis. In the case of the statistics shown in Figure 8-9, the x-axis values are Qtr 1, Qtr 2, and so on.

To define the x-axis you select Series from the Graph menu and then select X-Axis Series, which is one of the last options on the menu. You are prompted to enter the values as coordinates. You highlight the cells containing the x-axis data (cells B3 through E3 in this case) or type the coordinates, just as you did with the 1st Series command. When you press ENTER to confirm the x-axis coordinates, you are returned to the Graph menu. The coordinates are shown on the menu for reference purposes.

You can have from 1 to 8192 separate data points on the x-axis, if they are stored in a column; or from 1 to 256, if they are stored in a row.

However, you will encounter limitations of display space, which may make more than 30 data points difficult to see. In such cases, you do not need to enter any x-axis coordinates. Quattro Pro 3 will simply show a check mark for each set of data.

Viewing the Graph

To produce a basic graph, all Quattro Pro 3 needs is at least one series of values. A set of x-axis values helps only to clarify the chart. When you have entered the values for the volume spreadsheet, you can go ahead and view the graph. The Graph menu contains the View option. When you select View, your screen switches to graphics mode and displays the latest version of the graph you are working on. You cannot change the figures represented in the graph while you are viewing it. After you have viewed a graph, press ENTER or ESCAPE or SPACEBAR to return to the menu you left. The graph view of the volume statistics graph at this point is shown in Figure 8-18.

Although this graph still needs a title to describe what the bars represent, it is important to see how much work has been done so far. Quattro Pro 3 has totaled the figures for each quarter and represented the total as a large bar. It has proportionately divided the bar according to each class of traveler. The scale on the left has been selected to accommodate the largest quarterly volume total. The x-axis values—in this case, the labels Qtr 1, Qtr 2, and so on—are shown along the bottom. At this point the graph also lacks a legend. You create a legend by naming the series values. The Fast Graph command does this automatically by using the labels next to the series value cells. When you are constructing a graph manually, any legend text that you want displayed has to be entered one series at a time. You may also want to enter text for titles and to describe the x- and y-axes.

Adding Text

As you can see from Figure 8-19, there are several areas of the graph to which you can add text. These were diagrammed in Figure 8-3. These pieces of text are fixed to specific points of the graph and should not be confused with the free-floating text that can be added with the Annotate feature, which is described towards the end of this chapter.

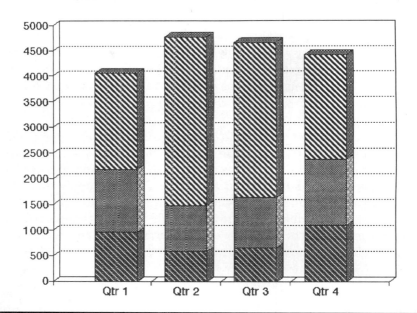

Figure 8-18. *Quarter volume graph*

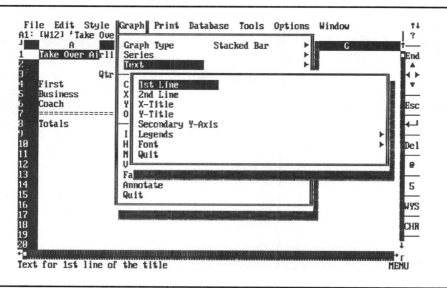

Figure 8-19. *The Text option*

Text Sources

All of the text added to a Quattro Pro 3 graph can be supplied by worksheet cells. This capability was used by the Fast Graph feature to label the first graph. Using a cell reference for text, rather than simply typing the text, has the advantage of being easy to update. As you saw in Figure 8-6, altering the name from World Cruise to Mega-Cruise automatically updated the graph.

To manually enter text for the graph you select the appropriate item on the Text menu and then type the text you want displayed in the graph, or type the coordinates of the cell containing the label you want used as text in the graph, preceded by a backslash (\). Thus, to supply the title Take Over Airlines as the 1st Line of the graph title, you would enter \ **A1**. Note that there is no facility for pointing to cells to enter their coordinates in the Text menu. Furthermore, the cell references are not dynamic. If you move the label from A1 to B1, Quattro Pro 3 will not know, and the label will essentially disappear from the graph.

Title Text

Most graphs need a title. To supply one you first select Text from the Graph menu. The item called 1st Line is the one that heads the graph. Select 1st Line from the Text menu and type the text you want, such as **Take Over Airlines**, in the box provided, as shown in Figure 8-20. Alternatively, since this same text has been entered as a label in worksheet cell A1, you can type \ **A1**. The title can be 39 characters long. You can use BACKSPACE to correct any errors as you type. If you want to edit the title, the LEFT and RIGHT ARROW keys move the cursor through the text of the title. You can insert new characters to the left of the cursor just by typing them. Pressing ESCAPE while you are typing a title removes the text you have entered. Pressing ESCAPE with nothing on the title edit line returns you to the Text menu. When you have typed the title correctly, press ENTER to confirm it. Quattro Pro 3 returns you to the Text menu, where all or part of the text of the title is visible. This helps you to keep track of text you have entered. Note that when you use a cell reference for text, the cell reference and not the text itself is visible on the Text menu.

You can add a 2nd Line title, such as Volume by Class, or type \ **E1** to use the text from the worksheet. Text to label the x-axis is called the X-Title. In the case of the graph in Figure 8-18 this could be Current Year.

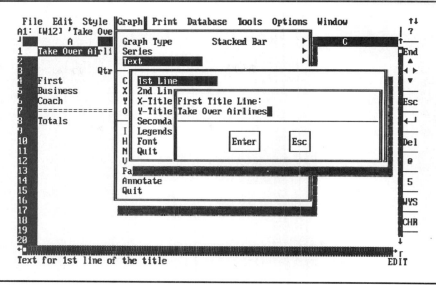

Figure 8-20. *The 1st Line option*

The Y-Title labels the y-axis, and the graph in Figure 8-18 should include text that explains what units of measurement are displayed, in this case Passengers. While the x-axis title may sometimes be omitted, a y-axis title is often essential to properly document the graph. Note that if you use a second y-axis, as described later in this chapter, then you can label it with the Secondary Y-Axis option.

All of these pieces of text are limited to 39 characters. You can see the graph from Figure 8-18 labeled in Figure 8-21. Note that this figure was produced by using a screen print program, and not the Graph Print option on the Print menu. Since the clarity and dimensions of displayed graphs vary according to display types, this graph may not be an exact replication of what you will see on your screen. Also note that the style of lettering used is the default—the font options for your lettering may be different.

The Legend

The one element still lacking in the graph in Figure 8-21 is an explanation of what the different data values represent. You cannot tell from the graph which shading represents which class. The key to a graph is its legend,

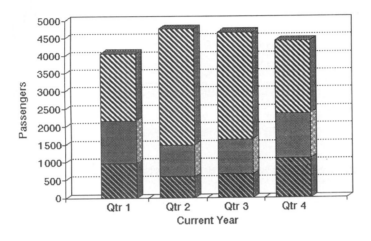

Figure 8-21.   *Labeled graph*

which you set through the Text Legend option. The legend text for each series consists of either manually entered text, or a reference to a cell where the text can be found. When you select Legends from the Text menu you will be shown a list of six series, one for each of the maximum six sets of values. You enter text here as you do with the other text items. To label the first series, the First Class passengers, you pick 1st Series, and either type the text **First Class** or use the cell reference \A4. Remember that the first series appears at the bottom of a stacked bar graph.

The Text Legend menu also includes the Position option, which lets you decide between displaying the legend at the Bottom of the graph, to the Right of it, or not at all. The default setting is at the Bottom, so that as soon as you enter some legend text a legend will be displayed below the actual graph. You select None from the Position menu to turn off the legend display without erasing the text that you have entered in the legend series. By switching between None and one of the other two choices for Position you can turn the legend on and off. Note that the Annotate feature, described later in this chapter, allows you complete freedom to place the legend wherever you like on the graph.

The maximum number of characters you can enter as the legend text for a series is 19. The number of characters of legend text displayed by the graph will vary according to the dimensions and proportions of the graph. Tall, narrow graphs can accommodate only nine or ten characters in the legend, while wide graphs can show the full 19. After typing the legend text and pressing ENTER, you can proceed to the other series and name them accordingly. After setting up the legends, you can view the results by pressing the F10 key. The resulting graph will look like the one pictured in Figure 8-22.

Fonts

You may notice that the text of your titles is displayed in a different typeface, or font, from that seen in Figure 8-22. There are many different fonts available for graphing, including all of those available for enhanced spreadsheet printing (described in Chapter 5). You can adjust the font settings for each piece of text in the chart by using the Font option on the Text menu. When you select Font from the Text menu you see these choices:

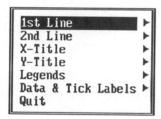

Text in each of these areas of the graph can be individually adjusted to achieve the best visual effect. All of the options are the same as in the Text menu, except for Data & Tick Labels. These are the numbers that Quattro Pro 3 adds to the y-axis to document the scale of the graph.

When you select any of the options on the Font menu you are shown a menu of four characteristics that can be adjusted to alter the displayed and printed appearance of your graph, as follows:

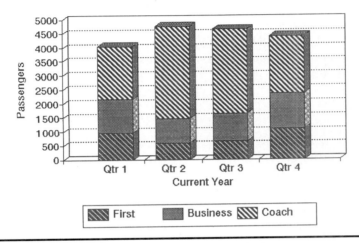

Figure 8-22.   *Graph titles and legend (in bottom location)*

Note that selecting the Color option, which leads to a list of colors that can be assigned to the text, does not affect the printed version of your graph unless you have a color printer.

The Typeface option on the font characteristics menu leads to a list of available typefaces, with the current selection already highlighted. The list includes the Bitstream fonts, plus the Hershey fonts listed here:

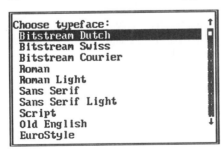

In addition, there may be typefaces for specific printers such as those available to LaserJet users. To see the full range of typefaces, scroll down the list. To assign a typeface you highlight your choice and press ENTER. To leave the list without altering the current typeface setting you press ESCAPE.

When you have chosen a typeface you will also want to assign a point size. The Point Size option leads to a list that goes from 8 point to 72 point. To give you an idea of the relative size of these measurements, take a look at Figure 8-22. The 1st Line title is in 36 point and the 2nd Line is in 24 point. The x-axis title is in 18 point.

The Style option allows you to select from the following list of font styles:

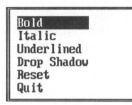

```
Bold
Italic
Underlined
Drop Shadow
Reset
Quit
```

Some items may have the word "On" next to them, indicating that the style has been chosen for the current piece of text. You can turn on one or more of the items by highlighting and pressing ENTER, or by typing the first letter.

The Bold and Italic options are useful for adding emphasis to a piece of text. The Underline option causes the text to be displayed with a line below it. The Drop Shadow option places a shadow behind letters to highlight them. The Reset option allows you to turn off all of the attributes.

You can see the effects of font choices while you are still in the menu structure just by pressing F10. While it may take you a while to get used to the effect of different sizes on the text of your graph, you will find that an appropriate choice of font will enhance your graph's appearance and effectiveness.

Graph Keys

When you have designed a graph and returned to READY mode, any changes you make to the cells that make up the x- axis values or the series values will be reflected in the graph and visible the next time you view it. You can try this now by leaving the Graph menu, either with ESCAPE or the Quit option, and typing a new number, 333, for First Class passengers in the third quarter. To see the change that this new number has made to the graph, you can either choose View from the Graph menu, or from READY mode press the Graph key (F10), which displays the current graph.

You can have only one graph at a time in memory, and this graph is referred to as the current graph. The next key you press will return you to the Graph menu if you used the Graph View command, or to READY mode if you viewed the graph from READY mode with F10.

The F10 key works either in READY mode or MENU mode, whether or not you are using the Graph menu. Bear in mind that when you have no graphs defined in a worksheet, pressing F10 will cause Quattro Pro 3 to display a blank screen with the message "No series defined." The one exception to this is if you select Text as the Graph type but define no series values. In this case you get a blank graph screen on which to place text with the Annotate feature.

There is one special key to use while viewing a graph and that is the / key. This activates Quattro Pro 3's Annotate feature, which is a complete drawing program built into the Graph feature. With this feature, described later in the chapter, you can enhance your graphs with a virtually unlimited range of images. You can even use Annotate to create pictures that are not graphs but shapes and symbols, like the ones in Figure 8-23, that can be printed from Quattro Pro 3 or inserted into spreadsheets. However, before exploring these exciting possibilities it is important to learn the mundane but vital commands needed to save and organize your work with graphs.

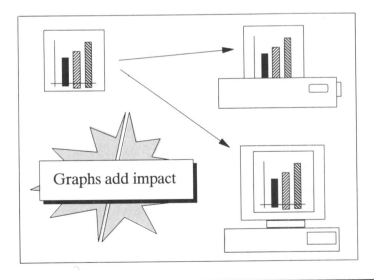

Figure 8-23.   *Pictures created by using Annotate*

Naming and Storing Graphs

Having viewed your graph and decided that it is acceptable, you might be tempted to rush to print the graph. But before proceeding, you should take a moment to save your work. So far, none of your graphing work has been stored by Quattro Pro 3. The settings for the x- and y-axes, your titles, the choice of font, and so forth are still only in memory. You must issue the File Save or File Save As command to save the worksheet and the graph settings.

Storing Graph Names

If you design a graph and then store your worksheet, you will be able to see the graph the next time you retrieve the file simply by pressing F10, or by using the Graph View command. Having built one graph, however, you may wish to go on to create another. Since Quattro Pro 3 can have only one graph in memory at a time, changing the graph settings at this point would alter the graph you just designed. To store the collection of settings that together produce the graph you have just viewed so that you can recall them later, you assign a name to the graph, much the same as you do when naming a block of cells. Select Name from the Graph menu and you will see the seven options: Display, Create, Autosave Edits, Erase, Reset, Slide, and Graph Copy.

Select Create and you will see a list of any previously stored graphs. Whether or not there are any previously stored graphs, you will be prompted with "Enter graph name:". You can highlight one of the existing names and press ENTER to replace that graph with the current one, or you can simply type a new name and press ENTER. Here you can see that a couple of graphs have already been named:

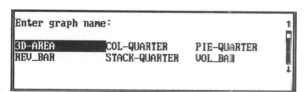

When you have entered a name, you are returned to the Graph menu. If you want to see a previously named graph, select Name again, and then select Display. Finally, select a name from the list. You can remove names from the list with Erase or completely remove all graph names with Reset.

The Reset command requires that you answer Yes or No to the question "Delete all named graphs?", since the command is a destructive one, wiping out all named graph settings.

The Graph Name Create command attaches a name to whatever graph is current. If you display a graph called BAR with the Name Display command and then make changes to it, you must be careful if you want to keep the changes. If you use Name Create and select BAR, that will update the BAR graph to reflect the changes. But you must do this before you display another graph or the changes will be lost. Alternatively, you can set the Autosave Edits option to Yes. This will ensure that changes made to a named graph are stored under that name.

An exciting option on the Graph Name menu is Slide. Using this option you can create a *slide show* with Quattro Pro 3. This consists of a series of graphs displayed one after the other. See the section "Slide Shows" in Chapter 13 for more on this command.

The last option of the Graph Name menu is Graph Copy, a powerful tool for users who need to create a lot of graphs. With Graph Copy you can paste a graph from one spreadsheet into another. Linking cell references are automatically created for you. You can use the graph as is, or edit it. This allows you to transfer a whole range of graph settings from one set of data in one spreadsheet to a completely different set of data in another.

Suppose you are working on a spreadsheet to predict revenue for the next year for Take Over Airlines. You want to use this revenue spreadsheet as the basis for a presentation to the board of directors. You know that in the spreadsheet containing last year's volume figures there was a super graph of volume by class of passenger. You want to use that volume graph in the revenue projection spreadsheet but do not want to import all of the figures. You can use Graph Copy to paste the graph into the revenue projection spreadsheet, just as you would a block of cells. First you open the spreadsheet containing the graph you want to use, in this case, the volume spreadsheet. Then you issue the Graph Copy command and select from the list of named graphs that is displayed. When you have entered the name of the graph you want to copy you are asked to indicate the target spreadsheet, the one into which the chosen graph will be pasted. In this case, you indicate the revenue projection spreadsheet. Simply select the spreadsheet, either with SHIFT-F6 or the Window Pick command, and then press ENTER to complete the Graph Copy command. The graph is now a named graph in the revenue projection spreadsheet.

You must move to the target spreadsheet and issue the Graph Name command to actually see the graph. Select Display and you will see the copied graph named in the list. Select the graph and it will be shown, and made the current graph. You can keep the graph as is, or change the settings. For example, if you like the style of the graph, you can change the data series to cells within the current spreadsheet and then give the new graph a different name. This allows you to copy the style of graphs from one worksheet to another. Note that unless you edit the copied graph it will continue to draw its data from the source worksheet. This means that when you load the worksheet containing the copied graph you will get the chance to select one of the Link options (Load supporting, Update Refs, or None). Either choose Load Supporting to open the file that supplies the data for the copied graph, or Update Refs to read the correct current values for the linked graph. If you choose None, the supporting links will be temporarily disabled.

Remember, even though you have assigned a name to a graph you still must save the worksheet file to store the graph names on disk. Also bear in mind that placing graphs in worksheets with Graph Insert command also has a bearing on graph changes. In effect, a graph inserted in the worksheet becomes the current graph if you enter the Graph menu while your cell selector is within the inserted graph. For example, if you have inserted the graph called BAR in A21..H30, you will see Graph A21:BAR and similar notations in all of those cells. If you press F10 or select a command from the Graph menu while your cell selector is in one of these cells, then BAR will become the current graph. However, if you return to the READY mode and move your cell selector to a nongraph cell, the previous current graph will be reinstated.

Storing Graph Files

There may be times when you want to store a graph as a *picture file*, which contains the necessary data for other programs to read the graph as an image and display it, edit it, or print it. To save a graph in this type of file, you print it to a file with the Graph Print option on the Print menu. You then use the Write Graph File option, which is described in the next section.

Finer Points of Graph Printing

When you have stored the worksheet containing the current graph settings, you can proceed to print the graph. You do not have to store before printing, but it is advisable. The Graph Print option on the Print menu prints out the latest version of the current graph if the Destination setting is Graph Printer. You should press F10 once more before printing to make sure that the graph you are about to print is the correct one.

Telling Quattro Pro 3 About Printers

When you select Graph Print from the Print menu you will see a menu listing the following: Destination, Layout, Go, Write Graph File, Name, and Quit. The Destination is normally set to Graph Printer and the name of the printer model will be shown, as you can see in Figure 8-24. The Layout option leads to a submenu of settings that describe how you want the graph sized and placed on the page. The Go option actually initiates the printing process. The Write Graph File option is for creating files from graphic output.

Figure 8-24. *Graph Print Destination*

Destination

When you select Destination from the Print menu, you can choose to send the graphic output to one of three places: File, Graph Printer, or Screen Preview. The last option, Screen Preview, shows you what the graph will look like when printed, including the dimensions and placement on the page. The preview system for graphs works in the same way as that for spreadsheets (described at the end of Chapter 5).

If you want to store a Quattro Pro 3 graph as a text file that can be printed later or used by another program, select File as the destination of the print operation. Quattro Pro 3 prompts you to enter a file name of up to eight letters for the graph. When you enter the file name, Quattro Pro 3 sets the destination to which a PRN file containing a data image of the current graph would be written. To create this graph, execute the Graph Print Go command. An alternative file format for storing graphic images is the EPS type, which you can create by using the Write Graph File option on the Graph Print menu.

Write Graph File

To store your graph in a special file that can be read by other programs, you select Write Graph File from the Graph Print menu. The options are EPS, PIC, Slide EPS, and PCX. The EPS format is Encapsulated Post-Script. This can be read by a number of other programs, and can be printed on a printer that understands the PostScript page description language, such as the Apple LaserWriter. For example, when you are using the TOPS network to connect IBM PCs to Apple Macintoshes and LaserWriters you can use the TOPS commands to send your EPS file to a LaserWriter on the network. The EPS format preserves all of the graph's visual qualities; however, none of the graph file formats are dynamic. This means that once a graph is written to a file it does not automatically change when the worksheet that generated the graph is updated.

The PIC format is compatible with Lotus 1-2-3, which enables 1-2-3 to print Quattro Pro 3 graphs. However, 1-2-3 graphs are limited in scope. Thus, features unique to Quattro Pro 3—such as special fonts, free-floating text, and drawn objects—are lost when a file is stored in the PIC format. The Slide EPS format is used when sending files to a slide preparation 35mm service bureau, as described in your Quattro Pro 3 manual. The PCX format allows the graph to be edited and used by paint programs such as PC Paintbrush or Microsoft Paint running under Windows 3.

To create a specialized file of either of the two types, you select the correct type from the list. For example, to create an EPS file you select EPS from the Write Graph File menu and then enter a file name of up to eight letters. Quattro Pro 3 will add the EPS extension. When you press ENTER the file is created on disk.

Layout

When you have selected Graph Printer as the Destination on the Graph Print menu and picked Go, Quattro Pro 3 prints the current graph with the current page layout. The default page layout produces a graph that covers the width of a regular sheet of paper and is positioned halfway between the top and bottom of the paper.

While the default setting is acceptable in many cases, there will probably be times when you want to alter the size and shape of the finished graph. You do this with the Layout option of the Graph Print menu. As shown in Figure 8-25, the Layout menu lets you define the dimensions of the printed

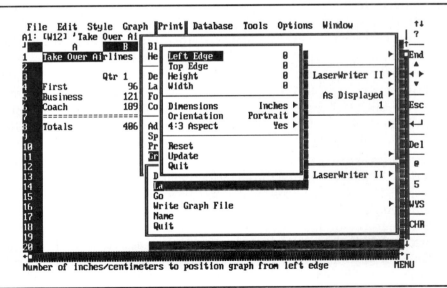

Figure 8-25.   *The Layout menu*

graph in either inches, which is the default, or centimeters. The Left Edge setting indicates the graph's left margin, the number of inches or centimeters from the left edge of the paper. The Top Edge setting indicates the top margin, where Quattro Pro 3 should start printing the graph.

In Figure 8-25 you can see that the dimensions of the graph are not defined. The effect of a setting of 0 for the edges, height, and width is to tell Quattro Pro 3 to fill the page with the graph. If you do enter height and width measurements Quattro Pro 3 gives you the option of either preserving a standard ratio of width to height (4:3) or allowing the actual ratio of height to width measurements to determine the proportions of the finished graph. For example, if you enter 4 inches for both height and width then Yes for the 4:3 Aspect option on the Layout menu, Quattro Pro 3 will not print the graph as a square. Instead the rectangular shape of the graph is preserved within the space you have allotted. For example, a graph that is laid out as 4 inches by 4 inches will have an x-axis side that is 4 inches long, but the y-axis side will be about 3 inches. However, if you select No for the 4:3 Aspect option, Quattro Pro 3 will scale the graph to the dimensions you have specified, and in this example, you will get a graph that is literally square.

You will find that some printers take a long time to produce full-page graphs, particularly at high resolution. Consequently, you may want to limit their size when printing the first few versions until you have the design ready for a final printing. Note that in their standard configuration, the HP LaserJet II and some other laser printers cannot accept a full graphics image at 300 dots per inch. They must print full-page graphs at 150 dpi or print half-size graphs at 300 dpi. (A LaserJet requires 1MB of memory to print a full-page graph at 300 dpi.)

The Orientation setting on the Layout menu is where you choose between the default (the Landscape placement of the image at right angles to the print path) and the alternative, which is Portrait, or vertical placement. In Figure 8-26 you can see a diagram—drawn with Quattro Pro 3—of the difference between Landscape and Portrait. If you print the graph in Portrait orientation, the height measurement is the y-axis of a stacked bar graph and the width measurement is the x-axis. In Landscape orientation the height measurement is the x-axis and the width is the y-axis.

Go

With the Destination and Layout information recorded, you can initiate printing with the Go command on the Print menu. Since your printer or

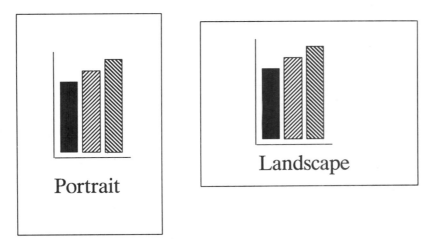

Figure 8-26. *Choices of graph orientation*

plotter has to translate the screen image into a series of dots or pen strokes, some time can pass before the image of the graph appears. The "Now Printing" message appears along with the message "Ctrl-Break to stop". Quattro Pro 3 will stop printing the graph if you press CTRL- BREAK. Do so if you realize you have made a mistake and do not want to complete the printing.

Several items that affect printing of graphs are located within the Options Hardware Printers menu. The Options Hardware Printers menu has an item called Plotter Speed. This lets you adjust the speed of your plotter. You may need to do this because some surfaces you plot onto, such as plastic overheads, accept ink better at lower speeds. When you select Plotter Speed, you can enter a value from 0 to 9, with 0 being the fastest, or current speed.

When you select a PostScript printer model, you will see two options for each paper size: Normal and Patterns. The Patterns options will print graphs in which the shading matches the hatch patterns of your graph; the Normal option allows the PostScript printer to substitute its own shading.

Changing Graph Types

The examples so far in this chapter have featured the default graph type, Stacked Bar. There are ten more types of graph available in Quattro Pro 3 and you can mix types within a graph. The type of graph is easily changed and does not require that you select the values to be graphed all over again. Once you have selected appropriate values, you can see them graphed in each of the different graph types. The main types of graph were shown earlier in Figure 8-11.

Bar Types

Four of the Quattro Pro 3 graph types are variations of a bar graph. The stacked bar graph you have seen so far is a good way to show relative performance across the x-axis for cumulative values. For example, you can clearly see in Figure 8-22 that total volume varied from quarter to quarter.

To see the plain bar graph, select Graph Type from the Graph menu and then select Bar. This version of the graph can then be displayed with the View option or the F10 key. It will look like the graph shown in Figure 8-27. Each piece of data is represented by a separate bar. This graph makes gauging the overall performance in each quarter more difficult, but it makes comparing the relative performance per quarter in each class somewhat easier. Notice that the scale for a bar graph does not need to be as large as that of the stacked bar graph shown earlier. Quattro Pro 3 automatically adjusts the y-scale.

The third type of bar graph produced by Quattro Pro 3 is the Rotated Bar, shown in Figure 8-28. This chart is very effective when you want to highlight the performance of different categories. The viewer's eye is immediately drawn to the longest bar. Note that the x-axis is the vertical axis in a rotated bar graph.

The fourth type of bar graph is called Column, which is also known as the 100% bar. This graph type displays a single column that gives a percentage breakdown of a single series of values. If you select Column for the same series used in Figure 8-28, you will get a breakdown of the first series—the volume of First class passengers—by quarter, as shown in Figure 8-29. Seeing a chart of the percentage of annual volume attained in each quarter is probably not that useful. The percentage breakdown that you would probably like to see is the total volume for the year according to

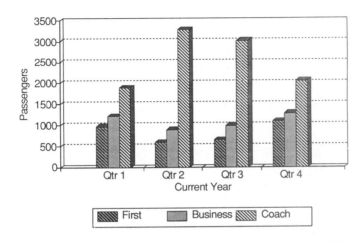

Figure 8-27.   *The graph as a bar type*

class. For this task the column graph is ideal, although the series needs to be redefined. The first series would be cells F4..F6 of the worksheet. There would be no other y-axis series. Column charts do not use legend text. Instead, you use the x-axis series to label the data. Thus, the x-axis series would be cells A4..A6. When the graph is drawn, the percentage breakdown of the total will be provided next to the names, as you can see from the resulting graph on the left of Figure 8-30. Notice the similarity of a column graph to a pie chart. A column graph is essentially a rectangular pie chart. The shading of column charts is actually controlled by pie chart commands.

Pie Charts

The pie chart is an effective image when you want to display the proportional distribution of values within a single whole. Like a column graph,

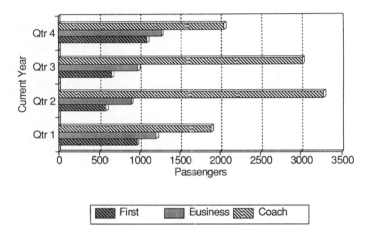

Figure 8-28.   *Rotated bar graph*

the pie chart is a one-dimensional graph; it uses only one series of values. If you were to select Pie as the Graph Type for the series graphed in Figure 8-27 or 8-28, you would see the breakdown of the first data series; that is, the First Class volume broken down between quarters. What you probably prefer is to show the total volume for the year broken down by class. This is done by redefining the first series as cells F4..F6 of the worksheet. There would be no other y-axis series. You would use the x-axis series to label the data. Thus the x-axis series would be A4..A6. As you can see from the results on the right of Figure 8-30, the percentage breakdown of the total is provided next to the names. This is one of the many elements of a pie chart that can be changed, as described in the following section, "Customizing Graphs." Both pie charts and column charts are controlled by the Pies command on the Customize Series menu.

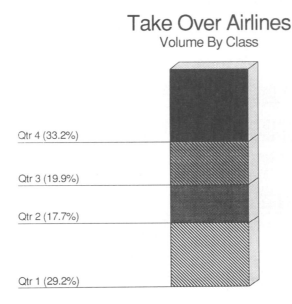

Take Over Airlines
Volume By Class

Qtr 4 (33.2%)

Qtr 3 (19.9%)

Qtr 2 (17.7%)

Qtr 1 (29.2%)

Figure 8-29. *Column graph*

Line Graphs

When you want data values to appear as points, and lines to be drawn connecting the points, then you need the line graph type. This is used effectively for showing changes in data over time, as in the chart seen in Figure 8-31, which graphs the volume figures. You can use different symbols for the *markers* that represent data points, or you can turn them off and just use lines to connect the points. Alternatively, you can turn off the lines and just use markers for the data. You make these changes through the Customize series command. Note that in Figure 8-31 the second title is printed in drop shadow text.

Area Graphs

When you want to represent data as an expanse of space rather than as a line or bar, then you can use the area graph, an example of which is shown

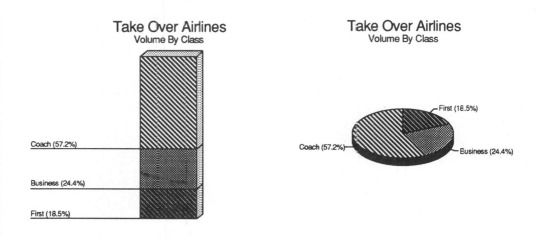

Figure 8-30. *Column graph and pie chart*

in Figure 8-32. Note that this type of chart does not allow accurate comparison of relative series values but does give a strong visual impact.

Hi-Low Graphs

To graph stock price and trading in other commodities in the classic format of hi-low charts, you select the Hi-low option. In its basic form this graph uses two series, one for the highest price during each trading period and the other for the lowest. Each pair of prices is represented by a vertical line from the high number down to the low number. Two further series can be added for the closing price and opening price of the period. These are represented by small horizontal lines, as shown in Figure 8-33.

Text Graphs

The diagrams in Figures 8-23 and 8-26 were created with the feature in Quattro Pro 3 known as the Graph Annotator. This allows you to place

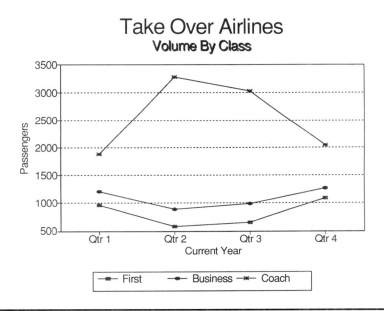

Figure 8-31. *Line graph*

free-floating text, arrows, shapes, and symbols on a graph. You can actually choose a type of graph, Text, that does not require a data series. This allows you to use a blank graph area for designs created entirely by the Graph Annotator. The Annotate feature is described in greater detail at the end of this chapter. In Chapter 13, you can read how to use Annotate and other commands to create slide shows.

3-D Graphs

You will find some very effective graph types grouped under 3-D Graphs at the bottom of the Graph Type menu, or under the 3-D Graphs icon if you are working in graphics display mode. There are four 3-D Graphs: Bar, Ribbon, Step, and Area. You can see a 3-D Bar graph in Figure 8-34. Note that instead of being displayed next to each other as in an ordinary bar

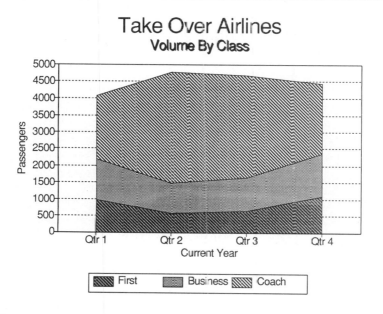

Figure 8-32.　*Area graph*

graph, the bars are ranked across a third axis. This is what distinguishes 3-D Graphs from the mere impression of perspective used by Quattro Pro 3 when drawing other graph types, as seen earlier in Figures 8-27 and 8-30. The perspective used in regular graphs is a setting adjustable from the Graph Overall menu, where the Three-D option can be set to Yes or No. The default setting is Yes.

The 3-D Graphs can be very effective in conveying information and are visually striking, a cut above ordinary charts. In Figure 8-35 you can see a 3-D Step graph of the same data as in Figure 8-34. A step chart is essentially a bar chart with no spaces between the bars, giving an impression of solid data.

There are some tricks to using 3-D Graphs effectively. In particular, attention should be paid to the selection of each data series since the first series is the one shown at the back of the graph, that is, further along the

Figure 8-33. *Hi-low graph*

third axis. You will note that in the regular stacked bar chart seen in Figure 8-22 and earlier, the series were as follows:

1st Series	First
2nd Series	Business
3rd Series	Coach

While this led to a slightly top-heavy set of bars, the results were still legible. If you were to use the same settings for a 3-D bar chart, the smaller bars of the Business and First series would be lost behind the much higher volume of the Coach series. You will need to review the data you plan to show in a 3-D Graph and give some thought to the selection of series. In

Figure 8-34. *A 3-D bar graph*

this example the series were changed to the following to produce the graphs seen in Figures 8-34 through 8-37:

1st Series   Coach

2nd Series   Business

3rd Series   First

Another area requiring attention in 3-D graphs is the placement of the legend. You will note that the graphs in Figures 8-34 and 8-35 both have the legend in the bottom right corner. This is the only legend location permitted in a 3-D Graph. However, you can leave out the legend and use alternative means to label the graph. In Figure 8-36 you can see a 3-D Ribbon graph that has no legend. The Ribbon graph is effective for showing

Figure 8-35.   *A 3-D step graph*

changes over a period of time, as in a line chart, but with more visual interest.

The text describing the series was added by means of Interior Labels, a command on the Customize Series menu. The three names for the legend were placed in cells E11 through E13, as shown here:

	B	C	D	E
11				Coach
12				Business
13				First

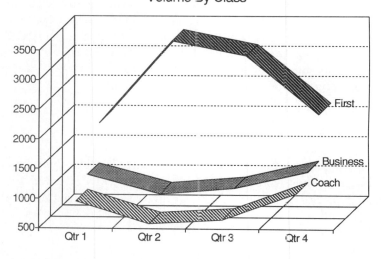

Figure 8-36. *A 3-D ribbon graph*

From the Customize Series menu the Interior Labels command was used to select this area of the worksheet to label the graph, as follows:

Series	Cell Block	Location
1st	B11..E11	Right
2nd	B12..E12	Right
3rd	B13..E13	Right

The Location setting determines the position of the labels with respect to the data points. The relative position of the labels in the Cell Block determines how far along the x-axis the labels will be placed. The Text Legends Position command was used to turn off the regular legend.

There is one more 3-D Graph type, the Area graph, an example of which is shown in Figure 8-37. This is an effective type for use with cumulative data or situations where you can rank each series according to size. Note that the 3-D Area graph is not automatically cumulative, that is, the series are not added together or stacked, as they are in a regular Area graph. Also note that the second series of the graph in Figure 8-37 was given an empty shading to produce the "wire frame" effect.

XY Graphs

The XY graph is mainly used to show the distribution of values, and thus it is helpful when you are analyzing statistical data. XY graphs are described in the context of other Quattro Pro 3 statistical features in Chapter 9.

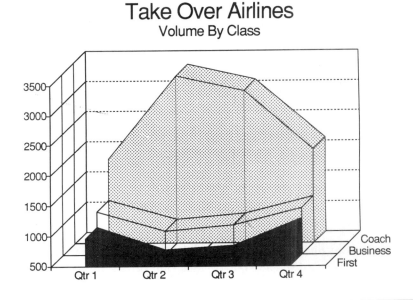

Figure 8-37.   *A 3-D area graph*

Customizing Graphs

Quattro Pro 3 is so rich in features for customizing graphs that an entire book could be devoted to the subject. Just about every aspect of a chart can be fine tuned to your personal whim. There are two main approaches to customizing graphs with Quattro Pro 3. You can use the Annotate feature, described later in this chapter, and you can use the Graph menu, as described in this section. You have already seen that text can be presented in a variety of typefaces, styles, and sizes. The four items in the second section of the Graph menu are used to customize other aspects of a graph: Customize Series, X-Axis, Y-Axis, and Overall.

Customize Series

In Figure 8-38 you can see the Customize Series menu displayed. The first option allows you to select the colors for each of the six series on the graph. When you select Colors you are shown a list of the series with their current color settings. When you select a specific series, a range of possible colors appears from which to choose. This appears as a palette, as shown in Figure 8-39, if you are using graphics mode. The current choice is outlined and you can use your mouse or the arrow keys to move the selection box to another color. Click the mouse button or press ENTER to select the color of your choice. If you are not using graphics mode the color choices appear as a list, as shown in Figure 8-40.

The Fill Patterns option lets you pick a pattern to be used in the bars of bar graphs, the areas of area graphs, and the slices of pie charts. There are 16 different patterns to choose from and they appear as a palette, as shown in Figure 8-41, if you are using graphics mode. Otherwise, the choices are listed as shown in Figure 8-42.

The Markers & Lines option allows you to control the appearance of line and XY graphs by varying three elements for each of the six series. You can vary Line Styles, Markers, and Formats. The eight choices for lines are: Solid, Dotted, Centered, Dashed, Heavy Solid, Heavy Dotted, Heavy Centered, and Heavy Dashed. The ten choices for Markers are: Filled Square, Plus sign, Asterisk, Empty Square, an X, Filled Triangle, Hourglass, Square with X, Vertical Line, and Horizontal Line. The four possibilities for the Formats in a line or XY chart are Lines, Symbols, Both (lines and symbols), or Neither (no lines or symbols). Given so many options

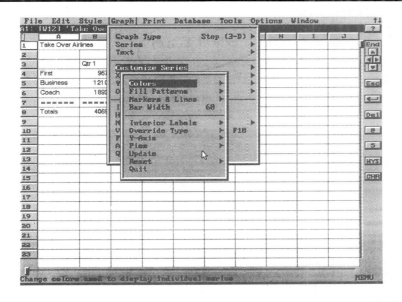

Figure 8-38.   *The Customize Series menu*

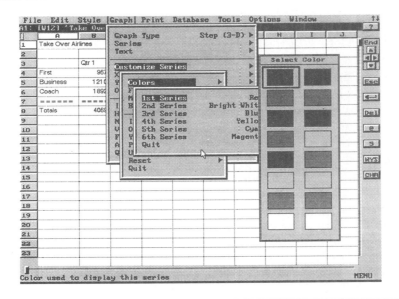

Figure 8-39.   *The color palette in graphics mode*

File Edit Style Graph Print Database Tools Options Window
A1: [W12] 'Take Ove
J   A
1 Take Over Airli   Graph T   Bar   ▶   G
2   Series   Black   ▶
3   Qtr   Text   Blue   ▶
4 First   Green   ▶
5 Business   Customi   Cyan   ▶
6 Coach   X   Red   ▶
7 ===============   Y   Colo   Magenta   ▶
8 Totals   O   F   Brown
9   M   D   White   Red
10   I   B 2   Gray   Green
11   H   3   Light Blue   Blue
12   M   I 4   Light Green   Yellow
13   V   O 5   Light Cyan   Cyan
14   F   Y 6   Light Red   Magenta
15   A   P Q   Light Magenta
16   Q   U   Yellow
17   Re   Bright White
18   Quit
19
20
← Color used to display this series   MENU

Figure 8-40. *The Colors menu*

Figure 8-41. *The Fill Patterns palette in graphics mode*

Figure 8-42. *The Fill Patterns menu*

you do not have to be a great mathematician to figure out that the total number of design combinations for line graphs is astronomical.

When you are creating a bar graph, the spacing between bars may not be to your liking. You can use the Bar Width option on the Customize Series menu to alter the spacing. You can make the thickness of the bars anything from 20%, which is really skinny, to 90%, which leaves virtually no gap between the bars. When you select Bar Width, just type in the desired number and press ENTER.

Y-Axis Customizing

There are times when the automatic scale applied to the axes by Quattro Pro 3 does not give the desired effect. On the right side of Figure 8-43 you can see the effect of graphing First Class volume figures with an upper limit on the y-axis of 2000. This makes the performance look pretty poor compared to the graph on the left. Both graphs use the same numbers, but the graph on the left uses the automatic scaling of the y-axis whereas the

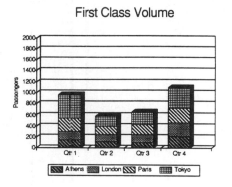

Figure 8-43. *Relative y-axis scales*

one on the right has had the y-axis customized. This was done because the company goal is 2000 First Class passengers per quarter. This adjustment puts the performance into a different perspective.

You adjust the y-axis by selecting Y-Axis from the Graph menu and using the options shown in Figure 8-44. The Scale setting is either Automatic, which is the default, or Manual. When you alter the other settings on the Y-Axis menu to create a customized scale you can turn this scale on by selecting Automatic, or turn it off by using Manual.

The Low and High settings determine the boundaries of the scale, normally from 0 to a round number larger than the largest number you want to graph. A typical example of setting the graph's *origin* (the beginning point of the y-axis) is seen in weekly charts of average stock prices. These are often shown with an origin larger than 0 so as to emphasize the day-to-day variation of the figures. You can see an example of this in Figure 8-33, where the origin is set at 45. Note that area and stacked bar charts cannot have their origin made less than 0.

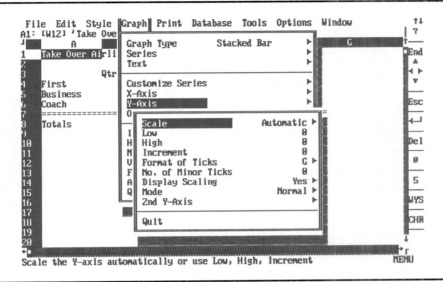

Figure 8-44.   *Customize Y-Axis options*

The Increment affects the numeric gap between the values on the y-axis scale. For example, for the numbers graphed in Figure 8-43 the automatically selected values for the y-axis were 0 to 1200 in 200-unit increments. The manually adjusted graph on the right of Figure 8-43 also uses 200-unit increments.

The Format of Ticks is a rather strange sounding option that is in fact very important. The numbers on the y-axis can be formatted using any of the worksheet formats, such as Currency, Fixed, and so on. For example, in the previous illustration, the Comma format is used to place commas as thousands separators. This format will also put negative numbers in parentheses.

The No. of Minor Ticks option allows you to create small lines on the y-axis scale instead of numbers. For example, if you set the increment to 50 you will have this series of numbers: 0, 50, 100, 150, 200, and so on. If you request a No. of Minor Ticks setting of 1, then Quattro Pro 3 will skip every other number, showing 100, 200, and so on, and place tick marks at 50, 150, and so on. Every third scale number is displayed by using a setting of 2.

When Quattro Pro 3 graphs large numbers that run into the thousands or millions, those units are displayed as text on the axis and the actual axis numbers are adjusted accordingly. You can turn off the display of this text if you want, by selecting No for Display Scaling. Although some graphs may appear to need no explanation of the scale, you should use this option to avoid graphs that are deceptive or hard to read.

When you are dealing with large numbers or scientific data you may want to use a logarithmic scale rather than a normal scale. To turn the y-axis scale to log mode, select Mode and then Log. Select Normal to go back to a regular scale. Be sure to document the use of a logarithmic scale on the graph to avoid confusion.

Quattro Pro 3 allows you to set a second y-axis for mixing graph data. When you do this you can completely customize the second axis by choosing the 2nd Y-Axis option. You can also use this option to turn off the display of scaling for the second y-axis. An example of a graph with dual y-axes is given later in this chapter.

X-Axis Customizing

There are times when you also want to customize the x-axis. In Figure 8-33 you saw a graph of stock prices. The x-axis consists of a series of dates from column B in the worksheet that generated the graph. These dates are all seven days apart. If every date was displayed on the x-axis, they would be unreadable. There are two approaches to clarifying the x-axis when it is crowded. You can have the x-axis series represented on two rows instead of one, and you can skip some of the values. The latter approach was taken in Figure 8-33 where only every fourth date was shown.

You typically use the X-Axis option on the Graph menu to adjust the x-axis when it consists of numbers and the graph type is XY. Customizing the x-axis may be redundant when the x-axis series is labels, as is the case when graphing quarterly volume. You can see from Figure 8-45 that the X-Axis options closely match those on the y-axis menu. The Scale can be set to Automatic to have Quattro Pro 3 design the x-axis or you can turn on your own design by setting the Scale to Manual and using the other menu options. The Alternate Ticks option is set to Yes when you need to use two rows for your x-axis data. The No. of Minor Ticks option is adjusted to replace labels in the x-axis with minor tick marks. In the example in Figure 8-33, this was set to 3 to produce a date every fourth label.

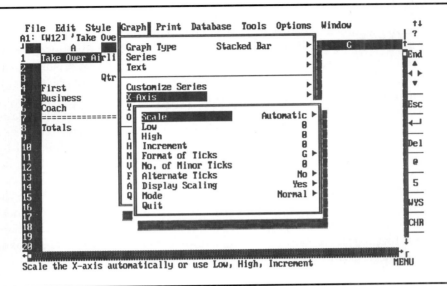

Figure 8-45. *Customize X-Axis options*

Overall Customizing

The options for Overall customizing are Grid, Outlines, Background Color, Three-D, Color/B&W, and Drop Shadow Color, as shown here:

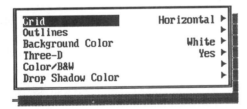

The Color/B&W option was used in creating the graphs in this chapter. When you select Color/B&W you can choose either Color or B&W. When you pick B&W the colors in your graphs are turned to black and white so that you can print in black and white as opposed to color. The nice part of the Color/B&W command is that after you have used B&W you can turn the color back on and Quattro Pro 3 will reinstate all of the default color choices. Do not select the B&W option if you have customized colors that you want to save.

The Grid option allows you to place lines on your graph. You can use Horizontal, Vertical, or Both. Use the Clear option to remove the lines. The grids you create can be customized by choosing Grid Color, Line Style, and Fill Color. The Fill Color is the color that lies behind the bars in a bar graph.

The Outlines option is used to put boxes and other demarcation around three elements of the graph: Titles, Legend, and Graph (the entire chart, including text and legend). Each of these elements can be outlined with the following: Box, Double-line, Thick-line, Shadow, 3D, Round Rectangle, or Sculpted. The last choice for an outline is None, to turn off the outline. The 3D option draws a perspective box behind an object to give it an appearance of depth. The Shadow option is rather effective for text and was used in Figure 8-10. The Sculpted option creates a box like those used for menus in WYSIWYG mode.

The Background Color option on the Overall menu simply lets you choose the color used for the background of the graph, while the Three-D option adds perspective lines to the chart box to give an impression of depth. You can see the effect of Three-D on a pie chart in Figure 8-30 and again in Figure 8-46.

Customizing Pies

There is a whole series of settings that you can use to customize pie charts like the one shown in Figure 8-46. This chart has the Overall option called Three-D set to Yes. The first slice of the pie is exploded from the rest, and the labels show the data values. To adjust a pie chart you first select Customize Series from the Graph menu and then Pies. The Pies menu shows you the various aspects of pie charts that can be altered to fit your preferences, as follows:

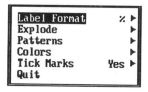

In addition to Explode, you can select Patterns to fill the pie slices, Colors to change the color displays of the pie chart, and the Label Format, which will be discussed shortly. You can also add or remove lines called Tick Marks between labels and slices.

When you select Explode from the Pies menu, you are shown a menu of slices 1 through 9. The 1st slice is the leftmost or topmost value in the 1st Series; in Figure 8-46, this is Athens. If you select 1st Slice, you can see the way Quattro Pro 3 records your explosion preference. The Explode choice is normally set to Don't Explode. To change this setting, highlight Explode and press ENTER or type **E**. This tells Quattro Pro 3 to display the first slice offset from the rest, as is the case in Figure 8-46.

When you select Label Format from the Pies menu, you have four options: Value, %, $, and None. The Value option is the one used in Figure 8-46. The % option, which is the default setting, was used in Figure 8-30. If the values are dollars you can use the $ option, which displays the actual values preceded by a dollar sign. Alternatively, you can suppress any value display by selecting None.

Remember that the title for a pie chart will probably be different from that used for other graphs of related data. You can use the Text option from the Graph menu to enter a correct title.

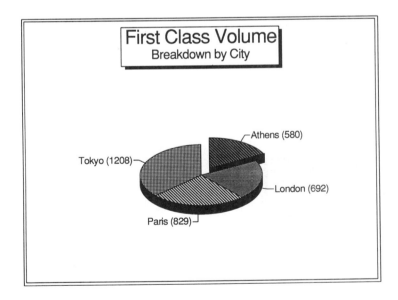

Figure 8-46. *Pie chart in 3-D*

Updating and Resetting Custom Features

If many of the aspects of the graph you are designing are different from the previous one, you can selectively reset those aspects through the Reset option on the Customize Series menu shown in Figure 8-38. Selecting Graph will completely erase the graph settings, so use it with care.

Interior Labels

The graph in Figure 8-47 shows the First Class volume figures in a rotated bar graph. The remarks for each city are displayed on the graph by means of the Interior Labels option. Such a display can be helpful and also enhances the graph's visual effect.

When you select Interior Labels from the Series menu, you can select each series in turn and specify the spreadsheet coordinates of the data to be used to identify points of the series on the graph. The labels for your

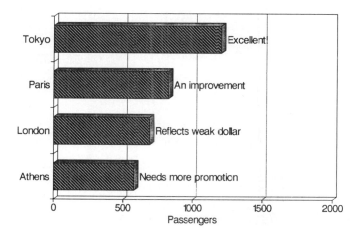

Figure 8-47. *Remarks as interior labels*

graph can be the values in the chart; they can be any set of numbers or labels. For example, you could use the city names to label the bars by using the cells that are the X-Axis series. Alternatively, as in Figure 8-48, you can enter into the worksheet a series of remarks about the values represented in the chart and then display them as interior labels. The labels in column G have been selected as labels for the graph. The results are as shown in Figure 8-47. Note that you do not have to label every data point. If you erased cells G5, G7, and G8, but still used the block G5..G8 for the interior labels setting, the graph would only show the comment for London.

When you have entered the cell coordinates for interior labels, you are prompted for the position of the labels on the graph. Your choices are Center, Left, Above, Right, Below, or None. The None option suppresses display of that set of labels. When you have chosen an appropriate position, you are returned to the Interior Labels menu to work on the next series. The labels in Figure 8-47 are shown with a position setting of Right. Also note that the graph has customized y-axis settings that elongate the graph to make room for the labels.

Figure 8-48. *The Interior Labels option*

Multiple Graph Types And Y-Axes

In Figure 8-43 you saw two graphs of passenger volume. The one on the right was customized to show that the passenger volume was not as great as it might appear in the graph on the left, relative to expectations. You might want to create a graph that shows the expectations or goals relative to performance. You can see an example of this in Figure 8-49. The total volume for each quarter is shown as a bar, while the goal for the quarter is shown as a line.

To create this graph from the worksheet in Figure 8-50 you need to establish the totals in cells B10..E10 as the first series and the goal figures in B13..E13 as the second series. The x-axis series is cells B3..E3. If you already have data series established you can use the Graph Customize Reset command to delete the previous series settings. You highlight the series you want to reset and press ENTER. Bear in mind that this action cancels the series coordinates but does not change such items as graph type

Figure 8-49. *Combined bar and line graph*

and graph text. Also bear in mind that the Graph option on this menu removes all graph settings including text.

Having established the correct data series you can select Bar as the Graph Type. This will show both series of data as bars. In order to show the first series as bars but the second as a line you need to use the Customize Override Type menu shown here:

This menu shows each of the six series and the current type setting for the series. At first these are all the defaults, meaning whatever you have selected as the current graph type. If you select one of the series you can then choose between Default, Bar, and Line. In this case, Line will be chosen for the second series. The results are shown in Figure 8-49.

While the ability to mix graph types increases your options for making a clear presentation of the facts, it does have limitations. You cannot mix stacked bar, pie, column, or area graphs. You can mix only line, mix marker, and bar graphs. Mixing graph types does not get around the problem posed by mixing numbers of completely different types. For example, what if you wanted to add the profit figures to the graph in Figure 8-49? These numbers, in row 16 of the worksheet in Figure 8-50, are in dollars and bear little relation to the other numbers. To help you graph such unrelated numbers, Quattro Pro 3 provides the ability to add a second y-axis.

To graph the profit numbers on a second y-axis you first add cells B16..E16 as the third series. Then you select the Y-Axis option on the Customize Series menu. This allows you to assign each series to either the Primary or the Secondary axis, as shown here:

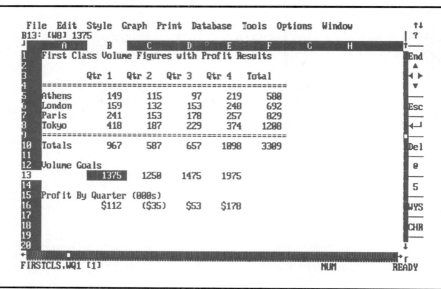

Figure 8-50. *Spreadsheet showing goals*

The third series is assigned to the second axis. Since the current graph type is bar, the profit will initially appear as a bar. To change this to a more suitable line type you would use the Override Type command on the Customize menu, selecting Line for the third series. The results are shown in Figure 8-51.

Note that the graph in Figure 8-51 has been customized slightly from the default settings. The Fill Patterns option on the Graph Customize menu was used to clarify the bars for the first series. The Marker and Lines option on the Customize Series menu was used to alter the third series display. First, the Line Styles command was used to alter the style of line for the series, in order to distinguish it from the goal line. Then the Markers option was used to make asterisks the symbol for the profit line. The Text Secondary Y-Axis command was used to add the words Dollars (000s) to the graph. The actual scale of the secondary axis was set automatically by Quattro Pro 3 but the 2nd Y-Axis command from the Customize Y-Axis menu was used to change the format of the numbers to Currency with zero decimal places. Finally, the Overall command was used to add boxes

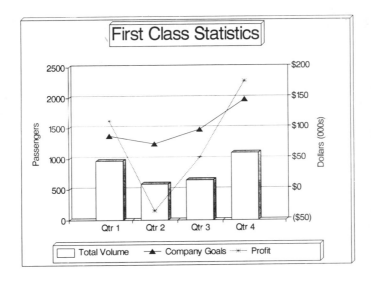

Figure 8-51. *Using a second y-axis*

around the legend, the title, and the entire graph. The box style was set to 3D as was the overall style of the graph.

By the careful mixing of features as shown in this example it is possible to use Quattro Pro 3 to graph most information in an attractive and effective manner. When you want to go further in your customization, you can use the Annotate feature described next.

Annotation—The Finishing Touch

The Graph Annotate feature in Quattro Pro 3 is really a full-featured built-in drawing program. You can use it to turn ordinary worksheet-generated graphs into stunning visuals, or even to create drawings that are not related to figures in the spreadsheet. In this area of Quattro Pro 3, a mouse—while not mandatory—is certainly a great plus, making quick work of drawing and coloring shapes and lines, as well as moving elements of the graph and performing cut-and-paste operations.

The Annotate Screen

You can see the Annotate feature at work in Figure 8-52, where a piece of text is being added to a stacked bar graph. Note that this level of customizing goes beyond the use of interior labels. The text that has been added here can be floated to any point on the graph, resized, or even enclosed in a variety of box styles. The elements of the graph that you have created with the other graph commands can also be moved about. The legend can be moved to a new location, as can any graph text.

There are two ways to get to the Annotate feature. When you view a graph you can press the / key. You can also use the Annotate option from the Graph menu. In both cases the current graph is placed into a window

Figure 8-52.   *Text added by using Annotate*

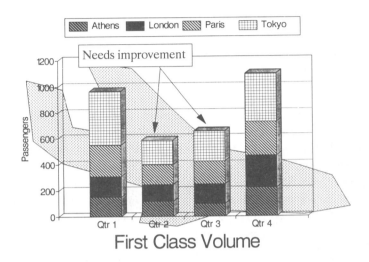

Figure 8-53. *Graphics created by using Annotate*

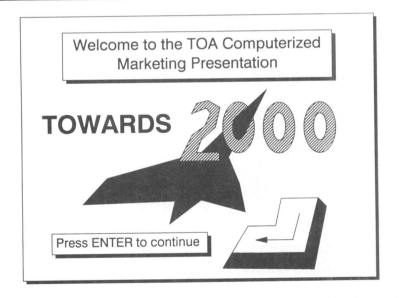

Figure 8-54. *A text chart*

and a panel of tools is provided. If you have used paint or draw programs with a mouse before, then the operation of the Annotate feature will be familiar. Basically, you click on the pointer box labeled P in the top-left corner of the screen to make your mouse or cursor keys act as the selector. Then you click on objects in the graph to select them, or press the TAB key to move from one item to another.

You click on the various tools in the top menu bar to select them and draw lines, polygons, rectangles, and circles by the click-and-drag method. Each object in the graph has a set of handles on it (the small boxes around the boxed text in Figure 8-52). If you point to one of these boxes and then click and drag you can alter the size and shape of the object. If you click within the selected object you can move it to another location on the screen. The menus and palettes on the right side of the screen are used for editing the colors, patterns, and other attributes of the objects you select. You click on the Clipboard, the second box, when you want to copy and paste elements of the graph and move them to the front or back of the picture. You also use this tool to paste pictures from the clip art files (with the extension CLP). You can click on the Text tool to type free-floating text for the graph.

In the lower part of the screen a very helpful set of instructions guides you through the appropriate actions and provides keystroke alternatives to the mouse commands. In Figure 8-53 you can see the way that the Annotate feature transforms a good but basic graph into a stunning visual. The legend was moved to the top of the chart; the title was moved to the bottom. A piece of boxed text was added, along with two arrows. Then a polygon in the shape of an aircraft was drawn and placed below the main graph area using the Clipboard. In Chapter 13 you will find further discussion of this feature and how it can be applied.

Annotated Text Charts

When you want to use the Annotate feature to create charts like the ones shown earlier in Figures 8-23 and 8-26 that are not based on any numbers in a worksheet you simply open a new worksheet and select Text as the graph type. You can then select Annotate and a fresh canvas appears, ready for you to add text, shapes, or whatever you desire. The capability to perform these actions from within what is ostensibly a spreadsheet program makes Quattro Pro 3 one of the most versatile software packages around. In Figure 8-54 you can see an example of a text chart, which shows that the term really does not do justice to the results. This graphic can even be inserted into a spreadsheet to make a very interesting effect.

9 Dates and Advanced Commands

Quattro Pro 3 can treat dates and times mathematically, allowing you to quantify time-related information and manipulate it for spreadsheet and database applications. This chapter begins by explaining how dates and times are handled. After that, some of the more advanced commands provided in the Tools menu will be examined, including Advanced Math, What-If, Frequency, and Solve For. The Advanced Math command includes regression, matrix arithmetic, and optimization. Since they can plot regression lines, XY graphs will also be discussed in this chapter. You will find that Quattro Pro 3 provides powerful tools for the analysis of data, solution of mathematical problems, and visual presentation of results.

Dates as Numbers

Several of the examples in earlier chapters used dates produced by Quattro Pro 3's date arithmetic feature. The program is designed to perform math with dates and times. To read a date (such as April 1, 1990) as something that has value, the date must be converted to a number. Quattro Pro 3 performs this conversion by calculating the number of days between the date involved and the end of the last century. This is the date's *serial number*. Thus, January 1, 1900 is date number 1. Move ahead 1000 days and you have September 27, 1902. Man first walked on the moon on day number 25, 404, otherwise known as July 20, 1969.

When dates are converted to numbers, two dates can be compared and their difference calculated. Chapter 2 provided a calculation for how many days you have been alive. More typical applications are scheduling projects, dating and sorting records, and calculating loans. Date arithmetic is also useful for producing a series of dates, such as a row with the names of the months or a column of payment due dates.

Entering Dates

How do you tell Quattro Pro 3 to convert a date to a number? After all, if you type April 1, 1990 and press ENTER you create a label, since the letter *A* is a label indicator. There are several ways to enter a date as a number in Quattro Pro 3.

Entering Dates with *CTRL-D*

The easiest way to enter a date into a spreadsheet is to press CTRL-D before typing the date and then enter the date in one of the standard formats. In Figure 9-1, CTRL-D was pressed at cell A3 before **4/1/90** was typed.

The mode indicator in the lower right of the screen indicates DATE to let you know that you have pressed CTRL-D. All you need to do is type the date and press ENTER. The effect of CTRL-D is seen when the date is entered. You will see **04/01/90** on the worksheet, as shown in Figure 9-2. If you were to type **4/1/90** without pressing CTRL-D, Quattro Pro 3 would divide the number 4 by 1 and then divide the result by 90, producing 0.044 in the cell (assuming a format with three decimal places). The CTRL-D approach to entering dates works very well. You can enter the date in any of the standard formats:

01-Apr-90	DD-MMM-YY
01-Apr	DD-MMM (assumes current year)
Apr-90	MMM-YY (assumes first day of the month)
04/01/90	MM/DD/YY
04/01	MM/DD (assumes current year)

Figure 9-1. *Entering date*

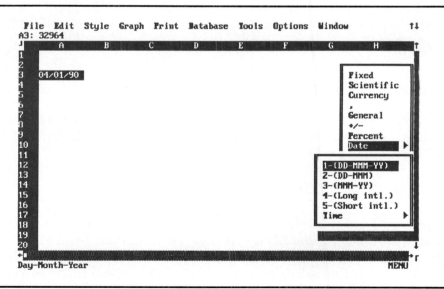

Figure 9-2. *Date and Numeric Format screen*

For example, if you press CTRL-D and then type **Apr-90, Apr-90** will display. The assumptions that Quattro Pro 3 makes when part of the date is missing are current year and first of the month. The current year is read from your computer's system clock. You can type month names in any mixture of capitals and lowercase and you do not need to type leading zeroes for date numbers. The CTRL-D method can also be used with the @NOW function described later.

While the CTRL-D method produces a date in a readable form in the worksheet cell, the cell content displayed on the status line is simply a serial number. In Figure 9-2 **32964** is displayed, which corresponds to 04/01/90. This is one of the standard date formats. The formats can be reviewed on the Style Numeric Format Date menu, which is also displayed in Figure 9-2.

You can change the format of the cell to one of the other formats by using the Style Numeric Format command and selecting Date. However, bear in mind that the first format, DD-MMM-YY, produces a date too wide for the default column width of 9 characters, so all you would see in A3 are asterisks. The asterisks mean Quattro Pro 3 is attempting to display **01-Apr-90**, which is 9 characters. Since the date is a value, and Quattro Pro 3 allows only eight digits of a value to be displayed in a 9-character column, the result is the series of asterisks that tell you to change the format or column width. You need only enlarge the column by one character to see the full date. If much of your work includes dates, you can change the default column width to 10 by using the Options Formats Global Width command.

Entering Dates with Functions

In addition to the CTRL-D method, there are several other ways to create a date. One that parallels the approach used in 1-2-3 is the @DATE function. This function has the syntax

@DATE(YY,MM,DD)

where YY is a numeric value between 0 and 199, MM is a numeric value between 1 and 12, and DD is a numeric value between 1 and 31.

The @DATE function returns the serial number of the date specified with year, month, and day arguments. Thus, @DATE(90,12,25) returns the value 33232, or 25-Dec-90. Since Quattro Pro 3 can handle dates well into the next century, the year 2000 is referred to as 100, 2001 is 101, and so on. The highest date available is December 31, 2099, referred to as @DATE(199,12,31).

The number created by @DATE can be a whole number of days plus a fraction of a day expressed as a decimal. The whole number (to the left of the decimal point) in a date serial number is the number of days from January 1, 1900 up to the date referenced in the formula. The fractional portion of a date serial number is used for the time functions, which are discussed later in this chapter.

To display a date's serial number in a date format, you use the Style Numeric Format command and select one of the date formats. This command suppresses the numeric display, showing instead the date in its more common form (1-Jan-87 instead of 31778). Any illegal dates—for example, @DATE(87,2,29)—return ERR as their value. This date corresponds to February 29, 1987, which is invalid since 1987 was not a leap year.

Another method you can use to enter dates in Quattro Pro 3 is the @DATEVALUE function. You may sometimes work with spreadsheets that contain dates entered as labels. This often happens when data is transferred to Quattro Pro 3 from another program and the date values are converted to text in the process. The @DATEVALUE function produces a serial date value from a string of text or labels. This function has the syntax

@DATEVALUE(*DateString*)

where *DateString* is a string value in any valid date form. An example would be the label '25-Dec-90.

If the value in *DateString* is not in the correct format, an ERR value is returned. There are five valid formats for labels to be read as values with the @DATEVALUE function:

■ DD-MMM-YY (25-Dec-90)

■ DD-MMM (25-Dec) (assumes the current year)

■ MMM-YY (Dec-90) (assumes the first day of the month)

■ MM/DD/YY (12/25/90) Long International, the system default

■ MM/DD (12/25) Short International, the system default (assumes the current year)

Provided they are written in these formats, dates entered as labels can be converted to values. You can display the resulting date values in standard date formats with the Style Numeric Format Date command. If you want to include the string in the function statement directly, you must enclose it in quotes. Thus, @DATEVALUE("25-Dec-90") returns the value 33232, which can be formatted to 12/25/90 using the D4 date format. The statement @DATEVALUE(A1) returns the same value if A1 contains the label 12-Dec-90. For further discussion of strings and their conversion to values, see Chapter 10.

Date Arithmetic

When dates are stored as values, you can perform arithmetic with them. A typical application of this is tracking accounts receivable. Figure 9-3 shows an accounts receivable list for Take Over Airlines. The names of

```
 File  Edit  Style  Graph  Print  Database  Tools  Options  Window          ↑↓
F1: (D1) [W11] @TODAY
J         A          B          C       D       E         F              ↑
1  TOA Accounts Receivable List                   As of:  14-Jun-90      ▪
2
3  Note: all past due amounts due subject to Late Fee of:      12.00%
4
5     Company      Amount    Payment  # of Days  Late    Date Last
6      Name         Due      Due Date Past Due   Fee     Contacted
7  ==================================================================
8  SYS Assoc.       845.76   05/07/90    38      10.57   06/01/90
9  DATA, Ltd.       719.34   05/23/90    22       5.20   06/02/90
10 Tridata, Co.     403.56   05/16/90    29       3.85   06/01/90
11 Softduo, Inc.    345.48   04/25/90    50       5.68   06/02/90
12 Amerwest, Ltd.   315.76   05/24/90    21       2.18   06/01/90
13 PER, Inc.        132.75   05/29/90    16       0.70   06/03/90
14 Advper, Inc.     123.43   05/27/90    18       0.73   06/01/90
15 Calcpro, Ltd.    197.48   05/06/90    39       2.53   06/03/90
16 Unouni, Inc.      51.82   05/23/90    22       0.37   06/04/90
17 Ultflex, Inc.    272.21   05/16/90    29       2.60   06/05/90
18 COMP, Inc.       124.43   04/25/90    50       2.05   05/24/90
19 VIA, Inc.        273.58   05/24/90    21       1.89   06/01/90
20 Amernew Assoc.   224.73   05/29/90    16       1.18   06/02/90      ↓
←▬▬▬▬▬▬▬▬▬▬▬▬▬▬▬▬▬▬▬▬▬▬▬▬▬▬▬▬▬▬■▬▬▬▬▬▬▬▬▬▬▬▬▬▬▬▬▬▬▬▬▬▬▬▬▬▬▬→ r
ARMF5MAC.WQ1 [1]                                   NUM           READY
```

Figure 9-3.   *TOA Accounts Receivable*

companies, how much they owe, and when their payment was last due are displayed. Note that in cell F1 the @TODAY function has been used to keep the worksheet up to date, as shown by the cell identifier at the top of the screen. The @TODAY function reads your computer system's date from DOS and, if you have the system clock set correctly, will always show the current date.

The number of days that have elapsed between the date the payment was supposed to have been made and the current date is calculated in column D, # of Days Past Due. The figure in D8 is produced by the formula +$F$1–C8, which subtracts the due date in column C from the current date in cell F1, as shown in Figure 9-4. The cell reference to the current date in F1 was made absolute so that the formula could be copied to the other cells in column D.

The practical value of knowing exactly how many days late a payment is can be seen in column E, where the late fee is calculated. This figure represents interest on the amount due. The late fee is calculated by multiplying the number of days past due by 1/365th of the annual percentage rate shown in F3 in Figure 9-5. Thus, when a client is contacted about paying the amount owing, the accrued late fee can be stated.

Figure 9-4. *Days past due*

```
 File  Edit  Style  Graph  Print  Database  Tools  Options  Window        1↓
E8: (,2) +B8*D8*$F$3/365
        A           B          C         D       E        F
 1  TOA Accounts Receivable List                  As of:  14-Jun-90
 2
 3  Note: all past due amounts due subject to Late Fee of:      12.00%
 4
 5     Company     Amount     Payment  # of Days  Late    Date Last
 6      Name        Due      Due Date  Past Due    Fee    Contacted
 7  ========================================================================
 8  SYS Assoc.      845.76   05/07/90     38      10.57   06/01/90
 9  DATA, Ltd.      719.34   05/23/90     22       5.28   06/02/90
10  Iridata, Co.    403.56   05/16/90     29       3.05   06/01/90
11  Softduo, Inc.   345.48   04/25/90     50       5.68   06/02/90
12  Amerwest, Ltd.  315.76   05/24/90     21       2.18   06/01/90
13  PEN, Inc.       132.75   05/29/90     16       0.70   06/03/90
14  Aduper, Inc.    123.43   05/27/90     18       0.73   06/01/90
15  Calcpro, Ltd.   197.48   05/06/90     39       2.53   06/03/90
16  Unouni, Inc.     51.82   05/23/90     22       0.37   06/04/90
17  Ultflex, Inc.   272.21   05/16/90     29       2.68   06/05/90
18  COMP, Inc.      124.43   04/25/90     50       2.05   05/24/90
19  VIA, Inc.       273.58   05/24/90     21       1.89   06/01/90
20  Amernew Assoc.  224.73   05/29/90     16       1.18   06/02/90
ARMFSMAC.WQ1 [1]                                      NUM         READY
```

Figure 9-5.   *Interest calculation*

Date Series

You can use date arithmetic to create a series of dates. Consider the budget worksheet shown in Figure 9-6. This worksheet was developed in Chapter 5. At that time the names of the months in row 6 were simply typed as labels. However, the same data could be created more quickly by using date values. As values, the dates could be easily updated for next year's budget. To create a series of the names of the months with date values, you enter the date as the first day of the first month of the series. Since you can format dates with the MMM-YY format, entering **1/1/90** and changing the format to MMM-YY produces **Jan-90**. You can then add 31 days to this date to produce the first of the next month, **Feb-90**, and so on.

As you can see from Figure 9-6, the label JAN is about to be replaced by a date, January 1, 1990, entered as **@DATE(90,1,1)**. When this is entered, the value of the date is first shown as a date value. This will be changed to a readable date in a moment. In cell C6 the formula 31+B6 is entered to create a serial date that is 31 days greater than that in the cell to the left.

File Edit Style Graph Print Database Tools Options Window   ↑↓
[Enter] [Esc] @DATE(90,1,1)

	A	B	C	D	E	F	G	H
1								
2				Quattro Vadis Travel 4 Office Total:$122,131				
3								
4			90 Budget - Based On Monthly Growth Factor of				1.015	
5								
6		JAN	FEB	MAR	APR	MAY	JUN	JUL
7	POLK ST.							
8	Lease	350	355	361	366	371	377	383
9	Phones	230	233	237	241	244	248	251
10	Telex	110	112	113	115	117	119	120
11	Electric	120	122	124	125	127	129	131
12	Res. Rent	1,100	1,117	1,133	1,150	1,167	1,185	1,203
13	VAN NESS							
14	Lease	500	507	515	523	531	539	547
15	Phones	250	254	258	261	265	269	273
16	Telex	150	152	155	157	159	162	164
17	Electric	225	228	232	235	239	242	246
18	Res. Rent	1,200	1,218	1,236	1,255	1,274	1,293	1,312
19	UNION SQ.							
20	Lease	1,200	1,218	1,236	1,255	1,274	1,293	1,312

B6: ^JAN   VALUE

Figure 9-6.   *Budget worksheet*

In a moment this formula will be copied to the rest of the cells in row 6. However, since all of the date cells need to be formatted, and formats are duplicated by the copy process, the two date cells created so far will be formatted prior to the formula being copied. In Figure 9-7 you can see the third date format being selected. The resulting display of the dates is shown here:

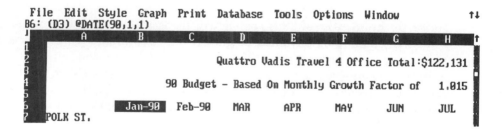

File Edit Style Graph Print Database Tools Options Window   ↑↓
B6: (D3) @DATE(90,1,1)

	A	B	C	D	E	F	G	H
1								
2				Quattro Vadis Travel 4 Office Total:$122,131				
3								
4			90 Budget - Based On Monthly Growth Factor of				1.015	
5								
6		Jan-90	Feb-90	MAR	APR	MAY	JUN	JUL
7	POLK ST.							

All that remains to complete the date series for all months is to copy the formula in cell C6 to cells D6..M6. The result is a series of month headings for the budget model. While the actual dates created by repeatedly adding

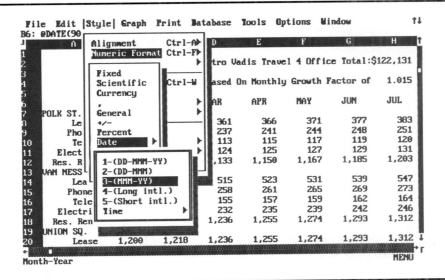

Figure 9-7.   *Formatting the date cells*

31 to the first of January are not the first of every month, because of the differing number of days in a month, the D3 format ignores the day of the month to give the date series just created an acceptable appearance.

Of course, the major advantage of entering dates in this manner is the ease with which they can be updated for next year's budget. By simply highlighting the starting date of the series in cell B6, pressing F2 to edit it, and changing @DATE(90,1,1) to @DATE(91,1,1), you can update the entire series to the months of 1991, as shown in Figure 9-8. The technique of repeatedly adding 31 days to a beginning date of January 1 will produce acceptable consecutive MMM-YY dates for about 54 months.

When the date series you want to create has to be more exact, showing the complete dates, you can proceed in several ways. Take the case of a payment schedule where you need a list of payment dates. Suppose that the schedule calls for 12 payments, one due every 30 days. To begin, the first date of the series is entered as April 1, 1990, with the statement @DATE(90,4,1) in cell A3. Cell A3 is then formatted to the D1 format. The next value, in cell A4, can be created by adding 30 to the starting date in A3.

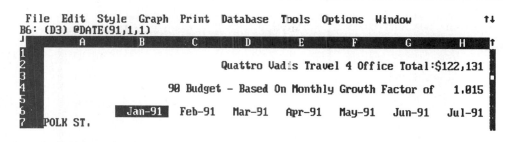

Figure 9-8. *Updated series*

This formula is then copied down the column to produce the results shown in Figure 9-9. This type of formula works well for such applications as a series of weekly meeting dates or biweekly pay days, where the interval between dates is a set number of days. Remember that a cell format is copied with the cell, so formatting before you perform the copy operation will save time. Alternatively, you can wait to format the entire date series until after it has been created; however, working with unformatted dates such as 32964, 32994, 33024, and so on is not always easy.

An alternative method of creating a regular series of dates is to use the Edit Fill command. To use this method, you enter the first date of the series as a function, as in @DATE(90,4,1). This function will display the number 32964 if you do not apply a date format to the cell. With the cell selector on the number 32964, use the Edit Fill command and highlight a block with the number of cells you need. Then use 32964 as the start value and the number of days between dates as the step value. You can use the number 73050, the largest valid date number, as the stop value. The resulting numbers can then be formatted as dates. Note that a date series created with the Edit Fill command is not interactive and will not update when the first date in the series is changed.

These methods of creating date series—adding a fixed number of days to the previous date, either by copying formulas or filling a block—work in situations where the interval between dates is fixed. Thus, in the previous example, you assume that the payment schedule works on a fixed cycle of 30 days. When the cycle is based on calendar months, the calculations become more complex because of the differing number of days per month. An example of how to work with this is given in the section "Date Part Functions."

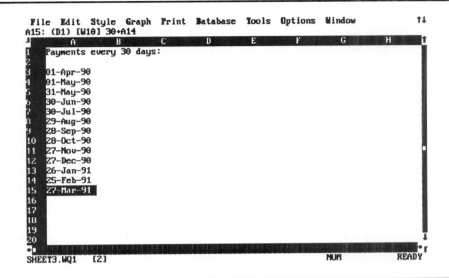

Figure 9-9.   *The complete series of dates*

Date Functions

In addition to simple addition and subtraction, there are a number of other ways to manipulate dates. You have already seen how the @TODAY, @DATE, and @DATEVALUE functions are used to create dates and convert labels to dates. There are also date functions that allow you to extract parts of a date value for specialized calculations.

Date Part Functions

Several Quattro Pro 3 functions are designed to extract part of a date from a date value. The @DAY function extracts the day of the month. It has the syntax

@DAY(*DateNumber*)

where *DateNumber* is a number under 73050.06249. This number represents the highest date possible, December 31, 2099.

The @DAY function converts the date serial number you supply as *DateNumber* into the number (1 through 31) associated with that day. Thus, the formula @DAY(A1) would return the answer 25, if A1 contained the number 33232, regardless of whether it is formatted as a date, or the formula @DATE(90,12,25).

The @MONTH function, which has the syntax

@MONTH(*DateNumber*)

returns the number (1 through 12) corresponding to the month of the year represented by *DateNumber*. Thus @MONTH(A1) returns 12 if the number in A1 is 33232 or A1 contains @DATE(90,12,25).

The @YEAR function returns the year of a date value and has the syntax

@YEAR(*DateNumber*)

The formula @YEAR(A1) would produce the answer 90, if A1 was any serial number or date within 90.

The date part functions can be used with cell references or in combination with other date functions. Thus, the formula @MONTH(@DATE(90,12,25)) returns the answer 12. You can combine date functions with other functions for some useful formulas, such as the one shown here in cell D44:

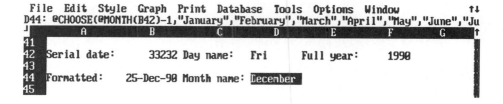

This formula lets you display the full name of the month represented by the date serial number in cell B42. None of the built-in date formats produce the full name of the month. This formula uses the @CHOOSE function (described in Chapter 4) to pick a name from the list of names that are typed as labels in the formula. As you may recall, the syntax of the @CHOOSE function is

@CHOOSE(*X*,Case0,Case1,Case2,Case*n*)

where *X* is the number of the case to be selected from the list of cases, and Case0, Case1, and so on are either numbers or labels.

Thus, the formula has the 12 months entered as the cases. Because they are labels, they are entered in quotes. The @MONTH(A1)-1 calculation returns a number from 0 through 11 for the case number, which the @CHOOSE function then reads into the cell.

A similar formula is shown here, where the name of the day of the week for the date number is returned by dividing the number by 7 and looking up the remainder (0-6) in a list of seven cases:

```
 File  Edit  Style  Graph  Print  Database  Tools  Options  Window        ↑↓
[Enter] [Esc] @CHOOSE(@MOD(@DATE(87,9,25),7),"Sat","Sun","Mon","Tue","Wed","Thu"
,"Fri")█
41
42  Serial date:      33232 Day name:   Fri      Full year:     1990
43
44  Formatted:    25-Dec-90 Month name: December
45
```

Another example of the date part functions is shown in Figure 9-10. This figure shows a date series for a loan repayment schedule that requires payment on the first day of every month. This series cannot use the +30 method used earlier, because of the varying number of days in a month. Instead, it uses the @CHOOSE function to pick the appropriate number of days of the month from a list. An @IF function statement is used for the second month number to determine if the year in question is a leap year and adjusts the number of days for February accordingly.

Time Functions

In addition to measuring calendar time, Quattro Pro 3 can calculate hours, minutes, and seconds. Calculating clock time can be done with the @NOW function, which is a more precise version of the @TODAY function. In the example shown in Figure 9-11, taken from the TOA Lost Baggage File, the date in cell E1 is created by the @NOW function formatted with the D4 format.

The number in cell G1 is the actual number created by the @NOW function. To read @NOW as a time and not a date, you simply format the

```
 File  Edit  Style  Graph  Print  Database  Tools  Options  Window        ↑↓
[Enter] [Esc]  +I44+@CHOOSE(@MONTH(I44)-1,31,@IF(@MOD(@YEAR(I44),4)=0,29,28),31,3
0,31,30,31,31,30,31,30,31)█
41
42        Date Series
43        every 1st:
44         01-Apr-90
45         01-May-90
46         01-Jun-90
47         01-Jul-90
48         01-Aug-90
49         01-Sep-90
50         01-Oct-90
51         01-Nov-90
52         01-Dec-90
53         01-Jan-91
54         01-Feb-91
55         01-Mar-91
56         01-Apr-91
57
58
59
60                                                                          ↓
←                          ■                                              →⌐
145: (D1) [W11] +I44+@CHOOSE(@MONTH(I44)-1,31,@IF(@MOD(@YEAR(I4         EDIT
```

Figure 9-10.   *Payments on the first*

cell containing @NOW with a time format, as is about to happen in Figure 9-12, where you can see the four time formats. They are reached from the Date Format menu you see when you use the Style Numeric Format Date Time command. There are two International formats, long and short, and these correspond to your selection from the Options International menu.

```
 File  Edit  Style  Graph  Print  Database  Tools  Options  Window        ↑↓
G1: [W9] @NOW
       A          B          C          D         E        F        G        H
1   TOA Lost Baggage File              Today: 06/14/90   Time: 33038.91
2
3
4   Passenger    Loss      Reported   Shift     Flying          Flight   Bag
5   Name         Date      Time       Duty   From     To        Number   Type
6   ==================================================================
7   James, H.    06/13/88   08:34 AM  Day    Paris    London     103  B5
8   Smith, N.    06/14/88   09:56 AM  Day    Rome     New York   112  C3
9   Jones, S.    06/14/88   01:23 PM  Night  London   Paris      134  A4
10  Young, F.    06/14/88   11:35 PM  Night  London   New York   136  C1
```

Figure 9-11.   *@NOW function*

Figure 9-12.   *Time formats*

The first time format produces a display that is too wide for the default column width of 9. (It actually requires a column 12 characters wide because it displays not only hours, minutes, and seconds, but also the AM or PM indicator). The second time format only requires a column of 9 characters.

The result of formatting cell G1 with the second time format is shown in Figure 9-13, where more of the Lost Baggage File is shown. Notice the AM indicator and the leading zero used in the time display.

You can also see that a time value is about to be entered into the worksheet in cell C10. This is an application of the @TIME function. Like the @DATE function, the @TIME function can be used to enter a time value so that Quattro Pro 3 can perform arithmetic with it. The syntax of the function is

@TIME(*HH*,*MM*,*SS*)

where *HH* is the hours (from 0 to 24), *MM* is the minutes (from 0 to 59), and *SS* is the seconds (from 0 to 59.99999).

```
 File  Edit  Style  Graph  Print  Database  Tools  Options  Window         ↑↓
[Enter] [Esc] @TIME(23,35,30)█
        A            B           C          D         E          F         G          H
1  TOA Lost Baggage File                      Today: 06/14/90      Time: 10:07 PM
2
3
4  Passenger     Loss        Reported    Shift     Flying                Flight    Bag
5  Name          Date        Time        Duty   From      To            Number    Type
6  =====================================================================================
7  James, H.    06/13/88    08:34 AM Day       Paris     London        103 B5
8  Smith, R.    06/13/90    09:56 AM Day       Rome      New York      112 C3
9  Jones, S.    06/13/90    01:23 PM Night     London    Paris         134 A4
10 Young, F.    06/12/90    ▓▓▓▓▓▓▓▓
11
```

Figure 9-13. *Formatted time display*

Because the @TIME function works on a 24-hour clock, the time 11:35:00 PM is expressed as @TIME(23,35,00). However, if you want to use the shorter time format that was applied to cell G1—shown in column C—you need to add 30 seconds to the time as it is being entered. Otherwise, Quattro Pro 3 will round down the display to the previous minute. Thus, the entry in cell C10 is @TIME(23,35,30) which is displayed as 11:35 PM.

Time values are used in such applications as recording customer loss reports or identifying losses not recovered within 12 hours. To add 12 hours to a time, you must bear in mind that the basic unit is a day, and that one day equals 24 hours. Thus, 12 hours is represented by 0.5, and 1 hour is represented by 0.04166 recurring.

If you have times that are currently entered as labels, you can convert them to time values with the @TIMEVALUE function. Like the @DATE-VALUE function, this process converts a string to a value if the string conforms to the standard time formats. The syntax of the function is

@TIMEVALUE(*TimeString*)

where *TimeString* is a label in one of the following formats:

HH:MM:SS

HH:MM

Long International

Short International

The International formats are specified with the Options International command. The string must be enclosed in quotes if it is included in the function statement directly. Thus, @STRING("21:39:52") returns the value 0.902685, which is 9:39 PM when formatted with the T2 time format. The statement @TIMEVALUE(A1) returns the same value if A1 contains the label 21:39:52.

Time Part Functions

Just as Quattro Pro 3 can extract parts of the date from a date value, so it can extract the elements of a time value. The time part functions are

@HOUR

@MINUTE

@SECOND

Thus, @HOUR(@TIME(10,30,00)) produces 10 and @MINUTE(A1) produces 30, if A1 contains the value @TIME(10,30,00) or the number 0.4375, which is the serial number of 10:30 AM.

Suppose you want to indicate the shift during which the lost baggage report was made. You could calculate this with a time part function. Suppose that there are two shifts, the day shift from midnight to noon, and the night shift from noon to midnight. There is a column for this information just to the right of the time record. The worksheet in Figure 9-14 shows a formula that uses the @HOUR function to evaluate the time in the cell to the left. The formula then uses the @IF function to return the label Night if the hour is less than 12 or the label Day if the hour is greater than 12.

Advanced Tools

There are four Quattro Pro 3 features grouped together on the bottom part of the Tools menu: Advanced Math (Regression, Invert, Multiply, and Optimization), Parse, What-if, and Frequency. These are not necessarily

```
 File  Edit  Style  Graph  Print  Database  Tools  Options  Window        ↑↓
D7: [W7] @IF(@HOUR(C7)>12,"Night","Day")
┌─────────────────────────────────────────────────────────────────────────┐
│      A         B        C         D        E         F        G       H   │
│ 1 TOA Lost Baggage File          Today: 06/14/90      Time: 10:09 PM      │
│ 2                                                                         │
│ 3                                                                         │
│ 4 Passenger   Loss     Reported  Shift    Flying             Flight  Bag  │
│ 5 Name        Date     Time      Duty     From      To       Number  Type │
│ 6 ========================================================================│
│ 7 James, H.   06/13/88 08:34 AM  Day      Paris     London      103 B5    │
│ 8 Smith, R.   06/13/90 09:56 AM  Day      Rome      New York    112 C3    │
│ 9 Jones, S.   06/13/90 01:23 PM  Night    London    Paris       134 A4    │
│10 Young, F.   06/12/90 11:35 PM  Night    London    New York    136 B4    │
│11 Chan, A.    06/11/90 03:05 AM  Day      Boston    London      721 B5    │
│12 Front, B.   06/11/90 03:07 AM  Day      Boston    London      721 C3    │
│13 Wong, E.    06/11/90 03:10 AM  Day      Boston    London      721 A4    │
│14 Dobbs, J.   06/11/90 03:13 AM  Day      Boston    London      721 C1    │
│15 Smith, J.   06/11/90 03:16 AM  Day      Boston    London      721 A4    │
│16 Grant, M.   06/11/90 03:19 AM  Day      Boston    London      721 C1    │
│17 Blass, M.   06/11/90 03:22 AM  Day      Boston    London      721 B5    │
│18 Smith, M.   06/11/90 03:25 AM  Day      Boston    London      721 C3    │
│19 Green, F.   06/11/90 03:28 AM  Day      Boston    London      721 C3    │
│20 Wong, S.    06/11/90 03:30 AM  Day      Boston    London      721 A4    │
└─────────────────────────────────────────────────────────────────────────┘
LOSTBAG1.WQ1 [2]                                           NUM          READY
```

Figure 9-14. *@IF function used with @HOUR*

more complicated or less used than other aspects of Quattro Pro 3, but they have specialized uses, particularly the Advanced Math options shown here:

The rest of this chapter reviews these specialized features, with the exception of Parse, which is covered in the next chapter.

Relating with Regression

When you have a large collection of related facts you may want to see how strong the relationship is between them. For example, you may want to evaluate the relationship between goods sold and the amount of money spent on advertising them, or see the connection between earnings and levels of education, and so on. One method of analyzing the connection between such facts is called *linear regression*. Quattro Pro 3 provides a built-in method for performing this through the Regression option on the Advanced Math menu. The subject of regression analysis is complex, and a complete discussion is beyond the scope of this book. A reference such as *Modern Business Statistics* by Ronald L. Iman and W. J. Conover (New York: John Wiley & Sons, 1983) provides complete coverage of all aspects of the field as they relate to typical business situations.

A Regression Example   Regression is a measurement of how different factors relate to each other. For example, how does the amount of advertising done by a company relate to its sales? Standard business philosophy states that the amount of advertising a company does is related to the sales level it achieves. Regression can help you determine the strength of this relationship in the case of your company.

Suppose you have compiled the marketing data shown in Figure 9-15. Column B is the number of full-page newspaper advertisements placed by

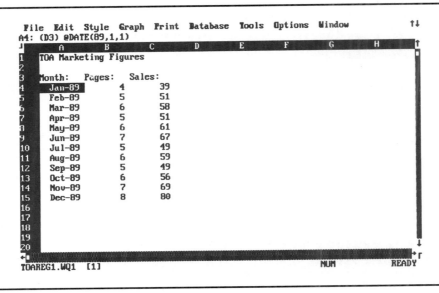

Figure 9-15.   *TOA Marketing Figures*

TOA in 1989 listed by month. The numbers in column C represent sales, in thousands, for those same months. You may want to know how these two sets of numbers relate. Once you measure the relationship, you can use that measure to predict future sales based on different levels of future advertising. In the figure, the months were produced by adding 31 days to the first month and formatting the cells with the D3 format.

Setting Up Regression When you select Regression from the Advanced Math menu, you see the menu shown in Figure 9-16. Note that before this menu was selected, the cell selector was placed in E3. This was done because the Regression command produces a table of results that occupies an area of the worksheet. It should be a block of blank cells set apart from the data being analyzed.

The first two items on the Regression menu refer to the variable factors in the regression calculation. The effect of the independent variable on the dependent variable is being calculated. In this case, Pages, in cells B4..B15, is the independent variable. Its effect on Sales, in cells C4..C15, the dependent variable, is what is to be calculated. Both variables must be

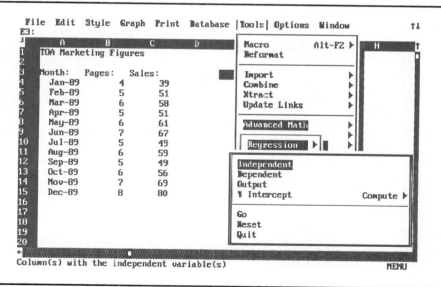

Figure 9-16. *Regression menu*

situated in matching columns and rows of the worksheet and must contain an equal number of pieces of data, as is the case in this example. When you select Independent and Dependent, you can enter the cell coordinates either by typing them or by pointing to them. (There can be more than one independent variable, as will be shown in a later example.)

Figure 9-17 shows the completed entries for the regression calculation in the expanded form of the menu. The independent and dependent variables have been defined. The Output block is referred to as E3..E3, although the results of the calculation will occupy four columns and nine rows. You need only define the top-left corner of the cells of the Output block. As you can see from Figure 9-17, the Go option is highlighted to tell Quattro Pro 3 to complete the regression calculation. The results are shown in Figure 9-18.

Regression Results   The result of a regression calculation is a column of numbers that represent the numeric relationships between the variables, and columns of labels describing these numbers. The heading Regression Output will appear more centered if you output to wider columns than the

Figure 9-17.   *Completed menu*

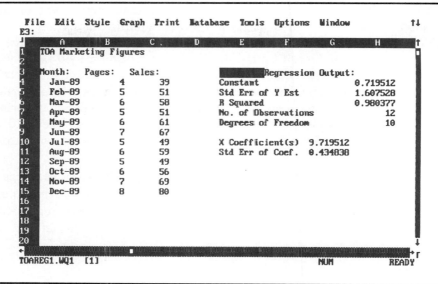

Figure 9-18.   *Results of regression*

default width of 9. Note that outputting to columns any narrower than 9 will make the data difficult to read.

Interpreting these results involves understanding numerous concepts from statistics. The No. of Observations is how many data points were observed for the variables, in this case 12, one for each month. Degrees of Freedom represents the number of observations minus one for each variable observed, in this case 10. The value R Squared is sometimes referred to as the coefficient of determination, a measure of the extent to which the variables are related, with 1 being the optimal value. In this example, where the sales are clearly very closely related to the pages, the value of R Squared is nearly 1.

The Std Err of Y Est is the estimated standard error of the Y values. With this you measure the certainty with which the independent variables predict the dependent variables. In general, the larger this measure, the less reliable the relationship between the independent and the dependent variables. This measure, like R Squared, is useful when deciding between different independent variables as predictors of the dependent variables. The Std Err of Coef gives an error measurement of the coefficients. The larger this measurement, relative to the X coefficient, the less certain the relationship between the variables. This measurement will often be smaller when more observations are included in the calculation.

Probably the most useful numbers in the regression output are the constant and the X coefficient. The constant can be described as the y-axis intercept of the regression line that describes the relationship between pages and sales. The X coefficient tells how much the dependent variable, sales, will change for a single unit increase in the independent variable, pages. As you can see in the output in Figure 9-18, this is close to 10, and most of the sales figures are, in fact, about ten times the pages figures.

Using Regression Results The constant and X coefficient readings can be used to predict the value of sales based on different numbers of pages. In Figure 9-19 a calculation has been entered in column D, representing the formula *Constant+X coefficient × Independent variable*; in this case,

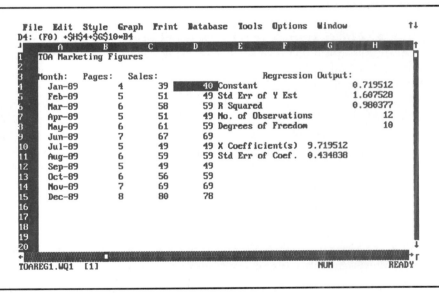

Figure 9-19. *Completed menu*

cell D4 is **$H$4+$G$10*B4**. This formula was copied down the column to produce the predicted results, which are fairly close to the real results. The value of this calculation can be seen when the pages are changed to the figures shown in Figure 9-20 and the sales for 1990 are predicted. Remember that the prediction shown here is only a statistical inference, not a guaranteed basis for a business decision. However, it is a suggestion that more advertising will produce more sales.

Multiple Variables You can include more than one independent variable in the regression calculation. An example of this is the analysis of the survey questionnaire shown in Figure 9-21. This set of questions was sent to all of TOA's corporate accounts. The worksheet shows a sample set of

Figure 9-20. *Adding predictions*

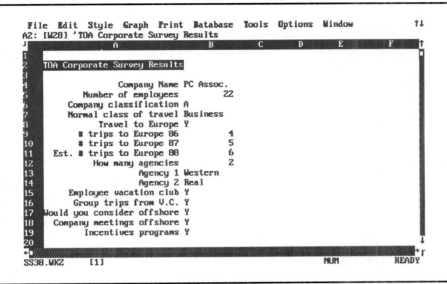

Figure 9-21. *Making predictions for 1990*

responses. The results of the survey were entered into the worksheet in tabulated columns, as shown here:

```
 File  Edit  Style  Graph  Print  Database  Tools  Options  Window        ↑↓
A22: [W17] 'PC  Assoc.
⌐        A        B        C        D        E        F        G        ↑
21 Company Name   Employees Code    Class     Europe  Europe 86Europe 87
22 PC  Assoc.         22 B         Business  y           4        5
23 Quadkilo, Inc.    420 C         Business  y          40       42
24 Multiper          167 B         Coach     n           0        0
```

The company names are in column A. Column B shows the number of employees at the company. The letters entered in column C refer to a code for the company's type of business. There are just over a hundred responses to the survey. The analyst wants to know if there is a significant relationship between the size of the company, as measured by the number of its employees; the type of business the company is in, as signified by the code; and the number of flights made to Europe in 1990, listed in column H. This means that the independent variables are columns B and C, and column H is the dependent variable. Before the Code data can be used in a regression calculation, however, it must be converted to its numeric values. This is done by adding a column to the left of the current column C and entering into that column a formula that converts the letter codes A through E into the numbers 1 through 5. A series of @IF statements can accomplish this, as shown here:

```
 File  Edit  Style  Graph  Print  Database  Tools  Options  Window            ↑↓
C22: [W9] @IF(D22="A",1,@IF(D22="B",2,@IF(D22="C",3,@IF(D22="D",4,@IF(D22="E",5,
⌐            A              B       C       D      E         F       ↑
21 Company Name          Employees Code #  Code  Class    Europe
22 PC Assoc.                  22     2 B    Businessy
23 Quadkilo, Inc.            420     3 C    Businessy
24 Multiper                  167     2 B    Coach    n
```

The new column C now contains numeric data. It is also adjacent to the other column that is used as an independent variable. This is a requirement when there is more than one independent variable. Here you can see the settings made on the Regression menu. Select Go to perform the calculation.

```
┌─────────────────────────────┐
│ Independent      B22..C124  │
│ Dependent        I22..I124  │
│ Output           P2..P2     │
│ Y Intercept      Compute ►  │
├─────────────────────────────┤
│ Go                          │
│ Reset                       │
│ Quit                        │
└─────────────────────────────┘
```

The result of this regression example, seen in Figure 9-22, shows two X coefficients, one for each of the independent variables. The measure of R Squared is 0.65642, which shows a moderate relationship between the two independent variables and the dependent one.

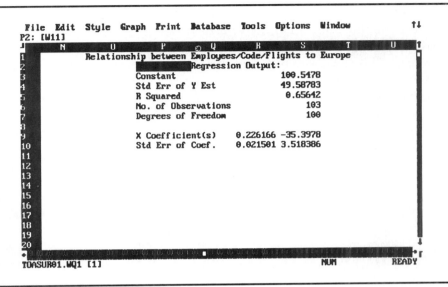

Figure 9-22. *Multiple regression results*

Frequency Distribution

When you are handling large quantities of data, such as that shown in the last example, you often need to analyze the distribution of the data. For example, someone might ask "How big are the companies who responded?" Measured in terms of employees, you could say that they range from 5 to 500, and you could see this from simply browsing column B. But this response would be rather vague. If you were to categorize the companies based on number of employees and count how many fell into each category, you would get a better understanding of the survey's respondents. This is the role of the Frequency command on the Tools menu.

Performing a Distribution To perform a frequency distribution with Quattro Pro 3, you need to supply two pieces of information. The first is the block of values that are to be categorized. The second is the column of numbers representing the range over which the values are to be distributed—the categories, as it were. The group of cells containing these category numbers is called the *bins block*, as though each number in the values block was tossed into the appropriate bin for counting. The result of the Tools Frequency command is a list of the totals of that count placed in the column to the right of the bin numbers.

To see this in action, consider the response to the TOA survey, which you want to analyze according to the number of employees at each company. First, a series of numbers for the bins block must be entered. The first number will represent from 0 to the number, so that 100 would represent from 0 to 100. For the employee numbers you could use 100 through 1000 in intervals of 100. This series of numbers can easily be entered with the Edit Fill command, as shown in Figure 9-23.

Be sure that the cells you use for the bins block have empty cells immediately to the right of them. When you select Frequency, you are first

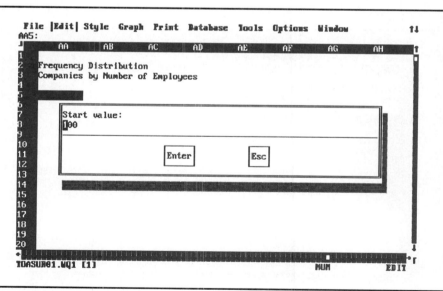

Figure 9-23. *Edit Fill*

prompted for the values block, in this case, cells B22..B124. As soon as you enter this, you are prompted for the bins block, as shown in Figure 9-24. Here you can see that the bin numbers range from 100 to 1000, and are being defined. When you enter the bins block, Quattro Pro 3 immediately responds with the count of numbers shown in Figure 9-25. From this result you can see that 35 of the companies responding to the survey had from 0 to 100 employees. There were 14 companies with 101 to 200 employees. These results provide a valuable picture of the survey data. Frequency distributions are a good basis for many graphs, an example of which is shown in Figure 9-26.

Improving the Distribution   Since the bin numbers are somewhat difficult to interpret, you can add a second column as shown in the worksheet in Figure 9-27. This is a list of sales figures for travel agents. The sales from column C are distributed in column H. The bin numbers are shown in column G. The numbers in column F show the range of numbers implied by the distribution performed by the Frequency command.

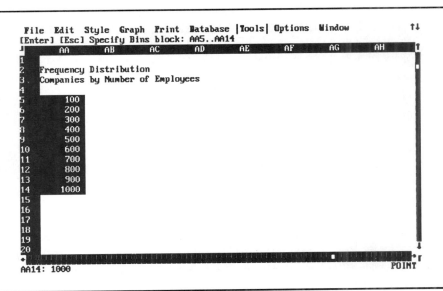

Figure 9-24.   *The bins block*

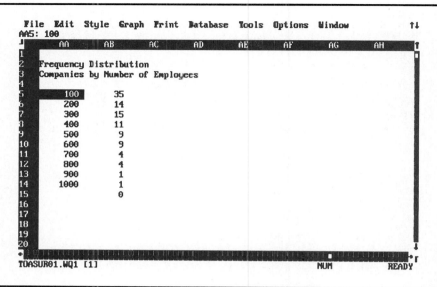

Figure 9-25. *The completed distribution*

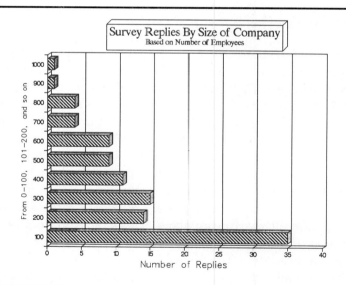

Figure 9-26. *Distribution graph*

```
File  Edit  Style  Graph  Print  Database  Tools  Options  Window          ↑↓
F4: [W10] 0
J    A        B        C        D       E      F         G          H        ↑
1
2            Quattro Vadis Sales Totals        Sales Levels        Number of
3                                              From:     To:         Agents
4    Agent  Office    Sales    Comm                  0    500,000        2
5    Sue    Union Sq. 687,450  41,247         500,001    600,000        3
6    Sam    Van Ness  586,780  35,207         600,001    700,000        1
7    Joe    San Mateo 876,900  52,614         700,001    800,000        2
8    Liz    Polk St.  878,590  52,715         800,001    900,000        6
9    Ann    Polk St.  768,545  46,113         900,001  1,000,000        1
10   Lee    Union Sq. 500,001  30,000                                   0
11   Ian    Union Sq. 849,050  50,943
12   Tim    Van Ness  459,870  27,592
13   Tom    Union Sq. 859,600  51,576
14   Ron    Van Ness  901,250  54,075
15   Sal    San Mateo 760,805  45,648
16   Pip    Polk St.  458,790  27,527
17   Jud    General   890,670  53,440
18   Jim    General   804,550  48,273
19   Rob    Polk St.  564,560  33,874
20
SALESTAT.WQ1 [3]                                    NUM           READY
```

Figure 9-27. *Improved bin numbers*

What-if Analysis

When making projections, you will want to experiment with values to see what different actions will result in. This is called *what-if analysis*. After you have established the formulas that relate the different cells in a worksheet, you can change the numbers upon which the formulas are based. For example, you can set up a worksheet to calculate sales for the next 12 months based on a starting volume of 2000 units increasing at 5% per month. By adding up the sales for the year, you can see what kinds of sales are possible with a 9% growth rate starting at 2000 units. By changing the starting figure, you can calculate sales beginning at 2500 instead of 2000. Then, you might want to create a table of total sales achieved by different starting numbers. Such a table is sometimes referred to as a *one-way data table* because it lists the results obtained from varying one factor in a calculation. You could create a *two-way data table* by varying both the beginning figure and the rate of growth. This kind of what-if analysis can be automated to a certain extent by the What-if selection on the Advanced menu.

A One-Way What-if Example Suppose you are thinking of buying a car. The spreadsheet shown in Figure 9-28 includes some of the calculations involved. The cells are shown in the text format to reveal the formulas they contain. The total price of the car is calculated and the down payment subtracted to show the amount you would need to finance.

The figures in D1, D2, and D3 show the principal, interest, and term of the loan. You may want to know how large the payments on the loan will be at different rates of interest. For example, the list of rates that begins at 10% in cell A11 could be extended all the way to 19% by the Edit Fill command, filling cells A11 through A20 with values starting at 0.1, incremented by 0.01 to stop at 0.19. The Percent format could then be applied to the cells. The formula in cell B10 simply refers to the loan payment calculation cell. This is the cell whose answers you want to see in the completed table.

You can see from Figure 9-28 that the What-if option has been chosen from the Tools menu. You can actually vary two items with the What-if selection by choosing 2 Variables. The Reset option simply clears any previous settings. The action performed by the first item on the menu, 1 Variable, is to replace one cell with cells from the left edge. This is what is needed to see the loan payment calculated for each rate of interest.

Figure 9-28. *Calculation formulas*

When you select 1 Variable, you are prompted for the block of cells to be used as the data table. In this case the block is cells A10 through B20, as shown in Figure 9-29.

The table is all of the numbers to be fed into the formula, plus the formula, represented in this case by +D5. When you have entered the data table block, the program prompts "Input Cell from column," meaning "Into which cell do you want to read the values from the left column of the data table?" In this case, the interest cell, D2, is the input cell, as shown in Figure 9-30.

When you have entered the input cell, the results are then tabulated. Quattro Pro 3 feeds each of the values from column A into cell D2 and reads the resulting answer in D5 into the table, creating the output shown in Figure 9-31. This output consists of numbers, not formulas, and so it is not interactive. Changing the terms of the loan on the spreadsheet would not cause any change in the cells of the data table. You must repeat the What-if command to take into account changes in the model. The data table is a quick way to perform a repetitive series of calculations, and pressing Table (F8) repeats the last table command.

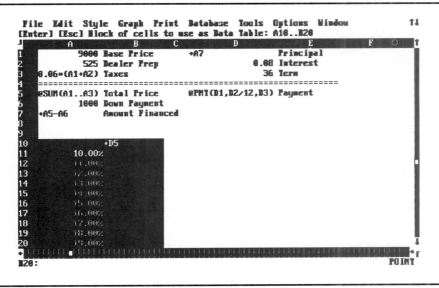

Figure 9-29.   *Marking the block*

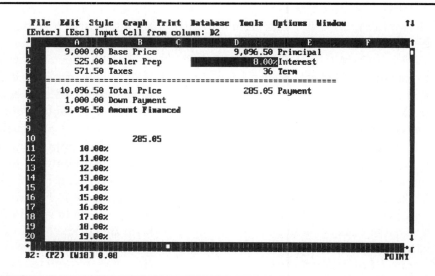

Figure 9-30. *Setting input cell*

Figure 9-31. *A What-if loan*

Two-Way What-if Calculations   The next step is a two-way data table, shown in Figure 9-32. This table shows the payments on the loan based on a variety of interest rates and five different payment terms. The table varies both the interest in D2 and the term in D3. The operation is performed by first setting the interest rates down the side of the worksheet and then the terms across the top. The What-if command is then selected from the Tools menu, and 2 Variables is chosen. The data table is defined as the block formed by the column of variables and the row of variables, A10 through F20, in this case. You are then prompted "input cell from Column," which is the interest in D2. Finally, you are prompted for the input cell from the top row, the term in cell D3, as entered in Figure 9-33.

The results are then created by Quattro Pro 3 as shown in Figure 9-32. You can use this table to decide what terms are best suited to your budget. You could easily produce a different table with various prices and interest rates to see how expensive a car you could afford to finance. Use the Reset command to clear out the current settings for the data table and input cells. Remember that the data table is not interactive and will not be updated when you change other factors in the model. You must reissue the What-if command to update the table, or press F8, the Table key.

```
 File  Edit  Style  Graph  Print  Database  Tools  Options  Window          ↑↓
 A10: (T) [W13] +D5
J      A          B          C          D          E          F         ↑
1    10,000.00 Base Price         10,156.50 Principal
2      525.00 Dealer Prep             9.00%Interest
3      631.50 Taxes                     36 Term
4   ================================================================
5    11,156.50 Total Price          322.97 Payment
6     1,000.00 Down Payment                                            ■
7    10,156.50 Amount Financed
8
9
10  +D5            12         24         36         48         60
11      10.00%    892.92     468.67     327.72     257.60     215.80
12      11.00%    897.65     473.37     332.51     262.50     220.83
13      12.00%    902.39     478.10     337.34     267.46     225.93
14      13.00%    907.15     482.86     342.21     272.47     231.09
15      14.00%    911.92     487.64     347.13     277.54     236.32
16      15.00%    916.71     492.45     352.08     282.66     241.62
17      16.00%    921.51     497.29     357.07     287.84     246.99
18      17.00%    926.32     502.16     362.11     293.07     252.42
19      18.00%    931.15     507.05     367.18     298.35     257.91
20      19.00%    935.99     511.98     372.30     303.68     263.47    ↓
 DT2WAY.WQ1   [3]                                    NUM         READY
```

Figure 9-32.   *Two-way data table*

```
 File  Edit  Style  Graph  Print  Database  Tools  Options  Window           ↑↓
[Enter] [Esc] Input Cell from top row: D3
 ┌─────────A────────────────B──────────────C─────────D──────────────E──────────F───────1
 1      10,000.00 Base Price                 10,156.50 Principal
 2         525.00 Dealer Prep                    9.00%Interest
 3         631.50 Taxes                          36 Term
 4 ==========================================================================
 5      11,156.50 Total Price                  322.97 Payment
 6       1,000.00 Down Payment
 7      10,156.50 Amount Financed
 8
 9
10  +D5                    12          24          36          48          60
```

Figure 9-33.   *Input cell*

Matrix Arithmetic

Two items on the Advanced Math menu, Invert and Multiply, provide you with tools for performing matrix arithmetic. If you know what the inverse of a matrix is and need to perform matrix arithmetic in your work, the following account of the Invert and Multiply commands will get you started applying Quattro Pro 3 to the task. If you are not familiar with inverting matrices, the following example will give you an idea of how they are used to solve practical problems.

Matrix arithmetic is used in linear programming, a technique for determining the optimal allocation of limited resources. This has practical application in many areas, notably economics, which has been defined as "the science that studies human behavior as a relationship between ends and scarce means which have alternative uses." Although a discussion of economic theory and linear programming concepts is clearly beyond the scope of this book, you can get an idea of how matrix commands work and how linear programming is applied with Quattro Pro 3 from a relatively simple example.

At Take Over Airlines, management needs to determine the optimal mix of cargo on a plane, choosing between packages and people. The data from which this mix must be calculated is the amount of fuel needed to fly each package and each person, plus the amount of handling time involved for each package and each person. This data is laid out in the worksheet shown in Figure 9-34.

The profit per package and person is also listed in the worksheet. The numbers are pure data, not formulas. You can, however, set up a similar worksheet very easily by setting the width of column A to 16 and the rest to 10. Enter the numbers as values. In cell F3, the words **Matrix Output** have been entered to label the results of the first set of calculations, which will be created by Quattro Pro 3's Invert command. The calculation that must be performed to determine the optimal mix of packages and persons involves the following equations:

$$2750*Packages+9250*Persons=80,000 \text{ Gallons}$$
$$3*Packages+2*Persons=40 \text{ Hours}$$

These equations will yield the number of packages and persons you should load to optimize allocation of the given resources. Once you have entered the data in the worksheet, as shown in Figure 9-34, you can have Quattro Pro 3 calculate an inverse of the matrix of numbers in B4..C5.

Matrix Invert   When you select Invert from the Advanced Math menu, you are prompted for the source block of cells. In this case the block is B4..C5. The cell coordinates can be pointed out or typed in, just as you do at other Quattro Pro 3 block prompts. The matrix to be inverted must be square; that is, it must have the same number of columns as rows. When you have entered the Source Block coordinates, you are prompted for a Destination Block. In this case F4 will be used. The Destination Block will be the same size as the Source Block, so you must use an adequate area of your spreadsheet for this. However, you need only point out the top-left corner

Figure 9-34.   *The cargo worksheet*

of the Destination Block. When you enter the Destination Block coordinates, the inverse matrix is produced, as shown in Figure 9-35.

This example shows how Quattro Pro 3's default General format displays long numbers. The number in cell F4 is -0.000076294277929. But since the column is only ten characters wide, the number is shown in scientific notation, standing for -7.63×10^5. Unless you need to observe the details of the inverse matrix results, you will probably want to leave the output cells in General format. Otherwise, you may have to use a format with a large number of decimal places and a wide column width to see the numbers.

Matrix Multiply   Having calculated the inverse matrix of the numbers, you can use the Advanced Math Multiply command to multiply the original resources of 80,000 gallons and 40 hours by the inverse matrix. The resources, which were the constants in the equations, constitute a matrix. The Multiply command allows you to multiply two matrices together. In this case the results will be the number of packages and persons that make the most efficient use of your limited resources. When you select Multiply from the Matrix menu, you are prompted to "Specify 1st Matrix," which will be the output of the inverse matrix, cells F4..G5.

When you enter these coordinates, you are prompted to "Specify 2nd Matrix," which will be the resources in D4..D5. After entering the second matrix coordinates you are prompted for a "Destination for cells." In this example cell B10 is named, as shown in Figure 9-36, where some additional labels have been added to identify the results. When you enter the destination coordinates, the results of the calculations are seen. In this case a mix of 10.03 packages and 5.67 persons is the most efficient use of the resources available.

Note that cells B10 and B11 in Figure 9-36 have been formatted to two decimal places with the Comma format. Since you cannot have 5.67 persons, you might want to display the result without any decimal places.

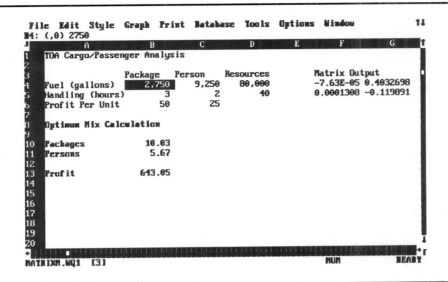

Figure 9-35. *The inverse matrix*

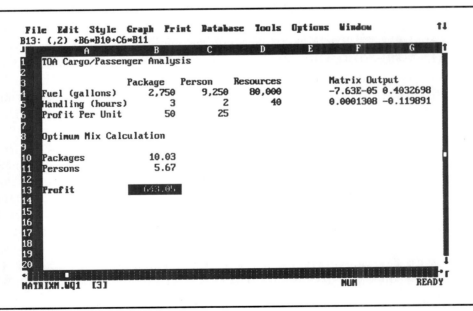

Figure 9-36. *Profit calculation*

However, if you are going to use the result in another calculation, you may want to use the @ROUND function to eliminate the decimal places.

In Figure 9-36 there is one additional calculation in the worksheet. This figure shows the amount of profit made by the mix determined in B10 and B11, using the profit figures from row 6. The formula +B6*B10+C6*B11 is used to multiply the per-unit profit by the optimal number of units. You might modify the formula as follows, in order to use whole units of packages and persons:

+B6*@ROUND(B10,0)+C6*@ROUND(B11,0)

XY Graphs

Since this chapter has discussed some advanced features of Quattro Pro 3 for analyzing and determining relationships between collections of data, this is an appropriate place to address the subject of XY graphs. This type of graph was not included with the other graphs in Chapter 8 because it is a specialized type. Used to plot the relationship between data points that have two coordinates, XY graphing can be used for such tasks as analyzing measurements and displaying regression lines.

Making an XY Graph

Figure 9-37 shows a worksheet of size and weight measurements for a number of packages. The weight is in kilos and the size is the sum of the length plus the circumference of the package in centimeters. These packages were picked at random from the airport loading dock in an effort to learn more about the relationship between package size and weight. You decide to graph the size of these packages relative to their weight.

If you set the weight figures in B2..B14 as the x-axis and the sizes in C2..C14 as the 1st Series Value, and use the Marker graph type, you get a graph like the one in Figure 9-38. Each measurement is displayed as a point on the graph, a square box in this case. The x-axis numbers are displayed in the order in which they exist in the worksheet. Although each package is graphed, the graph does not tell you much about the relationship between the two axes. However, if you change the graph type from

```
 File  Edit  Style  Graph  Print  Database  Tools  Options  Window          ↑↓
A1:
 」      A         B         C         D         E         F         G         H      ↑
1               Weight    Size
2                 1.6      19.0
3                 2.5      16.2
4       Parcel    3.5      22.5
5        Size     4.7      28.2
6         To      4.8      27.0
7       Weight    5.8      34.8
8       Sample    6.3      35.0
9                 6.7      40.2
10                7.0      43.5
11                8.0      47.8
12                8.9      53.4
13                9.3      55.8
14                9.9      59.4
```

Figure 9-37.   *Parcel data*

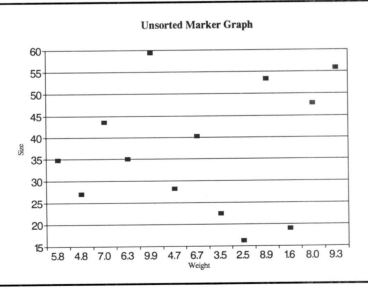

Figure 9-38.   *Unsorted Marker graph*

Marker to XY, the graph is much more informative, as you can see in Figure 9-39. This is because the XY graph sorts the data on the x-axis into order of magnitude. You can see a fairly strong relationship between the size and weight. As size increases, so does weight. If you were told a package weighed 6.5 kilos, you could guess that the size is probably 60 centimeters.

Graphing Regression

There is a close relationship between the display of data in an XY graph and the calculations in regression analysis. If you look at the revised TOA marketing figures shown in Figure 9-40, you will see the monthly advertising page count next to the sales for the month (in thousands) and the projected sales based on the regression analysis on the right. If the pages were graphed as the x-axis in an XY graph, and if the sales were graphed as the 1st Series value, you could see the relationship between them.

Figure 9-41 shows how this has been done. The actual sales are seen as boxes. The projected sales calculated from the regression figures are also

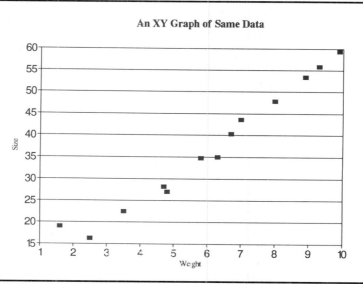

An XY Graph of Same Data

Figure 9-39.　*XY graph*

```
 File  Edit  Style  Graph  Print  Database  Tools  Options  Window              ↑↓
D4: (F2) [W10] +$H$4+$G$10*B4
J     A         B         C         D         E         F         G         H   ↑
1  TOA Marketing Figures
2  By Month  Pages     Actual    Estimated
3  for 1990: Planned: 89 Sales: 90 Sales:         Regression Output:
4     Jan-90    6.00     56.00     58.63 Constant                     9.120338
5     Feb-90    7.50     69.00     71.00 Std Err of Y Est             6.922244
6     Mar-90    8.00     80.00     75.13 R Squared                    0.668407
7     Apr-90    5.25     51.00     52.44 No. of Observations               12
8     May-90    6.75     61.60     64.82 Degrees of Freedom                10
9     Jun-90    7.25     67.00     68.94
10    Jul-90    5.00     49.00     50.38 X Coefficient(s)   8.251101
11    Aug-90    6.00     59.50     58.63 Std Err of Coef.   1.837782
12    Sep-90    5.50     73.60     54.50
13    Oct-90    4.25     39.30     44.19
14    Nov-90    5.25     51.00     52.44
15    Dec-90    6.75     58.90     64.82
16
17            Totals:   715.9      716
18                    Actual 89/Estimated 90
19
20                                                                              ↓
                                                                             ┌─┐r
TOAREG3.WQ1  [3]                                          NUM         READY
```

Figure 9-40.   *The updated marketing figures*

graphed, as the 2nd Series value, and displayed as a line rather than as data points. You can see that the data points produced by the regression calculation represent a straight line drawn to fit as closely as possible to the relationship between sales and pages.

Optimization

The Tools Advanced Math menu provides another tool for analyzing data in the context of a linear model. This is the Optimization command. This command, which actually performs sophisticated linear programming for you, is used to minimize or maximize a combination of variables, subject to various constraints. The calculations are based on data in your spreadsheet that you specify through a series of settings. In the context of Optimization, *constraints* are the limitations placed on your variables. The ability to deal with constraints makes optimization particularly useful in

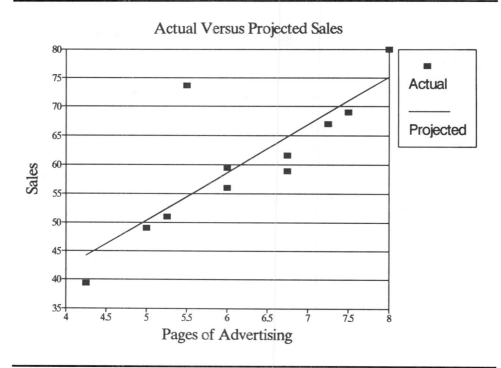

Figure 9-41. *Regression graph*

analyzing economic problems, since economics is based on the relationship between ends and scarce means that have alternative uses. Suppose you want to optimize a manufacturing operation. The resources available are a constraint, since you do not have endless supplies nor an infinite number of person-hours per month. Plant capacity is also a constraint since you cannot make an unlimited number of products.

The Scenario

For example, suppose you are a blacksmith running a smithy that makes knives, rapiers, daggers, and swords. To supply the royal army you need to make a minimum number of each item per month and this minimum is a constraint. You know that it takes so many ingots of steel to make each item: knives take 3, rapiers 4, daggers 2.5, and swords 6. If steel is in limited supply, then the maximum amount of steel available each month is also a constraint. For example, the smithy currently has an allocation of 600 ingots per month. Since person-hours are limited by the number of employees and how many hours they can each work per month, the time that can be allotted to making the weapons is a further constraint. For example, the smithy employs 12 people and they each work 40 hours per week, so 1920 hours are the most that can be applied to production. To begin to determine the total profit that can be made in this operation you might want to start with regular math and Quattro Pro 3's What-if capability. You might set up a model like the one shown in Figure 9-42, which analyzes making an equal number of each weapon.

You can see from row 5 in Figure 9-42 that to make a knife it takes 7 hours; a rapier takes 14, a dagger 10, and a sword 16. The amount of profit per item is listed on row 8. In cell D10 is a guess at the number of units of each item that will yield the greatest profit. This number is used in the

```
 File  Edit  Style  Graph  Print  Database  Tools  Options  Window          ↑↓
H15: (,0) @SUM(B15..E15)
      A        B        C        D        E     F      G          H        ↑
1  We Be Blades - Blacksmiths to the Royal Armory
2
3           Knife    Rapier   Dagger    Sword
4  Quantity per unit:
5  Hours        7       14       10       16       Total Hours:    1,920
6  Ingots       3        4        3        6       Total Ingots:     600
7  ==================================================
8  Profit       4        7        3        8
9
10 What if we make, of each:        30           Results:
11
12 Hours      266      532      300      600       Total Hours:    1,786
13 Ingots     114      152       95      228       Total Ingots:     589
14 ==================================================
15 Profit     152      266      114      304       Total Profit:     836
16
17
18
19
20
+                                                                          ↓
BASICOPT.WQ1 [2]                                    NUM           READY
```

Figure 9-42.   *Simple problem analysis*

multiplication formulas shown in Figure 9-43, where cells are displayed in text format. By simply entering a different number in D10, the blacksmith can see the effect on profit, as well as the total number of hours and ingots consumed. If the numbers exceed the constraints, as they do in Figure 9-43, then a lower number must be used. While this model is helpful in coming to grips with the problem, it cannot address all of the issues facing the blacksmith. For example, this approach does not recognize constraints and therefore cannot adjust all of the factors that can be adjusted to reach an optimal set of figures.

The Optimization Tool

As you can see from Figure 9-44, the Optimization menu is divided into three sections. (The menu is shown in the figure in the narrow form to make it more readable.) The first section of the menu is called Input Values, the second is Output Values, and the third is Commands. The Input Values section is where you specify cells or blocks of cells as input. These are the

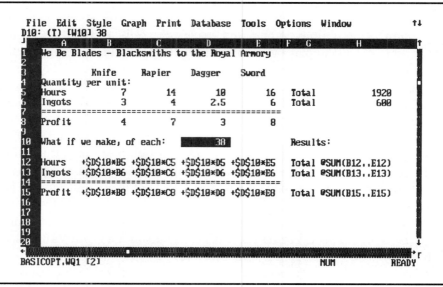

Figure 9-43. *Worksheet showing formulas*

```
 File  Edit  Style  Graph  Print  Database  Tools  Options  Window        ↑↓
A2: [W15]
         A         B       C       D      E      F      G       H      I
1  We Be Blades - Blacksmiths to the Royal Armory
2
3              Knife   Rapier  Dagger     ┌─────────────────────────────────┐
4  Smith Hours     7      14      10      │Linear constraint coefficients   │
5  Per Item        1       1       1      │Inequality/equality relations    │
6  Ingots Required 3       4     2.5      │Constant constraint terms        │
7  ====================================   │Bounds for variables             │
8  Profit/Weapon  $4      $7      $3      │Formula constraints              │
9  Minimum Supply 24      24      24      │Objective function               │
10 Maximum Volume 48      48      48      │Extremum                       ▸ │
11 ====================================   ├─────────────────────────────────┤
12 Recommended    Knife  Rapier  Dagger   │Solution                         │
13 Quantity        48      48      24      │Variables                        │
14                                         │Dual values                      │
15 Dual Values (2) 0.00   1.67   -0.33    │Additional dual values           │
16                Okay   Okay  Reduce     ├─────────────────────────────────┤
17                                         │Go                               │
18 ====================================   │Reset                            │
19 Max Profit    $872 Sum Product         │Quit                             │
20                                         └─────────────────────────────────┘
Range of coefficients for equality or inequality constraints        MENU
```

Figure 9-44.   *The Optimization menu*

cells on which Quattro Pro 3 performs the linear programming operation. In the Output Values section you specify the cells and cell blocks where Quattro Pro 3 is to place the results of the optimization, just as it outputs the results of regression. The third section consists of three commands. The Go command starts the search for the optimal solution. You must define the input value blocks and output value blocks before choosing this command. The Reset command clears all settings in the Input and Output Values sections of the Optimization menu so you can work on a different set of values or completely redefine your model. Note that the cell coordinates defined in the Input and Output Values sections remain defined in the current worksheet for future use. The Quit command returns you to READY mode.

Before running Optimization you need to designate certain cells of data in your spreadsheet. You do this with the items in the Input Values section of the Optimization menu. The variables in your model can be any real numbers that satisfy certain constraints or realistic limitations. The variables must also come within certain bounds. Figure 9-45 shows an

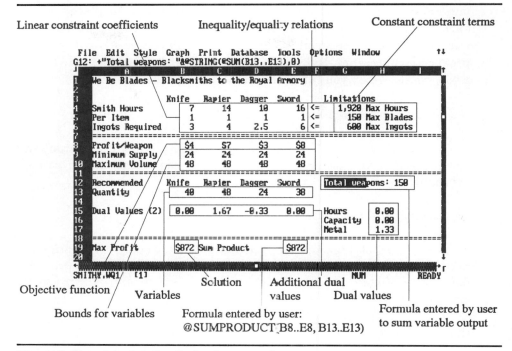

Figure 9-45. *Annotated optimization example*

optimization model designed for the smithy. The various parts of the model are annotated so that you can see where they fit in. The location of the various input and output items can vary from this arrangement. Each item will be explained as the model and the basic principles of optimization are described.

What Are Constraints?

With the first item on the Optimization menu, Linear Constraint Coefficients, you define the cells that contain the linear constraints on your model's variables. This matrix consists of one row for each constraint and one column for each variable. Constraints are limitations placed on the variables in your model; these limitations can be expressed as algebraic statements. In the blacksmith scenario you might be under royal decree to produce no more than 150 weapons per month, of whatever kind. This is a constraint, which you can describe as

knives + rapiers + daggers + swords <= 150

The smithy must produce at least 60 weapons per month to satisfy the basic needs of the armory. This is another constraint, which can be expressed as

knives + rapiers + daggers + swords >= 60

Remember that it takes so many ingots of steel to make each item: knives take 3, rapiers 4, daggers 2.5, and swords 6. But the smithy can obtain only 600 ingots of steel per month. This is also a constraint, which can be expressed as

(knives*3)+(rapiers*4)+(daggers*2.5)+(swords*6) <= 600

Since person-hours are limited by the number of employees and how many hours they can each work per month, the time that can be allotted to making the weapons is a fourth constraint. With 12 persons working 160 hours per month, this limitation can be expressed as

(knives*7)+(rapiers*14)+(daggers*10)+(swords*16) <= 1920

where 7, 14, 10, and 16 are the hours required to make the respective weapons.

Constraints are said to be linear when their algebraic statements express relationships in which variables are being added or subtracted in various combinations. This is the case in the previous statements.

k	+ r	+ d	+ s	<=	150
k	+ r	+ d2.5	+ s	>=	60
k3	+ r4	+ d2.5	+ s6	<=	600
k7	+ r14	+ d10	+ s16	<=	1920

In Figure 9-45 you can see linear constraint coefficients in cells B4..E6. The columns of this block represent the model's variables, while the rows represent the linear constraints.

Equality and Inequality of Constraints

The constraints on your model are said to be *equality constraints* when an exact figure must be attained. This would be the case if the smithy was ordered to produce exactly 72 blades a month, no more or less. Constraints can also be *inequality constraints,* as in the previous formulas where a minimum or maximum applies.

Each of the linear constraints within the model states that some combination of the variables is equal to (or greater than or less than) some constant value. With the Constant Constraint Terms menu item, you define a column with x number of entries, where x is the number of constraints in the model, that is, the number of rows in the matrix of coefficients. Each of the entries in this column is the constant term for one of the linear constraints in the model. In the model in Figure 9-45 you can see that this setting should be cells G4..G6.

If your model incorporates inequality constraints you must set up a column of labels that describe these constraints, such as >=. Then you enter the coordinates of the labels and the values in the Inequality/Equality Relations setting. You can use the symbols <, >, >=, <=, and <> to express inequality. Just type the label and press ENTER for a left-aligned label. You can also center or right-align these labels without affecting their functionality. You can even precede the symbol with spaces, and you can place any character after it for aesthetic purposes. Thus, the label entry

" < less than

is an acceptable right-aligned label for indicating "less than." If you do not specify a column of Inequality/Equality Relations labels, Quattro Pro 3 assumes all your model's constraints to be equality constraints, using the values in the Constant Constraint Terms setting.

Bounds for Variables

Just as the variables that represent the best solution to your model must satisfy certain constraints, they might also be required to fall within certain upper and lower bounds. For example, as the blacksmith running the smithy you are under royal decree not to produce more than 48 weapons per month of each kind. This is an upper bound for the variables knives, rapiers, daggers, and swords. However, the smithy is required to produce a minimum number of each weapon per month to satisfy the basic needs of the armory, say, 24 weapons. This is a lower bound for the variables knives, rapiers, daggers, and swords.

You specify the bounds by selecting a block with two rows, the first row being the lower bound and the second being the upper. The number of columns is the same as the number of variables. In the case of the smithy, new armory commitments require production of at least 24 of each weapon per month, but royal decree limits output to no more than 48 of each item. To represent these bounds, you would select a block of cells with the following values:

24   24   24   24

48   48   48   48

Your variables do not have to be bounded. For instance, the only restriction on a particular variable might be that it must be non-negative. This means that the variable's lower bound is 0, but it has no upper bound. If the smithy had no armory commitments, the only lower bound would be zero; it can produce none of a particular item, but it cannot produce a negative number of weapons.

You specify non-negative bounds by putting 0 in the lower-bound cell and leaving the upper-bound cell blank (or putting a label in it). Likewise, a blank or a label in a lower-bound cell means that the corresponding variable has no lower bound. If you do not specify any bounds for variables, Quattro Pro 3 restricts all your variables to non-negative real numbers.

Formula Constraints

Instead of specifying your model's constraints as a matrix of coefficients, you can specify them as formulas, which are required to be non-negative. For example, the constraint

$3 * A + 4 * B <= 18$

is essentially equivalent to the formula

$18 - (3 * A + 4 * B)$

To use the Formula Constraints menu item, you specify a block of cells that includes all of the formulas you want treated as constraints. Quattro Pro 3 must then find values for the variables such that the formula, when evaluated, is non-negative. The formulas must all be linear in the unknown variables.

Objective Function

In a model where there are more variables than constraints, there is usually more than one set of variable values that satisfies all the constraints. The objective of linear programming is to find the best solution among these sets. Generally, the best solution is one that yields some optimal value when plugged into a specific function. This specific function is called the *objective function,* and it is this function that Quattro Pro 3 optimizes when you choose Go on the Advanced Math Optimization menu.

For example, there might be three or four different combinations of knives, rapiers, daggers, and swords produced in the smithy that meet the monthly production constraints (more than 24, less than 48) and yet do not exhaust the monthly resources (600 ingots of steel, 1920 person-hours). However, the blacksmith is really motivated by another factor: the total profit per month. This profit is a linear function of the number of weapons produced each month:

Total Profit = (knife profit)+(rapier profit)+(dagger profit)+(sword profit)

(number of knives produced)= W (profit per knife) = \$4
(number of rapiers produced)= X (profit per rapier)= \$7
(number of daggers produced)= Y (profit per dagger)= \$3
(number of swords produced)= Z (profit per sword)= \$8

Objective Function = $4(W) + 7(X) + 3(Y) + 8(Z)$

With the Objective Function menu item, you specify a single row of cells containing the coefficients for the variables of your objective function. Use

Objective Function to mark the profit function: a single row that contains one cell for each variable in your model. (In this case, there are four variables—knives, rapiers, daggers, and swords.) This row must have x entries, where x is the number of variables in your model. In the example, the Objective Function row is row 8. You can omit the Objective Function block of cells if a suitable formula is in the Solution cell. To be suitable, the formula must be linear in the variables. In this case, the formula would be

@SUMPRODUCT(*Objective Function Row*, *Variables Row*)

Setting the Extremum

This item leads to a small menu, from which you select either Largest or Smallest for the optimal value for the objective function. In other words, you specify whether you want to maximize the objective function, such as the profit (choose Largest), or to minimize it, such as the cost of goods (choose Smallest). If you do not specify a value with this item, Quattro Pro 3 automatically chooses Smallest, minimizing the objective function.

Output Settings

Once you have specified the input data for the optimization, you need to designate the blocks where Quattro Pro 3 will place the output values, the results of the optimization. You do this with the items in the Output Values section of the Optimization menu. The row that you specify with the Variables command is where Quattro Pro 3 places the set of variable values that represents the best solution. This row must have N entries, where N represents the number of variables in your model. These output values, when plugged into the objective function, yield the optimal value for that function.

With the Solution command, you specify a single cell where Quattro Pro 3 will place the calculated value of the objective function. This optimal value is either a maximum or minimum, as with the Input Values Extremum menu item. You can also obtain the optimal value by leaving the Objective Function range unspecified and entering this formula in the solution cell:

@SUMPRODUCT(*Objective Function*, *Variables Row*)

In this case, *Objective Function* is the row you have specified with Objective Function in the Input Values section of the Optimization menu. If an objective function formula is in the Solution cell, Quattro Pro 3 will use it instead of the Objective Function row. *Variables Row* is the row of output variable values you have specified with Variables in the Output Values section of the Optimization menu.

Dual values allow you to determine how much the optimal value depends on the individual linear constraints and on the bounds for the variables. A *dual value* is the amount by which the optimal value of the objective function would be increased or decreased if one constant term or one bound is relaxed or tightened by one unit. Dual values are used for sensitivity analysis, for such tasks as determining how much a constraint or bound is restricting your profit or adding to your total cost.

In the Output Settings section of the Optimization menu you can specify two types of dual values, either for constraints or bounds. Dual Values is a column combining as many entries as there are constant terms in your model. Additional Dual Values, on the other hand, is a row combining as many entries as there are variables in your model. If you do not specify any Dual Values blocks, Quattro Pro 3 omits these calculations.

A small change in the constant term multiplied by the dual value for that constraint gives the resultant small change in the optimal value of the objective function. If the dual value corresponding to a constraint is 0, a small change in the constant term of that constraint will cause no change in the optimal value. If the dual value for a given constraint is 1.5, changing the constant term by 1 will change the optimal value by 1.5.

Interpreting bounds for dual values specified by the Additional Dual Values setting can be a little tricky. While only one dual value is associated with each variable, each variable can have two bounds. You need to be able to tell which bound of a variable, upper or lower, is affecting the optimal value of the objective function. If a variable's value is equal to one of its bounds, that bound is said to be active, and the dual value relates to that active bound. A small change in the active bound multiplied by the corresponding dual value gives the resultant small change in the optimal value. If a variable's dual value is 3, changing the active bound by 1 will change the optimal value of the objective function by 3. If, on the other hand, the variable's value does not equal either of its bounds, its bounds' dual value will be 0, and a small change in the bounds for that variable will not affect the optimal value.

Bear in mind that, as with the other Advanced Math operations, Quattro Pro 3 does not automatically recalculate the dual value results. If you change any of the input data, you will have to choose Tools Advanced Math Optimization Go again to get the correct solution and its related values.

Going for the Result

As the blacksmith you want to produce the combination of weapons that yields the most profit; satisfies the limitations of time, capacity, and metal; and meets your commitments to supply the armories as well as to obey the king. To review the terminology used here, remember the following:

■ The resource limitations are your constraints.

■ The amounts of each weapon manufactured are your variables.

■ The armory commitments and factory capacity are the lower and upper bounds on your variables.

■ The sum of the individual profits (total profit, which you want to maximize) is your objective function.

■ The unique combination of weapons that yields the largest total profit is the solution.

■ The most profit you can get (in terms of dollars) is the optimal value. This is calculated as the solution times the objective function.

In Figure 9-45 you saw one way to arrange the spreadsheet, using Optimization to find the best solution. Note that the formula in cell G12 is not part of the Optimization output, but merely an enhancement to sum up the number of weapons from the Variables output.

With your spreadsheet set up like the one in Figure 9-45, the next step is to designate the input settings. These are shown in Figure 9-46. Note that no formula constraints or objective functions are specified. After setting the various input and output blocks, you can use the Go command to get the results. You can then change any of the input factors and repeat the Go command to update the results. By combining the optimization command with the What-if command you can create a powerful analytical tool that presents results from a wide range of scenarios.

To test this particular model, consider what happens when peace breaks out, swords are banned, and there is a need for alternative products such as plowshares. The model can be altered to reflect the new constraints,

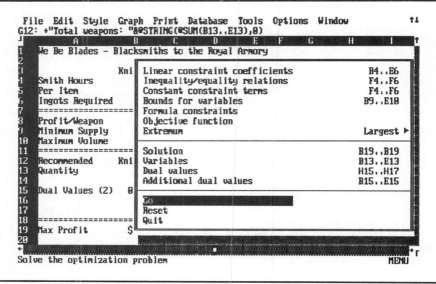

Figure 9-46. *The sample settings*

variables, and bounds. The results are shown in Figure 9-47. Note the addition of string formulas that interpret the results of the command. These are @IF statements that respond to the dual values. You can see that cell I17 displays the word **Increase** because the number in cell H17 is greater than 0.5. A value significantly greater than 0 in a dual value result means that an increase in the constraint (in this case, the 600 ingots) would increase the optimized figure (the profit). The formulas in B16..E16 analyze the additional dual values, letting the blacksmith know that the suggested output levels are acceptable. In Figure 9-48 you can see how the results of the first scenario appear when text formulas are added and some of the variables changed. For more on text formulas, see the next chapter.

Solving Equations

While Optimization can perform some very complex calculations, it is not the easiest of tools to use, particularly if you have just one equation to solve.

```
 File  Edit  Style  Graph  Print  Database  Tools  Options  Window        ↑↓
I17: @IF(H17>0.5,"Increase",@IF(H17>0,"Hold"," "))
└───────A───────B───────C───────D───────E──F──────G────────H───────I──────↑
1 We Be Blades - Blacksmiths to the Royal Armory
2
3                Knife   Rapier  Dagger Plowshares Limitations
4 Smith Hours       7       14      10       5 <=   1,920 Max Hours
5 Per Item          1        1       1       1 <=     250 Max Items
6 Ingots Required   3        4     2.5       2 <=     600 Max Ingots
7 =========================================================================
8 Profit/Item      $4       $7      $3      $3
9 Minimum Supply   24       24      24      36
10 Maximum Volume  48       48      48     100
11 =========================================================================
12 Recommended   Knife   Rapier  Dagger Plowshares Total weapons: 222
13 Quantity         48      48      26     100
14
15 Dual Values (2)  0.40    2.20    0.00    0.60  Hours      0.00
16               Okay    Okay    Okay    Okay     Capacity   0.00
17                                                Metal      1.20 │Increase│
18 =========================================================================
19 Max Profit        $905 Sum Product        $905
20
SMITH@PC.WQ1 [3]                                          NUM        READY
```

Figure 9-47. *The new scenario*

```
 File  Edit  Style  Graph  Print  Database  Tools  Options  Window        ↑↓
D10: [W8] 48
└───────A───────B───────C───────D───────E──F──────G────────H───────I──────↑
1 We Be Blades - Blacksmiths to the Royal Armory
2
3                Knife   Rapier  Dagger  Sword    Limitations
4 Smith Hours       7       14      10      16 <=   1,920 Max Hours
5 Per Item          1        1       1       1 <=     150 Max Blades
6 Ingots Required   3        4     2.5       6 <=     600 Max Ingots
7 =========================================================================
8 Profit/Weapon    $4       $7      $3      $8
9 Minimum Supply   24       24      24      24
10 Maximum Volume  48       48      48      48
11 =========================================================================
12 Recommended   Knife   Rapier  Dagger  Sword    Total weapons: 150
13 Quantity         48      48      24      38
14
15 Dual Values (2)  0.00    1.67   -0.33    0.00  Hours      0.00 Hold
16               Okay    Okay    Reduce   Okay    Capacity   0.00 Hold
17                                                Metal      1.33 Increase
18 =========================================================================
19 Max Profit        $872 Sum Product        $872
20
SMITHY.WQ1  [1]                                           NUM        READY
```

Figure 9-48. *Initial example with strings added*

For this reason, Quattro Pro 3 provides a simple but powerful new command, Solve For. This allows you to specify an answer to a formula and determine the appropriate value for one of the formula inputs. For example, consider a simple loan repayment calculation:

	A	B
1	Principal	5000
2	Interest	.12
3	Term	36
4	Payment	@PMT (B1,B2/12,B3)

The formula in B4 returns the amount required to pay off a loan of $5,000 paid in 36 monthly installments at 12.00% A.P.R. The answer, to two decimal places, is $166.07. Suppose you can only repay at $150 per month. This means you cannot afford to borrow as much as $5,000. However, you want to know the largest amount you can borrow given the same term and rate of interest. The Solve For command can tell you this very quickly.

Before using the Solve For command, it is a good idea to save your spreadsheet and to turn on the Undo feature (using Options Other Undo Enable). This allows you to experiment with the possible answers without disturbing the original data.

To solve the payment formula for a given payment you select Solve For from the Tools menu. You must provide three pieces of information: Formula Cell, Target Value, and Variable Cell. The cell information can be provided either by typing in a cell reference or by pointing to the cells in the worksheet. In this example the Formula Cell is B4 and the Variable Cell is B1. The Target Value is simply typed, in this case 150. After setting these three items you select Go. This tells Quattro Pro 3 to change the value in the Variable Cell so that the formula cell results in the number specified as Target Value, in this case 4516.13, when given to two decimal places.

If you select Quit from the Solve For menu, you can press ALT-F5 to change the contents of B1 back to the former value. In this manner you can switch between two possible values and see the effects in the formula cell. This is a basic example, but it shows the usefulness and simplicity of this command. You can apply Solve For to much larger models. In Figure 9-49 you can see the expense worksheet developed in Chapter 5. The figure for total expenses for the year is displayed in H2, which in turn refers to

File Edit Style Graph Print Database Tools Options Window   ↑↓
H4: (F4) [W9] [F4] 1.015

	A	B	C	D	E	F	G	H
1								
2					Quattro Vadis Travel 4 Office Total:			122,131
3								
4				90 Budget – Based On Monthly Growth Factor of				1.0150
5								
6		JAN	FEB	MAR	APR	MAY	JUN	JUL
7	POLK ST.							
8	Lease	350	355	361	366	371	377	383
9	Phones	230	233	237	241	244	248	251
10	Telex	110	112	113	115	117	119	120
11	Electric	120	122	124	125	127	129	131
12	Res. Rent	1,100	1,117	1,133	1,150	1,167	1,185	1,203
13	VAN NESS							
14	Lease	500	507	515	523	531	539	547
15	Phones	250	254	258	261	265	269	273
16	Telex	150	152	155	157	159	162	164
17	Electric	225	228	232	235	239	242	246
18	Res. Rent	1,200	1,218	1,236	1,255	1,274	1,293	1,312
19	UNION SQ.							
20	Lease	1,200	1,218	1,236	1,255	1,274	1,293	1,312

SOLVE4.WQ1   [1]   NUM   READY

Figure 9-49. *The expense projection*

N32 where there is an @SUM formula adding up all of the expenses. The expenses grow from month to month based on a factor, currently 1.015, recorded in H4.

As company comptroller you want to keep expenses down. You would like to know what rate of monthly increase would result in a total expense figure of only $115,000. You enter this as the Target Value in the Solve For menu, as shown in Figure 9-50. You then enter H2 as the Formula Cell and H4 as the Variable Cell. When you select Go you get the answer seen in Figure 9-51. If you have the Undo feature enabled you can easily switch back to the original value in H4 and try a different entry in Target Value. As you can see, this type of backward solving of equations is very useful when dealing with projections and what-if scenarios.

When you want to move on to solve a different formula, you can use Solve For Reset to clear the current settings. The Parameters command allows you to specify two settings: Max Iterations and Accuracy. Since Solve For works by repeatedly guessing the answer, the Max Iterations setting

```
File  Edit  Style  Graph  Print  Database  Tools  Options  Window          ↑↓
H4: (F4) [W9] [F4] 1.015
┌───┬─────────────┬──────┬───────┬────────┬──────────────────────────────────┐
│ J │      A      │  B   │   C   │   D    │ Macro          Alt-F2 ▶    H    ↑ │
│ 1 │             │      │       │        │ Reformat                         │
│ 2 │             │      │       │ Quattro Vadi ┌──────────────────────────┐ │
│ 3 │             │      │       │        │ I │ Formula Cell      H2..H2  │■│ │
│ 4 │             │      │ 90 Budget – Based On │ C │ Target Value      115000  │ │ │
│ 5 │             │      │       │        │ X │ Variable Cell     H4..H4  │ │ │
│ 6 │             │ JAN  │  FEB  │  MAR   │ U │ Parameters             ▶  │ │ │
│ 7 │ POLK ST.    │      │       │        ├───│ Go                        │ │ │
│ 8 │    Lease    │ 350  │  355  │  361   │ A │ Reset                     │ │ │
│ 9 │    Phones   │ 230  │  233  │  237   │ P │ Quit                      │ │ │
│10 │    Telex    │ 110  │  112  │  113   │ W └──────────────────────────┘ │ │
│11 │ Electric    │ 120  │  122  │  124   │ Fr                             │ │
│12 │ Res. Rent   │1,100 │ 1,117 │ 1,133  │ Solve For              ▶  1,203 │ │
│13 │ VAN NESS    │      │       │        │                                │ │
│14 │    Lease    │ 500  │  507  │  515   │                            547  │ │
│15 │    Phones   │ 250  │  254  │  258   │ 261   265    269     273       │ │
│16 │    Telex    │ 150  │  152  │  155   │ 157   159    162     164       │ │
│17 │ Electric    │ 225  │  228  │  232   │ 235   239    242     246       │ │
│18 │ Res. Rent   │1,200 │ 1,218 │ 1,236  │1,255 1,274  1,293   1,312      │ │
│19 │ UNION SQ.   │      │       │        │                                │ │
│20 │    Lease    │1,200 │ 1,218 │ 1,236  │1,255 1,274  1,293   1,312    ↓ │
└───┴─────────────┴──────┴───────┴────────┴────────────────────────────■───┘→r
Solve for the specified Target Value                                   MENU
```

Figure 9-50. *The Solve For menu*

```
File  Edit  Style  Graph  Print  Database  Tools  Options  Window          ↑↓
H4: (F4) [W9] [F4] 1.0041800701344
┌───┬─────────────┬──────┬───────┬───────┬───────┬───────┬───────┬────────┬──┐
│ J │      A      │  B   │   C   │   D   │   E   │   F   │   G   │   H    │ ↑│
│ 1 │             │      │       │       │       │       │       │        │  │
│ 2 │             │      │   Quattro Vadis Travel 4 Office Total: 115,000 │  │
│ 3 │             │      │       │       │       │       │       │        │  │
│ 4 │             │ 90 Budget – Based On Monthly Growth Factor of │ 1.0042│  │
│ 5 │             │      │       │       │       │       │       │        │  │
│ 6 │             │ JAN  │  FEB  │  MAR  │  APR  │  MAY  │  JUN  │  JUL   │  │
│ 7 │ POLK ST.    │      │       │       │       │       │       │        │  │
│ 8 │    Lease    │ 350  │  351  │  353  │  354  │  356  │  357  │  359   │  │
│ 9 │    Phones   │ 230  │  231  │  232  │  233  │  234  │  235  │  236   │  │
│10 │    Telex    │ 110  │  110  │  111  │  111  │  112  │  112  │  113   │  │
│11 │ Electric    │ 120  │  121  │  121  │  122  │  122  │  123  │  123   │  │
│12 │ Res. Rent   │1,100 │ 1,105 │ 1,109 │ 1,114 │ 1,119 │ 1,123 │ 1,128  │  │
│13 │ VAN NESS    │      │       │       │       │       │       │        │  │
│14 │    Lease    │ 500  │  502  │  504  │  506  │  508  │  511  │  513   │  │
│15 │    Phones   │ 250  │  251  │  252  │  253  │  254  │  255  │  256   │  │
│16 │    Telex    │ 150  │  151  │  151  │  152  │  153  │  153  │  154   │  │
│17 │ Electric    │ 225  │  226  │  227  │  228  │  229  │  230  │  231   │  │
│18 │ Res. Rent   │1,200 │ 1,205 │ 1,210 │ 1,215 │ 1,220 │ 1,225 │ 1,230  │  │
│19 │ UNION SQ.   │      │       │       │       │       │       │        │  │
│20 │    Lease    │1,200 │ 1,205 │ 1,210 │ 1,215 │ 1,220 │ 1,225 │ 1,230 ↓│  │
└───┴─────────────┴──────┴───────┴───────┴───────┴───────┴───────┴────────┴──┘→r
SOLVE4.WQ1    [1]                                     NUM           READY
```

Figure 9-51. *New expense projection*

determines how many times Quattro Pro 3 guesses before giving up. If your variable has only an incremental influence on your target value, then you may need to increase this setting from the default value (for example, using a target value of 100,000 in this example results in the warning message "Maximum iterations reached"). If you get this message you should try Solve For again, using a larger iteration setting. The Accuracy setting determines how close Solve For must get to a perfect answer before it stops guessing. The default value should be acceptable in most cases.

10 *Managing Text*

Although spreadsheets are designed primarily to manipulate numbers, in some situations you can use them to manipulate text as well. In this chapter several Quattro Pro 3 commands that apply to text will be examined, and Quattro Pro 3 will be used to produce paragraphs of text. Quattro Pro 3 can convert spreadsheet data to text files that can be read by word processors and can also read text files from other programs. This process of data exchange will be examined. Finally, the string commands that manipulate labels will be discussed.

Quattro Pro 3 as a Text Editor

Most spreadsheets require that you enter at least some text—words or phrases that describe the values in the model. Sometimes these pieces of text can be fairly lengthy. Consider the spreadsheet of projected expenses shown in Figure 10-1. The designer of this model felt that it was necessary to explain several of the assumptions at work in the calculations. This is a good practice to adopt, especially if the spreadsheet is going to be used or read by others.

```
   File  Edit  Style  Graph  Print  Database  Tools  Options  Window         ↑↓
   A1:
   ┌─────A────────B──────────C────────D────────E────────F──────────┐
   1                      Five Year Expense Projection
   2
   3   Quattro Vadis Travel       1988     1989     1990     1991
   4   ────────────────────────────────────────────────────────────
   5   Expenses Office Rents     36,000   39,600   43,560   47,916
   6            Equipment Leases  6,000   12,000   12,000    7,000
   7            Wages/Commissions 125,000 125,000 125,000 125,000
   8            Advertising      35,000   25,000   20,000   15,000
   9            Telex/phone       2,500    3,500    4,500    5,500
   10           Res. System       5,450    8,000    8,800    9,680
   11  ────────────────────────────────────────────────────────────
   12           Total           209,950  213,100  213,860  210,096
   13
   14
   15           Assumptions:
   16           1  Office Rent increases by 10% each year
   17           2  Equipment Leases represents the new computer
   18           system, acquired on a three year lease,
   19           commencing in mid-88.
   20
   └────────────────────────────────────────────────────────────────┘
   CHAP10EX.WQ1 [1]                                    NUM          READY
```

Figure 10-1. *Annotated expenses*

Entering Blocks of Text

Entering a piece of text, like assumption 1 in Figure 10-1, is simply a matter of typing a long label. You type the text and then press ENTER. Once you have entered the text, you may need to edit it, for which you use the F2 key, as described in Chapter 2. Remember that you can move your cursor through a long label by using the CTRL-RIGHT or CTRL-LEFT ARROW key combinations, which move the cursor five character positions to the right or left. Use CTRL-\ to delete to the end of the entry.

Text like that in assumption 2 is handled a little differently. It begins as a long label. When you type a label longer than 66 characters, Quattro Pro 3 actually moves the worksheet display down a line to make the text visible as you type it. This is shown in Figure 10-2. The program does not know that you are typing a series of words. Notice that the word *on* is split between two lines because the sixty-sixth character on the first line of the label is the *o* in *on*. Quattro Pro 3 does not perform the word processing function known as word wrap while you enter a long label. When you complete the label and enter it, the label initially spreads across the columns of the worksheet in a long, somewhat hard-to-read line of words.

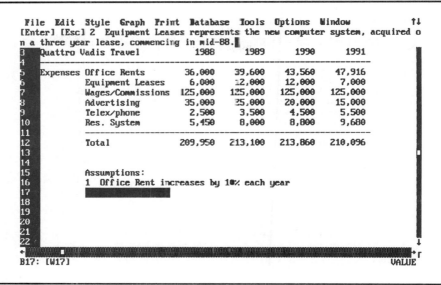

Figure 10-2. *Typing a long label*

You will usually want to format a long label like this into a paragraph. Quattro Pro 3 does this by breaking the long label into several shorter labels in a process called *block reformatting*. You perform this process with the Tools Reformat command, which wraps the text within an area of the spreadsheet that you designate. Place your cell selector on the cell containing the long label that you want to adjust to a more compact size, in this case B17. Select Reformat from the Tools menu and, when you are prompted for the block to be modified, point out the area into which you want the long label rearranged. In this case, the block of cells B17..E19 is highlighted, as shown in Figure 10-3.

The highlighted area should be empty except for the cell being reformatted. It should be as wide as you would like the paragraph to be and should stretch several rows below the original cell, so that there is room for the formatted text. When you press ENTER, the long label is divided into a series of shorter labels as wide as the block you highlighted. Notice that the label is divided without breaking the words. The results can be seen in Figure 10-1 and in Figure 10-4, where the second line of the second assumption is highlighted to show that it is indeed a label formed in the cell below the original label.

```
 File  Edit  Style  Graph  Print  Database ‖Tools‖ Options  Window          ↑↓
[Enter] [Esc] Block to be modified: B17..E19
J      A          B            C        D        E        F          ↑
1                         Five Year Expense Projection
2
3  Quattro Vadis Travel          1988     1989     1990     1991
4  ─────────────────────────────────────────────────────────────
5  Expenses Office Rents        36,000   39,600   43,560   47,916
6           Equipment Leases     6,000   12,000   12,000    7,000
7           Wages/Commissions  125,000  125,000  125,000  125,000   ■
8           Advertising         35,000   25,000   20,000   15,000
9           Telex/phone          2,500    3,500    4,500    5,500
10          Res. System          5,450    8,000    8,800    9,680
11 ─────────────────────────────────────────────────────────────
12          Total              209,950  213,100  213,860  210,096
13
14
15          Assumptions:
16          1  Office Rent increases by 10% each year
17          2  Equipment Leases represents the new computer system, acquired o
18
19
20                                                                    ↓
←▓▓▓▓▓▓▓▓▓▓▓▓▓▓▓▓▓▓▓▓▓▓▓▓▓█▓▓▓▓▓▓▓▓▓▓▓▓▓▓▓▓▓▓▓▓▓▓▓▓▓▓▓▓▓▓▓▓▓→ r
E19: [W10]                                                        POINT
```

Figure 10-3. *Reformat block*

```
 File  Edit  Style  Graph  Print  Database  Tools  Options  Window          ↑↓
B18: [W17] 'system, acquired on a three year lease,
J      A          B            C        D        E        F          ↑
1                         Five Year Expense Projection
2
3  Quattro Vadis Travel          1988     1989     1990     1991
4  ─────────────────────────────────────────────────────────────
5  Expenses Office Rents        36,000   39,600   43,560   47,916
6           Equipment Leases     6,000   12,000   12,000    7,000
7           Wages/Commissions  125,000  125,000  125,000  125,000   ■
8           Advertising         35,000   25,000   20,000   15,000
9           Telex/phone          2,500    3,500    4,500    5,500
10          Res. System          5,450    8,000    8,800    9,680
11 ─────────────────────────────────────────────────────────────
12          Total              209,950  213,100  213,860  210,096
13
14
15          Assumptions:
16          1  Office Rent increases by 10% each year
17          2  Equipment Leases represents the new computer
18          system, acquired on a three year lease,
19          commencing in mid-88.
20                                                                    ↓
←▓▓█▓▓▓▓▓▓▓▓▓▓▓▓▓▓▓▓▓▓▓▓▓▓▓▓▓▓▓▓▓▓▓▓▓▓▓▓▓▓▓▓▓▓▓▓▓▓▓▓▓▓▓▓▓→ r
CHAP10EX.WQ1 [1]                                     NUM        READY
```

Figure 10-4. *Reformatted label*

If you need to edit the text that you have reformatted into shorter labels, you highlight the cell containing the text to be edited and press F2. However, you should not make any line in the middle of a paragraph (such as line 18 in this example) much shorter or longer than it was before editing. Quattro Pro 3 will not automatically rearrange a paragraph of text after part of it has been shortened or lengthened, so you should keep editing to a minimum after reformatting. Nevertheless, you can compose short documents, letters, and memos from a series of long labels using the reformatting command. You can use a number of macros to simplify successive reformatting of text. Macros will be described in Chapter 11.

Figure 10-4 illustrates one small problem with reformatting: The numbers of the assumption are not set off from the text when the assumption is longer than one line. The Tools Reformat command cannot perform a paragraph indentation. However, you can solve this problem by approaching the text layout a little differently. By putting the assumption numbers in a separate column, either as values or right-aligned labels, you can set off the numbers from the text. This is shown in Figure 10-5. However adept you become with Quattro Pro 3, you cannot duplicate all of the editing features of a word processor. Fortunately, you can easily transfer information from Quattro Pro 3 to a word processing program.

```
 File  Edit  Style  Graph  Print  Database  Tools  Options  Window          ↑↓
A1:
J     A        B            C        D        E        F              ↑
1                    Five Year Expense Projection
2
3    Quattro Vadis Travel     1988     1989     1990     1991
4    ──────────────────────────────────────────────────────────────
5    Expenses Office Rents    36,000   39,600   43,560   47,916
6            Equipment Leases  6,000   12,000   12,000    7,000
7            Wages/Commissions 125,000 125,000 125,000  125,000
8            Advertising      35,000   25,000   20,000   15,000
9            Telex/phone       2,500    3,500    4,500    5,500
10           Res. System       5,450    8,000    8,800    9,680
11   ──────────────────────────────────────────────────────────────
12           Total           209,950  213,100  213,860  210,096
13
14
15           Assumptions:
16         1 Office Rent increases by 10% each year
17         2 Equipment Leases represents the new computer
18           system, acquired on a three year lease,
19           commencing in mid-88.
20
CHAP10EX.WQ1 [1]                                      NUM        READY
```

Figure 10-5.   *Indented text*

Printing to a File

The basic process for transferring words and numbers from Quattro Pro 3 to a word processing program is to create a special file that the word processor can read. Different word processing programs store their documents in different file formats. That is, the way in which the actual letters are stored on disk varies from program to program. However, all popular word processing programs can read files that are stored in ASCII, the American Standard Code for Information Interchange. One reason word processing programs can read information stored this way is that they communicate with printers in ASCII. Printers receive the letters and numbers of your documents as ASCII characters. In fact, that is how Quattro Pro 3 sends your spreadsheet cells to the printer. By diverting data intended for the printer to a file on disk, you can create an *ASCII file*, or *print file*, of the spreadsheet data. Quattro Pro 3 creates this file through the Print Destination command, which changes the target of the print block from the printer to a file. The file name usually has the extension PRN to distinguish it from other files. The data in the file is simply strings of letters, numbers, and spaces. Formulas are converted to their values and the values become text, including any formatting such as the dollar signs of the Currency format. The resulting file is often called a *text file*.

Suppose that you want to put the numbers from Figure 10-5 in a memo that you have been writing with your word processing program. Retyping the numbers from Quattro Pro 3 into a word processing document would be a chore, and errors could arise from inaccurate typing. Instead, you decide to export the figures as an ASCII file. To do so, you use the Print Block command to tell Quattro Pro 3 which cells of the worksheet are to be placed in the file.

Preparing for Printing

In order to make the data coming from Quattro Pro 3 easier for your word processor to read, you may want to use the Print Layout command to change some of the options prior to printing to disk. By selecting the Margins option from the Layout menu, you can change the left margin from 4 to 0 characters. This number will prevent Quattro Pro 3 from adding four spaces to the left of the data in the file. Similarly, entering 0 for a top margin will stop Quattro Pro 3 from adding lines to the top of the print block. The right margin setting needs particular attention, since the data in the file will be split into sections if you have set the right margin narrower than the width of the print block. In general, you will not want to use a right margin wider than 80 for a text file that will be read by a word processor that is using a normal 8 1/2-by-11-inch page. Otherwise, your text file will contain more data than will fit between the word processor's margins.

Completing the Print

Having selected the Print options you want to use, you can proceed to indicate the print block, the cells whose contents will be placed in the print file. You decide to use cells B3 through G12, as shown in Figure 10-6, because the numbers are the most important part of the worksheet and the rest of the titles can be added in the word processing document. You do not want to include any extra columns and rows in the print block, since they will only add empty space to the word processing document.

The next steps are to select Destination from the Print menu, then File. As soon as you select File, Quattro Pro 3 displays a list of existing PRN files. You can choose one of these names as the destination of the print block. If you select an existing name, the program asks if you want to

```
 File  Edit  Style  Graph │Print│ Database  Tools  Options  Window
The block of the spreadsheet to print: B3..G12
J            B          C         D         E         F          G
1                       Five Year Expense Projection
2
3      adis Travel      1988      1989      1990      1991       1992
4      ---------------------------------------------------------------
5      Office Rents     36,000    39,600    43,560    47,916     52,708
6      Equipment Leases  6,000    12,000    12,000     7,000          0
7      Wages/Commissions 125,000 125,000   125,000   125,000    125,000
8      Advertising      35,000    25,000    20,000    15,000     15,000
9      Telex/phone       2,500     3,500     4,500     5,500      6,500
10     Res. System      5,450     8,000     8,000     9,600     10,640
11     ---------------------------------------------------------------
12     Total            209,950   213,100   213,860   210,096    209,856
13
14
```

Figure 10-6. *The print block*

replace the data in an existing print file with new data or if it should append the new data to the old. Appending new data is useful for accumulating data from various parts of a spreadsheet or from different spreadsheets into one text file. You can also choose to cancel the overwriting of an existing file or to back up the data already in it to a file with the BAQ extension.

To create a new file in the current directory, you type the file name. If you want the extension PRN, you leave the extension blank and Quattro Pro 3 supplies it. Otherwise, you can enter a file name with an extension of your choice. Once you have selected or typed a name, that file name is written to the disk and space is set up to receive the print data. When you select Spreadsheet Print from the Print menu, the data is actually written into the file.

Editing the Results

Once you have created the print file, you can edit it with a word processor. Make sure that you have saved any necessary changes to your worksheet; then quit Quattro Pro 3 and load your word processing program. You can type text as you normally would, up to the point where the print file is to be included. Before issuing the command to read in the print file, you may want to set the margins wide enough to accommodate the incoming data. How word processors read in ASCII text varies. Some programs, such as WordPerfect 5.1, can simply read ASCII files with the Retrieve command. Others require a special command. In Figure 10-7, you can see the PRN file retrieved into a WordPerfect document. Note that the text "adis Travel" is left over from the long label in cell A3 of the worksheet. This can be edited out.

At this point the text is a series of characters and spaces. There are no tab stops inserted. If you want to import a table from Quattro Pro 3 into WordPerfect, you might prefer to use the Spreadsheet option on the Text In/Out menu. This allows you to import a group of spreadsheet cells as a WordPerfect table, or even to Link to a spreadsheet. The Link option creates a table in WordPerfect that is updated when the spreadsheet on which it is based is changed. This feature is supported in WordPerfect 5.1,

```
                         Quattro Vadis Travel
                              Memorandum
         To:      Fred

         From:    Sue

         Subject:  Five Year Expense Projection

              Here are the expense figures that you asked me to pull
         together:

         adis Travel        1988     1989     1990     1991     1992
         -----------------------------------------------------------
         Office Rents      36,000   39,600   43,56E   47,916   52,700
         Equipment Leases   6,000   12,000   12,000    7,000        0
         Wages/Commissions 125,000 125,000  125,000  125,000  125,000
         Advertising       35,000   25,000   20,000   15,000   15,000
         Telex/phone        2,500    3,500    4,500    5,500    6,500
         Res. System        5,450    8,000    8,800    9,680   10,648
         -----------------------------------------------------------
         Total            209,950  213,100  213,860  210,096  209,856

         D:\WP\DOCS\MEMO2F                    Doc 1 Pg 1 Ln 2.83" Pos 1.9"
```

Figure 10-7. *The PRN file in WordPerfect*

and Quattro Pro 3 spreadsheets are among those WordPerfect can read directly. You can see the worksheet in Figure 10-6 as a linked table within WordPerfect in Figure 10-8.

One category of data that is treated differently by word processing programs is the names and addresses used for *mail merging,* the customizing of a form letter with names and other information from a list. Some word processing programs—WordPerfect, for example—can read a name-and-address list from a spreadsheet file for mail merging if the file is saved in the DIF format. Accomplishing this is a specialized word processing function, and you should consult the word processor program manual or a detailed text about that program. Although Quattro Pro 3 may not be mentioned in the documentation, remember that a Quattro Pro 3 spreadsheet can be saved as a 1-2-3 worksheet by using the extension WK1.

```
                    Quattro Vadis Travel

                        Memorandum
To:       Fred

From:     Sue

Subject:  Five Year Expense Projection

      Here are the expense figures that you asked me to pull
together:

┌──────────────────────────────────────────────────────────────┐
│ Link:    C:\QUATTRO\DATA\CHAP10EX.WQ1                           │
└──────────────────────────────────────────────────────────────┘

┌─────────────┬──────────┬──────────┬──────────┬──────────┬──────────┐
│             │   1988   │   1989   │   1990   │   1991   │   1992   │
│             │          │          │          │          │          │
│─────────────│──────────│──────────│──────────│──────────│──────────│
│             │          │          │          │          │          │
│Office Rents │  36,000  │  39,600  │  43,560  │  47,916  │  52,708  │
│             │          │          │          │          │          │
│Equipment Leases│ 6,000 │  12,000  │  12,000  │   7,000  │    0     │
D:\WP\DOCS\MEMO2F1                              Doc 1 Pg 1 Ln 2.83" Pos 1.9"
```

Figure 10-8.   *Quattro Pro 3 spreadsheet as a WordPerfect table*

Text into Quattro Pro 3

Having seen how Quattro Pro 3 creates a text file that can be read by word processing programs, you will see next how Quattro Pro 3 reads text files into a spreadsheet. At times you may have useful information stored in files created by another program, but Quattro Pro 3 cannot read the format of those files. You might like to bring this information into a Quattro Pro 3 spreadsheet. One way of doing this is to convert the data into a text file by using the other program's equivalent of Quattro Pro 3's Print Destination File command.

Importing ASCII Text Files

Suppose your company has an accounting program for accounts receivable. You would like to take a spreadsheet of the accounts receivable with you when making calls. The accounting program should be able to print a text

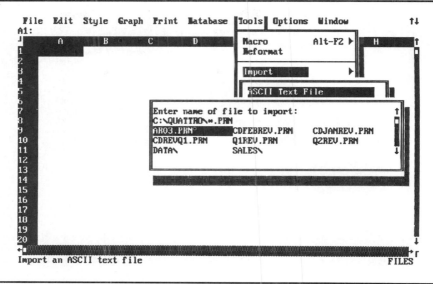

Figure 10-9. *Selecting a text file with Tools Import*

file to disk. In Figure 10-9 you can see the command in Quattro Pro 3 that you need to use, the Tools Import command, about to be issued with the cell selector in A1 of a blank worksheet.

You will probably want to try your first experiments with importing text files using a blank spreadsheet, since the data that is brought in can have unexpected effects on existing data in the spreadsheet. Your choices when importing files are ASCII Text File, Comma & "" Delimited File, and Only Commas. The ASCII Text option is for importing a file name that consists simply of lines of data separated by spaces, not punctuation. The Delimited File option is used for bringing in data from programs that create files in which the pieces of information are separated by either commas, quotes, or both. The Only Commas option is for files in which commas are used to separate sections of text.

When you issue the Tools Import ASCII Text File command, you must specify the name of the file. That file is then read into the worksheet at the current position of the cell selector, as shown in Figure 10-10. Note that Quattro Pro 3 assumes your text file will have the PRN extension. You can edit the file prompt to list other files.

```
     File  Edit  Style  Graph  Print  Database  Tools  Options  Window          ↑↓
     A4: 'SYS Assoc.        415.78   04/21/89           55       7.52   06/01/89
     ┘       A      B       C         D        E         F         G        H     ↑
     1         Company         Amount   Payment   # of Days   Late    Date Last
     2           Name            Due    Due Date  Past Due    Fee     Contacted
     3       ===========================================================================
     4     SYS Assoc.          415.78   04/21/89              55       7.52   06/01/89
     5     DATA, Ltd.          719.34   05/08/89              38       8.99   06/02/89
     6     Tridata, Co.        403.56   05/01/89              45       5.97   06/01/89
     7     Softduo, Inc.       345.48   04/10/89              66       7.50   06/02/89
     8     Amerwest, Ltd.      315.76   05/09/89              37       3.84   06/01/89
     9       ===========================================================================
     10        Total Due:    2,199.92                       48.20  (Days Late Average)
     11
     12
     13
     14
     15
     16
     17
     18
     19
     20                                                                            ↓
     ←■                                                                          ■→ ┌
     SHEET3.WQ1    [4]                                             NUM        READY
```

Figure 10-10. *Imported file*

The information in Figure 10-10 looks a lot like a spreadsheet, but if you carefully observe the contents of cell A4, you will see that it is one long label. There is no data in columns B, C, D, and so on. There are two techniques you can use to help Quattro Pro 3 make sense of data like this. The first is called *parsing*, which involves breaking up the lines of data according to a set of interpretation rules. The second approach is to use the string functions, described later in this chapter.

Using the Tools Parse Command

To give Quattro Pro 3 a set of rules by which to break up the long labels of data into separate cells of information, you place your cell selector on the first cell containing a label to be parsed. You then issue the Tools Parse command, which displays the menu shown in Figure 10-11. Next, select the third option, Create. This option inserts a new row into the worksheet above the current row. Quattro Pro 3 places a line of symbols, called the *parse line*, into this row, as shown in Figure 10-12.

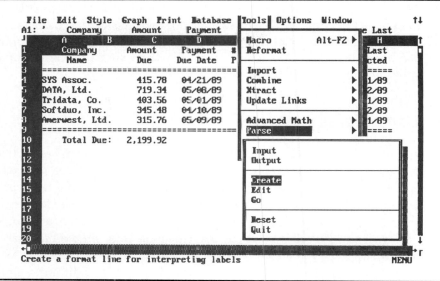

Figure 10-11.   *Parse menu*

```
File  Edit  Style  Graph  Print  Database  ▐Tools▌ Options  Window                    ↑↓
A1: |*****L>>>>>*****L>>>>*****L>>>>>***L*L>*L>>>****L>>*****L>>>*L>>>
   ┌────A───────B────────C────────D────────E───────F────────G────────H──────┐↑
  1 *****L>>>>>*****L>>>>*****L>>>>>***L*L>*L>>>****L>>*****L>>>*L>>>
  2   Company       Amount     Payment    # of Days   Late      Date Last
  3   Name          Due        Due Date   Past Due    Fee       Contacted
  4 ===========================================================================
  5 SYS Assoc.       415.78    04/21/89        55      7.52     06/01/89
  6 DATA, Ltd.       719.34    05/08/89        38      8.99     06/02/89
  7 Tridata, Co.     403.56    05/01/89        45      5.97     06/01/89
  8 Softduo, Inc.    345.48    04/10/89        66      7.50     06/02/89
  9 Amerwest, Ltd.   315.76    05/09/89        37      3.84     06/01/89
 10 ===========================================================================
 11    Total Due:  2,199.92                 48.20 (Days Late Average)
 12
 13
 14
 15
 16
 17
 18
 19
 20
SHEET3.WQ1  [4]                                    NUM OVR           FRMT
```

Figure 10-12.   *Parse line*

The symbols begin with the | character, which tells Quattro Pro 3 not to print this line. Several asterisks follow, indicating spaces in the label in the new row 2. The letter *L* stands for labels, and each of the labels on row 2 has been identified as such. The greater-than sign (>) stands for the number of characters in the labels.

Parse Editing

If you look closely at the way this parse line reads, you can see that the text # *of Days* has been read as three labels. However, these characters should be read as one label. This is why the Parse menu has the Edit option. There are many situations in which the parse line created by Quattro Pro 3 does not interpret the text as you would like it to. After all, it is a complex logical task to determine what parts of this long label should be placed in which cells.

When you are still at the Parse menu, you can select Edit immediately after issuing the Create command, and the menu will disappear so that you can make changes to the symbols. Notice that you are automatically placed into OVERSTRIKE mode, as indicated by the bottom status line message, OVR. The reason for this mode is that, although the symbols on the parse line may be wrong, there are just the right number of them to describe the line. Instead of adding and deleting symbols, you type the ones you want over the top of the incorrect ones. For example, suppose two sets of labels need to be changed because they have been erroneously read as multiple columns (and note the edited line in Figure 10-13). When you have edited the line, press ENTER to return to the Parse menu. You can also edit a parse line from READY mode by using the F2 key, since the parse line is simply a label.

Although the parse line in Figure 10-13 looks fairly good for the column heading labels, clearly the data on row 5 is significantly different from the top three lines. Consequently, the Parse command must be issued again to create a second parse line for the number rows. You do this by quitting the Parse menu and placing the cell selector in column A of row 5. This time when you select the Tools Parse Create command, the parse line will contain the letters *V* for value and *D* for date. If you had time data, you would see *T* for time. Note that dates and times are only read as such by the Parse command if they conform to the date and time formats shown in the last chapter. The greater-than sign (>) is used for the number of digits in the values and dates. By looking closely, you can see that the *V* and *L*

```
 File  Edit  Style  Graph  Print  Database |Tools| Options  Window                  ↑↓
A1: |*****L>>>>>*******L>>>>>*******L>>>>>****L*L>*L>>>*******L>>>*******L>>>*L>>>
J      A       B        C         D        E       F        G        H               ↑
1  *****L>>>>>*******L>>>>>*******L>>>>>****L>>>>>>>*******L>>>*******L>>>>>>>
2     Company      Amount     Payment    # of Days   Late      Date Last
3     Name         Due        Due Date   Past Due    Fee       Contacted
4  =================================================================================
5  SYS Assoc.      415.78     04/21/89       55       7.52     06/01/89
6  DATA, Ltd.      719.34     05/08/89       38       8.99     06/02/89
7  Tridata, Co.    403.56     05/01/89       45       5.97     06/01/89
8  Softduo, Inc.   345.48     04/10/89       66       7.50     06/02/89
9  Amerwest, Ltd.  315.76     05/09/89       37       3.84     06/01/89
10 =================================================================================
11    Total Due:   2,199.92                 48.20 (Days Late Average)
12
13
14
15
16
17
18
19
20
←□                                                                              →r
SHEET3.WQ1    [4]                                        NUM OVR           FRMT
```

Figure 10-13.   *Edited parse line*

are themselves counted in the numbering of the characters. The line you see on row 5 of Figure 10-14 has been edited to conform more closely to the data. The company name *SYS Assoc.* was originally read as two labels, which were changed to one label with the Parse Edit command.

Parse Completion

When the parse lines are acceptable (and it may take several attempts to perfect them) you must identify the input and output cells. The *input cells* are those that contain the data to be parsed including the parse lines, in this case cells A1..H12. The *output cell* is the top-left corner of the area of the spreadsheet you want the parsed data to occupy, in this case, cell A14. When you have specified the input and output cells, you can issue the Go command. The results are shown in Figure 10-15, where both of the parse lines used are completely visible. Although not all of the company names are readable because the column widths are currently set at the default of 9, you can see that the numbers were read as numbers and the dates as serial numbers. You can format the dates as described in Chapter 9. The

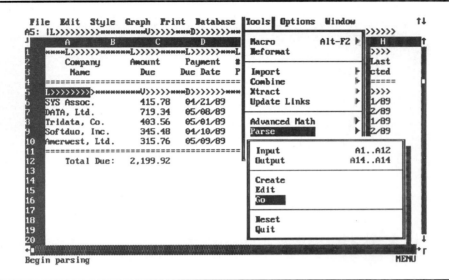

Figure 10-14.   *Parse Go command*

Figure 10-15.   *Parse results*

labels appear to be fine, although widening the columns will show that there are not enough equal signs. The == labels can be replaced with \=.

The one item that is likely to be problematic in parsing is the total line. It is not worth a separate parse line, since the formulas for the totals will need to be recreated anyway. A formula and the formatting of dates can be added later to complete the process.

Parsing text is not a particularly common operation for most spreadsheet users, but it can be a great time-saver when you need to work with data from other programs.

Text in Formulas

Text entered into a cell in Quattro Pro 3 is a label and has no numeric value. However, the program can still use labels in many formulas. This means that you can handle a variety of data in your spreadsheet. Text formulas are particularly useful when you are developing macro commands, as described in Chapter 12.

Labels in Logical Functions

You can use text in several of the @functions. As you saw in Chapter 9, Quattro Pro 3 can enter a label in a cell by means of an @IF formula. The formula

@IF(A1>1000,"Expensive","Cheap")

returns the answer "Expensive" if the contents of A1 are greater than 1000, or "Cheap" if not.

You can use text in the @CHOOSE function to supply a label for a number. Thus, the formula for typing the day of the week, described in the last chapter, used @CHOOSE to look up the words Saturday, Sunday, and so on. As with the @IF function, text in an @CHOOSE statement must be enclosed in quotes.

The @VLOOKUP function can turn a number into a label or vice versa. This function is useful for such applications as evaluating survey responses that are recorded as letters. A simple table, entered into a spreadsheet and named TABLE with the Edit Name Create command, can convert the letters *A* through *E* to the numbers 1 through 5:

A   1

B   2

C   3

D   4

E   5

The formula to return a number corresponding to the value in cell B5 would read @VLOOKUP(B5,TABLE,1).

The company names used in the survey example in Chapter 9 were imaginary names, created by looking up numbers in a table of typical names. In fact, the formula combined parts of names in the table to form new names. Combining text from separate cells is described in the next section.

Combining Labels

Quattro Pro 3 formulas can reference labels in other cells as well as values, as you can see in Figure 10-16.

The formula +B16 has been placed in cell B19. This formula cross references the name Emma from the list of names into the Availability Report. There are a number of situations where it is useful to relate label cells in this manner. Using the formula +C16 in cell C19, you could bring the last name into the cell next to B19.

If you are preparing an information report from a spreadsheet, you may want to connect the two names with just one space between them, as in Emma Wong. You might be tempted to use the formula +B16+C16 to do this, but that formula results in 0 because Quattro Pro 3 thinks you are trying to add two labels together, and labels have a value of 0. However, you can combine labels with the & sign. The formula +B16&B16 produces Emma Wong.

The & sign adds labels together. This process is called *concatenation*. Unfortunately, the two parts of the name have been completely concatenated without a space between them. You can add a space and other text such as words and punctuation to a concatenated formula by enclosing

```
  File  Edit  Style  Graph  Print  Database  Tools  Options  Window          ↑↓
B19: +B16
J      A      B        C      D      E        F      G        H               ↑
1
2             TGA On-Call Roster                    As of: 07-May-90
3
4             First  Last    Rank  Based    Standby  Notice Last Call
5             Joe    Smith     3   Rio      Yes         2   04/06/90
6             Alan   Chan      1   London   Yes         6   04/26/90
7             Sue    Wong      1   Paris    No          4   04/08/90
8             Jane   Folsom    2   Rio      Yes         3   04/23/90
9             Nancy  Blass     3   Paris    Yes         1   05/06/90
10            Peter  Green     6   Paris    No         10   05/04/90
11            Will   Right     2   London   No          2   04/14/90
12            Bill   Front     4   Paris    No          3   04/17/90
13            Jane   Dobbs     7   Rome     No          1   05/03/90
14            Mary   Grant     2   Tokyo    Yes         4   05/05/90
15            Nina   Smith     7   Paris    Yes         6   04/15/90
16            Emma   Wong      2   Rome     Yes         3   04/24/90
17
18            Availability Report:
19            Emma
20                                                                            ↓
←                                                                           → r
DBPRESRT.WQ1 [3]                                               NUM        READY
```

Figure 10-16.   *Referencing text*

it in quotes ("). You must add the text in quotes to the formula with an &
sign. Thus,

+B16&" "&C16

produces the desired result, shown in Figure 10-17.

The & sign is not acceptable as the first character in a formula, but you
can use it between cell references and strings of text in a formula. The
previous formula is simply three pieces of information: a cell reference,
B16; text placed in quotes, in this case, a space " "; and another cell
reference, C16. The formula begins with a + sign to let Quattro Pro 3 know
this is a formula. The & sign simply works as an addition sign for text data.
You can create some useful formulas by using these elements for cell
referencing (the & sign and the quoted text preceded by a + sign). In Figure
10-18 you can see that the Availability Report can take on the appearance
of a written statement using a string formula with the last two cells of the
staff list. If the list is sorted by the Standby column, in ascending order,
then the employees with "Yes" in this column will be at the bottom.

File Edit Style Graph Print Database Tools Options Window   ↑↓
B19: +B16â" "âC16

```
┌─┬──────A────┬───B────┬───C────┬──D──┬───E────┬───F────┬──G──┬───H────┬─┐
│1│                                                                       │
│2│           TOA On-Call Roster                    As of: 07-May-90      │
│3│                                                                       │
│4│           First     Last     Rank  Based     Standby  Notice Last Call│
│5│           Joe       Smith       3  Rio        Yes        2  04/06/90   │
│6│           Alan      Chan        1  London     Yes        6  04/25/90   │
│7│           Sue       Wong        1  Paris      No         4  04/08/90   │
│8│           Jane      Folsom      2  Rio        Yes        3  04/23/90   │
│9│           Nancy     Blass       3  Paris      Yes        1  05/06/90   │
│10│          Peter     Green       6  Paris      No        10  05/01/90   │
│11│          Will      Right       2  London     No         2  04/14/90   │
│12│          Bill      Front       4  Paris      No         3  04/17/90  ■│
│13│          Jane      Dobbs       7  Rome       No         1  05/03/90   │
│14│          Mary      Grant       2  Tokyo      Yes        4  05/05/90   │
│15│          Nina      Smith       7  Paris      Yes        6  04/15/90   │
│16│          Emma      Wong        2  Rome       Yes        3  04/24/90   │
│17│                                                                       │
│18│          Availability Report:                                        │
│19│          Emma Wong                                                    │
│20│                                                                      ↓│
└─┴───────────────────────────────────────────────────────────────────────┘
TOATEXT.WQ1  [1]                                            NUM        READY
```

Figure 10-17. *Improved concatenation*

File Edit Style Graph Print Database Tools Options Window   ↑↓
B19: +"Staff on standby include "âB15â" "âC15â" and "âB16â" "âC16â"."

```
┌─┬──────A────┬───B────┬───C────┬──D──┬───E────┬───F────┬───G───┬───H────┬─┐
│1│                                                                        │
│2│           TOA On-Call Roster                     As of: 07-May-90      │
│3│                                                                        │
│4│           First     Last     Rank  Based     Standby  Notice Last Call │
│5│           Joe       Smith       3  Rio        Yes         2  04/06/90   │
│6│           Alan      Chan        1  London     Yes         6  04/26/90   │
│7│           Sue       Wong        1  Paris      No          4  04/08/90   │
│8│           Jane      Folsom      2  Rio        Yes         3  04/23/90   │
│9│           Nancy     Blass       3  Paris      Yes         1  05/06/90   │
│10│          Peter     Green       6  Paris      No         10  05/01/90   │
│11│          Will      Right       2  London     No          2  04/14/90   │
│12│          Bill      Front       4  Paris      No          3  04/17/90  ■│
│13│          Jane      Dobbs       7  Rome       No          1  05/03/90   │
│14│          Mary      Grant       2  Tokyo      Yes         4  05/05/90   │
│15│          Nina      Smith       7  Paris      Yes         6  04/15/90   │
│16│          Emma      Wong        2  Rome       Yes         3  04/24/90   │
│17│                                                                        │
│18│          Availability Report:                                         │
│19│          Staff on standby include Nina Smith and Emma Wong.           │
│20│                                                                       ↓│
└─┴────────────────────────────────────────────────────────────────────────┘
TOATEXT.WQ1  [1]                                            NUM        READY
```

Figure 10-18. *Lengthy string formula*

The benefit of using a formula like this, rather than simply typing a statement, is that the cell references in the formula are dynamic. When members of the available staff change, the text is updated. When new names appear in B15 through C16, then they will also appear in the formula.

This means that you can create invoices, letters, and other documents that have the appearance of static text but are, in fact, dynamically related to the contents of the spreadsheet.

A simple example of this is shown in Figure 10-19, which is a list of travel agents and their sales figures. The list is sorted by sales, and the formula in cell A3 states that the two top agents are those whose names appear in cells A6 and A7. If the figures in the Sales column change and the list is re-sorted, the statement will still be correct. This occurred when it was discovered that Liz's sales figures were incorrect. The correct figure now places her at the top of the re-sorted list, as shown in Figure 10-20.

File	Edit	Style	Graph	Print	Database	Tools	Options	Window	↑↓

A3: [W9] +"The top two agents are "âA6â" and "âA7â"!"

	A	B	C	D	E	F	G
1		Quattro Vadis Sales Totals					
2							
3	The top two agents are Ron and Jud!						
4							
5	Agent	Office	Sales	Commissions			
6	Ron	Van Ness	$901,250	$54,075			
7	Jud	General	$890,670	$53,440			
8	Liz	Polk St.	$878,590	$52,715			
9	Joe	San Mateo	$876,900	$52,614			
10	Tom	Union Sq.	$859,600	$51,576			
11	Ian	Union Sq.	$849,050	$50,943			
12	Jim	General	$804,550	$48,273			
13	Ann	Polk St.	$768,545	$46,113			
14	Sal	San Mateo	$760,805	$45,648			
15	Sue	Union Sq.	$687,450	$41,247			
16	Sam	Van Ness	$586,780	$35,207			
17	Rob	Polk St.	$564,560	$33,874			
18	Lee	Union Sq.	$500,001	$30,000			
19	Tim	Van Ness	$459,870	$27,592			
20	Pip	Polk St.	$458,790	$27,527			

SALESTAT.WQ1 [1]   NUM   READY

Figure 10-19.   *The top agents*

```
 File  Edit  Style  Graph  Print  Database  Tools  Options  Window        ↑↓
A3: [W9] +"The top two agents are "&A6&" and "&A7&"!"
 J    A         B          C          D        E       F       G         ↑
1            Quattro Vadis Sales Totals
2
3   The top two agents are Liz and Ron!
4
5   Agent       Office       Sales     Commissions
6    Liz        Polk St.    $978,590    $58,715
7    Ron        Van Ness    $901,250    $54,075
8    Jud        General     $890,670    $53,440
9    Joe        San Mateo   $876,900    $52,614
10   Tom        Union Sq.   $859,600    $51,576
11   Ian        Union Sq.   $849,050    $50,943
12   Jim        General     $804,550    $48,273
13   Ann        Polk St.    $768,545    $46,113
14   Sal        San Mateo   $760,805    $45,648
15   Sue        Union Sq.   $687,450    $41,247
16   Sam        Van Ness    $586,780    $35,207
17   Rob        Polk St.    $564,560    $33,874
18   Lee        Union Sq.   $500,001    $30,000
19   Tim        Van Ness    $459,870    $27,592
20   Pip        Polk St.    $458,790    $27,527
SALESTAT.WQ1 [1]                                    NUM          READY
```

Figure 10-20. *The re-sorted sales*

Label Formulas to Labels

If you ever want to change a formula that results in a label to the label produced by that formula, you can use the Edit Values command. This command requires that you indicate the cell or block of cells that is being converted to values and a destination. The destination can be a separate area of the worksheet, if you want to preserve the original formulas; or the original cells themselves, if you want to convert them permanently to their result.

Numeric Formulas to Labels

In several situations you will find it useful to convert a numeric formula to a label. Suppose you have developed a lengthy formula containing numerous relative references to cell locations. The formula is correct but located in the wrong cell. When you copy or move a formula with the Edit commands, the relative cell references change relative to the new location of the formula. To prevent this from happening, you first convert the formula to a label and then copy or move it. Finally, you convert it back to a formula. The easiest way to do this is to highlight the formula in question, press F2 to edit the cell, press HOME to move the cursor to the beginning of the formula, and then type an apostrophe ('). When you press ENTER, the formula will appear as a left-justified label. To return the formula to active status, you reverse the procedure: edit the cell, press HOME, and delete the apostrophe.

This procedure is particularly useful when you enter a formula to which Quattro Pro 3 objects, that is, one containing a syntax error. If the formula is lengthy, the error might not be immediately apparent and you might need time to find it. If the formula contains a reference to a named block that has not yet been created, you will not be able to enter the formula, and you might think that you have to abandon the typing that it took to create the formula. This loss can be avoided if you press HOME to go to the beginning of the formula, type an apostrophe ('), and press ENTER to store the formula as a label. Then you can examine the formula, find the problem, and create any necessary block names before converting the label back to a formula.

String Functions

A specialized means of working with labels in formulas in Quattro Pro 3 is through the use of @functions specifically designed for manipulating text. These functions are called the *string functions* because a string in Quattro Pro 3 is a series of characters that results in a label and not a value. String functions are very valuable when working with data imported from other programs in the form of text files. They can also be used effectively with some advanced macro commands, as described in Chapter 12.

@CHAR

Earlier you saw that many programs can share information by using ASCII characters. There are 256 ASCII characters, numbered from 0 to 255. Many of them are symbols not found on the keyboard, such as graphics characters. The @CHAR function can display these codes in Quattro Pro

3. @CHAR returns the ASCII character corresponding to a given ASCII code. Its syntax is

@CHAR(*code*)

where *code* is a numeric value between 0 and 255. Since Quattro Pro 3 will truncate any values entered as *code* to an integer, you should always enter the *code* argument as an integer.

While you can refer to a standard ASCII table for numbers corresponding to the ASCII codes for each character, you can use the @CHAR function instead to create such a table within Quattro Pro 3. In Figure 10-21, the numbers 80 through 255 have been entered in alternating columns. The @CHAR function has been used to show the character corresponding to that code number. For example, the pounds sterling sign is code 156. You can print this as a reference for the codes, although some printers will not print all of the characters.

The usefulness of the @CHAR function depends on how much of your programming requires looking up ASCII codes, or on how much imagination you want to use in designing your spreadsheets. For example, the box around the assumptions in the Expense Projection shown in Figure 10-22

Figure 10-21. *ASCII table*

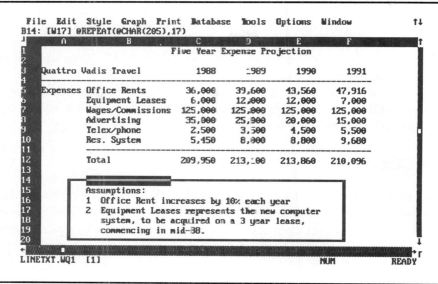

File Edit Style Graph Print Database Tools Options Window

B14: [W17] @REPEAT(@CHAR(205),17)

	A	B	C	D	E	F
1			Five Year Expense Projection			
2						
3	Quattro Vadis Travel		1988	1989	1990	1991
4						
5	Expenses	Office Rents	36,000	39,600	43,560	47,916
6		Equipment Leases	6,000	12,000	12,000	7,000
7		Wages/Commissions	125,000	125,000	125,000	125,000
8		Advertising	35,000	25,000	20,000	15,000
9		Telex/phone	2,500	3,500	4,500	5,500
10		Res. System	5,450	8,000	8,800	9,680
11						
12		Total	209,950	213,100	213,860	210,096
13						
14						
15		Assumptions:				
16		1 Office Rent increases by 10% each year				
17		2 Equipment Leases represents the new computer				
18		system, to be acquired on a 3 year lease,				
19		commencing in mid-88.				
20						

LINETXT.WQ1 [1]   NUM   READY

Figure 10-22. *Boxed assumptions*

was created with the @CHAR command and another string function, @REPEAT. Of course, you can use the Line Drawing and Shading commands on the Style menu to create boxes and other designs without using the @CHAR function.

@REPEAT

The @REPEAT function repeats a string of characters a specified number of times. Its syntax is

@REPEAT(*string,number*)

where *string* is a string value and *number* is a numeric value greater than or equal to 0. @REPEAT returns as many copies of the *string* as you specify with *number*. The result is a label.

While this function is somewhat similar to the repeating label prefix (\) that is used to produce dashed lines in a cell, the main difference is that with @REPEAT you can specify exactly how many times you want the string to be repeated. Also, the label prefix adjusts the number of repeated characters to fit the column, even when the width is changed. The @REPEAT function can display a fixed number of characters that does not change. When you specify a text string with @REPEAT, you must surround it by double quotes (").

The *number* argument in the @REPEAT statement can be a formula or a cell reference. This argument can be used to repeat a character or characters according to a variable factor.

@*CODE*

A reverse of the @CHAR function, the @CODE function tells you the ASCII code of a special character. Why would you want to know this? Sometimes data that you import from another program is corrupted by odd characters. Identifying them with the @CODE function could help you determine their origin. Its syntax is

@CODE(*string*)

where *string* is a string value, and the first letter is evaluated by @CODE to return the ASCII code.

As you have seen, converting results of the @CHAR function allows you to produce unusual characters yourself in a Quattro Pro 3 spreadsheet. You can determine the character's ASCII number by applying the @CODE function to it. Another way of producing special characters in Quattro Pro 3 is to type them and then press ENTER. You type them by using the ALT key together with the numeric keypad. The worksheet in Figure 10-23 shows the characters produced by holding down ALT and typing the numbers 155 through 196. You cannot use this method of making special characters for ASCII codes 0 through 28. This is because these codes are nonprinting characters that are used for control functions. In Figure 10-23, you can see that the @CODE function is being applied to cell B5. This tells you that the yen symbol is ASCII code 157.

You can use ASCII characters for making simple pictograms. A pictogram is a chart that represents numbers as pictures. In a pictogram one picture usually equals one unit of measure. For example, you can use the @REPEAT function to repeat the male symbol, @CHAR(11), as shown in Figure 10-24.

Figure 10-23. *Control characters*

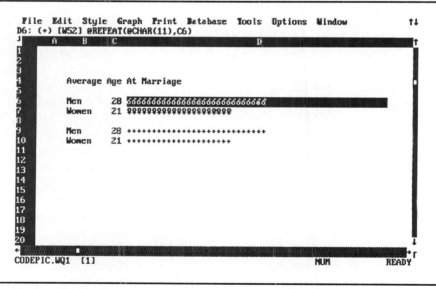

Figure 10-24. *Pictograms*

The upper bar shows the number 28 by repeating the male symbol 28 times. The lower bar shows the number 21 as the female symbol, which is @CHAR(12).

This method of making a chart is an alternative to selecting the +/– bar chart format from the Style Numeric Format menu. You can see the numbers 28 and 21 formatted with this style in the lower pair of pictograms in Figure 10-24.

@FIND

The @FIND function uses three arguments to find characters within a string. Its syntax is

@FIND(*substring,string,startnumber*)

where *substring* is a string value representing the target value to search for, *string* is a valid string value representing the source value to search within, and *startnumber* is a numeric value of 0 or greater representing the character position to begin searching with. The @FIND function returns the character position at which the first occurrence of the target was found.

The number 0 represents the first character in the string, the second is 1, and so on. Thus, @FIND("t",A1,0) returns the value 3 if A1 contains the label *Quattro Pro 3*, because the letter *t* first occurs at position 3. Note that the *startnumber* value tells the program to begin the search at that number of characters into the string. You will receive an error if the value of *startnumber* is more than the number of characters in *string* minus 1. You will also get an error if @FIND fails to find any occurrences of the *substring*.

Consider the spreadsheet in Figure 10-25, prepared by the Union Square office of Quattro Vadis Travel. The users in this office are new to spreadsheets and enter the agent name and office name as one long label, rather than as separate facts in separate cells. You need to convert the data to a more useful format.

This example will be used several times in the following sections to demonstrate string functions. The most likely source of problem entries like this is either a new user or a set of data imported from another program. The first three names of agents are exactly the same length, and all of the labels have a hyphen in them. The hyphen might help break the labels into their separate parts. You can use the @FIND function to measure the position of the hyphen, as shown in Figure 10-26.

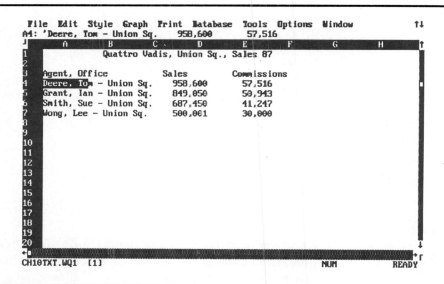

Figure 10-25. *Entries as long labels*

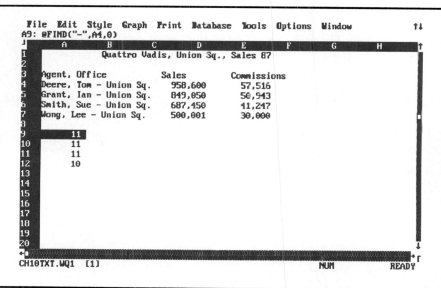

Figure 10-26. *@FIND results*

While this is not exactly vital data, it shows how the function can be used to compare labels, a function that might prove useful with larger collections of labels.

@EXACT

Another way to compare labels is to use the @EXACT function. This function has the syntax

@EXACT(*string1,string2*)

where *string1* is a string value or a reference to a cell containing a string, and *string2* is a second string value or cell reference.

The @EXACT function compares the values of *string1* and *string2*. If the values are exactly identical, including capitalization, it returns a value of 1. If there are any differences, it returns a 0 value. As you can see in Figure 10-27, the text in strings that you are comparing must be surrounded by double quotes.

Since @EXACT returns a value of 1, you can use it to activate mathematical calculations. Thus, agents who have not answered Yes in this example could be paid commissions times the value in column E. You can

```
 File  Edit  Style  Graph  Print  Database  Tools  Options  Window        ↑↓
H4: @EXACT(G4,"Yes")
J      A        B         C        D          E         F       G        H        1
1               Quattro Vadis, Union Sq., Sales 87
2
3  Agent, Office           Sales          Commissions        Report    Complete
4  Deere, Tom - Union Sq.   958,600        57,516            Yes            1
5  Grant, Ian - Union Sq.   849,050        50,943            Yep            0
6  Smith, Sue - Union Sq.   687,450        41,247            YES            0
7  Wong, Lee - Union Sq.    500,001        30,000            No             0
8
9
10
```

Figure 10-27. *The @EXACT function*

compare only the contents of label cells with @EXACT. If you attempt to compare one or more numbers or empty cells, the result is ERR. Label prefixes are ignored.

To compare strings or cell contents without regard for capitalization, you can use the @IF function. The @IF function is not case-sensitive. For example, @IF(A1=A2,1,0) will return a 1 value, meaning true, if the contents of the cells are the same but capitalized differently (for example, if A1 contained YES and A2 contained Yes). Another formula that you can use to check for a spelling match that disregards capitalization in a string is +D4="Yes", which returns 1 for both Yes and YES.

@REPLACE

You can use the @REPLACE function with four arguments to replace a string of characters within a label. The syntax is

@REPLACE(*string,startnumber,num,newstring*)

where *string* is a string value, the label to be worked on; *startnumber* is the character position to begin with; *num* is the number of characters to delete; and *newstring* is a string value, the characters to insert at the position marked by *num*. In Figure 10-28 you can see @REPLACE used to update the spelling of *Sq.* to *Square*.

This formula would not work for Mr. Wong since the twentieth character in his label is a period, not *q*. Thus, the result for him would be *Union Sqquare*. The @FIND function works well with @REPLACE to locate the first occurrence of *Sq* in order to replace it with *Square*. This can be seen in Figure 10-29, where the string *Sq* is being used as the place to make the replacement. The only time this would cause a problem is when an agent has a last name like Squib, since @FIND is looking for the first occurrence of *Sq* and would replace *Squib* with *Square* rather than *Sq* with *Square*. Other uses of @REPLACE are to add one string to the end of another. You do so by specifying as the *startnumber* a number that is one greater than the number of characters in *string*. To delete part or all of a string, specify " " as *newstring*. Remember that you can also use the Edit Search & Replace command to perform search-and-replace operations instead of @FIND and @REPLACE.

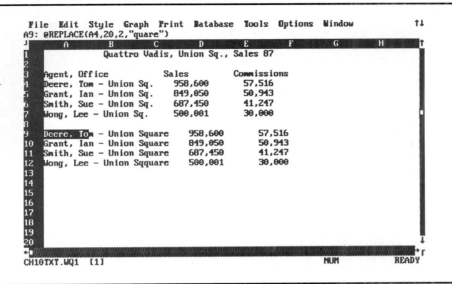

Figure 10-28.   *The @REPLACE function*

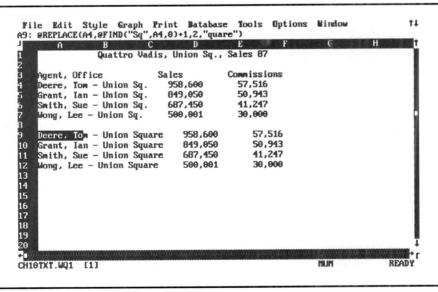

Figure 10-29.   *@FIND with @REPLACE*

@LEFT, @RIGHT, and @MID

The @LEFT, @RIGHT, and @MID functions are used to find strings of characters within labels based on the position of those characters. These functions follow the same basic syntax

@LEFT(*string,number*)

where *string* is a string value and *number* is a numeric value of 0 or greater.

The @LEFT function returns the leftmost characters of *string*, the number of characters returned being that specified by the *number* argument. In Figure 10-30, @LEFT returns the characters *Deere* from cell A4 since they are the five leftmost characters.

This function can be used to extract the agent names from the label where the agent name and office are mixed. However, the problem of varying label lengths appears once again due to cell A7. You can solve this problem by using the @FIND function. You use it to specify how far the reading of the leftmost characters must go. In this case, that is as far as the comma.

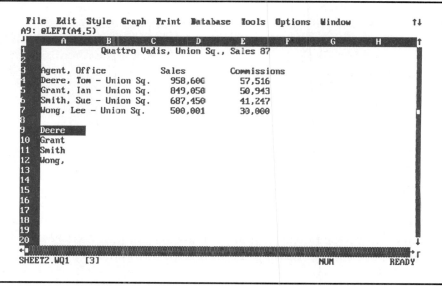

File Edit Style Graph Print Database Tools Options Window   ↑↓
A9: @LEFT(A4,5)

	A	B	C	D	E	F	G	H
1	Quattro Vadis, Union Sq., Sales 87							
2								
3	Agent, Office		Sales		Commissions			
4	Deere, Tom – Union Sq.		958,600		57,516			
5	Grant, Ian – Union Sq.		849,050		50,943			
6	Smith, Sue – Union Sq.		687,450		41,247			
7	Wong, Lee – Union Sq.		500,001		30,000			
8								
9	Deere							
10	Grant							
11	Smith							
12	Wong,							

SHEET2.WQ1   [3]   NUM   READY

Figure 10-30.   *The @LEFT function*

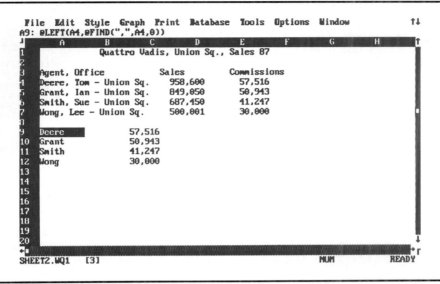

Figure 10-31.   *@FIND with @LEFT*

In Figure 10-31 the comma is being found by the @FIND function. The @RIGHT function is sometimes easier to apply, as is the case when you want to extract the commission figure from the labels.

The formula in cell C9 uses the function statement @RIGHT (C4,6) to extract the last six characters of the label, which is the commission figure in every case.

@TRIM and @LENGTH

The @TRIM function has the syntax

@TRIM(*string*)

It is used to remove any extra spaces from *string*. These extra spaces include the trailing spaces following the last nonspace character. It can also mean spaces preceding the first nonspace character plus duplicate spaces between words. Normal strings are not affected. If *string* is empty or contains a numeric value, the @TRIM function returns ERR. This function is particularly useful when you are working with data from other programs that pad some data to equal lengths by using trailing spaces.

The @LENGTH function is used to measure the length of a label. It uses the syntax

@LENGTH(*string*)

Thus, @LENGTH(A1) returns 13 if A1 contains the words *Quattro Pro 3*.

@LOWER, @UPPER, and @PROPER

These three functions change the case of a string. Their syntax is as follows:

@LOWER(*string*)
@UPPER(*string*)
@PROPER(*string*)

You can use @LOWER to turn a string into all lowercase characters. The @UPPER function returns all uppercase characters; that is, it capitalizes the string. The formula @UPPER(B4) returns YES if B4 contains either yes or YES.

To make the change permanent, you can use the Edit Values command to copy over the original label with the value of the formula. A more typical use of these three functions is to change an entire block of labels, which can save you some extensive editing.

The @PROPER function converts the first letter of every word in the string to uppercase and the rest of the characters to lowercase. In Quattro Pro 3 a word is defined as an unbroken string of alphabetic characters. The @PROPER function considers any blank spaces, punctuation symbols, or numbers as marking the end of a word. You can use the @PROPER function to produce better looking text from heavily capitalized text entries. Thus @PROPER(B4) returns "William Shakespeare" if B4 contains WILLIAM SHAKESPEARE.

In all three functions, numbers and symbols within the string are unaffected by the function. If the string is blank or is a numeric or date value, the result is ERR.

@STRING

Used to convert numbers to labels, the @STRING function has the syntax

@STRING(*x,decplaces*)

where *x* is a numeric value and *decplaces* is a numeric value between 0 and 15 representing the number of decimal places to the right of the decimal point. Thus, for example, @STRING(A1,0) converts 20.01 to a label, rounding it and then returning the decimal precision indicated by the *decplaces* argument. The label returned is 20.

You can use @STRING to convert a ZIP code entered as a number into a piece of text that can be concatenated with the rest of the address. This can be seen in Figure 10-32.

```
 File  Edit  Style  Graph  Print  Database  Tools  Options  Window        ↑↓
C26: [W25] +E20&", "&F20&"  "&@STRING(G20,0)
J                 C                      D                   E        F    G   ↑
1  Company                   Address                   City          ST  Zip
9  Control Systems, Inc      3150 Holcomb Bridge Road  Norcross      GA  30071
10 Cricchio Studio           2701 Gulfway Drive        Port Arthur   TX  77640
11 Fingerhut Corporation     440 Baker Road            Minnetonka    MN  55343
12 Good Samaritan Hospital   1111 E. McDowell Rd.      Phoenix       AZ  85006
13 Green River Comp Care     416 West 3rd Street       Owensboro     KY  42301
14 Itron Inc.                E. 15616 Euclid Ave.      Spokane       WA  99215
15 Larry D Noe, Attorney     PO Box 15                 Campbell      KY  42718
16 Leon & Bayless            500 Lexington             San Antonio   TX  78215
17 Marine Midland Bank       360 S. Warren St.         Syracuse      NY  13202
18 Martin V. Smith Assoc.    300 Esplanade DR. #2100   Oxnard        CA  93031
19 Maryknoll Fathers         224 SW 40th Street        Gainesville   FL  32607
20 Mt. Sinai Med. Center     Box 1000                  New York      NY  10029
21
22 Label:
23 Linda Coates
24 Mt. Sinai Med. Center
25 Box 1000
26 New York, NY  10029
27
ADDRESS1.WQ1 [4]                                            NUM        READY
```

Figure 10-32.   *The @STRING function*

@VALUE

The @VALUE function converts a label to a numeric value. The syntax is

@VALUE(*string*)

where *string* is a string value that can contain any of the arithmetic operators, but must not contain dollar signs, commas, or embedded spaces. One period, interpreted as the decimal place, is permitted, and leading and trailing spaces are ignored.

The @VALUE function—together with @DATEVALUE and @TIME-VALUE—is useful for converting data that was imported as text with the Tools Import command but was not automatically converted into values. You can also use this function to return values for numbers that have been turned into labels.

More Text Tips

The possibilities for text manipulation with Quattro Pro 3 are extensive. Using the string functions and text in formulas, you can handle many tasks beyond the traditional number crunching for which spreadsheets were originally designed. As a final example, consider the Quattro Pro 3 Business Name Generator shown in Figure 10-33. The plausible-looking company name in F11 was produced by the formula at the top of the screen. The @VLOOKUP function was used to look up a random number in the table of name parts from A1..D46. The table consists of a column of numbers roughly spaced across the possible value of @RAND, from 0 to 1.

Columns B and C are typical business names. Column D contains several types of companies repeated down the list. The @PROPER function is used to turn the actual business name into a capitalized word. The & sign is used to connect the three @VLOOKUP statements, and the comma and space separate the name from the type. By repeatedly pressing F2 to edit the cell containing the formula and then pressing ENTER, you can cause Quattro Pro 3 to reselect the random numbers and keep producing new combinations of names.

If you make the lookup table references absolute in the formula, you can copy the formula to many cells in a column to produce a list of possible

Figure 10-33.   *Name generator*

names. By extending the table with phrases that fit the kind of business for which you are trying to create a name, you can produce some very interesting results. The list of company names shown in the survey in Chapter 9 was produced by a formula of this kind. You can use @PROPER to alter the capitalization of the name, as shown in Figure 10-34. You can also use string formulas to simulate intercapitalization, the style so favored in the computer business by companies such as the WordPerfect corporation.

You can combine text formulas with the tremendous formatting capability of Quattro Pro 3 to achieve impressive results. For example, consider the finely printed certificate in Figure 10-35. This was produced by printing a Quattro Pro 3 spreadsheet. In fact, you can see the data that forms the basis of the certificate in Figure 10-20. The word "Liz" in Figure 10-35 was produced with a simple cell reference, +A6. The worksheet area occupied by the certificate can be seen in Figure 10-36. The WYSIWYG mode is used to display the formatting.

The block L2..P20 was formatted with Style Line Drawing. using the Outside and Double options. A variety of fonts was used in the wide, center-aligned column N. The formula in N15 was designed to produce a

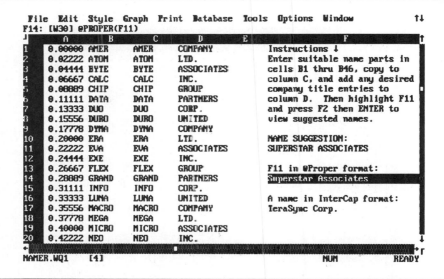

File Edit Style Graph Print Database Tools Options Window   ↑↓
F14: [W30] @PROPER(F11)

	A	B	C	D	E	F
1	0.00000	AMER	AMER	COMPANY		Instructions ↓
2	0.02222	ATOM	ATOM	LTD.		Enter suitable name parts in
3	0.04444	BYTE	BYTE	ASSOCIATES		cells B1 thru B46, copy to
4	0.06667	CALC	CALC	INC.		column C, and add any desired
5	0.08889	CHIP	CHIP	GROUP		company title entries to
6	0.11111	DATA	DATA	PARTNERS		column D. Then highlight F11
7	0.13333	DUO	DUO	CORP.		and press F2 then ENTER to
8	0.15556	DURO	DURO	UNITED		view suggested names.
9	0.17778	DYNA	DYNA	COMPANY		
10	0.20000	ERA	ERA	LTD.		NAME SUGGESTION:
11	0.22222	EVA	EVA	ASSOCIATES		SUPERSTAR ASSOCIATES
12	0.24444	EXE	EXE	INC.		
13	0.26667	FLEX	FLEX	GROUP		F11 in @Proper format:
14	0.28889	GRAND	GRAND	PARTNERS		Superstar Associates
15	0.31111	INFO	INFO	CORP.		
16	0.33333	LUNA	LUNA	UNITED		A name in InterCap format:
17	0.35556	MACRO	MACRO	COMPANY		TeraSync Corp.
18	0.37778	MEGA	MEGA	LTD.		
19	0.40000	MICRO	MICRO	ASSOCIATES		
20	0.42222	NEO	NEO	INC.		

NAMER.WQ1   [4]   NUM   READY

Figure 10-34. *The @PROPER function*

Certificate of Recognition

presented to:

Liz

from the

Polk St. Office

for sales in excess of

978,000

Signed: _____

Date: _____

Figure 10-35. *Finely printed certificate*

Figure 10-36.   *Worksheet area*

Figure 10-37.   *The rosette graphic in the Annotator*

round number slightly less than the actual sales figure in Figure 10-20, cell C6. The formula uses a negative value for the @ROUND function's decimal place argument:

@ROUND (C6-500,-3)

The -3 argument rounds up to the nearest 1000th so the -500 constant is used to make sure the result is actually the next lowest 1000th, as you can see from Figure 10-36.

The text "Polk Street Office" is supplied by the text formula +B6&" Office", which adds a space and the word *Office* to the name in B6. The print block that produced Figure 10-35 was L2..P20.

The rosettes were created from clip art (the file AWARDRIB.CLP) to which the number 1 was added. The clip art was added to a text chart in Annotate. The graph was named ROS1 and again ROS2. Two graphs had to be created since Quattro Pro 3 can only insert each named graph once. Using Graph Insert, ROS1 was placed in L3..M8, and ROS2 was placed in 03..P8. Note that a full screen graphic can be made small by inserting it in a small block. You can see the rosette graphic in the Annotator in Figure 10-37 (for more on Annotator see Chapter 13).

By combining text formulas, spreadsheet Style commands, and Graph Annotate work, you can produce a wide range of results that go far beyond the bounds of traditional spreadsheet work.

11 *Shortcuts and Macros*

As you become familiar with Quattro Pro 3 and apply it to more tasks, you will want to take advantage of several shortcuts to frequently used menu items, and to use macros to reduce repetitive typing. In this chapter you will read how to use, modify, and create Quattro Pro 3 Shortcuts; and how to record and use basic macros.

You may be somewhat in awe of the term *macros*, since they have traditionally been in the realm of power users and spreadsheet aficionados. However, with Quattro Pro 3 it is easy to create and use macros. Macros are no more complex than other spreadsheet tasks, and they do not require you to be highly proficient with everything else in the book to this point. If you plan on using more than a few macros, you should have a good grasp of naming blocks, described in Chapter 2. Perhaps the most important requirement for using macros is that you are already using Quattro Pro 3 for a task that you want to simplify or speed up.

In the Quattro Pro 3 menu system, the most commonly used commands are grouped in a logical way, making them easily accessible. The size of menus is kept manageable. Because different types of spreadsheet work require different sets of commands, however, you may often use commands that are several layers down in the menu structure. Quattro Pro 3 addresses this problem in two ways. First, you can create Shortcuts. A Shortcut allows you to use a single keystroke to select any menu item. The second approach, described in the next chapter, is to redesign the menu system. Quattro Pro 3 allows you to regroup and rename menu items to match your pattern of work with a feature called the Menu Builder.

Shortcuts

You may have noticed that several of the Quattro Pro 3 menus have notations on the right, such as the CTRL-S and CTRL-X on the File menu shown in Figure 11-1. These represent Shortcuts or *hot keys* that are already incorporated into Quattro Pro 3. A Shortcut allows you to access a menu item with a single keystoke, bypassing the menu system. Little mention has been made of these keys so far in order to concentrate on the purpose of the menu items rather than quick ways of selecting them. However, once you are familiar with what a particular menu item does you may want to start selecting it with the assigned Shortcut. You can see all of the preassigned Shortcuts listed in Table 11-1. Perhaps the most useful is CTRL-C for the Edit Copy command. This takes you directly to the Source Block prompt, ready to perform a copy operation. Another very convenient Shortcut when building worksheets is CTRL-W for Style Column Width. One Shortcut, CTRL-D, is rather special since it does not represent any single menu item, but is used to enter dates, as described in Chapter 9.

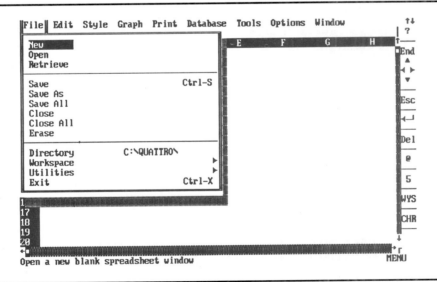

Figure 11-1.   *File menu Shortcuts*

Shortcut	Command
CTRL-A	Style Alignment
CTRL-C	Edit Copy
CTRL-D	Date Prefix
CTRL-E	Edit Erase Block
CTRL-F	Style Numeric Format
CTRL-G	Fast Graph
CTRL-I	Edit Insert
CTRL-M	Edit Move
CTRL-N	Edit Search & Replace Next
CTRL-P	Edit Search & Replace Previous
CTRL-R	Window Move/Size
CTRL-S	File Save
CTRL-T	Window Tile
CTRL-W	Style Column Width
CTRL-X	File Exit

Table 11-1.   *Default Shortcuts*

Creating Shortcuts

The more spreadsheet work you do, the more you will appreciate an opportunity to reduce keystrokes, and Shortcuts do just that. However, you may not like or use all of the preassigned Shortcuts. Fortunately, Quattro Pro 3 allows you to reassign or eliminate them. Suppose you are designing a large spreadsheet. You find you are repeatedly using the Window Options Locked Titles Both command to set titles in the worksheet. (Recall that this command freezes the cells above and to the left of the cell selector, so that row titles and column headings do not scroll off the screen when you move around the worksheet.) Using Quattro Pro 3's Shortcuts feature, you can execute the Window Options Locked Titles Both command with a single keystroke, such as CTRL-L. The same feature can be applied to the Window Options Locked Titles Clear command, assigning it to CTRL plus a different letter. This will enable you to set and remove titles with just two keystrokes instead of eight.

To make a shortcut for a menu item, you first highlight the menu item you want, as shown in Figure 11-2 where the Locked Titles Both command

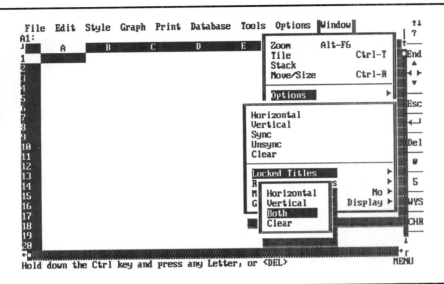

Figure 11-2. *Setting locked titles shortcut*

is highlighted. You then press CTRL-ENTER, and Quattro Pro 3 prompts you at the bottom of the screen for the keystroke combination to which you want this menu item assigned. Press the letter L, and the prompt disappears. The menu remains on the screen. The menu item you assigned to CTRL-L has not been selected, but the menu now shows the name of the assigned Shortcut, as seen in Figure 11-3. You do not have to select the menu item just to assign it to a CTRL-letter key combination. If you do not need the menu item at this time, press ESCAPE or CTRL-BREAK to leave the menu. Whenever you are ready to set titles in the worksheet, press CTRL-L. The command is instantly executed without any need to use the menu system.

Reassigning Shortcuts

To match the Locked Titles Both Shortcut you might want to assign Locked Titles Clear to a different CTRL-letter key combination, for example, CTRL-C. You do this by highlighting the Clear command on the Locked Titles menu and pressing CTRL-ENTER followed by CTRL-C. You can then clear titles

Figure 11-3. *Assigned shortcut* CTRL-L

simply by pressing CTRL-C. However, this new Shortcut conflicts with the preassigned use of CTRL-C for Edit Copy. In fact, you must first remove the current assignment of the CTRL-C shortcut before reassigning it to another task. To remove CTRL-C from Edit Copy you highlight Copy on the Edit menu and press CTRL-ENTER followed by DELETE. You will be prompted to press DELETE again to confirm the action.

If you highlight any menu item and press CTRL-ENTER, then DELETE, then CTRL-ENTER again, you can delete any of the Shortcuts by typing the letter, or ALL shortcuts by pressing DELETE.

Managing Shortcuts

If you try to reassign an existing Shortcut without first deleting the current assignment, Quattro Pro 3 will warn you "Shortcut key is already in use."

Quattro Pro 3 has no built-in means of displaying a list of current Shortcut assignments. However, you can see the Shortcuts on the menus from which they operate. You can use the Help system to find a list of the default or preassigned Shortcuts. Just highlight a menu item, press

CTRL-ENTER, and then press F1. This will take you to Help for Shortcuts and a list of Preset Shortcuts. This list does not change to reflect new Shortcuts you create or changes to existing Shortcuts. You might want to keep track of active Shortcuts by noting them on a piece of paper or in a worksheet file. If you share a PC system and Quattro Pro 3 with other users, you should inform them of the Shortcuts you have set up. This will help prevent problems that arise from accidental activation of a Shortcut. Quattro Pro 3 automatically records Shortcuts in the current configuration file. See Appendix A for more about configuration files.

Note that if you remove all Shortcuts, then use the Options Update command you will have to reinstall Quattro Pro 3 or manually recreate the Shortcuts to get them back. To remove all shortcuts you use CTRL-ENTER, DELETE, CTRL- ENTER, DELETE, while highlighting any menu item.

Macros

When you find yourself repeating the same keystrokes over and over, but they are not simply menu items you can assign to Shortcuts, then you need the power of macros. Originally developed for word processing programs as a way to record and play back frequently used phrases, macros store multiple keystrokes under a single key or name.

Macros in Quattro Pro 3

The macros you create in Quattro Pro 3 enable you to record and play back any series of keystrokes, including labels, numbers, formulas, menu choices, and even Shortcuts. For example, you could create a macro for setting titles in your worksheet. In addition to simply picking the Locked Titles Both command from the menu, the macro could move the cell selector to the correct cell prior to issuing the command, thus eliminating the need for you to position the cell selector yourself. If you have to format a lot of separate cells to Percent format you could create a macro to perform that action. You might have noticed that the Numeric Format option on the Style menu already has a Shortcut, CTRL-F. But this only takes you to the list of formats. If you assigned a Shortcut to the Percent format, you would still need to specify decimal places and select the block to be formatted. A macro can complete the whole command, including selection of decimal places, without having to go through the menus every time.

A Quattro Pro 3 macro can be defined as a set of keystrokes or instructions stored as labels. Numbers and letters are stored as numbers and letters; commands are stored as special symbols or words within brackets. For example, you can have a macro that consists of the label **Report**. This macro tells Quattro Pro 3 to type the letters **R-e-p-o-r-t**, then press ENTER (represented by the tilde symbol, ~). You can use this macro to enter the word "Report" into a cell. In fact, you can easily create this macro in a blank worksheet, as follows:

1. Place the cell selector in A1, type **Report**, then press ENTER. The cell identifier will show **'Report**~ as the contents of the cell.

2. Move the cell selector to A3, where the word "Report" will be typed by the macro.

3. Press ALT-F2 for the Macro menu shown in Figure 11-4. Select Execute from the Macro menu. You will be prompted for the cell coordinates of the block of macro commands that you want to execute.

4. Type or point to A1 and press ENTER. The word "Report" is entered in cell A3. You have just created and used your first macro.

Obviously, this is a simple example; the macro is of limited use and sophistication. Macros can consist of much longer instructions. When a macro contains many instructions, the instructions are placed on successive rows of the same column. A macro that consists of more than one line of instructions is executed by indicating the first cell in the macro. Quattro Pro 3 reads the instructions in that cell, then the instructions in the next cell down, and so on until a blank cell is encountered. One problem with the simple macro just described is that it is not particularly easy to use. Executing it involves several steps, including entering the location of the macro. You can make a macro easier to execute by using the Macro Name command to name the cell containing the macro. You can use several types of macro names.

Macros by Name

When you have attached a name to a cell containing a macro, you can use F3 to execute that macro. For example, if cell A1 were named RP with the

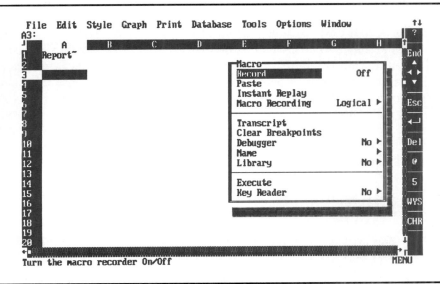

Figure 11-4.   *Macro menu*

Macro Name command, the macro could be executed more easily. To name
a macro and use the name to execute the macro, follow these steps:

1. Place the cell selector in the cell that contains the first line of the
   macro, in this case A1.

2. Press ALT-F2 for the Macro menu (you can also use the Macro command
   from the Tools menu). Select Name and then Create and type the name
   RP, as shown in Figure 11-5. Press ENTER.

3. Quattro Pro 3 prompts you to specify coordinates for the block, but it
   assumes the current cell, in this case A1..A1, as the block. This is
   correct, so press ENTER.

4. To execute the newly named macro, move to a blank cell into which
   you will enter the word "Report" and press ALT-F2. Select Execute and
   then press F3. You will see RP in the list of named blocks. Highlight
   RP and press ENTER. The macro in the cell named RP will execute.

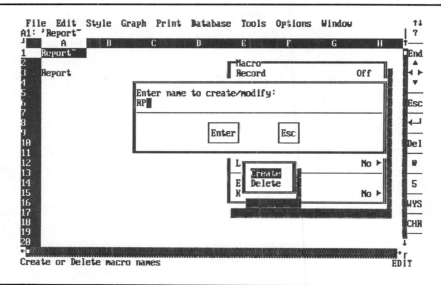

Figure 11-5.   *Naming a macro*

Macro Shortcuts

One Shortcut you can use to improve the macro-execution process is to assign the Macro Execute command to CTRL-E. To do this you must first delete CTRL-E as the Edit Erase Block Shortcut. To do this, highlight Erase Block on the Edit menu, then press CTRL-ENTER, followed by DELETE, and DELETE again. Now bring up the Macro menu from the Tools menu. Then highlight Execute and press CTRL-ENTER. Now press CTRL-E and the Execute command is assigned to CTRL-E.

You might wonder if it is not better to keep Edit Erase Block as CTRL-E, but in fact Edit Erase Block is a somewhat redundant command when you are familiar with Quattro Pro 3. An easier way to erase a block is to use the Extend key (SHIFT-F7) to select the block of cells and then press the DELETE key. This performs a block erase without using the menu system at all. With CTRL-E as the macro-execute key you can run your named macros very efficiently. Simply press CTRL-E followed by F3 and then select the macro name from this list.

If you want instant access to a macro, you should name the macro with a special combination of characters: the backslash (\) together with a letter. You can then execute the macro by holding down the ALT key and pressing the letter you used in the name. To make an instant macro, use the following steps, which describe the procedure in the case of the Report macro. This macro can be called \R, so that it can be executed with ALT-R.

1. Place the cell selector in the cell that contains the first line of the macro, in this case A1.

2. Select Name from the Macro menu, pick Create, and type the name \R. Press ENTER.

3. Quattro Pro 3 prompts you to specify coordinates for the block but it will assume the current cell, in this case A1..A1, as the block. This is correct, so press ENTER.

4. To execute the newly named macro, move to a blank cell and press ALT-R. The macro will execute.

Note that block names can overlap, as in this case, where the names RP and \R were both assigned to cell A1. Since \R is a block name, you can execute this macro with the Macro Execute command as well as with the ALT key. You can create 26 instant macros named from \A to \Z. These names are usually reserved for frequently used macros. The letter used in the macro name should have some mnemonic relationship to the action of the macro, such as \R for the Report macro.

Applying Macros

In practical applications, macros are used for common operations and repetitive tasks, particularly ones that involve many settings. Good examples are database operations and printing. You will recall that Quattro Pro 3 can remember only one Sort Block and one set of sort keys at a time. Similarly, the Print command can remember only one Print Block at a time. Sorting two different databases on the same spreadsheet or printing two different blocks of the spreadsheet involves changing a lot of settings. You can use macros to specify all of the details about two different sort or print jobs, reducing many keystrokes and many chances for error to just one accurate set of instructions.

You can even create macros that contain conditional statements. Such statements as If-Then-Else enable you to have a macro choose among several different actions based on user input or spreadsheet conditions. The ability to include special command language statements in macros transforms macros into the equivalent of a programming language. With this capability you can create custom menus, data input forms, and specialized applications. The Quattro Pro 3 command language and its use in macros is explained in greater detail in the next chapter.

Ways to Create Macros

When you consider creating practical macros you will quickly face the question of how to tell Quattro Pro 3 to perform typical actions such as Edit or END, or UP ARROW. You have seen that a macro is essentially a label or series of labels stored in a worksheet cell. When you created the macro to enter "Report" into a cell you used the tilde (~) to represent pressing ENTER. This is because you cannot type "ENTER" as a label. In fact, if you are typing a label and you press ENTER, what you are typing is simply entered into the cell. Consequently, there is a whole system of codes for those actions that cannot simply be typed as labels. These codes are listed in Table 11-2.

There are also special ways of describing menu actions in macros. If you wanted a macro to execute the Spreadsheet Print command you could use the characters "/PS" but Quattro Pro 3 has a better way than this, as you will see as you examine the different ways to create macros. The method you use for a particular macro will depend on the purpose of the macro, its level of complexity, and your level of familiarity with the macro process. You can combine all three methods of making macros when you are creating large macros.

Macro Recording

The simplest method of creating useful macros is to record them. Even novice users can make macros in this way to simplify commonly used tasks. Recording a macro simply means telling Quattro Pro 3 to keep a record of your actions while you use the program. This is done by placing the

Macro Equivalent	Key Represented	Macro Equivalent	Key Represented
Function Keys		**Movement Keys**	
{ABS}	F4	{HOME}	HOME
{CALC}	F9	{END}	END
{CHOOSE}	SHIFT-F5	{LEFT} or {L}	LEFT ARROW
{COPY}	SHIFT-F9	{RIGHT} or {R}	RIGHT ARROW
{EDIT}	F2	{UP} or {U}	UP ARROW
{FUNCTIONS}	ALT-F3	{DOWN} or {D}	DOWN ARROW
{GOTO}	F5	{PGUP}	PAGE UP
{GRAPH}	F10	{PGDN}	PAGE DOWN
{MACROS}	SHIFT-F3	{BIGLEFT}	CTRL-LEFT
{MARK}	SHIFT-F7	{BACKTAB}	SHIFT-TAB
{MARKALL}	ALT-F7	{BIGRIGHT}	CTRL-RIGHT
{MOVE}	SHIFT-F8	{TAB}	TAB
{NAME}	F3	{WINDOW*n*}	Selects window *n*
{NEXTWIN}	SHIFT-F6		
{PASTE}	SHIFT-F10		
{QUERY}	F7	**Status Keys**	
{STEP}	SHIFT-F2	{NUMON}	NUM LOCK
{TABLE}	F8	{SCROLLOFF}	SCROLL LOCK off
{UNDO}	ALT-F5	{SCROLLON}	SCROLL LOCK on
{WINDOW}	F6	{CAPOFF}	CAPS LOCK off
{ZOOM}	ALT-F6	{CAPON}	CAPS LOCK on
		{INS}	INSERT
		{INSOFF}	INSERT off
Other Keys		{INSON}	INSERT on
{BREAK}	CTRL-BREAK		
{BACKSPACE} or {BS}	BACKSPACE		
{DATE}	CTRL-D		
{DEL}	DELETE		
{DELEOL}	CTRL-\ (delete to end of line)		
{ESC}	ESCAPE		
{CLEAR}	ESCAPE		
{CR} or ~	ENTER		
{?}	PAUSE (for user input)		

Table 11-2.   *Macro Equivalents and Keys*

program in RECORD mode, and then typing the necessary keystrokes to perform the actions that are to be part of the macro. Quattro Pro 3 holds a record of the actions you carry out in memory, until you either paste the macro into a worksheet or record a new macro. You do not have to paste the recorded macro into a worksheet in order to use it. However, if you do paste the recording into a worksheet you can examine it, edit it, and add to it. For example, suppose you have recorded the following actions:

■ Move the cell selector to B4 with the GoTo key (F5)

■ Set both vertical and horizontal locked titles

The recorded macro would look like this:

```
{GOTO}B4~
{/ Titles;Both}
```

From this macro code you can see what the macro is supposed to do, and you can see that Quattro Pro 3 has provided the codes for special keys and menu items. In the next section a complete macro recording example will be presented.

Macro Writing

The sample macro that enters the word "Report" was created by simply writing it into a cell. When you become familiar with how macros work, you can use this method to write macros. Use Table 11-2 to find the equivalents that Quattro Pro 3 uses for common commands when you are writing macros. Remember to use a label prefix before such entries as @SUM when writing macros.

Macros from Transcript

The record of your keystrokes maintained by Transcript (described in Chapter 7) is compatible with Quattro Pro 3's macro terminology. Thus, you can call up the Transcript log and copy sections of the keystroke record to your spreadsheet. An example of the Transcript log is shown in Figure 11-6. The actions since the last file retrieve operation are linked by a line

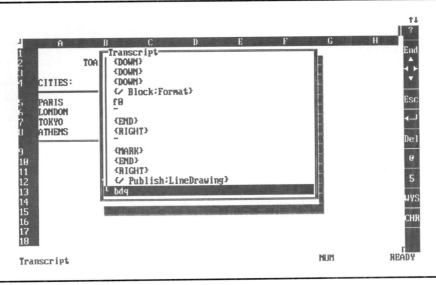

Figure 11-6.   *Transcript log*

in the left margin of the keystroke records. You can see that the line-drawing command was used in two instances since the file was retrieved. You could use this code to create line-drawing macros. You call up the Transcript log by using the Macro Transcript command. When the log is on screen, you can type / for the Transcript menu and mark a block for copying to the spreadsheet. This process is described in detail at the end of this chapter.

Recording a Macro

To see the macro-recording process in action and to get a better understanding for the potential of macros, try the example in the following section. This macro enters the current date in the worksheet.

Macro Design

Whenever you create a macro, you need to give some thought to what the role of the macro will be. You can use macros to enter values and labels, to select menu items, and to activate function keys. You can execute macros in READY mode, in EDIT mode, and from within the menu system. Of course, if you make a macro that works from READY mode, you must execute it in READY mode and not in the middle of a menu. Also, you need to be careful about the action of the macro and the cells it will affect. Keep in mind that there is a possibility of losing data through any of these actions: Copy, Move, Fill, Transpose, Output, Erase, or Delete. For example, if the macro is designed to perform a particular action on a cell, you must remember to move your cell selector to a suitable cell before executing the macro.

Suppose you need to enter today's date at several different places in a spreadsheet used for recording sales calls. If the choice of date format is not important, you can press CTRL-D, type **@NOW**, and press ENTER. This action enters the current date in the D4 format.

To enter the current date with the D1 format, you would type **@NOW,** press ENTER, and then format the cell using Style Numeric Format Date 1. Doing so requires a dozen keystrokes, and it is a tedious operation if you have to repeat it often. To make a macro to perform this task, you simply perform the steps once while Quattro Pro 3 is in RECORD mode. This operation is presented here in a sales call worksheet used by salespersons, and shown in the following illustration. Of course, you can try this operation in any practice worksheet.

1. Select any empty cell on a spreadsheet into which you want to enter the date. You may want to make sure that the column is at least ten characters wide, so that the date you are about to create can be seen properly.

2. To begin recording the macro, press the Macro key (ALT-F2) and select Record. This command begins and ends the macro-recording process. After you select Record, the Macro menu disappears and you are returned to the READY mode with the REC message in the status line.

3. Type **@NOW** and press ENTER. Then select Style Numeric Format Date. Select the D1 format and press ENTER to confirm that the current

cell is the one you want to format. The result is shown in Figure 11-7. The current date has been read from the system clock and formatted with the D1 format. The REC message is still displayed as the recording mode is still active.

4. Press ALT-F2 and select Record to end the recording. The REC message will disappear. Your macro is ready to use.

There are two ways to stop the macro recorder other than using the ALT-F2 key. You can select Paste from the Macro menu, or you can select Instant Replay. These options will be described next.

Instant Replay

As soon as you are back in READY mode you can use the macro that you have just recorded. Move the cell selector to an empty cell, press ALT-F2, and then select Instant Replay. The macro instructions are carried out, and the date is entered and formatted. Instant Replay plays back the most recently recorded macro. Quattro Pro 3 stores what you record in a small area of memory called a *buffer*. When you begin a new recording the contents of the buffer are cleared out to be replaced by the new recording. For this reason Instant Replay is best used for one-shot macros that you will not need again. Using Instant Replay saves you the trouble of naming a macro if you will need it only for a short while. If you like you can assign a Shortcut to Instant Replay to execute the recorded macro with a single keystroke.

Macro Paste

Another way to stop macro recording is to use ALT-F2 followed by Paste. This command allows you to paste the recorded macro into a worksheet where you can examine, name, and store it. In fact, before doing more work with the @NOW macro you have just created, you might want to take a look at the way it has been recorded by Quattro Pro 3. You can do this by selecting Paste from the Macro menu. You will be prompted for a name to create or modify, as shown in Figure 11-8. This is the name of the macro and the block of cells it will occupy. In this case, use the backslash and the letter *T* (for Today). Now press ENTER to confirm the name. Next, you will be prompted for the coordinates of the block of cells in which to store the

Figure 11-7. *Actions completed*

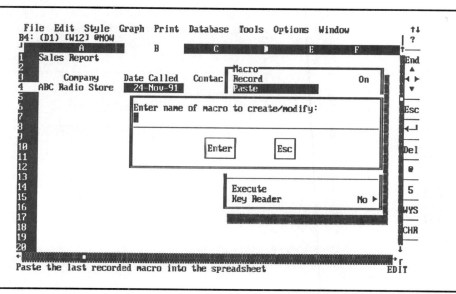

Figure 11-8. *Naming a recorded macro*

keystrokes that make up the macro. Quattro Pro 3 assumes you want to use the current location of the cell selector. This location is not correct, since the current position of the cell selector is the cell in which you actually want to enter the date. You change the cell coordinates by first unlocking them with ESCAPE.

Move the cell selector to an empty cell away from the rest of the worksheet—one that has at least two empty cells directly beneath it. For example, you could press HOME and then TAB. Using these keys is a quick way to move to a position away from the main work area with only two keystrokes. Press ENTER to confirm the location. You have now named the macro so that it can be executed with ALT-T. Before you use the macro, you might want to examine it.

An easy way to move to the cell you named to store the macro is to press the GoTo key (F5) and then the Name key (F3). You should see \T on the name list along with the names of any other blocks of cells that have been named in the spreadsheet. Highlight \T and press ENTER. Your cell selector will be placed in the top cell of the block you named \T. In Figure 11-9 you can see the record that Quattro Pro 3 made of your keystrokes while in RECORD mode. The first cell is the function @NOW, as you typed it, followed by the tilde (~), which is the macro language symbol for ENTER. Below this is a record of the menu items you chose. These are stated in terms that Quattro Pro 3 calls menu equivalents. Instead of simply saying /SND1, which were the actual letters for the menu items you selected, Quattro Pro 3 shows you the nature of the menu commands you chose.

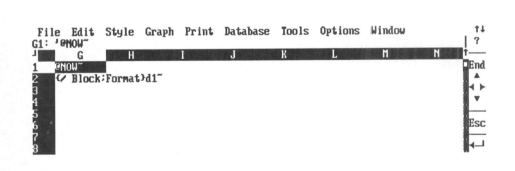

Figure 11-9. *Macro code*

To use the \T macro you have created, first place the cell selector on the cell into which you want to enter the date. Then press ALT-T and the date will be entered and formatted for you.

Macro-Naming Strategies

If you had named the macro using the word DATE instead of \T you could execute it by first using the Macro Execute command and then pressing F3 for a list of named blocks. Selecting DATE by highlighting it and pressing ENTER would execute the macro commands stored in that block. As was mentioned earlier, you can create as many as 26 instant macros named with ALT plus a letter *A* through *Z*. While this method limits you to 26 macros, you can use any valid block name for a macro and thus create an unlimited number of macros. The chances are that as your applications become more complex and your procedures more streamlined, you will use both macro-naming methods, together with Shortcuts. Thus, you could have 26 menu items assigned to CTRL-A/Z, 26 common operations assigned to ALT-A/Z, and then a selection of macros accessible with Macro Execute.

Expanding Macros

Recall that in the previous example, only cell G1 was named as \T. The macro record occupied more than one cell, however, so Quattro Pro 3 split the record of your keystrokes to prevent the creation of very long labels that are hard to read and edit. Since Quattro Pro 3 reads macros from the first cell, then from the next cell below that, and so on until it reaches an empty cell, you can easily add steps to the end of an existing macro. For example, when entering the date with the @NOW function, which was the purpose of the ALT-T macro described previously, you may want to add a step to convert the date in a function statement to a fixed date value.

The @NOW function returns the current date from your system clock. If you load the same spreadsheet the next day, the @NOW date changes. What you would probably want in a record of sales calls is a permanent date that does not change. You can set this with the Edit Values command. To add another set of instructions to the existing macro in G1 and G2 using the record method, follow these steps:

1. Place the cell selector in the cell that contains the @NOW function (B4 in this example). This location is where the actions to be recorded will be carried out.

2. Press ALT-F2 and pick Record to initiate the record feature.

3. You are now in RECORD mode. Use the Edit Values command and press ENTER to confirm that the cell containing the @NOW function is the one you want to transform into a value. Press ENTER again to copy the value to the same cell.

4. Press ALT-F2 and select Paste to terminate RECORD mode. Quattro Pro 3 prompts for the "name of macro to create/modify" and displays a list, as shown in Figure 11-10. Do not pick \T, but press ESCAPE once and then press ENTER. This will result in a prompt for a paste location.

5. Press ESCAPE to unlock the prompted coordinates, move the cell selector down to G3, and press ENTER. The recorded action is now pasted into the worksheet below the existing macro code.

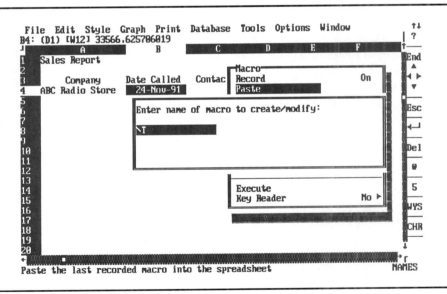

Figure 11-10. *Name macro prompt*

If you look at cells G3 and G4 now, you will see the action you just performed recorded as

{/ Block;Values}~~

Since this instruction is directly below the last cell of the \T macro, it will be read as part of the \T macro. You can now move to the cell into which you need to enter today's date and press ALT-T; the date will be entered and converted to a value that will not change when the worksheet is reloaded at a later date.

Note that you could have replied to the prompt in Figure 11-10 by typing a new name, such as **VALUE** or **\V**, which would then have been attached to the recorded code even as it became a part of the other macro. However, placing macros within macros is not recommended. If you want to use the code in G3 and G4 in a separate macro, the best approach is to copy it to another location, which brings up the question of macro management.

Macro Management

Since macros are such powerful and useful tools for spreadsheet users, once you start to develop them you will probably begin to accumulate many of them. Placement of macros within a worksheet, conventions used for assigning names, and sharing macros between worksheets are important factors to consider when organizing your macros.

Macro Placement

If you want to store additional macros close to the ones already entered into the worksheet, but you do not want them to become part of the existing macros, you should make sure that at least one blank cell separates each macro. In Figure 11-11 you can see that several more macros have been added in the same area of the worksheet as the \T macro. The macro in G7 is the Edit Values macro that turns a formula in a cell into a value. In cell G10 is a macro that widens the current column by one character, while

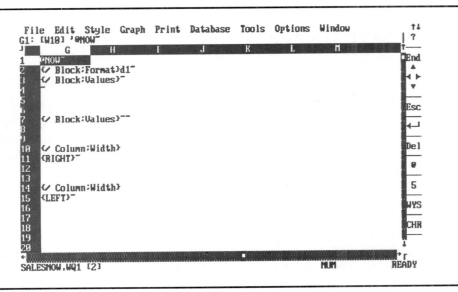

Figure 11-11.   *Additional macros*

the macro in G14 narrows the current column by one character. Because each of these macros is separate from the others, they are not activated by another macro.

Where you place macros on your spreadsheet not only affects how they relate to other macro instructions but also the rest of your work. Consider the location of the macros in the previous example, that is, to the right of the work area. This location is acceptable until you decide to delete a row from the work area. Since the macros and the work area are probably not going to be in view at the same time, it is all too easy to delete a row from the work area and accidentally delete a row of macro code. Since macros run until they encounter a blank row, even deleting a blank row or inserting a new row can cause problems for macros stored to the right of the work area. One way to avoid damaging these macros is to use the full movement of the cursor when you use the Row Delete or Row Insert command. You can press not only the DOWN ARROW key when deleting or inserting rows but also the RIGHT ARROW and the TAB keys. Doing so allows you to move to the right of your work area to check for macros before deleting or inserting the rows.

Another way to avoid problems for macros caused by deleting rows is to store the macros below the work area. In this way you are less likely to delete columns, and adding columns is less likely to disrupt a macro, since the instructions are stored in single columns. Some users like to place their macros above the main work area and to the left of the spreadsheet, that is, around the home position. Here they are safe from row deletion and easy to find. Such considerations are a part of worksheet aesthetics or spreadsheet design. The three preferred arrangements—below, to the right and below, and to the left and above—are shown in Figure 11-12. You will probably develop your own style of organizing your spreadsheets.

Organizing Macros

If you want to rearrange your macros within a worksheet, keep in mind that you can easily move a macro without affecting its operation by using the Edit Move command. This command retains the integrity of block names, so that Quattro Pro 3 knows where a named block is, even after it has been moved.

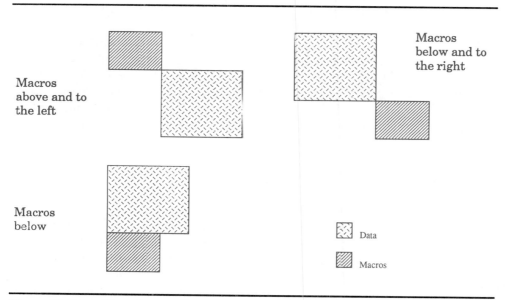

Figure 11-12. *Macro layout diagram*

When you are designing macros, remember that you can use the TAB and PAGE DOWN keys to quickly move your cell selector a number of columns and rows at a time. By using HOME before TAB and PAGE DOWN, you can consistently move to the same location from anywhere on the worksheet. Thus, if you are working in normal character mode with 20 rows per screen you can set up a macro area at cell A61 that you can reach from anywhere on the worksheet with just four keystrokes: HOME, PAGE DOWN, PAGE DOWN, PAGE DOWN. But keep in mind that while this method is convenient, it is unreliable if you have to add or delete many columns or rows. The series of cursor keystrokes you have been using to get to a specific area may no longer be accurate. This is also true if you switch to a different display mode with more rows per screen.

An alternative way of moving to a specific area is to name the area with the Edit Names Create command. In this example, to make moving directly to the area where you have stored the macros easier, you could assign the name MACROS to the entire macro storage area. Then you can move to the named block by pressing GoTo (F5), typing **MACROS,** and pressing ENTER. You could also use GoTo followed by F3 to list the names and then select the name from the list. (One way to move quickly to an important block is to name it with a block name, such as AAA, that is alphabetically prior to any other names you have used. In this way the name becomes the top name on the F3 list. Then you can move to the block with GoTo, F3, and ENTER.)

Using cursor-movement keys to move to a specific location can be a problem in macros themselves. When designing cursor movement into a macro the best approach to locating a specific area is first to name the cell in the top-left corner of the area you want to get to and then, in the macro instruction, to use {GoTo} and the block name. Subsequent changes to the location or size of the block will not affect the macro instruction.

Macro Layout

In addition to the possible danger to the macros in Figure 11-11 from deleting rows, there are other problems with the layout of these macros. You cannot see what their names are from looking at them. One way of finding out the names and locations of all named blocks in a worksheet is to use the Edit Names Make Table command. This command produces a 2-column list of the block names and their corresponding coordinates, as shown in Figure 11-13.

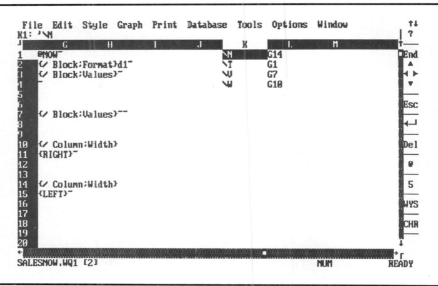

Figure 11-13. *Edit Names Make Table results*

In the figure, the Edit Names Make Table command was issued with the cell selector in K1. The table occupies columns K and L and as many rows as are needed to list all the current block names. You should always issue this command with enough room for the resulting table to appear; otherwise, the table will overwrite the contents of existing cells. Note that the table is not dynamic; that is, it is not linked to the Edit Names Create command and will not be automatically updated when new names are created.

As useful as the Make Table command is in many situations, particularly when you have many block names to keep track of, it does not really tell you what you want to know about the macros in the worksheet. Consider the layout of the macros shown in Figure 11-14. These macros were moved to an area of the spreadsheet below the main work area. This arrangement follows the 3-column convention that has been widely adopted by many spreadsheet users. The first column contains the block names of the macros. The second column contains the actual lines of macro instructions. The third column contains a series of labels briefly describing what each macro does. (Note that entering \T as a label requires a label prefix character.)

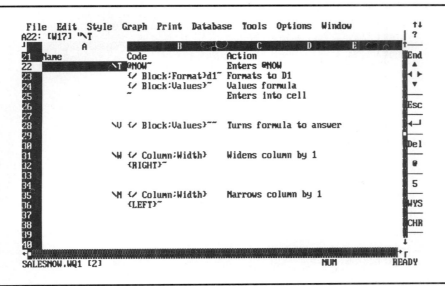

Figure 11-14.   *Three-column layout*

One reason for the popularity of this arrangement is that it works well with the Edit Names Labels command that assigns names to blocks based on labels in adjacent cells. For example, with the @NOW macro in cell B22 and the label \T in cell A22, as in Figure 11-14, you can use the Edit Names Labels Right command to name cell B22 as T. Similarly, you could use the Edit Names Labels Down command to attach the names Name, Code, and Action, to cells A21, B21, and C21. When you use the Labels command to assign names, you must include all the cells on the row or in the column that contain the names you want to use. Blank cells do not create blank names, they are simply ignored.

Macro Libraries

Macros stored in a regular spreadsheet are specific to that spreadsheet. Unlike Shortcuts, which can be recorded as part of the program settings with the Options Update command, macros initially consist of labels stored in the cells of a single worksheet. Macros are saved with that worksheet and are not immediately available when you move to a new worksheet. However, chances are that you will want to use some macros in many different worksheets. You can easily copy macros from one worksheet to another by using the Edit Copy command, but when you copy a named block from one worksheet to another the block name does not go with it. This means that to make a macro active in the worksheet to which it has been copied, you must issue the Edit Names command. If you use the 3-column layout you can use the Labels Right method described in the previous section.

Creating a Macro Library

You may want to collect macros from several worksheets into a single worksheet file called a *macro library*. A macro library is a very useful file to maintain in an office with several users developing Quattro Pro 3 macros. You can share macros and avoid duplication of effort if a common macro library is maintained. A prerequisite to this is adherence to some basic standards of layout such as the 3-column method. In Quattro Pro 3 a macro library is not just a useful collecting place for macros. You can open macro libraries so that the macros they contain can be used in other worksheets.

A macro library is a document that typically consists of nothing but macros. Whenever you execute a macro Quattro Pro 3 looks for the name of the macro in the current worksheet. If the macro you have called on is not there, the program looks to see if there are any open macro libraries. These are worksheets that are specially designated as libraries with the Macro Library command. Any worksheet can be designated as a macro library. To make a macro library out of a worksheet you must load the worksheet and make it current, and then execute the Macro Library command. This command gives you a Yes/No choice, as shown in Figure 11-15. Choose Yes and then save the worksheet. From now on, whenever this worksheet is loaded Quattro Pro 3 will look to it for macros that are not in the current worksheet.

There is no special name for a macro library document; you can use any worksheet name. When more than one macro library is open, Quattro Pro 3 will look into them in the order in which they were opened. Remember, Quattro Pro 3 only looks outside of the current worksheet for a macro if

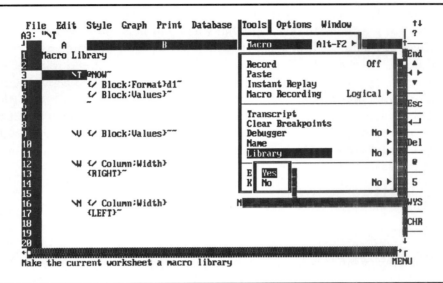

Figure 11-15. *Macro library command*

the current worksheet does not contain the macro you have asked to execute.

Applying Macro Libraries

There are numerous advantages to placing most of your macros into one or more macro libraries. Earlier, the question of protecting and preserving macros was discussed. From an organizational point of view, macros are much safer from accidental corruption when they are stored separately in a macro library, and they are generally easier to keep track of.

Since Quattro Pro 3 allows you to have more than one macro library, you can develop libraries for specific types of work. A macro library for spreadsheet design work could contain 26 instant macros plus many others that you have developed to speed design work. When it comes time to move on to data entry you can close the design macro library and open the data entry macro library, containing 26 different instant macros plus other macro routines. You can save a macro library as part of a workspace so that it is available immediately when you get down to work. You can use some special macros, described later in this chapter, in a macro library to initiate a whole chain of events and provide real power over your Quattro Pro 3 environment.

Macro Control

Quattro Pro 3 contains numerous features for controlling macro execution. You can use these features to determine why a macro does not work the way you expect it to.

Stopping Macros

If you give the command to execute a macro and the effects immediately appear to be different from what you expect, you may want to stop the macro. You do this with CTRL-BREAK (CTRL-SCROLL LOCK on some keyboards). When you press CTRL-BREAK during macro execution, Quattro Pro 3 responds with "Macro Error at *Location.*" *Location* is the cell containing the macro instruction that was interrupted. This message appears at the bottom of the screen. To remove the error message and return to READY mode, just press ESCAPE. You can pause a macro by pressing CTRL-NUMLOCK. Press any key to then resume macro execution.

Debugging Macros

Since Quattro Pro 3 macros execute quickly, it may be hard to tell what goes wrong when a macro misbehaves and it may be hard to stop the macro before it is completed. For this reason, Quattro Pro 3 provides a DEBUG mode of macro execution. This mode is both a sophisticated tool for identifying errors in advanced macro programming and a simple way of seeing your macro run one step at a time. Using the Macro Debugging menu, you can set *breakpoints* in the macro—points at which Quattro Pro 3 will pause during playback. These breakpoints allow you to see sections of the macro at a time.

As an example of how the macro debug feature can help in a relatively simple macro, consider the worksheet in Figure 11-16. This worksheet is

Figure 11-16. \S *macro in trouble*

a monthly expense projection. The expenses are listed in columns by month. The columns are being summed on row 11 using an @SUM formula like the one in B11. The macro visible on the worksheet is designed to sum a column. The macro is supposed to do this by first typing the @SUM function and the opening parenthesis. The macro then moves the cell selector to the top of the column, anchors the block to be summed at that point with a period, and includes all the cells down to the bottom of the column. Finally, a closing parenthesis is added and the formula is entered in the cell with a tilde.

The idea behind the \S macro is that the user will place the cell selector in C11 and press ALT-S to activate the macro and sum the column. But as you can see from Figure 11-16, the results are not as expected. Cell C11 contains the formula @SUM(C10..C8192), which is not only incorrect but also a circular formula, as noted by the message CIRC at the bottom of the screen. The debug feature should help show where the problem lies.

To activate DEBUG mode, press the Step key (SHIFT-F2). The message DEBUG appears at the bottom of the screen. From this point until you reissue the SHIFT-F2 command, any macro you execute will cause the debug windows to appear. Before executing the macro you want to debug, however, you should make sure that the conditions are correct. For example, in the case of the worksheet in Figure 11-16, the incorrect formula needs to be deleted from cell C11 before the macro is retried. If you then issue the command to run the sample macro \S that needs to be debugged, Quattro Pro 3 opens up two windows in the lower half of the screen, as shown in Figure 11-17. In the upper window, called the *debug window*, Quattro Pro 3 shows the location of the macro you are executing and places the cursor on the first instruction. (The apostrophe is not an instruction, merely the label indicator.) The lower window, the trace window, shows you any trace cells that you have specified. This feature is used in advanced debugging, which is described in Chapter 12.

The SPACEBAR is used to play back the macro one step at a time. Pressing the ENTER key tells Quattro Pro 3 to run the macro until the next breakpoint. For a simple investigation of a malfunctioning macro you will not need to set breakpoints; you can use the SPACEBAR to play back the macro one step at a time. (Breakpoints are discussed further in Chapter 12.)

In Figure 11-18 you can see that the problem with this macro has become apparent. The END, UP ARROW combination took the cell selector only to cell C10, and the END, DOWN ARROW combination is about to take the cell selector to the bottom of the worksheet. You can abort the macro at this

File	Edit	Style	Graph	Print	Database	Tools	Options	Window	↑↓

C11:

	A	B	C	D	E	F	G
1							
2							
3		JAN	FEB	MAR	APR	MAY	JUN
4	POLK ST.						
5	Lease	350	355	361	366	371	377
6	Phones	230	233	237	241	244	248
7	Telex	110	112	113	115	117	119
8	Electric	120	122	124	125	127	129
9	Res. Rent	1,100	1,117	1,133	1,150	1,167	1,185
10	==
11	TOTALS	1,910					
12							
13							

```
┌DEBUG WINDOW───────────────────────────────────────────────────┐
│                                                                │
│ [CPRINTFA]E16: @SUM(<END><UP>,<END><DOWN>)~                     │
│ [CPRINTFA]E17:                                                 │
│ ─TRACE WINDOW──────────────────────────────────────────────── │
│                                                                │
│                                                                │
└────────────────────────────────────────────────────────────────┘
```

CPRINTFA.WQ1 [1]   NUM   MACRO READY

Figure 11-17. *The DEBUG screen*

Figure 11-18.   *The problem revealed by DEBUG*

point by typing **/** for the Macro Debugging menu shown in Figure 11-19. Select the Abort option from the menu to return to READY mode. Note that this action does not reverse the effect of SHIFT-F2, which will continue to cause macros to be executed in DEBUG mode until you press it again. The other options on the Macro Debugging menu will be examined in Chapter 12, which explores more advanced macro applications.

Special Macros

A macro consists of instructions stored in a series of spreadsheet cells. You enter the instructions as labels, using either the exact keys you press to enter a command, as in **/FR** for the File Retrieve menu command; or menu equivalents, as in {/File;Retrieve}. The menu equivalents are used by Quattro Pro 3 when it records your commands, both in the macro RECORD mode and the Transcript log. You execute macros instructions with the

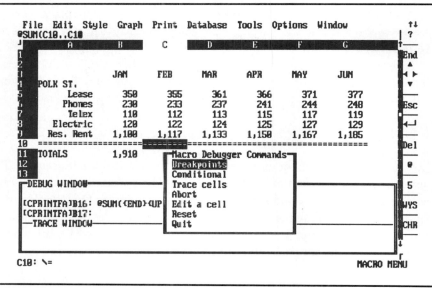

Figure 11-19. *The DEBUG menu*

Macro Execute command, either by pointing at the first cell in the macro or by looking up its name with the F3 key. You can create an unlimited number of named macros that you can select with ALT-F2 and F3. You can create 26 instant macros named \A through \Z. You activate these macros by pressing the ALT key and the letter. In addition to these, there are several special types of macros that you can use.

Automatic Macros

You can have Quattro Pro 3 activate a macro as soon as the file in which it is stored is retrieved. This *Startup macro* is normally called \0, but you can use a different name, such as FIRST, as long as you record your choice with the Options Startup and Options Update commands. The Startup macro works well with the autoload file, which is a worksheet file that is retrieved from disk as soon as you load Quattro Pro 3. The name of the file that the program looks for when it is loaded is normally called QUAT-TRO.WQ1, but you can change it to another name (such as FIRST.WQ1) by using the Options Startup menu. If you create a Startup macro in a worksheet named as the autoload file, you can initiate any series of events that macros can control.

A simple application of the Startup macro feature is to have Quattro Pro 3 display a list of files every time you load the program. To do this, enter the label '/FR or

{/ File;Retrieve}

into an empty worksheet and name the cell as the Startup macro, \0. Then save the file using the name QUATTRO.WQ1 or whatever name you have selected as your autoload file. When you next start up Quattro Pro 3, the first thing you will see is a list of files from which to select. Note that the label '/FR is the exact key equivalent of the command, while the words in braces are the menu equivalent of the command.

Command-Line Macros

If you want to load Quattro Pro 3 and then a particular spreadsheet, you can do so without using the autoload feature. Type the name of the file after the name of the program when you are loading from the DOS prompt or the command line. For example, suppose you have to respond to an urgent request for a price quote. Your pricing calculations are in a file called PRICING.WQ1. You have turned on your PC and are at the DOS prompt ready to load Quattro Pro 3. Simply type

Q PRICING

and press ENTER. The program will load and immediately retrieve the pricing worksheet.

You can go one step beyond this by naming a macro on the command line as well. Thus, if you have a macro in the PRICING worksheet called QUOTE that is a series of steps to produce a price quote, you could type

Q PRICING QUOTE

at the DOS prompt and press ENTER. The program would then load itself, the worksheet, and the macro. This level of flexibility, together with the speed with which Quattro Pro 3 loads, opens a wide range of possibilities for your applications. For example, you could set up several different DOS batch files to load Quattro Pro 3 together with different worksheets. (DOS batch files are described in Appendix A.) The automatic and command-line macro-loading options take on particular significance when you work with the macro commands described in the next chapter.

You can also load a workspace from the command line. You do this by specifying the full name of the workspace file, as in

Q PRICING.WSP

which loads a workspace called PRICING.WSP. If this workspace includes a worksheet that has been designated as a macro library, and includes an autoexecute macro, then you can initiate a whole series of events from the command line.

A Macro-Executing Macro

When you have created a number of named macros and want a quick way to execute them, you can develop a macro that will help you select one macro from a macro list. You could create this macro-executing macro by entering the label

{/ Name;Execute}{NAME}

into a blank cell. If you use the Edit Names Create command to name this cell with an instant macro, possibly \M for macro executing, the next time that you need to execute a named macro, you can simply press ALT-M. The macro uses the Macro Execute command and the F3 function {NAME} to display a list of named macros from which you can choose.

Macro Writing and Editing

As you have seen, there are several ways to create macros in Quattro Pro 3. You can record your keystrokes. You can use sections of the log of your keystrokes recorded by Transcript, as described later in this chapter. You can also write the macro yourself, using your knowledge of Quattro Pro 3 to compose a set of keystrokes. You can combine sections of macros that you have written with sections produced by the other methods. Writing or editing macros becomes more important as your macros become more complex. The chances are that you will need to edit lengthy macros to improve their performance, streamline their arrangement in the worksheet, or correct bugs in their operation.

Composing Macros

Before composing a macro, it is helpful to make notes of the operations you want the macro to perform and sketch out the required steps. When you enter the macro instructions into the worksheet, remember that you can use either direct keystrokes for menu selections or the menu equivalents. Thus, you could enter a macro to convert the current cell into a value as /EV or

{/ Block;Values}~~

While the first approach might seem quicker, it is more difficult to read. The second approach does not require that you memorize all of the menu equivalents. You can look these up by using ALT-F3 and selecting /Commands from the menu. The commands are logically grouped together and easy to find.

Often you will be able to put together a macro from several sources. For example, you can use the record method to capture the keystrokes for part of an operation and then add those recorded keystrokes to the rest of the macro with the Edit Move command. When you are combining macro instructions, you may want to use several of the techniques described here.

Repeating and Abbreviating

When you use the record method to capture keystrokes, you sometimes get rather cumbersome lines of instructions like this one:

{/ Block;Copy}{DOWN}{DOWN}{DOWN}{DOWN}{DOWN}{RIGHT}{RIGHT}

Quattro Pro 3 records each cursor movement as a separate keystroke, repeating the keystroke representation over and over. However, you can refer to a series of repeated keystrokes by the name of the key representation and a number. That is, the key representation takes a numeric argument enclosed within braces, as in {DOWN 5}. You can use this system with any of the macro key representations listed in Table 11-2 except for {CR} and {MENU}.

The number used as the argument can be a number you type in or a number in a cell referenced by the cell coordinate or a block name. Thus, {DOWN A1} causes the DOWN ARROW action to be repeated five times if A1 contains the number 5 or a formula that results in 5. Likewise, the instruction {DOWN TIMES} causes the action to be repeated five times if the block TIMES contains the number 5 or a formula that results in 5.

You can further shorten your macros if you refer to the arrow keys as follows: DOWN as {D}, UP as {U}, LEFT as {L}, and RIGHT as {R}. Also, you can use {ESC} instead of {ESCAPE} and {BS} instead of {BACKSPACE}. Thus, {DOWN 5} becomes {D 5} and the lengthy instruction just given can be reduced to this:

{/ Block;Copy}{D 5}{R 2}

This abbreviated version is easy to read and much more compact. However, you will probably want to look carefully at the use of multiple cursor-movement keystrokes in your macros. In general, you will find macros more reliable if you use block names wherever possible, instead of the pointing method of identifying cell coordinates.

Splitting Macro Lines

At times you may not be able to reduce the length of recorded macro instructions by using the abbreviation method. However, you may still want to split the macro line into more manageable sections. One way to do this is to copy the line that needs to be split and then edit both versions. For example, you might want to split the following line:

{/ Sort;block}{BS}.{END}{RIGHT}{END}{DOWN}

To split this line of instructions, first copy the line from its current cell to the one below it (assuming that the cell you are copying to is empty or contains expendable data). Then highlight the original instruction and press F2 to edit it. Use the BACKSPACE key to erase all the text to the right of the period. Then press ENTER to return the edited line to the cell. Move your cell selector to the copy of the original line and press F2 to edit it. Press HOME and then press DELETE to remove all of the text up to and including the period. Press ENTER to return the edited contents to the cell. The resulting cells will look like this:

{/ Sort;block}{BS}.

{END}{RIGHT}{END}{DOWN}

You now have the macro instruction in two short labels rather than one long one. This technique often helps to make macro instructions more manageable.

There may also be times when it is prudent to combine lines of macro code. For example, earlier in Figure 11-11 you saw that Quattro Pro 3 recorded a single tilde on one line at the end of a macro. This was later added to the line above to make the macro easier to copy and keep together.

Transcript Macros

The Transcript feature keeps track of all your keystrokes while you are using Quattro Pro 3. It saves the keystrokes to a log file on disk so that you can reconstruct your work after a power outage or a serious operator error. The format in which Transcript records your keystrokes is the same as that used in macro recording. You can actually copy sections of the Transcript log to your worksheet for use in macros.

Using the Transcript Log
For Macros

If you have loaded Quattro Pro 3 and have performed an operation that you would like to incorporate into a macro, you can access the Transcript log of your actions by using the Tools Macro command or by pressing the Macro key (ALT-F2). From the Macro menu, select Transcript. A window showing the Transcript log will open in the middle of the screen. You can see this window in Figure 11-20, which shows an accounts receivable worksheet in which a new column for Total Owed is being added. The most recent actions are at the bottom of the list. You use the UP ARROW or LEFT ARROW key to scroll back up through the log to view earlier actions. Mouse users can click the mouse pointer on the word Transcript to produce the Transcript log. Hold down the mouse button to continuously scroll up the list.

The line in the left margin of the Transcript window marks the activity since the last File Retrieve, Open, Save, or New command or since the last time Transcript saved the log. Transcript uses the files you save on disk as a basis for the re-creation of your work in the event of data loss. You can see the File Retrieve command in Figure 11-21, where the log has been scrolled and the Transcript menu activated by typing /.

Suppose that you copy the new formula created in cell G9 of the accounts receivable worksheet down to the bottom of the model, using the END key. Having performed the action you would like to make a macro out of it. Press

Figure 11-20. *Transcript window*

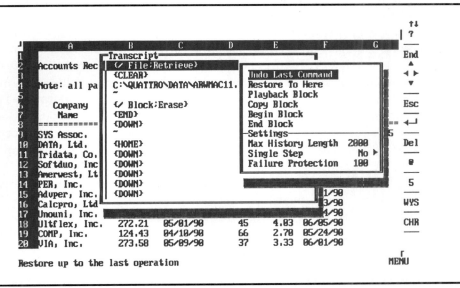

Figure 11-21. *The Transcript menu*

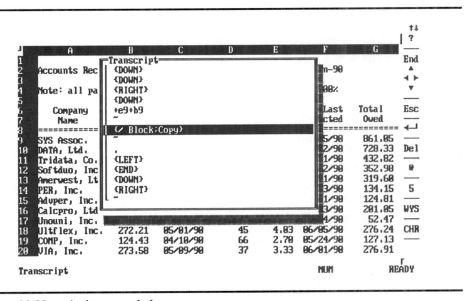

Figure 11-22. *Action recorded*

ALT-F2, select Transcript, and you will see that the action has been recorded, as shown in Figure 11-22, where it occupies the last two lines of the log. To copy a section of the log to your worksheet, first place the highlight bar on the first line of instructions you want to copy, as was done in Figure 11-22. Then type / for the Transcript menu. Select Begin Block from the menu. The menu will disappear and leave a triangle marking the beginning point of the block. You can move the highlight bar to the last line of the section you want to copy. Type / and select End Block. This marks all of the commands chosen from the beginning to the end of the block with a triangle, as you can see in Figure 11-23.

Having marked the block of Transcript code, type / again and select Copy Block from the Transcript menu. You will be returned to the worksheet and prompted for a macro name to create or modify, as shown in Figure 11-24. This allows you to name the worksheet cell into which you are about to paste the Transcript code. You can enter a name if you have one picked out already, or just press ENTER to continue with the copy operation without naming the destination cell. When you press ENTER or enter a name you will be prompted for a cell location, just as you are when you use the Macro Paste command. You can paste the code into the current worksheet or into a macro sheet by entering the worksheet name in

Figure 11-23. *Block marked*

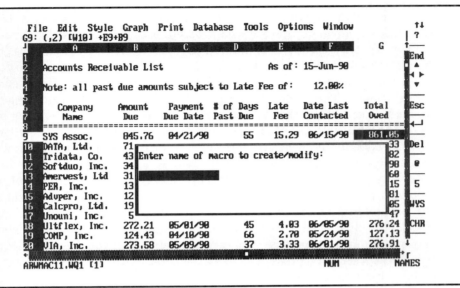

Figure 11-24.   *Name prompt*

brackets before the address. After specifying the first cell of the block to which you want the instructions copied, press ENTER and the copy is

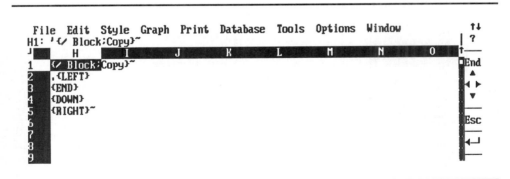

Figure 11-25.   *Posted Transcript code*

completed. In Figure 11-25 you can see the results of copying from the Transcript Log with H1 as the destination.

Bear in mind that the destination cell must be above enough empty cells to accommodate the number of lines you are copying into the worksheet. The Transcript log records the copy action as a Macro Paste and remembers the block markers. You can move these to other parts of the Transcript log with the Begin Block and End Block commands.

Other Transcript Commands

The Undo Last Command option at the top of the Transcript menu is useful when you do not have the regular Undo feature activated. To use this command and the Restore To Here command successfully, maintain your position in the spreadsheet before issuing the command. When you issue the Restore To Here command Quattro Pro 3 carries out all of the actions since the last file save or retrieval. If you make an error and then move all over your worksheet trying to fix it before remembering Transcript and selecting Restore To Here, you can get unexpected and chaotic results. It is best to use this command as soon as you realize you have made a mistake.

You might wonder how far back you can go to get code for macros from the Transcript log. Notice the Settings section of the Transcript menu in Figure 11-21. The Max History Length option is currently set at 2000 lines. This is how many lines of instructions Transcript will record before discarding line 1. You can increase this setting to store more of your actions, resulting in larger Transcript log files on disk, or you can shorten the setting to conserve space. The maximum setting is 25,000 lines. To change this setting, simply highlight the menu option and press ENTER. Note that adding to Max History Length increases the memory area used by Transcript.

In Figure 11-21 you can see that the option called Single Step is currently set to No, meaning that if you use the Playback Block command the code in the log will be played back one step at a time, similar to the DEBUG mode of macro execution. Setting this option to Yes provides a greater level of control when playing back Transcript with the Restore To Here or Playback Block commands.

Under the Transcript settings, the Failure Protection option refers to the number of lines recorded before Transcript saves the log to disk.

Currently this is set to 100. Failure Protection carries the same limit as the Max History Length, 1 to 25,000. If you decrease this number you will notice more disk activity, but recovering from a disaster will likely be more complete. Bear in mind that the Undo feature will reverse some actions if you use it immediately, providing a front line of defense ahead of Transcript.

12 *Further Macros and Macro Commands*

This chapter explores the more advanced aspects of creating Quattro Pro 3 macros, including automatic macros and macro libraries. You will learn about the macro commands that allow you to create menu-driven applications with Quattro Pro 3. You will see examples of macros that prompt for user input and review advanced @functions, such as @CELL. You will also learn how to customize the actual program menus of Quattro Pro 3, using the Edit Menus command to cut and paste menu items and arrange them the way you want, thus developing a unique program interface.

Macro Commands

In addition to using macros for a fixed set of instructions that replicate keystrokes as if they were entered manually from the keyboard, you can use special macro commands to access features and functions that are not available from the keyboard. The following sections discuss the theory of macro commands and review the individual commands. These range from {BEEP}, which sounds your computer's beep to alert the user, to {GET-LABEL}, which prompts for user input, to {MENUBRANCH}, which branches to the data for a custom menu.

The Role of Macro Commands

The basic purpose of macro commands is to add logic to macros, thus enabling you to create macros that evaluate conditions and choose between different courses of action based on parameters you specify. For this reason the macro commands are a lot like programming statements. This does not mean that macro commands are just for programmers. Typical power users are quite capable of taking advantage of this facility, either to simplify their own work or to prepare Quattro Pro 3 applications for others. However, the macro commands do permit you to develop macros to such a high level of sophistication that complete texts have been devoted to programming in macro command languages. Since the Quattro Pro 3 macro commands closely follow the syntax and format of the 1-2-3 macro command language you will find that texts on that subject are generally applicable to Quattro Pro 3. You should bear in mind that there are some commands in Quattro Pro 3 that do not exist in 1-2-3 Release 2, and that the design of Quattro Pro 3 has alleviated the need for some of the programming steps necessary in 1-2-3. These differences will be pointed out as the commands are described in this chapter.

Using the {BRANCH} Command

A simple, yet typical situation where a macro command can be very effectively applied is the need to repeat a series of operations. Suppose you have a column of values that need to be rounded to two decimal places. You edit the first cell and place **@ROUND(** in front of the value. Then you place **,2)** at the end of the value and enter the new information into the cell. You could use a macro called \R to do this:

\R {EDIT}{HOME}@ROUND({END},2)~

After performing this action on one value you would move down to the next. Alternatively, you can add this movement to the macro. Since the DOWN ARROW key enters data from EDIT mode you could amend the macro to read:

\R {EDIT}{HOME}@ROUND({END},2){DOWN}

If the column of values is long, you will need to repeat the macro many times. Instead of repeatedly executing the same macro, you can incorporate this repetition into the macro by means of the macro command {BRANCH}. The {BRANCH} command tells Quattro Pro 3 to go to a new cell and read the instructions from there. Like @functions, many of the macro commands require arguments. Include these within the braces, separated from the name of the command by a space. Connect multiple arguments with commas, just as you do in @functions.

The following \R macro tells Quattro Pro 3 to go back and repeat the macro. When the first line of code is read the second line tells Quattro Pro 3 to return to the first, the actual cell named \R:

\R {EDIT}{HOME}@ROUND({END},2){DOWN} {BRANCH \R}

Once you execute \R the macro will loop continuously until you stop it. You can stop the macro with CTRL-BREAK or pause it with CTRL-NUM LOCK. Although this is a fairly crude way of controlling macro execution, it is simple to implement.

Using the @CELL Command

The @CELL command and its companions, @CELLPOINTER and @CELLINDEX, are very useful in macros when you need to get information about a cell. For example, suppose you want to know whether cell A1 is blank. There are several methods you could use, but the simplest is @CELL("type",A1). This returns b if the cell is blank, v if it contains a value, or l if it contains a label. The codes you can use in the @CELL commands and more examples of the function are provided later in this chapter. The information returned by the @CELL function covers address, row, column, contents, type, prefix, protection status, width, and format.

Bear in mind that the @CELL response itself may be a label, so an {IF} or @IF statement using @CELL may need to refer to the result as a string in quotes, like the "b" in this formula, which returns VACANT if A1 is blank:

@IF(@CELL("type",A1)="b","VACANT","OCCUPIED")

Using the {INPUT} Command

Many macros are designed to make a worksheet easier for novices to use. Often, you would like a macro to prompt the user for the required pieces of data. An example of this is shown in Figure 12-1 where an automobile loan is being calculated. Cells E8 through E10 are formatted with text format to show the calculations that they perform. The calculations all stem from the price of the automobile. A macro has been designed to ask the customer the price on which they want to base the loan. In Figure 12-2 you can see some of the macro code. The first line of the macro places the price of the automobile into the cell named PR, using the {GETNUMBER} command.

A {GETNUMBER} statement needs two pieces of information: the text of the prompt or question, enclosed in quotes; and the location into which to place the response. This location can be a cell coordinate or a block name. Block names are preferable since they are more constant than cell references. When you activate this macro you are prompted with

When you type a number and press ENTER, the number is placed into the designated cell, E3. If you enter something other than a number, you get an ERR message.

Finding Commands

You can use Quattro Pro 3 to look up macro commands as you are writing macros. The Macro key (SHIFT-F3) shows a list of different types of macro commands, as shown in Figure 12-3. The commands that prompt for user input are called the *interactive commands*. If you select Interactive from the SHIFT-F3 list, you will see the possibilities shown in Figure 12-4. Highlight the one you want to use in your macro and press ENTER to place it on the edit line. In the case of user-input commands, you can use a whole series one after the other to prompt for all of the variables in the loan

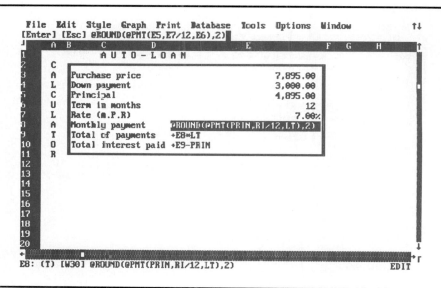

Figure 12-1. *Auto loan calculator*

Figure 12-2. *Macro code*

Figure 12-3. *Macro commands*

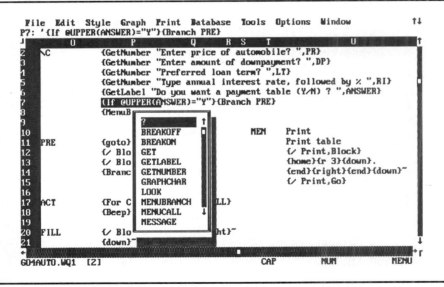

Figure 12-4. *Interactive commands*

calculation. The {GETLABEL} command you see in Figure 12-4 handles label input in a continuation of the \C macro. This command has been set up to place the response in a location stated as a named block, ANSWER.

Using the {IF} Command

The example is designed so that the responses to the price, down payment, and term questions of the loan calculation are placed in their respective cells. The {GETLABEL} command asks the user if he or she wants to see a payment table, and places the response in a cell named ANSWER. The next line of the macro, on row 7 of the worksheet, evaluates the contents of the ANSWER cell, using the very powerful {IF} command. This command is used to make the macro evaluate a specific condition before proceeding. Like the @IF function, it is followed by a condition statement. If the cell named ANSWER contains the label Y, then the macro branches to a macro cell called PRE. The {BRANCH} command moves the flow of the macro to the cell specified in its argument. If the condition is not True, then the macro continues with the next line, which is a {MENUBRANCH} command.

Another Branch Macro

The PRE macro in Figure 12-2 is activated if you type **Y** in response to the prompt in line 6 for a payment table. The instructions in PRE create a payment table. This is done by first exposing a block of cells called CALC (whose contents were previously disguised with the Hide format) as shown in Figure 12-5. These are the titles and first two lines of calculations in the payment table. After resetting the format of those cells so that they can be seen, the macro branches to ACT.

Using the {FOR} Command

The macro called ACT, shown in Figure 12-6, uses the {FOR} command to control repetition of a task. In this case the task it repeats is a macro called FILL, which copies a line of the payment table once. The {FOR} command has several arguments. The first is the location of the counter, in this case a cell named COUNT. The second argument is the starting number to be

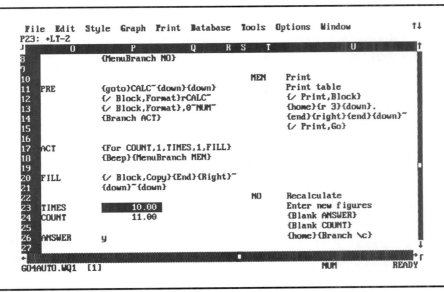

Figure 12-5.   *Exposed cells*

placed in the counter. The next argument is the stop, the total number of times the command repeats, in this case the cell called TIMES. Located at P23, this cell is the number of periods in the term of the loan, minus two because of the lines already entered and hidden in the worksheet. The

Figure 12-6.   *The {FOR} command*

fourth argument is the step, the amount to increment the counter after each iteration. The last argument is the cell address or block name containing the cell routine to be executed. The result of a complete execution of the \C macro, in which the user responded **Y** to the payment table question, is shown in Figure 12-7.

Evaluating Input

When you are designing applications to be used by others, there are many factors to consider that do not arise when you are simply creating macros for your own use. For example, the macro command used to prompt for the payment table in the loan calculation model might have been written as

{If ANSWER="Yes"}{Branch PRE}

This would require that the user enter three characters, thus increasing the chance of mistakes. The {IF} command is not case-sensitive, so **YES** and **yes** will be accepted as well as **Yes**. You could make the response requirement a single letter to simplify the user's role by requiring Y or N.

```
 File  Edit  Style  Graph  Print  Database  Tools  Options  Window        ↑↓
A1: [W4]
 J    A B    C       D       E    F  G    H        I         J          ↑
 1    C               A U T O - L O A N
 2    C
 3    A    Purchase price     7,895.00      # Payment  Interest   Balance
 4    L    Down payment       3,000.00      1 423.55     28.55   4,500.00
 5    C    Principal          4,895.00      2 423.55     26.25   4,102.70
 6    U    Term in months          12       3 423.55     23.93   3,703.09
 7    L    Rate (A.P.R)         7.00%        4 423.55     21.60   3,301.14
 8    A    Monthly payment      423.55       5 423.55     19.26   2,896.84
 9    T    Total of payments  5,082.60       6 423.55     16.90   2,490.19
10    O    Total interest paid  187.60       7 423.55     14.53   2,081.17
11    R                                      8 423.55     12.14   1,669.76
12                                           9 423.55      9.74   1,255.95
13                                          10 423.55      7.33     839.73
14                                          11 423.55      4.90     421.07
15                                          12 423.55      2.46       0.00
16
17
18
19
20                                                                        ↓
 ←□▪▪▪▪▪▪▪▪▪▪▪▪▪▪▪▪▪▪▪▪▪▪▪▪▪▪▪▪▪▪▪▪▪▪▪▪▪▪▪▪▪▪▪▪▪▪▪▪▪▪▪▪▪→ r
 G04AUTO.WQ1  [1]                                  NUM         READY
```

Figure 12-7. *Completed command*

There is actually a redundant function in the statement used in this example:

{If @UPPER(ANSWER)="Y"}{Branch PRE}

The @UPPER function, which turns the contents of ANSWER into capitals, is not required since {IF} evaluates y and Y as the same response. However, there may be situations where you would like to maintain tight control of the input to ensure accuracy. You can demand an exact response by using @EXACT, as in

{If @EXACT(ANSWER,"Yes")}{Branch PRE}

Here, the user would have to type **Yes** to proceed. Entering **YES** would not be acceptable.

Providing Feedback

In Figure 12-6, the {BEEP} command is used in the ACT macro. This sounds the beep when the payment table is completed. Tasks that take more than a few seconds to complete and keep the user waiting can benefit from a {BEEP} to alert the user of the task's completion.

Menus Created by Macros

Following the completion of the ACT macro in the loan payment example, the macro branches to a menu by using the {MENUBRANCH} command. One of the most popular uses of the macro commands is to create customized menus within a spreadsheet to simplify its operation, either for yourself or for other users. You can place macro menus in macro libraries to make them available in any worksheet. Figure 12-8 shows the menu named MEN that is called from within the loan calculation macro. This menu offers the user three choices: printing the loan table, changing the figures in the loan calculation, or saving the worksheet.

Writing Macro Menus

Macro-generated menus follow the same format as regular Quattro Pro 3 menus, with a vertical list of the options, descriptions of the options at the top of the screen, and the first letter method of selection. Quattro Pro 3 automatically places the menu on the screen in a suitable location, based on the position of the cell selector when the menu is invoked, as well as the size of the menu. To let you know that you are still in the middle of a macro, and not in a Quattro Pro 3 menu, the program automatically displays the MACRO message at the bottom of the screen.

When the user selects one of the items on the menu in Figure 12-8, macro commands are activated to carry out the menu item. You can easily create such a menu to operate macros in your worksheets. However, remember that this menu is part of this worksheet, not a part of the overall Quattro Pro 3 menu system. You can use the Edit Menus command to splice macros into the system menu, as described later in this chapter, but the macros remain specific to one spreadsheet. You can place macro menus in a macro library if you would like to access them from any spreadsheet.

All of the instructions that make up the menu macro in Figure 12-8 are shown in Figure 12-9. Each menu item is in a separate but contiguous

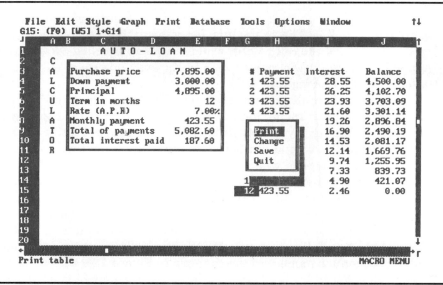

Figure 12-8. *The MEN menu*

Figure 12-9.   *Menu macro code*

column, listing the parts of the macro on consecutive rows. The first row is the name of the item as it is to appear on the menu. Quattro Pro 3 can normally display about 12 menu items in a single level of a menu macro out of a total of 256. The actual number of menu items displayed depends on the position of the cell pointer when the macro is called. Quattro Pro 3 dynamically adjusts the menu size to fit the available space on the screen and to avoid obscuring your work.

You can create multiple-level menus just as in the Quattro Pro 3 menu system itself. Each menu item at the same level should begin with a different first letter if you want to be able to use the first-letter method of picking them. The second line is the explanation of the item that appears at the top of the screen when the item is highlighted. In 80 x 25 display mode, menu item names can be up to 55 characters long, and the explanation line can be up to 72 characters long. (In normal practice, make the menu name brief and the explanation lengthier.) Below the explanation text are the macro commands that are executed when an item is chosen. To refer to a menu like this in a {MENUBRANCH} command the top-left cell of the menu is named. In the example in Figure 12-9 the cell is T10.

Note that in cell U13 of Figure 12-9 the command {r 3} is used instead of {right}{right}{right}. This is an abbreviation that you can use with all of the direction commands. It helps to shorten the macro and makes it easier to change should the number of repetitions be incorrect.

You can see from Figure 12-9 that the placement of macros in adjacent columns stipulated by the menu macro command syntax could make it difficult to see all of the commands on a given line, particularly if you could not widen the columns. However, this is not a problem for the execution of the macro since Quattro Pro 3 does not care if the entire command is visible.

Macro Menu Control

When the user selects any one of the menu items in the example in the last two figures, the commands beneath that item are executed and Quattro Pro 3 returns to the READY mode. Alternatively, you could refer the macro back to the menu for more choices. You would accomplish this with the command

{MENUBRANCH MEN}

at the bottom of each item. If you take this approach you will probably want to include an option to quit the menu.

Another example of a menu macro is shown in Figure 12-10, where an employee database has been set up with a four-item menu offering the options Enter, Sort, Print, and Quit. The Quit option takes the user out of the menu and back to the READY mode. Most of the menu macro cells are shown in Figure 12-11. Notice that each menu item except Quit leads the user to a second menu. For example, the Sort option leads to SORTMENU. The sort macro uses block names instead of cell references when identifying the sort blocks. This makes the macro easier to read and minimizes its length.

Menu Types

There are several approaches to creating customized menus in Quattro Pro 3. There are the menus you create with macros and there are the system menus that you access with the / key. You can also create a type of menu using graphics, as described in Chapter 13. The Edit Menus command described in detail later in this chapter is used to modify the system menu structure. Although the system menu structure can be modified, it remains

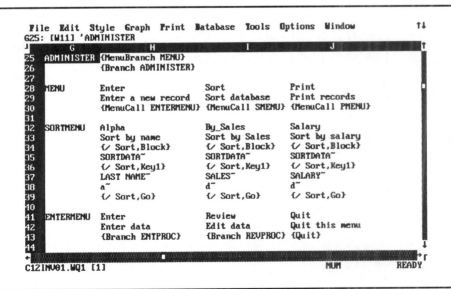

Figure 12-10.   *Menu macro*

```
File  Edit  Style  Graph  Print  Database  Tools  Options  Window        ↑↓
G25: [W11] 'ADMINISTER
     G         H              I               J
25  ADMINISTER {MenuBranch MENU}
26            {Branch ADMINISTER}
27
28  MENU      Enter          Sort            Print
29            Enter a new record  Sort database   Print records
30            {MenuCall ENTERMENU} {MenuCall SMENU} {MenuCall PMENU}
31
32  SORTMENU  Alpha          By_Sales        Salary
33            Sort by name   Sort by Sales   Sort by salary
34            {/ Sort,Block} {/ Sort,Block}  {/ Sort,Block}
35            SORTDATA~       SORTDATA~        SORTDATA~
36            {/ Sort,Key1}  {/ Sort,Key1}   {/ Sort,Key1}
37            LAST NAME~      SALES~           SALARY~
38            a~             d~              d~
39            {/ Sort,Go}    {/ Sort,Go}     {/ Sort,Go}
40
41  ENTERMENU Enter          Review          Quit
42            Enter data     Edit data       Quit this menu
43            {Branch ENTPROC} {Branch REVPROC} {Quit}
44
C12INV01.WQ1 [1]                              NUM         READY
```

Figure 12-11.   *More macro code*

constant between worksheets; that is, it is not worksheet-dependent. This is an important difference from the macro menus you create with the {MENUBRANCH} and {MENUCALL} commands, such as the one shown in Figure 12-10. These macro menus, which consist of a series of macros in consecutive columns, are created in one worksheet. While they can be shared by making the worksheet that contains them into a macro library, the library must be open for them to work, so they are still worksheet-dependent. By using the autoload file and the \0 macro you can have Quattro Pro 3 load directly to a macro library and a macro menu. However, this menu is still specific to a worksheet, unlike items that are part of the system menu tree that you can customize with the Edit Menus command.

Flow Control

On row 28 of Figure 12-11 you can see the beginning of the set of instructions called MENU. These are the menu item names. Below them are the descriptions of the items and the actions each one performs. Notice that the first three items lead to further menus by means of the {MENUCALL} command. This differs from the {MENUBRANCH} command in that the flow of the macro returns to the macro stated as the {MENUCALL} argument after the actions in the menu have been completed. This serves to keep the user within the menu structure. The fourth item on the MENU menu is Quit. This provides a direct (and easy to pick) route out of the menu and back to the READY mode. The menu created by the MENU macro was shown earlier in Figure 12-10. Most of the contents of SORTMENU, called by the second option on the menu, are shown in Figure 12-11. As you can see, SORTMENU is a series of database sort actions to rearrange the data according to LAST NAME, SALES, and so on. The cells in the database have been named SORTDATA.

The ENTERMENU code can be seen in Figures 12-11 and 12-12. The first option, Enter, is the most important. It leads to the ENTPROC macro, a series of prompts for data. The data is placed in a vertical set of cells named ENT1, ENT2, and so on, located elsewhere in the worksheet. The entry of data is followed by a move with the {GOTO} command to view the cells where the data has been placed. The user is prompted to respond **Y** or **N** to the question "Is the data correct?" The response is placed in a cell called DYN.

You can see in Figure 12-12 that the {IF} command is employed to check the user's response. The @CELL function is used to determine the contents

Figure 12-12.   *The ENTERMENU code*

of DYN. If the response is **Y**, then the macro proceeds with the {BRANCH} command following the {IF} statement. This leads to the PUT macro, which places the user input from ENT1, ENT2, and so on into the database. The combined data entry cells ENT1 through ENT5 are called ENTRY. The PUT macro inserts a blank row into the database called SORTDATA, and then transposes the vertical list of entered data from ENTRY into the SORTDATA block. After new data has been entered the macro loops back to the first menu, ADMINISTER, where the user can choose to sort the expanded database or add more data.

You can see that menu instructions like those in Figure 12-12 can become crowded. In fact, the instructions for the Review option in column I were curtailed so that all of the Enter option could be seen. There is certainly not room to annotate the steps in the menu macro when it is arranged this way. Furthermore, you may already have several macros in a worksheet and want to add a menu to access them, yet you do not want to move the macros around. One solution is to place most of the menu item code in a separate area and direct flow to it from the third line of the menu macro. The following arrangement provides menu access to macros called PD and SD:

Print	Sort	Quit
Print data	Sort data	Leave the menu
{BRANCH PD}	{BRANCH SD}	{QUIT}

If the user picks Print, the PD macro is executed. If the user picks Sort, the SD macro is executed. If the user picks Quit, the macro ends, whether it was called with {MENUBRANCH} or {MENUCALL}.

Subroutines

An alternative to this approach is to call on macros with a subroutine command. In its simplest form, this is the name of the macro in braces, as in {PD}, entered on a line by itself. When Quattro Pro 3 encounters this statement in a macro it looks for the macro called PD and executes it. The difference between a subroutine and a branch is that the macro flow after a subroutine is back to the place from which the subroutine was called, whereas flow after a branch does not return but continues in the new direction. The subroutine is normally referred to as {*subroutine*} in lower-case to indicate that the only argument is a variable. You can actually add data to a subroutine, a technique described later under the heading "The {*subroutine*} Command."

In the case of {BRANCH PD}, the flow is directed to PD when the user picks Print and it terminates there (unless the menu itself was generated with {MENUCALL}, which essentially runs menu choices as subroutines; or unless the PD macro redirects the flow). In the following example the selection of List runs a macro called SORT_DATA and then the PRINT_DATA macro. The SORT_DATA macro does not have to contain any statements directing macro flow. Quattro Pro 3 automatically returns to the line after the SORT_DATA call in the macro.

List
Sort and print list
{SORT_DATA}
{PRINT_DATA}

Note that Quattro Pro 3's ability to refer to macros by full block names makes it easy to read and write macro statements, particularly as they begin to approach a programming language in their complexity of flow control. However, it is important to make a distinction between names used to refer to blocks of data cells, names used for macros, and the names of macro commands. You may want to establish some conventions for naming to help you distinguish between the various parts of macro code. As you can see from the examples so far, block names, macro names, and macro commands can all be given in either upper- or lowercase. This means you could use a system such as all uppercase for block names, all lowercase for macro names, and initial capitals for macro commands. Also, you should avoid using two part names for blocks or macros, unless you connect them with an underline. For example, SORT_DATA is better than SORT DATA, because the latter is ambiguous and might be taken to mean two blocks, SORT and DATA.

One of the main appeals of the {*subroutine*} command is that it provides the ability to assemble macros from reusable parts. Thus, the SORT_DATA macro might be a sorting operation that is used in several other macros. Instead of repeating the same code each time sorting is required, the SORT_DATA macro can simply be referenced as a subroutine. A simple subroutine can store commonly used commands such as the standard steps for printing:

{CALC}   Recalculate spreadsheet

{/ Print;Align}   Align printer

{/ Print;ResetAll}   Reset printer settings

Placing this macro in a subroutine called PRE_PRINT would enable you to insert these commands into any print macro in the spreadsheet with the simple statement {PRE_PRINT}.

Links and Flow

When you are designing and running more complex macros you need to consider the question of current cell location. The macro command {GOTO}B52~ directs Quattro Pro 3 to make B52 of the current worksheet the current cell. This means that the next action will affect cell B52 of the worksheet. This is radically different from the command {BRANCH B52} which directs macro flow to cell B52 of the worksheet. You might want to think of macros as establishing two movable pointers, one being the regular cell selector, the other being a macro cell selector. As the macro executes, both pointers are moved. The regular cell selector goes from one cell to another based on the macro commands, while the special macro pointer goes from cell to cell of macro code, based on the rules of flow and any subroutine or branching commands.

This concept of two independent pointers is particularly important in multiple spreadsheets. Before the advent of linked spreadsheets and macro libraries, a subroutine could only call macros from the current spreadsheet. However, when you are running macros from a macro library file, additional questions about macro flow need to be addressed. A standard method of operation with Quattro Pro 3 is to keep macros in a library file that has been saved with a Tools Macro Library setting of Yes. With the library file open, any open worksheet can call macros from the library. If you press ALT-M while SALES.WQ1 is the current worksheet and there is a macro named \M in an open library file called MACLIB.WQ1, that macro is run. (If there is a macro called \M in the SALES.WQ1 worksheet, that macro will run first, giving you an opportunity to preempt your library macros on special occasions.)

When the \M macro in MACLIB.WQ1 is running, the flow of command moves the macro pointer through the library worksheet. The regular cell pointer is maneuvered in the regular worksheet. However, there is nothing to stop the macro from using links, either for worksheet actions or macro flow. The command {GOTO}B52~ tells Quattro Pro 3 to make cell B52 the current cell of the current worksheet, whereas {GOTO}[BUDGET]B52~ makes cell B52 of the open worksheet BUDGET.WQ1 the current cell. The macro command {BRANCH [MACLIB1]B52} directs macro flow from the current macro library to the worksheet called MACLIB1. You can even direct flow to the worksheet that called up the macro to begin with. This is done by referring to the worksheet with empty square brackets. For example, if you execute \M while SALES.WQ1 is current and \M runs from a macro library, but you want to direct flow to a section of code at cell B100 of SALES.WQ1, you use {BRANCH [ ]B100}.

If you bear in mind the difference between the active cell of the worksheet and the current location of the macro pointer, you can keep track of macro action even while crossing several worksheets. However, you will probably find it easier to put most subroutines in one place, rather than skip from worksheet to worksheet. One advantage of running macros from a macro library is that you can copy to your favorite library subroutines that you have developed in other worksheets. You can name these and then pull them into new macros whenever you need them with the {*subroutine*} command.

Syntax of Macro Commands

Having explored the ways in which some of the more popular macro commands are used, it is time to review all of the commands. Quattro Pro 3's macro commands can be categorized in several ways. There are those that do not have arguments, and those that do. Both types include a keyword in braces. Subroutine calls are an exception since they invoke another macro, making the name of the called macro (rather than a keyword) the item that is placed in the braces. The format of the nonargument commands is simply a keyword enclosed in braces, { }. These braces are recognized as label indicators by Quattro Pro 3. A subroutine call also follows this pattern except that the characters inside the braces represent a macro name instead of a keyword. The format of the argument type of command consists of the keyword followed by a blank space and a list of arguments separated by commas. As with @function arguments, no spaces are allowed between or within arguments. The entire statement complete with arguments is enclosed in the braces.

Screen and Response Commands

You can use macro commands to control updating of the display screen and the Quattro Pro 3 control panel. If you leave such commands turned on, you can follow the progress of the macro on-screen; when you turn them off, the screen does not change. The macro commands in this group also allow you to customize the mode indicator and to give audible feedback to the user.

The {BEEP} Command

The {BEEP} command produces a sound from your computer's speaker, somewhat like the one Quattro Pro 3 makes when you press an invalid key (such as BACKSPACE in the READY mode). The format for the {BEEP} command is {BEEP *number*}, where *number* is an optional argument that you can use to affect the tone of the sound. The *number* argument can have any value from 1 to 4; 1 is the default value when no number is specified.

You can use the beep to alert the operator to an error, indicate that you expect input, periodically show that a macro is still functioning during a lengthy set of instructions, or signify the conclusion of a step. Try using several beeps of different tones to really grab attention, and to distinguish between actions. Since each PC seems to make a different sound in response to the {BEEP} command, you may want to test your system's beeper. This is easy to do in a blank spreadsheet with the value **1** entered in A1 and the following formula entered in B1:

+"{BEEP "&@STRING(A1,0)&"}"

This formula produces the result {BEEP 1} in B1 and is an excellent example of how string functions can be used to generate dynamic macros, that is, macros that depend on the contents of other cells. Now enter the numbers **2**, **3**, and **4** in cells A2, A3, and A4. Copy the formula from B1 to B2..B4. Your spreadsheet should look like this:

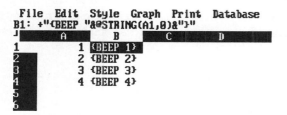

```
 File  Edit  Style  Graph  Print  Database
B1: +"{BEEP "&@STRING(A1,0)&"}"
         A           B           C           D
1          1  {BEEP 1}
2          2  {BEEP 2}
3          3  {BEEP 3}
4          4  {BEEP 4}
5
6
```

Now use the ALT-F2 key or Tools Macro menu to select Macro Execute and then point to B1 as the cell to execute. You will hear all four tones from your computer's speaker. By varying the number in column A you can compose short jingles that add a personal touch to your macros. (Try the sequence 1,1,2,2,3,3,2, which sounds like "Twinkle Twinkle Little Star" on some systems.)

The {INDICATE} Command

The {INDICATE} command allows you to customize the mode indicator in the lower-right corner of the screen, which normally says READY. The format of the {INDICATE} command is

{INDICATE *string*}

where *string* is any character string. Actually, the screen can show only five characters for the mode indicator, so {INDICATE} will use only the first five characters of the string. You can blank out the indicator by using an empty string (that is, {INDICATE ""}). You can return the indicator to READY mode by omitting the string argument (that is, {INDICATE}). Another way of blanking out the mode indicator is to adjust the colors of the status line so that the text is not visible.

The indicator you establish with {INDICATE} remains in effect until you use the command again, either to establish a new setting or to return it to the default, READY. In fact, the {INDICATE} setting continues beyond the completion of a macro. Setting the indicator to PAUSE in a macro causes the word PAUSE to remain on the screen even if you are back to the READY mode. Use {INDICATE} without any argument to restore Quattro Pro 3's normal indicator display at the conclusion of the macro.

The {INDICATE} command is useful if you have a series of menu selections. You can use it to supply a string that reflects the menu selection, providing positive feedback as to the user's selection. Thus, the command {INDICATE "SORT"} can be inserted near the beginning of a macro that performs a sort operation. The user can then see that Sort has been selected.

The {PANELOFF}
And {PANELON} Commands

These two commands control redrawing the control panel, the upper and lower areas of the screen that normally show you the progress of an action or command. The format for the {PANELOFF} command is simply {PANELOFF}. The {PANELON} command restores the default setting, instructing Quattro Pro 3 to update the control panel with each instruction executed. The format for the {PANELON} command is {PANELON}. These commands have no arguments.

You can use these commands to temporarily obscure the details of a macro's execution. After a macro reads the {PANELOFF} command, the entries on the input line are not visible as they are typed by the macro. When the macro reads {PANELON} the normal display is restored. One reason for these commands was to control the annoying screen jitters that occurred when 1-2-3 executed macro instructions, particularly those involving menu choices. This is less of a problem in Quattro Pro 3 since the menu equivalents bypass menu selection. The commands are still useful if you do not want the operator to be aware of the macro code being run. Even if a user invokes DEBUG to slow down the operation of the macro so that the instructions can be read, the control panel will not be updated while {PANELOFF} is in effect.

The {WINDOWSOFF} And {WINDOWSON} Commands

The {WINDOWSOFF} command freezes the entire screen, except for the control panel. It has the format {WINDOWSOFF}. The {WINDOWSON} instruction returns the normal mode of screen updating and has the format {WINDOWSON}. Neither command uses an argument. Like the panel commands, the window commands reduce the flicker that occurs on the screen with some macro instructions. They can also speed execution of long macros, since Quattro Pro 3 does not have to redraw the screen every time the macro moves the cursor or changes data. You can use {PANELOFF} and {WINDOWSOFF} together with {INDICATE "WAIT"} to flash the WAIT message and simply suspend further screen change until a macro is complete. Of course, you should use {WINDOWSON} near the end of a macro to have the screen updated with the current results.

Interactive Macro Commands

When you want user input during a macro's execution, you need to use the interactive macro commands. These commands can streamline data entry and add flexibility to macro designs.

The {?} Command

The {?} command is one of the most convenient and powerful of the macro commands, and it is often the first macro command that users learn beyond simple replaying of keystrokes. Its purpose is to allow the operator to enter information from the keyboard. This command has no arguments and uses the simple format {?}. Place this at any point in a macro where you need to obtain information from the user. After a macro encounters a {?} command, program control is handed to the user who can type a label or number, make a menu selection, or highlight an area of the spreadsheet. However, as soon as the user presses ENTER, the macro resumes control. For this reason, the {?} is followed by an ENTER (~ or {cr}) to actually enter or confirm the user input.

If you want to prompt for input of values or labels, then {GETNUMBER} and {GETLABEL} are more useful. These commands provide prompts as a part of the instruction to clarify the exact information you want. {GET-NUMBER} tests the response to see if it is indeed a number. If you use the {?} instruction, you can use an instruction before it to place a prompt message in the current cell. For example, this instruction places the cell selector in the cell called AGE, enters the message "Type Age and Press Enter," and then replaces that message with the number when the user types it and presses ENTER:

{GOTO}AGE~Type Age and Press Enter~{?}~

One disadvantage of such a macro is that the user is free to access the menu system (and potentially destructive options) as long as they don't press ENTER. Some power users would say that {?} is better suited to your own macros than to applications for beginning users.

The {GET} Command

The {GET} command is designed to accept the entry of a single character from the keyboard. The format of the {GET} command is {GET *location*} where *location* is the storage location for the single character you enter from the keyboard. Thus, you could use {GET ANSWER} to place the response letter Y or N into the cell named ANSWER. The response to {GET} can be any key, letter, number, or function key. This command is yet another option to consider when you need to incorporate keyboard input in a macro. For example, you could use the following to prompt for a single-letter piece of information:

Type Y/N
{GET ANSWER}

{ESC}

The text **Type Y/N** will appear on the input line. The next character typed will be placed in ANSWER. The input line will be cleared.

The {GETLABEL} Command

You use the {GETLABEL} command to handle entering a label from the keyboard in response to a prompt message. The format for the {GET-LABEL} command is {GETLABEL *prompt message, location*}. The *prompt message* argument is a word or words. The *location* is the cell into which the label is placed when the user presses ENTER. You must enclose the prompt text in double quotation marks if you use a comma or a semicolon because these characters are used as argument separators (as in {GET-LABEL "Enter Name:",D1}). You must include a space at the end of the prompt text if you want a space to appear between the text and the cursor on the input line.

The length of text in the prompt is limited by the space at the top of the screen, which is used by the macro when it displays the {GETLABEL} instruction. If you use a string longer than 76 characters, the text will wrap to the next screen line and may be difficult to read since Quattro Pro 3 will not wrap the text of the prompt by complete words. However, you can use spaces after the 76th character to push text onto the next line, and you can use up to three lines at the top of the screen for the prompt. The prompt text string can be stored in a separate cell and referenced if you construct the macro as a formula. Thus

+"{GETLABEL "&C3&"?,E3}"

will give you the prompt "Last Name?" if cell C3 contains the label **Last Name**. This is very convenient when you have a series of field names and want to provide prompts for each one.

The *location* argument in {GETLABEL} is a reference to the cell, block, or block name where the information entered from the keyboard will be stored. Up to 80 characters will be accepted as input. If a named block is supplied for the argument, the character string entered will be stored in the upper-left cell of the block. The {GETLABEL} command stores your entry as a left-justified label in the specified location. This is true regardless of the current default label alignment setting. If the entry is a number it is still stored as a label.

The {GETNUMBER} Command

The {GETNUMBER} command is very similar to the {GETLABEL} command and is used to elicit numeric information from the user in response to a prompt message. The format for the {GETNUMBER} command is {GETNUMBER *prompt message, location*}. The rules for the *prompt message* argument are the same as for {GETLABEL}. The elements of the prompt text string can be stored in a separate cell and referenced by constructing the macro as a formula. When you use a whole series of data cells, your formula can even determine whether to use the {GETLABEL} or {GETNUMBER} command. Thus, the formula

+"{GET"&@IF(@CELL("type",D3)="v","NUMBER","LABEL")&"}"

returns {GETNUMBER} if cell D3 contains a value, or {GETLABEL} if it contains a label. You can combine that result with a formula to produce the prompt message from a label in cell C3:

+"{GET"&@IF(@CELL("type",D3) ="v","NUMBER","LABEL")&"
"&C3&"?,D3}"

This formula will give you the {GETLABEL} prompt "Last Name?" if cell C3 contains the label **Last Name** and D3 contains a label. The formula gives you the {GETNUMBER} prompt "Age?" if C3 contains the label **age** and D3 contains a value. This is very convenient when you have a series of labels for a column of mixed number and label data and you want data entry macro prompts for each.

The {GETNUMBER} rules for the *location* argument are the same as for {GETLABEL}. However, if the user enters a label in response to a {GET-NUMBER} prompt the response in the location cell is ERR, produced by the @ERR function. This makes for a convenient method of trapping entry errors. If you follow a {GETNUMBER} command with an {IF} command you can direct the flow of the macro to an instruction in another cell if the user does not enter a number. For example, in

{GETNUMBER Age? ,ANSWER}
{IF @ISERR(ANSWER)}{BEEP}{BRANCH MESSAGE}

the macro flow goes to MESSAGE when the content of ANSWER is @ERR. Of course, MESSAGE could be a loop back to the {GETNUMBER} command but it could also be an error-message display routine. There is more on @ISERR and related functions later in this chapter.

The {LOOK} Command

The {LOOK} command is similar to {GET}, except that if a macro uses {LOOK} the user can type the entry ahead and the macro will still find it. This is because {LOOK} checks the keyboard buffer for data and places the first character from this buffer into the location defined in the command. The format of the {LOOK} command is {LOOK *location*}. The *location* argument refers to a cell used to store the character from the keyboard's typeahead buffer. If {LOOK} finds the buffer blank, it blanks the location cell. Whereas the {GET} instruction suspends macro execution while waiting for a response, {LOOK} does not. This makes {LOOK} suitable for use in a loop where you want to give the user some time to respond before the application is aborted.

The {MENUBRANCH} Command

As you saw earlier in this chapter, the {MENUBRANCH} command diverts macro flow to a set of cells into which you have placed the data required to build a custom menu. The format of the {MENUBRANCH} command is {MENUBRANCH *location*}, where *location* is the upper-left cell of the area used for menu storage. Information for the customized menu must be organized according to certain rules.

The top row of the menu area must contain the words used for the menu items, entered one per cell, in contiguous columns. Each of these words should begin with a different character, just as in Quattro Pro 3's menus, if you want to be able to pick from the menu by pressing the first letter of an item as well as using the point and ENTER method. (If you use menu items with the same first letters Quattro Pro 3 will pick the first of the similar items when you press the duplicated letter: from a menu consisting of Erase and Extract, pressing **E** will pick Erase). Menu-selection words can be up to 55 characters long, but remember that the longer the word, the wider the menu, and thus the more obtrusive it will be. You can have up to 256 items in a menu although you will only be able to see 13 different items in the menu box (the rest can be scrolled into view).

The second row of the menu area contains the expanded description for each menu choice that will display at the top of the screen when you highlight the menu selection. Since these are explanations they are likely to exceed the width of the column into which they are entered, particularly as they will occupy contiguous columns. Unsightly as this is, it will not affect macro performance.

The third row of the menu instructions contains the actual macro instructions for each choice in the column with the menu item and description. These instructions begin in the cell immediately under the description. They can extend down the column or branch to a subroutine. The subroutine approach makes for cleaner design since macro instructions in contiguous columns can be hard to read, edit, and annotate.

The {MENUCALL} Command

The {MENUCALL} command works like {MENUBRANCH}, but whereas a macro using {MENUBRANCH} ends when the code for the selected option completes, {MENUCALL} returns control to the statement following {MENUCALL} in the main code for the macro, and execution begins again at that location. This has the effect of locking the user into the menu system, returning them to a menu rather than dumping them when the action they chose from the menu is complete. The format of the {MENUCALL} command is {MENUCALL *location*}, where *location* is a cell address or block name that represents the upper-left cell in the area for menu storage. The rules for the menu building are the same as those for {MENUBRANCH}.

The {WAIT} Command

The {WAIT} command is the "hold-up" command. With {WAIT} you can stay the execution of a macro until a stated time. The format of the command is {WAIT *time serial number*}, where *time serial number* is a decimal value that represents the serial number for the time of day when you want execution to resume. Suppose you want users to read a lengthy instruction on the screen. You need to pause the macro long enough for this information to be read, say 45 seconds. This can be accomplished by the following instruction:

{WAIT @NOW+@TIME(0,0,45)}

The wait value is computed by adding a time value to the value returned by @NOW. This results in a measured delay. The instruction adds the desired 45 seconds to the current time and waits until that time is reached before continuing execution. The mode indicator will say WAIT while Quattro Pro 3 is waiting.

Program-Flow Macros

Normally, a macro is read line by line, proceeding down a column from the cell that bears the macro name. However, you can redirect flow in many different ways, branching to other locations or calling subroutines, with the program-flow macro commands.

The {BRANCH} Command

The {BRANCH} command transfers the flow of a macro to a new location. The format of the {BRANCH} command is {BRANCH *location*}, where *location* is a cell address or block name that tells Quattro Pro 3 where the next instruction to be executed by the macro is stored. The {BRANCH} command is often combined with the {IF} command to change the flow of execution based on a test condition. The classic example of this combination is the loop controller, shown here in a macro called CENTER that turns a column of values into a centered label:

```
{EDIT}{HOME}^~{DOWN}~
{IF @CELLPOINTER("type")="b"}{QUIT}
{BRANCH CENTER}
```

After the edit is performed the macro moves the cell selector down one cell. The {IF} command tells Quattro Pro 3 to check the cell currently occupied by the cell selector and return the cell's type. If this is **b** for blank (as opposed to **v** for value or **l** for label) the macro will quit. If the cell is not blank the macro will branch, or loop, back to its beginning, the macro called CENTER.

Remember that {BRANCH} controls macro flow, not cell selector positioning. Do not confuse {BRANCH} with {GOTO} since {GOTO} repositions the cell selector without affecting the execution of the macro. {BRANCH} moves the macro's execution flow but does not move the cell selector.

The {QUIT} Command

The {QUIT} command, used to terminate a macro, has no argument. You simply include {QUIT} as the last line of the macro you want to terminate. Although it can be said that macros automatically stop when they get to a blank cell, this is not strictly true. If a macro has been called by {*subroutine*} or {MENUCALL}, then Quattro Pro 3 returns to the calling point when it gets to a blank line. Placing a Quit option that uses {QUIT} in a {MENUCALL} menu thus provides the user with a way out of the menu. Placing a {QUIT} command at the end of a macro called by a subroutine ends both the subroutine macro and the one that called it. You will also find {QUIT} useful as a value at the end of an {IF} command. When the {IF} condition evaluates as True, the macro—including all subroutines—terminates.

The {RESTART} Command

The {RESTART} command cancels the execution of the current subroutine. This command also cancels all pointers or calls in the macro that reference the subroutine to prevent return. The {RESTART} command has no arguments. Placing this command anywhere within a called subroutine will immediately cancel the call, complete the routine, and continue executing from that point downward. In the process, any upward pointers to higher-level routines are cancelled.

The {RETURN} Command

The {RETURN} command is used to return from a subroutine to the calling routine. Used in conjunction with {MENUCALL} and {*subroutine*}, this command has the same effect on macro flow as a blank cell. This command has no arguments. When Quattro Pro 3 reads {RETURN} in a called subroutine it returns the flow of control back to the instruction beneath the one that called the subroutine. The difference between {RESTART} and {RETURN} is that the latter does not cancel upward pointers. The difference between {QUIT} and {RETURN} is that {RETURN} continues processing after returning to the call point, whereas {QUIT} actually ends the macro at the point where it is encountered.

The {subroutine} Command

This is the command that calls a specific macro subroutine. The format is {*subroutine argument1,argument2,argumentN*}. The subroutine is a macro name. The arguments, and there may be many of them, are values or strings to be passed to the subroutine. These arguments must have corresponding entries in a {DEFINE} statement.

The {*subroutine*} command is a great way to recycle common sections of macro code in a spreadsheet and to spread out macro sections for clarity. Remember that unless the macro called by the {*subroutine*} command ends in {QUIT}, program flow returns to the line below the one on which the {*subroutine*} command was placed.

The {BREAKOFF} And {BREAKON} Commands

The {BREAKOFF} command is used to disable the CTRL-BREAK key function, thereby preventing the interruption of a macro. The format of the command is simply {BREAKOFF} with no arguments. The {BREAKON} command reinstates the CTRL-BREAK key's function so that you can press CTRL-BREAK to interrupt a macro. The format of the command is {BREAKON} with no arguments.

Normally, CTRL-BREAK can be used to stop a macro. It will display ERROR as a mode indicator. When you press ESCAPE, you can proceed to make changes in the worksheet from the READY mode. However, when you have designed an automated application and want to ensure its integrity by maintaining control throughout the use of the worksheet, you will want to disable the Break function by placing {BREAKOFF} in your macro. Be sure you have tested the macro before doing this; the only way to stop a macro that contains an infinite loop and {BREAKOFF} is by turning off the computer.

You may choose to disable the Break function during part of a macro and then restore its operation for a later section, such as printing or data entry. In any case, the Break function is automatically restored at the end of a macro.

The /X Macro Commands

In early versions of 1-2-3 the original concept of macros as a typing alternative was augmented by special macro commands that all began with /X. The earliest form of the macro-command language, these commands provided limited logic and program-flow control for macro execution. Still functional in 1-2-3 Release 2 and in Quattro Pro 3, each one now has a macro language equivalent. Refer to that equivalent for a full explanation of the /X commands. Unlike the macro language commands, the /X commands are preceded by a slash (/) and are not enclosed in braces. There is no space between the command and its arguments. The command is followed by a tilde (~) to actually enter the command.

The /XC Command

The /XC or "call" command corresponds to the {*subroutine*} command. The format for the /XC command is /XC*location*~ where location is the address or block name of a cell containing the subroutine that you are calling. After /XC executes the routine or when it encounters the /XR or {RETURN} statement at the end of the routine, control will return to the macro line following the /XC instruction.

The /XG Command

The /XG command is the {BRANCH} command, directing the flow of a macro by branching to a new location containing the commands that will be entered next. The format of the /XG command is /XG*location~* where *location* is the address containing the commands that you want executed next.

The /XI Command

The /XI command is the equivalent of the {IF} command. The format for the /XI command is /XI*condition~true*. The *condition* argument is a comparison of two values in cells or a formula. If the condition evaluates as True, the macro will execute the instructions on the same macro line as the /XI statement. If the condition is False, the next instructions executed will be on the macro line that follows the condition. The *true* argument is any valid macro instruction. For example, to tell a macro to beep if A1 is greater than 100 you would enter

/XIA1>100~{BEEP}

The /XL Command

The /XL command is equivalent to {GETLABEL}. It causes Quattro Pro 3 to wait for the operator to input a character string from the keyboard and then to store the entry in a specified location. The format for the /XL command is

/XL*prompt message~location*

The *prompt message* argument is a message of up to 39 characters that prompts the user for label input.

The /XM Command

This is the equivalent of the {MENUBRANCH} command, directing flow of the macro to a set of cells that form a custom menu. The rules for the custom menu are the same as for the {MENUBRANCH} command.

The /XN Command

The equivalent of the {GETNUMBER} command, /XN uses the format /XN*prompt message~location* to prompt the user for numeric input and enter it in the cell specified as *location*. If the user enters a label instead of a number the *location* cell will return ERR.

The /XQ Command

Used to terminate a macro, the /XQ command is the same as {QUIT} and is normally used at the end of a macro to ensure that it terminates correctly.

The /XR Command

The equivalent of the {RETURN} command, the /XR command returns the flow of a macro to the point at which it was called as a subroutine. There are no arguments to this command.

The Cells Commands

Quattro Pro 3 groups the following macro commands as cells commands because they let you manipulate values and strings stored in spreadsheet cells. You can use these commands to blank out a section of the spreadsheet or to store a value or a string in a cell. These are also the commands that you can use to recalculate the worksheet in row or column order.

The {BLANK} Command

A macro command alternative to the Block Erase menu option, {BLANK} erases a block of cells on the worksheet. It has the format {BLANK *location*} in which *location* is the address of a block of cells or a block name. Generally used to clean out a data entry area ready for new data, you will find {BLANK} effective when a macro has to reuse an area of the worksheet. Use a block name rather than the cell coordinates as the argument for better control and remember that {BLANK} does not reset cell formatting information; it just removes the contents.

The {CONTENTS} Command

The {CONTENTS} command copies the contents of one cell into another, converting to a label of specified format and width in the process. The correct syntax of the {CONTENTS} command is {CONTENTS *destination,source,width,format*}. The *destination* argument is the location where you wish the resulting label to be stored, stated as a cell address or a block name. The *source* argument is the cell address or block name of the value entry you want copied into *destination* as a label. The *width* and *format* arguments are optional. Thus, the command

{CONTENTS A1,B1}

would take the number 2001 from the fixed-format (0 decimal places) cell A1 and copy it into B1 as the left- aligned label 2001.

The *width* argument is only required if you want to control width or specify format. It determines the width of the resulting label, so omitting it lets Quattro Pro 3 use the width of the source location. The *format* argument provides control over the appearance of the value copied into the *destination*. Thus, the command

{CONTENTS A1,B1,12,34}

copies the same 2001 into B1 as $2,001.00 with three leading spaces. This

Number	Format
0...15	Fixed, 0-15 places
16...31	Scientific, 0-15 places
32...47	Currency, 0-15 places
48...63	Percent, 0-15 places
64...79	Comma, 0-15 places
112	+/–
113	General
114	DD-MMM-YY (D1)
115	DD-MMM (D2)
116	MMM-YY (D3)
117	Literal
118	Hidden
119	HH:MM:SS AM/PM (T1)
120	HH:MM AM/PM (T2)
121	Full International Date (D4)
122	Partial International Date (DS)
123	Full International Time (T3)
124	Partial International Time (T4)
125	General

Table 12-1.   *Width and Format Number Arguments for {CONTENT}*

is because 12 is the specified cell width and 34 is the code for currency format with two decimal places. The codes used for the different formats in the {CONTENTS} command are listed in Table 12-1.

The {LET} Command

The {LET} command assigns a value to a location in the spreadsheet using the format {LET *location,value: type*}. This saves a macro from having to move the cell selector to a location to enter data. The *location* argument is the address or block name of the cell where you wish to store the value or label. (Specifying *location* as a multi-cell block means that the upper-left cell in the block will be used.) The *value* is the data you want assigned to the *location*. Quattro Pro 3 will try to assign a numeric value but if it cannot it will assign a string. Use the optional *type* argument to control how the value is handled. Thus, the command

{LET A1,101}

places the number 101 in cell A1. The command

{LET A1,101:string}

places the left-aligned label 101 in cell A1. Of course, you can use cell references for the value argument. Note the use of a colon for the argument separator.

The {PUT} Command

Unlike {LET}, which accepts only a cell address, {PUT} allows you to place a value in a location by selecting a row and column offset within a block. The correct format for the {PUT} command is thus {PUT *location, column,row,value:type*}. The block of cells, identified by cell addresses or a block name, into which you want to place the data are stated in the *location* argument. The *column* argument is the column number of the cell within the block you want to use for the data (as in other Quattro Pro 3 commands, such as @VLOOKUP, the first column in the block is column 0). The *row* argument works the same way, with the first row being 0. Thus the command

{PUT A1..C5,0,0,20:string}

places the left-aligned label 20 in cell A1. The command

{PUT A1..C5,1,1,Help}

places the label Help in cell B2.

The {RECALC} Command

The {RECALC} command recalculates the formulas within a block you specify, proceeding rowwise within the block. The format for the {RECALC} command is {RECALC *location,condition,iteration*}. The block to be recalculated is specified as *location*. The *condition* is an optional argument, specifying a condition that must be evaluated as True before the block is no longer recalculated. While the *condition* evaluates to False, Quattro Pro 3 will continue to recalculate the worksheet. Used in conjunction with *iteration*, which specifies a maximum number of iterations, the *condition* stops recalculation short of the maximum number of iterations if it evaluates to True.

The point of this command, and the companion command {RECALC-COL}, is to avoid unnecessary delays in processing data. When a worksheet gets large it is normal to make recalculation manual instead of automatic. New entries do not cause dependent data in the rest of the spreadsheet to be updated. Instead, this is done by returning to automatic calculation or pressing the Calc key (F9). While this key recalculates the entire worksheet, the {RECALC} and {RECALCCOL} commands evaluate just a portion, which takes far less time. Use {RECALC} when the area you are recalculating is below and to the left of the cells referenced by the formulas in the area. Use {RECALCCOL} when the area you are recalculating is above and to the right of the cells referenced by the formulas in this area. Use these commands prior to printing a report to ensure that the reported data is correct, while avoiding a lengthy delay caused by updating the entire spreadsheet. (If the formula to be calculated is both above and to the left of cells with new values, you must use the Calc key.)

The {RECALCCOL} Command

The {RECALCCOL} command recalculates the formulas within the specified block, just like {RECALC}, except that it proceeds column by column. The format is {RECALCCOL *location,condition,iteration*} using the same argument definitions as {RECALC}.

The File I/O Macro Commands

The file I/O macro commands provide you with a means of manipulating data in a disk file, somewhat like the sequential file-handling capabilities you get in the BASIC programming language. In your macros, these commands allow you to read and write data in ASCII files. This is a fairly advanced activity, and one which has the potential to corrupt valuable data files if not handled correctly, so the file control commands should be used with care.

Using I/O Commands

The I/O commands work with ASCII or text files. These are files like the ones created by the Quattro Pro 3 Print command when the Destination setting is File. Such files are sometimes used for exchanging information between programs that cannot read more sophisticated file formats, such as WRl or DBF.

A typical application of these commands would be when you want to write information, one line at a time, to a text file. The following macro code writes the contents of cell A21 to a file called INFO.DAT:

```
{OPEN "INFO.DAT",M}
{FILESIZE SIZE}
{SETPOS SIZE}
{WRITELN A21}
{CLOSE}
```

The macro opens the file to be modified, reads the size of the file in bytes into a cell called SIZE, and then positions the byte pointer at the end of the file. The byte pointer is like an invisible cursor within the disk file you open. When a file is first opened, the byte pointer is located at the first character of the file. Any reading from or writing to the file occurs at the location of the byte pointer. You can position the byte pointer with {SETPOS}.

Each of the file manipulation commands is described in the following sections.

The {CLOSE} Command

The {CLOSE} command closes a file that was opened with the {OPEN} macro command. It takes no arguments. This is one of several commands that enable macros to read from files on disk and write information to disk files.

The {FILESIZE} Command

The {FILESIZE} command has the syntax {FILESIZE *location*}. It records the size of an open file, stated as a number of bytes, in the cell specified as *location*, which can be a cell or range name.

The {GETPOS} Command

The {GETPOS} command has the syntax {GETPOS *location*}. It records (in the cell specified by the *location* argument) the byte pointer's current position. The position is read as an offset number; the first character of a file is 0, the second is 1, and so on.

The {OPEN} Command

The {OPEN} command has the syntax {OPEN *filename,access mode*}. The {OPEN} command opens a file named as *filename* for reading, writing, or both. The *access mode* argument is one of four characters:

W   Opens a new disk file to which you can write information. This is potentially dangerous, since there is nothing to stop you from overwriting an existing file. Be sure that the *filename* argument does not refer to a file that you want to preserve.

M   Opens an existing file so that you can modify it. This allows you to use the read and write commands. It, too, is dangerous; what you write to a file will overwrite existing data if the byte pointer is not positioned at the end of the file.

R   Opens a file so that you can read information from it. This is the safest form of file access, since it prevents writing to the file.

A   Opens a file and automatically positions the file pointer at the end of the file.

The {READ} Command

The {READ} command has the syntax {READ *byte count,location*}. The {READ} command copies the number of characters, specified by the *byte count* argument, from the file to the cell specified by the *location* argument. The command starts reading at the current position of the byte pointer.

The {READLN} Command

The {READLN} command has the syntax {READLN *location*}. This command copies a line of data from the file to the cell specified by the *location* argument. The command starts reading at the current position of the byte pointer and stops at the end of the current line.

The {SETPOS} Command

The {SETPOS} command has the syntax {SETPOS *file position*}. This command sets a new position for the byte pointer in the currently open file. If you read the file size and use this as the *file position* argument, you will locate the end of the file and be able to add data to it. Bear in mind that the first position is 0 (zero), the second is 1 (one), and so on.

The {WRITE} Command

The {WRITE} command has the syntax {WRITE *string*}. It copies characters into an open file at the byte pointer's current location. The *string* argument can be a single cell or a named single-cell range. The command does not add a line feed at the end of what is written.

The {WRITELN} Command

The {WRITELN} command has the syntax {WRITELN *string*}. The {WRITELN} command copies characters into an open file. The *string* argument can be a single cell or a named single-cell range. The command adds a line feed sequence at the end of the string of characters as it writes the string to the file. Thus, you can use a series of {WRITELN} statements to add successive lines of data to a file.

Utility Commands

There are a couple of commands that make it easier for the macro writer to handle the chores of documentation and design. These allow you to insert comments and blank lines in your macros.

The {;} Command

When you want to place a comment in a macro you can do so with the {;} command. Entering {;**This line is a comment**} in a macro allows the comment to appear in the spreadsheet but not to affect the way the macro runs. The macro skips this line during execution. This is useful for documenting macros, particularly where space considerations prevent the use of comments to the right of the code cells.

The {} Command

To skip a cell completely during macro execution you can use { }, which lets a macro come as close as possible to containing a blank cell without stopping. This is sometimes useful when you want to have two macros arranged so that comparable commands are in adjacent cells but one macro is not as complex as the other, as in this example:

Enter	List
Enter data	Sort and print list
{ENTER}	{SORT_DATA}
{}	{PRINT_DATA}
{QUIT}	{QUIT}

System Menu Building

The Quattro Pro 3 command language is not the only way you can develop a custom menu system with Quattro Pro 3. The entire Quattro Pro 3 menu structure is designed so that it can be redesigned. This means that you can make custom menus that are not specific to just one worksheet or macro library.

The MU Files

The Quattro Pro 3 menu system is stored in a file called QUATTRO.MU. You can copy and modify this file. For example, you do not need to have the same set of items on the main menu bar as the program comes with. In fact, two complete sets of menus different from the standard Quattro Pro 3 menus are provided along with the program. The file 123.MU contains a menu system that will be familiar to users of 1-2-3. The file Q1.MU contains menus that are similar to those in the original version of Quattro.

As you can see in Figure 12-13, which shows the main menu displayed by the 123.MU menu system, the menu still has the look of the regular Quattro Pro 3 menu. If you have a mouse installed, the mouse palette will

Figure 12-13. *The 1-2-3 menu*

be displayed. Some items are named differently and the commands are grouped differently, however. For example, the Edit Erase command is found on the Range menu, shown in Figure 12-14. This command is functionally equivalent to the 1-2-3 Range Erase command. To change from one menu system to another, you can use the Options Startup command and select Menu Tree.

Menu files all have the extension MU. You can select the MU file you want by highlighting it and pressing ENTER. Your choice appears in the Menu Tree setting for you. As soon as you exit the Options menu, the new menu tree will be in place. If you are using the Quattro Pro 3 menu tree, you can write your choice of menu system to the configuration file, using the Update command on the Options menu. When you exit from Quattro Pro 3 and reload the program, the new menu system you selected will be in effect. To change the menu tree while using the 1-2-3 menus, use Worksheet Global Default Files. The Worksheet Global Default Update command will record your choice.

In addition to the 123.MU file and Q1.MU file that come with Quattro Pro 3, you can create your own MU file containing your personalized menu system. This is discussed in the following sections.

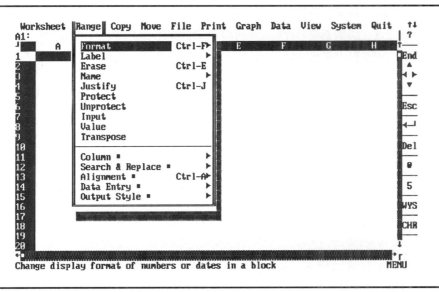

Figure 12-14.   *Edit Erase as Range Erase*

Customizing Menus

Quattro Pro 3 is written so that the actions it performs can be requested by several different methods, not simply by a specific set of keystrokes. This allows you to use menu equivalents in macros. The same design feature allows you to choose your own names for the program's actions and then access them from a menu that is arranged to suit the way you work. You define menu items and cut and paste menus by using the Edit Menus command from the Options Startup menu (in some earlier versions of Quattro Pro this feature was referred to as the Menu Builder, and it is also sometimes called the menu editor).

The Edit Menu Windows

To use the Edit Menus command, select the Options Startup command and pick Edit Menus. Quattro Pro 3 takes a moment to read the current menu file into memory, showing a bar graph of the task's progress. You then get a screen like the one shown in Figure 12-15. In the center of the screen, in the Menu Tree window, you see the top level of your current menu system. The one that is shown in Figure 12-15 is the default Quattro Pro 3 menu. The middle window is the current window, so designated by the double-line border. The window above it is the Current Item window, which defines whatever item is highlighted in the Menu Tree window.

The Current Item window displays the six different fields of information by which Quattro Pro 3 defines each menu item. The Desc field stores the description of the menu item that appears at the bottom of the screen when you are using the menu tree. There are two forms of Action for each menu item: General and Specific. Items that lead to further menus have no Specific action. Most menu items can be selected and so carry the entry Yes in the Selectable field. However, some items are placed just for show, like the lines dividing the menus into parts, and these are not selectable. All items that can be selected have an action that they perform After Selection. In the case of the File item on the main menu, the After Selection setting is Quit, which is the case for all items that lead to further menus. You can select items on menus by a key letter. The Menu Key field stores this letter, which is F in the case of the File menu.

In the Menu Tree window there is a highlight bar that you can move up and down the menu to highlight different items. All items preceded by a plus sign have submenus, or child menus. When an item is highlighted,

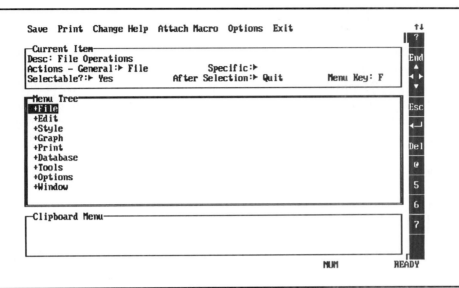

Figure 12-15.   *Using the Edit Menu feature*

you can press the numeric plus key to show the corresponding child menu branching to the right. Thus, the Edit option on the top level shows the options on the Edit menu to the right, as seen in Figure 12-16. You can use the RIGHT ARROW key to move to this set of items and then DOWN ARROW to move down the list. In Figure 12-16 you can see that the Copy item has both a General action, Block, and a Specific action, Copy. Note that the lines on the menu are separate items. To shrink a set of submenus back under the parent item, press the minus sign (–) on the numeric keypad while the Menu Tree window is active and you are highlighting the parent item. Thus, to put the Edit menu items back under Edit, you highlight Edit and press minus.

The third window in the menu editor is the Clipboard menu, which is a place to store items that have been cut from the menu structure. Using the middle and bottom window you can alter the placement of items on the menu tree by performing cut-and-paste operations, rearranging the menu items to suit your taste.

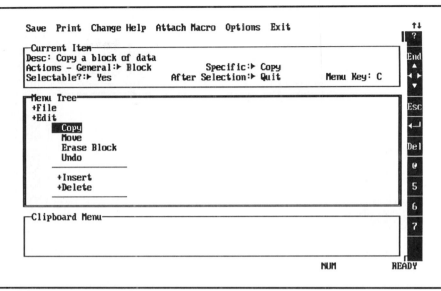

Figure 12-16. *The Edit menu child menus*

Moving a Menu Item

Suppose that you want to move the Database commands to the Tools menu. You do this with a cut-and-paste operation. The first half of the cut-and-paste involves highlighting in the middle window the menu item you want to move, in this case Database. Then you press the DELETE key to remove the highlighted item from the Current menu to the bottom window, where it is stored, as you can see in Figure 12-17. The paste half of the operation involves first highlighting the item in the bottom window that you want to insert back into the tree. If you move only one item at a time, this item will already be highlighted, as seen in Figure 12-17. With the middle window active you move to the new location for the Database item, above Macro in the Tools menu. To do this you highlight Tools, type the numeric +, and press RIGHT ARROW to highlight Macro, as shown in Figure 12-18. Now you can press INSERT to insert the item from the Clipboard.

All of the child menus of a command are moved with it, as you can see by expanding the newly placed item, as shown in Figure 12-19. Once an item is pasted it disappears from the Clipboard menu. Using this

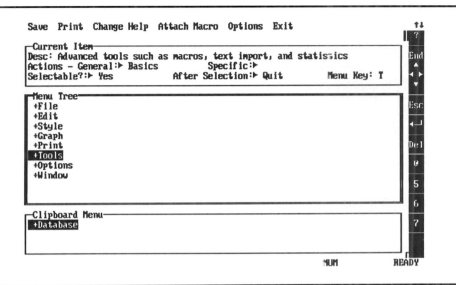

Figure 12-17.   *A menu item clipped*

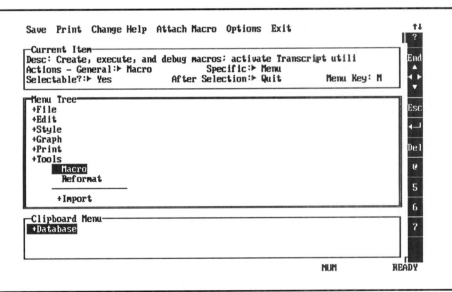

Figure 12-18.   *The Tools menu expanded*

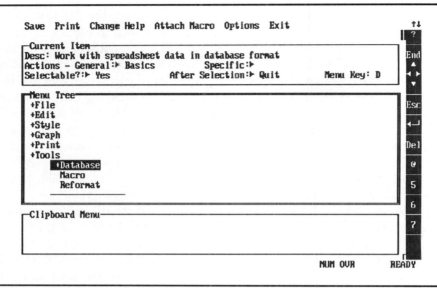

Figure 12-19. *The Database item pasted*

technique, you can rearrange items that are already defined. Items that have been cut are shown in the bottom window to remind you that they have been cut and need to be pasted or they will be lost when you save the new menu tree.

Defining Menu Items

When you are in the top window of the menu editor you can edit any of the items. By pressing the SPACEBAR while highlighting any entry except Desc and Menu Key, you get a menu of possible choices. For example, suppose that you want to add an item called Copy on the main menu, right after Tools. First, make the Menu Tree window active, and then place the highlight bar *below* Tools. Press ENTER and a space will appear. Now press F6 to move to the Current Item window to define this new item.

In the first field of the Current Item window, Desc, you could type **Copies a cell or block of cells**. After typing this entry, press ENTER.

When you move the cursor to the General field, using the TAB key, you can press the SPACEBAR to see a list of actions, as shown in Figure 12-20. You want to pick Block. Notice that the top of the menu shows a generic menu equivalent for the commands, which is further evidence of the link between Quattro Pro 3's macro language and the menu structure. When you move to the Specific field, the list that is displayed by pressing the SPACEBAR is more specific, showing a list of Block operations from which you can select Copy, as shown in Figure 12-21. Leave the Selectable field entry as Yes and move to After Selection. Pressing the SPACEBAR here lists three options entitled What to do next. The self-explanatory choices are Stay, Quit, and GoTo Parent. The Copy command should Quit after being used. You can then move to the next field and type **C** for the Menu Key.

The new menu item is almost completed, but it still lacks a name. In fact, as you enter **C** as the Menu Key Quattro Pro 3 will remind you that the letter must refer to a named item on the menu. Press F6 to move to the Menu Tree window, type **Copy** in the empty slot, and press ENTER. The result is shown in Figure 12-22. Do not worry about the plus sign—this command does not get one as it does not lead to a child menu. In the Current Item window Quattro Pro 3 has entered C for the Menu Key.

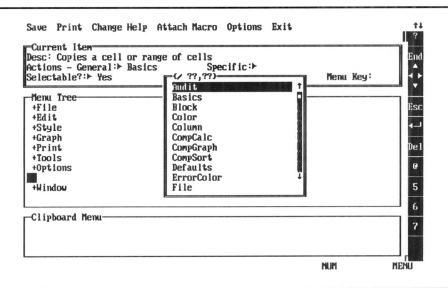

Figure 12-20.   *General action list*

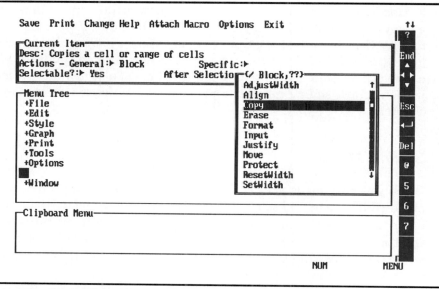

Figure 12-21. *Specific action list*

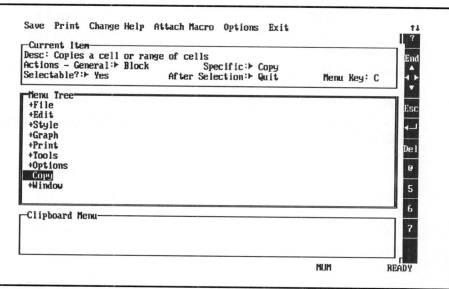

Figure 12-22. *Defining copy on the main menu*

This is the basic procedure for defining new menu items. There is still a Copy option under Edit on this menu tree. Of course, if you simply want to move Copy from the Edit menu you can use the cut-and-paste procedure just described. Defining new menu items is useful when you want to add a specialized command in several places. You will also use this procedure when you are adding macros to menu trees, as described later in this chapter.

Saving Menus

When you have made your changes to the menu structure, type / for the menu editor menu and select Save. You will see a submenu requesting a name for your new menu system. When you type a name and press ENTER, Quattro Pro 3 will save the menu, which takes a little while. You are still left in the menu editor. Select Exit from the menu to return to the regular worksheet window.

When you are picking a name for a new or modified menu tree, avoid using one of the existing names from the list of MU files unless you are sure you want to replace an existing menu file. Quattro Pro 3 will warn you before replacing an existing menu tree. You do not want to accidentally replace the QUATTRO.MU file with a faulty menu tree menu—one that does not include all of the options you need. If you damage the QUATTRO.MU file you can recopy it from the original Quattro Pro 3 disks.

You activate the new menu system with the Options Startup Menu Tree command. As soon as you select your new menu file from the list and quit the menus, the new menu tree will be in place, as you can see here:

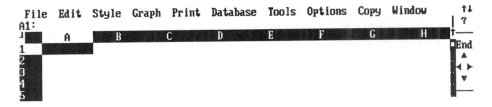

For this reason, your menu designs should always include the Startup Menu Tree command as well as the Edit Menus command, even if they are disguised as something else to prevent novice users from getting to them. You will have a hard time changing back to the original menu tree if you do not include these items. However, if you do not pick Update from the

Options menu your choice of menu file will not be recorded. This means that you can call up a special simplified menu tree for a novice user, possibly using a macro. When the user is done, Quattro Pro 3 will revert to the original menu tree. If you do get stuck in a menu that has no Menu Tree option, you can get back to square one by recopying the RSC.RF file into your Quattro Pro 3 directory from the original program disk. Indeed, if you are going to do a lot of experimenting with menu designs you might want to place a copy of your RSC.RF file in another directory in readiness for this eventuality.

Adding Macros
To the Program Menu

Quattro Pro 3 lets you use the menu editor to add the running of a macro to the program menu structure. The ability to call macros from the main menu system adds greatly to your ability to create customized menu-driven applications with Quattro Pro 3. Users can be prompted to enter and manipulate information by means of a set of specialized program and macro menus.

Figure 12-23 shows a customized program menu that includes the option Administer. This option was inserted into the menu tree with the menu editor, but the action it performs is not a normal program action. When Administer is selected, a macro called ADMINISTER is executed. There must be a macro with that name currently loaded, either in the current worksheet or in a macro library. If there is no ADMINISTER macro available when Administer is selected, nothing happens. The AD-MINISTER macro was shown in Figure 12-11, where it was used to initiate a macro menu system.

To create a system menu item that executes a macro command you first select the Edit Menus option on the Options Startup menu. When the current menu is loaded you use the cursor keys to move around the Menu Tree window and locate the menu to which you want to add the macro command. Insert a new menu item by positioning your cursor on the menu item below which the new item is to appear. Press ENTER to insert a new line and type a menu name for the item. This does not have to be the same as the name of the macro, although using the same name may make it easier to keep track of the program flow. Press F6 to get to the Current Item pane of the menu editor screen. Enter a description of the menu item. In the General field enter **Name**. In the Specific action field enter **Attach**. Then type / for the menu editor menu and pick Attach Macro.

```
 File  Edit  Style  Graph  Print  Database  Administer  Tools  Window      ↑↓
A1: [W17] 'Employee I.D. #
J          A            B              C          D          E             ↑
1   Employee I.D. #       Last Name      First Name  Salary    Sales        ▓
2          10701 Rue            Mick         24        300
3          10702 Wading         Les          27        330
4          10703 Figone         Fred         22        240
5          10704 Jones          Karen        18        320
6          10705 Forte          Steve        33        200
7          10706 Baxter         Andrew A.    26        210
8          10707 Torres         Lisa         23        250
9          10708 Abenojar       Bill         29        220
10         10709 Herzberg       Brian        27        310
11         10710 Chang          Charly       24        330
12         10711 Ruess          Berni        23        180
13         10712 Willock        Sam          23        200
14         10713 McKenna        Sharon       22        300
15         10714 Muller         Mario        33        300
16         10715 Kobuchi        Joseph       19        310
17         10716 Matsumoto      Owen         30        200
18         10717 Romfo          Erin         24        230
19
20                                                                          ↓
←                                                                        →r
Enter, update, sort, and print database                            MENU
```

Figure 12-23. *The Administer item on the menu*

In the Attach Macro box, type the name of the macro as it is recorded in the worksheet, enclosed in curly braces. You can see this being done in Figure 12-24. Press ENTER to confirm the name. The box will disappear and the key letter will be selected.

Now that you have added the macro to the system menu you can save the new menu tree. By selecting the new tree with the Options Startup Menu Tree command and then picking Update to record this change in the default or RF file, you can use the new menu in the current session and when you reload Quattro Pro 3. When you pick the macro item from the new menu, Quattro Pro 3 will look for a macro with the appropriate name in the current worksheet. If it does not find a macro with the correct name in the current worksheet, it will look for the macro in any open macro library worksheet. When the macro is found, Quattro Pro 3 will execute it. For example, you could have several different worksheets all containing a macro called ADMINISTER. The Administer item on the / menu would activate any one of them, depending upon which worksheet was loaded and current, even if they each contained different commands.

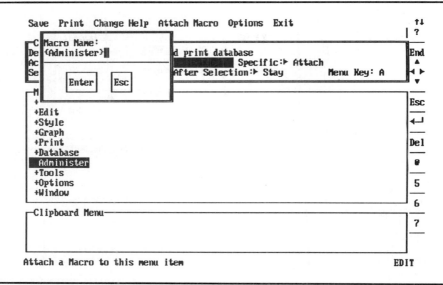

Figure 12-24. *Attaching a macro*

Edit Menu Options

There are several options that you can use when you are designing a menu system that affect how the menu will work. If you select Options from the menu editor menu you can see these options listed, as shown in Figure 12-25. These options will be invoked whenever the menu structure you are designing is in use.

Files and Macros

The name of the autoload file that you want this set of menus to use can be specified. For example, you could enter **AUTO123.WK1** if you were using 1-2-3 style menus. Also, the default file extension can be specified. The 123.MU file uses WK1 in this setting. The Macro Recording option allows you to choose between Logical, the Borland-style menu equivalents, or Keystroke, the 1-2-3 style. Note that you can record macros in Logical

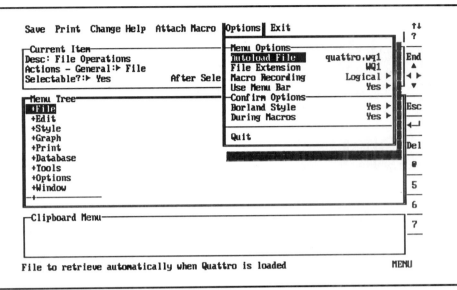

Figure 12-25.   *Menu Builder Options*

style even if you are using a 1-2-3-style menu. This allows your macros to run under Quattro Pro 3 even when a different menu tree is in effect.

Use Menu Bar

This option lets you turn on and off the menu bar across the top of the Quattro Pro 3 screen. When set to No you will find that there is no menu on the screen until you type /, at which point the main menu pops up as a vertical list, as shown in Figure 12-26. Note that the name at the top of the menu tree is the first part of the MU file that is current at the time. If you save a set of menus as STEPHEN.MU, then STEPHEN will be the name of the main menu. You could put your company name there to customize Quattro Pro 3. In addition to Yes or No, you can use a third menu bar option: Compatible. This tells Quattro Pro 3 to use a pop-up menu and move the highlighting up and down the menu when you use the LEFT and RIGHT ARROW keys.

```
A1: [W17] 'Employee I.D. #
```

Figure 12-26. *The pop-up vertical menu*

Confirm Options

Quattro Pro 3 normally displays a confirmation menu when you attempt an operation that will result in a loss of data, checking to see what actions you have performed and whether your work is saved. For example, you are prompted when you are retrieving a file or resetting block names. You can set the Borland-style option to No to be compatible with 1-2-3.

The During Macros option is normally set to Yes to prompt for confirmation while macros are being run and recorded. To make macros compatible with 1-2-3, set this option to No. Remember that when you want to record macros compatible with 1-2-3, you change to the 123.MU menu tree, then set Macro Recording to Keystrokes, and finally alter the Confirm Options to No.

Remember

Although not shown on any menu, there is one more feature of menu operation that you can adjust in Quattro Pro 3. This is the Remember feature. When Remember is set to Yes, Quattro Pro 3 remembers the last item you picked from a particular menu. For example, when Remember is in effect and you pick the Edit Insert Columns command, the next time you activate the menu the Edit command will be highlighted. When you pick Edit, the Insert command will be highlighted. When you pick Insert, the Columns command will be highlighted. This means that you can type / and press ENTER ENTER ENTER to repeat the Edit Insert Columns command. This saves you a lot of time, particularly with commands like Style Numeric Format Percent. Instead of having to find Percent on the list of Numeric Formats, Remember will take you there if that was the last format you picked.

Some tricks are useful when the Remember feature is in effect. Do not use the Quit option on a menu to leave the menu. Use CTRL-BREAK, which takes you directly back to the READY mode from just about any menu level. For example, when you pick Go from the Database Sort menu and you want to do more sorting after editing your list, exit the Sort menu with CTRL- BREAK. Then you can type / and press ENTER ENTER ENTER to repeat the Sort command. If you had used Quit to leave the Sort menu, then that would be the remembered choice when you went back there. While some users prefer each menu selection to revert to the default top item, others enjoy the speed of repetition that the Remember feature provides.

To activate the Remember feature you must issue the following macro command in the spreadsheet area:

{/ Startup;Remember}

When you execute this command as part of a macro you will get a Yes/No option box. Select Yes and Quattro Pro 3 will now remember your menu choices for the rest of the current session. To activate Remember without using the option box use

{/ Startup;Remember}y~

Advanced Functions

A complete set of macro menus to enter, review, sort, and print data is a fairly involved undertaking. The elements that make up such a system were illustrated in the earlier examples in this chapter, some of which used a set of advanced Quattro Pro 3 @functions that can be very useful in more complex macros. Sometimes called the miscellaneous functions, these advanced functions allow you to perform such operations as data entry checks and macro control.

The @CELL Functions

The @CELLPOINTER, @CELL, and @CELLINDEX functions return information about a cell. The type of information produced by the function depends on the code specified in the function statement. The cell about which information is returned, in the case of @CELLPOINTER, is the cell that the selector currently occupies. In the case of @CELL, the cell is the one referred to by a cell reference or the one in the top-left corner of a named block referred to by name in the function statement. For the @CELL-INDEX function, the cell is the one referenced by the specified column and row of a defined block. The syntax is as follows:

@CELLPOINTER (*Code*)

@CELL (*Code,Cell*)

@CELLINDEX (*Code,Block,Col,Row*)

The *code* argument is a string that determines the information about the cell that the function references. There are nine of these codes, as shown in Table 12-2. With careful use of these codes, particularly when combined with the {IF} command and @IF function, you can extract valuable information about cells of the worksheet for use in macros. Remember that if you use a block name to refer to the cell required in the @CELL function, the cell addressed will be the one in the top-left corner of the block. Since the cell used by the @CELLPOINTER function is the current cell, this function is useful for controlling looping macros. For example, the following macro, called ROUND, turns a column of formulas into results rounded to one decimal place:

```
{EDIT},1){HOME}@ROUND(
{CALC}{DOWN}
{IF @CELLPOINTER("type")="v"{Branch ROUND}
{Quit}
```

Code	Response
address	The absolute address of a cell
row	The row number of cell (from 1 to 8192)
col	The column number of the cell (from 1 to 256 corresponding to columns A through IV)
contents	The actual contents of the cell
type	The type of data in the cell: b if the cell is blank v if the cell contains a number or any formula l if the cell contains a label
prefix	The label-prefix character of the cell: ' if label is left-aligned ^ if label is centered " if label is right-aligned | if cell starts with that character \ if label is repeating
protect	The protected status of the cell: 0 if the cell is not protected 1 if the cell is protected
width	The width of the column containing the cell: (between 1 and 240)
format	The current display format of the cell: Fn is Fixed (n=0-15) En is Exponential (n=0-15) Cn is Currency (n=0-15) + is +/- (bar graph format) G is General Pn is percent (n=0-15) D-D5 is Date 1=DD-MMM-YY 2=DD-MMM 3=MMMY 4=MM/DD/YY,DD/MM/YY, DD.MM.YY,YY-MM-DD 5=MM/DD,DD/MM,DD.MM,MM-DD D6-D9 is Time 6=HH:MM:SS AM/PM 7=HH:MM AM/PM

Table 12-2.   *Codes Allowed by the @CELLPOINTER and @CELL Functions*

Code	Response
	8=HH:MM:SS-24hr, HH.MM.SS-24hr, HH.MM.SS-24hr, HHhMMmSSs
	9=HH:MM:-24hr, HH.MM.-24hr, HH,MM,HHhMMm
	T is Show Formulas (Text)
	H is Hidden
	, is Commas used to separate thousands

Table 12-2.   *Codes Allowed by the @CELLPOINTER and @CELL Functions* (continued)

The first line of the macro edits a cell and places the @ROUND statements around the existing formula. The second line calculates the formula and then moves down to the next cell. The third line of the macro checks whether the next cell is a value and, if it is, the macro loops to the beginning. If the cell is a label or is blank, and therefore not a value, then the macro quits. Note that the response to the function as well as the code must be identified with quotes.

The @@ Function

Another function that responds with information about cells is the @@ function. The @@ function can play a valuable role in more complex macros, since it returns the contents of a cell that is referenced as a label in another cell. Thus, @@(A1) returns the answer 10 if A1 contains a reference to a cell that contains the number 10—either the label A1 or a label that is the name of a block, the top-left cell of which contains 10.

The @COLS And @ROWS Functions

When you need to know how many columns or rows there are in a block of cells, you use the @COLS and @ROWS functions. Thus, @COLS(DATA) returns the response 7 if DATA is the name given to cells A1..G20. The response to @ROWS(DATA) would be 20.

The @N and @S Functions

Some spreadsheet programs cannot work with formulas that include cells containing labels or string values. The labels are not zero values and so can cause an ERR message to result from the formula. The @N function returns the numeric value of the cell or the top-left cell of the block that it references. Thus, @N(DATA) returns the value 5 if the top-left cell of DATA contains a 5 or a formula that results in 5. If the top-left cell of DATA contains a label, the result will be 0. Since Quattro Pro 3 already considers labels to be zero values, there is not much need to use this function in a Quattro Pro 3 spreadsheet. However, the function is available to provide compatibility with other spreadsheet programs. The companion to @N is @S, which returns the string value of the cell it references. Thus, @S(DATA) will return Name if the top-left cell of DATA contains the label Name or a string formula that results in Name. If the same cell contains 5, @S will return the empty label " ", which appears as an empty cell.

The Utility Functions

When you need to know the amount of regular and expanded memory available, you can use the Options Hardware command and read the screen. However, you can retrieve the same data into a spreadsheet cell with the @MEMAVAIL and @MEMEMSAVAIL functions. These functions are useful in macros when you need to check whether there is enough room for an operation to be performed or simply check that free memory is not getting too low. For example, the statement

{IF @MEMAVAIL/146389.20}{/ Block;Copy}DATANEW

would cause the macro to execute the Copy command only if there was more than 20% of the total memory free. The number 146389 is the total amount of memory, as you can read from the Options Hardware menu using @CURVALUE, described in a moment. Of course, if you have expanded memory installed, you will need to include that information in the equation (you can use @MEMAVAIL+@MEMEMSAVAIL). If you have no expanded memory in your system, the @MEMEMSAVAIL function responds with NA.

The @CURVALUE function has the very powerful ability to return the current value of any menu item that stores a value or setting. The menu item you want to read is defined by the arguments used in the @CUR-VALUE statement, which takes the form:

@CURVALUE("*general action*","*specific action*")

These arguments are the menu equivalents listed in the Quattro Pro 3 manual and by the SHIFT-F3 key, under / Commands. They are also found when using the menu editor. The items must be entered in quotes but capitalization is optional. For example, to read the current value of Normal Memory in the Options Hardware menu you use

@CURVALUE ("Basics","ShowMem")

The response to @CURVALUE is always a string, so it may need to be converted if it is to be used as a number or cell reference. Not all menu items have values that can be read, but the ability to read some, such as circular cell references, can be very useful in more sophisticated macros. To return the address of a cell occupied by a circular reference, you would use the command

@CURVALUE("Audit",ShowCirc")

True and False Tests

In some spreadsheet designs you may need to test whether a statement or condition is true or false. Quattro Pro 3 represents a true statement as 1 and a false statement as 0. Thus, A1>99 results in 1 if A1 contains any number larger than 99, or 0 if A1 contains a number less than 99 or a label (labels have a 0 value). The more likely place to find true/false tests is in an @IF statement, such as @IF(A1>99,1,0). Since this statement is somewhat difficult to read, you can use

@IF(a1>99,@TRUE,@FALSE)

The @TRUE and @FALSE functions return the responses 1 and 0 respectively and require no arguments.

The @IS Functions

@ISERR and @ISNA are true/false functions that give you the means to check whether a formula or cell entry results in either the ERR or NA response, respectively. These functions take the form @ISERR(*value*) and @ISNA(*value*), where *value* is a cell reference or a formula. The @ISERR function returns the response 1, meaning true, if *value* results in ERR, as is the case with @ISERR(1/0) or @ISERR(A1/A2), where A2 contains the value 0.

A typical application of the @ISERR function is shown in Figure 12-27, where a formula avoids the problem of dividing one column of numbers by another when some of the cells in the columns might be empty or contain zeroes. Thus, the division of total sales by the number of agents would result in an ERR message in cell D8 if the formula was simply C8/B8. The added @IF function uses @ISERR to turn the ERR result into the string of text "Not Available."

Another application of the @ISERR function is shown in Figure 12-28, where it is used in a data entry macro that completes the simple order form in the upper half of the screen. The {GETNUMBER} command places ERR

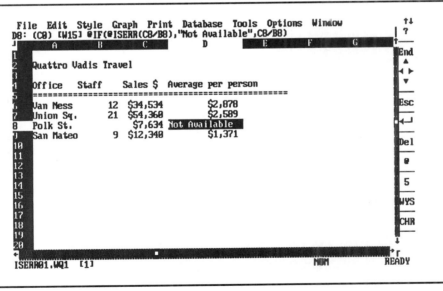

Figure 12-27.   *An @ISERR formula*

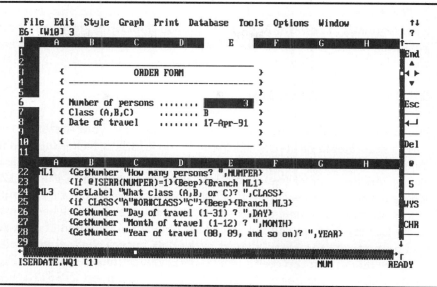

Figure 12-28. *Using @ISERR in data entry*

in the destination cell if the user enters a label instead of the requested number. The macro code at B23 causes Quattro Pro 3 to beep and repeat the {GETNUMBER} command if the user accidentally enters a label.

Notice the other test in this macro in cell B25. The {IF} statement causes a beep and a repeat of the preceding {GETLABEL} prompt if the user enters a label less than A or greater than C. This statement restricts valid responses to the A, B, or C requested in the {GETLABEL} prompt. This line is an example of the # sign being used to join two conditions. The statement

CLASS>"A"#OR#CLASS

evaluates as true if the contents of the cell named CLASS are either less than A or greater than C. You can also use #AND# to join two conditions. In this way, both conditions must be met for the result to prove true. The operator #NOT# can be used to preface a condition to negate it. Thus, #NOT#CLASS"C" would work just as well in cell B25.

The @ISNA function is used in the same manner as @ISERR, but is used less frequently. The value NA is less common than ERR, since few formulas give this result unless you design them that way. However, an example would be the statement

@ISNA (@MEMEMSAVAIL)

which returns 1 if you have no expanded memory in your system.

The statements @ISNUMBER(*value*) and @ISSTRING(*value*) are used in Quattro Pro 3 to test whether the referenced value is a number or a string. An example of these functions at work is shown in Figure 12-29, where a set of cells in column B is being used to receive data about a piece of lost baggage. The first piece of data, Passenger Name, has been entered in B5 and the Note in column C states "Okay." This method of data entry and prompting uses formulas next to the data entry cells to flag entries as they are made. You can see the formulas revealed in text format in Figure 12-30. Cell C5 evaluates to "Okay" because the statement @ISSTRING(B5) results in 1. In cell B6 there is a blank label, a simple apostrophe. This causes the message "Enter number" to be displayed as the result of the formula in C6 because @ISNUMBER produces 0 when it is applied to a cell containing a label. Of course, all the user sees is a note that the information for Date Lost must be a number rather than a label.

Note that the blank entry form should start with no entries in cell B6 or in cells B8 through B10. There should be blank labels in B6 and B7 to create the "Enter" prompts.

Protection and Input

The worksheets in Figures 12-28 and 12-29 are typical examples of a spreadsheet used for data entry. If there is much data to be entered, the person doing the entry may be accomplished at the keyboard but inexperienced with spreadsheet operation. To prevent accidental deletion or overwriting of important cells in a worksheet, you may want to take steps to protect your worksheet.

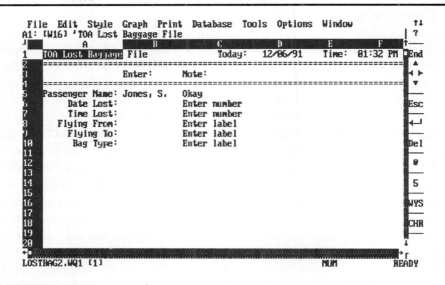

Figure 12-29. *Data entry check*

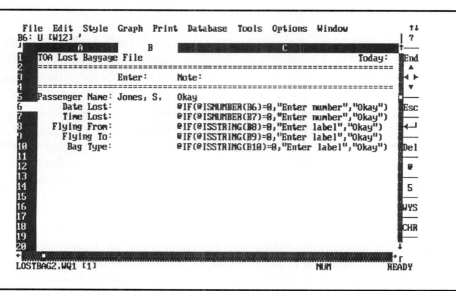

Figure 12-30. *Data entry formulas*

Complete Protection

To completely protect a worksheet, you use the Options Protection Enable command. This command prevents any cell of the worksheet from being changed. You use this feature in a number of situations. For example, when you share your PC with others, you may worry that someone will accidentally retrieve one of your worksheets and damage it before realizing they have the wrong file. Of course, password protection (described in Chapter 7) will prevent such file retrieval, but a less drastic step is to enable protection prior to saving the worksheet. The only way someone can alter your data is by turning off protection. Removing protection is done for the entire spreadsheet with Options Protection Disable. However, you can use Style Protection Unprotect to allow access to specific cells or groups of cells. When you enable protection for the entire worksheet, you will see the code PR in the cell descriptor of all cells, except those that have been unprotected by the Style Protection Unprotect command. Unprotected cells will show the code U.

Partial Protection

To turn on default protection and then remove it for specific blocks of cells is exactly what you need when turning over a spreadsheet to an inexperienced user. Quattro Pro 3 highlights the unprotected cells to make it easier to see which cells can accept data. The formulas and macros that run the worksheet are safe from damage while the data cells are clearly displayed. (If you try default protection and then block unprotect on your system and cannot see a different shading, try adjusting your monitor's contrast control and check the settings under Options Colors Spreadsheet.)

If you want to do more to restrict a user's access to a spreadsheet, you can use the Database Restrict Input command to define an area of the spreadsheet beyond which the cell selector cannot be moved. This area must coincide with a block of unprotected cells in an otherwise completely protected worksheet. When the Database Restrict Input command is issued, the top-left cell of the Input Block is placed in the top left of the screen and the cell selector is placed in the first cell that is unprotected.

At this point the cursor keys will not move the cell selector beyond the bounds of this block. However, pressing ESCAPE will remove this movement restriction, so you should keep in mind that an input area will not keep prying eyes away from confidential areas of a spreadsheet.

Advanced Macro Notes

You can see that extensive use of the macro commands and advanced functions in Quattro Pro 3 can take you into areas that are not mere spreadsheet usage but applications development and programming—areas that are beyond the scope of this book. However, the macro-building methods that you have seen here contain the basic principles on which you can build complete customized systems. If you bear in mind some basic rules, you will be able to assemble sophisticated systems of commands as your confidence with macros increases.

One Step at a Time

When you have an idea for a complex macro or series of macros, try developing the ideas in a fresh worksheet with test data, rather than in the large worksheet in which they will eventually be applied. Testing helps ensure against accidental data loss as well as making the success of the macro logic easier to assess. Once you are comfortable with the basic structure, you can apply it to large sets of real data. You should also avoid making any single macro too large. This is particularly true in the case of menu macros. Just because the {MENUCALL} and {MENUBRANCH} commands require the menu options to be in consecutive columns does not mean that the entire macro for each menu option needs to be below the menu. You can use a {BRANCH} command as the first line of macro code for each menu item, directing flow from the menu macro to code for each item that is stored in a separate area of the worksheet. An example of this is shown in Figure 12-31.

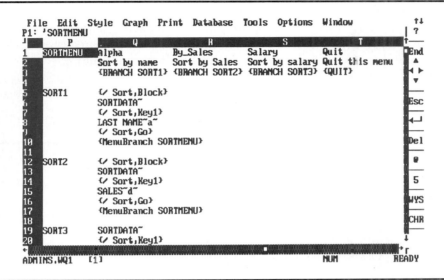

Figure 12-31. *Organization of menu with branches*

One Line at a Time

One simple feature of Quattro Pro 3's macro environment is that you can execute a macro without naming it. All you need to do is simply point at it. To test the last three lines of a 10-line macro, you can use Tools Macro Execute, place your selector on the third to the last line of the macro, and press ENTER. This avoids the need to create temporary macro names just to test certain steps. If you assign the Shortcut CTRL-E to the Tools Macro Execute menu item you can execute macro code very quickly.

To check only one line of a macro, you can temporarily insert a blank row below the line you want to check to prevent the macro from continuing.

Debug

Do not forget the DEBUG command (SHIFT-F2), which will, at the very least, provide you with single-step macro execution. To see the macro execute in single-step mode, you repeatedly press the SPACEBAR. While you are executing a macro in DEBUG mode, you can type / to get the Macro Debugger menu shown in Figure 12-32. The Edit a cell option allows you to edit the cells of the macro and thus avoid errors that you have noticed during execution. You select Quit from the Debugger menu to return to macro execution in DEBUG mode. If the macro appears fine during DEBUG playback, you can let it run to completion by pressing ENTER. To assist in problem-solving when a macro is not running properly, you can use the tools provided on the Debugger menu.

Breakpoints   In addition to the single-step feature, you can set breakpoints to control macro execution. These are blocks or cells of macro code at which the macro should pause during execution. Breakpoints are an easier way of testing sections of larger macros than inserting blank cells after the last line you want to execute. By pressing ENTER during DEBUG playback, you can run the macro to the next breakpoint. As many as four breakpoints can be set from the Macro Debugger menu. If you want the breakpoint to be effective only on a repetition of the macro, you can set a pass count for the breakpoint. Use Reset from the Macro Debugger menu to clear the breakpoints.

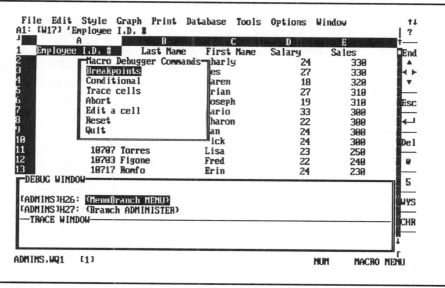

Figure 12-32.   *Macro Debugger menu*

Conditional   If you want a macro to run until a particular condition is met, you can use the Conditional option on the Macro Debugger menu to point to a cell in which you have entered a logical formula. An appropriate logical formula would be one that returns 1 for true and 0 for false. Thus, a cell containing the formula A>199 could be used to make the macro playback pause if it caused A1 to exceed 99.

Trace Cells   If you are concerned with the macro's effect on particular cells of the spreadsheet, you can identify four trace cells that will be monitored in the Trace Window during macro execution in DEBUG mode. This method is very helpful for running a large macro that affects diverse areas of the worksheet.

Transcript Help

Bear in mind that Transcript will not be recording while you record a macro. When you are involved in critical operations, you may want to adjust the Transcript Failure Protection setting to reduce the number of keystrokes between saves from 100 to a smaller number. Use the Tools Macro Transcript command to display the Transcript log and then type / for the Transcript menu. Select Failure Protection and enter the number you want. Press ENTER and then ESCAPE to clear the menu. A very small number, such as 5, will mean that Quattro Pro 3 slows down, saving to disk every five keystrokes. But a number like 25 is a good compromise between slow response and maximum recall in the event of a mistake or an equipment problem.

Full-Screen Effects

When you are managing a large number of macros, you may want to set up a menu from which to select groups of macros to be brought into the current worksheet. The menu in Figure 12-33 shows one method of organizing a large number of choices. When the user has highlighted the desired file, ALT-M is pressed to initiate a Tools Combine of that file. The ALT-M macro, shown in Figure 12-34, copies the name to a cell called CHOICE, which forms part of the macro instructions.

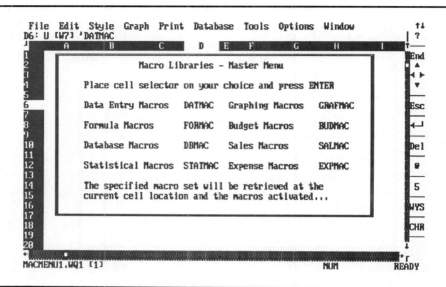

Figure 12-33. *Macro choice menu*

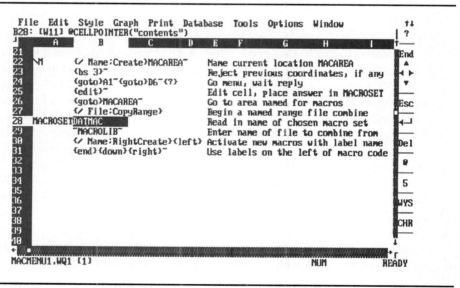

Figure 12-34. *The ALT-M macro code*

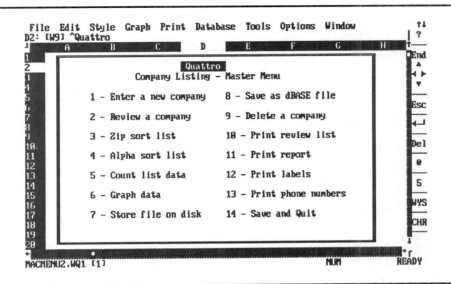

Figure 12-35.   *Large menu*

The large menu design can be used with other macro choice techniques. In Figure 12-35 a large menu offers the user 14 options. Each number on the menu represents a different macro, which is chosen by typing the number of the desired option. A menu like this is effective as a first screen, activated by a Startup macro (\0). Figure 12-36 shows the code that uses this menu. After the cell selector is positioned by a pair of {GOTO} statements, the user is prompted by a {GETNUMBER} statement: "Enter the number of your choice:." The response is placed in the cell called TEST. The series of {IF} statements branch to the chosen macros—ENTER, REVIEW, and so on. This approach can be used in a number of different situations where the choices fit into a normal Quattro Pro 3 menu. (Remember that in a normal {MENUBRANCH} menu, Quattro Pro 3 allows 13 menu choices to be shown at once, and more can be incorporated into the menu, although the user will have to scroll down the list to see them.)

The slight pause while Quattro Pro 3 evaluates the {IF} statements in macros like this might become annoying. An alternative approach that provides faster response and far less code is shown here:

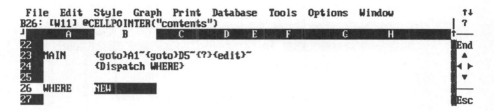

The {DISPATCH} command is used to direct macro flow to the cell called WHERE. This cell contains a formula that reads the contents of the cell currently occupied by the cell selector. This macro employs a menu screen like that shown in Figure 12-37 to present the user with options that are actual subroutine names that can be highlighted. When the user presses ENTER, the contents of the currently highlighted cell are read into WHERE and thus used in the macro.

Notice the {?}, which is the pause for the user to move the cell selector and press ENTER. This command is followed by the code {edit}. This causes Quattro Pro 3 to update the @CELLPOINTER function in the WHERE cell. If this is omitted, WHERE may retain the cell selector's previous location and the macro will branch improperly.

Figure 12-36. *Macro code*

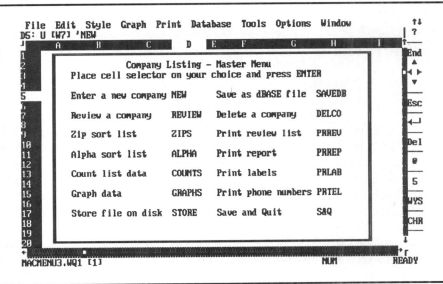

Figure 12-37.   *Menu of subroutines*

The macro names on the menu can sometimes be normal names, but in a large model where many names are used up you may be forced to make do with approximate choices, as shown in Figure 12-37. The fact that the names are not proper words is offset by the descriptions that accompany each one on the menu. You might want to elaborate on this menu system by using the Form Input command. When global protection has been turned on and the choice cells have been unprotected, the area from D5 to H17 becomes a Form Input area to restrict the user's movement to the choice cells.

An Opening Number

When a novice user application begins, it should make the operator comfortable with the program. You can do this by careful use of the Startup macro (\0) and screen positioning. This is an excellent way to use the wide-screen menus shown in Figures 12-35 and 12-37. However, you can accentuate a regular Quattro Pro 3 macro menu to make an effective opening. In Figure 12-38 the user is shown the first menu and told how to

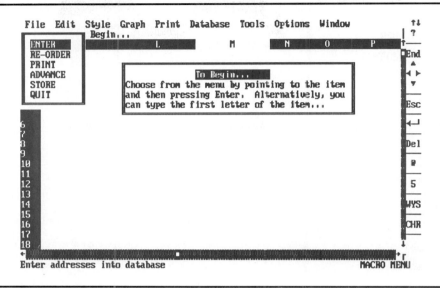

Figure 12-38. *Opening menu*

use it. This was achieved by the {GOTO} command, first to the top-left corner of the screen, and then to the highlighted label. The menu was then called. Note that Quattro Pro 3's menu positioning means some changes for those used to designing for 1-2-3's horizontal menu. Here the designing has positioned the box accordingly. This design could be improved by stating the application's name in the first screen for user reassurance.

While You Wait

Power users hate to wait, and one should assume the same for novice users. It is certainly prudent to let users know when they have initiated a procedure that takes time. The screen shown in Figure 12-39 is an example of this. The macro that performs the printing simply moves the cell selector to this screen before issuing the {/ Print;Go} command. Similar screens are advisable when the user saves the file. You might want to add an extra warning if the application is written for floppy-disk users, letting them know it is important not to remove the disk until the save process is complete.

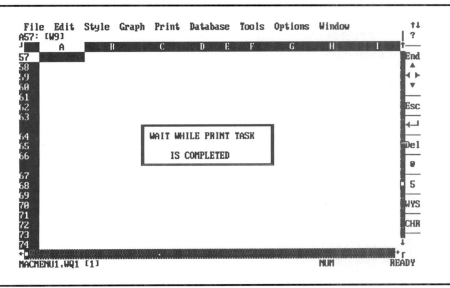

Figure 12-39.   *Print wait screen*

A Message System

As an alternative to the previous techniques for displaying messages and
menus, you can use text graphs. Graph message screens are not simply for
use in presentations. By using the {GRAPHCHAR} command you can get
user input while a graph is displayed and use this to branch to a series of
macro instructions. For more on this technique and the design of graph
buttons, turn to the next chapter.

13 *Special Features*

This chapter takes a closer look at some of the more interesting features of Quattro Pro 3. The chapter begins with a look at how Paradox and Quattro Pro 3 can work together to manage information. Then several aspects of presenting information are examined. Quattro Pro 3's ability to produce high quality text charts is detailed. The Annotate feature is reviewed in depth, and you will see how to use clip art and simple drawing techniques to greatly enhance graphs that are then combined into a professional presentation. The creation of slide shows is covered, together with ideas for graph buttons with which you can put together self-paced presentations. By combining graph buttons with macros you can create visually effective custom menus that can form the basis of a tailor made information system.

Working Together: Paradox and Quattro Pro 3

While Quattro Pro 3 has considerable power to organize and manage information, there are some applications which require the use of software with even more powerful database management capabilities. One such program is Paradox from Borland International, the makers of Quattro Pro 3. Paradox manages information in *tables,* which are column and row listings that look similar to Quattro Pro 3's databases.

709

About Paradox

Paradox has the ability to sort and search up to two billion records, and the size of the database that can be handled is limited only by disk space, not by the amount of RAM in your computer. Because it is a relational database manager, Pardadox can work with several databases at once, based on links established between different fields. For example, your company's order desk may use a database that lists all customer orders, recording the customer name in a field called Customer. A separate database may be used by the credit department to keep track of customer addresses, contact names, and credit information, with the name of the customer recorded in a field called Name. Suppose you want a list of all orders over a certain size placed in a particular month together with the names and addresses of the customers who placed them. Paradox can create an answer table that pulls this information together based on query criteria and a link between the Customer field in the order database and the Name field in the accounting database. A third database could be involved, perhaps accounts receivable, to reduce the answer table to those companies who had paid for their orders. This answer table can either be treated as a temporary collection of information, or it can be saved, sorted, and queried as though it were a new database.

In addition to the ability to relate large collections of information, Paradox is particularly well-suited to network operations where numerous users are adding, editing, and searching records. Paradox can also relate to databases on larger sytems, such as minicomputers and mainframes, using Structured Query Language (often abbreviated as SQL and pronounced "sequel"). SQL is a standardized system for requesting information from a large database. Using SQL Link (a separate product), Paradox can gather information from SQL database systems. Where Quattro Pro 3 shines is in the analysis of data and the preparation of presentation-quality graphics and slide shows. As you might imagine, it is possible to establish a very close working relationship between Paradox and Quattro Pro 3, thereby using the best features of both programs. If you have access to both Paradox and Quattro Pro 3 on your computer you can:

■ Read Paradox database files directly into a Quattro Pro 3 spreadsheet, using File Retrieve, File Open, or Tools Combine.

■ Extract specific records from a Paradox table into Quattro Pro 3 based on criteria, using Data Query Extract.

■ Access Quattro Pro 3 from Paradox, and switch between the two programs with a single keystroke (you must have Paradox 3.5 or later to do this).

In the following sections you will read how to work with Paradox and Quattro Pro 3. It is assumed that you already have some knowledge of Paradox (the Paradox documentation contains an excellent *Quick Guide to Paradox* that is written for spreadsheet users, and you will find all you need to know about the basic operation of Paradox in *Paradox Made Easy* from Borland/Osborne McGraw-Hill).

Reading Paradox Database Files

If the Paradox table you want to work on is not too large you can read it directly into Quattro Pro 3. The simplest approach is to open the table from within Quattro Pro 3 using the File Retrieve or File Open commands. The only limits to the size of table that Quattro Pro 3 can read are the amount of conventional and expanded RAM available and the limitations of the spreadsheet, that is, 256 fields or columns and 8191 records or rows.

Using File Open Simply select File Open and then press ESCAPE to edit the file specification for *.W?? to *.DB (Paradox tables have the extension DB). This enables you to show Paradox tables in the File Open list, as seen in Figure 13-1. Alternatively, you can use the File Manager to list DB files and select from the list. When you open a DB file with Quattro Pro 3 the field names appear on row 1, and the records are listed on rows 2 and below. The field names are in uppercase, the widths of the field columns are set, and dates appear in D4 format, as shown in Figure 13-2. Numbers that were formatted in the Paradox table retain their formatting in the Quattro Pro 3 worksheet. In addition, you will find that the first data cell in each field has been named, just as though the Database Query Assign Names command had been issued. Note that there are no Database Query settings in place in the file.

You can treat this worksheet just like a normal Quattro Pro 3 worksheet. You can edit, calculate, graph, query, and sort the data. However, you should be careful when using the File Save command to resave the file under its original name. When you issue the File Save command and the file has a DB extension Quattro Pro 3 will save the file as a table, reading

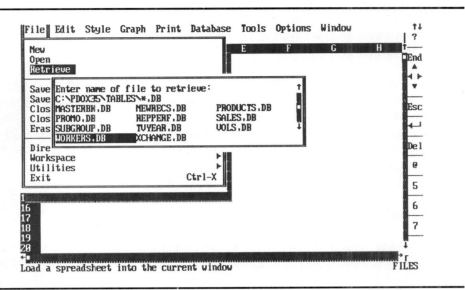

Figure 13-1.   *Paradox tables listed by File Open*

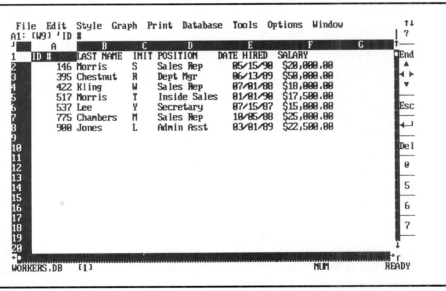

Figure 13-2.   *A Paradox table in Quattro Pro 3*

the closest text cell to A1 as the first field name and extrapolating a field and record structure from there. If you have added cell entries such as titles and calculations outside the table structure, then Quattro Pro 3 may have difficulty reading the worksheet back into a DB file. In a situation like this you can use the Tools Xtract command to specify the exact cells you want Quattro Pro 3 to store as a Paradox table. When you use File Save or Tools Xtract and specify a DB extension, Quattro Pro 3 presents a brief menu to allow you to review and change the file structure and confirm writing the DB file.

For more on the Tools Xtract command, see Chapter 7. In some situations using the original DB filename may confuse Paradox, as when the table has special relationships with other Paradox tables, and you may be prevented from completing the command by the error message "Cannot save without destroying family files." In this case you can save the worksheet as a table under another name.

Using Tools Combine   An alternative to using File Open to read a Paradox table is to use Tools Combine. This allows you to read Paradox data into an existing Quattro Pro 3 worksheet at the current cell. For example, in Figure 13-3 you can see the user is about to complete the Tools Combine Copy File command by selecting a Paradox table called WORKERS.DB. This file will be read into cell B31 and as many cells below and columns to the right as there are records in the chosen table. As you can see from Figure 13-4, the incoming data does not alter the current column width settings, which may need to be changed to make the new data legible. Block names are not attached to the new data, but the date format is automatically assigned.

The Tools Combine command also lets you import specific information from a Paradox table. This is done by choosing the Block option instead of the File option. When you choose Tools Combine Copy Block, Quattro Pro 3 prompts for a block name or coordinates. You can describe the section of the Paradox table you want to import by using block coordinates. For example, the file WORKERS.DB is 6 columns wide and 8 rows long. Consequently it can be described as A1..F8. If you only want to read in a list of names you could use Combine Copy Block and specify B1..C8. Obviously you have to know the structure of the Paradox table to make a selection like this, and you can only use a single contiguous group of cells per combine operation. You cannot specify two blocks at once, but you could perform two combine operations to bring in two separate parts of the table.

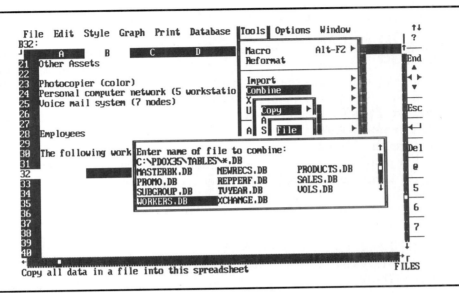

Figure 13-3. *The Tools Combine Copy command*

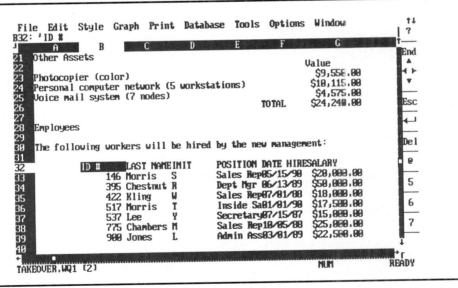

Figure 13-4. *Paradox data combined into a worksheet*

Extracting Specific Records from Paradox

While the Tools Combine command allows a certain amount of discrimination when reading records from a Paradox table, the Data Query Extract command gives you complete control over the reading of Paradox records, using the same system of criteria that you saw in Chapter 3 when selecting records from a Quattro Pro 3 database. Suppose that in the worksheet in Figure 13-5 you only want to read from WORKERS.DB the records of workers with salaries less than $20,000. Furthermore, you only want to read in the name, position, and salary fields. You set this up just as if you were performing a Data Query Extract on a Quattro Pro 3 database. You need to define the criteria table, as well as the database and output blocks.

The Output Block   First you enter the names of the fields that you want in the output. You can see this has been done in Figure 13-6 where the column widths have been adjusted to make the incoming data easier to read and the Database menu has been activated. After selecting Query, you select Output to define the area that the incoming records will occupy. This must include the field names (matching capitalization is not necessary). In this case you might choose D31..G40 since you know there will only be a few names. If you are not sure of the number of records that will only be a few names. If you are not sure of the number of records that will be read you can use just the field names as the output block, in this case D31..G31. However, if you use this approach you should be sure that all cells below the field names are clear of data because they could be overwritten by the incoming records.

The Criteria Block   There is one criterion in this case, a value in the salary field of less than 20,000. To create the criteria table you use an empty area of the worksheet and enter **Salary** as the field name. Below this you enter the criterion formula, which references the Paradox database as though it were another worksheet, as shown here:

Salary

+[C:\PDOX35\TABLES\WORKERS.DB]SALARY

When you enter this formula Quattro Pro 3 will read the file that you specify. This ensures that the file and field name are accurate. If they are

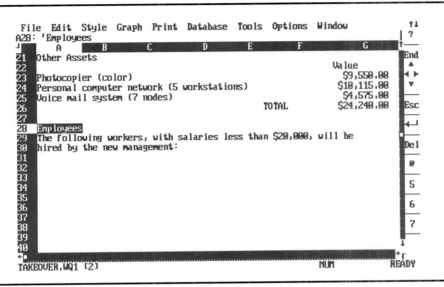

Figure 13-5. *Worksheet to receive Paradox data*

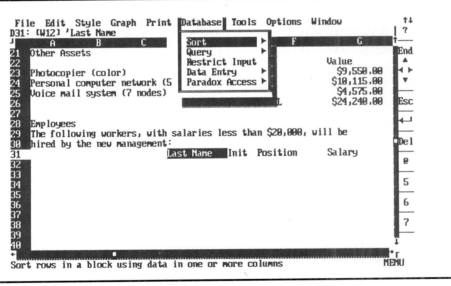

Figure 13-6. *Prepared worksheet with output range*

not you will be given an error message and the chance to alter the reference. If the reference is correct Quattro Pro 3 may shorten it to just the filename, indicating that it already knows the correct drive and directory. You use Database Query Criteria Table to specify the two cells containing the field name and formula.

The Database Block Now you can use the Database Query Block command to tell Quattro Pro 3 the name of the file you are querying. To do this you type the name of the file and then a "fake" cell reference, as in

[C:\PDOX35\TABLES\WORKERS.DB]A1..A2

If Quattro Pro 3 can find the file you are referencing it accepts this entry as the database block setting, and may abbreviate the path and directory description, as in Figure 13-7. The coordinates A1..A2 are used by Quattro Pro 3 to register the fact that this is a set of records. You use A1..A2 regardless of the size and structure of the Paradox database you are extracting from.

The Extract In Figure 13-7 you can see the completed settings for the extract operation. All that remains is to issue the Extract or Unique command. You can see the results in Figure 13-8. This method of reading data from Paradox enables you to limit the information coming into Quattro Pro 3 to just those records and fields you need. For more on criteria see Chapter 3.

Remember that the entries in the criteria table must reference the file and field name of the Paradox table. If you need to specify a range of records use the multiple field name approach. For example, to extract the records of all persons hired in 1988 and 1989 you would use the following as your criteria table:

Date Hired	Date Hired
+[WORKERS.DB]DATE HIRED<32874	+[WORKERS.DB]DATEHIRED>32142

The numbers 32874 and 32142 represent the dates 1/1/90 and 12/31/87, respectively.

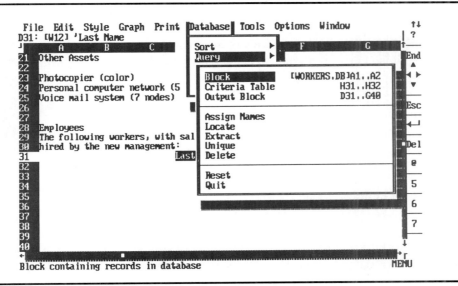

Figure 13-7. *Completed Database Query Extract settings*

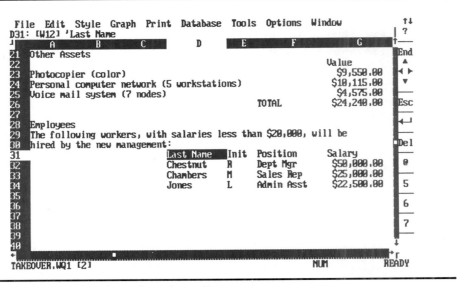

Figure 13-8. *Results of Database Query Extract*

Accessing Quattro Pro 3 from Paradox

All of the techniques discussed for accessing Paradox data can be carried out without using the Paradox program itself and are useful for anyone who has to read DB files with Quattro Pro 3. However, if you have both Quattro Pro 3 and Paradox on your system, you can switch between the two programs with a single keystroke (you must have Paradox 3.5 or later to do this). The Paradox Access command on the Quattro Pro 3 Database menu lets you run Quattro Pro 3 from within Paradox, automatically load a Paradox table into a spreadsheet, work with the table in Quattro Pro 3, and then return to Paradox, without having to close either program. There are several advantages to Paradox-Quattro Pro 3 switching:

- By using the Paradox SQL Link you can bring SQL-hosted data (residing on mainframes, minicomputers, or OS/2 servers) into Quattro Pro 3 spreadsheets.

- By using Quattro Pro 3's presentation and publishing features you can graph, print, and present Paradox data, including that pulled from SQL sources, and even turn it into a slide show.

- By using Paradox's powerful Query by Example feature (QBE), you can easily select records instead of using a criteria table in Quattro Pro 3. The Answer table of selected data that Paradox creates, equivalent to the output block in Quattro Pro 3, can be automatically imported into Quattro Pro 3.

- By using the Paradox sort commands you can perform sorts on data before bringing it into Quattro Pro 3, thus avoiding the Database Sort command.

- By using macros in Quattro Pro 3 or scripts in Paradox you can automate many repetitive or time-consuming tasks.

Running Paradox Access   To use Paradox Access, you first load Paradox, then switch to Quattro Pro 3 by pressing CTRL-F10. To switch back to Paradox you press CTRL-F10 in Quattro Pro 3 or choose Go from the Database Paradox Access menu. To be able to perform this operation you need a fairly powerful system, the minimum specifications of which are

■ *Paradox 3.5 or later* You will also need Paradox SQL Link if you want to access SQL data.

■ *At least two megabytes of RAM* Quattro Pro 3 needs 512K of RAM when run alone and 640K when installed for network use.

■ *An 80286 processor* An 80386, 8036SX, or 80486 procesor would be even better.

To work with very large spreadsheets in Quattro Pro 3, you might need additional expanded memory.

Before you use Paradox Access, there are several aspects of your system's configuration that should be checked. If the following steps for invoking Paradox Access do not work, refer to the section in Appendix B on Paradox Access. The best way to run Paradox Access is to run the PXACCESS batch file, which Quattro Pro 3 installed for you in the program directory. The file contains the following lines:

```
share
paradox -qpro -leaveK 512 -emK 0
```

As you can see, PXACCESS.BAT starts Paradox with a number of command line options. Most of the options concern how much memory Paradox uses. Usually the default settings in PXACCESS.BAT give optimum performance, but in some cases you might be able to improve performance by editing the file. Check the Paradox Access section in Appendix B for details.

After you run PXACCESS.BAT, Paradox starts and runs as usual. When you want to switch to Quattro Pro 3, press CTRL-F10; Paradox opens Quattro Pro 3 and passes control to it. If Paradox cannot open Quattro Pro 3, you will get the message "Can't load Quattro Pro." The first item to check is whether Quattro Pro 3 is on your DOS path in your AUTOEXEC.BAT file. If you do not start Paradox correctly (that is, by using the batch file or entering its contents directly), Paradox beeps when you press CTRL-F10. Exit Paradox and begin again by using the PXACCESS batch file. Note that pressing CTRL-F10 is the same as running a new PAL command called TOQPRO (PAL is the Paradox Application Language, somewhat like the macro command language in Quattro Pro 3). The TOQPRO command transfers control to Quattro Pro 3 and tells it the path to the user's private directory so that Quattro Pro 3 can find the file ANSWER.DB. This file is where Paradox stores the results of any queries. By allowing you to load ANSWER.DB directly into Quattro Pro 3 as you move from Paradox to the spreadsheet program, Paradox Access makes it very easy to query tables in Paradox and then analyze the results with Quattro Pro 3.

If you want to start Quattro Pro 3 whenever you run Paradox, create a Paradox startup script, INIT.SC, and keep it in the same directory as the Paradox system files. This file should contain the TOQPRO command. If this INIT.SC script exists, Paradox immediately transfers control to Quattro Pro 3 at startup. To automatically load a file when you first switch to Quattro Pro 3, use the qpro command-line option with an argument in the format shown here:

paradox -qpro [*filename macroname /options*]

The *filename* argument is the name and path of a spreadsheet, workspace, or .DB file that you want Quattro Pro 3 to open on startup. The name specified here automatically loads only when you transfer to Quattro Pro 3 for the first time. Subsequent transfers will load the file you specify with Quattro Pro 3's Paradox Access Load File command, as described in the next section.

The *macroname* argument is the name of a macro to run when Quattro Pro 3 opens the named file. The */options* argument refers to any of the regular Quattro Pro 3 command-line options, except for the /X option, which is disabled in Paradox Access. Note that the square bracket must be present.

Quattro Pro 3 and Paradox SQL Link   If you have SQL Link installed with Paradox, you can use Quattro Pro 3 to access data on a SQL database server. However, make sure that you have installed Paradox correctly for your SQL server, using the SQLINST program, as described in the SQL Link *User's Guide*. Bear in mind that switching to Quattro Pro 3 breaks your SQL connection and rolls back any uncommitted transactions. If you have changed the setting of Tools SQL Preferences AutoCommit to Off, be sure you save your changes before switching. See the SQL Link *User's Guide* for more about these commands. You should not attempt to load a SQL Link replica table into Quattro Pro 3 (you will get the error message "Cannot access SQL replica file" if you try).

Queries on SQL data can create huge Answer tables. If Quattro Pro 3 does not have enough memory to load the full Answer table, it warns you that there is not enough memory, and loads as much as it can starting at the first record.

The Database Paradox Access Command To control how Paradox Access works with Quattro Pro 3 you use the Paradox Access command from the Database menu in Quattro Pro 3. The Paradox Access menu consists of the following three options:

Go
: This switches you to Paradox. If you have done some work in Paradox already, you return to the point where you left off. Your Quattro Pro 3 session closes, but is not lost. If you switch back to Quattro Pro 3, you will be returned to where you were when you left.

Load File
: This specifies the file that automatically loads when you switch to Quattro Pro 3. The file can be a spreadsheet or a Paradox table. The default setting is ANSWER.DB. Even though you can enter a pathname here, Quattro Pro 3 knows to look in your private directory to find ANSWER.DB and any other Paradox temporary table, as well as in the current directory for all other tables and files. This command is appropriate only when Autoload is set to Yes.

Autoload
: This specifies whether the file named with Load File is automatically brought into Quattro Pro 3 each time you switch from Paradox to Quattro Pro 3. The default is Yes.

If the file you specify with Load File is a spreadsheet with a startup macro assigned, the startup macro runs every time you switch from Paradox to Quattro Pro 3 (you assign a startup macro with Options Startup, Startup Macro). If you started Paradox with the command-line option -qpro [*filename*], as described previously, the file specified by *filename* autoloads instead of the file entered with the Load File command. This is true only for the first transfer to Quattro Pro 3. Subsequent transfers to Quattro Pro 3 automatically load the file specified with the Load File command. If Autoload is set to Yes, the Options Startup Autoload File command is ignored. While you can change the settings of Load File and Autoload at any time, the Go command will work only when Quattro Pro 3 is run from within Paradox (you must start Paradox with the -qpro option, as incorporated in the PXACCESS.BAT file, before switching to Quattro Pro 3).

In addition to the commands on the Database Paradox Access menu, the Options Other Expanded Memory command also affects Paradox Access. For best use of memory, set this to Both. If you are running on a network be sure the Options Other Paradox commands are set correctly. Bear in mind that if you make a change to these settings, you must exit Quattro Pro 3 and reload the program for them to be active.

When you are done with your work in Quattro Pro 3, just press CTRL-F10 to return to Paradox. You don't have to close your spreadsheet files or choose File Exit. In fact, you can leave everything just as it is. If you later return to Quattro Pro 3 from Paradox your workspace will be just as you left it. If there are unsaved changes in Quattro Pro 3 when you quit Paradox, you will be asked if you want to save these changes before quitting to DOS. If you want to include switching to Paradox in a macro, use {/ Paradox;SwitchGo}, which is equivalent to pressing CTRL-F10.

Paradox Tables   In Figure 13-9 you can see a Paradox database of flight information for Take Over Airlines. This information has been pulled, by SQL Link, from the mainframe computer that tracks every detail of TOA reservations and flights. You want to analyze the performance of TOA during 1992 and so have used SQL to pull selected pieces of data from the mainframe program. Each record in Paradox consists of a flight number, destination, and the number of passengers who travelled on the flight, broken down into three classes: First, Business, and Coach. Off the right

```
Viewing Tuyear table: Record 1 of 627                        Main
```

TUYEAR	FLIGHT	DATE	DEST	FIRST	BUSINESS	COACH	
1	520	1/01/92	Rome	7	13	111	**
2	420	1/02/92	London	19	31	199	**
3	521	1/02/92	R-Base	8	17	141	**
4	620	1/03/92	Tokyo	13	18	58	**
5	820	1/03/92	Cairo	5	6	90	**
6	421	1/04/92	L-Base	15	26	163	**
7	720	1/04/92	Athens	5	11	89	**
8	821	1/05/92	C-Base	4	5	77	**
9	920	1/06/92	Paris	21	28	183	**
10	621	1/06/92	T-Base	18	23	76	**
11	921	1/07/92	P-Base	17	25	170	**
12	721	1/07/92	A-Base	6	12	99	**
13	520	1/08/92	Rome	6	12	104	**
14	420	1/09/92	London	19	31	199	**
15	521	1/09/92	R-Base	7	13	110	**
16	620	1/10/92	Tokyo	14	19	62	**
17	820	1/10/92	Cairo	6	7	103	**
18	421	1/11/92	L-Base	19	31	143	**
19	720	1/11/92	Athens	7	13	113	**
20	821	1/12/92	C-Base	5	6	96	**
21	920	1/13/92	Paris	20	27	174	**
22	621	1/13/92	T-Base	13	18	57	**

Figure 13-9.   *Paradox table*

of the screen there is also a Total field that shows the total number of passengers, plus a Revenue field, that shows the gross receipts from the flight. Suppose that you want to use Quatttro Pro 3 to analyze First Class traffic in the first quarter. You do not need details of flight numbers or revenue, just the flight destination, date, and the number of First Class passengers. Instead of dumping the entire database into Quattro Pro 3, you can first sift out the appropriate data with Paradox, using the Ask command.

Assuming that you have loaded Paradox with PXACCESS and have used the View command to select the desired table, you can use the Ask command to specify the information you need. First press F10 for the Paradox menu and then select Ask. You need to tell Paradox the table to be queried. Press ENTER to view a list of tables, and the table you are currently viewing is highlighted. Press ENTER to select it. You will see a list of the fields in the table with space to enter your criteria, as shown in Figure 13-10 where the criteria have been entered. In the DATE field you can see the following formula, used to specify records with a DATE entry in the first quarter:

>=1/1/92, <=3/31/92

```
√ [F6] to include a field in the ANSWER; [F5] to give an Example      Main  ═▼
    ═══FLIGHT═══           ═══DATE═══           ═══DEST═══         ═══FIRST═══
                     √ >=1/1/92, <=3/31/92 │                 │                 │

 TUYEAR──FLIGHT────────DATE──────────DEST─────FIRST───BUSINESS────COACH──
     1      520      1/01/92      Rome          7         13        111    **
     2      420      1/02/92      London       19         31        199    **
     3      521      1/02/92      R-Base        8         17        141    **
     4      620      1/03/92      Tokyo        13         18         58    **
     5      820      1/03/92      Cairo         5          6         90    **
     6      421      1/04/92      L-Base       15         26        163    **
     7      720      1/04/92      Athens        5         11         89    **
     8      821      1/05/92      C-Base        4          5         77    **
     9      920      1/06/92      Paris        21         28        183    **
    10      621      1/06/92      T-Base       18         23         76    **
    11      921      1/07/92      P-Base       17         25        170    **
    12      721      1/07/92      A-Base        6         12         99    **
    13      520      1/08/92      Rome          6         12        104    **
    14      420      1/09/92      London       19         31        199    **
    15      521      1/09/92      R-Base        7         13        110    **
    16      620      1/10/92      Tokyo        14         19         62    **
```

Figure 13-10. *Paradox criteria*

Select the fields that you want in the resulting Answer table by pressing F6. This places a check mark in the field. You can now press F2 to execute the query. The resulting Answer table can be seen in Figure 13-11. If you now press CTRL-F10 to switch to Quattro Pro 3, this data will appear there, ready for you to work on, as shown in Figure 13-12. If you need to save the analysis you perform in the worksheet you can store it as a WQ1 file using File Save As.

To understand how Paradox Access affects Answer tables, you need to be aware of the characteristics of Paradox temporary tables. There are twelve temporary tables, including Answer. You can use Paradox Access to open any temporary table in addition to any regular table to which you have rights. Table 13-1 lists the temporary tables and their contents. Remember that temporary tables are just that: Paradox deletes them when you exit. Paradox often overwrites temporary tables. For example, it generates a new Answer table whenever you make a new query. Simply switching back and forth between Paradox and Quattro Pro 3 does not, however, affect temporary tables. Temporary tables do not reside in the

```
Viewing Answer table: Record 1 of 156
ANSWER       DATE            DEST        FIRST
      1     1/01/92       Rome             7
      2     1/02/92       London          19
      3     1/02/92       R-Base           8
      4     1/03/92       Cairo            5
      5     1/03/92       Tokyo           13
      6     1/04/92       Athens           5
      7     1/04/92       L-Base          15
      8     1/05/92       C-Base           4
      9     1/06/92       Paris           21
     10     1/06/92       T-Base          18
     11     1/07/92       A-Base           6
     12     1/07/92       P-Base          17
     13     1/08/92       Rome             6
     14     1/09/92       London          19
     15     1/09/92       R-Base           7
     16     1/10/92       Cairo            6
     17     1/10/92       Tokyo           14
     18     1/11/92       Athens           7
     19     1/11/92       L-Base          19
     20     1/12/92       C-Base           5
     21     1/13/92       Paris           20
     22     1/13/92       T-Base          13
```

Figure 13-11. *Paradox Answer table*

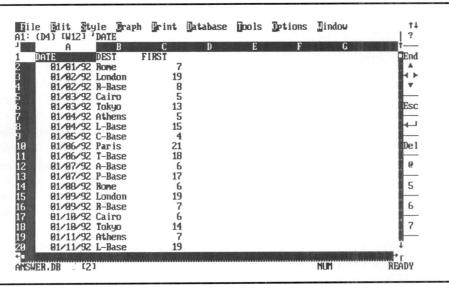

Figure 13-12.   *The results in Quattro Pro 3*

Name	Content
Answer	Results of a query
Changed	Unchanged copy of changed records
Crosstab	Results of a crosstab operation
Deleted	Deleted records
Entry	New records for a table
Family	Reports and forms for a table
Inserted	Inserted records
Keyviol	Records with duplicate key values
List	List of tables, scripts, files, network users, or locks
Password	Auxiliary passwords
Problems	Unconverted records
Struct	Table definition

For more information on the contents of these temporary tables, refer to the Paradox *User's Guide.*

Table 13-1.   *Paradox Temporary Tables*

working directory. Unlike your working tables, they are written to your private directory. This means they will not appear in the file list when you choose File Open, for example, because that list shows your working directory, not your private directory.

Paradox tells Quattro Pro 3 where your private directory is so it can open ANSWER.DB, STRUCT.DB, and the other necessary files. Both the Autoload command and the regular File commands can open any of the temporary tables, but because all files in a private directory are locked, you cannot save these tables as is. You can, however, edit and save a temporary table in a different directory and under a different name by choosing File Save As. Because of the strict locking rules for private directories, make sure your Paradox working directory and private directory are different. If they are not, use the Custom Configuration Program in Paradox (Script Play Custom). Choose Defaults SetDirectory to permanently change the location of your Paradox working directory.

Word Charts

When the time comes to present the information you have organized with Quattro pro 3 you will find it has capabilities that go far beyond those normally associated with a spreadsheet program. Later in this chapter the creative abilities of Annotate and Slide Show commands will be explored. Quattro Pro 3 even improves upon the basic spreadsheet ability to line up text in columns. This is appreciated by a wide range of users, from the secretary typing up a budget from a rough draft, to the salesperson who has a sales presentation to make. Word processing programs often make heavy going of columns, requiring mastery of complex commands. A spreadsheet offers a simple way of typing up lists that maintain a strict column and row format, such as the one shown in Figure 13-13. Quattro Pro 3 has special features to dress up such information.

Quattro Pro 3 for Professional Text

The text in Figure 13-13 was simply typed into the worksheet. The figures in column W are summed in cell W51, but otherwise there is no calculation going on in this collection of information. To dress up the text, perhaps to

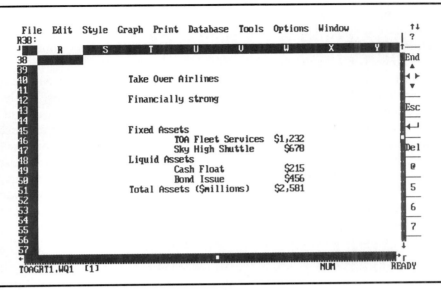

Figure 13-13. *Basic list typed into worksheet*

use it as part of a presentation, you could add bullet characters, as shown in Figure 13-14. The characters in column S are simply the letter "o" centered in the column. The characters in column T are the ASCII character 175, created by holding down ALT and typing **175** from the numeric keypad (not the row of numbers across the top of the keyboard). These characters are centered in the column. While this effect looks better, the bullet characters will simply print as characters when the cells are printed. Even if you use Graph Printer as the Print Destination the results will not be particularly eye-grabbing.

Instead of ordinary characters in your text you might want to use one or more of Quattro Pro 3's seven special bullet characters. These are shown in Figure 13-15, which was printed directly from a spreadsheet. These bullet characters are graphic symbols that can be placed in spreadsheet cells. The bullets only print as images when you use Graph Printer as the Print Destination for the Print Spreadsheet command.

You enter a bullet as a coded label that Quattro Pro 3 translates into an image during printing. For example, a style 1 bullet is created by the code

\bullet 1\

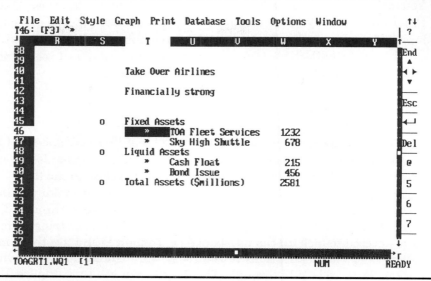

Figure 13-14. *Simple bullets added*

Quattro Professional Bullet Styles:

Bullet Style	0	□ Empty square
Bullet Style	1	■ Filled square
Bullet Style	2	☑ Checked square
Bullet Style	3	✓ Check mark
Bullet Style	4	▢ Shadow box
Bullet Style	5	☑ Checked shadow
Bullet Style	6	● Filled circle

Figure 13-15. *Special bullet characters printed*

You must enter this preceded by a label prefix (', ", or ^); otherwise, Quattro Pro 3 will assume you are using the cell fill character (\). You can enter a bullet code into a cell on its own or you can combine it with other text. You can even use a bullet code in a string formula. For example, to combine the word Present with the number 5 bullet you can enter

'\bullet 5\ Present

Note that the apostrophe must be typed, and that there is a space between the second backslash and the text that follows. This space is not mandatory, but without one the bullet would print too close to the text.

A string formula using the bullet code was used to make the list of printed codes in Figure 13-15. A column of numbers, from 0 through 6, was entered in column D, beginning at row 21. In column E, string formulas were entered to pick up the numbers from column D and use them in the bullet code. The descriptions of the codes were stored further down the worksheet in cells B29 through B34. As you can see from Figure 13-16, bullet 0 was created on row 21, with this formula:

+"\bullet" &"\"&" "&B29

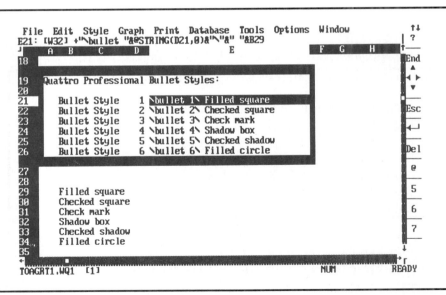

Figure 13-16.   *Bullet text formula*

This formula was copied from E21 to E22 through E27. This produced a list of codes, with descriptions. Notice the use of &" "& to create a space in the resulting label.

There are some minor inconveniences when using bullet codes. As you can see from Figure 13-16, they do not look pretty when you are working in character mode. However, when you switch to WYSIWYG mode you will see them. Bullets are hard to line up with text unless you give them their own column. As you can see from Figure 13-15, the amount of space between the bullet and the following text varies, leaving the text improperly aligned. The solution is an arrangement like that shown in Figure 13-17, where you can see bullets applied to the worksheet in Figure 13-14. These bullets are in their own columns, and so can be aligned accurately. You can then vary the printed location of the bullet within the column by using the left, right, and center label prefixes (', ", ^). In Figure 13-18 you can see the text from Figure 13-17 printed. Notice that the second bullet in the first column has been centered. Also notice that a different font has been applied to the first two lines of the text.

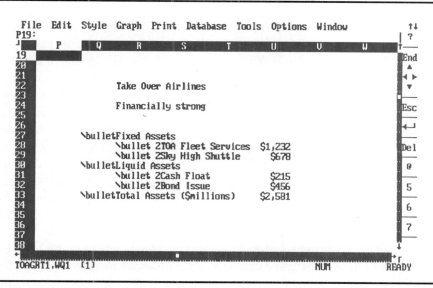

Figure 13-17. *Bullets in separate columns*

Take Over Airlines

Financially strong

☐ Fixed Assets		
☑	TOA Fleet Services	$1,232
☑	Sky High Shuttle	$678
☐ Liquid Assets		
☑	Cash Float	$215
☑	Bond Issue	$456
☐ Total Assets ($millions)		$2,581

Figure 13-18.   *Printed version of the worksheet in Figure 13-17*

Adding Style

In earlier chapters you saw how the Style commands could be used to dress up text in Quattro Pro 3. You can use Style Line Drawing to add single, double, or thick lines that go over, under, or around labels and numbers. The Style Shading command allows you to add several levels of gray to areas of your printouts. With the Style Font command you can vary the appearance of printed text, as shown in Figure 13-18. By combining these commands you can create impressive text charts and reports. For example, Figure 13-15 was printed from Quattro Pro 3 using the Style Line Drawing command with the thick line option to create the box around the text. You can see how this line appears in the worksheet itself by looking at Figure 13-16. In Figure 13-19 you can see an example of a text chart printed from Quattro Pro 3 using a combination of bullets, lines, and fonts.

An alternative approach to creating text charts with Quattro Pro 3 is to use the Graph Annotate command. This provides more creative freedom, including the ability to enliven charts with images from a clip art library.

Figure 13-19. *Text chart with lines, bullets, and different fonts*

The Power to Annotate

The Graph Annotate feature in Quattro Pro 3 allows you to create text charts and embellish graphs of spreadsheet data. In fact, Annotate is a full-featured drawing program capable of producing striking visual effects. A complete description of what can be done with Annotate could support a whole book, or at least several more chapters than will fit in this book. However, the following examples should give you an idea of what can be accomplished with this feature.

Exploring the Annotator

As you saw in Chapter 8, Annotate adds text and shapes to graphs created with the Graph command and displayed by Graph View, Graph Name Display, or the Graph key (F10). To access the Annotate feature you display a graph and then press the / key to bring up the Annotate screen. Alternatively, you can select Annotate from the Graph menu, which tells Quattro Pro 3 to display the current graph in the Annotate screen.

You do not have to add text or shapes to an existing graph. As you can see from Figure 13-20, the Annotate screen can be set up as a blank drawing board. To do this you should first make sure any existing graphs are named and saved, then use the Customize Series command on the Graph menu and select Reset followed by Graph to clear the current settings. You can now set the Graph Type to Text, which requires no series values to be established, and then select Annotate. Your screen should now look like the one in Figure 13-20.

The menu of icons across the top is called the Toolbox. The large blank rectangle is your canvas, where you will place text and shapes created with the Annotate tools. Each item you create is referred to as an *object*. The area on the right of the screen is called Properties. It allows you to change the appearance of the objects you create.

To activate the Toolbox menu you press the/key. You will see the outline of the boxes change. You can now press LEFT or RIGHT ARROW to highlight the tool you need, and then press ENTER to activate it. This places a thick line around the tool. Alternatively, you can activate the menu and then

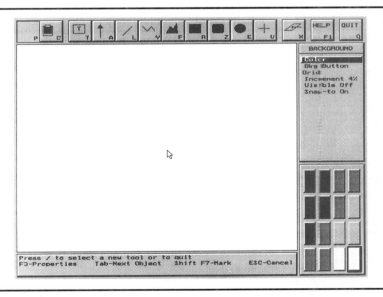

Figure 13-20.   *Annotate screen*

type the letter that appears in the tool icon. Mouse users can simply click on the desired tool. The tools are described in Table 13-2.

As you highlight different tools in the Toolbox you will see the Properties area change. The top half of Properties lists attributes applicable to the

Tool	Function
P (Pointer)	Selects objects (you can also use TAB and SHIFT-TAB to select objects in turn).
C (Clipboard)	Copies and pastes objects within current graph to/from clip art files. Also used to move objects to top or bottom layer.
T (Text)	Creates text and graph buttons (text will be boxed unless Box Type is set to None).
A (Arrow)	Draws straight line arrows at any angle.
L (Line)	Draws straight lines at any angle.
Y (Polyline)	Draws jointed lines or curves (by holding down SHIFT or enabling SCROLL LOCK).
F (Polygon)	Draws many-sided shapes or curved shapes (by holding down SHIFT or enabling SCROLL LOCK).
R (Rectangle)	Draws rectangular shapes with sharp corners.
Z (Round Rectangle)	Draws rectangular shapes with rounded corners.
E (Ellipse)	Draws circles and ovals.
V (Line)	Draws straight vertical or horizontal lines.
X (Link)	Links drawn objects to series within a graph so that they move with that part of the graph.
F1 (Help)	Displays help information about Annotate.
Q (Quit)	Quits back to full-screen display of graph (unless Annotate was accessed with the Annotate command from the Graph menu, in which case it quits back to the Graph menu with no graph display).

Table 13-2. *Tools in the Annotator*

Key	Function
ARROW keys	Move or resize a selected element or group of elements.
TAB	Moves the pointer clockwise around the elements in the drawing area.
SHIFT-TAB	Moves the pointer counterclockwise around the elements in the drawing area.
SHIFT-F7	Selects elements in the drawing area; use in combination with TAB and SHIFT-TAB to select multiple elements.
SHIFT	Used with a mouse, the SHIFT key held down as you click on elements in the drawing area selects multiple elements that are not connected.
DELETE	Deletes a selected element or group of elements; if used with a mouse, point and press DELETE to delete one element.
PERIOD (.)	With an element or group of elements selected, the period anchors the selected area and allows you to resize it. The lower right-hand corner is the default corner, which will extend or contract the element as you press ARROW keys or move the pointer with the mouse. To resize the area using a different corner, press the period repeatedly to cycle around the corners of the selected area.
HOME, END	Moves the corners of a selected area diagonally.
PAGE DOWN, PAGE UP	Moves the corners of a selected area diagonally.
F2	With an element selected, enters MOVE mode so you can reposition the element; for a text element, enters text editing mode.
CTRL-ENTER	In text editing mode, wraps inserted text to a new line.
BACKSPACE	Used to erase characters and line breaks in text editing mode.
SLASH (/)	Activates the Toolbox.
F3	Activates Properties.
F10	Redraws the Graph Annotator screen.
ESCAPE	Returns to the drawing area from Properties or the Toolbox; with a selected element in RESIZE mode, switches to MOVE mode.

Table 13-3.   *Keys Used in Graph Annotator*

type of object that the selected tool creates. The lower half shows the available choices. When you highlight a tool the name appears in the Properties area (except for the Clipboard), which reflects the name of the currently selected object. When the Pointer is selected the Background properties can be changed, including the color and the optional grid that may help you align objects.

The Toolbox menu is in several parts. The first two items are Pick and Clipboard. When the Pick option is active you can select items within the canvas area. To do this you place the mouse pointer over the item and click, or you draw a selection box around the object by dragging the pointer across the screen. Keyboard users can select each object in turn by pressing TAB when the Pointer is active. The Clipboard allows you to copy and cut items that have been selected, and also to move them to the top or bottom when there are overlapping items. The Cut To, Copy To, and Paste From commands allow you to export and import images in clip art files. These files have the extension CLP, and a number of them are included with Quattro Pro 3. The next nine menu items are the drawing tools for such shapes as lines, arrows, polygons, filled polygons, rectangles, and circles. The last three menu items are Link, Help, and Quit. When you select Quit you are presented with the results of your annotation, drawn full screen. You can then press ESCAPE to return to the worksheet, or / to return to the Annotator.

Drawing a Shape

Suppose you want to draw a free-form object, or a polygon. Press /, and then highlight the icon marked F and press ENTER (or type F). This places a cross on the screen, which is your pointer. To begin the shape, you move the pointer to the place on the screen where you want to begin, using the mouse or cursor keys. The specific actions of the cursor keys are listed in Table 13-3. To anchor the beginning point, click the mouse button or type a period (referred to as MouseDown and Dot, respectively, by the help section at the bottom of the Annotate screen). You can then move the pointer to begin drawing a line from the fixed point in the direction that you are moving the pointer. To fix the next point of the polygon you press ENTER again. You can press ESCAPE to cancel the action or type / to change tools. When you have completed the polygon you press ENTER twice, and Quattro Pro 3 closes up the object's outline, as shown in Figure 13-21. If you want your polygon to include curves, you can hold down SHIFT while

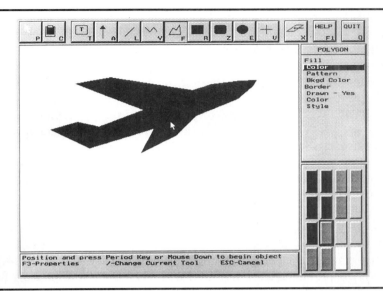

Figure 13-21.   *Completed polygon*

dragging the mouse pointer. This will produce free-form curves. When you release SHIFT the tool draws straight lines again. This also works with the Polyline tool. Alternatively, you can activate curves by pressing SCROLL LOCK once. The tools will draw curves until you press SCROLL LOCK again.

If you want to draw rectangular shapes, then you should use the Background option called Snap-to. When you turn Snap-to on, the lines and shapes you draw will adhere to a fixed grid. You can see this grid if you turn on the Visible option in the Background tool. The coarseness of the grid can be adjusted. The default setting is 4%. A greater percentage will create a coarser grid.

Enhancing the Shape

Once an object has been drawn you can enhance it by changing its attributes. This is done by using Properties, the menu to the right of the main area that lists Fill, Border, and so on. Before you use Properties, you need to select the object you wish to change. You can do this by typing / to change tools and then selecting Pick, the first item on the left of the menu. Then point and click on the object with the mouse or press TAB to select the object. If there is more than one object on the canvas, pressing TAB selects each one in turn. A set of handles appears around a selected item, as you can see in Figure 13-22. These are used to move and size the object, as described in Table 13-4.

To alter the attributes of an object, activate Properties by pressing F3. When you press F3 the box around Properties becomes a double line and you can highlight an item that you want to alter, such as the Pattern used to fill the polygon object. The items on the menu vary according to which object is selected. For example, when a polygon is selected the two main categories are Fill and Border. To change the filling of the shape you press DOWN ARROW to move the highlight to Pattern and then press ENTER (or click on it with the mouse). The palette in the lower half of Properties is activated and you can use the arrow keys to move the highlighting to the attribute you want. The filling of the selected object will not change as you move from one pattern to another, but when you have highlighted the pattern you want, press ENTER or click the mouse, and the object is then filled with the chosen pattern, as shown in Figure 13-23. Note that the NO pattern means the shape will be given no filling. You can change the color as well as the pattern of the filling.

Figure 13-22.   *Selected item with handles*

1. Any selected object has eight handles, one on each corner and four in between the corners. These are used to alter the size of objects.

2. A handle that is not on a corner can be dragged to increase/decrease the size of the object in one direction, inward or outward from that side.

3. A handle that is on a corner can be dragged to increase/decrease the vertical and/or horizontal size at the same time.

4. If you have difficulty selecting a small object with a mouse, press TAB or SHIFT-TAB to cycle the selection handles through all objects in turn.

5. If you drag a handle all the way across an object you will flip the object on one or more axes. This allows you to create matching objects (for example to make two identical wings for a plane: create one wing, copy and paste, and drag one handle on the copy across the object so that it is the mirror image of the original.)

6. Adjusting the size of a boxed text object does not alter the text size, just the dimensions of the surrounding box. (Use the Font property to alter text size).

7. If you have selected a group of objects they can be sized and otherwise adjusted as a single object by pressing F7. This gives the group eight handles, as described above.

Table 13-4.   *Using Object Handles in the Annotate Screen*

Figure 13-23.   *Filling with a pattern*

You can proceed in this fashion to alter the attributes of the object. You press ESCAPE or click in the main section of the window to return to creating new objects. You can move the current object with the cursor-movement keys, or by clicking with the mouse to select the object and then dragging it to a new location. You can choose a new tool from the menu to make a new object, such as lines, arrows, rectangles, rounded rectangles, or even text that is discussed next.

Adding Text

You could add the letters TOA to the plane in Figure 13-23. When you select the Text tool you can type text at a selected point on the screen. To create a second line of text you press CTRL-ENTER. You press ENTER to complete the text object. When you enter text, it is initially boxed in a rectangle. You can alter the attributes of this box, adding shading for example, or you can remove it. As you can see from Figure 13-24, you can alter the font of the text by using a selection process similar to that used when selecting fonts for your spreadsheet entries. When you have selected a font Quattro Pro 3 may take a moment to draw the necessary screen font for you. This only happens the first time you use a particular font.

To edit text that you have already created, you first select the text object and then press F2. This places an edit cursor after the last character of the text. You can use the UP and DOWN ARROW keys to move from line to line in the text. The LEFT and RIGHT ARROW keys move the edit cursor through the text.

Using the Shape

When you want to see the drawing at full size you type / to activate the menu and pick Quit. This takes you to the full-screen graph view if you entered Annotate by typing / while viewing a graph. If you entered Annotate with the Graph Annotate command, Quit will return you to READY mode, and you can press F10 to view the graph. From here you can press ENTER to return to the worksheet. It is important to use the Graph Name Create command to save the work you do with Annotate.

There does not need to be any entry in the worksheet to support a text graph or drawing. However, you can use drawings effectively with worksheets that contain text and numbers. For example, you could en-

Figure 13-24. *Changing the font*

hance the presentation of facts about TOA by inserting the drawing into the worksheet. To do this you use the Insert command from the Graph menu. The procedure is the same as for inserting a numeric graph (described in Chapter 8). You select a named graph from the list provided and then indicate a block of cells for the graph to occupy.

WYSIWYG mode inserted graphs appear with impressive effects, as shown in Figure 13-25. Note that a circle and some clouds were added to the basic filled polygon to make the chart shown. The results of printing from this spreadsheet, including the inserted graph and the text with bullet characters, is shown in Figure 13-26. Remember that to print the inserted drawing and text together you must include both in the Print Block. Bear in mind that when you insert a drawn graph into a spreadsheet, the entire graphic is placed. You cannot place objects smaller than the full graph view screen. While the Graph Insert command reduces the graph to fit the block of cells you define for it, the text in the spreadsheet will need to be placed outside of the insert block to be visible and printable. The graph can be inserted over text or numbers, but these will be hidden in the display and in any printout of that section of the worksheet.

Note that you must be in graphic display mode to see the graph in your worksheet. In character mode the inserted graph appears as a permanent-

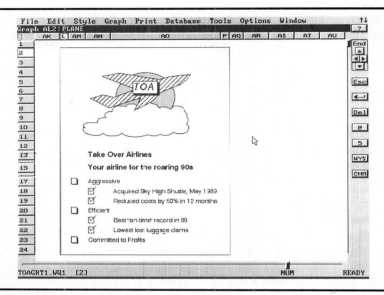

Figure 13-25. *Viewing the inserted graph*

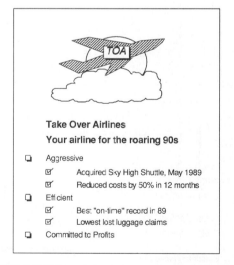

Figure 13-26. *Printed results*

ly highlighted blank block of cells. You may find that Quattro Pro 3's response time slows down when you are in graphics mode and have inserted one or more graphs into a worksheet. Furthermore, keeping track of cells that contain special formats, lines, and fonts can be cumbersome when you are engaged in writing formulas and setting up numerical analyses. For this reason you might want to consider placing highly formatted entries in a special worksheet and feeding data to that worksheet from a less intensely formatted worksheet, using linked cell reference formulas. This allows you to work quickly on one worksheet while providing correct numbers to the presentation worksheet.

You can use the Annotate feature for such projects as organization charts and flow diagrams. Figure 13-27 shows an example of an organization chart. All that you need for such a chart are a few lines and boxed text entries. The shadow attribute was selected for the boxes and the center attribute was chosen for the text with the Justify option. Although freeform drawing with Annotate is fun as well as practical, one of the primary uses of the feature is to enhance graphs. Figure 8-53 in Chapter 8 shows an ordinary graph made much more interesting with the addition of objects from Annotate.

Figure 13-27.   *Organization chart printed from Quattro Pro 3*

Power Slide Shows

The Graph Name Slide command in Quattro Pro 3 adds a new dimension
to spreadsheet graphics, giving you the ability to develop self-running
presentations based on your Quattro Pro 3 graphs. A series of graphs are
displayed one after another like a slide show. Quattro Pro 3 takes the
information about each graph from a list of graphs. You can develop your
own slide shows fairly easily or view one put together by another Quattro
Pro 3 user.

Making a Slide Show

A slide show actually consists of two columns of information entered into
the worksheet. The first column contains the graph names. The second
column contains a list of numbers that indicate the length of time, in
seconds, that each graph is to be displayed. In figure 13-28 you can see a
slide show arranged in columns A and B. The first slide, called INTRO, is
identified in cell A13 and is to be displayed for ten seconds. The names you

Figure 13-28.   *Slide show instructions*

use in the first column are those assigned to your graphs with the Graph Name Create command. The graphs must be named in the current worksheet, although you can display graphs from the current worksheet that use data supplied by other worksheets.

When you issue the Graph Name Slide command you must identify the block of cells containing the slide show instructions. In Figure 13-28 the block is A13..B18. When you enter the coordinates the show begins. Each slide is displayed in turn, for the specified period of time. You can make the display self-paced by having the user press a key to advance to the next slide. You do this by entering **0** in the second column instead of a number of seconds. When Quattro Pro 3 encounters a graph name with 0 for the display time, such as the CONCLUDE graph in Figure 13-28, it waits until a key is pressed before going on to the next graph.

Suppose you have created a number of Quattro Pro 3 graphs that you want to use to highlight points in a sales presentation. Printed versions of the graphs form part of your handout. However, you would like to display the graphs during your speech for extra impact. You have a large-screen monitor connected to your PC so that the graphs can be seen properly, but you are nervous about having to type a series of instructions every time you want to move to a new graph. This is where the slide show feature comes in.

Instead of having to type a series of Graph Name Display commmands, and having to pick the correct graph name each time, you can use the slide show list to control your graphs. This avoids the F10 key and the constant need to return to the Graph menu. When a slide show is running you cannot tell that the program is actually a spreadsheet. If you need to break out of a slide show while it is running, perhaps to resume manual control of graphs, you can always press CTRL-BREAK. If Quattro Pro 3 encounters a graph name that does not exist in the current worksheet, then it goes on to the next graph in the list. To provide complete control over a slide show and automate the process even further you can use macro commands, as described in the next section. Before using a slide show in a live presentation, always do a dry run to make sure the graphs appear as you want them to. This will also ensure that all the fonts required by the graphs have been built; otherwise, the slide show will pause while fonts are built, which detracts from the professional appearance of the show.

Slide Show Macros

The ability to start a slide show with a macro and to make slide displays dependent upon keystrokes gives you the ability to make some very sophisticated presentations with Quattro Pro 3. Slide shows are activated by the macro command

{/ Graph;NameSlide}

This is followed by the coordinates of the slide show instructions. Typically, you will use a block name for this to simplify matters. The following macro will present a slide show stored in the block named SALES as soon as the worksheet is retrieved:

\0 {/ Graph;NameSlide}SALES~

To make self-paced presentations you can use text graphs that contain instructions together with the {GRAPHCHAR} command, which returns user input during graph display. Figure 13-29 shows an instruction graph that was created with the Annotate feature and named INTRO1. The following macro code is used to display it and handle user input:

```
SLIDES              {/ Graph;NameUse}INTRO1~
                    {GRAPHCHAR RESPONSE}
                    {If RESPONSE="1"}{Branch VOLMAC}
                    {If RESPONSE="2"}{Branch REVMAC}
                    {Branch NEXT}
```

When the macro SLIDES is executed, the INTRO1 graph is displayed and Quattro Pro 3 waits until the user presses a key. The {GRAPHCHAR} command places the user's response in a cell named RESPONSE and the {IF} statement evaluates the contents of this cell. If the user presses 1, then the macro branches to code called VOLMAC. If the user presses 2, then the macro branches to code called REVMAC. If the user presses any other key, then the macro continues to the last line, branching to NEXT. The macro VOLMAC looks like this:

VOLMAC   {/ Graph;NameSlide}VOLUME~
                                     {Branch SLIDES}

The block named VOLUME contains the data for a slide show. The macro REVMAC is similar and looks like this:

REVMAC   {/ Graph;NameSlide}REVENUE~
                                     {Branch SLIDES}

There must be a cell named RESPONSE for the macro to work. The code loops the user back to the instruction screen until a key other than 1 or 2 is pressed. The {GRAPHCHAR} command is very useful for displaying graphs that act as menus. You can also use it with the {MESSAGE} command to get user response from a screen message. The {MESSAGE} command is discussed later in this chapter.

Figure 13-29. *Graph giving instructions*

Graph Buttons

As you can see, the {/ Graph;NameUse} and {GRAPHCHAR} commands can be combined to create an interactive macro to display graphs, although the macro code required can get quite complex. The alternative method of displaying a series of slides, the Graph Name Slide command and its macro equivalent, is simpler, but it is strictly linear, only capable of displaying a series of graphs one after the other (you can press BACKSPACE during a slide show to go back one slide in the list, but this halts the slide show until another key is pressed). In Quattro Pro 3 the graph display system supports branching, allowing the user to choose what comes next. The feature that makes this possible is graph buttons. These can be used independently of the Graph Name Slide command.

You place a graph button on a graph using Annotate. Each graph button can "call" another named graph, causing it to be displayed. Graph buttons are simply boxed text objects that have the Graph Button option activated. When you have created and selected a boxed text object in Annotate you will see that Graph Button is one of the properties for that object. If you select Graph Button you are shown a list of named graphs for the current worksheet. The graph you select from the list is the one that is displayed when the button is activated. When a graph containing buttons is being displayed a user can click on any button to display the graph named by that button. You can see an example in Figure 13-30, where there are three buttons, each leading to a different graph. Typically you will have some text on the graph that explains to the user how the graph buttons work. Note that you do not have to activate the buttons with a mouse. The first letter of the button text can be used to activate the button (for example, in Figure 13-30 you would press **F** for the graph of First Class volume).

This ability of graphs to call other graphs gives you tremendous flexibility when developing presentations. If you are going to present a series of graphs/slides to an audience, the connections between graphs will make it much easier for you to navigate your way through the material, and give you the impressive ability to jump between connected graphs without having to cycle through a whole stack. If you are creating a presentation that users will view at their own pace, you can link related screens together in a way that gives the viewer an active rather than a passive role, making the experience more enjoyable, and thus considerably more memorable. Indeed, with Quattro Pro 3 you have "hypertext" capabilities that go far beyond a simple sequence of images. Hypertext is

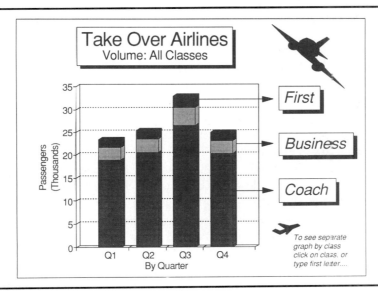

Figure 13-30.   *Graph of all classes with three buttons*

a way of presenting information that depends upon multiple links between associated items, using lateral as well as linear connections.

Applying Graph Buttons

The key to a successful hypertext presentation using graph buttons is planning. The first step is to decide what graphs you need to make. Then you can use either pencil and paper, or a Quattro Pro 3 graph, to sketch a flow chart of the graphs, as shown in Figure 13-31. This will help you decide how many buttons each graph needs and which graphs each button will call. The flow chart does not have to be fancy, but it can be quite complicated. In Figure 13-31, which shows the buttons used in Figure 13-30, there are only four graphs involved: one for all classes combined, and one for each of the three classes graphed separately. As you can see, even this simple arrangement requires a total of six graph buttons.

After you have decided on the flow of graphs, create and name each graph that is to be used by a graph button. This must be done before the buttons can be properly set up. However, you do not have to perfect each graph before you set up the buttons. (In fact, when you choose Graph

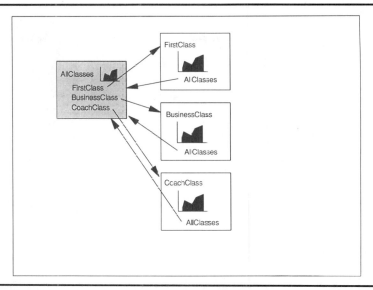

Figure 13-31. *Flow chart for graph button*

Button from the Properties list for Boxed Text in the Annotate feature, you can type in a graph name that does not yet exist, but you cannot use the button properly until a graph has been given that name.) Any graph can be safely worked on later *if* you remember to use the Name Create command after making changes.

When you have made the graphs you can place the buttons on them. Remember that a graph button is essentially a boxed text object. Also bear in mind that boxed text can be displayed without a box, turning it into free-floating text. You can make a graph button out of text you have already added to a graph by selecting the text and then choosing Graph Button from the Properties list (you cannot directly attach a graph button to standard chart text). You can also create a fresh piece of text to be used as a graph button, and you can even create "blank" buttons to be used with icons, such as the coffee cup on the "Pause the show" button in Figure 13-32. Note that the sculpted look of the buttons in Figure 13-32 was drawn in. You can also use the sculpted style for buttons that match those of Quattro Pro 3's WYSIWYG mode.

To create a blank button you select the text tool and choose None for the Box Type. Then, instead of typing characters, you press the SPACEBAR a number of times to create a shape of the size you want (select a large font

Figure 13-32. *Menu graph with "Pause" button*

size to give the box height). When you press ENTER you will have a clear rectangle that you can place over an icon. Choose Graph Button in the usual manner and enter the name of the graph that you want the button to call. This technique allows you to "hide" a graph button within a graph, so that, for example, each of the four bars in Figure 13-30 could lead to a pie chart of the appropriate quarter.

In Quattro Pro 3 you can also create a "default" button from the background of your graph. The Background properties include Bkg Button, so you can create a button that is effective whenever the user clicks on part of the graph that is not specifically designed as a button. This allows a form of error trapping in your slide shows.

The graph you see in Figure 13-32 is essentially a graphic menu. This gives you some idea of how you can place user controls into the series of graphs you are presenting. The series may be started by the Graph Name Display command. The first graph might look something like Figure 13-33, giving the user instructions. The graph in 13-30 would be selected by the Begin button. The graph in Figure 13-32 might be universally referred to as "Other" and referenced by buttons on many of the charts, such as the one in Figure 13-34, which is the Business Class breakdown, displayed

Figure 13-33. *Opening graph with instructions*

Figure 13-34. *Graph of Business Class volume*

when the user clicks the Business button in Figure 13-30. Note the way the bars are filled with images of passengers. This type of histogram is created by using the Graph Customize Series menu to select Blank as the Fill Pattern for the series. The image is then drawn with Annotate. The drawing can be quite large when first created, then reduced in size to fit the columns before being duplicated using the Clipboard Copy and Paste commands.

Graph Button Strategies

As you can see, the ability to branch from one graph to another opens up a wealth of possibilities. The previous example can be set up without using the slide show command. The presentation simply begins when the first graph, Figure 13-33, is displayed. However, this type of presentation requires user input at every screen to trigger the next graph.

Another simple application of buttons is to include a button-equipped graph in a slide show. This allows the user to choose between several different sequences, but also allows some graphs to be displayed automatically, on a timed basis, rather than having to wait for user input.

For example, suppose that you have graphs of volume figures and revenue figures for all classes of passenger and for each of the three classes. You create a beginning graph called OPENING, as shown in Figure 13-35, which gives the user a choice between volume and revenue figures. The slide show cells might appear as in Figure 13-36.

When the show begins the OPENING graph is displayed until the user selects one of the two buttons, leading either to TOTAL_REV or TOTAL_VOL. If the user selects Revenue, the TOTAL_REV appears, for a limited time, before leading to the next graph in the list, FIRST_REV. The BUSIN_REV and COACH_REV graphs then appear in timed sequence, followed by OPENING, which stays on screen until the user makes a selection. If the user selects Volume, either before or after viewing Revenue, then TOTAL_VOL appears, for a limited time, before leading to the next graph in the list, FIRST_VOL. The BUSIN_VOL and COACH_VOL graphs then appear automatically, followed by OPENING, which stays on screen until the user makes a selection. Note that the OPENING graph is required in the middle of the sequence, otherwise the flow would proceed from Revenue through all revenue *and* volume graphs while the Volume option would only show volume graphs.

Figure 13-35. *Opening graph with revenue/volume choice*

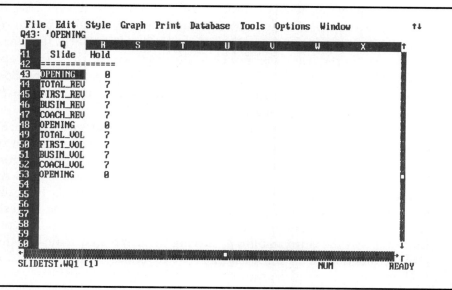

Figure 13-36. *Slide show entries*

Further Slide Show Effects

Several new slide show features were added in Quattro Pro 3, notably visual and audio slide show transition effects that can be used in slide shows and with graph buttons. Normally, when one slide replaces another, the first slide disappears and the second one is drawn on screen. This transition gets the job done, but it is not very exciting. If a slide is complicated, the drawing process can be slow and there is the possibility that the viewer's attention will wander. In Quattro Pro 3 you can use special visual slide transition effects to move from one slide to another while holding and even heightening the viewer's attention.

There are the 24 transition effects in the following categories:

■ Horizontal wipes (single and double edged)

■ Vertical wipes (single and double edged)

■ Spirals

■ Dissolves

The full range of transition effects is listed in Table 13-5. Each has a range of speeds at which it can operate. You set up these visual effects by entering the appropriate number in a third column added to a slide show block. A fourth column is used to determine how long it will take for the effect to make the transition from one slide to the next, that is, the speed of the effect. In Figure 13-37 you can see two columns, Effect and Speed, added to the earlier slide show to control the transition effects (the fifth column, Sound, will be discussed in a moment).

This expanded table means that the OPENING screen appears spiralled in from the edges (effect 17), very quickly (Speed 0). On instruction from the user the slide TOTAL_REV is painted, spreading out from the center like an iris opening (effect 12), taking a few seconds to do so (speed 4). After 7 seconds' hold, FIRST_REV appears over the top of TOTAL_REV like a barn door closing (effect 7), also taking a few seconds (speed 4). The show progresses in this manner according to the parameters in the table. Entering 0 in the third column or leaving the cell blank indicates that a visual transition effect is not assigned to that slide.

Note that the speed measurement is relative to the hardware you are using and to the type of effect. For example, a speed of 4 for effect 12 results in about 4 seconds of transition time. A speed of 4 for effect 17 results in a

Effect #	Speed Range	Description
1	0	Cut (instantaneous)
2	0	Switch to black, then new image
3	0-16	Wipe from right
4	0-16	Wipe from left
5	0-16	Wipe from bottom
6	0-16	Wipe from top
7	0-16	Barn door close (right/left to center)
8	0-16	Barn door open (center to right/left)
9	0-16	Barn door (top/bottom to center)
10	0-16	Barn door (center to top/bottom)
11	0-16	Iris close
12	0-16	Iris open
13	0-16	Scroll up
14	0-16	Scroll down
15	0-16	Vertical stripes right
16	0-16	Stripes right and then left
17	0-16	Spiral in
18	0-16	Dissolve, 2x1 rectangles
19	0-16	Dissolve, 2x2 squares
20	0-16	Dissolve, 4x4 squares
21	0-16	Dissolve, 8x8 squares
22	0-16	Dissolve, 16x16 squares
23	0-16	Dissolve, 32x32 squares
24	0-16	Dissolve, 64x64 squares

Table 13-5. *Slide Show Transition Effects*

13-second transition. This is simply because some effects are more complex than others.

Transition effects also allow you to overlay one slide with another rather than simply replace it. Entering the transition effect number as a negative indicates that the transition effect will be used to overlay the current slide with the next slide. For example, if you enter −19 in the third column of your slide show, the new slide is overlaid on the existing one using a slow dissolve. This opens up terrific possibilities for presentations. Suppose you have a text chart summarizing a series of points you want to make. The complete chart consists of a title line and three bulleted items. As you create the chart you name a copy at each stage, as follows:

■ Title only—CHART0

■ Title with first point—CHART1

■ Title with first and second points—CHART2

■ Title with all three points—CHART3

Your slide show can then present CHART0, the title. When you are ready to make your first point you transition to CHART1 as an overlay. Since the title in CHART1 is in exactly the same place as in CHART0, it does not appear to change. The effect gives the appearance of the first point being written onto the chart. The same happens when the second point is overlaid by a transition to CHART2, and so on.

Although slide transition effects are difficult to describe in print, they look very effective in a presentation. Figure 13-38 shows you how some of

```
 File  Edit  Style  Graph  Print  Database  Tools  Options  Window         ↑↓
Q43: 'OPENING
J         Q         R      S        T          U          V        W       X    ↑
11      Slide     Hold  Effect    Speed      Sound
42    ==================================================
43    OPENING      8      17        8   DRUMS.SND
44    TOTAL_REV    7      12        4   FANFARE.SND
45    FIRST_REV    7       7        4
46    BUSIN_REV    7       7        4
47    COACH_REV    7       7        4
48    OPENING      8      11        6   APPLAUSE.SND
49    TOTAL_VOL    7      23        4   FANFARE.SND
50    FIRST_VOL    7       7        4
51    BUSIN_VOL    7       7        4
52    COACH_VOL    7       7        4
53    OPENING      8      11        6   APPLAUSE.SND
54
55
56
57
58
59
60
←                                                                           →
SLIDETST.WQ1 [1]                                              NUM      READY
```

Figure 13-37. *A slide show with visual and sound effects*

Transition from slide 1 to 2

The barn door effect

Diagonal wipe effect

The iris effect

Figure 13-38.	*Diagram of visual effects*

these effects operate, but the best way to get to know them is by experimentation.

Since the slide show transition effects place a heavy demand on video memory, Quattro Pro 3 displays them in EGA resolution even if you have a VGA graphics adapter. This does not seriously impair the appearance of the slides. When you give the command to start a slide show, Quattro Pro 3 checks the slide show block to see if it contains a third column. If it does, Quattro Pro 3 automatically switches your display to 640x350 EGA resolution, then returns it to the previous resolution when the slide show is over.

The finishing touch for Quattro Pro 3 presentations is sound effects. These can be incorporated in slide shows, graph buttons, and macros without additional equipment. The sound effects are digitized sound files stored on disk with the extension SND. You can use sound effects in the following ways:

■ Slide show (enter the sound file name in the fifth column of the slide show block, as shown in Figure 13-37).

- Graph button (after the visual effect speed, insert a semicolon and the filename).

- Macro (use the {PLAY filename} command).

Quattro Pro 3 assumes the sound file is in the program directory and the filename extension is SND, unless you specify otherwise. You can see a sound effect column in the slide show in Figure 13-37. You can usually tell the nature of the sound effect from the file name. For example, file THANKYOU.SND is likely to be someone saying "Thank you."

Playing sounds makes extra demands on your PC hardware. If the sounds are distorted or fail to play, remove unnecessary items from your computer setup. Sounds might not work if your system is logged onto a network, if RAM-resident programs are running, or if you're running Quattro Pro 3 under Windows in Enhanced mode. These limitations are not that severe when compared to the terrific quality of sound the system provides, even through the small speaker on a normal PC (if you have facilities for an external speaker the results are quite dramatic). For serious presentations you are likely to use a dedicated PC that will not need to run programs that interfere with the sound system. Quattro Pro 3 is shipped with several sound files, including FANFARE, THANKYOU, and APPLAUSE.

Transition effects and sounds can be attached to graph buttons even if the graphs containing the buttons are not part of a Quattro Pro 3 slide show. Quattro Pro 3 uses semicolons as delimiters to distinguish which type of effect is requested. To attach special effects to a graph button, use the following syntax:

Slide;Hold;Effect;Speed;Sound

where *Slide* is the name of the graph, *Hold* is the length of time it is to be displayed, *Effect* is the type of transition, *Speed* is the rate of transition, and *Sound* is the name of an SND file. For example, you could attach OPENING;2;19;2;DRUMS to a graph button. When you click the button, a slow dissolve (effect 19) at speed 2 will fade in a graph called OPENING, which will display for 2 seconds. The transition will be accompanied by the DRUMS sound effect. If a graph button with special effects is used in a slide show, the number of seconds to display the next graph is ignored, but the visual and sound effects you specify on the button will be used. You can skip any item of the syntax by stacking semicolons with nothing between them (for this reason you should avoid semicolons within graph names).

If you use visual effects in graph buttons that are not in a slide show block, Quattro Pro 3 cannot automatically slip into 640x350 EGA resolution to display the effects. When using graph buttons that call various graphs or macros with effects, you should manually set Options Hardware Screen Resolution to 640x350 EGA before you begin the presentation.

By creating a macro to launch a presentation driven by graph buttons, you can automate the process of setting the screen resolution to 640x350 EGA before you begin your presentation. Simply begin the macro by changing screen resolution, then call the first graph of your presentation.

Graph Button Macros

Both the automated slide show technique and the user-prompted named-graph approach can be further enhanced with macros. You can use {/ Graph;SlideShow} to launch a slide show. From that point until the end of the show, the slide show feature takes control of user input. The only keys that are allowed are:

CTRL-BREAK	Terminates the show and returns you to the worksheet.
letters	The first character of any graph button text, which displays the slide attached to that button and branches to that part of the show.
any other key	Ends the slide show if the last slide is displayed; otherwise it triggers the next sequence of slides.
BACKSPACE	Freezes the current slide if on timed display; otherwise backs up one slide in the series.

Note that you can use the right mouse button instead of BACKSPACE. If you prefer to exercise more direct control over the flow of charts and the handling of user input, you can start a button-driven presentation with {/ Graph;NameUse}. You can trigger the display of graphs with graph buttons, and even use graph buttons to run macro commands. Graph button macros give you almost unlimited power to control a series of events using the simplest of user interfaces: clicking a mouse.

A graph button macro can either be a named macro from the current worksheet or an open macro library, or it can be a separate piece of macro code up to 80 characters in length. You will recall that when you select Graph Button from the Properties list you are prompted for a graph name. In fact, you can type a macro name instead, or even a piece of macro code. For example, suppose you want to give viewers of a presentation the ability to print out a graph. You create a piece of boxed text on the graph that says Print. This will be the print button. You select Graph Button and enter {/ GraphPrint;Go} instead of a graph name. When the user clicks this button the currently displayed graph will be sent to the printer.

Note that graphs running in slide shows cannot utilize graph buttons for macros. When using a graph button to run a macro, Quattro Pro 3 returns to spreadsheet mode to execute the macro. Unless the macro specifically redisplays a graph, Quattro Pro 3 will not pass control back to graphics mode.

Of course, you will probably want to include a command that returns the user to the presentation after the print task. For example, this code displays the OPENING graph after the print task:

{/ GraphPrint;Go}{/ Graph;NameUse}OPENING~

If you wanted to provide the print feature on a lot of graphs you might want to set up a print macro in the worksheet like this:

```
GPRINT          {/ GraphPrint;DestIsPtr}
                {/ GraphPrint;Go}
```

This macro, called GPRINT, makes sure that the print destination is set to the graphics printer before beginning the print operation. To run this macro from a graph button you would enter {GPRINT} instead of a graph name. Note that named macros must be enclosed in curly braces for Quattro Pro 3 to recognize them when called from graph buttons.

A simple technique for returning the user to the current graph is to use a temporary name for the graph. For example, to have the GPRINT macro print the current graph and then redisplay it, you can use the following lines of code:

```
GPRINT          {/ Graph;NameCreate}CURRENT~
                {/ GraphPrint;DestIsPtr}
                {/ GraphPrint;Go}
                {/ Graph;NameUse}CURRENT~
```

This stores the currently displayed graph under the name CURRENT so that it can be recalled. It is still safely stored under its original name as well.

Graph button macros can be used to execute complex procedures beyond presentations. Indeed, with Quattro Pro 3 it is possible to use the macro ability of graph buttons to create mouse-operated, menu-driven information systems that even computer shy executives can use. In Figure 13-39 you can see what an executive information system might look like, dressed up in a graph menu. The Retrieve data button runs a macro that downloads current information from Paradox into the worksheet, based on parameters supplied by the user as the macro runs. The Analyze data button places the user in the spreadsheet area and carries out several calculations. The Chart data button displays a standard set of charts created from the data. Finally, the Home menu button takes the user to a screen where the current session can be saved, reports printed, and so on.

Another example can be seen in Figure 13-40 where a map of the world, copied from the clip art file WORLDMAP.CLP, is used as the basis for accessing information about each of the airline's destinations. To use the clip art that comes with Quattro Pro 3, you use the Paste From command

Figure 13-39. *Information system menu*

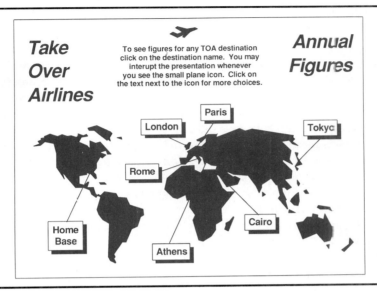

Figure 13-40. *A graphic menu with clip art*

on the Clipboard. To learn more about the clip art library, paste the 1-README.CLP file into a blank graph. To store your own creations as clip art to be used in other graphs simply select the object or group of objects and use the Copy To command on the Clipboard. You will then be prompted for a name for the file. To move an object out of the current graph and into a file use Cut To instead of Copy To. In Figure 13-40 the world map was adjusted and the polar subcontinents were removed. Each city name added to the map then had a graph button macro attached to it, leading to details of that city.

Messages Without Pictures

Users with systems that do not have the graphics capability needed to make the most of annotated images and graph buttons may want to explore the {MESSAGE} command. This can be used to display boxed message text that appears over the top of your regular work area, as opposed to a graphic screen. Messages to users can be displayed during macro execution. The {MESSAGE} command can display the message text for a period of time or until a key is pressed. The {MESSAGE} command takes the form

{MESSAGE *Block,Left,Top,Time*}

where *Block* is the cell or cells occupied by the message text, *Left* and *Top* are the screen coordinates for the message box, and *Time* is the length of time for the message to be displayed. The block coordinates must be wide enough for the whole piece of text to be displayed. For example, in Figure 13-41 you can see a macro called MESS01. This can be called by another macro when a message needs to be displayed. The macro refers to a message block called MSGA. This is actually cells B62..G62. If you use a smaller block, the message will be truncated. This means that you cannot simply name MSGA with the Edit Names Labels command. To display the message called MSGB in Figure 13-41, you would have to name cells B64..F65 as MSGB.

The macro MESS01 produces the results shown in Figure 13-42. The boxed message stays on the screen for 15 seconds, as defined by the formula @NOW+@TIME(0,0,15). The macro that calls this routine is suspended for that period of time, as indicated by the WAIT message in the lower right of the screen. If you enter 0 for the time, then the macro pauses until the user presses a key, at which point the macro continues with whatever code is on the next line. The screen coordinates of the message displayed in

Figure 13-41. *Message macro*

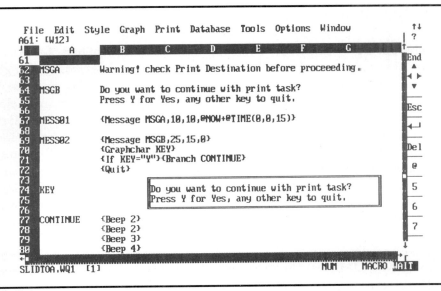

Figure 13-42. *Message macro with question*

Figure 13-41 are ten characters from the left of the screen and ten rows from the top, as defined by the *Left* and *Top* arguments. This locates the top left of the box.

By combining {MESSAGE} with the {GRAPGCHAR} command you can display messages and get user responses. Figure 13-42 shows a macro called MESS02, which displays the message shown in the figure, and waits for user response. When the user types **Y** the macro branches to CONTINUE, which in this case is a test macro of beeps. If the user presses any other key, the macro quits. Note that both lower- and uppercase **Y** are acceptable as a response. Also note the position of the message box, which is further across the screen and lower down than the one in Figure 13-41, as indicated by the screen coordinates of 25,15.

The {MESSAGE} and {GRAPHCHAR} commands make for convenient single-key user input routines. A series of {IF} staements can be used to evaluate a whole range of inputs and branch to different macro routines, making this yet another means of providing a menu for users. The {MESSAGE} command can also be useful in presentation macros when the user needs to be returned to the worksheet during macro execution. A reassuring message can be displayed momentarily to assure the user that the graphics will reappear in a moment.

Presentation Tips

Given the power of Quattro Pro 3's graphic commands you may well decide to use it for preparing presentations. To ensure that your presentation is a success bear in mind the following design guidelines and presentation tips.

Keep It Simple

With Quattro Pro 3 you can produce excellent graphs as long as you follow the golden rule of graphics: Keep it simple. Use several separate graphs instead of placing too much on one graph. Remember that the key elements of a good graph are:

- Unity
- Balance
- Contrast
- Meaning

If your graphs contain all four elements, they will be an effective means of communicating information. In the rush to add visual interest to everything that passes for information in today's office it is possible to end up with "chart junk." This is when someone goes over the top in dressing up an otherwise clear and understandable chart. If you feel the urge to add drawings and clip art to a chart, step back after each addition and ask yourself if it really adds to the impact and clarity of the information being presented.

The Value of Text

In some situations there is no substitute for a number chart or data table. This is essentially a printed report with the numbers in the spreadsheet arranged in columns and rows with titles and totals. When you need to provide extensive detail as well as summary information, then a spreadsheet printout is sometimes the best type of report to use. As you have seen in this chapter, there are several techniques that enable you to make charts with Quattro Pro 3 without using the graph commands. Particularly when it comes to word charts, Quattro Pro 3's publishing features allow you to organize your words and print them out in attractive designs.

When you have the chance to use color in presenting information you should heed the words of Aristotle about painting: "The most brilliant colors, spread at random and without design, will give far less pleasure than the simplest outline of a figure." If you do not have a color display or printer you are not as limited in your presentation abilities as some would suggest. Effective use of shading, fill patterns, and fonts can create stunning designs, which are usually cheaper to reproduce than color. Do not go to great lengths to produce charts in color unless there is a real need for them to be in color.

Slide Shows

When you have a lot of graphs to display you can use the slide show feature in Quattro Pro 3 to make presentations with your PC. How you actually mount the show depends upon the facilities at your disposal. You may have a large monitor, an overhead adapter, or other wide screen systems. Some of these systems have limited resolution and palettes. The first design consideration in such cases is to know what the final display method will be. Then you can choose your colors and fonts based on the way they look to the audience, not how they appear to you on your PC.

If you look at how television news programs use text and images you will see that they keep them simple to compensate for the fuzziness of TV images. If you have to use a fuzzy display system avoid putting text directly over images, and choose bright colors. Text can be seen better as light on a darker background, or when outlined in black to separate it from other images.

A good method of reinforcing your message and avoiding complete disaster when equipment fails during a presentation is to make printouts of all your slides and have them ready as handouts. These need not be in color, but having them closely match your slide show will increase the staying power of your message.

The Human Factor

Always remember that the key to a good presentation is not equipment or even handouts, it is the presenter. Computers and audio-visual equipment can be very effective, but without a good speaker they are a waste of money. A good speaker can get the message across even if the equipment fails, the handouts are late, and the room is cold and drafty. A good speaker will be warm, affable, and talk direct to the audience, making eye contact with as many people as possible. A lively and humorous approach is usually the most effective, particularly if the subject matter is essentially dry. A good speaker will enunciate clearly and adjust speed and volume to the specific audience, so that they feel this is a presentation made specially for them, not something you have done a dozen times already. Practice your presentation to friends and colleagues before going live, and when presenting to a real audience try for a relaxed demeanor. You will find that any time you step onto a platform you automatically create an impression of authority that can carry you through moments of hesitation.

Conclusion

This book has taken you from the basics of spreadsheet operation to the sophistication of graphics, macros, and even custom menus. You should not expect to retain everything you have seen on first reading. In many ways, the tremendous power of a program like Quattro Pro 3 is equivalent to that of an entire programming language, which students may take several semesters to study. You should not expect to learn or use all of Quattro Pro 3's capabilities right away. Unlike most programming languages, however, Quattro Pro 3 is easily applied to practical tasks almost immediately. You can also have fun with Quattro Pro 3, designing impressive graphs, charts, and drawings. Many examples of Quattro Pro 3 at work are given throughout the book, but the best way to become familiar with Quattro Pro 3 is to consider the tasks you perform in your own work and try to apply Quattro Pro 3 to them. By using Quattro Pro 3 you will get to know Quattro Pro 3, and you will become more productive and creative in the process.

A Installing Quattro Pro 3

Quattro Pro 3 uses sophisticated programming techniques to make installation and startup a simple process despite the wide variety of hardware
on which the program runs. Using the commands on the Options menu you
can adjust most aspects of the way in which the program runs, as described
in Chapter 6. However, to further integrate Quattro Pro 3 into your
personal computer system, you may want to employ some of the techniques
described on the following pages. This appendix also provides tips for
mouse users.

Basic Installation

Quattro Pro 3 arrives on a number of floppy disks that contain compressed
files. You install Quattro Pro 3 by using the INSTALL program on the
first disk (the one that has the serial number on it). Since the INSTALL
program requires quite a large amount of memory, run it when you have
booted up your PC, and do not have any programs loaded.

To begin, place the first disk in your floppy disk drive. At the DOS prompt type **A:** and press ENTER (if you are using drive B, type **B:**). Now type **INSTALL** and press ENTER (if you are using a black and white monitor type **INSTALL/B**). Answer the questions the INSTALL program asks about the source drive and the hard disk directory you want to use. The necessary files from disk 1 will then be transferred to the hard disk, and the next disk will be requested. You will be asked which style of menus you want to use. The normal choice is QUATTRO.MU, the regular Quattro Pro 3 menus. This is highly recommended. Check Chapters 6 and 12 if you want to alter menus, and consult Appendix B if you want to operate Quattro Pro 3 in 1-2-3 mode.

When all of the files have been copied, Quattro Pro 3 will ask you to enter a company name and user name to identify your copy of the program. Also, you must enter the serial number from disk 1. Then you can choose a printer to use with Quattro Pro 3. Note that you can add other printers later using the Options Hardware command. To complete the installation, Quattro Pro 3 asks you if you want to create any fonts. Creating at least a basic set of fonts is a good idea since this prevents too many Building font delays when you start using the program. However, you can build a group of fonts after you have installed Quattro Pro 3 by loading the worksheet called INSTALL.WQ1. This automatically operates a font-building macro for you.

When the installation is complete, place the original disks in a safe place. Load Quattro Pro 3 and check that the Options Startup Directory is set to the directory you want to use for your data files. Use Options Update to make the choice permanent. Alternatively, you can leave this setting blank and load Quattro Pro 3 from the data directory of your choice whenever you begin a session. To be able to do this, the Quattro Pro 3 directory must be in your PATH statement. For more on directories and paths see the next section.

Enhanced Installation

After completing the initial installation process for Quattro Pro 3 using the INSTALL program on the first program disk, there are several steps you can take to make Quattro Pro 3 more convenient to use. While not essential to the program's operation, these steps may be of interest to experienced users, particularly if they are setting up Quattro Pro 3 for less-experienced users.

Configuration File Enhancement

To efficiently use Quattro Pro 3 on your system you may need to fine tune the way the system, not just Quattro Pro 3, is configured. One file that greatly affects system performance is CONFIG.SYS. Remember that when your computer starts up, it looks to the floppy disk in drive A for DOS. If DOS is found on the disk in drive A, it is loaded into RAM. If not, the system looks to the hard disk, drive C, if you have one installed. If DOS is found on drive C, it is loaded into memory. One of the first pieces of information DOS looks for when it is loaded is the configuration file, CONFIG.SYS. This file contains information about how your system is configured.

If DOS does not find a CONFIG.SYS file it assumes certain default conditions. However, you will need to establish some settings with CONFIG.SYS when running Quattro Pro 3. In fact, Quattro Pro 3's INSTALL program can update the CONFIG.SYS file for you during initial installation. The two settings that affect Quattro Pro 3 involve two aspects of the way DOS manages information in RAM: buffers and files.

The number of buffers (temporary holding areas into which DOS can put information your programs use) is normally five. The number of open files that DOS can keep track of is normally eight. By increasing these settings with a CONFIG.SYS file, you can improve the speed with which DOS manipulates information in your system. A setting of 20 for buffers and 20 for files is often used. The settings are established by placing the following instructions in the CONFIG.SYS file:

BUFFERS = 20
FILES = 20

The instructions can be upper- or lowercase letters. They are placed one instruction per line. This may have been done to your system when you installed Quattro Pro 3; however, it is a good idea to check out the CONFIG.SYS file on your system.

You can check whether your system has a CONFIG.SYS file by typing the command **DIR *.SYS** at the DOS prompt while in the root directory of your hard disk or on the floppy disk with which you start your system. If you find a CONFIG.SYS file, you can examine its contents with the TYPE command, as in

TYPE CONFIG.SYS

If you plan to change the CONFIG.SYS file or create a new one, you should copy the original file to another file, such as CONFIG.OLD. You do this at the DOS prompt with the command

COPY CONFIG.SYS CONFIG.OLD

A new CONFIG.SYS file can then be created with the DOS COPY command. Type the following at the DOS prompt:

COPY CON CONFIG.SYS

After this press ENTER. The ENTER key gives you the first line for an instruction. Type the instruction, for example, **FILES = 20**, and then press ENTER for another line. After the last line of instruction, press F6 and then ENTER again. The file will be written to the disk. (Pressing F6 produces the CTRL-Z code, which DOS reads as meaning end-of-file.) This CON-FIG.SYS file is a pure ASCII file. You could also create one with SideKick's Notepad, WordStar in the non-document mode, and many other word processors, such as Borland's Sprint, that can save text in ASCII format.

Hard Disk Enhancement

The Quattro Pro 3 installation program places the program files in a hard disk subdirectory, typically called QPRO, or QUATTRO. A hard disk directory system for a computer running Quattro Pro 3 and WordPerfect might look like the one shown in Figure A-1, drawn with Quattro Pro 3's Annotate feature. Note that the directory containing Quattro Pro 3 is called QPRO. You may use other names, such as Q3, or QUATTRO. Substitute the name you are using for QPRO in the following examples.

Navigating Directories   For DOS to find either a program file or a data file, you must specify a path for it to follow. For example, the path to the worksheet file called PROJECT.WQ1 in the SALES subdirectory of Quat-

Figure A-1. *Hard disk directory system*

tro Pro 3 is \QPRO\SALES\. To identify files accurately on a hard disk, the path to the file becomes part of the file name. Thus, the full name of the PROJECT.WQ1 file is

C:\QPRO\SALES\PROJECT.WQ1

In order to navigate a hard disk with one or more subdirectories, you might want to change the uninformative C prompt, which tells you only that you are using drive C, to the C:\ prompt, which shows not only the current drive but also the path and the current subdirectory (in this case the root, or main directory). This more informative prompt will always tell you what subdirectory you are in. If you move into the Quattro Pro 3 subdirectory, the prompt will read

C:\QPRO>_

(If your hard disk is not drive C but drive D or E or any other valid letter, just substitute that letter for C in the instructions that follow.)

To change the prompt to a more informative version, type **PROMPT PG** at the C prompt. When you press ENTER you will see the drive letter, the path ($P) to whatever subdirectory you are in, and the greater-than sign ($G). Now change your location to a subdirectory such as the one for Quattro Pro 3. Type

CD \QPRO

and press ENTER. You will see your prompt change. To change your current location back to the root directory, type

CD\

and press ENTER.

Quattro Pro 3 data files should be kept in a separate directory from the program files. To create a subdirectory called QWORK directly below the root directory, type

MD \QWORK

and press ENTER. To create a subdirectory called MYWORK below the Quattro Pro 3 directory, type

MD \QPRO\MYWORK

and press ENTER. If you want to copy all the files from a disk in drive A into this new directory, you can move into the subdirectory by typing

CD \QPRO\MYWORK

pressing ENTER, and then entering

COPY A:*.*

Alternatively, you could type

COPY A:*.* C:\QPRO\MYWORK

from the root directory.

Using Batch Files Unfortunately, DOS forgets the helpful PROMPT command when you turn off the system. To solve this problem, you use batch files, which are collections of instructions to DOS that are delivered in a group or batch. A batch file has the extension BAT and is activated by typing the first part of the file name excluding the period and extension. For example, the file P.BAT might contain the following lines:

```
PROMPT $P$G
DIR/W
```

Typing **P** and pressing ENTER would tell DOS to change the prompt and then list the files in the current directory.

Every system can have a batch file called AUTOEXEC.BAT, which DOS looks for when the system starts up. For example, you might want to go straight to Quattro Pro 3 every time you turn on your computer. The following AUTOEXEC.BAT file on the hard disk would accomplish this:

```
DATE
TIME
ECHO OFF
PROMPT $P$G
CD \QPRO
Q
```

To create this batch file, you copy the instructions from the keyboard directly into a file by typing

```
COPY CON AUTOEXEC.BAT
```

at the DOS prompt. Pressing ENTER gives you the first line for an instruction. Type the instruction (DATE), and press ENTER for another line. After the last line of instruction, press F6 and press ENTER again. The file will be written to the disk. This file is a pure ASCII file. Note that you can add items to the last line of this batch file that cause Quattro Pro 3 to load specific worksheets or configurations, as will be described shortly.

The PATH Statement Consider what happens when you type the name of a program file at the DOS prompt and then press ENTER. First, DOS looks for a file in the current directory that has the name that you have entered, plus one of the valid program file extensions (COM, EXE, and BAT). For example, if you enter **Q**, DOS looks in the current directory for a file called Q.COM, Q.EXE, or Q.BAT. If such a file is found in the current directory, then DOS loads it. If such a file is not found in the current directory, then DOS returns the rather unfriendly message "Bad command or file name," *unless* your system has a PATH setting in effect.

The PATH setting is created by the PATH command, which you issue at the DOS prompt. The PATH setting tells DOS which directories should be searched for a program file when it cannot be found in the current directory. For example, the following command tells DOS to look in the root directory of drive C and the \DOS subdirectory, as well as the current directory:

PATH = C:\;C:\DOS

Note that the two directory statements are separated by a semicolon. The following statement tells DOS to look in the same directories, plus the Quattro Pro 3 program directory:

PATH = C:\;C:\DOS;C:\QPRO

This means that you could enter **Q** while in a directory called QWORK and DOS would still load Quattro Pro 3 even though the program files are stored in a directory called QPRO.

You can use the PATH command at the DOS prompt at any time. If you simply enter **PATH** then DOS tells you what the current setting is. If you enter **PATH** followed by the equal sign and one or more directory names, then those directories become the current path setting, superseding the previous setting. Typically, a PATH statement is incorporated in the AUTOEXEC.BAT file to set the various paths required for the programs you normally run. You may want to add your Quattro Pro 3 program directory to the PATH statement in your AUTOEXEC.BAT file to allow you to start Quattro Pro 3 from anywhere on your hard disk.

If you have not used the Directory command from the Options Startup menu to record a preference for a data directory, then Quattro Pro 3 will assume that you want to list files in the directory that was current when you entered **Q** to start the program. This means that if you are in the QWORK directory when you enter **Q** and you have QPRO in your current path, then Quattro Pro 3 will list files in QWORK when you use the File Retrieve or File Open commands. This gives you the flexibility to load

Quattro Pro 3 from different data areas depending upon the files you are going to use. You can always issue the File Directory command to specify a different temporary data directory.

If you use the Directory command from the Options Startup menu and then use the Options Update command, Quattro Pro 3 will present the same data directory regardless of where you load the program from. To remove a directory preference so that Quattro Pro 3 will use the directory that was current when the program was loaded as the data directory, you do the following:

1. Select Directory from the Options Startup menu.

2. Press ESCAPE to clear the current setting.

3. Press ENTER, select Quit, and then select Update.

A Batch File Menu System

If you have a hard disk, you can easily move among different programs stored on the hard disk by using a series of small batch files and a message file. The following sections show how this is done.

Message Files

A message file is simply an ASCII file that contains text you want DOS to display. If you use the TYPE command together with the name of an ASCII file, DOS reads the text from the file to the screen. By preceding this command with the CLS command, which clears the screen in DOS, you can achieve a display such as this:

Main Menu

==

1 Run Quattro Pro 3

2 Run WordPerfect

3 Use Backit program

Type the number of your choice and press ENTER.

You can display this message any time you return to DOS from another program by writing a batch file called Z.BAT, shown here:

```
ECHO OFF
CD \
CLS
TYPE MENU.MSG
```

This changes the directory back to the root (CD \), clears the screen (CLS), and types the message ("TYPE MENU.MSG").

If you write a batch file called 1.BAT that starts Quattro Pro 3, you can load Quattro Pro 3 simply by pressing 1 and ENTER. The 1.BAT file might look like this:

```
ECHO OFF
CD\QPRO
Q
Z
```

If the 1.BAT file that starts Quattro Pro 3 also runs the Z.BAT file after Quattro Pro 3, you have created a loop from the menu to Quattro Pro 3 and back. You could set up other batch files such as 2.BAT and 3.BAT to load other programs such as WordPerfect (2.BAT) and Backit (3.BAT).

You may want to place these batch files in a special subdirectory. Most systems have a subdirectory called DOS, which is to used store the DOS files. If you place your batch files in a subdirectory, make sure that your AUTOEXEC.BAT file uses the PATH command to let DOS know where to look for a batch file if it does not find it in the current directory. If you place the Z.BAT file in the \DOS subdirectory, and then include this subdirectory in the PATH command in your AUTOEXEC.BAT file, as in

PATH = C:\;C:\DOS;C:\QPRO

then DOS will always be able to find Z.BAT. Thus, you will always be able to return to the root directory and the menu from anywhere on the disk by pressing Z and then ENTER at the DOS prompt. You can easily adapt this system to your own needs by substituting the commands for other software programs and expanding the list.

Improving Menus

Programs on your PC have the ability to display line and corner characters that can be used to create boxes. Some word processing programs, like WordPerfect and DisplayWrite, can perform an operation called Cursor Draw, in which boxes made of lines are easily drawn around text. If saved as ASCII files, these boxes can be displayed with the TYPE command. The boxes help make attractive menus. An example of an enhanced menu is seen in Figure A-2.

Alternative Menus

A command to load Quattro Pro 3 can be given with an accompanying worksheet name, so that as soon as the program is loaded, the worksheet

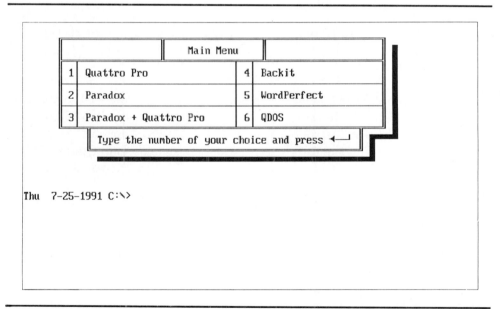

Figure A-2. *Enhanced batch file menu*

is retrieved from disk. For example, if you enter the following at the DOS prompt in the Quattro Pro 3 directory

Q SALES

then Quattro Pro 3 will load, followed by the worksheet SALES.WQ1, if there is a worksheet called SALES in the default directory with the default extension. This ability can be used in batch files to load Quattro Pro 3 in several different ways. You can set up a menu like this to offer a choice between different Quattro Pro 3 configurations:

Quattro Pro 3 Menu

==

1   Run Quattro Pro 3 for Pricing

2   Run Quattro Pro 3 for Budget Analysis

3   Run Quattro Pro 3 with no file

   The file 1.BAT used to activate this menu contains the instruction

Q PRICING.WQ1

so that Quattro Pro 3 loads the pricing worksheet as soon as the program loads. The 2.BAT file loads Q BUDGET.WQ1 and so on. You could use a variation of these instructions to load Quattro Pro 3 for different users. Bear in mind that the file you call needs to be available to Quattro Pro 3. To help ensure this you can use a more specific request such as

Q C:\DATA\SALES.WQ1

   You can set up this menu system in your QPRO directory. To use this system, the batch file called from the Main Menu to load Quattro Pro 3 contains the command ECHO OFF, followed by

```
CD \QPRO
CLS
TYPE Q.MEN
```

The file Q.MEN is the menu of Quattro Pro 3 choices.

Parameter Passing

Another useful technique in batch file construction is to add a parameter to the file. This can then be replaced by a value that you provide when you use the batch file. This is similar to the technique Quattro Pro 3 uses when loading. When you enter **Q** followed by a file name to load Quattro Pro 3 you are passing a parameter, in this case, the file name. If you create a batch file called 3.BAT that looks like this

```
ECHO OFF
CLS
Q %1
Z
```

then you can load Quattro Pro 3 with a worksheet by entering

3 filename

The %1 entry in the batch file is parameter 1. The nice feature of parameters is that they are optional. Thus, you can enter **3** on its own just to load Quattro Pro 3, or **3** followed by a space and a file name to load Quattro Pro 3 and a file.

Managing Shortcuts and RF Files

You may want to use batch files to manipulate Quattro Pro 3 configuration files. Quattro Pro 3 uses a special configuration or resource file to store basic definitions that specify the way the program is to be run. The file where the default settings are stored when you use the Options Update command or assign Shortcuts is called RSC.RF. You can create additional configuration files that all contain different sets of defaults. To create a file other than RSC.RF, first copy the current RSC.RF to a new file. For example, use the command

COPY RSC.RF MY.RF

Now load Quattro Pro 3 with the command

Q/dMY.RF

at the DOS prompt. Using /d and the RF file name loads the RF file that you specify, meaning in this case that changes made to the configuration will be stored in MY.RF. Now make the changes you want to the Shortcuts and program options. Use the Options Update command to make sure that the current default settings are stored in the configuration files. The next time you load Quattro Pro 3 you can either use the program defaults by typing **Q** to start the program, or you can use your own defaults by loading with the command

Q/dMY.RF

You can specify both a resource file and a worksheet on the command line, as in

Q/dMY.RF PIE

to load your RF file plus the worksheet PIE.WQ1.

By using batch file language with a parameter you can establish a batch file to run Quattro Pro 3 that looks like this:

```
ECHO OFF
CLS
Q /d%1.rf %2
```

If you call this file QP.BAT you can load Quattro Pro 3 with a special RF file and a worksheet called PIE by simply entering

QP MY PIE

By incorporating batch file code like this into a menu system you can provide users with a choice between default settings. For example, for those who like to use Quattro Pro 3 in 1-2-3 emulation mode you can set up a configuration file to run Quattro Pro 3 in 1-2-3 mode, as discussed in Appendix B.

About Mice

Quattro Pro 3 has complete mouse support built into the program. You can use a mouse to select cells and menu items, as well as to draw shapes with the Graph Annotate feature.

Mouse Installation

If you have connected a mouse to your system and installed it correctly, a mouse palette should appear when you load Quattro Pro 3, as seen on the right of Figure A-3. A mouse pointer should also appear, either as an arrow if your display is in graphics mode or as a small rectangle if not. If the mouse palette and pointer do not appear, check the installation instruc-

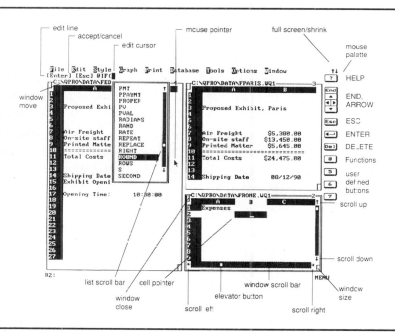

Figure A-3.   *Mouse points*

tions for the mouse. For example, mice require that a special program called a device driver be loaded or installed for DOS to recognize the mouse. This means that you either have to enter something like **MSMOUSE** at the DOS prompt before the mouse is recognized, or add a line to the CONFIG.SYS file, described earlier in this appendix, such as

DEVICE = MSMOUSE.SYS

If you have performed the necessary hardware and software installation of the mouse and Quattro Pro 3 still does not recognize it, check the mouse test program that comes with most mice. You may have a conflict between different devices that is affecting the mouse port or mouse card.

Mouse Actions

The areas of the screen used by the mouse are shown in Figure A-3. There are three actions you can perform with a mouse:

Point — Move the mouse pointer to a particular location, such as a menu item or a button on the mouse palette.

Click — Press down the mouse button and then release it. This usually selects whatever the mouse pointer is pointing at. For example, "click on Del" means to place the mouse pointer on the Del button, and then press the mouse button and release it.

Drag — Place the mouse pointer in one location, press down the mouse button, and hold it down while moving the mouse pointer to another location. This is used to select a group of cells or move the elevator button.

The Mouse Palette

The mouse palette consists of a number of screen buttons that you can click with the mouse to issue certain commands. The question mark button (?) is equivalent to pressing F1 for Help. The four arrows labeled End are equivalent to pressing END followed by one of the four arrow keys, as described in Chapter 1. The Esc button is equivalent to pressing ESCAPE. The button marked with the crooked arrow is the ENTER button, equivalent to pressing the ENTER key. The Del button represents the DELETE key, and the @ button is the same as pressing ALT-F3 for a list of @functions. Buttons 5, 6, and 7 can be customized to carry out keystrokes or macros, as described in Chapter 6. When you first install Quattro Pro 3, mouse button 6 is set up as WYS to activate WYSIWYG mode, and button 7 is CHR and switches you to character mode.

Scroll Bars and Elevators

When you are using a mouse each worksheet window and menu list has scroll bars that you can use to move through the list or around the worksheet. The vertical scroll bars have an up arrow at the top and a down arrow at the bottom. Clicking on these moves the highlighting up or down one line at a time, respectively. The horizontal scroll bars on worksheet windows have left and right arrows that can be clicked to move one column at a time. To move around more quickly you can point to the elevator box within the scroll bar and drag it along the bar. This moves the highlighting relative to the list or worksheet area. For example, if you drag the elevator box to the middle of the vertical scroll bar the highlighting will be moved to the middle of the list or halfway down the occupied area of the worksheet.

To move through a list or worksheet a section at a time you click in the gray area of the scroll bar. As an example, if 20 rows of the spreadsheet are visible in the current spreadsheet window, then clicking in the gray area below the elevator box in the vertical scroll bar will scroll the screen 20 rows.

Selecting and Sizing

You select items from lists and menus by pointing to them and clicking. To close a menu or list click anywhere outside of it. When you are editing data on the edit line you can click on the [Enter] or [Esc] button to either enter or cancel your editing, respectively. To edit a particular cell you first click on the cell and then click on the input line to get into EDIT mode (which is why there is no F2 button on the mouse palette).

The upward and downward pointing arrows in the upper right of the screen alter the size of the current worksheet window. The upward arrow always expands the window to full screen. The downward arrow reduces the window to either half-screen size, or, if you have previously altered the window size, to the adjusted size. You can drag the square in the bottom right of the worksheet window around the screen to alter the window size and shape. Drag the file name in the top left corner to move the window. Clicking the box in the top left of the worksheet window is equivalent to issuing the File Close command.

About Memory

To get the most out of Quattro Pro 3 on your personal computer you need to understand how your system uses memory. For those who are already familiar with the terms *RAM, expanded memory,* and *extended memory,* the important point to note about Quattro Pro 3 is that it prefers expanded memory. You can alter the way Quattro Pro 3 works with RAM by using the Options Other Expanded Memory command, described later in this section.

Types of Memory

There are two types of memory in a PC, Read Only Memory (ROM) and Random Access Memory (RAM). While some people refer to disks as a third type of memory, it is easier to think of disks as storage rather than memory. ROM holds instructions, permanently burned into the chips, that your computer uses immediately after the power is turned on, even before a disk is read. RAM is where all of the instructions for the programs that the computer is to execute are held prior to being carried out. RAM is also where data is held before it is stored onto disk. When you turn off your computer you wipe out the contents of RAM.

In a typical personal computer session with a typical piece of application software, such as Quattro Pro 3, memory works like this:

1. You turn on the computer. Almost immediately instructions are read from ROM. This includes the testing of memory that gives the numeric display in the top left of the screen, as well as the BIOS (Basic Input/Output System) instructions that lay the ground rules for the

exchange of information between different parts of the system, such as keyboard, display, disks, and so on.

2. The ROM instructions tell the computer to look to the drive(s) to find software on disk. When the computer finds a disk with DOS on it, DOS is read into memory. DOS actually consists of several parts, the two most important being the hidden system files and the command processor, COMMAND.COM. After COMMAND.COM is loaded DOS looks for two special files that tell it about the computer, CONFIG.SYS and AUTOEXEC.BAT. The CONFIG.SYS file is a list of settings for DOS to use, plus instructions about any special equipment that is part of the hardware configuration. The AUTOEXEC.BAT file is a list of instructions about what DOS should do first, like set the date and time and display a menu of programs.

3. As manager of the flow and storage of information, DOS then allows you to issue an instruction that loads an application, such as Quattro Pro 3 (this is known as an application program, as opposed to an operating system program or utility program, because it applies your system to a useful task). When you issue the command, Quattro Pro 3 is read from disk into RAM. DOS remains in RAM as well.

4. While using the application you enter some numbers or text from the keyboard. This is held in RAM.

5. You issue the program's save instruction, and a copy of the spreadsheet in RAM is stored on disk, but remains on screen as well for further editing.

6. When you are done editing you resave the file, replacing the old version on disk with the new one, and then exit Quattro Pro 3, which removes both text and the program from RAM.

Memory Size

The preceding story is simple enough *if* you have enough RAM to hold both DOS and Quattro Pro 3. How much is enough and how much have you got? Like file storage space on disk, RAM is measured in bytes and kilobytes. You can tell how much RAM is in your computer by using the CHKDSK command from the DOS prompt. To do this you type **CHKDSK** and press ENTER. The results will look something like this:

```
Volume TOWER 386 created Jun 16, 1990 8:23a
33449984 bytes total disk space
569344 bytes in 57 hidden files
69632 bytes in 26 directories
26648576 bytes in 1139 user files
2048 bytes in bad sectors
6160384 bytes available on disk
655360 bytes total memory
146496 bytes free
```

Most of the information is about the current disk and the files on it, but the last two lines are about memory. The memory referred to is "normal" RAM. To run Quattro Pro 3 a computer needs at least 512K of normal RAM. With 512K of RAM in your PC, Quattro Pro 3 will be able to handle modest spreadsheets. Your capacity to handle larger worksheets increases when you have 640K of RAM.

Depending on market conditions, RAM can be a fairly inexpensive commodity, and it is definitely worth upgrading to at least 640K. The benefits in speed and capacity will be reflected in your use of other programs as well as Quattro Pro 3. Due to the different types of information that make up spreadsheets, including values, calculations, and formatting, it is not really possible to give an upper limit to the size of spreadsheet Quattro Pro 3 can handle with 640K of RAM. Suffice it to say that Quattro Pro 3 can work better with more memory. The question is how to add more memory to your system in such a way that Quattro Pro 3 can recognize it.

As you have seen, if you type **CHKDSK** at the DOS prompt and press ENTER you will see a report on memory. This indicates the total amount of memory recognized by DOS, plus what is left after accounting for the space occupied by such information as the COMMAND.COM file. When the IBM PC was first introduced it came with 65,536 bytes or 64K of RAM. This was considered a lot of RAM at the time. Since the power users back then had 64K machines, the designers of DOS figured that ten times that much would be sufficient "user RAM" for DOS and any future applications; hence the figure of 640K, which is the maximum amount of user RAM that DOS can recognize. Although this sounded like a reasonable limit at the time, users kept demanding more features from software, and each new wave of programs required more RAM. New functions have been added to DOS, which used to occupy less than 30K but now requires about 80K. In addition to DOS and regular application programs, a new breed of software, called TSRs or Terminate-and-Stay-Resident programs, gained popularity and consumed RAM. A TSR program, such as the original Borland SideKick, is loaded into memory after DOS but before application software and stays there as you unload one application and then load another. This way, a TSR program can offer the same features, such as a notepad or clipboard, within whatever application you are using.

There is also pressure on memory space from users' thirst for more exotic hardware. The designers of the original PC and DOS could not anticipate every type of storage system, communications equipment, and hardware interface that was to be developed for PCs. Equipment like removable hard disks, FAX boards, and MIDI interfaces simply did not exist then. However, DOS was designed so that someone who designed a new piece of equipment could also write a piece of software that told the PC how to relate to that equipment. This specialized software is called a *device driver*, and many products for the PC come with a device driver. The problem with device drivers is that they are loaded into memory when the computer starts up, right after COMMAND.COM. You cannot use such equipment as Bernoulli boxes without these drivers occupying space in memory.

So, this is how the 640K limit of DOS came to be such a squeeze: bigger and better applications and versions of DOS, plus TSR software and specialized equipment. Add to this the growing need to network computers together, which requires memory resident network software, and you have the situation known as RAM-CRAM: not enough memory to do all the things you want to do.

Memory Architecture

You might wonder why DOS has not been altered to recognize more than 640K of RAM. The answer lies in the original design of the PC and what many users have seen as the necessity to keep each new wave of PC designs compatible with the last. The problem begins with *addresses*. In order for a computer to keep track of the data it handles it needs to know where the data is. The location of each byte that is going to be processed needs to be defined. This is done by assigning a unique address to every byte. Think of a delivery person attempting to make deliveries: if every customer has a unique address the job of locating them is made much easier. In a computer each piece of data that is processed has to pass through memory.

Every address in memory has to be coded in binary code. If you have eight digits, or bytes, to work with you can come up with 256 unique addresses. With 16 bits you can create 65,536 unique addresses.

The 8088 chip, the central processing unit that was at the heart of the first PCs, had the capacity to use 20 bits for addressing. This was a function of the physical design of the chip. This results in a maximum potential number of addresses of 1,048,576. This is exactly 1 megabyte of addresses or addressable memory. The 8088 chip can thus be said to have a 1 megabyte address space. However, not all of this space can be used by programs that you load from disk. Some of the area needs to be reserved for information passing through memory from and to displays. There also needs to be room to address the BIOS, which controls how the pieces of hardware communicate with each other. To allow for these factors IBM engineers preallocated 640K for programs and 384K for system overhead. Remember that this 640K is the limit of user RAM. In addition to this user RAM, there is the memory area occupied by ROM.

The total amount of ROM and RAM that a PC can work with is limited by the type of chip that is running the system. The chip must move data and program code in and out of memory. The Intel 8088 and 8086 chips can address up to 1024K, or 1 megabyte, of memory. This space is made up of the 640K of RAM, plus 128K reserved for use by video boards, plus 256K reserved for the system ROM (640K + 128K + 256K = 1024K = 1MB). Therefore, beyond the 640K of user RAM the rest of the PC's 1MB total address space is reserved for system operations, a 384K range of memory locations where the CPU finds data or instructions for its own use. The space from 640K to 768K is for video buffers, the data used to draw and redraw the screen display. Optional or installable ROM modules, such as those used by hard disk controllers and enhanced graphics boards, fit between 768K and 896K. The computer's own built-in ROM that starts the computer is addressed from 896K to 1024K.

The 8088/8086 processors can thus see a total memory space no bigger than 1024K, of which no more than 640K can be RAM. Even if you have more than 640K worth of RAM chips, DOS will not recognize it. However, the address area above 640K is rarely full. An 80-column, 25-line text display uses 4K of video memory. The Monochrome Display Adapter occupies just the area from 704K to 708K. Only the most colorful EGA and VGA modes fill or exceed the 128K assigned to video. Also, only IBM's PS/2 models, not PCs or ATs, use all the address space above 896K for system ROM. Having vacant space in high memory can come in handy. With a

64K gap amidst the video buffers and BIOS routines, the use of EMS, expanded memory, is possible. EMS is described in a moment.

While the early 8088 chip stops at 1MB of RAM, the 80286 chip introduced in the PC AT can address 16MB. The 80386 chip can address as much as four gigabytes (4096MB). RAM above the 1MB boundary is fairly simple to deal with compared with the busy addresses below it. Known as *extended memory,* this upper area of RAM is simply additional space for 80286 or 80386 systems running OS/2, Xenix, or some 80386-specific software. Unfortunately, an 80286 or 80386 using DOS runs in something called *real mode,* which has the same 1MB address limit as the 8088. This was designed into the chip for backward compatibility with earlier computers. The 8088-based PCs were around so long that hardware designers built their peripherals to take advantage of the addresses above 640K. Altering the limit would affect your ability to use many popular hard disk controllers, video boards, and so on.

There is an alternative mode that can be addressed by operating systems other than DOS. This is called the *protected mode,* and it can use large extended memory spaces. Some DOS programs, such as Paradox 3.5, and some utilities, can work with extended memory. For example, many PC ATs come with 384K of actual RAM memory installed beyond 640K, but DOS normally cannot use it. An AT with 1MB of built-in RAM gives the same CHKDSK report of available memory as one with 640K. Some 1MB systems use the extra memory as *shadow RAM,* loading a copy (or shadow) of slow video and BIOS ROM code into RAM for quicker performance. Shadow RAM makes screen displays more responsive, especially for graphics, but will not stop ordinary DOS programs from displaying "Out of memory" messages.

EMS Architecture

In contrast to the simple linear addressing of extended RAM, expanded memory relies on a technical trick known as *paging,* or *bank-switching.* This takes a "window" within the region visible to the processor (the 8088's 1MB address space) and swaps different areas, or pages, of expanded memory in and out of that space as needed. What happens is that an unused 64K section of the memory between 640K and 1024K is used as the address for a larger area, like a mail drop that is one stop on the postal route but that has boxes for lots of customers. The CPU is fooled into operating within this virtual space on data whose real, or physical, address may be many megabytes away.

Simple bank-switching is nothing new, but EMS is a sophisticated scheme. It involves hardware and software working together—the extra RAM and memory-mapping hardware on an EMS board, combined with a software driver added to your CONFIG.SYS file. This driver, the expanded memory manager (EMM), lets DOS and your applications recognize the paged memory. Given at least 64K of contiguous, vacant address space above 784K (one of the unused gaps), EMS creates a page frame holding at least four 16K pages. The memory manager can map any 16K segment, anywhere within expanded RAM, into any of these pages, fielding CPU requests while preventing collisions among multiple programs and among data areas.

The original Expanded Memory Specification, EMS 3.2, supported 8MB of expanded memory, mostly as workspace for spreadsheets and other data files. AST and other firms modified that standard to create the Enhanced Expanded Memory Specification (EEMS), which can swap more pages, including some below the 640K line as well as in the page frame above it. This helps environments such as DESQview shuffle programs in and out of conventional memory. Now EMS 4.0 has surpassed the EEMS standard. With EMS 4.0 you get support for up to 32MB at 8MB per expansion slot. This is swapped into pages almost anywhere below 1MB, and it has many more functions and routines for executing program code as well as handling data.

Understanding the difference between expanded and extended memory can take some effort, but there is a simple rule to follow when installing RAM in your system for use with Quattro Pro 3: configure as much memory as possible as expanded. Quattro Pro 3 can make use of expanded memory but not extended. Many memory boards can be configured as either extended or expanded. Even if you have an extended memory board you may find software that allows the extended memory to be treated as expanded.

The Memory Crunch

Now that you know why memory is organized the way it is in a PC, you can evaluate some techniques for getting around the limits imposed by this state of affairs. After taking steps to maximize the amount of memory in your system, and configuring as much of it as expanded memory as you can, you may still run into memory problems, typically when you have loaded Quattro Pro 3 and then built a very large worksheet. Quattro Pro 3's VROOMM feature allows you to keep building very large worksheets by reducing the amount of memory used by the program itself. The Virtual Real-time Object-Oriented Memory Manager is a technology designed by Borland to allow software to perform more efficiently under the 640K limitations of DOS. Programs written to run under VROOMM are composed of small modules that can be quickly loaded into memory as needed, allowing more room for data in memory. However, at some point the amount of disk access that this process requires will slow you down. Moving from one cell to the next will require a disk read, and this is the point at which you really need more memory.

You could also run into a memory problem trying to load Quattro Pro 3 after you have just installed and loaded a new piece of memory-resident software such as a network program. Try some of the following techniques to cope with the memory crunch.

Slimming Your CONFIG.SYS File Computer systems that have been around for a while can accumulate a lot of unnecessary additions. You may have noticed this in the case of disk files—dozens of files that have been on a hard disk for ages, but nobody is sure why. A similar thing can happen to your CONFIG.SYS file. Some applications add information to CON-FIG.SYS when they are installed, and some hardware requires that lines be added to CONFIG.SYS. If the application or hardware falls into disuse it can be removed, but the additions to CONFIG.SYS may remain. Devices loaded in CONFIG.SYS can take up precious memory, so you should remove ones you no longer need. Make sure you know why the items in your CONFIG.SYS file are there.

Mapping Out Your Memory A valuable tool for checking what you have in memory and where it is located is a utility program called a memory mapper. There are several of these available from bulletin boards, such as IBMNET on CompuServe. Some of these programs are free once you have downloaded them; others are shareware, which you pay for later if you decide to use them. If you are doing extensive work with memory—for example, configuring several different machines—then a program of this kind is very helpful.

Hardware/Software Solutions   Since 80386 systems have the capacity to address larger memory areas and have better memory-management functions built into their hardware, you can use software solutions to achieve results on an 80386 that require hardware solutions on earlier systems. An example of this is 386MAX from Qualitas. With 386MAX you can treat extended memory as expanded, access high DOS memory, and perform other tricks. Using programs of this nature requires that you coordinate several aspects of your computer system: video display, hard disk controllers, and network interface card. There are a lot of optional commands with 386MAX that allow you to alter the way it runs in order to avoid conflict with other programs. In some situations problems with high memory will require extensive analysis to resolve conflicts. For example, there are some VGA cards, such as the FastWrite VGA from Video7, that use up an area of memory often used by memory-swapping routines. If you load the VGA BIOS into RAM as described in the VGA utilities manual you can get around this conflict, but you will need to coordinate memory addresses with your memory expansion software.

Another memory management product is QEMM-386, from Quarterdeck Office Systems, makers of DESQView, a multitasking windows environment for DOS-based machines. While you can run DESQview on just about any PC, on 386-based machines DESQview is most commonly used in conjunction with QEMM-386, Quarterdeck's 386 Expanded Memory Manager. QEMM-386 has two major functions. First, like 386MAX, it can transform extended memory into expanded memory (LIM EMS 4.0 and EEMS 3.2), which can then be accessed by programs designed to take advantage of expanded memory, as well as by DESQview, which can use it to create virtual DOS environments for simultaneous operation of multiple programs. Second, it can map RAM into the unused addresses between 640K and 1MB and allow a user to load TSR modules into it, thus making more conventional RAM available to applications.

Expanded Memory Use Within Quattro Pro 3   The extra work of shuffling data through the DOS memory window into expanded RAM means that EMS RAM responds less quickly than RAM below 640K. For this reason Quattro Pro 3 allows you to make some trade-offs when using expanded memory. The Options Other Expanded Memory command provides these options:

Both

Spreadsheet Data

Format

None

The Both option allows EMS to be used for all types of worksheet information, permitting the largest possible models. The Spreadsheet Data option is the default setting, which limits EMS use to just formulas and labels, giving faster response than Both. The Format option is the fastest operation you can get while still making some use of EMS. The None option shuts off EMS so that your worksheet responds faster, although it cannot grow as large as when one of the other three options is used. Try changing your selection in this area when you need to increase worksheet capacity or program response times.

B Networks, Paradox, And Other Programs

Quattro Pro 3 has exceptional capabilities when it comes to getting along with other programs. This appendix explains how to set up Quattro Pro 3 to work on a network. There are tips for combining Quattro Pro 3 on the same system as Paradox, and for exchanging files with other programs such as 1-2-3.

Quattro Pro 3 and Networks

Quattro Pro 3 operates well in network environments. Users can share program files and fonts. User screen and menu preference files can be stored locally. Each user's default setting files can be stored in the same directory as private data files.

Network Installation

Installing Quattro Pro 3 for use on a network gives you the advantages of shared data access and reduced file storage requirements. By storing program files, including fonts, on a central file server equipped with a large hard disk, network users without hard disks can still make full use of

Quattro Pro 3. Expensive peripherals, such as laser printers and tape backup units, can be attached to the server, so that many users can benefit from them. Bear in mind that you must purchase a copy of Quattro Pro 3 for every network user of the program (except those using the network at different times). Instead of buying the full Quattro Pro 3 package for each user you can buy the Quattro Pro LAN which allows you to add one concurrent user to the network (since each copy of Quattro Pro 3 has its own unique serial number, and these are registered on the network, the program will know if more users attempt to run Quattro Pro 3 on the network than there are serial numbers).

Installing Quattro Pro 3 for network use is not particularly difficult although you should be familiar with DOS directories and commands, and with the workings of the network operating system. Quattro Pro 3 can be used with Novell Advanced NetWare version 2.0A or later, 3Com 3Plus version 1.0 or later, and any network fully compatible with either of these systems. You should use DOS 3.1 or higher.

In Figure B-1 you can see the type of file server directory structure recommended to run Quattro Pro 3 on a network. There are three basic requirements:

System file directory	For the main program files (use QPRO, with the subdirectory FONTS for shared font files)
Shared data directory	For shared spreadsheet files (use QPRODATA)
Private directories	For each Quattro Pro 3 user to store their own defaults and private data files (use subdirectories of a single directory called QPROPRIV)

You can vary the names of private directories to match your needs, but you will find installation easier if you do not stray too far from this model.

You can see that in addition to the directories for program files, you will also create private directories for each user, beneath the directory QPROPRIV. Each user's private directory will contain that person's Quattro Pro 3 private data files and program defaults (screen colors, hardware settings, and so on). While it is possible for two users to share a private directory this is not recommended because they could overwrite each other's defaults. The arrangement in Figure B-1 has QPROPRIV as a subdirectory of the root, with each user's directory beneath it. Each user should have full read/write/create rights to his or her private directory. If you prefer, you can place each user's private directory on their local hard disk, on their home directory on the network, or on a floppy disk. (The best

Figure B-1. *File server directory structure*

location for a user's private directory depends on the speed of his or her local hard disk and that of the network server: when a lot of users are accessing files on the network at the same time, it may be faster to retrieve files from the local hard disk unless it is an older, slower model).

In addition to the INSTALL.EXE program that is used in regular installations, network installation makes use of the following files:

QPUPDATE.EXE	Lets you enter the serial numbers for all other copies of Quattro Pro 3 that you want to run on the network. Use QPUPDATE if you need to add additional Quattro Pro 3 network users, or to remove a serial number from the network.
QPRO.SOM	Contains all of the serial numbers you've pledged for network use; it contains the path to the QPRO.NET file.
QPRO.NET	Controls the user count, so that the number of concurrent users cannot exceed the total number of serial numbers dedicated to run on the network.

MPMAKE.EXE	Creates personal menu preference (.MP) files, which indicate run time settings and whichever menu tree(s) each user will work with.
MU files	Let users work with Quattro Pro 3 via alternate menu trees. These menu files will reside on the network server in a shared directory, so all users can access them.
MP files	Contain the user's menu preferences. Users should store MP files on local hard disks to save disk space.
RF files	Contain Quattro Pro 3 default settings; the file RSC.RF is shipped with Quattro Pro 3, but each user can customize their RF file however they want.

The following steps cover the basic procedure for installing Quattro Pro 3 on your network:

1. Create a shared network directory to contain the Quattro Pro 3 program files (QPRO). The INSTALL program will need to copy files into QPRO, so it should not be made read-only until after installation.

2. Create a shared network directory for data files (QPRODATA). This will hold shared spreadsheet files; users who need these files should have read/write/create rights to QPRODATA. (If you need additional shared data directories at any time you will find it convenient to create them now.)

3. Install the Quattro Pro 3 software in the QPRO directory. Using the disks from a single-user Quattro Pro 3 package, run the INSTALL program as described in Appendix A. You will enter company name and the serial number from the label on Disk 1.

4. When asked if you are going to use a network, respond Yes. When asked for the location of QPRO.NET specify the full DOS path to the shared data directory QPRODATA. (While INSTALL can create QPRO.NET in whatever server directory you specify, the shared data directory is recommended because Quattro Pro 3 needs read/write access to this file.)

5. If you want to build fonts for your users ahead of time, choose Final and pick the desired set of fonts from the list (bear in mind that this step will take several minutes).

6. When prompted for other hardware and default information, answer according to the computer you are actually installing onto. These defaults can be customized later on for each user's computer.

7. When INSTALL returns you to DOS, switch to the QPRO directory and enter QPUPDATE. Then, enter the serial numbers of all copies of Quattro Pro 3 you want to dedicate to network (concurrent) use.

8. Establish a private directory beneath QPROPRIV for each Quattro Pro 3 network user. We recommend you place private **directories** beneath QPROPRIV; wherever they are, make sure users have read/write/create access to their directories.

9. For each user, create an MP file for his or her menu preference. Network users have the usual choice of menu trees: QUATTRO.MU, the normal Quattro Pro 3 menu tree; 123.MU, the 123-compatible menu tree; and Q1.MU, the old Quattro 1 menu tree, *not* the Quattro Pro 1 menu tree. From an administrative perspective it will be easier to support users if they all use the same menu tree. Store each user's MP files in his or her private directory. Do not store MP files in the QPRO directory. To create each MP file, from the QPRO directory use the following syntax:

   MPMAKE *QQQ.MU DIRECTORY* \

   where *QQQ.MU* is the name of the menu file they want to use and *DIRECTORY* is where to write the MP file containing this information (this directory must be in the user's PATH statement). For example, here is the command to create an MP file for the regular Quattro Pro 3 menu tree and place this MP file in Pam's private directory:

   MPMAKE   F:\QPRO\QUATTRO.MU   F:\QPROPRIV\PAM\

10. Create a default (RF) file in each user's private directory. To do this you first copy the RSC.RF file from QPRO into each private directory. Afterwards, you must delete the RSC.RF file from the QPRO directory (if you do not, Quattro Pro 3 will read the RF file in QPRO instead of the RF file in the user's private directory).

11. Now you can make the QPRO directory read-only to prevent anyone messing with the program files which no longer needed changing. If

your network software cannot make the QPRO directory read-only while keeping the FONTS subdirectory read-write, you should use the DOS ATTRIB command to make the program files read-only (for example, ATTRIB +R *.*). Users should only be able to open files and search in this directory, not change files.

12. Modify each user's CONFIG.SYS file where necessary. The CONFIG.SYS file in the root directory of each user's computer should contain the following statement:

FILES=20

For more on the FILES parameter, see Appendix A.

13. Add the SHARE command to each user's AUTOEXEC file or network log-in script.

14. Add (or change) the PATH statement in each user's AUTOEXEC.BAT or other network log-on file to include paths to his or her private directory and to QPRO. You must add the PATH statement after the log-in commands, and the path to QPRO must appear after the path to the private directory. For example, the last lines of AUTOEXEC.BAT might look like this:

F:LOGIN ADMIN\PAM
PATH F:\QPROPRIV\PAM;F:\QPRO

The first line, F:LOGIN ADMIN\PAM, logs Pam onto the Admin network. After the log-in statement, the PATH statement defines the paths to the Quattro Pro 3 directories.

You can now restart each computer to put the revised CONFIG.SYS and AUTOEXEC.BAT files into effect. Start Quattro Pro 3 at each computer to ensure the installation is working correctly. Quattro Pro 3 automatically detects each computer's hardware setup, so all users should be able to run Quattro Pro 3 regardless of monitor type.

While in the program, you can change default settings (see the next section), or exit and let users make their own changes. Now everyone is ready to use Quattro Pro 3. If you entered six serial numbers during this process, you should be able to start Quattro Pro 3 on six workstations concurrently. Make sure each user has a copy of the documentation and knows the location of the Quattro Pro 3 directories.

Bear in mind that if users want to switch from one menu tree to another, they must have separate MP files for each. Also, you must set up a path to each user's private directory and the QPRO directory. Quattro Pro 3 must know where the QPRO directory is in order to read the program files, and it must know where the QPROPRIV directory is in order to read and write each user's Quattro Pro 3 defaults.

Network Upgrades from Quattro Pro Version 1

If you have been running an earlier version of Quattro Pro 3 from your network server, you already have directories containing the previous program files, defaults, fonts, and data files. You will need to make substantial changes to upgrade to Quattro Pro 3. You must upgrade all copies of Quattro Pro version 1 to version 3 because version 3 monitors user count on a network, and requires version 3 serial numbers to do so.

You must delete the Quattro Pro version 1 program files before installing the version 3 program files. To do this without erasing spreadsheet data files, go into the existing Quattro Pro program directory and check for any spreadsheet, graph, or personal files. You can use the DOS DIR command to list all files with the extension .W??. This will catch all .WQ1 and .WQ! files, but if users have assigned other file extensions to their data files, check for these as well. Copy any data files you find to a data directory, such as QPRODATA. Since version 1 fonts may not be compatible with version 3, which features improved font files, delete existing font files. After verifying that all data files are safely stored in a separate directory, delete all files in the existing Quattro Pro program directory.

Now move to the RESOURCE subdirectory, which the Network Administrator's Guide in version 1 recommended creating. It should contain the MU files from version 1. These files are not compatible with version 3, so delete them and remove the RESOURCE directory. Now switch to the QPRORES directory, which the Network Administrator's Guide in version 1 recommended creating. Delete the contents of this directory, which are RF files, and then delete the directory. All that should remain is the Quattro Pro program directory (which should be empty), the QPRODATA directory (with its shared data files), and the QPROPRIV directory (with its subdirectories containing private data files). You can now proceed with the regular installation steps given earlier.

Network Printing

If you encounter extraneous blank pages before and after printing to a network printer, go to the Options Hardware Printers menu and choose Device Parallel 1 or Parallel 2. Do not use the logical device options LPT1 or LPT2. The Parallel 1 device is equivalent to LPT1 and Parallel 2 is equivalent to LPT2. If your network printers are installed using LPT3, LPT4, or LPT5, you must redefine these options for LPT1 or LPT2 and use Parallel 1 or Parallel 2 Device options within Quattro Pro 3.

Paradox Access

Before you use Paradox Access, the feature that allows you to switch between Paradox and Quattro Pro 3 with the CTRL-F10 key, there are several configuration items you will need to check, and several that you can alter to improve performance.

Configuration

The FILES setting in CONFIG.SYS must read at least FILES=40. If you start Quattro Pro 3 and get an error message stating that there are not enough file handles available, you must increase this number (remember that you need to reboot your computer for this setting to take effect; see Appendix A for more on CONFIG.SYS).

You also need to run the SHARE command from the DOS prompt for Paradox and Quattro Pro 3 to work together. The SHARE command loads a memory-resident module that allows file sharing and locking. Add this command to your AUTOEXEC.BAT file to avoid running SHARE each time you want to run Paradox Access. If SHARE is already loaded DOS gives you the message "SHARE already installed." You must also make sure that the directory containing Quattro Pro 3 is in your current PATH. You may want to add the directory to the PATH command in your AUTOEXEC.BAT file.

You should not have Quattro Pro 3 and Paradox program files stored in the same directory. There is no problem keeping both DB and WQ1 data files in the same area, but because of the strict locking rules in Paradox for private directories, make sure that your Paradox working directory and private directory are different (if you are already using Paradox on a network without any difficulty then it is likely that your working and private directories have already been set correctly).

To alter the Paradox working directory choose Defaults SetDirectory after running the Paradox Custom Configuration Program (this is a special script file, called CUSTOM.SCR, supplied with the Paradox program; to run it you choose Script from the main Paradox menu, then select Run and enter **Custom**). Choose Ok to permanently change the location of your Paradox working directory. Quattro Pro 3 respects all Paradox locks. For more information on locking and private directories, see your Paradox documentation.

When running Quattro Pro 3 from within Paradox, you must run Paradox in protected mode. You can set this as a default using the Paradox Custom Configuration Program. If you are using Paradox on a stand-alone system, that is, not as a network server, you still need to follow some network configuration procedures. First run the Paradox NUPDATE.EXE program, configure the network type to OTHER, and specify a path for the PARADOX.NET file. On a stand-alone system this file can be placed anywhere on your hard disk where both Paradox and Quattro Pro 3 can find it.

Next run Quattro Pro 3 and choose Paradox Access from the Options Other menu. Choose OTHER for the network type, and specify the same path you used in NUPDATE.EXE for the PARADOX.NET file. Press ESCAPE until you return to the main Options menu, then choose Update to save this configuration to disk. Exit Quattro Pro 3 and load Paradox with PXACCESS. You should now be able to retrieve Paradox DB files while running Quattro Pro 3 from within Paradox. In Figure B-2 you can see a suggested file and directory layout for running Quattro Pro 3 and Paradox on a non-networked system.

Loading Up

The best way to start Paradox with Quattro Pro 3 access is to use PXACCESS.BAT, which comes with Quattro Pro 3. The PXACCESS.BAT batch file contains these lines:

SHARE

PARADOX -qpro -leaveK 512 -emK 0

Figure B-2.   *File and directory layout*

In most cases, you will not need to change the contents of the PXACCESS batch file. However, if you want to include command line options for Quattro Pro 3 you can edit them into PXACCESS.BAT. For example, to load the file SALES.WQ1 with Quattro Pro 3 you would enter

PARADOX -qpro [SALES] -leaveK 512 -emK 0

Alternatively, you can place a batch file parameter in the command line which can then accept different files, as in

PARADOX -qpro [%1] -leaveK 512 -emK 0

which allows you to enter the command PXACCESS SALES to load the SALES worksheet.

If your computer has more than 2MB of extended memory you might want to edit PXACCESS.BAT to alter some parameters and improve performance. The first line of PXACCESS.BAT loads the SHARE module, and the next line starts Paradox with the command line options necessary for using Paradox Access. The -qpro command sets up Paradox for use with

Quattro Pro 3. You must use this option when you use Paradox Access. The leaveK 512 statement prevents Paradox from using 512K of extended memory, reserving it for a memory manager program to convert to expanded memory. Once it is converted, Quattro Pro 3 can use it, as long as the -emK 0 option is included. This option prevents Paradox from using any expanded (EMS) memory, so that Quattro Pro 3 can use it.

You might want to alter these settings to make more memory available for Quattro Pro 3. With an 80386-class computer, you probably have a memory manager device driver like QEMM-386 from Quarterdeck Office Systems. Such programs convert the onboard extended memory (which Paradox prefers) to expanded (which Quattro Pro 3 prefers). In this case, set leaveK to about 1MB less than the total, and keep -emK set to 0. With an 80286 AT-class computer, you may or may not have expanded memory installed through an expansion card (like the Intel AboveBoard or the AST Rampage card). If you have an expanded memory card, you can set -leaveK to 0 and keep the -emK option as is.

Remember that Quattro Pro 3 needs at least 384K of conventional memory to run, which is what -qpro provides. Quattro Pro 3 also needs all the expanded memory it can get, which is what the other options provide. When using Paradox Access, the Quattro Pro 3 /X command-line option (which lets Quattro Pro 3 use 512K of extended memory) is disabled. If Quattro Pro 3 cannot run at all, your computer might not have enough conventional memory available. In that case, try removing any RAM-resident (TSR) programs you have loaded. If your computer has no expanded memory available (either because there is none installed or because Paradox is using all the extra memory), Quattro Pro 3 will still be able to run, but only using small spreadsheets. If Quattro Pro 3 shows signs of running out of memory, such as failing to load all entries of a spreadsheet, increase the -leaveK setting to free up more expanded memory. For best use of memory, in addition to the commands on the Database Paradox Access menu, set the Options Other Expanded Memory option in Quattro Pro 3 to Both.

Relating to Other Spreadsheets

Quattro Pro 3 is similar in some respects to other electronic spreadsheet programs such as Lotus 1-2-3 and Microsoft Excel. The actual arrangement of data in Quattro Pro 3, Excel, and 1-2-3 is very similar, because all three programs use indexed columns and rows for managing data. However, there are considerable differences in terminology. The arrangement of indexed columns and rows in an electronic spreadsheet produces a collection of boxes, or *cells*. A cell is named or indexed by the column and row forming the cell. Thus, column B, row 3 is named cell B3. When a contiguous group of cells must be acted on collectively, it is called a *block* in Quattro Pro 3. In 1-2-3 a group of cells is called a *range*. Excel uses the term range as well but generally refers to *selected cells* rather than ranges. Commands that affect a group of cells are handled differently by the three programs. Excel and Quattro Pro 3 gather many block-related commands into an Edit menu. Formatting of grouped cells is handled by the Style commands in Quattro Pro 3, and the Format commands in Excel. In 1-2-3 there is a main menu item called Range that covers most commands affecting a group of cells, both formatting and editing. However, two editing commands for ranges, Copy and Move, are presented on the main menu.

When a command affects the entire spreadsheet, 1-2-3 refers to it as *global*. In 1-2-3 the Global commands are a subset of Worksheet commands. Even the program defaults are handled by the /Worksheet Global menu. Quattro Pro 3 refers to commands that affect the whole spreadsheet as Options, as does Excel. Quattro Pro 3 distinguishes between default settings made for a particular worksheet and those written to the configuration file permanent settings. This is done with the Options Update command. The global commands in 1-2-3 and their equivalent default settings in Quattro Pro 3 are as follows:

1-2-3 Global Commands	**Quattro Pro 3 Settings**
/Worksheet Global Column-Width	Options Formats Global Width
/Worksheet Global Format	Options Formats Numeric Format
/Worksheet Global Recalc	Options Recalculation
/Worksheet Global Protection	Options Protection

Interfacing

Both Quattro Pro 3 and Excel allow you to use a mouse to select cells and issue commands. Excel does this through the Windows operating environment whereas mouse support is an integral part of Quattro Pro 3. Both

Quattro Pro 3 and Excel allow you to select cells before issuing commands that affect those cells, whereas 1-2-3 requires you to issue a command and then select the cells. In fact, Quattro Pro 3 can operate in both modes. While all three programs use menu bars across the top of the screen, the 1-2-3 menu bar is only present when you press the / key. In Quattro Pro 3 and Excel the main menu bar normally remains on screen and you then pull down vertical menus of additional commands.

Both Quattro Pro 3 and Excel allow you to add or subtract items from the menu system, including macros. In Quattro Pro 3 this is done with the Options Startup Edit Menus command. This command also allows you to alter the style of menu between the normal pull-down style and pop-up menus that only appear when the menu is activated. You can adjust the width of Quattro Pro 3 menus to either display settings or hide them. You can even tell Quattro Pro 3 to remember the last item you picked from the menu, allowing rapid repetition of commands.

File Sharing

To use a 1-2-3 Release 2.01 or 2.2 worksheet in Quattro Pro 3, all you need to do is select it from the list of worksheet files. Quattro Pro 3 automatically translates the file into a Quattro Pro 3 worksheet. When importing a 1-2-3 Release 2.2 file that contains linking, the link references are converted to Quattro Pro 3 syntax. However, formatting done with the Allways add-in is not translated. To save a file with 2.2 linking in the Quattro Pro 3 format simply give the file a WQ1 extension. If you keep the WK1 extension when you save the file, Quattro Pro 3 asks you how you want to handle the file saving. You have three options: No, Yes, and Use 2.2 Syntax. The No option aborts the Save and you are warned that the file has been removed from the disk. The Yes option saves the file, but converts all links to their end result. The third option, Use 2.2 Syntax, saves the file and preserves 2.2 syntax, but only for single cell references. For Quattro Pro 3 to use macros in a 1-2-3 worksheet you can either set up Quattro Pro 3 with the 1-2-3 menu, as described in the next section, or you can set the Key option on the Quattro Pro 3 Tools Macro menu to Yes. To share files with users of Excel you can also use the WK1 format, which can be read by both Excel and Quattro Pro 3. For a complete list of file formats that can be read and written by Quattro Pro 3, see Table B-1.

Obviously, there are some situations in which Quattro Pro 3 cannot directly store your worksheet as a WK1 file. When you use a Quattro Pro

WKS	Lotus 1-2-3, Release 1A
WK1	Lotus 1-2-3, Release 2.01 and 2.02
WKE	Lotus 1-2-3, Educational Version
WRK	Lotus Symphony, Release 1.2
WR1	Lotus Symphony, Release 2
WKQ	Earlier versions of Quattro
WQ1	Quattro Pro (all versions)
WKP	Surpass
WK$	SQZ (Lotus 1-2-3, Release 1A)
WK!	SQZ (Lotus 1-2-3, Release 21)
WR$	SQZ (Lotus Symphony, Release 1.2)
WR!	SQZ (Lotus Symphony, Release 2)
WKZ	SQZ (Earlier versions of Quattro)
WQ!	SQZ (Quattro Pro all versions)
DB	Paradox
DB2	dBASE II
DBF	dBASE III, III PLUS, and IV
RXD	Reflex (early versions)
R2D	Reflex (Version 2)

Note: Not all programs that import or export DIF files use exactly the same file format. Quattro Pro 3 supports the DIF file format developed by Software Arts Products Corporation and used by VisiCalc. Files in other versions of DIF may not be readable by Quattro Pro 3 and some programs may not read DIF files from Quattro Pro 3.

Table B-1.   *File Formats Read/Written by Quattro Pro 3*

---

3 feature that has no equivalent in 1-2-3, then that feature is lost when the file is saved in 1-2-3 format. This affects those @functions that Quattro Pro 3 supports but 1-2-3 does not. When you save a file containing such functions, Quattro Pro 3 will warn you that it is about to convert an unknown function to a value and you are given a chance to cancel the file save operation and use a Quattro Pro 3 format instead. Table B-2 shows a list of Quattro Pro 3 @functions that should not be used in a worksheet you are saving in 1-2-3 format. When you are exchanging files between Quattro

@CELLINDEX	@HEXTONUM	@PAYMT
@CURVALUE	@IPAYMNT	@PPAYMT
@DEGREES	@IRATE	@PVAL
@DSTDS	@MEMAVAIL	@RADIANS
@DVARS	@MEMEMSAVAIL	@STDS
@FILEEXISTS	@NPER	@SUMPRODUCT
@FVAL	@NUMTOHEX	@VARS

Table B-2.   *Quattro Pro 3 @Functions to Avoid When Exporting to 1-2-3*

Pro 3 and 1-2-3 you will need to pay particular attention to macros. See the following section on sharing macros for more details.

Quattro Pro 3 and 1-2-3

The differences between Quattro Pro 3 and 1-2-3 can be minimized for the user by implementing the emulation features that Quattro Pro 3 provides. You may want to do this either to run 1-2-3 macros or to minimize retraining employees who already know how to use 1-2-3. In the long run you will probably find that users of 1-2-3 adjust quite happily to the Quattro Pro 3 menu system without using the 1-2-3 emulation features. However, if you do wish to make Quattro Pro 3 emulate 1-2-3, for example to run 1-2-3 macros, then the following steps should be followed.

The 1-2-3 Menu

Quattro Pro 3 provides a menu tree that will be familiar to users of 1-2-3. Found in the file 123.MU, this menu set appears much like the Quattro

Pro 3 menus, but options have names to match the 1-2-3 menu system and the commands are grouped differently. The Quattro Pro 3 Edit Erase command, for example, is found on the 1-2-3 Range menu, as the Range Erase command.

The 1-2-3 menu can be selected for use with Quattro Pro 3 during the installation process. If you did not select the 1-2-3 menu tree during installation you can still run Quattro Pro 3 in 1-2-3 mode by starting the program with this special command:

Q123

This command tells Quattro Pro 3 to use a special configuration file called 123.RF. This file contains settings that cause Quattro Pro 3 to emulate 1-2-3. For more on using RF files with Quattro Pro 3, see Appendix A.

You can also switch to the 1-2-3 menu tree after loading Quattro Pro 3 with the regular menus. If you would like to switch menu trees during a session, you can use the Options Startup command. You can also use this command if you selected the 1-2-3 menu system during installation and would like to try the regular Quattro Pro 3 menu. When you select Options Startup you will see from the menu the name of the current menu file. Normally, this is QUATTRO.MU, the regular Quattro Pro 3 menu tree. Select Menu Tree from the Startup menu and you will see a list of currently available menu files, including 123.MU. When you highlight 123.MU and press ENTER, you will be returned to READY mode and the 1-2-3 menu will be visible across the top of the screen.

The 1-2-3 menu in Quattro Pro 3 remains on screen at all times, like the regular Quattro Pro 3 menu. However, you still have to press / to activate it. When the 1-2-3 menu is activated, the word Worksheet is highlighted, just as in 1-2-3, and you can select items by either the first letter method or the highlight and ENTER method. Take a moment to explore the 1-2-3 menu tree. Some commands look slightly different. For example, the System command in 1-2-3 itself takes you immediately to DOS, whereas in Quattro Pro 3's 1-2-3 emulation mode the System command requires that you make a further menu selection before reaching DOS. You will also notice that the 1-2-3 menu tree has some items that are not found in 1-2-3 itself. These items are marked by small boxes next to their names in the menu list.

To make your menu tree file selection permanent you need to use the Options Update command. Under the 1-2-3 menu tree this command is Worksheet Global Default Update. When you select Update, Quattro Pro

3 writes your choice of menu system to the configuration file. When you exit from Quattro Pro 3 and reload the program, the new menu system you selected will be in effect.

Comfort Features

If you are using Quattro Pro 3 in 1-2-3 mode you will probably want to make Quattro Pro 3 save files in a 1-2-3 file format. If you install 1-2-3 emulation during installation, load Quattro Pro 3 with the Q123 option, or change from the Quattro Pro 3 menu tree to the menus in 123.MU, then the default file extension is automatically changed to WK1. You can alter this extension, for example to the SQZ version of the 1-2-3 format, by using the Worksheet Global Default Files command in the 1-2-3 menus, or Options Startup from the Quattro Pro 3 menu tree.

Borland designed Quattro Pro 3 so that it does not prompt you to save data before it executes the Erase or Exit command if you have already saved the data. However, because erasing block and graph names can waste hours of work, Quattro Pro 3 always prompts before completing an Edit Names Reset or a Graph Names Reset command. If you are familiar with 1-2-3, then you will know that this approach to name resetting and file saving is different from that used by Lotus. If you are comfortable with the Lotus-style confirmation prompts, you can use them. To make the change while using the Quattro Pro 3 menu tree, use the Options Startup Edit Menus command and select Options. Select Borland Style and change the setting to No. Use the Worksheet Global Default Files Edit Menus command in the 1-2-3 menu tree to switch to Lotus-style save and reset prompts. Select Options, then Borland Style, and change the setting to No. This is done automatically when you switch to 1-2-3 menus.

You will notice that while you are using the Edit Menus command there is another Confirm Options setting on the Options menu called During Macros. Setting this option to Yes preserves the Borland style of confirmation during the recording and execution of macros. Changing this option to No helps you to successfully share macros with 1-2-3. This option is automatically set to No when you invoke the 1-2-3 menus.

Sharing Macros

There are major differences between 1-2-3 and Quattro Pro 3 in the area of macros. When making macros in Quattro Pro 3 you do not have to use lists of actual keystrokes when replicating menu choices. For example, suppose that you want to print the cells you have named TOTAL. In 1-2-3 the macro code would be

```
/PPRTOTALAG
```

This is compact, but far from obvious to decipher. If you happened to use /PFRTOTALAG by mistake, the macro could have unpleasant effects. In the menu equivalent approach used by Quattro Pro 3 the macro would look like this:

```
{/ Print;Block}TOTAL~
{/ Print;Align}{/ Print;Go}
```

This is very easy to read and debug. Since Quattro Pro 3 records macros for you it takes no longer to create than the 1-2-3 version. The style of macro recording normally used by Quattro Pro 3 language is called Logical. The 1-2-3 style is called Keystroke.

When it comes to sharing macros, Quattro Pro 3 offers two ways to run macros made with 1-2-3. You can load Quattro Pro 3's 1-2-3 menu tree to run your 1-2-3 macro. Alternatively, you can set the Key option on the Tools Macro menu to Yes. Quattro Pro 3 can record macros that 1-2-3 can run, but only if you record them with the 1-2-3 menu tree in place and the Keystroke style of macro recording in effect, instead of the usual Logical or menu equivalent style. The style of macro recording is set by the Worksheet Macro Macro Recording command in the 1-2-3 menu tree. This is automatically set to Keystroke when you invoke the 1-2-3 style menus. In the regular Quattro Pro 3 menu tree the command is Tools Macro Macro Recording. Of course, for your macros to be compatible with 1-2-3 you cannot use any of the menu items or macro commands unique to Quattro Pro 3. These are listed in Table B-3.

Note that Quattro Pro 3 macros recorded with the Logical style will run regardless of the menu tree that is in place. This means that you can be using the 1-2-3 style menu and still run a Quattro Pro 3 macro developed under the normal Quattro Pro 3 menu. Since Quattro Pro 3 allows you to run macros from libraries, this feature gives users of the 1-2-3 menu tree access to macros developed by regular Quattro Pro 3 users. To make a macro library, first open the worksheet containing your collected macros. Use the Macro Library command and set the option to Yes, then save the

Menu Items

Worksheet	Macro
Worksheet	Undo
Range	Column
Range	Alignment
Range	Output Style
Range	Data Entry
Range	Search & Replace
File	New
File	Open
File	Workspace
File	!SQZ!
File	Update Links
Print	All Final Quality options
Graph	Instant Graph
View	All options

Macro Commands

{;}	{GRAPHCHAR}	{NUMON}
{BACKTAB}	{INSOFF}	{PASTE}
{CAPOFF}	{INSON}	{READDIR}
{CAPON}	{MACROS}	{SCROLLOFF}
{CHOOSE}	{MARKALL}	{SCROLLON}
{CLEAR}	{MARK}	{STEPOFF}
{COPY}	{MESSAGE}	{STEPON}
{CR}	{MOVE}	{STEP}
{DATE}	{NAME}	{TAB}
{DELEOL}	{NEXTWIN}	{UNDO}
{FUNCTIONS}	{NUMOFF}	{ZOOM}

Table B-3.   *Menu Items and Macro Commands to Avoid When Exporting Macros to 1-2-3*

file. As long as the file is open you can use macros that are in it, even if the library file is not the current worksheet.

Added Features

Several features found in Quattro Pro 3 are not found in 1-2-3 Release 2.01. These features have been incorporated into Quattro Pro 3's 1-2-3 menu system where appropriate. They include the Worksheet Macro command and such Graph commands as Area and Rotated Bar. Note that saving graphs in worksheets with the WK1 or WKS format removes color information about the graph. Use the regular WQ1 format to retain color settings.

There are some Quattro Pro 3 features that are not part of the menu system that 1-2-3 users need to know about. These include the use of the DELETE key for deleting the contents of a cell (the equivalent of /Range Erase ENTER in 1-2-3) and the Undo key (ALT-F5). The CTRL-D date entry method, the rest of the Shortcuts feature, and the ability to assign menu items to CTRL keys should also be pointed out to 1-2-3 users switching to Quattro Pro 3. The use of the Record feature and Transcript for macro making is part of Quattro Pro 3 that experienced 1-2-3 users will want to explore. The function keys are largely used in the same way in Quattro Pro 3 and 1-2-3. Exceptions in Quattro Pro 3 are the following:

- ALT-F2 for macro options

- F3 to activate the menu (in addition to /)

- ALT-F3 to list @functions

- SHIFT-F3 to list macro commands

- ALT-F5 to undo your last action

- ALT-F6 to zoom a window

Also note the use of the plus key on the numeric keypad to expand menus, and the use of the minus key to contract them. Expanding menus shows the current settings of items when they exist. Contracting menus makes them less obtrusive. These keys make for more flexible and informative uses of menus than in 1-2-3, where many of the current settings cannot be seen from the menu.

C Support and Printer Information

Technology as powerful as that used by today's personal computers is not always easy to understand and is bound to give rise to questions. This appendix provides some suggestions for when you run into problems using Quattro Pro 3, along with some tips on using printer setup strings.

Getting Support

When you are facing a problem using Quattro Pro 3, one of the first steps to take is a break. Give yourself a few minutes away from the computer to relax; you can then return to the problem in a better, and often clearer, frame of mind. If that does not help, trying asking fellow workers for their suggestions. Describing the problem to someone else can often help you see the solution. Be sure to check relevant sections in the manual. Check the spelling and syntax of any formulas, functions, or macro commands you are using. Refer to the index of this book for the relevant subject. If you still do not have an acceptable answer, consider the following sources of support.

Written Support

Do not underestimate the venerable process of putting the problem into words and putting those words on paper. This process can sometimes solve the problem as you think it through. If you still need help, send the problem, together with any printouts, screen prints, plus the software version and the serial number from the front of the original program disk to the following address:

Borland International, Inc.
1800 Green Hills Road
P.O. Box 660001
Scotts Valley, CA 95066-0001

While this is not the fastest way of finding support, it is sometimes the best way, particularly if you feel you need to present printed data from the program.

On-Line Support

If you have a modem and communications software, you should consider subscribing to CompuServe, the on-line information bank. Here you will find the Borland Applications Forum (accessed with GO BORAPP from the CompuServe prompt). The Forum contains answers to many common questions, a few of which are included at the end of this appendix. The Forum also has many useful Quattro Pro 3 worksheet files that you can copy, and a message and discussion system for exchanging views and news with other Quattro Pro 3 users. Many computer stores and bookstores sell sign-up packages for CompuServe, or you can write to

CompuServe Information Service, Inc.
P.O. Box 20212
Columbus, OH 43220

Note that CompuServe is available via a local phone call in many countries, so although it is operated from somewhere in the United States, it is a valuable support system for users around the world.

Registration

If you have just bought Quattro Pro 3, be sure to fill out and return the user registration card in the front of the manual. Registering your software protects your investment in it and ensures that you will hear of upgrades and related product announcements. For information about the latest version of the program, plus complimentary products as they become available, write to Borland at the address just provided.

Printer Setup Strings

To obtain the desired effects when printing, you may need to send certain codes to your printer. Although Quattro Pro 3 has a built-in system for communicating font and layout information to your printer, you may want to send specific print instructions. You can do this with a setup string, a special code that your printer understands. Note that you should only use setup strings in draft mode printing, not when the Print Destination setting is Graphics Printer.

In a setup string you tell the printer to use such features as condensed pitch and italic print. A setup string consists of one or more ASCII character codes, which are translated from the printer control codes listed in your printer's user manual. For example, some models of the Hewlett-Packard LaserJet printer understand the code

\027E\027(s16.66H)

to mean compressed print (17 pitch). You can enter a setup string with the Print Layout Setup String command, or you can place the string in the worksheet by entering it in a cell in the leftmost column of the Print Block, and preceding it with two of the special label prefix characters, as in

| | \027E\027(s16.66H)

When Quattro Pro 3 encounters this entry it will send the print instruction to the printer. Quattro Pro 3 will not print the line on which the entry occurs, which means that you should not place the code in a row that you want to print. The code does not have to be in the first row of the Print

Block and you can use several codes in the same Print Block, for example, to turn on condensed print, and then turn it off again. (Note that you can use the | | code alone to cause a row to be hidden during printing.)

Each printer recognizes its own set of control codes. The following tables list ASCII codes for several different printers. To enter a command for a printer other than those listed, refer to your printer's user manual for the control code or what is sometimes called an *escape code*.

Printer control codes can be sent in several forms. Most begin with the ESCAPE or ESC character, which is entered as \027. This is followed by further codes that are either entered as a \ followed by a number, or as a simple character like *E*. The first 32 ASCII codes do not have keyboard equivalents. Thus, your printer manual might tell you to use ESC,18, which is entered as \027 \018. Using the @CHAR function in Quattro Pro 3, you can check the character equivalent for the codes you are using. The formula @CHAR(069) returns E, which tells you that the code \027 \069 is the same as \027E, which may appear in your printer manual as ESC,E.

You can enter more than one code in a setup string as long as the printer supports it and the entire string does not exceed 254 characters. For example, a printer may be able to print near letter quality, bold, and elite pitch characters but may not be able to print italicized characters in near-letter-quality mode.

Setting Up the LaserJet

The HP LaserJet is found in many of today's offices. You can produce excellent reports using a LaserJet with Quattro Pro 3 if you follow a few basic guidelines. For normal 8.5-by-11-inch paper you should set the page length at 60 lines. For normal 10-pitch printing, use a left margin of 5 and a right margin of 80. Alternatively, set the margins using inches as the dimensions.

Always use Print Adjust Printer Align before each print job. You may find that the last page of the printout is not ejected from the printer. You can eject the paper by using the printer's control panel. Press the ON LINE button to take the printer offline; then press FORM FEED, followed by ON LINE. Alternatively, you can cause a page eject with a setup string in the worksheet. Place either the label | |\012 or | |\027E in a cell of the leftmost column of the Print Block (below the last line of data but within the Print Block) to cause a page eject. This code should be the only item on the row it occupies.

Index

{;} command, 672
{?} command, 653-654
{} command, 672
@@ function, 691
& sign, combining labels with, 562-563

A

@ABS function, 178-179
Abs key (F4), 256-257
Absolute cell references, 113, 256-257
Accelerated Cost Recovery System
   (ACRS), 210, 219
Active drive, 23
Addresses, memory, 791
Advanced criteria for queries, 139-145
Advanced functions, 688-696
Aggregate functions, 171-178
Aligning labels, 31, 78-79, 297-298
Analytical sorting, 128
Annotate feature, 16, 442, 478-481,
   545-546, 733-744
     changing fonts, 742
     drawing a shape, 737-744
     example graphic, 584
     table of keys used in, 736
     table of tools, 735
     using object handles, 739-740
Annotate screen, 734
Area graphs, 454-455, 457, 462

Arguments, function, 36, 168
Arithmetic functions, 178-182
ASCII, 126
ASCII tables, 305, 568
ASCII text files, 550
     importing to Quattro Pro 3,
      554-556
Aspect ratio, 320
Asterisk effect, 68-69
Autoload files, 392-393
Autoload macro, 314, 619-620
Automatic column width, 86
Automatic editing, 61
Automatic file loading, 313-314
Automatic file save, 52-53
Automatic linefeed, setting, 324
Automatic macros, 314, 619-620
Automatic recalculation, 299
@AVG function, 176

B

Background recalculation, 103, 299
BACKSPACE key in data entry, 58
Bank-switching, 793
Bar graphs, 451-453, 459
     and line graphs combined, 475
Basic installation (Quattro Pro 3),
   771-772
Batch file menu system, 779-784

823

M

The manuscript for this book was prepared and submitted to Osborne McGraw-Hill in electronic form. The acquisitions editor for this project was Elizabeth Fisher and the technical reviewer was Harriet Serenkin.

Text design by John Christgau and Lance Ravella, using Schoolbook for text body and Helvetica for display.

Cover design by Bay Graphics Design Associates, Inc. Book printed and bound by R.R. Donnelley & Sons Company, Crawfordsville, Indiana.

Osborne McGraw-Hill

**Computer
Books**

(800) 227-0900

You're important to us...

We'd like to know what you're interested in, what kinds of books you're looking for, and what you thought about this book in particular.

Please fill out the attached card and mail it in. We'll do our best to keep you informed about Osborne's newest books and special offers.

YES, SEND ME A FREE COLOR CATALOG
of all Osborne/McGraw-Hill computer books.

Name:_____Title:_____

Company:_____

Address:_____

City:_____State:_____Zip:_____

I'M PARTICULARLY INTERESTED IN THE FOLLOWING(*Check all that apply*)

I use this software:
- ❏ Lotus 1-2-3
- ❏ Quattro
- ❏ dBASE
- ❏ WordPerfect
- ❏ Microsoft Word
- ❏ WordStar
- ❏ Others_____

I use this operating system:
- ❏ DOS
- ❏ OS/2
- ❏ UNIX
- ❏ Macintosh
- ❏ Others_____

I rate this book:
❏ Excellent   ❏ Good   ❏ Poor

I program in:
- ❏ C
- ❏ PASCAL
- ❏ BASIC
- ❏ Others_____

I chose this book because...
- ❏ Recognized author's name
- ❏ Osborne/McGraw-Hill's reputation
- ❏ Read book review
- ❏ Read Osborne catalog
- ❏ Saw advertisement in _____
- ❏ Found while browsing in store
- ❏ Found/recommended in library
- ❏ Required textbook
- ❏ Price
- ❏ Other_____

Comments_____

_____

Topics I would like to see covered in future books by Osborne/McGraw-Hill

include:_____

_____

Print **ISBN** from the back cover here: 0-07-881   -

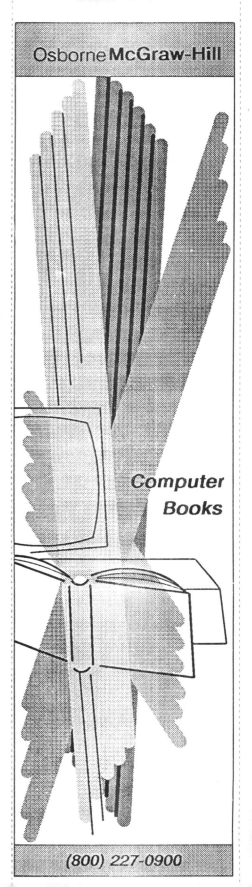

Osborne **McGraw-Hill**

Computer

Books

(800) 227-0900